IFIP Advances in Information and Communication Technology 442

IFIP – The International Federation for Information Processing

IFIP was founded in 1960 under the auspices of UNESCO, following the First World Computer Congress held in Paris the previous year. An umbrella organization for societies working in information processing, IFIP's aim is two-fold: to support information processing within its member countries and to encourage technology transfer to developing nations. As its mission statement clearly states,

> *IFIP's mission is to be the leading, truly international, apolitical organization which encourages and assists in the development, exploitation and application of information technology for the benefit of all people.*

IFIP is a non-profitmaking organization, run almost solely by 2500 volunteers. It operates through a number of technical committees, which organize events and publications. IFIP's events range from an international congress to local seminars, but the most important are:

- The IFIP World Computer Congress, held every second year;
- Open conferences;
- Working conferences.

The flagship event is the IFIP World Computer Congress, at which both invited and contributed papers are presented. Contributed papers are rigorously refereed and the rejection rate is high.

As with the Congress, participation in the open conferences is open to all and papers may be invited or submitted. Again, submitted papers are stringently refereed.

The working conferences are structured differently. They are usually run by a working group and attendance is small and by invitation only. Their purpose is to create an atmosphere conducive to innovation and development. Refereeing is also rigorous and papers are subjected to extensive group discussion.

Publications arising from IFIP events vary. The papers presented at the IFIP World Computer Congress and at open conferences are published as conference proceedings, while the results of the working conferences are often published as collections of selected and edited papers.

Any national society whose primary activity is about information processing may apply to become a full member of IFIP, although full membership is restricted to one society per country. Full members are entitled to vote at the annual General Assembly. National societies preferring a less committed involvement may apply for associate or corresponding membership. Associate members enjoy the same benefits as full members, but without voting rights. Corresponding members are not represented in IFIP bodies. Affiliated membership is open to non-national societies, and individual and honorary membership schemes are also offered.

Shuichi Fukuda   Alain Bernard
Balan Gurumoorthy   Abdelaziz Bouras (Eds.)

Product Lifecycle Management for a Global Market

11th IFIP WG 5.1 International Conference, PLM 2014
Yokohama, Japan, July 7-9, 2014
Revised Selected Papers

Springer

Volume Editors

Shuichi Fukuda
Keio University, Systems Design and Management
4-1-1, Hiyoshi, Kohoku-ku, Yokohama, 223-8526, Japan
E-mail: shufukuda@gmail.com

Alain Bernard
École Centrale de Nantes, Laboratoire IRCCyN UMR CNRS 6597
1, rue de la Noë, 44321 Nantes Cedex 3, France
E-mail: alain.bernard@irccyn.ec-nantes.fr

Balan Gurumoorthy
Indian Institute of Science, Centre for Product Design and Manufacturing
and Department of Mechanical Engineering
Bangalore 560012, India
E-mail: bgm@mecheng.iisc.ernet.in

Abdelaziz Bouras
Qatar University, Department of Computer Science and Engineering
P.O. Box 2713, Doha, Qatar
E-mail: abdelaziz.bouras@qu.edu.qa

ISBN 978-3-662-45936-2 ISBN 978-3-662-45937-9 (eBook)
DOI 10.1007/978-3-662-45937-9
Springer Heidelberg New York Dordrecht London

Library of Congress Control Number: 2014956963

Typesetting: Camera-ready by author, data conversion by Scientific Publishing Services, Chennai, India

Printed on acid-free paper

Springer is part of Springer Science+Business Media (www.springer.com)

Preface

The International Conference on Product Lifecycle Management started in 2003 and since then, it has been held yearly around the world and has served to exchange and discuss the most up-to-date information on product lifecycle management among academia and industry.

Product lifecycle management, also known as PLM, is an integrated business approach to the collaborative creation, management, and dissemination of engineering data throughout the extended enterprises that create, manufacture, and operate engineered products and systems.

This is the official conference of the IFIP Working Group WG 5.1 "Global Product Development for the Whole Lifecycle" (`www.ifip-wg51.org`) and PLM 2014 was held in Yokohama, Japan, as its 11th international conference under the theme of "Product Lifecycle Management for a Global Market".

A doctoral workshop was held prior to the conference. PhD candidates presented their on-going works and received feedback from mentors. Four plenary keynote presentations from academia and industry were made during the conference days. In addition to the academic presentations of the conference, a day was devoted to industry panels and presentations from various sectors of industry in Japan. This industrial presence has characterized the conference since its creation and serves to establish continuous ties between academia and industry.

This book, organized in 12 chapters, is composed of selected papers presented at the PLM 2014 conference. It is part of the *IFIP Advances in Information and Communication Technology* (AICT) series that publishes state-of-the-art results in the sciences and technologies of information and communication.

In addition to this conference, the *International Journal of Product Lifecycle Management* (IJPLM) is the official journal of the WG 5.1 (`www.inderscience.com/ijplm`).

Sincere thanks go to all authors, participants, and those who helped to organize and run the conference.

We hope this book serves to make a step forward in this exciting area of PLM and we look forward to meeting you at the next PLM conference in Doha, Qatar, during October 19–21, 2015 (`www.plm-conference.org`).

November 2014

Shuichi Fukuda
Alain Bernard

Organization

The conference is promoted by the International Federation for Information Processing (IFIP) Working Group 5.1 on Global Product Development for the Whole Lifecycle (`www.ifip-wg51.org`).

Conference Chair

Balan Gurumoorthy	Indian Institute of Science, India

Steering Committee

Debasish Dutta	Purdue University, USA (Chair)
Abdelaziz Bouras	Qatar University, Qatar
Balan Gurumoorthy	Indian Institute of Science, India
Chris McMahon	University of Bristol, UK
Henk Jan Pels	Technische Universiteit Eindhoven, The Netherlands
Louis Rivest	ETS, Montreal, Canada
Klaus-Dieter Thoben	BIBA University of Bremen, Germany

Program Chairs

Shuichi Fukuda	Keio University, Japan
Alain Bernard	Ecole Centrale de Nantes, France

Program Committee

El Abderrazak	Ouafi UQAR, Canada
Rober Amor	University of Auckland, New Zealand
Romeo Bandinelli	University of Florence, Italy
Alain Bernard	Ecole Centrale de Nantes, France
Nikolaos Bilalis	Technical University of Crete, Greece
Abdelaziz Bouras	Qatar University, Qatar
Manfred Breit	University of Applied Sciences and Arts Northwestern FHNW, Switzerland

Nopasit Chakpitak	Chiang Mai University, Thailand
Jonathan Corney	University of Strathclyde, UK
Umberto Cugini	Politecnico di Milano, Italy
Jean-Christophe Cuillière	UQTR, Canada
Steve Culley	University of Bath, UK
Frédéric Demoly	Université de Technologie de Belfort-Montbéliard, France
Namchul Do	Gyeongsang National University, South Korea
Debasish Dutta	Purdue University, USA
Waguih ElMaraghy	University of Windsor, Canada
Benoit Eynard	Université de Technologie de Compiègne, France
Sebti Foufou	Qatar University, Qatar
Shuichi Fukuda	Keio University, Japan
Augustin Gakwaya	Université de Laval, Canada
Marco Garetti	Politecnico di Milano, Italy
Michele Germani	Università Politecnica delle Marche, Italy
Walid Ghie	UQAT, Canada
Samuel Gomes	Belfort-Montbéliard University of Technology UTBM, France
Ning Gu	University of Newcastle, Australia
Balan Gurumoorthy	Indian Institute of Science, India
Nathan Hartman	William Purdue University, USA
Sébastien Henry	Université Lumière Lyon 2, France
Paul C. Hong	University of Toledo, USA
George Huang	University of Hong Kong, Hong Kong
Greg Huet	Ecole Polytechnique Montreal et Bombardier Aéronautique, Canada
Jafar Jamshidi	University of Coventry, UK
Hannu Kärkkäinen	Tampere University of Technology, Finland
Yves Keraron	KRCF, France
Dimitris Kiritsis	EPFL Lausanne, Switzerland
Samir Lamouri	Arts et Metiers ParisTech, France
Florent Laroche	Ecole Centrale de Nantes, France
Julien Le Duigou	Université de Technologie de Compiègne, France
Sang Hu Lee	Kookmin University, South Korea
Jiping Li	Dalian Polytechnic University, China
Jong Gyun Lim	Samsung Electronics Co., South Korea
Borhen Louhichi	ETS Montréal, Canada
Wen Lu	National University of Singapore, Singapore
Richard Malak	Texas A&M University, USA
Johan L. Malmqvist	Chalmers University of Technology, Sweden

Tuomo Uotila	LUT, Finland
Sandor Vajna	Magdeburg University, Germany
Darli Vieira	QTR, Canada
Jennifer Whyte	University of Reading, UK
Paul Witherell	NIST, USA
Bob Young	Loughborough University, UK
Yong Zeng	Concordia University, Canada
Linda Zhang	IESEG School of Management, France
Yufeng Zhang	Cambridge University, UK

Local Organizing Committee

Takashi Maeno	Keio University (Chair), Japan
Masaru Nakano	Keio University, Japan
Hidekazu Nishimura	Keio University, Japan
Hideki Aoyama	Keio University, Japan

Table of Contents

Design and Education

Naval Engineering and Shipbuilding

Aeronautical and Automotive Engineering

Industry and Consumer Products

Interoperability, Integration, Configuration, Systems Engineering

Change Management and Maturity

Knowledge Engineering

Knowledge Management

Service and Manufacturing

New PLM

Building Information Modeling (BIM) for Facilities Management – Literature Review and Future Needs

Mehmet Yalcinkaya and Vishal Singh

Department of Civil and Structural Engineering, Aalto University, Finland
{mehmet.yalcinkaya,vishal.singh}@aalto.fi

Abstract. Facilities management (FM) is a discipline comprising of various operations, activities and maintenance services to support the main functions of an in-use building or facility. It demands comprehensive sets of information about the facility. While various FM information systems are currently being used to manage such information, the multifarious graphical and non-graphical information stored in Building Information Models (BIM) from the pre-use phase have not been sufficiently integrated in existing FM systems. BIM, with its visualization, interoperability and information exchange capabilities, can streamline FM activities. Hence, use of BIM for FM has gained global research interest. This paper analyzes this trend based on qualitative analysis of the state- of-art literature on the topic. In particular, this paper scrutinizes the nature of BIM and FM within their variety of functions and interactions. The analysis concentrates on the value-adding potential of BIM and reports the findings to designate the benefits of BIM for FM, and assess potential challenges that are hindering the effective use of BIM in FM.

Keywords: Building information modeling (BIM), facilities management (FM), asset management (AM).

1 Introduction and Background

The operation and maintenance phase of a construction project is the main trigger that increases the total life-cycle cost. Studies show that the total life-cycle cost of a project is five to seven times higher than the initial investment costs [1] and three times higher than the construction cost [2]. According to National Institute of Standards and Technology (NIST), the lack of interoperability among various model-based applications cost $15.8 billion, of which, $10.6 billion (two-thirds) of this cost is attributed to O&M phase [3]. The majority of building information traditionally comes from paper based documents. The handover of information takes several weeks for collection of relevant and up-to-date information [5]. Another NIST report states that "an inordinate amount of time is spent locating and verifying specific facility and project information from previous activities.

S. Fukuda et al. (Eds.): PLM 2014, IFIP AICT 442, pp. 1–10, 2014.

Much valuable data associated with the design, construction, and operation of a facility is lost during its life span" [9]. Therefore, information is the most emerging necessity for FM [4], since it requires tremendous amount of information for efficient O&M of the facilities [5, 6, 7]. Further, facility managers encounter the issue of quality and timely-access to information for O&M activities [8], and the need for more efficient methods to manage the information [5].

In BIM a digital representation of the building process can be used to facilitate the exchange and interoperability of information in digital format [10]. It is expected that the BIM data is captured and used across the entire project life-cycle. While BIM has been predominantly used in design and construction purposes for many years due to its visualization and coordination capabilities, there is an ascending interest in professionals to use BIM in FM activities. Whatever graphical and non-graphical data of the facility is collected in BIM during the project life-cycle can be used for various FM activities such as commissioning and close out, quality control, energy management, and maintenance and repair [11]. While there are other computer aided facilities management (CAFM) applications in which various data related with space management, assets, move management, O&M is created, updated, and pushed for FM activities, the sources of information in these systems vary during the project life-cycle, leaving information handover processes inefficient [11]. BIM, in that case, has the potential to be a catalyst to improve efficiency by establishing the relationships between FM and other disciplines.

Although BIM is emerging and gaining acceptance in design and construction phases [11, 12], a recent survey of UK construction industry [13] suggests that only 39% of construction professionals are using BIM, only 54% are aware of BIM, three quarters of people believe that industry is not clear enough about BIM, and only 27% of people trust BIM. Moreover, a recent global market research shows that 36% of the BIM-using contractors are currently in the low and medium level BIM engagement whilst 11% are at a very high BIM engagement level [14]. There are some pioneering organizations that push the usage of BIM for FM. However, people still have been unable to recognize and quantify the benefits of BIM for FM [13]. The requirements for successfully utilizing BIM for FM are not clearly understood [11] in terms of interactions and interrelations between BIM and FM. This paper reviews BIM and FM literature to understand their functions, interrelations and interactions. The review focuses on identifying the gaps, and assessing the value adding potential and potential challenges in using of BIM for FM.

2 Data Collection and Research Methodology

The source of research data is the collection of academic papers from various construction science, information technologies, and facilities management journals; technical reports from research institutes; book chapters; theses and dissertation studies; conference proceedings, and; white papers and newsletters from leading BIM software companies. These papers and articles were classified in terms of BIM, FM and BIM based FM (BIM&FM) literature. Therefore the interactions of the papers from different backgrounds were identified during the qualitative analysis. A sample tabular representation of literature tracking is presented in Table.1. The findings reported in this paper are based on qualitative analysis. Keywords were assigned to the reviewed papers based on their focus and main contents. The analysis should highlight which BIM issues come more often for FM? What are the gaps? And, what are the key concepts and potential research areas?

Table 1. Sample tabular representation of literature tracking and review

Number	Document Type	Keywords	BIM	FM	BIM&FM
1	Journal Paper	Lifecycle, Benefits of BIM, Building Design, etc.			•
2	Book Chapter	Early Integration, FM Practices. etc.		•	
...	...	...			

The second step of the analysis is classification of the keywords with respect to the assigned paper's discipline (BIM, FM or BIM&FM), Table 2. Therefore, the frequency of each assigned keywords is distributed for each discipline. This step of the analysis would show the associated subjects of papers and missing gaps of BIM implementation in FM.

Table 2. Distribution of keywords across different subjects

Keywords/Frequency	Total	BIM	FM	BIM&FM
Information Exchange/Sharing	23	3	2	18
Lifecycle	14	2	2	10
...	...	...	...	...

3 Results from the Analysis

Initially 98 documents were reviewed under disciplines of BIM, FM and BIM&FM. After the completion of review, the documents were re-evaluated and 11 of them were eliminated as they contributed very little to the topic. Thus the content analysis was performed on 87 papers. During the review, 57 keywords were identified and assigned to the papers.

Distribution of keywords based on Table 1: Figure 1 shows the frequency of occurrence of keywords across all disciplines. As shown in Figure 1, information exchange/sharing, life-cycle, data integration/interoperability, maintenance practices, early integration to facility design and decision support are the most frequently discussed keywords in the reviewed literature. Most frequent keywords were determined by percentile assessment, and the keywords with less than 50 percentile were not considered for discussion in this paper.

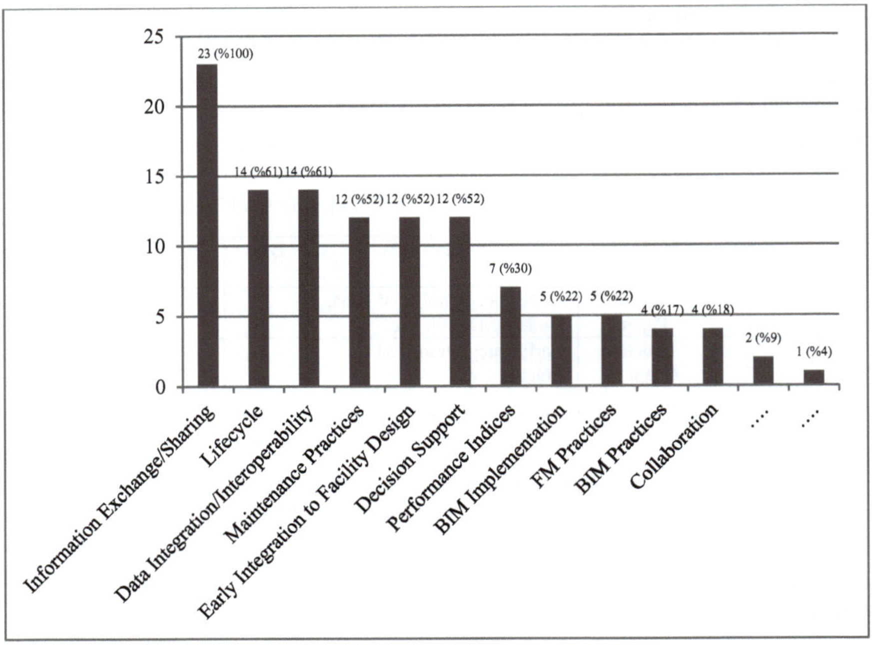

Fig. 1. Frequency of assigned keywords to the documents

Keywords vs. Discipline based on Table 2: Based on the analysis using Table 2, the frequency of assigned keywords and interrelations between each discipline is presented in Figure 2.

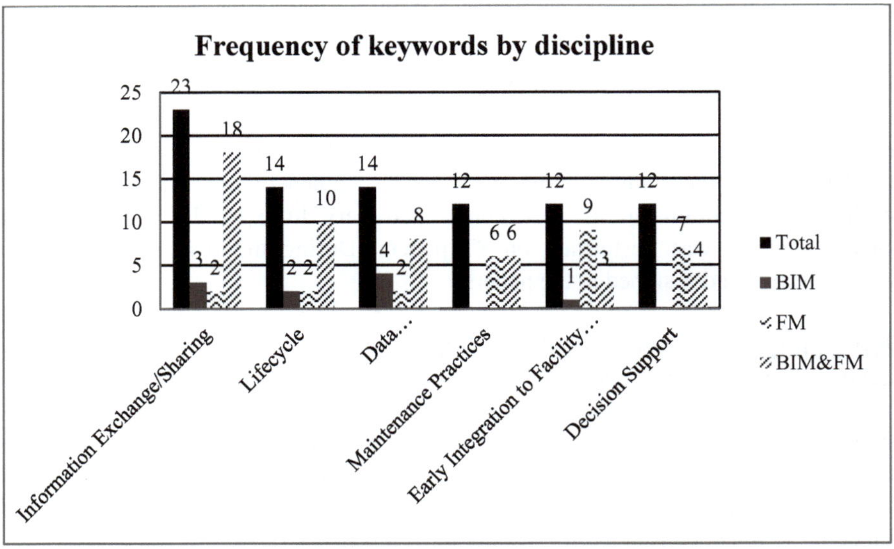

Fig. 2. Keywords and interrelations with each discipline

Table 3 shows the overlap of keywords across these disciplines. The numbers shown in parentheses represent the frequency of the keywords. For example "Data Integration/Interoperability (4-2)" in row two, column three, indicates that the keyword "Data Integration/Interoperability" was assigned four times to BIM based papers, and two times to FM based paper.

Table 3. Interrelations of different disciplines for assigned keywords

	BIM	FM	BIM & FM
BIM		Data Integration/Interoperability (4-2) Decision Support (1-7) Information Exchange/Sharing (3-2) Life-Cycle (2-2)	Data Integration/Interoperability (4-8) Decision Support (1-4) Information Exchange/Sharing (3-18) Life-Cycle (2-10)
FM			Data Integration/Interoperability (2-8) Decision Support (5-4) Early Integration to Facility Design (9-3) Information Exchange/Sharing (1-18) Life-Cycle (2-10) Maintenance Practices (6-6)
BIM&FM			

As shown in Table 3 when BIM and FM literature is compared, the keywords "*data integration/interoperability*" (4) in BIM; and "*decision support*" (7) in FM are the most frequent ones. When BIM and BIM&FM literature is compared, the keywords "*data integration/interoperability*" (4) in BIM; and "*information exchange/sharing*" (18) in BIM&FM are the most frequent ones. Finally when FM and BIM&FM literature is compared, the keywords "*early integration to facility design*" (9) in FM; and "*information exchange/sharing*" (18) in BIM&FM are the most frequent ones.

4 Keywords and the Reported Issues

Information Exchange and Transfer: Interoperability and Decision Making

BIM can be considered as a product, a process and a FM life-cycle management tool. Therefore, it is important for organizations to look at what they want out from BIM, and how. For an organization that implements FM functions and wants to use BIM in FM practices, it needs to consider several aspects connected to processes and usage of BIM prior to implementation. The findings of this review are directed towards identifying the basic minimum requirements to facilitate BIM for FM.

The data integration and information exchange for FM is mostly based on the integration of different IT tools. CAFM systems commonly use and integrate various building information. However, the re-usability of data in CAFM systems and the fragmented nature of construction industry make the information transfer challenging [18]. To overcome this problem, such systems which can integrate 3D BIM models and FM information in a database are being developed [18] as a knowledge-based BIM system [19] that enables better decision making. Since existing CAFM systems have inadequate capabilities and functions for collecting the building information pushed from various stakeholders and different phases of the project life-cycle, BIM based applications are being developed to simultaneously collect the data from different stakeholders and transfer this information to the facility manager in a cloud environment [20] to enable the mobility of facility manager during the FM activities. For such FM functions, BIM can act as a virtual database application. However, BIM is not enough by itself to collect and transfer the facility data simultaneously. To overcome this BIM systems need to integrate and communicate with technologies such as radio frequency identification (RFID). RFID provides wireless sensor technology to track and monitor the assets and building environment. The integration of RFID systems with BIM applications [21] through database servers and cloud services [22] provides access to the run-time data of the assets in a facility via either desktop or mobile devices.

A construction project involves different applications for various tasks such as architectural modeling, engineering analysis, and construction management. Despite technological advancements, the existing BIM systems or other IT based software applications are mostly implemented in isolation. There is also a lack of interoperability between systems. Therefore, sharing the data in such a heterogeneous environment becomes complicated. In addition, it is still not clear which facility data should be transferred by whom, when the related data should be transferred, and how [11]. To overcome this problem in terms of technology and strategy, several studies have been reported in the literature. A common interoperable computational environment such as extensible markup language (XML) has been proposed to facilitate the exchange, transfer, archival and re- usability of facility data through different database and software systems, and web-based environments [23]. However, XML may not be adequate for the all practices of construction industry which rely on several processes, people and products. The development of industry foundation classes (IFC) began in 1990s and it is still on going. IFC provides a framework for the digital representation of building design, engineering, construction, and operation data to facilitate information exchange between different BIM software. However, the information that is transferred with IFC contains lots of other information which are not needed for FM activities. Therefore, it should be filtered and modified for FM purposes. In response to this need to filter the information, the COBie (construction buildings information exchange) specification was developed to provide a structure for the lifecycle capture and delivery of facility information needed for FM purposes [24].

COBie is a simplified non-geometric subset of IFC [14] and can be created in IFC format or Excel [25]. COBie data includes rooms (spaces) and zones of the facility, equipment and its location, submittals, instructions, tests, certificates, maintenance, safety and emergency plans, start-up and shut-down procedure and resource data for the related activities [11]. Although there is an agreement about the requirement of COBie for structuring the facility data [26], COBie does not provide details on what information is to be provided, when, and by whom [27], and it has been found to be complex and unclear to use [28, 29]. At the same time, FMie (facility management information exchange) specifications are being developed by buildingSMART to link and exchange facility information more efficiently with the latest version of IFC [30].

Traditionally, the focus has been on the data that is created or updated during design and construction phases, but for effective FM practices, as-built data is needed. An accurate as-built model of the existing facility meets the owner's requirements and provides the best value [31]. The technology to produce as-built data (e.g. 3D laser scanning) needs to be integrated with other FM technologies and transferred through BIM process. Most existing technologies are not able to satisfy the integration and interoperability requirements between different systems.

Early Integration to Facilities Design

Successful implementation of FM functions depends on the identification of major requirements, functions and communications of the development at the earliest possible time [32]. Facilities design comprises the details of structural, architectural and MEP disciplines which elicit graphical and non-graphical information about the related facility. Considering the principle "begin with the final process in mind"; and FM needs and integration of owner/end-user and facility manager at the early design could potentially be worthwhile for the FM activities [33].

Another common subject mentioned in literature is the early integration of FM process to facilities design. Early engagement of FM could potentially reduce the needs for major repairs and alterations that will otherwise occur at the operational phase [34, 35] and will add value to the facility by establishing less rework and efficient control for supply chain. Facility managers have to identify the components' location and get access to the attributes and data relevant documents and maintenance information of the components. However, due to difficulty of altering the main structure and core service areas in the operational phase, it is hard to implement design process by considering operational conditions; and also most of the time designers do not care much about the factors in building maintenance [36]. Facility managers should also provide past maintenance information of facilities for the design team as a feedback. Since facility managers have a daily contact with users and obtain in-depth knowledge about the special needs for the facility, a knowledge transfer framework should be developed based on a combination of knowledge push from building operation, knowledge pull from building design [37]; and assumptions and specific facility requirements that are used as the input of design process [38]. The framework should also identify client's/end-user's organizational objectives while seeking to maximize the operational efficiency of the facility. The benefits of the integration of facility manager to facility design can decrease the cost of procurement due to reduction of rework in design and construction. Since the end-user/client requirements should be considered during the early phases, the facility can be better suited and more responsive to the needs, more attractive to potential users. BIM can be used as a potential tool. Implementation of BIM throughout design and construction stages, with the owners' and facility managers' data requirements in mind could provide an opportunity for facility managers [11]. However, one of the biggest challenges for BIM enabled FM practices is to define these data requirements, and to identify by whom and when the data should be provided through the project lifecycle. Although the data requirements are defined in the early phases, it is hard to follow these requirements due to dynamic and fragmented nature of a construction project. In addition to data requirements, interoperability and automated electronic data delivery are important for leveraging BIM in FM. Recent studies have attempted to clarify the information requirements and information transfer frameworks for facilities and asset management [39, 40]. However, the companies should configure and adopt their existing management strategies with respect to these frameworks for the individual projects. Recent developments such as COBie [26] and FMie [30] facilitate and provide solutions to transfer up-to-date facility information from different phases of the project lifecycle. Apart from them, CAD technologies, building automation systems (BAS) and CAFM tools are other potential systems to collect and transfer the required FM information between maintenance and operation, and design phases [41]. Another challenge can be summarized with the cost issue. During the construction of a facility, the client/end-user looks for the most cost effective solutions. This situation may make the design considerations and actions which are evaluated by facility manager, less important. Therefore, facility managers may become less powerful than the decision makers during the facility design. This can be explained with the contradiction between commercial priorities of the client and the operational requirements of the facility [42].

5 Conclusion

BIM practices for planning, design and construction phases have been discussed and researched in the literature. Understanding the existing status of BIM for FM with the challenges and value-adding potential is fundamental at the early stage of a project. In this paper, the challenges and important aspects of BIM for FM are analyzed through a literature review. The findings from the review provide evidence that there is an agreement about the value and potential of BIM in FM. This research shows that the value of BIM in FM practices are mainly for:

- Automated data process and information transfer from the early stages of the project to the operation and maintenance phases,
- Increasing the efficiency of work orders and decision making process by access to real-time as well as previously stored graphical and non- graphical data.

However, there are several challenges that are hindering the effective use of BIM in FM. These include:

- The interoperability between BIM and different FM (CAFM, BAS, etc.) technologies
- The lack of clear requirements for the implementation of BIM in FM through early stages of the project
- Despite the documentation in [39] and [40], challenges exist in identifying clear roles, responsibilities and collaboration requirements of project team to provide and exchange the necessary information due to the traditional implementation practices and the adoption process
- Integration of as-built information with BIM and FM technologies
- Complexity and limitations of information exchange frameworks such as COBie that need to be clearer and more usable.

Among the other issues, due to the evolving nature of the BIM for FM field, and the different structures in the existing FM technologies, organizations should not fit their FM processes to suit a particular technology for decision making which would otherwise result in a continuous effort of adaptation. Instead, they should define the dynamics of their FM strategies and adapt the related specifications of BIM aspects, which suit their individual organizational and operational strategies.

References

[1] Lee, S.-K., An, H.-K., Yu, J.-H.: An Extension of the Technology Acceptance Model for BIM-based FM. In: Construction Research Congress 2012 Construction Challenges in a Flat World, ASCE, pp. 602–611 (2012)

[2] BIM Task Group. The Government Soft Landings Policy (2012), http://www.bimtaskgroup.org/gsl-policy-2 (accessed January 12, 2014)

[3] N. GCR, Cost analysis of inadequate interoperability in the US capital facilities industry, National Institute of Standards and Technology (NIST) (2004)

[4] Atkin, B., Brooks, A.: Total facilities management (2009), http://Wiley.com

[5] Teicholz, P.: BIM for Facility Managers (2013), http://Wiley.com

[6] Wang, Y., Wang, X., Wang, J., Yung, P., Jun, G.: Engagement of Facilities Management in Design Stage through BIM: Framework and a Case Study. Adv. in Civ. Engg. 13, 1–8 (2013)

[7] Janus, K.: The relationship between FM and IT. In: May, M., Williams, G. (eds.) The Facility Managers Guide to Information Technology, IFMA 2012, pp. 1–3 (2012)

[8] Sabol, L.: BIM Technology for FM. In: Teicholz, P. (ed.) BIM for Facility Managers, 1st edn., pp. 17–45. John Wiley & Sons, New Jersey (2013)

[9] NIST, Cost analysis of inadequate interoperability in the U.S capital and facilities industry, http://fire.nist.gov/bfrlpubs/build04/art022.html (accessed December 23, 2013)

[10] Eastman, C., Teicholz, P., Sacks, R., Liston, K.: BIM handbook: A guide to building information modeling for owners, managers, designers, engineers and contractors (2011), http://Wiley.com

[11] Becerik-Gerber, B., Jazizadeh, F., Li, N., Calis, G.: Application areas and data requirements for BIM-enabled facilities management. Journal of Construction Engineering and Management 138(3), 431–442 (2011)

[12] Sabol, L.: Building Information Modelling and Facility Management, Design and Construction Strategies, http://dcstrategies.net/files/2_sabol_bim_facility.pdf (accessed: September 21, 2013)

[13] NBS National BIM Report (2013), http://www.thenbs.com/pdfs/NBS-NationlBIMReport2013-single.pdf (accessed: May 17, 2013)

[14] McGrawHill Smart Market Report (2013), http://bradleybim.files.wordpress.com/2014/01/2014_business_value_of_bim_for_construction_in_global_markets_smr_2014_.pdf (accessed January 25, 2014)

[15] Lane, T.: Tune in to BIM for FM (2013), http://www.building.co.uk/bim/bim-in-practice/tune-in-to-bim-fm/5055672.article (accessed October 23, 2013)

[16] BIM-FM Workshop. Aalto University, Civil and Structural Engineering, BIM Research Initiative, Espoo-Finland (2013), https://wiki.aalto.fi/display/ABIM/BIM+and+Facilities+Management (accessed January 12, 2014)

[17] Madritsch, T., May, M.: Successful IT implementation in facility management. Facilities 27(11/12), 429–444 (2009)

[18] Motawa, I., Almarshad, A.: A knowledge-based BIM system for building maintenance. Automation in Construction 29, 173–182 (2013)

[19] Wang, S., Xie, J.: Integrating Building Management System and facilities management on the Internet. Automation in Construction 11(6), 707–715 (2002)

[20] Jiao, Y., Wang, Y., Zhang, S., Li, Y., Yang, B., Yuan, L.: A cloud approach to unified lifecycle data management in architecture, engineering, construction and facilities management: Integrating BIMs and SNS. Advanced Engineering Informatics (2012)

[21] Shen, W., Hao, Q., Xue, Y.: A loosely coupled system integration approach for decision support in facility management and maintenance. Automation in Construction 25, 41–48 (2012)

[22] Ko, C.-H.: RFID-based building maintenance system. Automation in Construction 18(3), 275–284 (2009)
[23] Teague, T., Palmer, M.E., Jackson, R.: XML for Capital Facilities. Leadership and Management in Engineering 3(2), 82–85 (2003)
[24] East, E.W., Nisbet, N.: Analysis of life-cycle information exchange. In: Tizani, W. (ed.) Proceedings of the International Conference on Computing in Civil and Building Engineering, vol. 30 (2010)
[25] Sabol, L.: BIM Technology for FM. In: Teicholz, P. (ed.) BIM for Facility Managers, 1st edn., pp. 17–45. John Wiley & Sons, New Jersey (2013)
[26] Open BIM Network. "Open BIM focus" – COBie, issue 4 (October 2012)
[27] East, E.W., Carrasquillo-Mangual, M.: The COBie Guide: a commentary to the NBIMS-US COBie standard. Engineering Research Dev. Center, Champaign, IL, U.S (2013)
[28] Anderson, A., Marsters, A., Dossick, C., Neff, G.: Construction to Operations Exchange: Challenges of Implementing COBie and BIM in a Large Owner Organization. Construction Research Congress, 688–697 (2012)
[29] Gnanaredham, M., Jayasena, H.S.: Ability of BIM to satisfy CAFM information requirement. In: The Second World Construction Symposium 2013: Socio-Economic Sustainability in Construction (2013), http://suranga.net/publications/2013_bim_cafm.pdf (accessed: June 9, 2014)
[30] Facility Management information exchange (FMie) (2012), http://www.nbef.no/fileadmin/Styret/Styremoeter/Styremoete-2012-2/120302FMie-Project-proposal_Rev_0_9_STS.pdf (accessed: January 5, 2014)
[31] Woo, J., Wilsmann, J., Kang, D.: Use of as-built building information modeling. Construction Research Congress 1, 538–547 (2010)
[32] Edum-Fotwe, F.T., Egbu, C., Gibb, A.: Designing facilities management needs into infrastructure projects: case from a major hospital. Journal of Performance of Constructed Facilities 17(1), 43–50 (2003)
[33] Kasprzak, C., Ramesh, A., Dubler, C.: Developing Standards to Assess the Quality of BIM Criteria for Facilities Management, AEI 2013@ sBuilding Solutions for Architectural Engineering, ASCE, pp. 680–690
[34] Jaunzens, D.: Adding value through facilities management, http://projects.bre.co.uk/design/Download/management.PDF (accessed: January 18, 2014)
[35] Nutt, B., McLennan, P.: Facility management: risks and opportunities, Blackwell Sc. (2000)
[36] Arditi, D., Nawakorawit, M.: Designing buildings for maintenance: designers' perspective. Journal of Architectural Engineering 5(4), 107–116 (1999)
[37] Jensen, P.A.: Design interaction of facilities management: a challenge of knowledge transfer. Architectural Engineering and Design Management Journal 5, 124–135 (2009)
[38] Erdener, E.: Linking programming and design with facilities management. Journal of Performance of Constructed Facilities 17(1), 4–8 (2003)
[39] BIM Task Group, Employer's information requirements core content and guidance notes, http://www.bimtaskgroup.org/wp-content/uploads/2013/04/Employers-Information-Requirements-Core-Content-and-Guidance.pdf. (accessed June 03, 2014)
[40] British Standards Institute, Specification for information management for the operational phase of assets using building information modelling, http://shop.bsigroup.com/upload/Construction_downloads/PAS1192-3%20final%20bookmarked.pdf (accessed June 03, 2014)
[41] Bröchner, J.: Integrated development of facilities design and services. Journal of Performance of Constructed Facilities 17(1), 19–23 (2003)
[42] Enoma, A.: The role of facilities management at the design stage, http://www.arcom.ac.uk/-docs/proceedings/ar2005-0421-0430_Enoma.pdf (accessed August 10, 2014)

Maintenance of Facilities and Aircrafts: A Comparison of IT-Driven Solutions

Karoliina Parhiala[1], Mehmet Yalcinkaya[2], and Vishal Singh[2]

[1] Aalto Design Factory, Aalto University, Finland
[2] Department of Civil and Structural Engineering, Aalto University, Finland
{karoliina.parhiala,mehmet.yalcinkaya,vishal.singh}@aalto.fi

Abstract. Building Information Modeling (BIM) can significantly impact both new as well as existing architecture/engineering/construction (AEC) projects. It can provide a virtually simulated and large integrated database that can be leveraged not only in design and engineering, but also in planning and management operations, and facilities maintenance. Although most of the BIM tools are now mature enough to use in various phases of project lifecycle, they have been primitive and under-developed for many years. The concepts underpinning BIM have been around since the 1960s through various manufacturing industries such as automotive, ship building or aerospace. In the aerospace industry, especially in aircraft design and manufacturing, the concept similar to BIM is a Digital Mock-Up (DMU). It is both a tool and a product of engineering. As in BIM, aircraft's DMU is also a comprehensive digital product representation that is used to simulate the use, behavior and performance of a finished aircraft. While BIM and DMU are used for different industries and products, they do share similarities and differences. This paper briefly describes BIM and DMU technologies and their context, specifically focusing on implementation of these two technologies for operation and maintenance (O&M).

Keywords: Building Information Modeling, BIM, Digital Mockup, DMU, Configured Digital Mockup, cDMU, Maintenance.

1 Introduction

From the phases of the lifecycle of any type of manufacturing project, the operations and maintenance (O&M) phase is the longest one and is expected to cover previous costs of its lifecycle phases and to produce profits for its owner. O&M could be defined as "*all actions that have the objective of retaining or restoring an item in or to a state in which it can perform its required function to ensure related business operations are efficient in terms of using the optimum resource as needed, and meeting customer requirements. These actions include the combination of all technical and corresponding administrative, managerial and supervision activities*" [1]. O&M services include different activities with respect to the nature of the related industry. The critical aspect to achieve the objectives of O&M services is information management and application of state-of-art technologies to the related industry.

S. Fukuda et al. (Eds.): PLM 2014, IFIP AICT 442, pp. 11–20, 2014.

This paper presents two state-of-art IT-driven approaches towards product lifecycle management (PLM); Building Information Modeling (BIM), specifically developed for architectural/engineering/construction (AEC) and Digital Mock-Up (DMU) applied in mechanical engineering, especially in aviation industry. The paper describes BIM and DMU technologies and presents logical and functional similarities of them in product development and finally focuses to implementation of these two systems for O&M phase of the associated products' lifecycle, especially to the maintenance of these products.

2 IT-Driven Solutions for PLM: DMU and BIM

a Digital Mockup (DMU)

Digital Mock-Up is a **terminology** used for 3D representation of a product. It is **composed of** *3D Models,* Computer Aided Design (CAD) native and/or visualization data, and *Configuration Metadata.* The metadata is *Product Structure* with parent-child relations and positioning information, and *Attributes* for lifecycle management. Attributes are all the business and technical information of the product. This means that besides including the data of products' parts, it holds information at least on *work sharing, industrial flow, regulations of authorities, change process and configuration management.* DMU is more than a CAD file. DMU integrates data from engineering, manufacturing and maintenance, and uses the data to simulate various industrial processes, uses, behavior and performance of the finished product [2].

Barring a few exceptions, e.g. [2], there are limited academic studies on DMU, and nearly all of the knowledge on DMU comes from aviation industry. Most outspoken on **using DMU** in their product development process has been the aircraft manufacturer Airbus S.A.S [3]. Therefore, the concept of DMU is presented through an example of DMU at Airbus. For Airbus, DMU is the **source of all the original product information** and the **binding reference** in all Airbus's operations. But first of all, it was created to service the design and engineering processes. Everybody, inside and outside Airbus, subcontractors and suppliers are to be working with

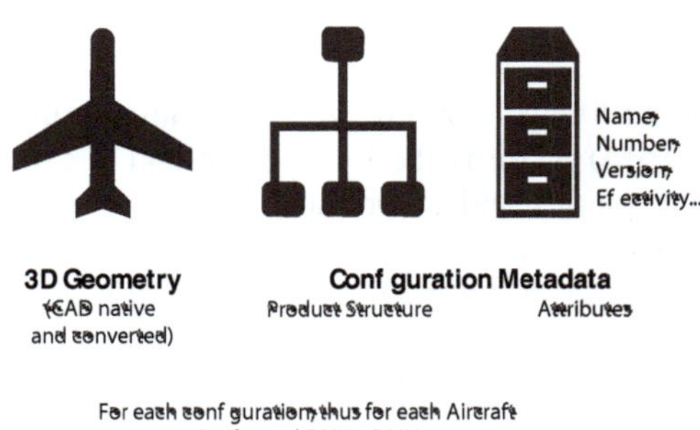

Fig. 1. Definition of the Configured Digital Mock-Up at Airbus [4]

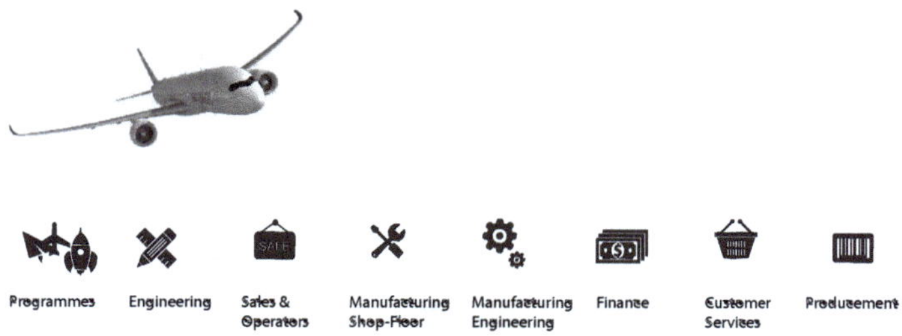

Fig. 2. Different disciplines extract their views from the Aircraft [3]

the same DMU, from the same, shared database and access the latest information possible [4]. DMU at Airbus is presented in the figure 1. The DMU can be accessed through several different views. This way, the user can not only access the data that is relevant to his/her work, but the connection of the data still remains within the product structure. [5] Different views are represented in Figure 2.

DMU starts at the design phase from where on, the whole lifecycle of the aircraft can be envisioned [5]. It is used for aircraft representation, assist the communication and decision making throughout whole lifecycle of the aircraft. With the DMU, different kinds of scenarios to visualize and test various design solutions, for example cockpit ergonomics, are created. For aircraft performance and structural analysis, the DMU provides behavior simulations already in the early stages of the development. To reduce physical prototypes to minimum, the DMU is utilized to simulate and optimize the work in manufacturing factories, validate the transport concept and plan the final assembly line. [4]

For each product configuration, hence each aircraft configuration, the DMU is called *Configured Digital Mock-Up* (cDMU). As customers are usually ordering more than one aircraft with the same configuration, the first configured and manufactured aircraft of the order is called ***Head of Version*** (HoV). Aircraft manufactured later with the same configuration are copies of the HoV. The cDMU is designed only for HoV, but then copied and linked to all aircraft with the same configuration. This results that every aircraft manufactured has its own cDMU [4].

b Building Information Modeling (BIM)

BIM represents both the technology as well as the process of digital representation of a facility through the use of object-oriented, data-rich, models potentially across the planning, design, construction and operation phases of the facility. In that sense, unlike DMU with its clear meaning, the **terminology** BIM is interchangeably used to represent the digital representation (Building Information Model), the process (Building Information Modelling), and increasingly the approach to managing the technology and the process (Building Information Management). Nonetheless, the BIM model can be viewed, extracted and analyzed by different stakeholders and user groups to manage, simulate and analyze various aspects of the project for improved decision making, operations and maintenance of the facility [6, 7].

BIM model is also composed of *3D Models,* native CAD files and/or visualization data, and *Configuration Metadata.* The metadata is *Product Structure* with parent-child relations and positioning information, and *Attributes* that are the main identifiers for model management such as object types, ownership and history. BIM also allows additional Attributes to be added, which can include information about the business and technical information of the objects. This means that besides including the geometric and specifications of the objects in the model, it is possible to add information that can be intelligently used for workflow management, procurement and regulations by defining relationships between such attributes. However, **unlike DMU** such attributes and information on *work sharing, industrial flow, regulations of authorities, change process and configuration management* are rarely, if ever, included in current BIM models. Thus, BIM can be configured and modified regarding the project/task requirements with the potential support of external software and hardware.

Similar to DMU, BIM is expected to be the **source of all the project information** linked through a shared database. It is expected that in an ideal BIM project the different stakeholders such as the designers, client, contractors, subcontractors and suppliers can with a shared BIM model and access the latest information possible [8]. The use of a shared database in BIM ensures that the different model views and data can be checked and updated for consistency [9].The model can be used to demonstrate the entire building lifecycle from conceptual design to demolition (Figure 3) [10]. Thus, materials' quantity takeoff can be extracted, work definitions and sequences can be defined, so the actual construction progress can be simulated in a virtual environment [11].

However, unlike the **Airbus example**, where Airbus is clearly the client, manager and coordinator of the DMU through the development stages, the fragmented nature of the construction industry means that the handling of BIM model is much more fragmented and complex in the construction sector. The issues of ownership and management of BIM model across the different phases remain unclear to most players in the industry. As a result, when compared to the role of Airbus in the development DMU, the following generic points can be stated about BIM: (1) BIM discussion has exploded as much in academic research in construction as it has gained the attention of the industry, (2) The role of clients as champions of BIM is critical to the implementation and use of BIM in practice [12], (3) Unlike, the aerospace industry that has very few, but dominant global players, in the fragmented construction sector the government agencies, regulatory authorities and public clients across different regions have also had to play an important role in **binding** the use of BIM across different phases of construction projects in the corresponding regions [13].

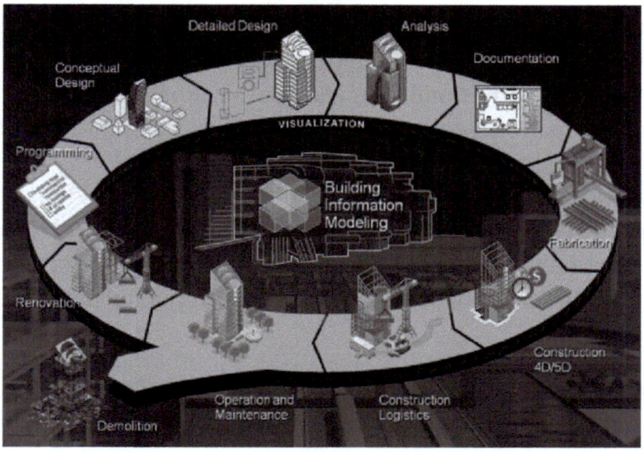

Fig. 3. BIM implementation through building lifecycle [10]

The discussion on **versioning** aspect of DMU and cDMU also highlights the following key differences in the context and scope of BIM in construction sector, vis-à-vis the use of DMU in the aerospace sector: (1) Unlike the aerospace sector, designs in construction projects are typically unique and rarely re-used for multiple instances. This means the concepts of Model Versions in BIM are entirely different to Model Versions in DMU. Instead, versioning in BIM is typically associated with aspects such as levels of detail (LOD), solution alternatives and different stages of model development, (2) Since versioning in BIM is more about model coordination within the same project rather than across different instances of the product, instead of the concept of ***Head of Versions***, typically the concepts of ***Reference Models*** is used in BIM development. Typically the *Reference Model* from one discipline is used to coordinate the models of all the other disciplines to ensure version compatibility, and (3) Unlike the aerospace industry where the DMU can be directly used as for fabrication, the lack of automation from design to fabrication in construction industry means that the *Reference Models* typically vary across the different phases of the construction projects. In the design phase, the architecture model is typically the *Reference Model*, while in the construction phase, the construction model may become the *Reference Model*. Similarly, it is expected that the as-built model of a facility should become the *Reference Model* in the maintenance phase. However, the use of as-built models is rare in practice. The lack of automation between design and fabrication also explains why the LOD is an important aspect of BIM models, because a very BIM model may not always be necessary or desirable [14].

In summary, on conceptual level both DMU and BIM are identical in their object-oriented approach, but the differences between them result from the context and products they are created, which have their own metadata requirements. However, the benefits of both IT-solutions in product development are similar, which are fundamentally derived from the way in which the user groups can contribute to the shared data model, and edit information [10] [3]. The most common benefits of DMU [3] [5] and BIM [11] include:

- Improved coordination in design through visualized object-oriented data technology which enables improved design management and change control
- Ability to perform simulation and optimization products' performance
- Ability to perform cost performance analysis and cost impact of any change in design and manufacturing process
- Reduction in manufacturing risks through identification of manufacturability issues early in the design process, early detection of clashes and simulating the cost and time effect of any change in design process.
- Creation of operation and Maintenance information database

3 Use of Models in Maintenance of End Product

a. Aircraft Continuing Airworthiness Management

Aircraft continuing airworthiness is managed by Continuing Airworthiness Management Organization (CAMO). As stated in European Aviation Safety Agency's aviation directives for maintenance organizations [15], *"Continuing Airworthiness means all of the processes ensuring that, at any time in its operating life, the aircraft complies with the airworthiness requirements in force and is in a condition for safe operation"*. CAMO usually is the operator of the aircraft, whether the aircraft is owned or leased. The organization itself is not responsible for the actual maintenance work, but ensures that all needed maintenance and repairs are performed as demanded. Actual maintenance work is done by authority approved maintenance organization [16].

Aircraft maintenance consists of scheduled and unscheduled maintenance. Unscheduled maintenance is corrective maintenance; repairs of defects. Scheduled maintenances aim is to prevent decline of the aircrafts airworthiness. Scheduling is based on aircraft's flight hours, flight cycles and overall time in service [17]. To have the ability to execute the maintenance to secure aircraft's airworthiness, a wide set of data on aircraft and its maintenance procedures is needed. This data can be divided to maintenance data, and aircraft configuration and condition data. *Maintenance data* is the collection of documents to regulate and guide the aircraft maintenance. It includes aviation authority issued requirements, airworthiness directives and technical data provided by OEM. *Aircraft configuration and condition data* is general identification information on aircraft and components installed on it. It describes the status of airworthiness directives and history of defects, maintenances and modifications. Records of operational data are also part of aircraft's condition information [5]. Regulated by the authorities [18], the OEM provided technical data should be followed, as shown in Table 1:

Table 1. OEM Technical data to be provided, as per the regulations [18]

Aircraft Description	Instructions for maintenance	Operation
Aircraft specifications to that detailed level that the maintenance can be carried out properly **Descriptions and installations** of aircrafts products and systems Structural pictures of aircraft with allowable working areas and access plates **Information for structural fasteners**	**Aircraft servicing information**, including access points, tools and materials Information for maintenance scheduling for each part of the aircraft, with frequency and extent of the maintenance activities Airworthiness limitations for damage-tolerance and fatigue evaluation **Dissembling and assembling information** of parts in the aircraft Troubleshooting instructions for malfunctions **Detailed instructions for special inspection methods**, like non-destructive testing Protective treatments after inspections Electrical wiring interconnection systems continued airworthiness instructions List of tools needed	Aircrafts operation and control instructions with procedures in special situations Instructions for ground operations, weighting and balancing

DMU in Aircraft Maintenance

The subject of utilizing the DMU in aircraft maintenance, or any product maintenance, has not been widely addressed. To open a discussion on how the DMU could be deployed in aircraft continuing airworthiness management, a master's thesis was written on the topic. The thesis approaches the topic from user's point of view by conducting interviews with two CAMOs [5]. Results of that thesis are presented here.

Data management to secure aircraft continuing airworthiness isn't a new subject; it is a mandatory requirement from aviation authorities. For that reason, sophisticated maintenance management software have been developed and used to manage aircraft configuration and condition, and maintenance data. However, current challenge with those data, especially OEM provided technical data, is that it represents aircrafts in parts. Having a full 3D-model of the whole aircraft would enable the aircraft parts to be examined in their actual context, the aircraft. This visual and spatial information gives better view on the part locations and access to them. Better visualization improves accuracy of maintenance planning and troubleshooting by facilitating the location of components, estimation of man-hours for maintenance tasks, and analysis of potential defects. This would reduce Aircraft on Ground (AOG) -time and make CAMO's operations more efficient.

The key challenges to the deployment of DMU in aircraft airworthiness management are limited resources, competence, time and money. To be able to use DMU as a reliable reference, it should be kept updated so as to correspond to the aircraft configuration and condition at any given point of the aircraft's lifecycle. Another challenge arises from the ownership of the DMU and that the DMU is the core competence and intellectual property of the OEM.

b. Facilities Maintenance

Facilities maintenance is the continuous process of service provision required to maintain a facility and its environment through its service life. These services encompass the entire activities required to assure that the built environment will perform the functions for which a facility was designed and constructed [19]. O&M phase of a construction project typically includes scheduled, preventive and emergency maintenance activities of major building systems. Managing the maintenance of facilities can be difficult on the O&M phase owing to various types of equipment and facilities. Furthermore, it is inconvenient for maintenance staff to maintain those facilities by relying on paper-based documents.

In contrast to the aviation industry, which has the legal obligation to regulate the maintenance of both private and passenger aircrafts and their lifecycle information, such practices and regulations are not common in construction industry. Although many governmental organizations have the responsibility to maintain their buildings, there is no obligation to maintain private buildings. Nonetheless, manuals and strategic maintenance guidelines may be agreed upon through contractual agreement between the owner and contractor. These manuals and guides typically describe the basic information requirements for effective maintenance activities, such as:

- Architectural and structural components of the facility like ceiling surfaces, floor coverings, roofing, and walls.
- Design details, floor plans, spaces and zones, and as-built drawings.
- Environmental considerations, required tools and equipment for safety issues, safety instructions of building systems.
- Equipment lists, descriptions, maintenance and repair guides, operation manuals.
- Preventive maintenance schedules, procedures, logs, troubleshooting guides, removal and replacement instructions of building systems, warranty information.
- Operation instructions of building systems, operation logbooks, start-up and shut-down procedures, emergency operating instructions.
- Descriptions of all systems in buildings, assembly and components diagram, utility connections and cutoff plans.

The listed information requirements are rarely applied to that extent, because of the difficulties to structure and digitally hand them over to a centralized source. As reported by National Institute of Standards and Technology (NIST), "an inordinate amount of time is spent locating and verifying specific facility information from previous activities. Much valuable data associated with the design, construction and operation of a facility is lost during its lifecycle" [20].

BIM in Facilities Maintenance

BIM can provide a shared resource and information sets about a facility's structure, functions and technical systems (mechanical, electrical, plumbing, lighting, etc.), including product manufacturers, if available and added to the model. However, construction contracts rarely stipulate providing or using these potential information in BIM models for maintenance activities, and hence, there are very cases on the actual use of BIM for facilities management. Instead, there are many other technologies that can also exchange the facility data. Building automation systems (BAS) or Building Management Systems (BMS) most often handle the operation of building mechanical, electrical, plumbing (MEP) and lightening systems. Integrated Work Management Systems (IWMS) or Computerized Maintenance Management Systems (CMMS) support maintenance activities, work orders, space management, personnel management, etc. However, the exchange and re-usability of the data in these systems and the fragmented nature of AEC industry make the information transfer among project stakeholders challenging, especially through BIM [21].

Therefore, an important point for the success of BIM for facilities maintenance activities is an accurate and structured specification of the BIM data and interoperability of BIM and maintenance software. Construction Operations Building Information Exchange (COBie) has been developed for O&M data handover [22]. COBie is a rapidly evolving standard to capture information, such as zones, rooms (spaces), equipment and components, tests and certificates, safety and emergency plans, start-up and shut-down procedures, etc. in BIM electronically during design and construction, to provide it to facility managers in a spreadsheet format. It can potentially eliminate the inefficient process of transferring large amounts of paper based documents or electronic data within facility management systems (CMMS, BAS, etc.). To establish the common practice and adoption of BIM-based maintenance management, contractual agreements are needed to stipulate the use and update of COBie data by the project stakeholders. In addition, the COBie standards and templates need further maturity and integration with different BIM applications.

4 Conclusion

This paper presents a comparison of BIM and DMU, two different IT-driven solutions applied in AEC and aviation industry respectively. In this paper O&M phase of the specified industries' products (buildings and aircrafts) are reviewed, and BIM and DMU's value adding functions are discussed. It is proposed that even if the industries and their related domains/products are different, both BIM and DMU apply similar functions for their individual products. However, it is important to understand and analyze the specific circumstances during each domain's lifecycle to figure out the specific needs, strategies to apply related IT-driven solutions. For both solutions, number of issues and potential improvements arise in 3D visualization and data management features of related software applications. Potential improvements by means of visualization, data collection/updating and information transfer may ease the BIM/DMU based activities during lifecycle, and make it more efficient.

Future work should include the application of both BIM and DMU for different phases of the lifecycle by highlighting specific workflow issues. Since O&M phase of both industries include various types of data coming from design and production/construction phases, the specific information requirements for O&M should be clarified and data/information transfer between these phases may also be a potential area to search.

References

[1] European Federation of National Maintenance Societies, http://www.efnms.org/

[2] Dolezal, W.R.: Success Factors for Digital Mock-ups (DMU) in complex Aerospace Product Development. Technische Universität München, Genehmigten Dissertation, Munich, Germany (2008)

[3] Airbus SAS, Setting new standards with the A350 XWB Digital Mock-Up, http://videos.airbus.com/video/dc6bd25e7f3s.html (accessed: January 11, 2014)

[4] Parhiala, K.M.: Utilising Configured Digital Mock-Up in Aircraft Continuing Airworthiness Management. Aalto University School of Engineering, Master's Thesis, Espoo, Finland (2014)

[5] Garbade, R., Dolezal, W.R.: DMU@ Airbus—Evolution of the Digital Mock-up (DMU) at Airbus to the Centre of Aircraft Development. In: The Future of Product Development, pp. 3–12. Springer, Heidelberg (2007)

[6] Associated General Contractors of America. The Contractor's Guide to BIM, 1st edn., http://www.engr.psu.edu/ae/thesis/portfolios/2008/tjs288/Research/AGC_GuideToBIM.pdf (accessed: October 14, 2013)

[7] Innovation, CRC Construction. Adopting BIM for facilities management: Solutions for managing the Sydney Opera House. Cooperative Research Center for Construction Innovation, Brisbane, Australia (2007)

[8] Singh, V., Gu, N., Wang, X.: A theoretical framework of a BIM-based multi-disciplinary collaboration platform. Automation in Construction 20(2), 134–144 (2011)

[9] Dispenza, K.: The daily life of building information modeling (BIM), http://buildipedia.com/aec-pros/design-news/the-daily-life-of-building-information-modeling-bim (accessed: January 25, 2014)

[10] Khemlani, L.: Top criteria for BIM solutions, http://www.aecbytes.com/feature/2007/BIMSurveyReport.html (accessed: September 6, 2013)

[11] Coates, P., Arayici, Y., Koskela, K., Kagioglou, M., Usher, C., O'Reilly, K.: The key performance indicators of the BIM implementation process. In: The International Conference on Computing in Civil and Building Engineering, Nothingham, UK, June 30-July 2 (2010)

[12] Gu, N., London, K.: Understanding and facilitating BIM adoption in the AEC industry. Automation in Construction 19(8), 988–999 (2010)

[13] Maintenance Organisation Approvals – PART-145. Acceptable Means of Compliance and Guidance Material. Luxembourg: European Aviation Safety Agency (2012) ISBN 978-92-9210-121-3

[14] Continuing Airworthiness Requirements – PART-M. Acceptable Means of Compliance and Guidance Material. Luxembourg: European Aviation Safety Agency (2012) ISBN-13 978-92-9210-123-7

[15] Aubin, B.R.: Aircraft Maintenance: The art and science of keeping aircraft safe. In: Society of Automotive Engineers, Warrendale, PA (2004)

[16] Certification Specifications and Acceptable Means of Compliance for Large Aeroplanes. CS-25. Luxembourg: European Aviation Safety Agency, June 14, 2012 (2013)

[17] Whole Building Design Guide, Facilities operation&maintenance, http://www.wbdg.org/om/om.php (accessed: January 19, 2014)

[18] NIST, Cost analysis of inadequate interoperability in the U.S capital and facilities industry, http://fire.nist.gov/bfrlpubs/build04/art022.html (accessed December 23, 2013)

[19] Madritsch, T., May, M.: Successful IT implementation in facility management. Facilities 27(11/12), 429–444 (2009)

[20] East, W.: bSa Construction Operations Building Information Exchange (COBIE): Means and Methods, The National Institute of Building Sciences (2012)

Towards a BIM Approach for a High Performance Renovation of Apartment Buildings

M. Aldanondo[1,*], A. Barco-Santa[1], E.Vareilles[1], M. Falcon[2], P. Gaborit[1], and L. Zhang[3]

[1] Toulouse University – Mines Albi, Albi, France
[2] TBC Générateur d'Innovation, Colomiers, France
[3] IESEG Business School Paris, France
michel.aldanondo@mines-albi.fr

Abstract. Building renovation is a key issue for energy saving in the future. The goal of this article is to show how this traditional activity can be industrialized thanks to a BIM supported process. The critical needs are explained and the proposed BIM presented.

Keywords: BIM, Energy renovation, Industrialization, Process, Design.

1 Introduction

The goal of this communication is to present the first elements that allow to set up a Building Information Model (BIM) and associated process for the renovation of apartment buildings that target high energy performance. This modeling problem appears in a large French multi-partner project called CRIBA that aims to industrialize building renovation in order to reduce energy consumption. In a second section the critical needs of renovation and relevant BIM will be explained and justified. Then the main ideas of the renovation solution proposed by the CRIBA project will be presented in a third section. The fourth section deals with the modeling propositions for the BIM.

2 BIM for Renovation: A Set of Various Cascading Needs

We present and characterize the renovation needs in a first step. Then the reasons that push towards the industrialization of the renovation process are explained. Finally the relevant BIM need is introduced.

2.1 Need for High Energy Performance Renovation

The global contribution from buildings (residential and commercial) towards energy consumption has steadily increased. Buildings account for around 20% and 40% of the total final energy consumption in developed countries: 37% in the EU [1], 36% in the USA [2] and 31% in Japan [3]. Nowadays, it has exceeded industry and

* Corresponding author.

S. Fukuda et al. (Eds.): PLM 2014, IFIP AICT 442, pp. 21–30, 2014.

transportation sectors. Growth in population, enhancement of building services and comfort levels, together with the rise in time spent inside buildings assure the upward trend in energy demand will continue in the foreseeable future. Reducing energy consumption of the building sector is therefore one of our century challenges.

In several countries, research works are carried out on the efficient measures to take in order to reduce energy consumption of the building stock. Most states set regulations to improve the energy performance of new buildings. Huge progresses have been realized in the materials and in the building processes. Thus it is now possible to build very low consumption buildings at reasonable costs. However, the annual rate of construction of new dwellings is only 1.1% in Europe [4]. At current rates, it would take nearly a hundred years to upgrade the energy efficiency of the existing building stock. It is therefore indispensable to renovate the existing buildings to reduce their energy consumption.

2.2 Need for the Industrialization of the Renovation Process

Nowadays, energy-efficiency renovation activities are currently still at the craftsman stage. Most of the time, the measurement are taken on site, then the materials are cut on demand directly on the building site in order to fit. The frames (windows, doors, solar modules...) are adjusted on site with waste of materials. Finally, cladding is attached according to the architect expectations. Most of these activities are achieved on the building site with a very low degree of anticipation. As a result, the effectiveness of the working site is low, the energy efficiency of the renovation is questionable and renovation costs tend to increase.

If you consider for example that there are about 20 million apartments in France, half of which were built before 1975 (when the first energy regulation was issued), that means that there are around 400 000 energy-inefficient buildings to renovate. Given these figures, it is clear that the building renovation process cannot remain at the craftsman stage and needs to be considered as an industrial activity. The main idea behind this industrialization is to distinguish: the existing building analysis, the renovation design, and the components production, from the renovation assembly on the building site. This allows to design, to prepare and to produce all the renovation components in factories with some anticipation allowing waste reduction and some optimization concerns. Then, all components are moved towards the building site for renovation assembly with a minimum of adjustments or fitting.

2.3 Need for a BIM to Support the Renovation Process

The industrialization need and the volume of renovations under consideration require three key elements:

- A technical concept allowing insulation by the assembly of off-the-shelf modular components with a minimum of specific components,
- A chain of stakeholders including renovation owner, renovation designers, architects, modular component suppliers, and on the building site installation teams,
- A digital engineering chain that can provide aiding tool for supporting each task of the renovation process [5].

We mean by digital engineering the entire chain of digital tools, ranging from initial scans and building analyses (required before renovation for measurement and specification of the existing building) up to the detailed plans of the renovated building (once renovation has been carried out) which will be supplied to the owner or building managers for maintenance and future adaptations.

Given this goal, it is obvious that the renovation process is collaborative. Thus all the stakeholders will need to share data, information and knowledge at the various steps of the renovation process. Furthermore, as explained in [6] most of the times they will want to use their own specific software tool (scanning package, computer aided design, finite elements, heating simulation, cost estimators, computer aided manufacturing, transport optimization, project manager…). In order to guaranty a minimum of consistency, it is necessary to share a same renovation model between all the stakeholders and therefore to support the whole process with a Building Information Modeling software (BIM software) [6]. Although if numerous studies have examined these tools for new builds, very few have looked at their use in renovation, however [5] or [7] can be consulted. Thus the goal of this article is to propose the first modeling elements relevant to a BIM dedicated to the renovation of apartment buildings that target high energy performance. This is achieved with respect to the key propositions relevant to BIM solutions like Open BIM, 4D or 5D-BIM as explained in [8]. Naturally these modeling elements are strongly dependent of the technical concepts used for renovation. Thus, the third section will present the renovation concept of the CRIBA project and the fourth one the modeling propositions.

The technical concept is quickly described, and then the compromise associated to the each specific solution design is discussed. Finally the renovation process is described introducing the BIM need.

3 The Proposed Technical Concept and Relevant Process

The technical concept is quickly described and then a compromise associated to the each specific solution design is discussed. Finally the renovation process is described introducing the BIM need.

3.1 Proposed Technical Concept

This industrialization is based on an external new thermal envelope which wraps the whole buildings. The envelope is composed of prefabricated rectangular multi-functional panels and fastener devices that are used to fix the panels on the facade. In this article we do not consider the technical concept associated to the roof and relevant modeling elements.

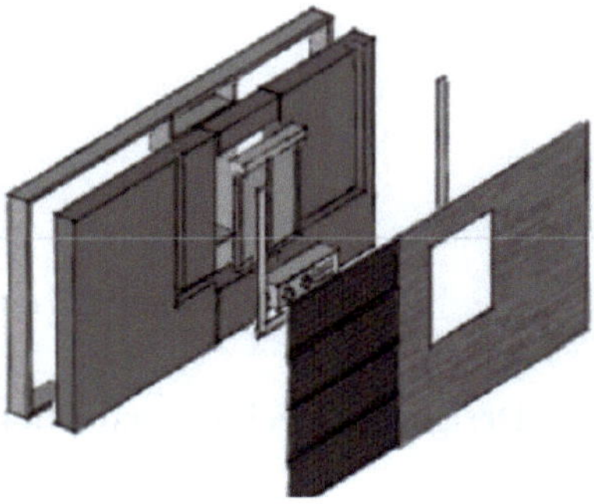

Fig. 1. Technical concept

A multi-functional panel includes a wood structure, insulation material, and cladding. Some of them, as shown in Fig. 1, may include windows, doors, solar modules and even balconies (all these elements are call from now frames). The length of these panels can vary between 1 and up to 13 meters while the width is between 1 and 3 meters. These sizes limits result from the transportation and manufacturing constraints. Two types of fastener devices can be used. When the facade is of good quality, meaning that it can be loaded, each panel is attached on two (and up to four) single fasteners that are themselves directly fixed on the wall as on the upper part of figure 2. This kind of single fastener varies according to their load bearing capacity and the distance between the facade and the panels. When the facade is not strong enough, each panel is attached on a vertical metal profiles that runs all along the facade thanks to a simple fastener as on the lower part of Fig. 2. The metallic profile is attached to the wall with previous single fasteners. In some hard situations, metallic profiles may require concrete foundations. To give an order of magnitude a panel weight can vary between 200 kgs and 2000 kgs mainly according to size, thickness and cladding.

The main interests of this concept are: (i) it can be adapted to any facade quality, (ii) renovation can be processed with people remaining living in the building, (iii) insulation quality and thickness selections allow using this concept with various climate conditions.

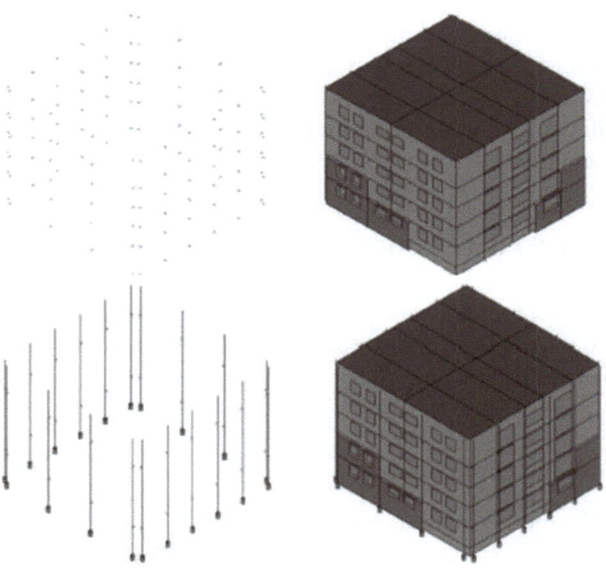

Fig. 2. Fasteners for good and poor quality facade

3.2 Designing Specific Renovation

Each renovation problem is specific and each renovation design is a kind of compromise. In order to minimize the average heat transfer coefficient of the façade, quantified in W/(m^2•K), it is necessary to design panels as large as possible. Because energy waste is mainly concentrated around joins between panels. But when panels become large, their weight become high also and the facade is not always able to support them. Thus designing a specific renovation is often a compromise between panel sizes and fastener devices or how to maximize energy efficiency while respecting the facade acceptable load. Given these elements, the renovation process can be now described and discussed.

3.3 Proposed Renovation Process and Identification of BIM Stakeholders

The renovation process can be decomposed in the five sub-processes (Sp-i) starting with first dimension analysis up to renovation reception by the building owner.

Sp-1: Building geometry generation.

On the existing building the first sub process consists of getting the building geometry. Most of the time laser scanning techniques are used and produce a raw cloud of points representing the building. This cloud is processed thanks to more or less autonomous techniques and provides a first building model with a reference plane for each facade and a set of various plane shapes. This step is critical for model accuracy and renovation quality because all downstream activities rely on this first building model. Then a human user or geometry designer enriches this model. He annotates the shapes according to three types:

- Frames gathering: windows, doors, balconies that will be included in the panel,
- Object that will cross the panel: electrical boxes, antenna… that will require a hole in the panel,
- Object that will be taken off the facade before renovation assembly and attached again after as: rain gutters, street lights... They will be included in the preparation and in the finish operations of the 5th sub-process.

Sp-2: Building analysis and renovation requirement characterization.

This sub process collects and adds four sets of information's to the previous geometry thanks to various stakeholders:

- First the robustness of the facade is analyzed by a structure expert. The reference plane of the facade is split in the three kinds of rectangles: load-bearing wall, slab nosing, and remaining areas as shown in Fig. 3. Each rectangle is analyzed in order to provide an acceptable load that will be used for fastener positioning. Each rectangle is annotated with an acceptable load and a platitude characteristic.
- Secondly the actual heat transfer performance level for each of the previous rectangle is measured with some kind of infra-red devices. This will be used for the definition of the heat transfer coefficient of the panel and relevant insulation characteristics.

Fig. 3. Structure analysis

- Thirdly, requirement or goal in terms of heat transfer coefficient is provided for each facade building. This will of course affect the selection of insulation thickness and type but also the frame energy performances.
- Lastly, requirements in terms of panel cladding must be collected. They can affect panel weight but also panel dimensions.

Sp-3: Renovation specific design.
Given previous information, it is now possible to define or more accurately configure the renovation. As explained in [9] renovation specific design can be considered and solved as a configuration problem. This sub-process generates two results:

- A bill of material of the renovation gathering the parameterized components fasteners and panels with dimensions, positions and all specific properties,
- An assembly process describing all the operations necessary to the assembly sequence that should be followed on the building site.

Sp-4: Production or manufacturing of the components of the specific renovation.
Following the previous step, the component suppliers (panels and fasteners) finalized the detailed design (with detailed BOM for the panel) and manufacture the parameterized component. They also prepare the packaging for transportation.

Sp-5: Renovation assembly on building site.
This sub-process is the most critical. If previous sub-processes have been undertaken correctly, it should ran smoothly, if not it will be necessary adjust and modify supplied components. Six kinds of task have to be planned:

- Facade preparation, removing object that must be taken off and facade cleaning,
- Transportation of fastener devices,
- Fixing all fasteners (with metallic profile if necessary) on the facade,
- Transportation of panel according to assembly sequence,
- Panel assembly on already fixed fasteners,
- Facade finish, some gasket can be added, fixing object that were removed.

Of course the sub-processes Sp-4 and Sp-5 must overlap in order to avoid huge panel inventory. A hard and not easy scheduling problem exists here. Finally after the renovation assembly, the reception by the building owner can occur and the maintenance of the building with its new renovation can start. Of course panel can be damaged and of course changed if necessary. It is clear that all this process must be supported by a BIM software and relevant model. The final section proposes adequate modeling elements.

4 BIM Propositions

BIM propositions are attached to each façade. Thus before detailing the façade, we first present how upper level objects of the hierarchy are defined.

4.1 Main Objects from Building site to the Facade

Four levels of abstraction are considered providing four objects that take part in the renovation. Some properties are attached to each of them.

- Working site: Is the bigger spatial division in the renovation. It is commonly referred by a name and brings attached crucial aspects for the renovation process, e.g., accessibility constraints and weather. Such entity is divided into blocks. A working site is characterized by: (i) a wind level, (ii) a level of accessibility for heavy truck..
- Block: Is a set of buildings which are usually attached by a common wall. A block has also accessibility constraints which as the same time has an impact on the panel sizes possibilities.
- Building: This is the actual place where apartment are arranged. It is the host of several facades and has dimensions (height and width). It is also characterized with space availability in order to park a truck or for some inventory purposes.
- Facade: A facade is a composition of apartments along with its doors, windows and so on. A reference plane (introduced in section 3.) will be attached to each façade..

These four elements are characterized by various referential and coordinate. We consider in the following the reference plane of the facade.

4.2 BIM Information and Knowledge

Five sets of information and knowledge (IK-i) are attached to each façade. They are associated with the five previous sub-processes.

IK-1: <u>Initial façade geometry</u> that can contain:

- IK-1.1 is the cloud of points that can be obtained by laser scanning. If the geometry is provided with a CAD file, this first element is not necessary.
- IK-1.2 is the reference plane of the façade. This plane is either extracted from the cloud or from the CAD file. It is a vertical plane tangent to the façade at a minimum distance of 2 cm of the façade. This plane corresponds with the back of the panels or the back of the vertical metallic profiles. A referential is attached to each reference plane. The plane has the height and the width of the façade. For simplicity we assume rectangle facades.
- IK-1.3 is the set of frames. Each frame is characterized by a type with sub-types (windows, door, balcony…) dimensions (w,h) and positions (x,y) in the reference plane.
- IK-1.4 is the set of objects that will cross the panels. Each of them is characterized by a type (electrical boxes, antenna..), a 2D shape defined with a position (x,y) on the reference plane.
- IK-1.5 is the set of objects that will be taken off and attached to the panels. Each of them is characterized by a type (rain gutters, street lights...), a 2D shape defined with a position (x,y) on the reference plane and a weight because they will be supported by the panel.

IK-2: building analysis and renovation requirements that can contain

- IK-2.1: is a set of rectangles that corresponds with the intersection of load-bearing wall and slab.
- IK-2.2: is a set of rectangles that corresponds with the slab nosing minus IK-2.1.
- IK-2.3: is a set of rectangles that corresponds with the load-bearing wall minus IK-2.1.
- IK-2.4: is a set of rectangles that corresponds with the remaining areas of the façade.

Each rectangle of these four elements is characterized by:

- dimensions (h,l) and positions (x,y),
- an acceptable load per meter/square estimated by structure engineer,
- a (min,max) distance between reference plane and façade if a cloud is available extracted from the BIM,
- a heat transfer level measured or estimated by a thermic engineer.
- IK-2.5: is an expected global heat transfer level for the whole façade, it is a requirement established by the owner and the thermic engineer. When you have this parameter for each façade, you can compute the global energy performance of the building.
- IK-2.6: is a set of rectangles (or sometimes shapes) provided by the architect that corresponds to the cladding of the façade. Cladding is characterized by a weight and sometime dimensions.

IK-3: Renovation description that represents all the component of the BOM of the renovation:

- IK-3.1: is a set of single fasteners (panel/façade, without metallic vertical profiles),
- IK-3.2: is a set of single fasteners (profile/facade, with metallic vertical profiles),
- IK-3.3: is a set of simple fasteners (panel/profile, with metallic vertical profiles),

All these fasteners are characterized by a type, positions (x,y), an acceptable load. Single fasteners have also a maximum acceptable overhang compatible with the distance between reference plane and facade.

- IK-3.4: is a set of vertical profiles, characterized by dimensions (x,y) and positions (x,y).
- IK-3.5: is a set of multi-functional panels, characterized by dimensions (x,y), panel thickness, positions (x,y), insulation type, and insulation thickness. If a frame is present: frame type (windows, door,...), dimensions (x,y) and positions (x,y). A panel is also characterized by its weight and its heat transfer coefficient.

Renovation description shows also the assembly process. Globally each physical component belonging to IK3-i (i=1to5) has an assembly order. This information can be processed with BIM-4D solutions in order to detect conflicts as explained in [10] It is admitted that for a façade, all fasteners must fixed before starting panel mounting.

IK-4: Component detailed descriptions are mainly used for panel and fastener detailed description that depends on the component suppliers. Detailed parametric CAD design of each component must be provided by the supplier. They will be scaled at the good dimensions and located at the good positions defined in IK3 and included in the BIM.

IK-5: Renovation assembly description is mainly used to describe where each physical component has been effectively mounted and if possible when. In a perfect world with no hazards, this information set should match IK-3 and IK-4.

The renovation process, the main stakeholders, the information and knowledge feeding the BIM are synthetized in the figure 4. The storage of information and knowledge is following the IFC standard [11] in order to offer, even if not full proof, some sharing and interoperability possibilities.

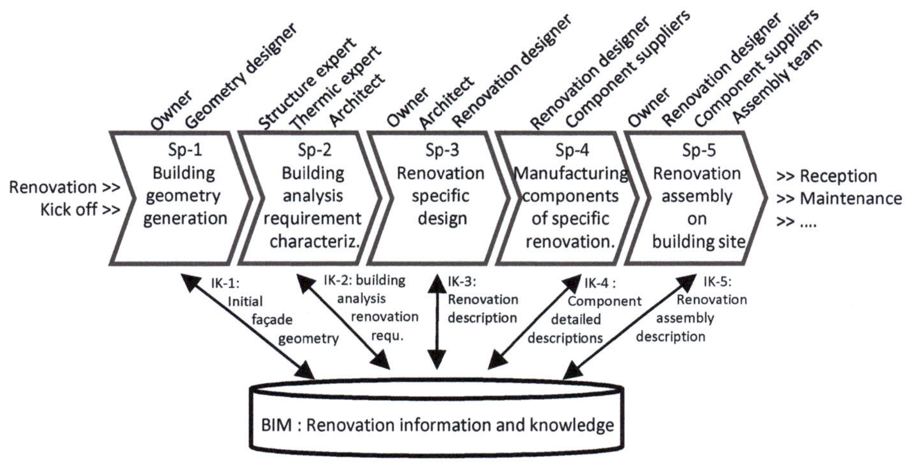

Fig. 4. Renovation process and relevant BIM

5 Conclusions

The goal of this article was to present the first elements allowing proposing a Building Information Model (BIM) and associated definition process for the renovation of apartment buildings that target high energy performance. The needs for energy renovation, industrialization of the renovation, digital engineering chain supported by BIM software have been explained. Then the technical concept defined during the CRIBA project for the renovation solution was presented. It is based on a set of off-the-shelf modular components (parametric or standard). Then the renovation process and associated information and knowledge have been proposed. At the present time, a numerical mockup of this engineering chain is in development and the renovation of a real working site gathering 4 blocks of 110 apartments will start this summer in the south of France.

References

1. Perez-Lombard, L., Ortiz, J., Pout, C.: A review on buildings energy consumption information. Energy and Buildings 40(3), 394–398 (2008)
2. U.S. Green Building Council. New Construction Reference Guide (2013)
3. The Energy Conservation Center. Energy Conservation Handbook. Japan (2012)
4. Poel, B., van Cruchten, G., Balaras, C.A.: Energy performance assessment of existing dwellings. Energy and Buildings 39(4), 393–403 (2007)
5. Juan, Y.K., Gao, P., Wang, J.: A hybrid decision support system for sustainable office building renovation and energy performance improvement. Energy and Buildings 42(3), 290–297 (2010)
6. Eastman, C., Teicholz, P., Sacks, R., Liston, K.: BIM Handbook, 2nd edn. Wiley (2011)
7. Martinaitis, V., Kazakevičius, E., Vitkauskas, A.: A two-factor method for appraising building renovation and energy efficiency improvement projects. Energy Policy 35(1), 192–201 (2007)
8. Popova, V., Juoceviciusa, V., Migilinskasa, D., Ustinovichiusa, L., Mikalauskasb, S.: The use of a virtual building design and construction model for developing an effective project concept in 5D environment. Automation in Construction 19, 357–367 (2010)
9. Vareilles, E., Langhoff, C., Falcon, M., Aldanondo, M.: Interactive configuration of high performance renovation of apartment buildings by the use of CSP. In: Proceedings of the 15th Int. Configuration Workshop, Vienna, Austria (2013)
10. Zhang, J.P., Hu, Z.Z.: BIM- and 4D-based integrated solution of analysis and management for conflicts and structural safety problems during construction: 1. Principles and Methodologies, Automation in Construction 20, 155–166 (2011)
11. Howard, R., Bjork, B.C.: Building information models-experts' views on BIM/IFC developments. In: Proceedings of the 24th CIB-W78 Conference, Maribo, Slovenia (2007)

Similar Concepts, Distinct Solutions, Common Problems: Learning from PLM and BIM Deployment

J.R. Jupp[1] and Vishal Singh[2]

[1] University of Technology, Sydney
[2] Aalto Univeristy
Julie.Jupp@uts.edu.au, Vishal.Singh@aalto.fi

Abstract. This paper describes the similarities and differences between Product Lifecycle Management and Building Information Modelling concepts, focusing on integration issues relative to their methods, information systems, effects and criticisms. In this literature based discussion, the authors show that the two concepts share fundamental similarities but are distinct in their scope and level of integration as well as maturity of process and workflow management. The paper highlights several common problems and aims to provide guidance for deployment initiatives.

Keywords: Building information modelling, product lifecycle management, business processes, information systems, information technologies.

1 Introduction

A variety of lifecycle management concepts enabled by advances in business process integration and information technology (IT) have been developed in various sectors. In manufacturing sectors, Product Lifecycle Management (PLM) has evolved to provide platforms for the creation, organization, and dissemination of product-related knowledge across the extended enterprise [1]. In the construction sector, a renewed focus on lifecycle processes is emerging within the BIM (building information modelling) paradigm, an object oriented approach to creating, managing and using construction project data. Whilst both are relatively new concepts, PLM stands as a more established approach, seeing steady uptake since the mid-1990s. BIM has only recently become the accepted term for the production and management of a built asset's information throughout design, construction and operations [2].

Recently comparisons have begun to relate PLM and BIM concepts, contrasting the functionalities and capabilities of their methods and systems, see [3, 4, 5]. These studies are beginning to examine their similarities and differences; however a number of open questions remain relative not only to their concepts, methods, and systems but also their intended effects and criticisms. In reviewing the literature, the authors present a comparative analysis that explores these questions to provide a broader account of PLM and BIM relative to the unique structural characteristics of each sector. The remainder of the paper is divided into four sections. Sections 2 and 3 review PLM and BIM concepts, information systems, effects and criticisms. Section 4 compares and discusses their main attributes and shared problems, before closing the paper with a discussion and summary of research contribution.

S. Fukuda et al. (Eds.): PLM 2014, IFIP AICT 442, pp. 31–40, 2014.

2 Product Lifecycle Management

Stark [6] broadly describes PLM as simply the activity of managing products effectively across their lifecycle. Understanding the evolution of PLM is helpful to expounding Stark's definition. Emerging from product data management (PDM), which provides data management capabilities [7, 8] PLM extends beyond the engineering aspects of a product to provide a shared platform for the creation, organization, and dissemination of all product-related knowledge across the extended enterprise [1]. PLM is thus a strategic business approach to the collaborative creation, management and exchange of product lifecycle information [9].

2.1 Concept and Methods

The general idea behind PLM is to serve up-to-date *data*, *information* and *knowledge* in a secure way to all people who are part of the product lifecycle [10]. Information is produced by a variety of participants at different levels of detail in diverse functions inside and outside a firm [11]. Complexity increases when moving from data towards knowledge, with data and information easier to store, describe, and manipulate [1]. The range of data, information and knowledge across an extended enterprise must be integrated correctly throughout the lifecycle. Various methods, systems and engineering tools are required to organize, store, access, convert and exchange these different forms correctly and seamlessly. Consequently generating appropriate data, information, and knowledge structures is critical [8]. IT infrastructure is therefore central to PLM, including hardware, software, and Internet technologies, and underlying representation and computing languages. In manufacturing industries, the product lifecycle is typically divided into three distinct phases: beginning/middle/end of life (BOL/MOL/EOL). PLM transverses these phases and assists a corporation and its extended enterprise in meeting functional- and data- level requirements [12]. Together numerous methods, systems and engineering tools form the systems architecture of a PLM solution. Currently, these are mostly deployed in the BOL phase to support design and development. However the application of IT in MOL and EOL phases is increasing as customer needs and technologies mature [10].

PLM functionality is achieved via 'system components', including the IT Infrastructure as well as a Product Information Modelling Architecture (PIMA), a Development Toolkit, and a set of Business Applications [11]. PIMA includes product ontology and interoperability standards. A development toolkit provides the means for building Business Applications and extends PLM functions to include kernels (e.g. geometry), visualization tools, data exchange standards and mechanisms, and databases. Business applications provide PLM functionalities to process corporate intellectual capital [11]. There are different types of functional- and data- level requirements of PLM system architectures. According to Jun [12], the *functional-level requirements* of PLM are defined by the large amounts of structured and unstructured data that are created, updated, transferred, removed, reused and stored in several application systems across the extended enterprise. The requirements for handling this include: real-time data acquisition, closed-loop information flow, interoperability between devices and application systems, integration with existing systems and services and the collaborative environment [12]. *Data-level requirements* relate to product and product-related data (e.g., business, maintenance and expiration data). For seamless interface between product and product-related data requirements surround the use of standardized data, data interoperability, product information traceability, data encryption, and user authentication [12].

2.2 Information Systems and Technologies

Depending on the level of integration, implementation and system architecture, the deployed information systems may include: Systems engineering (SE), Product design, Product and portfolio management (PPM), Engineering data management (EDM), Manufacturing process management (MPM), PDM, Enterprise resource planning (ERP) and and supply chain management (SCM). To limit the scope of this discussion, our review utilizes Crnkovic's PLM integration taxonomy [13] to rationalize the information systems utilized. Crnkovic defines three levels of integration: full, loose and no integration.

Full Integration: A package with all functions using common structures, data, user interfaces and application programming interfaces (APIs). The integration model has a layered architecture. The lowest tier is the data repository layer, which includes databases, file systems and information models [13]. The middle tier is the business layer, with tools and services to support business logic. The uppermost tier is the user interface layer. All layers are connected to each other using standardized APIs. A single database for all the data is superior in terms of data quality, because loss of data in exchange between systems is reduced and duplication is low [13].

Loose Integration: The different information systems operate more independently and store data in their own repositories. The information models in the repositories are different and can only be accessed from native tools. Information exchange between tools is carried out by additional interoperability functions. The advantage is that it does not require a common information model and enables the use of tools from different vendors. Disadvantages stem from the lack of a common information model, requiring interoperability functions, through middleware mechanisms acting as a 'middle layer' in PLM integration. Data inconsistencies pose a risk.

No Integration: All data transfers are done manually, increasing the risk of data inconsistencies, human error, and the lack of standardization in information models. The data update routines such as import and export functions need to be well defined.

2.3 Effects

As companies use PLM in different ways, the extent of its effects is contingent on the field of business and level of integration. The business case for PLM is usually linked to the reduction of operational level information systems and an increase in operational excellence [10]. Manufacturers can speed up the realization of complex products. Product engineers can shorten implementation and engineering change approval cycles across the extended design team. Purchasing agents can work more effectively with suppliers to reuse parts. Executives get a high-level view of all important information, from details of the manufacturing line to parts failure rates culled from warranty data and field information [14]. The effects of PLM may also include staff reduction, data integration, standardization, access to timely and complete information, improving customer service, creative and collaborative work methods; customization of products based on complex customer desires, lead-time reduction, prototype cost reduction, and reduction in late product changes [10].

PLM centres on the BOM (bill of materials), with methods, processes and legacy tools needing to be modular, follow standards and be reusable [11]. PLM integration must be flexible to react to changes in the market, organization structure, business processes, product and tools. Consequently data, processes and software should ideally be aggregated to reduce system complexity [15] and the use of open data standards is crucial. Numerous standards have emerged for the horizontal and vertical integration of PLM systems. MIMOSA and ISO are two leading bodies that develop such standards employed in PLM [31]. Examples include the STEP-*Standard for the exchange of product model data* (ISO 10303), covering data exchange through life. There are ongoing efforts to make STEP universally available using XML and UML standards. MIMOSA's OSA-EAI (OSA for Enterprise Application Integration) and OSA-CBM (Open System Architecture for Condition Based Maintenance) are also established and utilised [16].

2.4 Criticisms

There are several unique challenges related to business process and technological integration relative to the PLM concept, as documented in several case studies, see e.g., [10, 14, 15]. Many criticisms of PLM can be traced to: (a) failings in PLM technology; (b) 'elusive standard engineering processes' as the foundation for PLM; (c) organizational issues; and (d) dynamic environments.

Failings of PLM Technology: PLM solutions lack maturity; this is mostly due to high levels of technical complexity and incomplete data standards. Whilst PLM's functional footprint is improving, it is common to require multiple proprietary solutions to address each company's needs spanning the development lifecycle. PLM solutions are typically a complex collection of tools that are often loosely connected [15]. Depending on the overall architecture, the functionalities of systems and tools used might overlap causing redundancies, rework and data quality deterioration. Also, data standards and corporation-wide integration architectures are ongoing development activities and are not fully established [10, 15].

Elusive Standard Engineering Process: Whilst the development process may be viewed as standard across product groups and businesses, once details of how a company actually develops a product (how decisions are made, who is involved at various stages, how partner collaborations are executed, etc.), the nuances of a company's product development practices become visible [15]. The practices of seemingly similar product development and engineering processes can differ wildly across companies and between products developed in the same company.

Organizational Issues: Due to the diversity of engineering tools and subsystems there is a tendency to delegate PLM deployment to engineering executives, who traditionally manage technology rollouts [15]. This approach works for choosing point solutions, e.g., CAD tools, but studies show that it does not work well for enterprise-wide integration platforms [14, 15]. The main criticism being that different business functions generate and deal with product data in disparate ways. Related criticisms include: improper executive management expectations, frustrated end-users, high implementation costs, and evasive returns on investment [15].

Dynamic Environments: The systems and practices that underlie lifecycle management are continuing to undergo significant changes. New and emerging IT, rapid globalization of businesses, and evolving core functions such as collaborative design and outsourced manufacturing force companies to continually re-examine their product development practices, which can be costly and time consuming [6, 10].

3 Building Information Modeling

BIM is an object oriented approach to creating, managing and using various geometric and non-geometric data in a construction project. While conceptually BIM can be used across all the phases of a project lifecycle, starting from design to the demolition of the built environment, in practice, the level of integration and maturity of BIM usage across different phases is contingent on multiple factors defined relative to products (both the design artefact and tools), processes (e.g. operational, methodological, business, legal) and people (e.g. organizations, stakeholders, culture).

3.1 Concept and Methods

The evolution of BIM can be traced to simultaneous developments across CAD and information systems; both facilitated by progress in computing power, the emergence personal computers and the internet. The development of the BIM concept and methodology can be explained on the basis of four attributes: 1) representation, 2) information management, 3) inbuilt intelligence, analysis and simulation, and 4) workflow management.

Representation is integral to design, and it has driven the development of BIM in at least two ways. Firstly in terms of design cognition; as processing capabilities improved, computational tools moved from 2D drafting to 3D models, making visualization and working with complex geometries possible. This move from *symbolism to virtualization* initially led to photo-realistic renderings (based on solid geometry) and later to intelligent object-oriented models (replacing solid geometry). Second, at the level of communication and collaboration; representations used across multidisciplinary design teams demand greater specification of easily comprehended and disambiguated information. This requires higher levels of detail and accuracy in the geometric and non-geometric information contained in object-based models.

While representation and visualization is also part of documenting project-related information, it is equally important to be able to record, manage and use all other forms of building-related data, information and knowledge generated across the project lifecycle. Accordingly, document and information management capabilities that were developed in pre-BIM tools (as an independent set of specifications, documents and spreadsheets), have merged and evolved with BIM applications as information that is typically embedded, appended or linked to object-based models. Linking between all forms of geometric and non-geometric data is a critical aspect of BIM. Consequently, traditional users of electronic document management systems - such as contractors and project managers - have the expectation that BIM provides similar information management capabilities, with the added advantage of visualization. In construction, this typically takes the form of a BIM model server (see [17] for a discussion). Depending on the level of BIM implementation and maturity these systems may or may not be enabled in the project environment.

The object-oriented premise of BIM enables integration of CAD and information management capabilities. In doing so, it is possible to intelligently link different objects with relationships and constraints, allowing various forms of automated analysis and simulation, ranging from environmental and structural analysis to cost estimating and construction scheduling. Various forms of building compliance 'checks', such as interference and clash detection, are now common. Increasingly, BIM applications are becoming knowledge-based systems with more and more domain knowledge being integrated. Consequently, the number of BIM applications is expanding rapidly, each catering to different discipline-based requirements.

With the complexity, intelligence and number of BIM applications growing, information and workflow management is critical. Given the richness of building-related and project-related information it is desirable to design and plan the project and discipline-specific workflows. Design process optimization is receiving growing attention in recent efforts to model information flow and develop BIM workflow management frameworks, leading to new cloud-based approaches (see e.g., [19]).

3.2 Information Systems and Technologies

BIM shares many characteristics with PLM. The platforms supporting BIM resemble Crnkovic's [14] loose or no integration levels. Technologically, some of the key characteristics of BIM are: 1) Open data standards, 2) Centralised and decentralised BIM, 3) Information exchange standards, and 4) Data and information structures.

To achieve interoperability between BIM applications, open file formats such as the Industry Foundation Class (IFC) have been developed. IFC files can be viewed in most applications but modifications have to be undertaken in the native format and converted back to IFC. This process is error prone. Even if most geometric data can be completely exchanged, the intelligence is often lost in the transformation. Another information exchange method is sharing data through middleware or APIs, however this requires that different links are established between each application.

The BIM database can either be centralized or decentralized. In a centralized approach, information from e.g., a central IFC-based model must be exported, modified within a native format and imported back into the central model using IFCs. This 'roundtrip' is often not a viable option due to interoperability issues [20]. Singh *et al.* [17] highlight the challenges of system and sub-system integration in a centralized BIM-server approach. Due to this complexity, a decentralized, distributed information management approach is increasingly being considered [20]. In a decentralized approach, collaboration can occur at two levels: (1) within a single organisation or discipline using similar tools, and (2) across different discipline-specific models shared and combined using IFCs. IFC standardization has adopted a 'use case centred' approach [21]. Different use cases and information exchange requirements are specified in Information Delivery Manuals (IDM). IDMs together with other model management protocols have given rise to a variety of policy documents such as BIM Management, Coordination and Execution Plans [22].

Object-based building models include both non-modifiable internal data structures, and information structures that enable model management. NBIMS (National BIM Society) lists three potential reference standards that can be used to structure model information; IFC, as discussed above, the Construction Specifications Institute (CSI) OmniClassTM, and CSI IFDLibrary [23]. OmniClass provides a standardized basis for classifying information created and used by the North American AEC (Architectural, Engineering and Construction) industry. The IFD initiative, based on ISO standards and driven by buildingSMART, aims to find a way to create and catalogue a data dictionary of building objects and bring disparate sets of data into a common view of the construction project or asset. In addition to reference standards, a variety of *metadata* is also contained in the BIM model, e.g., information related to object creation and history. A recent development in BIM systems is towards distributed transactional models, e.g. the DRUM concept [20], which aims to create a mechanism to manage linked partial models such that building information can still be distributed.

3.3 Effects

Effects of BIM are visible both at micro (project and organization) and macro (industry and national) levels. The potential benefits of BIM are best exploited through collaborative engagement of different stakeholders from early stages of the project. Accordingly, new forms of project delivery practices are emerging such as Integrated Project Delivery (IPD) – an alliance-based relational contracting approach that aims to align the interests, benefits, roles, risks and responsibilities of all project stakeholder [24]; Big Room – a multidisciplinary BIM coordination office [25]; and 'knotworking' – occasional collocated and intense design sessions when distributed design teams physically get together to make rapid progress [26]. Furthermore, with increasing BIM maturity, its role and scope is expanding to different aspects and domains across the building lifecycle and specific topics for BIM, such as BIM for: facilities and operations management, lean construction, prefabrication, and safety.

At a macro level governments across many countries are mandating the use of BIM to facilitate productivity gains in the AEC sector. Among the various challenges in realizing these mandates is training enough BIM skilled and literate personnel.

3.4 Criticisms

BIM has received criticism on various issues, especially concerning, (1) data transfer and systems integration, (2) ill-defined terminology, scope and purpose, and (3) unstructured implementation processes.

Data Transfer and System Integration: There are gaps in using BIM smoothly between conceptual design to detail design, design model to construction model, as-designed to as-built data, etc. These interfaces need to be resolved for effective BIM usage. Also, the integration of BIM with advanced structural analyses techniques such as Finite Element Method has remained a challenge. While open standards have progressed significantly over the last two decades, the commercial interests of software vendors have also stunted the pace of development around interoperability.

Terminology, Scope and Purpose: The term and concept of BIM is unclear for many, with *M* in BIM being used interchangeably for models (product), modelling (process), and management (process). This needs to be resolved for stakeholders to reach a shared understanding on what they are committing to. Furthermore, the scope and purpose of BIM in a project is rarely defined clearly, leaving uncertainties about aspects such as the level of detail, information flow and modes of exchange of information across stakeholders, data transfer, model ownership and handover.

Unstructured Implementation Processes: One of the primary challenges to addressing macro level issues is to understand and plan around the key factors that drive and determine how and where BIM efforts are concentrated. For example, in Finland, the earliest BIM developments that were piloted in 1994, focused on later lifecycle management [27]. However, as the pilot project led to greater interest in BIM, direct and immediate benefits were seen by design consultants and contractors. The resulting market forces led to BIM development concentrating on design and construction phases, while work in facilities and later lifecycle management came to a standstill. In recent years this development is seeing a revival, e.g., developments have looked to establish definition of as-built datasets for FM [28], and the introduction of the COBie initiative (Construction Operations Building information exchange) for the exchange of IFC-based FM data [29].

4 Discussion

PLM and BIM share some similarities regarding lifecycle management objectives and the nature of their practice-based criticisms, however they differ in critical areas concerning their underlying methods, scope of business, technological and enterprise integration, and their intended effects. This sections attempts to elucidate these similarities and distinctions so that valuable learning opportunities may be identified.

Similarities exist in the key objectives of PLM and BIM, which include functionalities that support and manage the creation, release, change and verification of product-related information. PLM and BIM platforms typically provide for the same core functions: management of design and process documents and models, development and control of BOM records, provision of electronic file repositories, inclusion of document and model metadata, identification of model content for compliance and verification, provision for workflow and process management for change approvals, control of multi-user secured access, and data export controls. However it should also be noted that whilst BIM platforms have designed to cover these areas, their level of IT maturity and process sophistication appears to be behind that of most PLM system architectures.

Like PLM, BIM aims to integrate people and data processes throughout the design, construction and operation of a product (or built asset). However it has only been in the last five to seven years that an increasing focus on the application of BIM throughout the whole building lifecycle has emerged and the significance of business systems and business process integration been acknowledged. The literature surveyed reveals a growing number of studies that consider a range of building lifecycle management issues, where much of this research has sought to bridge the interface between AEC processes and the activities of facility operations and management. BIM servers are now being developed to provide a large integrated data- and knowledge-base that can be leveraged not only in design and engineering but also in planning and management of component fabrication, construction operations, and facilities maintenance [30]. Thus research efforts to 'close the loop' and develop the BIM concept for business process integration for the whole building lifecycle are increasing. This increasing scope, functionality and value of BIM is a consequence of platform expansion targeting collaborative processes, shared resources and decision-making to support the whole lifecycle [4].

The adoption of a lifecycle perspective in any sector depends on multiple factors. Depending on the size, cost and complexity of an engineered product or built asset the design and production will normally adhere to discrete stages to form a system lifecycle. In construction, IT implementations that span project or life cycle stages are less established than in manufacturing sectors such as aerospace. The speed and breadth of adoption of IT across the extended enterprise is also greater in these sectors. PLM in manufacturing is therefore a more proven lifecycle integration solution. In construction, even despite BIM-enabled IPD approaches, the flow and management of information is still not fully integrated among all stakeholders. In developing and advancing the BIM concept it is therefore imperative to adopt an ecosystem approach to mapping the network of interacting AEC actors, corporate business processes, project processes, activities, methods and technologies.

References

1. Ameri, F., Dutta, D.: Product Lifecycle Management: Closing the Knowledge Loops. Computer-Aided Design & Applications 2(5), 577–590 (2005)
2. Venugopal, M., Eastman, C.M., Sacks, R., Teizer, J.: Semantics of model views for information exchanges using the industry foundation class schema. Advanced Engineering Informatics 26(2), 411–428 (2012)
3. Ford, G., Bartley, T., Igba, J., Turner, A., McMahon, C.: Product Life Cycle Data Management: A Cross-Sectoral Review. In: Bernard, A., Rivest, L., Dutta, D. (eds.) PLM 2013. IFIP AICT, vol. 409, pp. 58–67. Springer, Heidelberg (2013)
4. Aram, S., Eastman, C.: Integration of PLM solutions and BIM systems for the AEC industry. In: Proceedings of 30th International Symposium of Automation and Robotics in Construction and Mining, Montréal, pp. 1046–1055 (2013)
5. Jupp, J.R.: Incomplete BIM implementation: Exploring challenges and the role of product lifecycle management functions. In: Bernard, A., Rivest, L., Dutta, D. (eds.) PLM 2013. IFIP AICT, vol. 409, pp. 630–640. Springer, Heidelberg (2013)
6. Stark, J.: Product lifecycle management: 21st century paradigm for product realization. Springer (2011)
7. PLM Interest Group. PLM vs PDM Definition, `http://www.plmig.com/welcome/stdpdmdefn.shtml` (retrieved February 2014)
8. Mostefai, S., Bouras, A., Batouche, M.: Data Integration in a PLM Perspective for Mechanical Products. Intl. Arab Journal of Information Technology 2(2), 141–147 (2005)

9. CIMdata, All About PLM (2014), http://www.cimdata.com/en/resources/about-plm (retrieved February 2014)
10. Terzi, S., Bouras, A., Dutta, D., Garetti, M., Kiritsis, D.: Product lifecycle management – from its history to its new role. Intl. J. of PLM 4(4), 360–389 (2010)
11. Sudarsan, R., Fenves, S.J., Sriram, R.D., Wang, F.: A product information modeling framework for product lifecycle management. Computer-Aided Design 37, 1399–1411 (2005)
12. Lee, B., Suh, S.: An architecture for ubiquitous product life cycle support system and its extension to machine tools with product data model. Int'l J. of Adv. Manuf. Tech. 42(5-6), 606–620 (2009)
13. Crnkovic, I., Asklund, U., Persson Dahlqvist, A.: Implementing and Integrating Product Data Management and Software Configuration Management. Artech House Inc., Norwood (2003)
14. Vainio, V.: Comparative Research of PLM Usage and Architecture, Masters Thesis, Tampere University of Technology (2011)
15. Hewett, A.: Product Lifecycle Management: Critical Issues and Challenges in Implementation. Inf. Tech. and Product Dev., Annals of Inf. Sys. 5(1), 81–105 (2009)
16. Koronios, A., Nastasie, D., Chanana, V., Haider, A.: Integration Through Standards: An Overview of International Standards For Engineering Asset Management. In: Fourth International Conference on Condition Monitoring, Harrogate, UK (2007)
17. Singh, V., Gu, N., Wang, X.: A theoretical framework of a BIM-based multi-disciplinary collaboration platform. Automation in Construction 20, 134–144 (2011)
18. Panchal, J.H., Fernández, M.G., Paredis, C.J., Allen, J.K., Mistree, F.: Designing design processes in product lifecycle management: Research issues and strategies. In: ASME 2004 Int'l. Design. Eng. Tech. Conf., pp. 901–913 (2004)
19. Rezgui, Y., Beach, T., Rana, O.: A governance approach for BIM management across lifecycle and supply chains using mixed-modes of information delivery. J. of Civil Eng. & Mgmt. 19(2), 239–258 (2013)
20. Törmä, S., Granholm, L.: Managing building information as a set of interrelated partial models. Espoo: Working paper (2011)
21. BuildingSMART. MVD Process (2012), http://buildingsmart.com/standards/mvd/mvd-process (retrieved February 2014)
22. Holzer, D.: BIM's seven deadly sins. Intl. J. of Arch. Comp. 9(4), 463–480 (2011)
23. NIBS, US National BIM Standard: Version 1, Part 1: Overview, Principles and Methodologies (2007), http://www.wbdg.org/bim/nbims.php (retrieved February 2014)
24. American Institute of Architects, Integrated Project Delivery: A Guide. CA Council (2007)
25. Dolan, K.A.: Building A Hospital Out Of Bits And Bricks. FORBES 186(5), 36–38 (2010)
26. Engeström, Y.: Knotworking to create collaborative intentionality capital in fluid organizational fields. Advances in Interdisciplinary Studies of Work Teams 11, 307–336 (2005)
27. Björk, B.C., Löwnertz, K., Kiviniemi, A.: ISO DIS 13567: Proposed Intl. Standard for Structuring Layers in Computer Aided Building Design. ITcon 2, 32–55 (1997)
28. Teicholz, P.: Owner BIM for FM Guidelines. In: Teicholz, P. (ed.) BIM for FM. Wiley (2013)
29. East, W.E.: Construction Operation Building Information Exchange. USACE ERDC (2007)
30. Beetz, J., van Berlo, L., de Laat, R., Bonsma, P.: Advances in development and application of an open source model server for building information. In: Proc. of CIB W078-W102, France (2011)

BIM and PLM: Comparing and Learning from Changes to Professional Practice Across Sectors

J.R. Jupp[1] and M. Nepal[2]

[1] University of Technology, Sydney
[2] Queensland University of Technology
Julie.Jupp@uts.edu.au, Madhav.Nepal@qut.edu.au

Abstract. This paper explores the effects of PLM and BIM on professional practice. It draws on existing literature documenting the experiences of both communities of practice to explain shifts in professional boundaries. A review of case study based literature compares the nature of changes triggered by PLM and BIM relative to the new activities, roles/responsibilities and knowledge competencies, and supply chain relationships. The paper synthesises these changes and reflects PLM and BIM experiences against each other so as to contrast the continuing evolution of professional practice and lessons learned.

Keywords: Professional practice, roles and responsibilities, knowledge competencies, stakeholder relations.

1 Introduction

With the increasing use of building information modelling (BIM), architectural, engineering and construction (AEC) professionals are experiencing radical changes to working practices. BIM as a newer technology and approach reflects many of the changes, challenges and opportunities triggered by the introduction of Product Lifecycle Management (PLM) in manufacturing sectors almost two decades ago. In particular, changes to professional practice relative to the new activities, roles/responsibilities, knowledge competencies, and supply chain relationships triggered during the implementation of PLM, appear to reflect many characteristics reported in the literature on the adoption and deployment of BIM in construction.

The differences between BIM and PLM chiefly surround their capacity for technical and organizational integration, leading to differences in their approach to data governance and information management [1, 2]. These characteristics together with sector-based structural differences highlight differentiators relative to discipline-based technology applications – e.g., differences in tools, BIM/PLM platform specification, and data specifications and requirements through-life. However BIM and PLM also share a number of similarities relative to their approach to data sharing, project management, organisation of teams around deliverables and timelines, and object-based visualisation activities. Similarities in the challenges that follow on from these characteristics may provide fertile grounds for sharing lessons learned. Challenges can be seen to stem from the new activities that are changing the nature of

S. Fukuda et al. (Eds.): PLM 2014, IFIP AICT 442, pp. 41–50, 2014.

professional roles and responsibilities at both the firm and project level. These changes not only require the development of new technical skills but importantly new knowledge competencies and stakeholder relationships.

This paper presents an investigation into BIM and PLM and their common ground relative to changes in working practices. The experiences of the BIM and PLM communities reflected in case study research can be used to understand the practice-based issues challenging each sector. From an industry perspective, construction industry still in the early phases of adoption and therefore it stands to benefit most in learning from case studies of PLM and professional practice. However whilst by comparison the application of PLM in the manufacturing sectors is more established, PLM is still seen as a recent concept and therefore also stands to benefit from lessons of BIM implementation due to the construction sector's (arguably) more challenging structural and organizational attributes. The paper proceeds with a review of relevant literature that reports on the nature of the practice-based changes triggered by the PLM and BIM concepts relative to new professional activities, roles/responsibilities and knowledge competencies, and stakeholder relationships. The paper then synthesises the changes to professional practice and reflects the two experiences against each other so as to discuss the continuing evolution of professional boundaries and identify lessons for each industry. The paper closes with a summary of perspectives reflected in the literature.

2 PLM and New Working Practices

The manufacturing industry has in the past decades seen rapid advances in the deployment of PLM. The three main concepts of PLM are to enable: (1) Universal, secured, managed access and use of product definition information; (2) Maintenance of the integrity of that product definition and related information throughout the life of the product; and (3) Management and maintenance of the business processes used to create, manage, disseminate, share, and use the information [3].

2.1 New Activities

The PLM concept emerged from Product Data Management (PDM) to primarily manage design files created by CAD tools and since PLM tools have evolved [3]. The services offered have expanded to cover product definition and design phases as well as manufacturing and operations. This expansion has led to PLM systems acting as a hub connecting intangible asset information (i.e. virtual design products and analysis activities) to physical assets information managed by systems, such as Enterprise Resource Planning (ERP) and Customer Relationship Management (CRM). With enhanced PLM system capabilities new processes, activities and tasks for project engineers, management, and administration staff have resulted. These surround the capture, management, and preservation of information for the entire product portfolio of a company rather than a single project or product as use to be the case.

Further, a common feature of PLM processes concern changes to activities relative to the organization and its systems and conventions [4]. The implementation of PLM in an organization is an extensive change process which is typically divided and managed in a series of smaller stages [4]. It requires various changes to strategic and operational (process-oriented) level activities as well as to IT system activities. These new activities must be carefully planned and coordinated. To that end, PLM information systems have undergone significant changes and cycles of evolution in the last three decades, from static, closed, standalone routine data processing activities to integrated knowledge and information management for the entire product portfolio. These new activities also surround advances in CAD/CAM/CAE tools, data exchange platforms, visualization and modelling systems such as parametric tools [5].

In some applications of PLM, the user community has grown to cover the entire supply chain so as to include designers, suppliers, manufacturing partners, customers and other partners. PLM integrates with mechanical, electrical and software configuration management systems [5]. From such levels of integration new processes, methods and ways of working have emerged, together with new interfaces between engineering design teams and PLM administrators [6]. Furthermore, traditionally manufacturing approaches have not considered customer and supplier activities as part of the value creation process, and are merely value extracting processes [7]. In a PLM approach a company will more explicitly play some part throughout a product's life and potentially develop a more service-oriented approach.

2.2 New Roles/Responsibilities and Knowledge Competencies

PLM focuses on the entire life cycle of a product. As such, PLM isn't the responsibility of just one functional unit or department but rather a whole organization. PLM deployment requires that the PLM implementation team work closely with the cross-functional business teams for example, people from purchasing, order management, sales and marketing, and inventory management [6]. PLM systems can be an enterprise-wide initiative, requireing close integration of products, data, applications, processes, people, work methods, and equipment from across the supply chain [8]. PLM deployment in supply chains raises significant changes to roles and responsibilities and as a result, it is central to deployment initiatives that the roles and responsibilities of a company's product development team be determined at the outset. Likewise responsibilities in relation to partnering companies and their role in the process must be carefully considered [6]. A number of new responsibilities within existing traditional roles can be identified in the PLM literature as well as how these roles are shared between administration executives (typically with an engineering background) and project engineers. Table 1 presents a summary of these new roles).

The shift of perspective from product delivery to a lifecycle approach represents a gap in knowledge for many manufacturing companies [6, 9]. Teaching institutions and professional bodies are seemingly behind in their alignment of current curriculums, assessments and accreditation relative to the needs of PLM and manufacturing industries. In the US this issue has been widely reported [see e.g., 10]. The call for versatile, cross functional employees that remain up-to-date with emerging technologies and are able to tackle the host of new responsibilities associated with through-life requirements and activities is common to both the aerospace and automotive sectors. Hutchins [11] notes that manufacturing professionals in North America are being asked to perform a range of tasks not traditionally included in their professional scope of works. The workforce lacks the capabilities needed to undertake these tasks successfully, and urges more diverse knowledge competencies [11]. The Society of Manufacturing Engineers has been researching "competency gaps" (specific capabilities that companies insist are lacking) and developing a 'Manufacturing Education Plan' [12]. Academia have also responded to the needs of the changing workforce from one that is 'task-oriented' to one of that is 'competency based' through the development of innovative curricula, such as Purdue University's initiative to develop a PLM-literate workforce [12].

Table 1. PLM - New/Changed Role and Responsibilities

Role	Responsibility
Project Manager	Direct implementation resources; Manage project schedules; Track Status; Resolve conflicts and issues
Business Process Owner(s)	Provide project priorities and objectives; Direct participation of resources; Resolve business process issues
Subject Matter Experts	Communicate current process; Provide information details; Support user community during rollout
IT System Support	Support site infrastructure; Extract legacy data; Provide technical expertise
Solution Architect	Analyze requirements; Configure application; Develop strategies for product lifecycle collaboration (including collaborative process planning)
Technical Consultant	Develop customizations; Provide technical expertise
Service Owner	Delivers and/or utilizes the expected business benefit, Manages service unit to deliver service benefits, Provides Subject Matter Experts to project

2.3 New Supply Chain Relations

A PLM approach attempts to uncover hidden relationships and rearrange the value network of actors. The most noticeable change in relations between different parties/stakeholders therefore stems from two fundamental changes to business focus. The first is the change in focus from a traditional product delivery business model to one that centres on the product in use, highlighting the role of the service owner and/or the customer role that the PLM concept is predicated on. This may extend the relations of a firm with suppliers or even include new relations with product customers as is the case in a product-service delivery model. The second shift in focus follows on from this and relates to a more strategic approach to intellectual property creation and intellectual property management of product information, from its initial conception to retirement [13 citing 3]. Following on from these two shifts in business focus which reveal new supply chain relations are a number of secondary factors such as the emergence of networked firms, changes in customer base, mass customization, and changes to the mode of production. These factors have accelerated changes in relations between suppliers, manufacturers and customers [14].

IT is the key enabler of PLM support in these new relational networks. However, most case studies report that manufacturing firms are only partially integrated 'islands of information' and still lack a holistic view of 'users of information' [14]. Further, the information systems underpinning PLM are said to be largely influenced by low levels of vertical integration [15], a lack of interoperability across complex and disparate tools, and a lack of a 'plug and play' approach to PLM deployment [14]. In an extended enterprise context, the benefits of PLM can only be realized when horizontal integration of several disparate systems is achieved so as to be able to support the wider partnering relations mentioned above.

3 BIM and New Working Practices

BIM is an emerging technology and collaborative process that in theory should facilitate the digital representation, exchange, use and reuse of all pertinent information about the life cycle of a facility from planning, design, construction, FM, and disposal [16]. In practice this is often only partially realised as a range of problems in 'closing the loop' persist across various lifecycle phases. Like PLM, BIM is a model-driven approach to construction, which relies on mastering new ways of working and integration and sharing of resources.

3.1 New Activities

Like approaches to PLM, BIM emphasizes open communication and information exchange, collaborative decision making, early participation and contribution of knowledge and expertise by downstream stakeholders (contractors and suppliers), and thus fosters greater levels of risk sharing [17]. BIM emphasizes integrated processes built around coordinated, reliable information about the life cycle of the facility. Consequently BIM introduces changes in working practices, both within an organization and across organizations [18], which are often difficult and painful.

Changes to BIM-enabled collaboration and multidisciplinary teamwork have emerged, with model-based collaboration becoming the norm in BIM deployment. The level of interaction is managed differently on projects according to required levels of technical and organizational integration [19]. Higher levels of interdisciplinary interaction and integration are often enabled by co-location arrangements which have spawned concepts such as the "Big Room" [20] and 'knotworking' [21]. Closer interdisciplinary collaboration between AEC stakeholders means that traditional role boundaries have become less distinct, and separations between responsibilities and areas of expertise are diminishing [18]. It also requires new project and technical management activities, such as new process management tasks surrounding the planning and execution of information protocols between stakeholders, and new model management activities surrounding the coordination of discipline specific datasets. New activities are also emerging onsite with the use of 3D and 4D models during fabrication and construction [22]. Most recently the activities of clients and facility managers have also begun to change with the use of the as-built model for operations and maintenance [23].

As was the case for PLM, these new AEC and FM activities have been initiated by advances in data exchange standards, new platforms and protocols and improvements to the visualisation and editing of information outside CAD and other modelling systems. Thus the community of users of BIM has also expanded to cover more of the supply chain, which includes designers, suppliers, manufacturing partners, and clients. From new coordination and integration demands, come new processes, tasks and activities that must be mastered across the design, delivery and operations team. Currently these new interfaces are being established mostly on an ad-hoc basis due to the project-based business focus of the sector.

3.2 New Roles/Responsibilities and Knowledge Competencies

Traditionally, AEC professionals have taken on separate and strictly defined roles, delineated by a precise scope of works with established discipline-based responsibilities. In defining roles, professional disciplines have sought to transfer risk to other parties formally in contractual arrangements [24]. Due to the interdisciplinary nature of BIM, traditional responsibilities relative to modelling, management, administrative and functional requirements are being challenged and professional boundaries being temporarily redrawn. Research indicates there is also a lack of clarity on whether new responsibilities need to be performed by one role or several, within an organisational framework or a project one [18]. In some case studies, the introduction of BIM is presented as simply an upgrade in the drawing production process from CAD to BIM. For these projects, the "BIM team", while described as a new function, is described as an up-skilled version of CAD operators [19]. In other case studies the need for new roles is well documented [25]. The proliferation of new roles may be seen as a reflection of the need for processes to allow different AEC stakeholders to contribute to model development [18]. Barison and Santos [26] have identified over 30 different job titles or descriptions for BIM specialists, with role variations and combinations depending on project size or professional affiliation. Table 2 summarizes the new roles and responsibilities identified from the literature. Whyte [27] suggests that different approaches to drawing and model development are to some extent 'institutionalised' in existing professional roles, with architects taking a direct lead in model production, and engineers conducting the fundamental design and analysis but passing instructions to technicians for transformation into the required models. This appears to be causing issues relative to process planning and control. Davies *et al.* [18] argue that BIM-related roles within contractor organisations have more freedom to redefine their responsibilities according to their core knowledge competencies. Contractors therefore appear to be maintaining their own institutional boundaries more readily.

There is growing consensus relative to industry requirements for new BIM knowledge competencies. Succar *et al.* [28] have proposed an integrated definition of BIM competencies which comprise of personal traits, professional knowledge and technical abilities. Construction industries worldwide are calling for the requirements of new abilities, activities or outcomes to be measureable against performance standards so as to hold education, training and/or development offerings to an acknowledged standard. Numerous BIM competency frameworks have been developed and categorised into useable competency taxonomies. Competencies are however too numerous, and potentially thousands of competency items would be required to satisfy an integrated BIM competency definition. The required knowledge competencies can generally be mapped to the new roles and responsibilities that have emerged (see Table 2). New competencies can also be identified relative to coordination requirements according to different information management functions.

Table 2. BIM - New Roles and Responsibilities

Role	Responsibility
BIM (Project) Manager	Including developing a BIM management plan, understanding data exchange protocols, understanding model progression specifications and document management. Provide project priorities and objectives; Direct participation of resources; Resolve business process issues
BIM Model Managers	Understanding data exchange protocols, Model auditing for model managers
BIM Contract Administrators	Including new skills in the contractual implications of using 3D models as a primary source of design information, administration and contract management
BIM System Support	Support site infrastructure; Extract legacy data; Provide technical expertise
Technical Consultant	Including technical skills relative to building information modelling (functional basics) as well as functional software skills relative to project execution, software applications, and model authoring
Client/ Facility Manager	Analyze operational requirements; specify requirements of as-built BIM model to be delivered for FM purposes.

3.3 New Supply Chain Relations

The procurement process and contractual arrangements of construction projects have considerable impact on how BIM is implemented throughout a project team, and on the resulting relations between parties. Under a traditional design-bid-build framework, BIM is more likely to be used in isolation by a single or a small group of design consultant/s, or in some cases, in the construction stage alone, as there is no incentive or support for collaborative engagement. More progressive arrangements such as alliancing and integrated project delivery (IPD) [29] can facilitate increased levels of collaboration and integration between design and construction roles [18]; particularly the increased involvement of contractor/subcontractors in the design phase of the project. Using such arrangements, BIM implementation increases levels of integration between collaborating stakeholders.

The emerging role of a third-party BIM specialist is also being used to assist different project partners with BIM implementation. While the use of such a person or team has the potential to bridge traditional role divisions or project stages, case studies to date (see [18-22]) suggest that it is most commonly seen in collaborative project frameworks. This highlights a significant difference between BIM and PLM initiatives where the introduction of a defined administrative PLM team appears to be a more significant and formal process, demanding new relations and where networks must be established with the product engineering team to ensure collaborative process planning and clearly defined data governance strategies.

4 Comparing BIM and PLM Experiences

There are a number of key differences between BIM and PLM concepts and their deployment and impact on professional practice. These differences also stem from the different structures, backgrounds and traditions of their respective industries. A comparison between the construction and manufacturing sectors inevitably highlights each industry's unique characteristics and any contrast between BIM and PLM should be mediated by differences in context. For example, the automotive and aerospace sectors are more globalised and consolidated industries; in contrast, the majority of construction projects remain rooted in local contexts where IT adoption is low in a highly fragmented industry [30]. Each sector also differs in terms of its technological intensity, which in turn affects the success of IT implementation. In construction, information modelling and management are challenged by lower levels of technological sophistication. In the product-centric companies that characterise manufacturing, the focus is instead on the overall business process and due to a more consolidated industry an enterprise perspective can be fostered more readily. PLM applications in aerospace and automotive sectors have also (arguably) gained more traction due to higher levels of supplier specialisation and technological expertise. This in turn means that suppliers compete on technical expertise as well as on cost.

In the last decade, widespread efforts have been undertaken to enhance various aspects of BIM ITs from their focus on internal modelling capabilities and software interoperability, to expand BIM's role to the entire lifecycle of a built asset. BIM servers are now being developed to provide a large integrated data- and knowledge-base that can be leveraged not only in design and engineering but also in planning and management of component fabrication, construction operations, and facilities maintenance. Hence, BIM's scope, functionality and value are only recently being expanded from modelling and simulation capabilities to a platform for collaborative processes and resourceful decision-making, aiming to support a whole life cycle approach. In contrast, PLM solutions have been serving as the basis for collaborative product definition, manufacturing, and service management for much longer. With PLM, companies think in terms of standard processes, standard data and standard systems that they, and the numerous suppliers, customers, and partners, can use to save an enormous amount of time and money [8]. A lack of process commonality and standardization usually results in non-standardized and suboptimal BIM implementations with a high cost of ownership being passed to AEC companies trying to implement such process-oriented integrations. This is a key lesson for the construction sector such that the support of PLM requires collaborative harmonization of a set of complementary and interoperable open standards and open source models that cover the full range of the products' life cycle [15]. However even from a PLM perspective, industry standards surrounding model based collaboration are not yet widely accepted and popular as a useful form of data storage due to the lack of information they hold [13]. Importantly, data exchange standards have been criticized for their inability to capture well-defined business processes, work flow patterns/ systems, and underlying business rules. For organizations of any sector, a key issue in the implementation of PLM or BIM is the transition processes required in adopting new standards, i.e. moving from the old to the new system.

In considering the transition process surrounding PLM and BIM deployment another key lesson concerns the fostering of new attitudes and perspectives towards collaboration and shared responsibility. PLM and BIM implementation must be driven by the requirements of product design processes rather than IT considerations, and therefore the bill of materials must remain at the centre of process requirements and workflow redesign. Such a perspective is arguably more difficult for AEC professionals to foster. BIM implementation challenges therefore centre on answering many of the same data exchange, business process and policy phasing problems that have faced PLM deployment. In overcoming these challenges a unifying solutions must be driven by product design requirements and focus on enabling both information and processes to be to acquired, managed and utilised across project and enterprise level systems. AEC professionals may therefore see further changes to practice. As BIM maturity levels increase across the construction industry a common end point with manufacturing industries may be realised with construction achieving greater rationalisation – including higher levels of consolidation in the supply chain, harmonisation in collaborative ways of working, increased use of 'IPD-type' procurement methods, and an increase use of collaborative process planning methods.

5 Conclusions

This paper provides a comparison of case study based research on the impact of PLM and BIM on the traditional practices of manufacturing and construction industries. The influence of these changes relative to new activities, roles/responsibilities, knowledge competencies and relationships within project and organizational contexts were reviewed. The comparison of PLM and BIM concepts and practice based changes aims to provide better understanding of the impact of their respective implementation. Irrespective of industry, managing these changes is critical to transition and must be planned for with appropriate commitment to process redesign, training and education, and development/use of industry standards. A useful direction for future research is to compare how each industry is supporting such commitments.

References

1. Jupp, J.R.: Incomplete BIM implementation: Exploring challenges and the role of product lifecycle management functions. In: Bernard, A., Rivest, L., Dutta, D. (eds.) PLM 2013. IFIP AICT, vol. 409, pp. 630–640. Springer, Heidelberg (2013)
2. Ford, G., Bartley, T., Igba, J., Turner, A., McMahon, C.: Product Life Cycle Data Management: A Cross-Sectoral Review. In: Bernard, A., Rivest, L., Dutta, D. (eds.) PLM 2013. IFIP AICT, vol. 409, pp. 58–67. Springer, Heidelberg (2013)
3. CIMdata, All About PLM (2014), http://www.cimdata.com/en/resources/about-plm (retrieved February 2014)
4. Kärkkäinena, H., Myllärniemia, J., Okkonena, J., Silventoinenb, A.: Assessing Maturity Requirements for Implementing and Using Product Lifecycle Management. In: The 9th International Conference on Electronic Business, November 30-December 4, pp. 669–678 (2009)
5. Rangan, R.M., Rohde, S.M., Peak, R., Chadha, B., Bliznakov, P.: Streamlining product lifecycle processes: a survey of product lifecycle management implementations, directions, and challenges. Journal of Computing and Information Science in Engineering 3, 227–237 (2005)
6. Hewett, A.: Product Lifecycle Management (PLM): Critical Issues and Challenges in Implementation. Inf. Tech. and Product Dev., Annals of Inf. Sys. 5(1), 81–105 (2009)
7. Prahalad, C.K., Ramaswamy, V.: Co-creation experiences: The next practice in value creation. Journal of Interactive Marketing 18(3), 5 (2004)
8. Stark, J.: Product lifecycle management: 21st century paradigm for product realisation, 2nd edn. Decision engineering. Springer (2011)
9. Ericson, Å., Larsson, T.: A service perspective on product development - towards functional products. In: 12th Intl. Product Dev. Mgmt. Conf., CBS, Copenhagen, DK (2005)
10. ACT Inc. A better measure of skills gaps: Utilizing ACT Skill profile and assessment data for strategic skill research (2011), http://www.act.org/research/policymakers/reports/abettermeasure.html (retrieved February 2014)

11. Hutchins, G.: SME Speaks: Manufacturing Engineers Must Reduce Competency Gaps. Manufacturing Engineering Magazine 132 (2) (2004), http://www.sme.org/MEMagazine/Article.aspx?id=31088&taxid=1427 (retrieved February 2014)
12. Fillman, S.A., Wilde, K.L., Kochert, J.F., Homan, S.R., Tomovic, C.L.: Entry-level engineering professionals and product lifecycle management: A competency model. Int. J. of Mfg. Tech. and Mgmt. 13(3/4), 306–311 (2010)
13. Cheung, W.M., Schaefer, D.: Product lifecycle management: State-of-the-art and future perspectives. In: Cruz-Cunha, M. (ed.) Enterprise Information Systems for Business Integration in SMEs: Technological, Organizational, and Social Dimensions, pp. 37–55. IGI Global, Hershey (2010)
14. Subrahmaniam, E., Rachuri, S., Fenves, S.J., Foufou, S.: Product lifecycle management support: A challenge in supporting product design and manufacturing in a networked economy. International Journal of Product Lifecycle Management 1(1), 4–25 (2005)
15. Rachuri, S., Subrahmanian, E., Bouras, A., Fenves, S.J., Foufou, S., Sriram, R.D.: Information sharing and exchange in the context of product lifecycle management: Role of standards. Computer-Aided Design 40(7), 789–800 (2008)
16. Eastman, C., Teicholz, P., Sacks, R., Liston, K.: BIM Handbook: A Guide to Building Information Modeling, for Owners, Managers, Designers, Engineers, and Contractors. John Wiley & Sons, Hoboken (2008)
17. Rezgui, Y., Beach, T., Rana, O.: A governance approach for BIM management across lifecycle and supply chains using mixed-modes of information delivery. Journal of Civil Engineering and Management 19(2), 239–258 (2013)
18. Davies, C., McMeel, D., Wilkinson, S.: Mapping roles in an altered landscape: The impact of BIM on designer-constructor relationships. In: Proceedings of CIB W78 30th Intl. Conf on Applications of IT in AEC Industry, Beijing, China, October 9-12 (2013)
19. Merschbrock, C.: Unorchestrated symphony: The case of inter-organizational collaboration in digital construction design. J. of Inf. Tech. in Const (ITcon) 17, 333–350 (2012)
20. Cohen, J.: Integrated project delivery: Case studies. AIA, Sacramento (2010), http://www.aia.org/aiaucmp/groups/aia/documents/pdf/aiab082051.pdf (retrieved February 2014)
21. Engeström, Y.: Knotworking to create collaborative intentionality capital in fluid organizational fields. Advances in Interdisciplinary Studies of Work Teams 11, 307–336 (2005)
22. Davies, R., Harty, C.: Implementing "Site BIM": A case study of ICT innovation on a large hospital project. Automation in Construction 30, 15–24 (2013)
23. Sabol, L.: Building information modeling and FM. In: IFMA World Workplace (2008)
24. Hughes, W., Champion, R., Murdoch, J.: Construction contracts: law and management. Routledge (2007)
25. Sebastian, R.: Changing roles of clients, architects and contractors through BIM. Engineering, Construction and Architectural Management 18(2), 176–187 (2011)
26. Whyte, J.: Managing digital coordination of design: emerging hybrid practices in an institutionalized project setting. Engineering Project Organization Journal 1(3), 159–168 (2011)
27. Barison, M.B., Santos, E.T.: An overview of BIM specialists. In: Tizani, W. (ed.) Proc. of Intl. Conf. on Comp. in Civil and Bldg Eng., p. 141. Nottingham University Press (2010)
28. Succar, B., Sher, W., Williams, A.: An integrated approach to BIM competency assessment, acquisition and application. Automation in Construction 35, 174–189 (2013)
29. American Inst. of Architects, Integrated Project Delivery: A Guide. CA Council (2007)
30. Green, S.D., Newcombe, R., Fernie, S., Weller, S.: Learning across business sectors: Knowledge sharing between aerospace and construction, University of Reading (2004)

Preliminary Study Impact of Building Information Modelling Use in Malaysia

W.I. Enegbuma[1], A.C. Ologbo[2], U.G. Aliagha[3] and K.N. Ali[1]

[1] Faculty of Built Environment
[2] Faculty of Management
[3] Faculty of Geoinformation Science
Universiti Teknologi Malaysia, 81310 Skudai, Johor
1wenegbuma2@live.utm.my

Abstract. The paradigm shift in the construction industry from 2D to Building Information Modelling (BIM) presents unforeseen challenges for new entrant construction industries. Experiences from advanced industry users of BIM shape the directions for future use. In Malaysia, BIM maturity is fast appreciating with increasing demand for efficiency and competitive advantages. However, adoption rate encounters resistance from several factors highlighted in previous research: people, process and technology. To improve on Information technology (IT) adoption models factors such as business process re-engineering, computer integrated construction and BIM adoption were considered for this research. This paper represents findings of an ongoing research, presenting the designed questionnaire to access perception of construction industry professionals (Architects, Quantity Surveyors, Engineers and Contractors) knowledge on BIM softwares and BIM attributes. Responses were derived from 120 construction professionals in the pilot phase of the research. The data is analyzed using SPSS for a descriptive overview of the most prominent BIM software usage. Smart PLS was utilized to analyze the path coefficient effects of each variable in the model. The Cronbach Alpha derived fell within an agreeable minimum threshold of above 0.60. The factors loaded appropriately to each variable. The path coefficient revealed people perception had the highest effect on collaborative processes, business process re-engineering (BPR) had the highest effect on BIM adoption and model variance R2 explained 24.6% of BIM adoption. The results will demonstrate the current state of BIM adoption in Malaysian construction industry complimenting current efforts to improve BIM awareness. At this stage, future research focuses on developing the second phase of the model and recommends towards extending and redefining the model with other mediating variables.

Keywords: Building Information Modelling (BIM), Construction Industry, Information Technology, Malaysia, Partial Least Square (PLS).

1 Introduction

Building Information Modeling is predominantly viewed as collaboration by different stakeholders at different phases of the life-cycle of a facility to insert, extract, update

S. Fukuda et al. (Eds.): PLM 2014, IFIP AICT 442, pp. 51–62, 2014.

or modify information in the model to support and reflect the roles of that stakeholder. The model is a shared digital representation founded on open standards for interoperability. BIM as the process of generating and managing building data during its life cycle. National Building Information Modeling Standard (NBIMS) views BIM as a digital representation of physical and functional characteristics of a facility [1]. The Malaysian Construction Industry Development Board (CIDB) ten-year construction industry master plan (CIMP) to refocuses on the strategic position and future direction of the industry breeding an innovative, sustainable, professional, profitable and world-class construction industry. Important to this study is the leverage on IT towards achieving the set vision of 2015. The dimensions to building information modelling (BIM) research is inexhaustible in fields of user perception, health and safety, costing, project management, green building, Off-Site Manufacturing (OSM), Integrated Project Delivery (IPD), self help housing and real estate [5] [6] [7] [8]. Information technology IT transforms and plays a vital role in how innovation affects project delivery in Malaysian construction sector. The Malaysian governments' aggressive drive to developed nation and exportation of construction services to India and South-East Asia intertwined with government-to-government projects favoured BIM propagation. Design technology is key to affordance of a project hence, choice and collaboration should commerce at the earliest stage. BIM implementation brings unsettling effect to technology, people and processes/policy, process and technology [9]. BIM implementation produces various impacts on both internal organisational culture and values; and external supply chain. Changes in delivery processes, shift from individual consulting to consultancy team, contractor involvement on projects, improved shared vision and trust amongst teams, rise in supply chain effectiveness, automatic building permission [10] [7] [8] [1]. Amidst such process improvement potentials through BIM also exists challenges to full system automation (knowledge; resistance; political engagement; technology capabilities; skills gaps; costs; new forms of contracts; legal issues; life cycle benefits; relevant training and data standards [11] [10] [7] [12]. This study presents pilot results for the Enegbuma and Ali [6] model aimed at plotting a path towards linking user perceptions of people, process and technology and focuses on how they react in strategic IT implementation for effective BIM penetration in the industry. Subsequent sections will delineate the variables of the BIM model, present the hypotheses, examine the data findings and discusses by re-visiting the earlier stated hypothesis.

2 BIM Penetration Model

People perception from previous research in BIM has highlighted the seemingly increasing effect of people dimension to BIM use [14] [2] [15-19]. This paper therefore defined people as the perception towards adapting to new BIM practices in the industry. BIM emergence offers an unsettling precedence to an already defragmented construction industry which offers less surety. New processes to enhance the construction process, electronic designs and construction professionals must acknowledge the individual risk associated with such a new technology. Boundaries of professional responsibility and work product are not clearly defined creating uncertainty for liability in a BIM model. The trend of older professionals still lagging behind while younger professionals lack experience in legal matters with a need for flexible legal form of agreement between construction teams to meet the rapid growth [14] [2] [15]. The emergence of local user Groups in various localities to discuss BIM concepts, softwares and products including information sharing on achievements has shown an adaptive response by people for BIM improvements [16]. Owner awareness is lacking in terms of information regarding successes of BIM by other competitive companies in operation, maintenance, repair and re-modelling. While, other seminar authors proposed a future expansion of current pedagogy in education of building professionals [17-18]. Hence the role of people perception is taken into consideration as it affects BIM penetration in the construction industry.

Process perception changes are inherent in affecting BIM use [13] [6] [1] [20] [21-23] [14] [19]. This paper defines such process thereof as how perception related to managing process changes in adapting to new BIM practices in the industry. Previous construction industry reports except the Latham 1994 report have ignored IT as an integral process in construction. However, emphasis on technology development alone places less attention to organisational and human issues. Furthermore, fewer staffs to regularly update BIM models and inadequate human resource training exist in the construction industry [20] [4] [21-22]. For smooth BIM implementation within an organisation strict consideration must be given to the long term goals of the organisation and requirement. Similarly, managing the cost of ownership can be actualised through BIM, with diligent improvement in BIM practices owners' BIM metamorphoses into a Business Intelligence Model placing it right within corporate mission and objectives. Similar to the CAD migration, BIM is faced with challenging bureaucracy by top management due to new risk and liability fears during model sharing [23] [14]. BIM implementation in the US coast guard achieved partial success. Full success was eventually marred by people's culture and senior leadership resistance to new methodologies; workflow changes; and technological innovation [3].

Technological Perception role presents significant impact on BIM use [25] [5] [26]. Owner push for faster product delivery improvement, safer construction environment, reduced construction cost, lean adoption to eliminate waste and proactive drive by industry professionals to assimilate new technology such as BIM [14]. Malaysian construction industry grapples in advanced IT and project management techniques which forms an essential part to high-tech and capital intensive construction [24]. McGraw-Hill construction report suggests that for BIM to strive and meet the challenges of the future, model objects needs to be readily available for smooth information extraction. Although, product library were created by software companies to represent generic components they lack enough data to represent the specifications of Building Product Manufacturers (BPMs). Knowledge of BIM software, inadequate reference material and component database provide challenges in BIM education in tertiary institutions. Inherent deficiencies in BIM specification provide inadequate differentiation between requirement for BIM deliverables and technology to deliver such information. Similarly, during hyper collaborative platforms such as BIM Storm, participants had to revert to do some manual communication [25] [5] [26].

Strategic IT Planning in line with industry transformation, from adversarial to cooperative thinking places more emphasis on business process. Construction industry is transforming into long term strategic planning to cope with the dynamic nature of economic, technological and social factors. Strategic IT usage though perceived with a degree of reluctance by the construction industry is currently transforming, as most business process were never designed but formed by ad hoc means. Research in labour and cost saving by Adam Smith and Fredrick Taylor provided an initiating argument towards a re-think of business process [27]. Sustainable competitive advantage is maintained though innovative process improvement and management reliant on IT to provide enabling environment [28]. ICT showed a positive and significant impact on the Malaysian economy from 1982 – 2004 which established a change from the norm of investments on agrarian economy to one of manufacturing and industrialisation [29]. Technology acceptance and usage has been studied extensively, expanding Fishbein and Ajzen Model of 1975, Fred Davies formulated the technology acceptance model (TAM). Fishbein and Ajzen Model explained the theory of reasoned action, which Davies conceptualised the existence of a response predicted by user motivation and influenced by external stimulus consisting of the system features and capabilities which triggered the use of a system. [30] perceived change to be structured and measured sets of activities designed for a specific product for various markets and clientele. In construction, process change from inception, project completion and FM stages provide benefits to clients in Malaysian construction industry. Business Process Re-engineering (BPR) drives organization to change their career paths, training, recruitment and policies [31]. Factors highlighted in driving BPR are organisational training, reward, communication, research and development [32]. This paper considers business process re-engineering and computer integrated construction aspects of strategic IT planning.

Collaboration in construction is defined as an agreement among specialist to share their abilities in a particular process, to achieve the larger adjectives of the project as a whole, as defined by a client, a community, or a society at large. Collaboration is working together in a seamless team for common objectives that deliver benefit to all. Collaboration is more effective when undertaken at the project inception stage [33]. Construction industry presents a rather unique approach to collaborating which when done ineffectively creates islands of automation [34]. Major challenges to effective collaboration exist in the construction industry due to independent working and taking decisions which affects the project team [35]. Issues bordering around undefined boundary between teamwork and collaboration including, unsolved issues of shared-understanding, alignment of purpose and shared meaning. Different educational upbringing, terminologies and adversarial contractual agreement further provides barriers to collaboration [36]. This paper adopts collaborative construction as a means improving BIM penetration in the industry.

BIM Penetration amongst other benefit derives competitive gains and future guiding policies of new systems. Communication of innovation over time amongst members of the same social systems over a period of time is often referred to as a product of complex social interaction. Social system acts as a determinant of socio-psychological processes within the social system [37]. Diffusion describes the acceptance and usage of new technology while innovation denotes a new product or process technology, or administrative. Innovation diffusion proposes new models of diffusion of new technologies with complimentary implications for increasing the rate of innovation in the industry. Furthermore, investigations identified four forces that drive innovation: competitive advantage, process problems, technological opportunity, and institutional requirements [38]. [39] argued that relative advantage, compatibility, complexity, observability and triability are determining factors for technology diffusion. The structural equation modelling path study towards improving innovation diffusion level within the architectural and engineering design (AED), delineated definitive pathways and practical strategies harnessed by the construction industry to derive outcomes from innovation via diagnosing and improving their existing innovation capability which invariably strengthen their business performance [37].

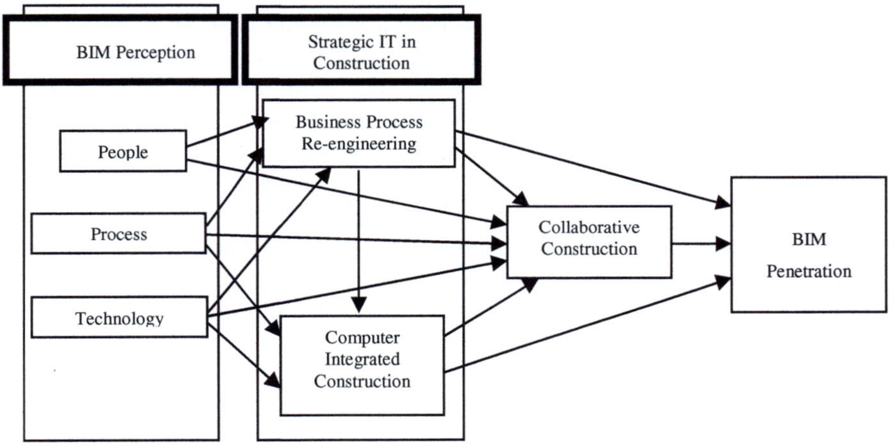

Fig. 1. Research Model and Hypothesis [1]

Table 1. Generated Hypothesis

H1	There is a positive relationship between People and Business Process Re-engineering
H2	There is a positive relationship between Process and Business Process Re-engineering
H3	There is a positive relationship between Technology and Business Process Re-engineering
H4	There is a positive relationship between Process and Computer Integrated Construction
H5	There is a positive relationship between Technology and Computer Integrated Construction
H6	There is a positive relationship between People and Collaborative Construction
H7	There is a positive relationship between Process and Collaborative Construction
H8	There is a positive relationship between Technology and Collaborative Construction
H9	There is a positive relationship between Business Process Re-engineering and BIM Penetration
H10	There is a positive relationship between Business Process Re-engineering and Collaborative Construction
H11	There is a positive relationship between Business Process Re-engineering and Computer Integrated Construction
H12	There is a positive relationship between Computer Integrated Construction and Collaborative Construction
H13	There is a positive relationship between Computer Integrated Construction and BIM Penetration
H14	There is a positive relationship between Collaborative Construction and BIM Penetration

3 Methodological Approach

In structural equation modelling, dual techniques separate the chosen method of analysis namely; covariance-based methods [40] or variance-based PLS-SEM approach [41]. Prevalent in strategic management research is the use of PLS-SEM approach, since this BIM pilot study targets a strategic approach to improving BIM penetration in the construction industry, PLS-SEM was chosen. BIM penetration construct represents a more variance-based (prediction oriented) approach [43]. Other aspects to fortify the methodology technique include increased level of statistical power in small sample size [44] and less rigid assumption [45]. Smart PLS 2.0 [46] was used in evaluating the path model and parameter estimation to evaluate the path weighting scheme [43]. The guidelines by [47] were followed in reporting the measurement model values and subsequent structural model. The constructs were measured by means of multiple items using a five-point Likert scale ranging from 1 (disagreement) to 5 (agreement) [48]. Due to inadequate specific research in contrition IT regarding BIM penetration, items to measure the constructs were reworded and some generated by the authors from previous literature. Hence the need arose to revalidate the reliability of items. Strict attention was placed on confining the multi-item measures to denote representatively the underlying construct.

4 Results and Discussion

The demographic nature of the respondents showed that Engineers made up 36.7% of the respondents. Male respondents were more with 73.3%. The age bracket of 25-35years was predominant by 66.7%. 36.7% of the respondents are originally from Federal Territory of Kuala Lumpur. 83.3% carry out their construction activities from the private sector. 53.3% represents the junior management community in the various establishments. 66.7% are qualified with a bachelor in the outlined fields of construction. 50.0% majority have been active in construction for 6-10years. 50.0% are registered in their various professional affiliations. 50.0% are of the opinion that their level of BIM involvement falls within the beginner class.

The initial pool of item amounted to 48 namely; People (RPPB) - 12, Process (RPP) – 7, Technology (RTP) – 6, Business Process Re-Engineering (RBPR) – 6, Computer Integrated Construction (RCIC) – 6, Collaborative construction (RCC) – 5 and BIM penetration (RSBP) – 6. The first stage of Alpha analysis via SPSS revealed a low Cronbach Alpha for constructs RPPB (0.606), RBPR (0.496), RCIC (0.546) and RCC (0.490). Subsequently, from the Item-Total Statistics item suggested to be deleted to raise the minimum alpha threshold were delete RPPB9, RBPR4, RCIC3 and RCC5 respectively. The final Cronbach Alpha for the constructs are above the minimum threshold of >0.60 [49].

The path diagram linking all constructs was drawn in Smart PLS and analysis initiated by PLS algorithm. The default PLS algorithm settings were utilised; weighting Scheme (Path Weighting Scheme), Data Metric (Mean 0, Variance 1), Maximum Iterations (300), Abort Criterion (1.0E-5) and Initial Weights (1.0).

In Smart PLS the factor loadings are derived from the outer loading result which showed low values <0.50. Lowest value loadings were deleted. Discriminant validity holds with all factors loadings in respective variables derived from the PLS cross loading. Convergence occurred at 9 iterations from the stop criterion changes. To derive an acceptable reflective measurement model, 2 steps have to be taken into consideration namely; reliability (reliability of construct measures indicator and internal consistency reliability) and validity (convergent and discriminant). Out of 33 items, four factors loaded below 0.7 recommended thresholds for factor loading but due to the stage in the research this factors were still considered and compared to the composite reliability for any stringent effects. Thus, the measurement model achieved a considerable level of indicator reliability levels. The composite reliability values revealed that all construct measures achieved a healthy score of above 0.7 which reflects a satisfactory level of internal consistency. For the convergent validity the AVE table was assessed denoting all construct scaled the 0.5 threshold. Discriminant validity was analysed through matching the cross loading values in Smart PLS which showed no construct cross loaded more than 0.2 of the leading item. Furthermore, the [50] specifications for discriminant validity was utilised. It specifies that the construct AVE should be higher than the correlation of all opposing constructs. All construct measure according to this measurement model assessment showed reliability and validity.

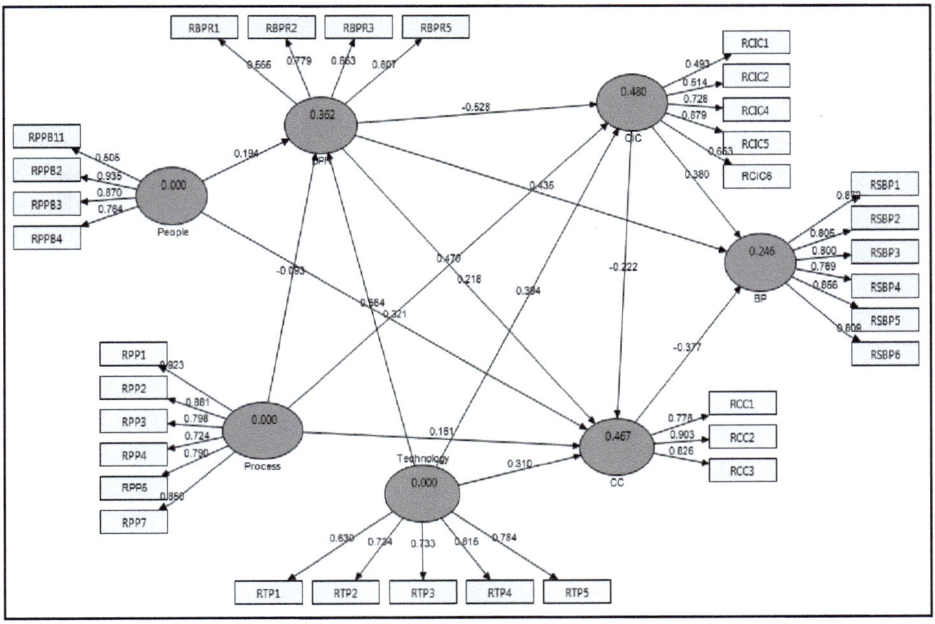

Fig. 2. Measurement Model

The structural model focuses on the relationships between the hypothesized various in the construction industry namely; BIM Perception (people, process and technology), Strategic IT Implementation (business process re-engineering and computer integrated construction), collaborative construction and BIM penetration. Figure 2 shows the results from SmartPLS using the earlier stated parameters. Following [42] recommendations, the central criterion for the structural model assessment is given by the coefficient of determination *R2*. The *R2* for BIM Penetration derived 0.25. *R2* for CC derived 0.47. *R2* for BPR derived 0.36. *R2* for CIC derived 0.48. The average value of *R2* depicts the models predictive validity [42]. From the path weights, 0.56 of technology represents the highest variable affecting BPR in the industry. 0.47 of process has d highest impact in CIC. 0.44 of BPR represented the highest impact on BIM penetration in the industry. The bootstrapping technique was later carried out to derive the level of significance [41] [42]. Figure 3 shows that most hypothesized relationships are significant except for the following; process –> CC (1.33, $p < 0.05$), process –> BPR (0.86, $p < 0.05$), BPR -> BP (0.80, $p < 0.05$), People -> BP (1.48 $p < 0.05$), Technology -> BP (1.50 $p < 0.05$) and Technology -> CIC (0.99 $p < 0.05$). The highest significance values occurred between technology and BPR (9.87, $p < 0.05$).

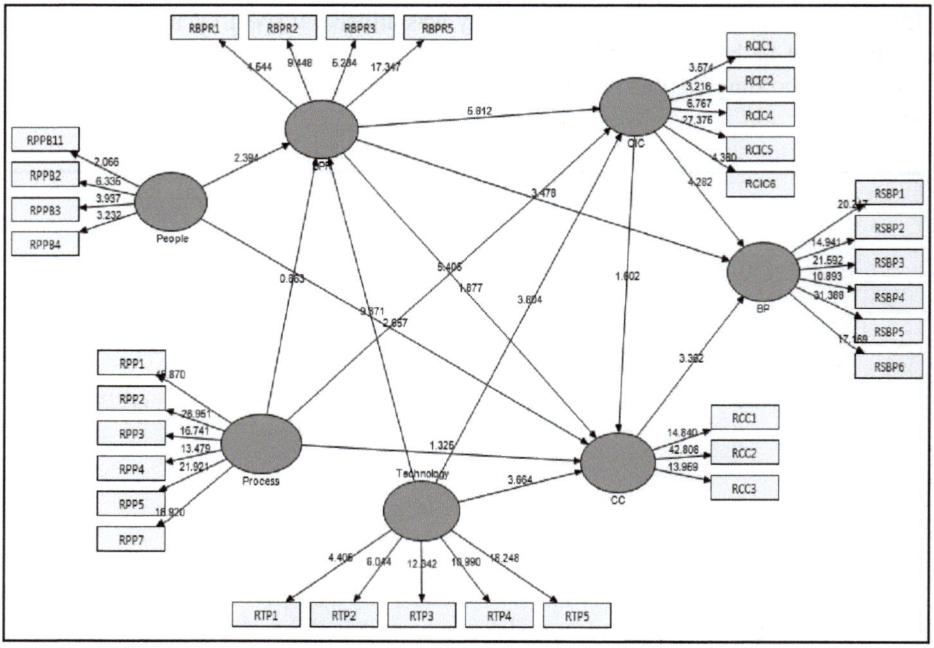

Fig. 3. Bootstrapping (T statistics, >1.96 significant at 0.05 at 95% confidence level)

5 Conclusion

This paper set out to examine the varying factors affecting BIM penetration in the industry, accomplished through an extensive literature study to define the key variables. The hypothesized model and subsequent hypothesis was presented. The instrument for the main study showed a healthy Cronbach alpha including achieving discriminant validity amongst the model variables. A test of the hypothesized variables showed most importantly that 24.6% of BIM penetration can be explained by the model considering the sample size. Seemingly, the effects of technology had a highest influence on BPR, conforming with previous standpoint that technology enabler's drive towards strategic innovation and leads to changes to traditional business processes [30] [27] [31] [51] [32]. In the long run therefore BPR weighed heavily on BIM penetration in the industry. Efforts such as seminars and conference to promote BIM by organisations such as CIDB, BQSM, RISM and software vendors sponsored by individual firms shows there is indeed a drive towards change [13]. How Malaysian construction industry professional view process change weighed heavily on CIC, thus follows prior research linking CIC to improvement in communication, planning, collaboration, and databases [52] [20]. These findings contribute immensely to the body of knowledge in the field of global BIM study as it present a total outlook on several variables determining BIM penetration in the industry. Prior research studied presented a division in various aspect of BIM research pointing to key limiting factors as people, process and technology [22] [14] [54] [5], further studies define technology adoption [55], similar to such limiting factors while this research combined other factors. [19] recommended a follow up research on BIM readiness in Malaysia from a more quantitative approach. This research provides numerical figures though with limiting sample size still in a pilot phase. The findings points a path for major managerial decision making choices as to which areas in the construction industry to improve upon. These bodies are not limited to Construction Research Institute of Malaysia (CREAM) and Construction Industry Development Board of Malaysia (CIDB), Malaysian BIM committee, Malaysia Engineer Boards actively in the fore-front for BIM total implementation. The interrelationship found in the model denotes that prompt attention be given to areas such as BPR in the industry. The successes from JKRs BIM pilot project (National Cancer Institute) will push for future changes in BPR in Malaysia [56] [19]. The results of this research explicate the strategic role of BIM and the ability of construction professionals to deal with the dynamics of BIM adoption and use. This research contributes to both theory and practice on BIM and technology adoption by developing and validating the research instrument. Future research will not only look into extension of the model but also seek to test various mediating variables and varied sample population testing.

References

1. Enegbuma, W.I., Ali, K.N.: Hypothesis Analysis of Building Information Modelling Penetration in Malaysian Construction Industry. In: Proceedings of CIB World Building Congress 2013, Brisbane, Australia, May 5-9 (2013)
2. Rosenberg, T.L.: Building Information Modelling (2006), `http://www.ralaw.com/resources/documents/Building%20Information%20Modeling%20-%20Rosenberg.pdf` (retrieved)
3. Hammond, D.M.: The BIM Balancing Act. Journal of Building Information Modelling. Fall 2008 issue, 12–14 (2008)

4. Rezgui, Y., Zarli, A.: Paving the Way to the Vision of Digital Construction: A Strategic Roadmap. Journal of Construction Engineering and Management 132(7), 767–776 (2006)
5. East, E.W.: Performance Specifications for Building Information Exchange. Journal of Building Information Modelling, Fall 2009 Issue, 18–20 (2009)
6. Enegbuma, W.I., Ali, K.N.: A Theoretical Framework for Building Information Modelling Penetration in Malaysian Construction Industry. In: Proceedings of Management in Construction Research Association (MiCRA) Post Graduate Conference, Kuala Lumpur, Malaysia (2012)
7. Hampson, K., Kraatz, J.: Modelling, Collaboration and Integration: A Case Study for the Delivery of Public Buildings. In: Proceedings of International Council for Research and Innovation in Building and Construction (CIB) World Building Congress 2013, Brisbane, Australia, May 5-9 (2013)
8. Hjelseth, E.: Integrated Approach for Development of Automatic Building Application Systems. In: Proceedings of International Council for Research and Innovation in Building and Construction (CIB) World Building Congress 2013, Brisbane, Australia, May 5-9 (2013)
9. Succar, B.: Building Information Modelling Framework: A Research and Delivery Foundation for Industry Stakeholders. Automation in Construction 18, 357–375 (2009)
10. Allen Consulting Group: Productivity in the Buildings Network, Built Environment Industry Innovation Council, Canberra, Australia (2010)
11. Hartmann, T., Fischer, M.: Applications of BIM & Hurdles for Widespread Adoption of BIM. CIFE Working Paper, CIFE, US (2008)
12. DIISR, Department of Innovation, Industry, Science and Research. Issues Paper: Digital Modelling & the Built Environment, Commonwealth of Australia, Aust. (2010)
13. A.K.N., Al-Jamalullail, S.N.N.I., Boon, T.C.: Building Information Modeling Awareness and Readiness: Among Quantity Surveyors and Quantity Surveying Firms. Royal Institution of Surveyors Malaysia (RISM), Selangor (2013)
14. Jordani, D.: BIM: A Healthy Disruption to a Fragmented and Broken Process. Journal of Building Information Modelling, Spring 2008 issue, 24–26 (2008)
15. Salmon, J.L.: The Legal Revolution in Construction: How collaborative Agreements, BIM and Lean Construction Methods Support Integrated Project Delivery. Journal of Building Information Modelling. Spring 2009 issue, 18–19 (2009)
16. Lega, A.: Synergy in the Sandbox. Journal of Building Information Modelling, Fall 2008 issue, 44–46 (2008)
17. Edgar, A.: Building Value through Building Information Innovation. Journal of Building Information Modelling, Spring 2008 issue, 38 (2008)
18. Henderson, L., Jordan, N.L.: A Modest Proposal for a Transdisciplinary Curriculum: for the Design, Construction, Management and Maintenance of Architecture. Journal of Building Information Modelling. Fall 2009 issue, 35–37 (2009)
19. Haron, A.T.: Organisational Readiness to Implement Building Information Modelling: A Framework for Design Consultants in Malaysia. PhD Thesis School of the Built Environment Faculty of Business, Law and the Built Environment, University of Salford Manchester, Salford (2013)
20. Aouad, G., Cooper, R., Kaglioglu, M., Sexton, M.: An IT-supported New Process. In: Betts, M. (ed.) Strategic Management of IT in Construction, pp. 363–375. Blackwell Science (1999)
21. Yan, H., Damian, P.: Benefit and Barriers of Building Information Modelling. In: 12th International Conference on Computing in Civil and Building Engineering (2008)

22. Liu, Z.: Feasibility Analysis of BIM Based Information System for Facility Management at WPI. Worcester Polytechnic Institute, Worcester, Massachusetts (2010)
23. Smith, D.: An Introduction to Building Information Modeling (BIM). Journal of Building Information Modelling. Fall 2007 issue, 12–14 (2007)
24. Ibrahim, A.R., Roy, M.H., Ahmed, Z., Imtiaz, G.: An Investigation of the Status of the Malaysian Construction Industry. Benchmarking: An International Journal 17(2), 294–308 (2010)
25. Jones, S.A., Lien, J.K.: Towards Interoperable Building Product Content. Journal of Building Information Modelling, Fall 2008 issue, 36–37 (2008)
26. Onuma, K.: Integration Today Using Open Standards: BIMStorm™, Rotterdam to Los Angeles and Beyond. Journal of Building Information Modelling, Spring, issue, 14–18 (2008)
27. Betts, M.: Strategic Management of IT in Construction. Blackwell Science Ltd., Oxford (1999)
28. Alshawi, M.: Rethinking IT in Construction and Engineering: Organisational Readiness. Taylor and Francis, London and New York (2007)
29. Kuppusamy, M., Shanmugam, B.: Islamic Countries Economic Growth and ICT Development: The Malaysian Case. Journal of Economic Cooperation 28(1), 99–114 (2007)
30. Davenport, T.: Process Innovation: Re-engineering Work through Information Technology. Havard Business School Press, Boston (1993)
31. Liang, Y., Cohen, E.: Business Process Re-engineering: An Overview. In: South-Central Small College Computing Conference, Amarillo, April 15-16, pp. 130–136 (1994)
32. Kohar, U.H.A., Senina, A.A., Ismaila, K.: The Cultivation of Organizational Innovation amongst Malaysian Bumiputera (Indigenous) ICT-Based Small Firms. Procedia - Social and Behavioural Sciences 40, 358–363 (2012)
33. Anumbe, C.J., Ugwu, O.O., Newnham, L., Thorpe, A.: A Multi-Agent System for Distributed Collaboration Design. Journal of Logistics Information Management 14(5&6), 355–366 (Special Issue on Softwares and Methods for Improving Decision-Making in Civil Engineering) (2001)
34. Sun, M., Aouad, G.: Integration Technologies to Support Organisational Changes in the Construction Industry. In: 7th ISPE International conference on Concurrent Engineering, Lyon, France, pp. 596–604 (2000)
35. Anumbe, C.J., Ugwu, O.O., Newnham, L., Thorpe, A.: Collaborative Design of Portal Frame Structures using Intelligent Agents. Automation in Construction 11(1), 89–103 (2002)
36. Lang, S.Y.T., Dickinson, J., Bucha, R.O.: Cognitive Factors in Design. Computers in Industry 48, 89–98 (2002)
37. Panuwatwanich, K., Stewart, R.A., Mohamed, S.: Critical Pathways to Enhanced Innovation Diffusion and Business Performance in Australian Design Firms. Automation in Construction 18, 790–797 (2009)
38. Mitropoulos, P., Tatum, C.B.: Forces Driving Adoption of New Information Technologies. Journal of Construction Engineering Management 126, 340–348 (2000)
39. Rogers, E.M.: Diffusion of innovations. Free Press, New York (1983)
40. Joreskog, K.G.: The LISREL Approach to Causal Model-Building in the Social Sciences. In: Wold, H., Joreskog, K.G. (eds.) Systems under Indirect Observation, Part I, pp. 81–100. North-Holland, Amsterdam (1982)
41. Hair, J.F., Hult, G.T.M., Ringle, C.M., Sarstedt, M.: A Primer on Partial Least Squares Structural Equation Modeling (PLS-SEM). Sage, Thousand Oaks (2013)

42. Henseler, J., Ringle, C.M., Sarstedt, M.: Using Partial Least Squares Path Modeling in International Advertising Research: Basic Concepts and Recent Issues. In: Okazaki, S. (ed.) Handbook of Research in International Advertising, pp. 252–276. Edward Elgar Publishing, Cheltenham (2012)
43. Henseler, J., Ringle, C.M., Sinkovics, R.R.: The Use of Partial Least Squares Path Modeling in International Marketing. Advances in International Marketing 20, 277–320 (2009)
44. Lu, I.R.R., Kwan, E., Thomas, D.R., Cedzynski, M.: Two New Methods for Estimating Structural Equation Models: An Illustration and a Comparison with two Established Methods. International Journal of Research in Marketing 28(3), 258–268 (2011)
45. Pinto, J.R., Rodrıguez-Escudero, A.I., Gutıerrez-Cillan, J.: Order, Positioning, Scope and Outcomes of Market Entry. Industrial Marketing Management 37(2), 154–166 (2008)
46. Ringle, C.M., Wende, S., Will, A.: SmartPLS 2.0 M3 (2005), `http://www.smartpls.de`
47. Chin, W.W.: How to Write Up and Report PLS Analyses. In: Vinzi, V.E., Chin, W.W., Henseler, J., Wang, H. (eds.) Handbook of Partial Least Squares: Concepts, Methods and Applications. Springer Handbooks of Computational Statistics Series, vol. II, pp. 655–690. Springer, Heidelberg (2010)
48. Diamantopoulos, A., Sarstedt, M., Fuchs, C., Sebastian, S., Wilczynski, P.: Guidelines for Choosing between Multi-Item and Single-Item Scales for Construct Measurement: A Predictive Validity Perspective. Journal of the Academy of Marketing Science 40(3), 434–449 (2012)
49. Cronbach, L.J.: Coefficient Alpha and the Internal Structure of Tests. Psychometrika 15, 297–334 (1951)
50. Fornell, C.G., Larcker, D.F.: Evaluating Structural Equation Models with Unobservable Variables and Measurement Error. Journal of Marketing Research 18(1), 39–50 (1981)
51. Too, E., Tay, L.: Implementing Construction and Real Estate IT Education: Needs and Strategy. In: Proceedings the 10th European Real Estate Society Conference, Helsinki, Finland (2003)
52. Arayici, Y., Ahmed, V., Aouad, G.: A Requirements Engineering Framework for Integrated Systems Development for the Construction Industry. ITcon 11, 35 (2005)
53. Arayici, Y., Aouad, G.: DIVERCITY: Distributed Virtual Workspace for Enhancing Communication and Collaboration Within the Construction Industry. In: European Conference on Product and Process Modelling in the Building and Construction Industry (ECPPM), Istanbul, Turkey, pp. 415–422 (2004)
54. Wong, K.A., Wong, K.F., Nadeem, A.: Government Roles in Implementing Building Information Modelling Systems: Comparison between Hong Kong and the United States. Construction Innovation 11(1), 61–76 (2011)
55. Taylor, S., Todd, P.A.: Understanding Information Technology Usage: A Test of Competing Models. Information Systems Research 5(2), 144–176 (1995)
56. Sani, R.: Modelling for Better Buildings. New Straits Times, 21 (August 16, 2010)

BIM for FM: A Case Support for Business Life Cycle

Ricardo Codinhoto[1] and Arto Kiviniemi[2]

[1] School of the Built Environment, The University Of Salford, The Crescent, Salford, M5 4WT, United Kingdom
r.codinhoto@salford.ac.uk
[2] School of Architecture, University of Liverpool, Liverpool, L69 3BX, United Kingdom
a.kiviniemi@liverpool.ac.uk

Abstract. Relatively little information exists about the use of BIM in the operation and maintenance of buildings. Reported cases of BIM adoption to support facilities management and lifecycle management reveals that the implementation of BIM for FM processes is, in general, limited to an experimental scale. Even large public owners who have been using BIM for managing their construction projects have not implemented it into their FM activities. Therefore, there is little evidence of the benefits of BIM in the operational phase. In addition, the challenges involved in shifting from traditional FM processes to new BIM-based processes are not well known. In this paper we document some of the issues involved in the adoption of BIM in FM and identify some applications, metrics and benefits related to its adoption. The findings are based on a case study carried out within a major re-development project in Manchester, UK. Results indicate a step rise in the level of awareness regarding potential benefits of BIM in FM activities and lifecycle information management.

Keywords: BIM, FM, Building Information Modelling, Facilities Management, Lifecycle Information Management.

1 FM and Product and Service Life Cycle

Modern Facilities Management (FM) conceptualisation recognises the importance of FM within the business life cycle. Traditionally, the FM function was widely described as involving clients, real estate and AEC teams, all planned around a cost factor to be spent on non-value adding activities such as the maintenance and cleaning of a building, and the provision of support services such as reprographics, reception, stationery [1], [2]. This view has changed considerably. For example, for the British Standards Institute (BSi) FM refers to "*the integration of processes within an organisation to maintain and develop the agreed services that support and improve the effectiveness of its primary activities*" [3]. The Institute of Asset Management (IAM) PAS 55-1:2008 also emphasises the importance of FM to the life cycle of products and services.

The effectiveness of many organisations is certainly dependent on the way its facilities are managed. Effectiveness can be measured in different ways that maintain

S. Fukuda et al. (Eds.): PLM 2014, IFIP AICT 442, pp. 63–74, 2014.

strong links with the mission, goals and objectives of the organisation, the influence of its stakeholders [4] and the profit in its operations. To succeed, businesses must recognise that the rising cost of occupying buildings, providing services to support operations and improving working conditions are fundamental factors impacting the business life cycle. As such, business pressures to improve quality, reduce cost and minimize risks continue to drive FM decisions [4]. If profitability is to be achieved, business owners must make strategic choices related to managing facilities.

It is argued that effectively planned facilities and supporting services can create significant business returns [4]. This can be seen through introducing professional FM methods to support increased efficiency [5], [6], on-going responsibility for the continuous operation of services [7] and a holistic view of the dynamics of the workplace amongst the product design and production of the physical workspace, and also between people and processes, and people and their environment [4].

Despite evidence existing to demonstrate the link between FM and an organisation's success, in practice FM is often seen as a 'fire fighter' service. It is not uncommon to see facilities managers taking a reactive approach in their activities, waiting for instructions before any action is taken. As a result, constantly emerging issues have to be remediated quickly without planned assessment of the best long-term solution [8]. This approach, in general, leads to poor service delivery, dissatisfied customers and loss of value to the organisation that does not operate efficiently. Generally, poor FM delivery is seen in organisations where the business strategy is not effectively aligned with building/asset/service management [9].

In this respect, the sought alignment between business and FM has been continuously evolving as a reflection of, amongst other things, the effectiveness of the information technology and communication systems within organisations [10], [7]. Effective information management forms a critical aspect in the ability of FM teams to coordinate processes so as to achieve the required output, [4] whilst providing valuable information to planners, designers and corporate decision makers [7].

However, the efficient utilisation of information, its management and its supporting technology in FM has been somewhat problematic [8], [10], [11]. Facilities managers can have access to a variety of data sources but the opportunities to utilise or manipulate data are frequently unexploited [8]. Often, systems designed to generate the necessary information required by senior executives to make decisions are lacking [4] with current solutions relying on the duplication of data leading to the over-processing of this data and information overload [8].

A way of resolving this challenge is to invest in appropriate information management resources. This investment should aim at making information processing easier [8] and it is important that facilities managers evaluate alternative simple and appropriate systems to ensure that they meet the organisation's needs [12]. By easing information overload, the FM team has a greater chance of knowing exactly what is expected of them, thus procedures such as work programmes, service level agreements, maintenance schedules, meeting schedules can be instituted [8].

In this respect, the use of building information modelling (BIM) has been investigated as a way to support the reduction of unnecessary processes through better integration of information in FM [13], [14]. However, whilst its use within the design and construction phase is well studied [14], its adoption for FM purposes is still embryonic, in general, due to a lack of skills in the sector [15].

An often-introduced claim is that BIM can be a powerful tool for facility managers to improve buildings' performance and manage operations more efficiently throughout their life cycle. Although this claim has been common since the early introduction of BIM, there is relatively little information about the real use of BIM in the operation and maintenance of buildings. Even most large public owners who have been early adopters of BIM, such as GSA, USACE or Senate Properties, have used BIM more in managing their construction projects than into their FM activities.

Indeed, the literature shows that very little has been implemented extensively in FM and even less has been measured in terms of improvements made due to BIM. In the following, twenty BIM FM related articles reporting on case studies were analysed to identify BIM capabilities implemented in case studies and also to identify the measures of success used that can be related to Return on Investment. As shown in Table 1, the application of BIM to FM has been focused on Hard FM to a great extent and in particular on the accuracy of 3D as-built models and the link to digital statutory/maintenance/supplier information available through online services.

Table 1. FM related BIM capabilities explored and implemented in the literature

Capabilities / Cases	[16]	[17]	[18]	[19]	[20]	[21]	[22]	[23]	[24]	[25]	[26]	[27]	[28]	[29]	[30]	[31]	[32]	[33]	[34]	[35]	[36]
Elimination of duplicated and inaccurate data through 3D modelling	• (I)													• (I)							
Analyse and simulate design to support preventive and reactive maintenance	• (I)	• (I)					• (S)			• (S)											
Life cycle costs and environmental analysis	• (I)																	• (I)			
4D as-built model containing construction process information			• (I)																		
3D as-built model				• (I)	• (I)		• (S)	• (I)						• (I)			• (I)			• (I)	
3D as-built model linked to estatutory/maintenance information						• (I)								• (I)	• (I)		• (I)		• (I)		
3D linked to cleaning schedule							• (S)														
3D linked to waste disposal schedule							• (S)														
Maintenance linked to expenditure history							• (S)														
Order/supply linked to inventory schedule							• (S)							• (I)	• (I)		• (I)		• (I)	• (I)	
Energy Simulation witin as-built								• (I)													
Maintenance schedule									• (S)	• (S)				• (I)	• (I)	• (I)					
Accurate as-built model											• (S)									• (I)	
Maintenance as-done record of event/problem description and solution												• (I)	• (S)						• (I)	• (I)	
Real-time, mobile resource location tracking													• (S)								
Facility condition analysis																• (I)					
Building Automation System																	• (S)				
Travelling path of maintenance																					• (S)

Implemented (I)
Simulated (S)

In regards to measures of success, *'a facility manager is responsible for making critical strategic, tactical, and operational facilities-planning decisions that affect the organization's business performance'* [17]. In this respect, a taxonomy of indicators of success in the implementation of BIM for FM purposes composed of a) financial indicators related to costs and expenditures associated with operation and maintenance, energy, building functions, real estate, plant, etc.; b) Physical indicators associated with the physical shape and conditions of the facility, buildings, systems, and components; c) functional indicators related to the way the facility and the buildings function and which express building appropriateness through space adequacy, parking, etc.; and d) survey-based indicators, which are based solely on respondents' opinion to surveys that are primarily qualitative in nature [37]. In this respect, Table 2 shows metrics used to identify benefits from adopting BIM for FM purposes across many case studies. To a large extent, most of the results obtained in the studies are based of the testimony of managers rather than from a systematic collection of information.

Thus, despite progress being made in terms of advancing the knowledge regarding the adoption of BIM for FM, very little hard evidence is reported in the literature regarding how effective or ineffective BIM based FM processes are in relation to solving FM problems so to justify BIM implementation. Despite the existence of positive testimony that BIM improves FM, a lack of diagnostics for FM problems and baseline measures, BIM in FM is still a solution looking for a problem.

Table 2. Metrics used to identify benefits from adopting BIM for FM

Baseline Measure	[16]	[17]	[18]	[19]	[20]	[21]	[22]	[23]	[24]	[25]	[26]	[27]	[28]	[29]	[30]	[31]	[32]	[33]	[34]	[35]	[36]
Better customer service	•																				
Better decision-making	•	•						•		•	•						•	•			•
Better cost forescast		•					•								•						
Improved data consistency			•		•		•	•				•				•	•		•	•	
Better access to information				•								•							•	•	
Reduced response time					• (S)																
Increased process efficiency						•								•							
Better planning							•								•	•					
Better AEC-FM Integration									•												
Reduction of maintenance failure											•										
Strealined processes											•						•		•	•	• (S)
Improved tracking of inventory													•		•	•					
Reduction of reactive maintenance															•						
Reduced cost of operations															•	•					
Reduced time of operations																• (S)		•			
Reduce effort of operations																					•

Implemented (•)
Simulated (• (S))

2 Case Manchester Town Hall Complex

This research was done in the context of the UK Government's BIM initiative. Further understanding of the key issues in migrating to BIM-FM is crucial to the development of general guidance. The research strategy was Case Study Research, carried out to investigate the use of BIM FM in the Manchester City Council Town Hall Complex (MCC THC) project and followed a previous investigation during the design and construction phase of the same project in 2011 [29], [39]. The tools and methods used for data collection included a literature review on FM and ICT related topics, and interviews with project team members and FM team members. It also involved the use of the NBIMS Capability Maturity Matrix [38], archival analysis of documentation and a workshop for data validation. The sources of evidence utilised included information extracted from the BIM alongside verbal and written explanations describing integrated processes as provided by six members of the FM team.

THC FM Structure: The FM services are organised in a distinctive way. At the macro level, services are divided between front and back-office activities. Within back-office services there are two categories, namely FM Support and Building Support. FM support refers to secondary activities that are directly linked to the provision of primary services. Building support, on the other hand is related to the overall maintenance of the fabric. In this category, there are three levels of 'maintenance': planned preventive maintenance, reactive maintenance and capital projects (i.e. major redevelopments of the facility). In relation to front-office services, there are two categories: housekeeping and customer support. Housekeeping, in general, refers to activities that are performed regularly such as cleaning and waste collection, whilst customer support refers to activities dealing directly with visitors and suppliers to the THC. A BIM was developed to aid building support activities in the main. ICT (hardware, software and systems management) is not managed in coordination with FM. According to the FM interviewees, this disconnection between FM and ICT is an extremely relevant barrier to the adoption of BIM for FM.

With regards to BIM, its depiction for the FM team consists of four systems: C-PAD, ArtrA, eDocuments and UE. C-PAD is the current system used for logging issues raised by end users and non-compliant technical audits. ArtrA, the software which serves as a user friendly interface to access 3D building information on BIM and a cloud-based repository of information (eDocuments), supports this process by making available electronic versions of documents such as statutory requirements and building data, maintenance reports, etc. In this respect, data structure (including building geometry) within ArtrA is hyperlinked to relevant documentation in eDocuments and vice-versa. The maintenance service provider uses the UE as their accounting system and discussions have started regarding the possibilities of increasing UE interoperability.

FM Problems: When the FM team was prompted to identify the benefits of BIM adoption during the initial stages of the research, quite often the answers were related to design and construction benefits such as automated clash detection, support for decision-making, automated costing. Even though these benefits were important for the project, their direct relationship with business core activities or FM was limited or nonexistent. As BIM awareness increased within the FM team the focus shifted to the identification of opportunities for FM service improvement (Table 3).

Table 3. FM problems potentially benefiting from BIM FM implementation

Problems
Data entry procedure was repeated in triplicate for reactive maintenance
Errors due to manual input of information within different system
Incompletion of planned maintenance due to delays in reactive maintenance
Time spent on finding correct information to support building maintenance
Lack of information regarding FM performance
Lack on links between back and front offices services
Errors in the statutory maintenance record due to symmetrical characteristic of the facility

BIM FM Maturity: The results presented here (Table 4) highlight the perspective of the FM team within MCC THC on the level of maturity of BIM as applied to the reactive maintenance process. Overall, these results show that high levels of maturity have been attributed to the areas directly related to graphical information development, whilst lower scores have been attributed to areas related to business functions. As argued by the FM team, business functions are not yet linked with FM results. The process for assessment used also revealed that the FM team still face a degree of uncertainty related to their understanding of the actual level of BIM maturity.

Data richness: interviewees agreed that BIM was established, but with only very basic data loaded. Their perception is that additional data has gradually been made available and that data is beginning to be accepted as an authoritative primary source.

Life-cycle view: data was gathered as it was made available throughout the project, however no single phase (design, construction and use) was totally authoritative or complete. One participant indicated that a fourth phase of the facilities lifecycle has been added and some information is flowing.

Table 4. Cumulative assessment of maturity from the FM team (reactive maintenance)

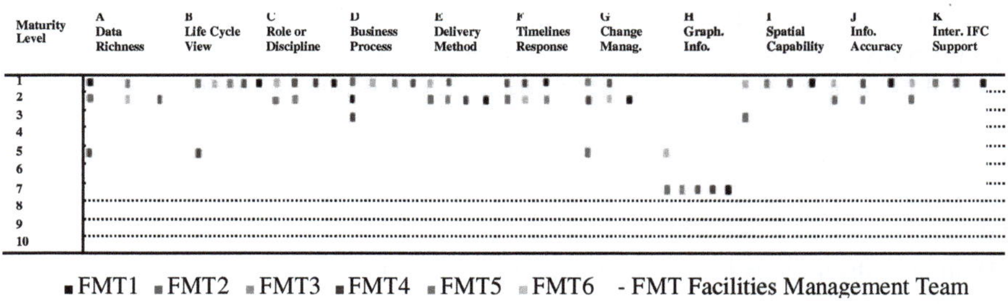

Roles or discipline: Roles apply to people's jobs at this level but no roles are fully supported through BIM. Contradicting this conclusion, two members of the FM team believe that the Service Resident Engineer uses BIM for entering data and via building geometry can access related documentation; for them his role is fully supported through BIM.

Business process: Business processes are not completely defined and therefore cannot be used to store information in the BIM. However, to a limited extent, cross-departmental integration has begun, as a few business processes are being designed to collect information to maintain the BIM in the organization.

Delivery method: Despite the BIM being accessible, it is not on a network and there is control over who can access it. This is to be kept this way until the FM team develops enough confidence to operate the BIM.

Timelines / response: The information is stored and managed only on the "room data sheet" through an external database in ArtrA Software. Currently, the system is not designed to reply to a set of pre-determined enquires. The model is under development and as such it is not completed or automated. However, reports can be generated from the service order request logs in C-Pad, and building geometry (in ArtrA) is linked to building documentation (in eDocuments), thus indicating some level of timeliness / response.

Change management: Awareness exists that there is change management process for BIM in place at project level, however there is lack of clarity regarding to whether this will be extended to the organisation.

Graphical information: Drawings are 3D object based and have intelligence. The MCC FM team has achieved this by using the software solution ArtrA (Figure 1). Within ArtrA, each asset, such as the MEP asset, has a location based asset identifier and a unique webpage reference generated by eDocuments. Currently, information provided via eDocuments is in non-intelligent PDF format. Visualisation of the model is possible in different packages; however, loss of intelligent information happens if functional model manipulation is needed.

Spatial capability: The facility is recognized in a worldview spatially and the common coordinate system was inherited from the architectural model. Despite the space not being spatially located in the real world according to a GPS/GIS system (as indicated in the CMM) the current system adopted constitutes a BIM capability.

Information accuracy: To date, electronic validation of information for internal spaces is available to a limited extent. This is due to limited interoperability, where in some instances data from information structure in one model is lost during exchange, thus leading to gaps and duplication in the information model where data has to be re-entered manually (Figure 1).

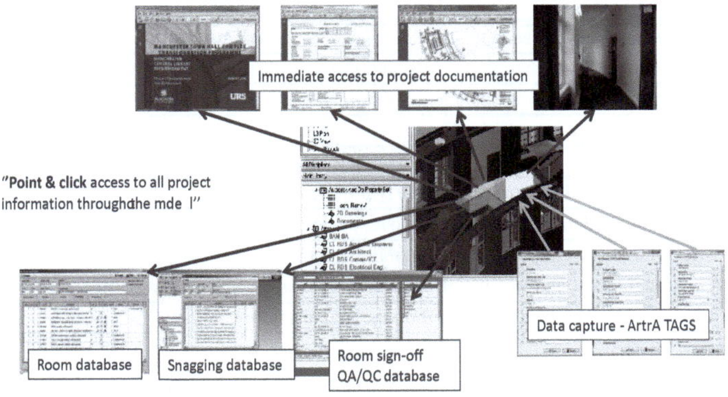

Fig. 1. ArtrA graphical information displays rich contextual information in a 3D model

Interoperability / Exchange support: some interoperability exists that is not yet automatic or seamless. Interoperability was achieved by using COBie for exchanging information from ArtrA (portable 3D intelligent data set), C-Pad (management) and eDocuments (archival register). These applications form a system linked via relationships that enables automatic updating of data and information. Data and information entry can be done from existing models, manually from archival documentation or survey. Key stakeholders within the facilities management team are tasked to author and review the information.

Overview: As expected, the overall results achieved by MCC Reactive Maintenance Services are low if analysed independently. That does not mean that MCC is not performing well in the implementation of BIM. Comparatively with the industry in general, the efforts put forward in the implementation are quite remarkable, considering that technology is not ready for full adoption, thus imposing a constraint in higher scores.

Barriers: the research identified many barriers that hindered the implementation of BIM in the THC project. Examples of the identified barriers include the necessary technical expertise to generate and operate BIM, readiness for a fast implementation, the completion of the model before completion of construction to assist hand-over activities, lack of organisational buy in and most importantly the separation of MCC ICT from FM. Table 5 shows the barriers to implementation identified during the research.

Benefits and Returns from BIM FM: several benefits were identified for all phases of the project (i.e. design, construction and use). With regards to the benefits for the design and construction phase, these were related to support to decision-making and the reduction of errors and risks on site. A series of simulations revealed that many potential gains in terms of time, human resources and finance can be achieved (Table 6). Above all, faster maintenance process will lead to shorter service disruption, thus enhancing the support to business core activities and customer satisfaction.

Table 5. Barriers to the implementation of BIM FM within the THC

Barriers
Technical expertise needed for the maintenance and updating of the BIM
Number of process changes made simultaneously
Risk of underperform whilst changing from current to BIM enabled process
Limited software interoperability
Lack of guidance, protocols and standards for BIM FM
Unclear BIM FM requirements at early project stages
Model incompletion at project hand over stage
Lack of clarity regarding model assembly and its relationship with FM processes
Lack of clarity regarding overall management system, KPIs and bechmark figures
lack of cross functional buy in wihtin the organisation

Table 6. Benefits and returns from BIM FM (Adapted from MCC, 2013)

Scenario	Traditional		BIM Enabled		Savings		
	Time	Man/hours	Time	Man/hours	Time	Man/hours	£
Ventilation motor replacement	4 weeks	14	1 day	3	27 days	11	£286.00
Alcove light replacement	6 weeks	10	1 day	2	40 days	8	£108.00
Extract duct - unknown water build up	12 weeks	23	1 day	10	92 days	13	£838.00
Public lift repair	5 weeks	16	2 days	6	32 days	10	£260.00
Ceiling leak in heritage area	3 days	14	1 day	3	2 days	11	£286.00

3 Discussion and Conclusions

A great deal of effort has been made in the UK towards the adoption of BIM within the construction sector. However, once construction is finished, the use of the large and rich amount of information generated within project phases has not been explored to the same extent. The literature in this area shows that, despite many attempts to BIM FM implementation exists, these are still piecemeal and FM cases showing extensive use of BIM are lacking. The identified challenge faced by facilities managers relates to the lack of integration and transparency across organisational functions. Integration seems to be discussed as the way forward for the sector and BIM has been considered as a facilitator of this process. However, the lack of evidence demonstrating its benefits generates scepticism within managers. Also, the lack of FM "terminology" and understanding about how it applies to FM (being most of the discussions around design and construction) also contributes to the promotion of misunderstood perspectives of how BIM supports FM, whilst paradoxically also generating inflated expectations. As identified through this research, the ownership of the implementation process is not yet in the hands of FM teams. Much effort is still made by design and construction teams to provide information modelling services to assist FM teams. In this regard, the clarification that roles and responsibilities do not automatically change with BIM implementation is crucial. However, an adequate system must be in place to support authoring of information at all instances. The maintenance of a performance baseline and a history of critical services that can support the prioritization of services are also fundamental.

Conversely to the FM sector in general, the initial findings indicate that MCC despite being at early stages of BIM implementation has progressed rapidly, positively pushing the boundaries of BIM adoption for FM purposes. It is clear from the research that the willingness of MCC to implement BIM and their vision in using BIM to improve FM has been paramount to this fast development. One of the most relevant changes is in the attitude of the FM team that became more process oriented and is seeking to identify process inefficiencies that could be mitigated by the adoption of BIM. In other words, the MCC FM team is not just following a trend, rather the team is focused on promoting continuous improvement by setting new standards for the management of facilities making use of BIM whenever appropriate. This approach is creating an MCC construction knowledge asset base - information assets that improve the future management of this and other projects. With the support of this research, the FM team became aware of their advanced position in relation to traditional FM practices as well as of the path for redefining the process model for FM in public building projects and further BIM implementation and development.

Acknowledgments. Our special thanks to the BIS for funding this research, and to Mark Bew (Chairman of the UK Government BIM Implementation Group) and Liam Brady (Town Hall Complex Client Programme Manager) for their support to the research collaboration between the University of Salford and Manchester City Council.

References

1. Thomson, T.: The essence of facilities management. Facilities 8(8), 8–12 (1990)
2. Tay, L., Ooi, J.T.L.: Facilities management: a 'Jack of all trades'? Facilities 19(10), 357–363 (2001)
3. British Standards Institute: Facility Management - Part 1: Terms and definitions: BS EN 15221-1:2006, vol. 44, 19p. BSI Standards Publication, London (2007)
4. Alexander, K.: Facilities Management: Theory and Practice. E & F N Spon, London (1996)
5. Amaratunga, D., Haigh, R., Sarshar, M., Baldry, D.: Assessment of facilities management process capability: A NHS facilities case study. International Journal of Health Care Quality Assurance 15(6), 277–288 (2002)
6. Lennerts, K., Abel, J., Pfründer, U., Sharma, V.: Reducing health care costs through optimised facility management-related processes. Journal of Facilities Management 2(2), 192–206 (2003)
7. Atkin, B., Brooks, A.: Total Facilities Management, Facilities, 3rd edn., vol. 12. Wiley-Blackwell, Oxford (2009)
8. Barrett, P.S., Baldry, D.: Facilities Management: Towards Best Practice, 2nd edn. Facilities Management, vol. 2. Wiley-Blackwell, Oxford (2003)
9. Amaratunga, D., Baldry, D.: A conceptual framework to measure facilities management performance. Property Management 21(2), 171–189 (2003)
10. Abel, J., Diez, K., Lennerts, K.: A Standard Database Model for Computer Aided Facility Management in Hospitals. In: Proceedings of the Joint International Conference on Computing and Decision Making in Civil and Building Engineering, Montréal, Canada, pp. 535–542 (2006)
11. Bainbridge, M., Finch, E.F.: Getting the attention the facilities manager deserves. Facilities 27(7/8), 277–290 (2009)
12. BIFM: The Good Practice Guide to Selecting FM Software, The Good Practice Guide, Hertfordshire, 22p. (2006)
13. Ballesty, S., Mitchell, J., Drogemuller, R., Schevers, H., Linning, C., Singh, G., Marchant, D.: Adopting BIM for facilities management: Solutions for managing the Sydney Opera House. Cooperative Research Centre for Construction Innovation. Report, pp. 1–32 (2007)
14. Eastman, C., Teicholz, P., Sacks, R., Liston, K.: BIM Handbook: A Guide to Building Information Modeling for Owners, Managers, Designers, Engineers, and Contractors. John Wiley & Sons, Inc., New Jersey (2008)
15. Cracknell, D.: Sector BIM Strategy: Improving BIM Education & Training, The Higher Education Academy, `http://www.heacademy.ac.uk/assets/documents/disciplines/built_environment/BIM/BIM_Skills_CIC_David_Cracknell.pdf` (accessed March 2014)
16. Innovation, CRC Construction: Adopting BIM for facilities management: Solutions for managing the Sydney Opera House. Cooperative Research Center for Construction Innovation, Brisbane, Australia (2007)
17. Lavy, S., Shohet, I.M.: Computer-Aided Healthcare Facility Management. Journal of Computing in Civil Engineering 21(5), 363–372 (2007)
18. Goedert, J., Meadati, P.: Integrating Construction Process Documentation into Building Information Modeling. Journal of Construction Engineering and Management 134(7), 509–516 (2008)

19. Khanzode, A., Fischer, M., Reed, D.: Benefits and lessons learned of implementing building virtual design and construction (VDC) technologies for coordination of mechanical, electrical, and plumbing (MEP) systems on a large healthcare project, 324–342 (2008)
20. Akcamete, A., Alkinci, B., Garrett Jr., J.H.: Motivation for Computational support for Updating Building Information Models (BIMs). In: Workshop on Computing in Civil Engineering, pp. 523–532 (2009)
21. Fruchter, R., Schrotenboer, T., Luth, G.P.: From Building Information Modeling to Building Knowledge Model. In: Proceedings of the 2009 ASCE International Workshop on Computing in Civil Engineering, Austin, TX, June 24- 27, pp. 380–389 (2009)
22. Onyenobi, T.C., Arayici, Y., Egbu, C.O., Sharman, H.K.: Project and facilities management using BIM: University of Salford relocation management to Media City (2010)
23. Woo, J., Wilsman, J., Kang, D.: Use of As-Built Building Information Modeling, Construction Research Congress, 538–548 (2010)
24. Ospina-Alvarado, A.M., Castro-Lacouture, D.: Interaction of Processes and Phases in Project Scheduling Using BIM for A/E/C/FM Integration, Construction Research Congress 2010: Innovation for Reshaping Construction Practices, pp. 939–948 (2010)
25. Hao, Q., Xue, Y., Shen, W., Jones, B., Zhu, J.: A Decision Support System for Integrating Corrective Maintenance, Preventative Maintenance and Condition-based Maintenance. In: Construction Research Congress, pp. 470–479 (2010)
26. Tang, P., Huber, D., Akinci, B., Lipman, R., Lytle, A.: Automatic reconstruction of as-built building information models from laser-scanned point clouds: A review of related techniques. Automation in Construction 19, 829–843 (2010)
27. Su, Y.C., Lee, Y.C., Lin, Y.C.: Enhancing Maintenance Management Using Building Information Modeling in Facilities Management. In: Proceedings of the 28th International Symposium on Automation and Robotics in Construction (2011)
28. Costin, A., Pradhananga, N., Teizer, J.: Integration of passive RFID location tracking in Building Information Models (BIM). In: EG-ICE, Int. Workshop, Herrsching, Germany, pp. 4–6 (2012)
29. Codinhoto, R., Kiviniemi, A., Kemmer, S., Da Rocha, C.G.: BIM Implementation: Manchester Town Hall Complex. SCRI Report Series 6 (2011), `http://live.scri.salford.ac.uk/wp-content/uploads/2011/12/MCC_Final_Research_Report.pdf`
30. Aladham, O., Gonzales, J., Grant, I., Harper, K., Kruger, A., Nannis, S., Patel, A., Snedeker, L.: Case Study 1: MathWorks. In: Teicholz, P. (ed.) BIM for Facility Managers. Wiley (2013)
31. Beatty, R., Kim, K.: Case Study 2: Texas A&M Health Science Center – A case study of BIM and COBie for Facility Management. In: Teicholz, P. (ed.) BIM for Facility Managers. Wiley (2013)
32. Aspurez, V., Lewis, A.: Case Study 3: USC School of Cinematic Arts. In: Teicholz, P. (ed.) BIM for Facility Managers. Wiley (2013)
33. Afedizie, E., Beatty, R., Hanselman, E., Heyward, E., Lawal, A., Nimer, E., Rosenthal, L., Siman, D.: Case Study 4: Implementation of BIM and FM at Xavier University. In: Teicholz, P. (ed.) BIM for Facility Managers. Wiley (2013)
34. Lewis, A.: Case Study 5: State of Wisconsin Bureau of FM, Division of State Facilities, Department of Administration. In: Teicholz, P. (ed.) BIM for Facility Managers. Wiley (2013)
35. Lewis, A.: Case Study 6: University of Chicago Administration Building Renovation. In: Teicholz, P. (ed.) BIM for Facility Managers. Wiley (2013)

36. Wang, Y., Wang, X., Wang, J., Yung, P., Jun, G.: Engagement of facilities management in design stage through BIM: framework and a case study. Advances in Civil Engineering (2013)
37. Lavy, S., Garcia, J.A., Dixit, M.K.: Establishment of KPIs for facility performance measurement: review of literature. Facilities 28(9/10), 440–464 (2010)
38. National Institute of Building Sciences. US National Building Information Modelling Standard, Version 1 – Part 1: Overview, Principles and Methodologies (2007), http://www.wbdg.org/pdfs/NBIMSv1_p1.pdf (last accessed November 2009)
39. Kiviniemi, A., Codinhoto, R.: Challenges in the Implementation of BIM for FM: Case Manchester Town Hall Complex. In: Proceedings: ICCCBE and CIB W078 2014, Disney World, Orlando, Florida, USA, June 23-25 (2014)

Fostering the Link from PLM to ERP via BIM

The AEC Industry in Transition

Dominik Holzer

The University of Melbourne, Australia

Abstract. This paper investigates approaches for linking Product Lifecycle Management (PLM) via structured data stemming from Building Information Modeling (BIM) to information systems that get applied for Enterprise Resource planning (ERP) across Architecture, Engineering and Construction (AEC). The author highlights key pathways for such integration, with a particular focus on the hurdles contractors, suppliers and manufacturers need to overcome to master their transition to BIM-enabled PLM and the associated ERP. Based on a case-study (Hickory Group), the paper analyses the opportunities for the strategic repositioning of a construction and manufacturing firm who combines PLM with BIM and ERP within its organisation.

1 Background to the PLM-ERP Integration

Expanding from product development and lifecycle planning into resource management is an approach that has steadily gained momentum since the introduction of ERP systems in the early 70s [1]. As a production-oriented sector, manufacturing benefits in particular from PLM-ERP linkages and consequently the use of well integrated information systems. Such systems assist the management of a broad range of processes relating to the product lifecycle. Similar to PLM, there is a number of core-activities specific to ERP. Being more transaction-oriented, these activities cover tasks such as resource planning, purchasing, storage, QA, change management, productivity management, HR, finances/payroll, and more. Common to most ERP systems (and similar to PLM) is the integration and management of data via a centralised server in a standardised format, in order to avoid data-duplication. With the progressing development of the World Wide Web, systems for ERP are increasingly becoming location agnostic, web-based, with information stored and accessed via cloud-based services [2]. If integration between PLM and ERP is desired, it is crucial for any organisation to create logic connections between product structure and production planning. A clear mapping of processes and points of connection is required to create bi-directional links between the two activities. Often the common point of connection is the Bill-Of-Materials (BOM) [3].

A key obstacle to the introduction of ERP to the construction industry can be highlighted as follows [4]: ERP systems provide scalable solutions that ideally help to manage information across an enterprise in its totality. On the other hand, the construction industry (and the support systems applied therein) is highly project-based. A large number of external stakeholders federate information on a temporary (project-dependent) level,

S. Fukuda et al. (Eds.): PLM 2014, IFIP AICT 442, pp. 75–82, 2014.

using a number of disparate information systems and formats. Establishing ERP systems in construction firms is therefore a task that needs to be considered specific to a highly dynamic project and production-based context [5]. Also, the effort for implementing PLM and ERP solutions in an organisation is difficult to justify in smaller or medium sized organisations (which are common in the construction sector)

2 BIM as an Enabler

In the past, efforts have been undertaken to link construction information and manufacturing data for construction to ERP systems. These efforts were mainly based on CAD output for documentation with added data/attributes to 2D documents. The proportion of valuable information-content that can easily be made available from 2D CAD to ERP is low. Consequently the use of 2D CAD is not best suited to tie in with the information-centric approach required to establish a clearly defined product structure. Research has been undertaken how to better manage the integration of product information in the construction process [6]. BIM provides such integration and its inclusion into planning and construction processes seems to promise increased connectivity between PLM and ERP [7].

It has now been over 10 years since BIM became officially accepted as the acronym across the construction industry to represent the breadth of approaches for object-based virtual modelling and building product models to encompass the entire building lifecycle. Up until that point (in 2003), variations of BIM had been applied across the construction industry globally in one way or another for 2-3 decades. By 2014, the adoption of BIM methods for the design and delivery of projects has increased substantially [8]. BIM is becoming ever more mainstream, driven by a number of key countries such as the US, UK, Singapore, Finland, Denmark, Norway, and Australia [8]. Many other nations follow this international trend where more and more developed countries are becoming knowledgeable in the implementation and application of BIM related processes, policies, training, and procurement. An ever growing number of construction sectors globally embrace the added benefits of a more integrated and streamlined way of operation[1].

Initially architecture and engineering firms were the first to adopt BIM to strengthen their in-house (lonely BIM) design/analyse/delivery methods. By nature, consultants operating with BIM tend to create 'Design Intent' BIM[2] (or LOD[3] 200/300) that serve design coordination without necessarily involving a description of the detailed

[1] McGraw Hill has issued a smart market report on: "The Business Value of BIM for Construction in Major Global Markets" in early 2014. The report outlines in detail how the construction sector in various developed markets globally has taken up BIM.

[2] The Consensusdocs 301 – BIM Addendum makes a clear distinction between design intent and construction BIM. It is the first standard contract document that globally addresses legal and administration issues associated with using BIM.

[3] The American Institute of Architects (AIA) 'E202-2008 BIM Protocol' was the first document to classify the progression of BIM into five major stages of development (LOD 100 – 500) ranging from conceptual modelling to construction and operation.

object to be installed by the trades. This approach has been complemented over the past few years with the production of 'Construction BIM' (LOD 400) as more and more contractors embrace BIM for detailed coordination and quantity take-off during construction and assembly. In order to achieve the required level of detail, contractors work with sub-contractors and suppliers who provide coordinated BIM that consider actual manufacturing for detailed assembly and the extraction of Bill-of-Quantities of actual equipment components. By incorporating coordinated object data from sub-contractors and suppliers into their delivery process, the construction industry moves towards system integration and process automation in an unprecedented way. The link from BIM data output to fabrication equipment either directly, or via a CAD/CAM interface is becoming more commonplace throughout a number of trades within the construction industry. Pre-fabrication and offsite assembly is on the rise globally.

The use of BIM is expanding with progressive convergence between information systems that logically tie into the data-rich environment it offers. In order to achieve data-integrity, the construction industry increasingly relies on standardised formats to structure BIM object data via Integrated Construction Information Systems (ICIS) [4]. On one end of the spectrum, BIM increasingly gets linked to geospatial data and GIS integration for City Information Modeling. BIM now plays an important role as a stepping stone to connect geometric information and spatial data from the building level, to a 'precinct' scale, and finally the overarching geospatial context (GIS). On the other end of the spectrum, BIM methods get applied for manufacturing and detailed assembly of construction components. On this component level, the construction industry (finally) comes to terms with the relevance of managing highly detailed virtual representations of the built artefacts. An increasing number of BIM objects are available via libraries and manufacturer/reseller's websites. Hand in hand with this development, BIM encompasses an ever larger number of stakeholders throughout the building lifecycle (social BIM) - in line with the initial ideals by its proponents [9].

3 The Relation between BIM, PLM and ERP

Despite a number of similarities, investigations into the PLM to ERP transition has rather occurred in parallel to (and not in conjunction with) the development of BIM over the past 3+ decades [5]. A key point of investigation therefore relates to the question of how to establish authoritative data that allows organisations to communicate between all three systems. Resolving the definition of authoritative data that cuts across product lifecycle, resource planning and building information modeling processes may lead to highly efficient sharing of data across these processes. Such integration would likely result in an increase of efficiency throughout a number of inter and intra-organisational business processes.

Only recently BIM has matured to a point where the construction industry starts to explore closer links between BIM, PLM and ERP on a mainstream level. There are four main reasons for this delay:

Firstly: detailed coordination of virtual building objects for construction is fairly new to the AEC industry (apart from a few exceptions) where subcontractors and trades only slowly start to embrace BIM. A manufacturing mindset is not always prevailing in the construction industry that is historically rooted in craft-based skills and the experience of its workers.

Secondly: the construction industry needs to overcome the hurdle of setting up and adopting protocols that enable interoperability and integrated data-sharing across a number of stakeholders.

Thirdly: Software linking data from object-oriented BIM assemblies directly to ERP systems has only recently become mature and available to the mainstream construction market.

Fourthly: Many firms in the AEC industry are small or medium in size [11]. Whereas BIM use has become common in these firms, the effort to implement PLM or ERP systems across those firms may seem too costly and undesirable

Still, many goals of BIM have strong overlap with the goals of both PLM and ERP. The application of BIM on construction projects aims at streamlining the information flow across the building lifecycle using high-fidelity data associated to virtual building components that represent their physical counterparts as closely as possible. Despite their traditionally different scope of service, there are manifold possibilities for connecting product data from design and engineering to PLM [12]. Agram and Eastman list the following five key areas of connection: System Configuration, Authoring Information, General Management Functions, Change Management & Synchronisation, and Data Visualization & Interoperability.

In the context of BIM, key to the integration between PLM and BIM is the ability to synchronise data between the PLM system and the BIM server, based on the definition of authoritative data. In order to achieve such an interface between BIM and PLM systems a logic for the creation, naming, tagging and management of object data (and the opportunities to interface this information with other server- based systems) has to be established across design and planning within an organisation. BIM objects include, category, type, and attribute definitions; parametric relations can be established to govern these definitions across the entire building-lifecycle and help optimise sustainable building design [9].

Other industries such as car-manufacturing or aerospace have long experienced the benefits of PLM and ERP use within their associated manufacturing sectors [10]. It is therefore no surprise that the first steps for integrating BIM with PLM and further with ERP in construction were facilitated by software environments that can also be found in parallel industries. Dassault Systèmes is a company that has steadily expanded such environments from industries like Aerospace and Financial Services to facilitate solutions within Architecture, Engineering and Construction. Their Logistics offering includes equipment placing, human modelling & simulation, material handling and flow to the site, cost & construction time estimation, just to name a few [13]. In 2008, Skanska was one of the first organisations to employ Dassault's Enovia™ PLM solution in conjunction with their BIM approach and the goals to further integrate it with ERP. Skanska has since done so for data management across the supply chain on a number of their projects – building on their PLM approach to establish authoritative data.

4 The Hickory Example

Most contractors and manufacturers that operate in the construction industry, have yet to explore the PLM/BIM/ERP integration [9] [14]. Those organisations that actively pursue a path of integration between PLM, BIM and ERP often see themselves entering unchartered territory.

In an attempt to draw from a practical example of PLM, BIM and ERP integration, the author has conducted research at one organisation in particular that actively promotes their supply-chain integration in the production of unitised building systems. The Victoria-based enterprise surrounding the Hickory Group is on the forefront of innovation and development in the Australian construction sector. Founded in 1991, Hickory combines a construction business with manufacture, plant hire, and more. Next to their conventional construction division, the Hickory Group oversees a division for prefabrication and assembly of building units (UB), as well as a division for the pre-fabrication bathroom pods as specialised building systems (SYNC). What distinguishes Hickory from most of their competitors in Australia is their strong focus on streamlining the fabrication processes of their production line, applying a manufacturing mindset rather than construction. This approach becomes most apparent within their UB and SYNC divisions where they collaborate with designers on new patents and innovative production methods. Over a period of 1 year, the author has conducted two site visits to the Hickory production facilities where he inspected the production line as well as interviewing Hickory staff, who form part of their drafting team, their process management group, their production management group, as well as the organisation's leadership.

Whereas BIM is based on disruptive technology for the delivery of design documentation and beyond, a transition to an ERP system affords the integration of highly disruptive technology to all sectors of their business. Challenges faced by Hickory on their path of embracing PLM and ERP relate to the fundamental changes required on their path to gain benefits from an introduction of related systems to their business. Segregated business units within the Hickory group were re-integrated in order to streamline data transfer across IT systems and management practices across different sectors of the enterprise. Such a move also allowed for increased standardisation naming conventions related to their resource planning and production processes.

Initiated by new leadership, Hickory recently expanded their competencies by employing new staff with manufacturing background. In addition, external consultants assist Hickory with a major overhaul of their internal project delivery processes. The overhaul goes hand in hand with the establishment of a new data-management strategy that covers the integration of PLM with ERP and BIM. The shift from a construction to a manufacture is manifest in a number of ways:

- A strong focus on frontloading the design effort in order to identify and validate detailed assembly requirements as early as possible
- Logical naming conventions that allow for fluent data transfer between PLM, BIM and ERP
- Knowledge engineering based on detailed analysis of prototypes and knowledge transfer further down the supply-chain

- A revised tool ecology with detailed specification of data-transfer and management.
- Introducing detailed process plans with clearly defined hold-points, complemented with progress checklists and identification of high-risk items.
- Consolidating separate information systems across the entire business into a centralised system for data storage and management with particular focus on the integration between PLM, ERP and BIM.

Key to the above activities is the establishment and assignment of authoritative ('master') data to those processes where most of the information is required. This approach involves upfront planning via PLM with the consequence that design changes can be traced and communicated directly to the BOM for production planning via their ERP (and in particular their Material Resource Planning - MRP). At the UB and SYNC divisions at Hickory, Autodesk's PLM solution Vault™ was chosen to facilitate this transition and manage the 'master' data. A third party technology consultancy was commissioned to revise the existing tool ecology and process map across the Hickory group. The consultancy established an implementation strategy in order to enable the streamlined integration of virtual 3D geometric construction objects in LOD 400 BIM (shop-drawing) level, their associated data for construction, and the organisation's ERP systems that ties the BIM/PLM data to the production process. The increasing information content incorporated into the 3D BIM for assembly provides the backdrop for data integration in Vault™. In order to streamline the transfer from BIM to the PLM system, Hickory has transitioned from using Autodesk's Revit™ to Inventor™ as their predominant documentation tool. It was identified that Revit™'s integration with Vault™ is insufficiently resolved to facilitate the level of authoritative data integration aspired to by Hickory. Inventor™ on the other hand has a stronger manufacturing focus than Revit™, with better integration to Vault™. BIM drafters at Hickory had to be up-skilled and new staff was hired in order to accommodate the revised workflow.

Risk analysis at UB and SYNC revealed that linking between ERP and BIM could not be achieved successfully on the first available project. Instead, UB at Hickory are gradually migrating their data storage and management from a spreadsheet-based approach to a centralised server, increasing the information content, value engineering, and data management[4] capabilities as they go. The Hickory team is gradually learning to adjust and refine the interfaces between the lifecycle planning and production processes, but there are great expectations for the streamlined interface to deliver major benefits to the business once major steps in the implementation have been accomplished.

5 Future Goals

The transition such as seen at Hickory exemplifies a major shift in thinking by local construction companies: The ultimate goal for integrating PLM with BIM and ERP

[4] Such as Kanban systems and change-tracking to increase automation.

does not merely lie in the streamlining of processes and the reduction of production/business cost. Much more than that, if lifecycle management, resource planning, and design can be connected via robust processes and high-fidelity data, a company could then export that 'system' and manufacture anywhere in the world. Design will need to be rationalised to a point where it can be realised through knowledge-engineering and related manufacturing processes. Mastering such an approach will allow a construction firm to positions itself as strong competitor on a global market, dramatically reducing production cost, increasing turnover of capital, and becoming manufacturers rather than remaining builders.

6 Conclusions

After 10 years of BIM use across the construction industry undergoes increasing convergence due to the efforts by various professions to establish the closest possible match between virtual representations of building components and their physical counterpart. BIM is now steadily expanding into other areas and its use has reached a level of maturity where data fidelity is sufficiently resolved that BIM output can interact with PLM systems and further drive the definition of Bills-Of-Material that feed into ERP processes and help to drive the production line.

The construction industry is still in early days of exploring the full potential of these connections. Any organisation aiming to make a transition towards greater synergies between their planning and production process using BIM, PLM and ERP, needs to account for a possible temporary drop in productivity. Re-skilling of staff (and likely also the employment of experts from other industry sectors), the re-organisation of established intra and inter-organisation processes, data integration between business sectors, and a revised tool infrastructure are just a few points in a long list of challenges such organisations are facing. Changing the mentality from a traditional mindset (that is at times still rooted in a craft-based industry) towards highly engineered manufacturing and production does not occur overnight.

Despite the obstacles, those organisations within the construction industry who innovate with a strong focus on supply-chain integration, pre-fabrication, rapid manufacture and assembly, have most to gain by embracing the possibilities for tight links between BIM, PLM and ERP. They will be able to position themselves as strong global players on a competitive market that will increasingly rely on manufacturing and automation.

Acknowledgments. The author would like to acknowledge the assistance from the Hickory Group as well as Memko in the development of this paper.

References

[1] Fitzgerald, A.: Enterprise Resource Planning. IEE Conference Publication 359, Institute of Electrical Engineers, London, UK, pp. 291–297 (1992)

[2] Wilkinson, P.: Online Resource: "Unit4 combining collaboration, ERP and BIM in the cloud, http://www.extranetevolution.com/2012/02/unit4-combining-collaboration-erp-and-bim-in-the-cloud/#sthash.dmlBT4ez.dpuf (accessed on February 16, 2014)

[3] Shilovitsky, O.: BOM: Apple of Discord between PLM and ERP? Online Resource, http://beyondplm.com/2013/09/17/bom-apple-of-discord-between-plm-and-erp/ (accessed on February 16, 2014)

[4] Mêda, P., Sousa, H.: Towards Software Integration in the Construction Industry – ERP and ICIS Case Study. In: Proceedings of the CIB W78 2012:29th International Conference, Beirut, Lebanon, October 17-19, pp. 304–313 (2012)

[5] Babič, N.Č., Podbreznik, P., Reboljêda, D.: Integrating resource production and construction using BIM. Automation in Construction 19, 539–543 (2010)

[6] Technia PLM Newsletter, The Construction industry in focus" Online Resource, http://www.technia.com/Section-News-Events/Newsletters/Nordic-PLM-Newsletter/Issue-1-20102/Jonas-Chronical/The-Construction-industry-in-focus/ (accessed on February 15, 2014)

[7] Cutting-Decelle, A.-F., Dubois, A.-M., Fernandez, I.: Management and Integration of Product Information in Construction: Reality and Future Trends. The Int. Journal of Construction IT 5(2), 19–46 (1997)

[8] SmartMarket Report, The Business Value of BIM for Construction in Major Global Markets. How Contractors around the world are driving innovation with Building Information Modeling. McGraw Hill Construction (2014)

[9] Eastman, C.: Building Product Models: Computer Environments Supporting Design and Construction. CRC Press, Boca Raton (1999)

[10] Cimalore, C.: ERP/PLM complement each other & facilitate a collaborative environment in design, engineering and manufacturing processes. Electronics Supply Manufacturing (2007)

[11] Ghosh, S., Negahban, S., Kwak, J.H., Skibniewski, M.J.: Integration of PLM Solutions and BIM Systems for the AEC Industry. In: Proceedings of the 30th ISARC, Montréal, Canada, pp. 1046–1055 (2011)

[12] Aram, S., Eastman, C.: Impact of Sustainability on Integration and Interoperability between BIM and ERP – A Governance Framework. In: Proceedings of the Technology Management Conference (ITMC), 2011 IEEE International, pp. 187–193 (2013)

[13] Dassault Systèmes: Logistics, Online Resource, http://www.3ds.com/industries/architecture-engineering-construction/business-processes/logistics/ (accessed on February 16, 2014)

[14] Barthorpe, S., Chien, H.J., Shih, J.K.: A survey of the potential for enterprise resource planning (ERP) in improving the effectiveness of construction management in the UK construction industry. International Journal of Computer Applications in Technology 20(1), 120–128 (2004)

The Turning Point: MEP Contractors as the Key to Achieving Lifecycle BIM

Sumit Oberoi and Dominik Holzer

Air Conditioning and Mechanical Contractors' Association (AMCA), Australia
The University of Melbourne, Australia

Abstract. Developments in the construction industry across a number of countries over the past decade suggest that the use of Building Information Modeling (BIM) is becoming the norm for the design and delivery of projects. As BIM increasingly enters a broad range of domains within the built environment, the importance of Specialist Contractors - and in particular MEP Contractors - as part of these developments begins to show. MEP Contractors form a crucial link in the information-chain to achieve life-cycle BIM. This paper investigates the shift to the role of MEP Contractors in the context of BIM. It analyses the structural changes within the contracting professions, and it highlights the impact of BIM enabled MEP Contractors on the construction industry as a whole. The paper scrutinises this development by example of the BIM-MEP^{AUS} initiative of the Australian Air Conditioning and Mechanical Contractors' Association (AMCA). Accounts from BIM-MEP^{AUS} illustrate the raise of the BIM-enabled MEP Contractors and thereby act as a reference for other international industry groups who may wish to follow their example.

1 Background to the Use of BIM in the Construction Industry

Research suggests that the construction industries in a number of developed countries waste some 30 per cent of their efforts through rework and inefficient practices [1] [2]. If that wasted effort were to be reduced, it would make a significant contribution to the construction industry's environmental footprint globally. If the changes required to achieve that reduction were also to flow throughout the supply chain then the improved output would be substantially higher. Embracing the ethos at the core of Integrated Project Delivery (IPD)[1] practices, modelling techniques and supply chain integration practices have proven to be pivotal for a number of industries to achieve notable productivity gains within the past forty years [3].

Although the use of BIM technology in the delivery of construction project is now becoming pervasive, significant fragmentation and adversarial business models in the

---

[1] IPD was first introduced by the California Council of the American Institute of Architects (AIA|CC) in 2007 as part of a publication tiled: *Integrated Project Delivery: A Working Definition.* A comprehensive summary of IPD principles can be found as an online resource by the AIA|CC: `http://www.aiacc.org/2012/06/05/integrated-project-delivery-a-history-of-leadership-advocacy-and-commitment/`

S. Fukuda et al. (Eds.): PLM 2014, IFIP AICT 442, pp. 83–90, 2014.

construction sector have prevented efficiency-gains to translate across the entire building life-cycle [4]. The predominant project-focus prevailing in the construction industry is creating impediments to innovation as ongoing projects do not incorporate systemic efforts towards innovation through rigid organisation practices [5]. The construction industry is consistently slow in adopting new project management and workflows practices that leverage technological advancements; in parallel, the manufacturing sector is also experiencing a decline[2]. Whilst the low productivity in the building sector can be partly attributed to the "one-off or bespoke" nature of construction activities with each project being essentially a prototype, there is a lack of focus on process improvement and collaborative integrated project delivery practices. BIM can bridge this gap, as the platform for construction innovation and specify a focus on process improvement and collaboration. Organisations such as building Smart alliance and the US National Institute of Building Sciences have been promoting the uptake of BIM and related technology since the mid-1990s, other industry bodies and institutes have followed their lead. Key organisations in the propagation of BIM within construction sectors globally have been the U.S. General Services Administration - mandating BIM for Spatial Program Validation on their projects since 2006 [6] and the 'Department of Veterans Affairs' (releasing a BIM Guide [7] in 2010) . In the UK, the National BIM Task Group has continuously been working on policies for the introduction of BIM on public sector projects. This combined industry/government funded organisation has laid out a roadmap for a gradual introduction of BIM requirements for projects procured via central government departments between 2011 and 2016 (& beyond). The Singaporean Building and Construction Authority (BCA) introduced an e-submission system for regulatory submissions based on BIM data back in 2008. The above examples merely represent the tip of the iceberg of recent industry/government initiatives to propagate BIM.

One notable aspect reflected in most of the approaches by the above industry bodies and organisations is their focus on BIM for architects and engineers. These consultants were the first to integrate BIM into their profession-specific work processes. Hence, BIM software initially mainly catered for architectural and engineering processes. A recent global industry study [8] points in the direction that, after several years of moderate change, Contractors are currently the most active industry group in adopting BIM. Annual growth rates in BIM uptake among Specialist Contractors in particular are excelling in a great number of industrialised countries. What influence has such transition on the required expertise and BIM-related capabilities by Specialist Contractors? How do associated industry bodies react to this challenge? How do they adopt their training regimes to foster BIM?

---

[2] As an example: Over the past 25 years, Australia's manufacturing sector's share of total industry gross value added (GVA) has declined from 16 per cent in the year to the June quarter 1986 to 10 per cent in the year to the June quarter 2011; Source: *Trends in manufacturing to 2020*, Future Manufacturing, Department of Innovation, Industry, Science and Research, Australia.

2 The Changing Skill Requirements for Specialist Contractors

Specialist Contractors in most developed countries are undergoing a major transition in their education from 2D drawing to object based 3D modelling. Current and novice professionals undergo dedicated BIM training as industries gears up to become BIM enabled [9]. A pivotal part of this education process is BIM advocacy and stronger awareness of the change in work practices by major industry bodies. Implementing BIM is more than picking up software skills; it is about acquiring communication and collaboration skills that enable and encourage stake-holders across the building life-cycle to deliver projects in an integrated way [9].

For Specialist Contractors this process-change means: preparing for early involvement in the design process and interpreting consultants' BIM for the purpose of creating BIM equivalent to the level of resolution inherent to traditional a shop drawings. Such translation requires prior definition of standards for information exchange and the generation of BIM content in order to comply with technical schedules. Research and Development into standard forms of information exchange between collaborators has been high on the list of organisations such as the buildingSmart alliance. Their Industry Foundation Classes (IFC2×4) format allows for the transfer of data-rich 3D models from one software platform to another (with little loss of data fidelity). At the same time the 'Construction Operations Building information exchange' (COBie), created by the U.S. Army Corps of Engineers and NASA [10], is developed as a standard framework of objects for information exchange to link construction data to facility management in a structured manner.

It becomes crucial to associate BIM components on a Specialist Contractor level with numeric product data (quantities, cost, servicing), to consider interfaces to computer aided manufacture (CAM) for rapid (& less waste) manufacture, and to facilitate the generation of O&M manuals that can be accessed by a facility's operator [11]. The Specialist Contractor can therefore advise the Facility/Asset Manager on how the Commission As-Built (CAB) will influence the operation of the building. Specialist Contractors who form part of this 'information supply chain' need to be more encompassing in terms of the tasks they are able to facilitate [11]. Depending on the project type, MEP equipment constitutes approximately 15-25% of construction cost [12]. Such numbers highlight the relevance of the work undertaken by the MEP Contractors in particular. MEP Contractors rely on a combination of 'Made-to-stock' and 'Engineered-to-order' components [13]. Whereas the former can usually be grouped and represented in an electronic product catalogues, the latter group requires specialist assembly and installation. Appropriating product information from MEP Contractors hence requires diligent mapping of production information and performance specifications. Further, MEP Contractors deal with process-planning and the sequencing of fabrication and assembly activities on and offsite, with substantial risk associated to estimating correct quantities and workloads for costing purposes [14].

3 Information-Richness Associated to MEP Contractor BIMs

The level of detail and precision Specialist Contractors and trades apply to design for fabrication is unparalleled compared to other parties involved on construction projects. The ConsensusDOCS 301BIM Addendum by the Associated General Contractors of America (AGC) BIM Forum [15] provides a clear distinction in definition between 'Design' and 'Construction' BIM.

Design BIMs contain the design/procurement/CAB (commissioned as built) technical schedules and provides a basic range of standard generic design models covering the major requirements of the designer's. Design data embedded in the BIM objects that are compiled during the design development stage includes the extraction of specification relevant data for the equipment schedules as well as system integration information. In current practice, there still remains room for improvement regarding the usefulness of Design Intent BIM passed on by some consultants to other stakeholders such as the Specialist Contractor [16]. There exists one related factor that impacts on an industry's ability to achieving life-cycle BIM: The lack of standardised BIM object libraries that facilitate the dialogue between consultants and those further down the supply-chain.

Construction BIMs on the other hand are manufacturer specific models which have both the design schedule and procurement schedule data completed. Models are dimensionally accurate sufficient for workshop detail drawings for manufacturing and installation purposes. In addition to their role as translators, MEP Contractors are also responsible to attach product details (data-sheets) for Operation and Maintenance (O&M) manuals associated to the geometrical information in BIM. Construction BIMs also need to consider the installation constraints and safe handling sequencing, as well as the spatial requirements for access and servicing during operation. In doing so, MEP Contractors link equipment information from construction to operation and maintenance; the abovementioned COBie format is one pathway to achieve such links. These 'as-maintained' BIMs can be accessed via the cloud and viewed on tablet devices that can extract the data on demand [9].

4 Responding to the Challenges: The BIM-MEP^{AUS} Initiative

Industry bodies representing Specialist Contractors and the trades have a responsibility to assist their members in mastering the transition to BIM. In this paper, the authors focus on the approach taken by the Australian 'Air Conditioning and Mechanical Contractors' Association' (AMCA) to support the development of bespoke standards and BIM content for their members through their initiative: 'BIM-MEP^{AUS}'.

The BIM-MEP^{AUS} initiative by the AMCA was started in early 2010 with the goal to investigate steps to introduce a 'BIM-all-the-way' life-cycle workflow to their constituency. The initiative started by conducting targeted research surveys among 15 of its key members across all Australian states. Based on their qualitative feedback, a discussion paper was released that led to the formation of a combined industry/academia steering committee consisting of 25 Australian BIM/MEP Contractor experts. Representatives of the BIM Steering Committee included representation from specialist building services contractors, consultants, architects, builders, equipment manufacturers and suppliers, and software vendors.

Targeted research by the BIM-MEP^{AUS} initiative identified a number of challenges related to the role of MEP Contractors in the context of life-cycle BIM: Participants in their research lamented the inadequate information content within 'Design BIMs' that were not set up with their estimating, fabricatable, installation and maintenance needs in mind by consultants. A trend is noticeable among mechanical Specialist Contractors: They increasingly take over modelling tasks that were traditionally performed by engineering drafters who would provide more than just the performance outline, scope of works and design intent of uncoordinated services routes and equipment to be installed.

Further, the BIM-MEP^{AUS} research revealed that the lack of standardisation within a number of construction industries has created barriers to the effective uptake and use of BIM. Concerns about the viability of BIM remain among a large number of MEP Contractors irrespective of a particular discipline; specific concerns include:

- Significant time and cost burden involved in customising BIM modelling software to suit both design and construction requirements.
- Lack of industry standards supporting BIM.
- Inconsistent interoperability between different BIM software packages.
- Poor consideration of the requirements for integrated project delivery.
- Limited BIM project and data management expertise within the industry.
- Reluctance to share the models by consultants and other trades.
- Not enough time allowed with Specialist Contractors to engage earlier.
- Client expectations of BIM for ongoing O&M are often not understood well.
- Consultants not educated to understand the fabricateable, installation and maintenance site constraints.

5 Bridging between 'Design Intent BIM' and 'Construction BIM'

In direct response to the challenges mentioned above, the BIM-MEP^{AUS} initiative proposes a 'BIM-all-the-way' design/construction/ (CAB) workflow. The BIM-all-the-way workflow enables a building to be designed and coordinated in a virtual environment before being built on site whilst also allowing best of breed fabrication software to be used for the manufacture and estimating. The workflow is fundamentally dependent on the use of managed content to deliver standard models which are certified to assure compliance with the technical schedules and functionality with the BIM-MEP^{AUS} add-in for BIM authoring software and fabrication software needed for manufacturing purposes and for procuring bought in equipment. There exists a range of opportunities for supplier-interaction amongst various businesses that link project components from various MEP Contractors together during off site assembly processes called modularisation for 'just in time' site deliveries.

The BIM-MEP^{AUS} approach can be adjusted to suite other trade contractors and their specific workflow. The combination of strong standards in parallel with the development of referring BIM content facilitates a fluid transition from the design phase to the construction phase, and ultimately to the fabrication phase. The following paragraphs highlight how this transition is currently facilitated through BIM-MEP^{AUS}.

Design Phase

Manufacturers should be able to promote vendor neutral 'Design' BIMs related to their respective trade (ideally hosted on an online repository). Examples of where this is likely to occur are where a new product is introduced into the market.

Where a manufacturer works with a designer/detailer, they would ideally have access to a framework for certification by their respective industry body. This should allow manufacturer models to be inserted in the design model. The design schedules generated will identify the manufacturer as either a nominated supplier, or approved or equal supplier as deemed appropriate by the designer.

Construction Phase

Once the key structural elements are determined and the 'Design' is clearly defined at the end of Design Development, it is envisaged that the trade installers will take custodianship of certified BIM components and will develop them to 'Construction BIM' model status, which will:

- incorporate the manufacturer models for the equipment selected;
- sufficiently resolve spatial coordination for general construction purposes;
- consider procurement data schedules;
- associate FM related data as part of commissioning (via COBie or similar)
- target commissioning data prior to commissioning commences; and

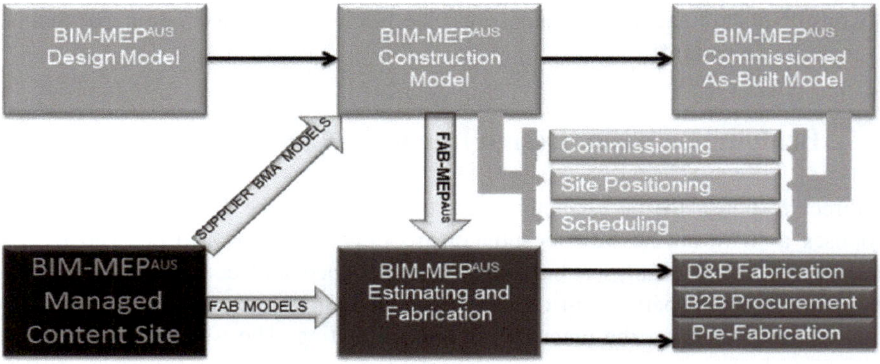

Fig. 1. Schematic diagram of the BIM-MEP^{AUS} workflow (Source: AMCA)

Fabrication Phase

Once the construction models are approved, it is envisaged that installers will convert them into Fabrication Models in cases where their workflow allows for this mode of delivery (e.g. for ducts and pipework). The level of automation that can possibly be applied to this process depends on predefined, knowledge-based semantic interpretation capabilities of the fabrication software in use.

Fabrication model can be used for a variety of purposes including construction detailing, fabrication and CAM routines for manufacture.

- Construction BIMs can get converted to fabrication models whilst retaining their geometry.
- Conversion back to a BIM Construction model will be possible.
- It results in greater opportunities to explore value-adding services.
- Data extracted to exchange onto the robotic site positioning layout equipment.
- The fabrication BIMs can be uploaded to the cloud and viewed on hand held tablet devices that can extract the data on demand for the installation teams.

6 Conclusions

BIM signifies a major cultural change for Specialist Contractors as it allows them to be more linked into the design process while simultaneously maintaining tighter control over fabrication and installation processes. As a result, Specialist Contractors are empowered to provide essential value-add to life-cycle BIM as they close the gap between design intent by consultants, construction scheduling and costing by head contractors, and O&M activities by owner/operators of a facility.

Leading Specialist Contractors are increasingly opting to link BIM to offsite fabrication. They thereby combine single or multiple trade models into virtual 'smart assemblies' to then assemble physical modules or units in controlled environments such as a factory floor. Offsite prefabrication has significant impact on time, material waste, cost and safety related matters. It reduces risk and offers more certainty about the quality of the assembly, the time required for installation, and 'just in time' deliveries. Cost savings are proving to be significant and principals and head contractors are likely to expect from their Specialist Contractors the ability to deliver such assemblies based on well-coordinated BIM.

In addition to the above, the industry is likely to experience a development towards further automation of assembly and construction with the use of robotic equipment that can directly interpret coordinated datasets provided by BIM. In order to streamline their production methods, trades can draw upon skills and expertise of parallel (e.g. car) industries where supply-chain integration and product lifecycle management (PLM) has been common for decades. Specifically, trades can draw upon the expertise from manufacturing offsite and applying a framework for prefabrication and modular strategies. Specialist Contractors and the trades thereby adopt sophisticated construction techniques and supply chain integration such as e-commerce linking or procuring equipment directly from a supplier from a BIM model. Mechanical BIM components that are set up with FM requirements in mind (using formats like COBie) will assist Specialist Contractors in bridging the gap between the construction and the operation & maintenance aspect of the facilities they work on.

Acknowledgments. This paper is partially based on an industry whitepaper the authors conceived for the Australian Institute of Architects and Consult Australia. The authors would like to acknowledge the assistance from the AMCA in authoring this paper.

References

[1] Gallaher, M.P., O'Connor, A.C., Dettbarn Jr., J.L., Gilday, L.T.: Cost Analysis of Inadequate Interoperability in the U.S. Capital Facilities Industry. NIST GCR 04-867, 194 (2004)

[2] Brown, K. (ed.): BIM: Implications for Government. CRC Construction Innovation, Commonwealth of Australia (2008)

[3] Teicholz, P.: Labor-Productivity Declines in the Construction Industry: Causes and Remedies (Another Look), AECbytes Online Resource (2013), http://www.aecbytes.com/viewpoint/2013/issue_67.html

[4] Smith, D.K., Tardif, M.: Building Information Modeling: A Strategic Implementation Guide for Architects, Engineers, Constructors, and Real Estate Asset Managers. John Wiley & Sons (2009)

[5] Taylor, J.E., Levitt, R.: Modeling Systemic Innovation in Design and Construction Networks, CIFE Technical Report #163, Center for Integrated Facility Engineering, Stanford University (2005)

[6] General Services Administration, BIM Guide For Spatial Program Validation, GSA (2007), http://www.gsa.gov/graphics/pbs/BIM_Guide_Series_02_v096.pdf (last accessed: June 6, 2014)

[7] Department of Veterans Affairs, The VA BIM Guide, v1.0 (April 2010), http://www.cfm.va.gov/til/bim/BIMguide/ (last accessed: June 6, 2014)

[8] McGraw Hill, 'SmartMarket Report', The Business Value of BIM for Construction in Major Global Markets, How Contractors around the world are driving innovation with Building Information Modeling. McGraw Hill Construction (2014)

[9] Specialist Engineering Contractor (SEC) Group, 'First Steps to BIM Competence, A Guide for Specialist Contractors', Specialist Engineering Contractor (SEC) Group (2013)

[10] East, E.W.: Construction-Operations Building information exchange (COBie), buildingSMART alliance, National Institute of building Sciences, Washington, DC. (2012), http://www.nibs.org/?page=bsa_cobie

[11] Dossick, C.S., Neff, G., Fiore-Silfast, B.: Implications of New Construction Technology for Western Washington Mechanical Contractors, PNCCRE Technical Report #TR001, University of Washington (2011)

[12] Ottaviano Study of Construction Cost in NY, HVAC Costs, Online Resource (1995), http://www.fullerheating.com/fhonline/hvac/commercial/information/hvaccost.html (last accessed: June 6, 2014)

[13] Eastman, C., Teicholz, P., Sacks, R., Liston, K.: BIM Handbook: A Guide to Building Information Modeling for Owners, Managers, Designers, Engineers and Contractors. John Wiley and Sons Ltd., Chichester

[14] Kieran, S., Timberlake, J.: Refabricating Architecture: How Manufacturing Methodologies are Poised to Transform Building Construction. McGraw Hill Construction (2004)

[15] ConsensuDOCS, 'ConsensusDOCS 301BIM Addendum', Associated General Contractors of America (AGC) (2008)

[16] Buildingsmart Australia, 'National Building Information Modelling Initiative'. Strategy: A strategy for the focussed adoption of building information modelling and related digital technologies and processes for the Australian built environment sector, Department of Industry, Innovation, Science, Research and Tertiary Education, Sydney (2012)

A Design Method for Product Upgradability with Different Customer Demands

Masato Inoue[1], Shuho Yamada[1], Tetsuo Yamada[2], and Stefan Bracke[3]

[1] Department of Mechanical Engineering Informatics, Meiji University, Japan
[2] Department of Informatics, The University of Electro-Communications, Japan
[3] Chair of Safety Engineering and Risk Management, University of Wuppertal, Germany
m_inoue@meiji.ac.jp

Abstract. A sustainable society requires changes in the traditional paradigm of mass production and consumption. Products such as personal computers and smartphones are discarded even though they are fully functional. This paper proposes a design method for product upgradability which satisfies various different customer demands to increase the product value and extend the value lifespan by exchanging components closely related to its deterioration in value. In addition, this paper also proposes a method that can specify future product performances, effective upgradable product components, and the side effects of upgrade on other product components. Finally, this paper discusses the applicability of our proposed design method by considering a vacuum cleaner and various different customer demands.

Keywords: Product upgradability, sustainability, customer demands, set-based design.

1 Introduction

The change of traditional paradigm of mass production and consumption is required for a sustainable society. Companies and nations are required to reduce their environmental loads [1]. Therefore, environmentally conscious product design is essential. Some of these design methods such as 3R including reuse, reduce and recycle, and upgradable product design method have been studied [2]. The upgradable product design method is intrinsically executed prior to the disposal of products. Shimomura et al. [3] proposed a method for upgrade planning based on the prediction of customer demands. Fukushige et al. [4] developed a prototype system for product upgradability based on 3D-CAD. However, the method nearly addresses only physical product performance without quantitative considerations of requirements such as cost and environmental load. Thus, this paper focuses on an upgradable product design method, which can treat concurrently physical product performance, environmental loads, and product cost. This method also considers uncertain product requirements and design information needed in the future at the time of upgrade. The authors assume that customers discard their products when the perceived value of their present product has deteriorated with time below a certain level relative to the

S. Fukuda et al. (Eds.): PLM 2014, IFIP AICT 442, pp. 91–100, 2014.

perceived value of new products in the market. In addition, this paper also proposes a method that can specify future product performance and functions, effective upgradable product components, and the side effects of upgrade on other product components. Finally, this paper discusses the applicability of our proposed design method by applying to a design problem of a vacuum cleaner design problem with different customer demands.

2 A Design Method for Product Upgradability

2.1 Purpose and Procedure of the Method

A design method for product upgradability seeks to design products that are capable of being adapted to future enhancements of product performance and functions at the early phase of design by predicting those product performance and functions that will be required at the time of upgrade. There are two basic classes of this method as follows:

(a) Upgrade by exchanging components
(b) Upgrade by adding components or modifying the structure of the product

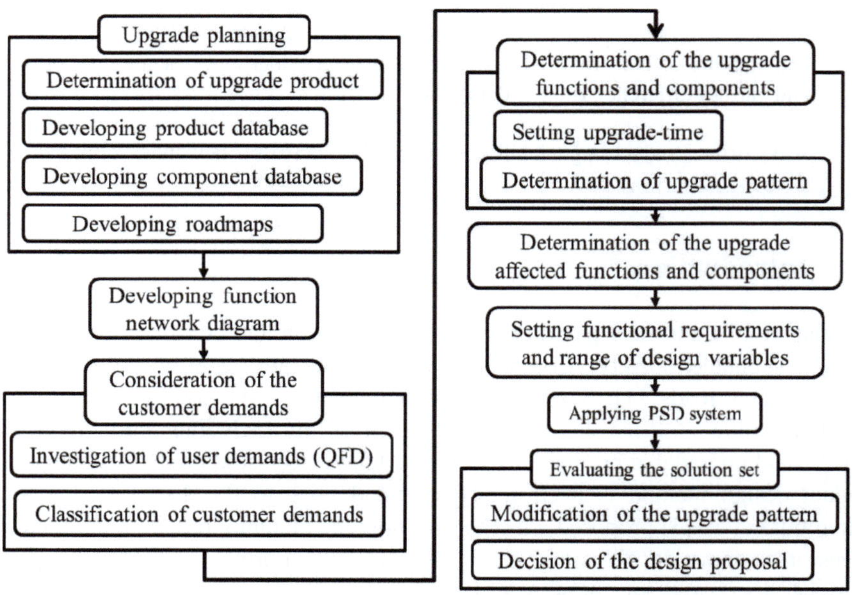

Fig. 1. Procedure of the proposed upgradable design method

This study focuses on the former class of the method (a). Because future enhancements of product performance and functions eligible for upgrade are to be predicted, the proposed method must include uncertain design information. Here, the uncertain design information is represented as a range value, and a preference set-based design (PSD) method [5, 6] is applied to estimate future enhancements of product performance and features eligible for upgrade. The PSD method can obtain a ranged set of design solutions. Figure 1 shows the procedure of the proposed method.

This paper defines two product lifetimes: durable life and value life [7]. The durable life is a measure of the duration over which the failure rate of a product or component remains below a defined threshold. Conversely, the value life is a measure of the duration that the product value perceived by the consumer remains above a defined threshold. Products such as personal computers and smartphones are usually discarded even though they are fully functioning. This situation derives from the condition where the value life is shorter than the durable life. Therefore, the primary purpose of our method is to reduce the extent of product disposal and the resulting environmental load by increasing the value life of products by exchanging components that have a relatively short value life or by adding new components in accordance with the description.

2.2 Upgrade Planning

Here, the authors establish the criterion of the upgrade time. Definition of the upgrade time is based upon several factors such as product upgrade cycle, disposal cycle, or administrative strategy. In addition, the product and component databases are created. These databases contain manufacturers, model numbers, launch times, and product and component performance and/or design variables such as capacity of storage, weight, and dimension. Based on these databases, the authors create product and component roadmaps that evaluate the temporal distributions of performance criteria and/or design variable values. The upgrade time and the product and component roadmaps are used for configuring the performance requirements of the products and components. Under conditions where a product has not yet been launched, roadmaps of similar products can be used for market prediction and for configuring performance requirements.

2.3 Developing the Function Network

A function network diagram illustrates the input and output relationships between performance criteria and product components. This diagram is used for the analysis of upgrade components. Figure 2 provides an example of a function network diagram for a vacuum cleaner. In this diagram, performance criteria and product components are represented by the individual graphics. The positive parameters are indicative of a condition where a higher or larger value represents better performance. Conversely, negative parameters are indicative of a condition where lower or smaller values represent better performance. The input–output relations between performance criteria and product components are connected by straight lines, and relevant design variables are described on these lines. Therefore, designers can easily search for components that are related to upgrade performance by following the input–output lines.

In case of a vacuum cleaner (cf. Figure 2), for example, the suction power is the chosen target for upgrade performance. The pertinent components affecting that performance are motor, turbine fan, body, or power unit. They represent candidates with regard to an upgrade possibility.

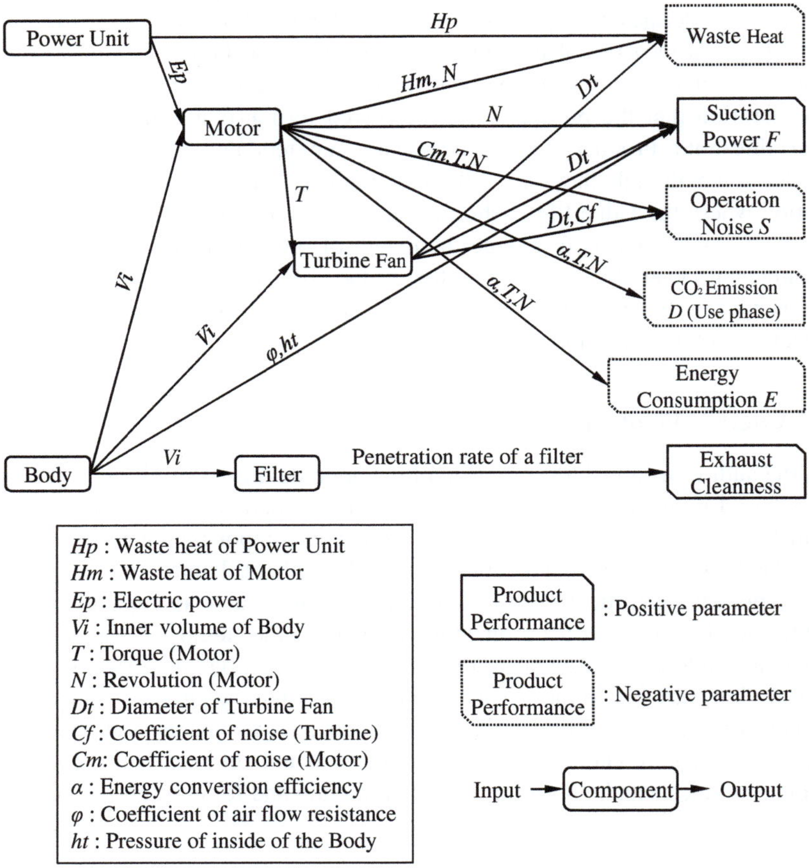

Fig. 2. Function network diagram of a vacuum cleaner and graphical representation of performance criteria (positive and negative) and product components

2.4 Consideration of Upgradable Performance Criteria and Components

Upgradable performance criteria are defined as a product performance upon which consumer emphasis is placed, as evaluated by application of quality function deployment (QFD) or, alternatively, those performance criteria, which have a short value life. Using the function network diagram, a designer searches for components that have close relationships with the chosen upgrade performance criterion and defines those as potential upgradable components. When a plurality of upgradable components are identified, the candidates should be narrowed down by considering the balance between upgrade performance criteria and possible upgrade affected performance criteria and components as described below.

2.5 Consideration of Upgrade Affected Performance Criteria and Components

Upgrade affected performance criteria indicate that the value of performance is changed by exchanging upgrade components. In addition, the authors define a component that has a close relationship with an upgrade affected performance criterion as an upgrade affected component. Upgrade affected performance criteria and components are identified in the same way as upgrade components by using the function network diagram. For example, a designer defines the performance of the suction power as the upgrade performance criterion and the turbine fan component as the upgrade component for the vacuum cleaner described in Figure 2. In this case, the waste heat and operation noise are defined as upgrade affected performance criteria because the upgrade of the turbine fan causes the diameter of turbine fan D_t and the coefficient of noise of the turbine C_f to increase. Therefore, the power unit and the motor emerge as upgrade affected components. Possible approaches for mitigating this condition can be developed such as building low-level waste heat and low-noise motor into the 1st generation vacuum cleaner, or developing and upgrading a motor that has high suction power, low-level waste heat and a low noise, simultaneously upgrading and changing the motor with the turbine fan. These approaches are narrowed down in the same way as that of the upgrade components.

2.6 Application of the PSD Method and the Evaluation of the Solution Set

This study applies the PSD method to the proposed method in order to obtain the range of required product performance and functions, and the range of the component design variables that can realize this performance and function range. To obtain these ranged design solutions, the equations and the range of the required product performance and functions and the design variables of the components are needed. The equations show the relationships between product performance and functions and component design variables. In the absence of equations, the designer should define approximate equations based on the performance parameters and design variables in the product and component databases.

Range of the required product performance and functions and the designer configurable range of design variables are configured in accordance with the distributions in the product and component roadmaps. A conclusive point-based design proposal is selected from the ranged set of design solutions and a preference number. Under conditions where the design proposal must be modified, the designer should search for the design proposal that satisfies the modified requirements from the ranged set of design solutions. However, in the absence of a design proposal in the ranged set of design solutions, the designer should define the required performance and design variables again and apply them to the PSD system.

3 Case Study: Application to the Design of a Vacuum Cleaner

3.1 Setting the Design Problem

This paper shows an application of the proposed method to a vacuum cleaner. According to the cycle of trade up to a new model, the authors hypothesize an upgrade time equivalent to approximately five years (for a consumer trade up proportion of 60%) from launch time of the 1st generation product. To understand the trend of performance requirements and design variables, the authors create databases for launched products and components. The product databases include the vacuum cleaners manufactured by three companies (Company A, B, and C) from 2005 to 2013. The component database includes motors manufactured by a single company in 2013 because there is no data for motors manufactured before 2012.

		Components										
Customer demands	Priority	Dust cup volume	Area of base	Total weight	Load of operation	Weight of controller	Exhaust velocity	Exhaust cleanness	Diameter of hose pipe	Suction	Power consumption	Operation noise
High suction power	**6.3**								3	9		
Easy to clean a narrow space	**6.2**									1		
Easy to clean	**5.9**		3	9	9	3				1	9	3
Easy to clean a wooden floor well	**5.1**									3		
Easy to store a cleaner	**4.9**	9	3									
Easy to operate a cleaner	**3.6**		3	9	3	3						
Low operation noise	**3.6**								3			9
Priority		7.8	7.6	15.0	11.2	5.0	3.8	11.4	5.2	14.8	9.3	8.8

9 : Strong relationship, 3 : Moderate relationship, 1 : Weak relationship

Fig. 3. Result of customer demands investigation. [Source: Kobayashi (2003), partially modified]

Figure 2 shows the function network diagram of the vacuum cleaner. Using the result of QFD as shown in Figure 3, this study defines the suction power F [W] as an upgrade performance that has a high level of value degradation. Using the information in Figure 2, the motor is configured as an upgrade component. In addition, the operation noise *S* [dB], the amount of CO_2 emission *D* [g], the energy consumption *E* [W], and total production cost as the performance criteria affected by the upgrade are defined. The product performance requirements and the range of design variables based on the product database and roadmap are configured. Finally, the ranged set of design solutions is calculated using the equations between product performance and design variables from the PSD system.

The range of the design variables can increase and decrease relative to the reference values that are assumed to be the design variables of the 1st generation product. The total production cost for the upgraded product has multiple relations with the costs for the upgrade components and the affected components (i.e., the motor and the turbine fan). The assumption is that the cost for the components increases relative to the difference between the design variables of the 1st generation (reference value) and those of the 2nd generation. Therefore, the cost for components (not including the motor and the turbine fan) is higher than components without the upgrade. This study assumes that if the range of the design variables decreases, then total production cost increases moderately than is the case for an increase in the range of the design variables. Figure 4 shows the relationship of the production cost for the product with and without the upgrade.

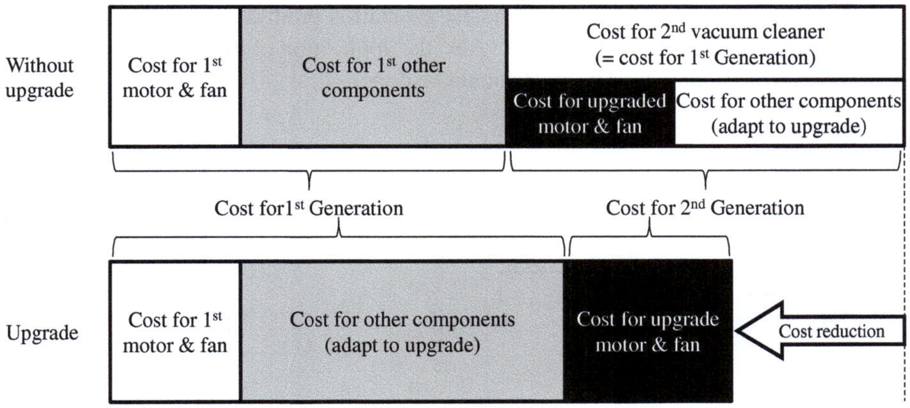

Fig. 4. Comparison of the product costs with and without the upgrade

In this application, the authors assume that the product performance and design variables of the components of the 2nd generation product without an upgrade are equal to the upgraded product's parameter. In addition, the authors assume that the cost of the 2nd generation without a product upgrade is equal to the 1st generation without a product upgrade.

This study classifies the customer demands into 3 types as follows:

(1) Performance preferable customer: the customer requires a high suction power
(2) Silence preferable customer: the customer requires a low noise
(3) Energy-saving preferable customer: the customer requires a low energy consumption

3.2 Discussions

With respect to the relation between the suction power and the power consumption, and the operation noise, Figure 5 compares the performance-oriented solutions (performance preferable customer), silence-oriented solutions (silence preferable customer), and ecology-oriented solutions (energy-saving preferable customer). Figure 5 indicates that ecology-oriented solutions satisfy the required performance for the silence preferable customer. The result indicates the designer can define the customer demands as the demands for the performance preferable customer and the energy-saving preferable customer.

In this study, a ranged set of product design solutions that include various performance criteria, cost, and environmental loads in use concurrently with the consideration of future uncertain design information are obtained.

Figure 6 shows the comparison of the cost for each customer demand. The results suggest that the total production cost of the upgraded product is reduced by about 25% compared with that of the product without upgrade, and that suction power satisfies the required range. Therefore, this study concludes that the proposed method can obtain a ranged set of product design solutions in consideration of performance criteria, cost, and environmental load for various customer demands. However, the designers should define the increasing rate of 1st generation production costs of the upgraded product that customers allow to consume because the 1st generation production cost of the upgraded product increases from 22.4% to 27.6%. Also the application of this increasing rate to the requirements of the upgraded product should be done.

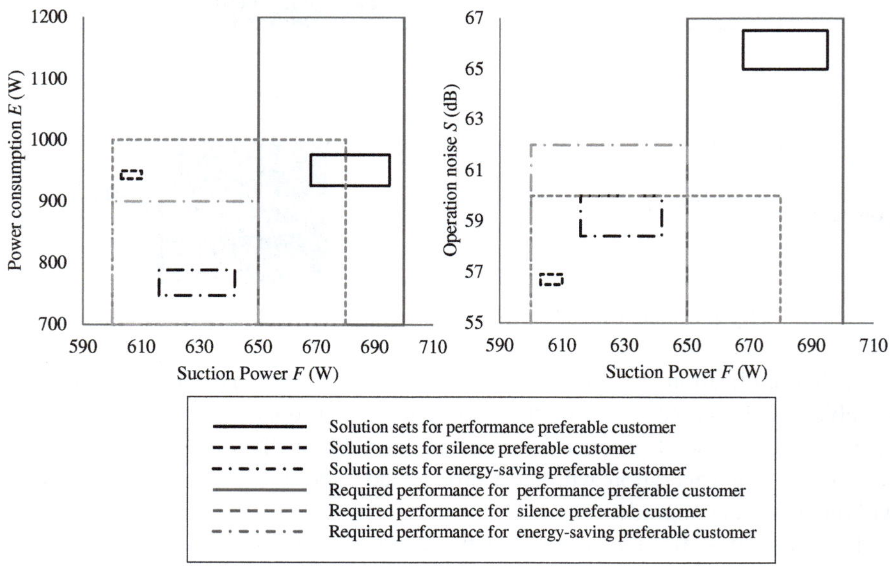

Fig. 5. Comparison of the solution areas of each customer demands

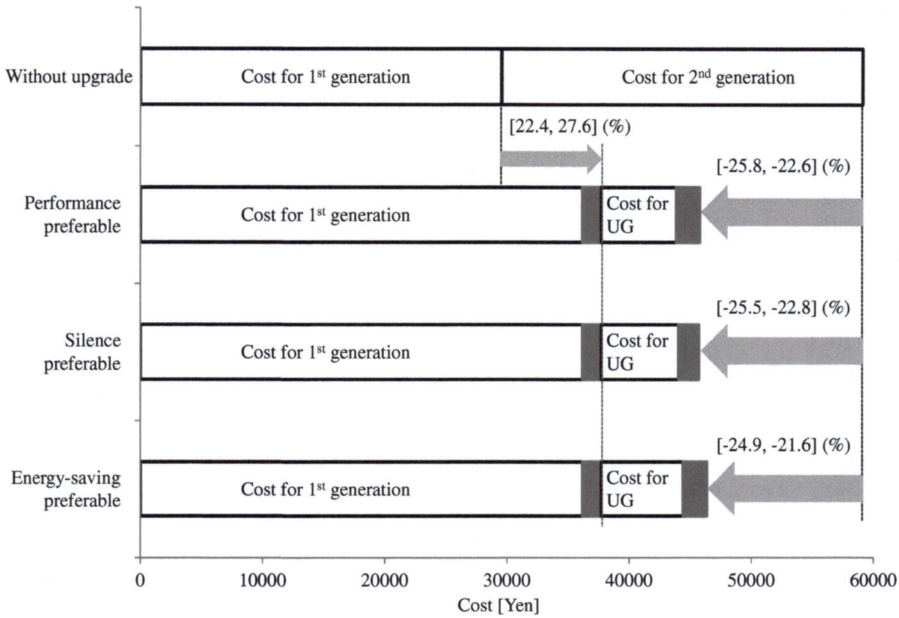

Fig. 6. Comparison of the cost for each customer demands

4 Conclusions

This paper proposed a design method that can obtain a ranged set of solutions that satisfies multiple product performance criteria, cost, and environmental load by considering uncertain design information for various customer demands. To obtain the ranged set of solutions, PSD method is applied to the proposed method that proposes to increase product value and extend product life by exchanging components whose value has diminished below a threshold value. In addition, the authors proposed the function network diagram to define the product performance criteria and components that possess a short value life. This paper showed the usefulness of this diagram by application.

In this paper, the ranged set of requirements that include future uncertainty is predicted arbitrarily based on the distribution of the product roadmap. Moreover, this prediction needs the designer's knowledge and experience. Therefore, predicting the ranged set of requirements logically is one of the subjects of future study. In addition, the authors also need to indicate the business model for familiarizing the concept of the product upgradability.

Acknowledgments. This work was partially supported by Research Project Grant by Institute of Science and Technology, Meiji University.

References

1. Ministry of the Environment in Japan: Kyoto Protocol Target Achievement Plan, Ministry of the Environment of Japan (2008)
2. Kobayashi, H.: Product Lifecycle Planning, pp. 103–130. Ohmsha (2003) (in Japanese)
3. Shimomura, Y., Kondoh, S., Umeda, Y.: Proposal of an Upgrade Planning Method for Upgradeable Product Design. Transactions of the Japan Society of Mechanical Engineers, Series (C) 72(713), 282–289 (2006)
4. Fukushige, S., Arino, M., Umeda, Y.: Computer-Aided Design for Product Upgradability under Geometric Constraints. In: Matsumoto, M., Umeda, Y., Fukushige, S. (eds.) Design for Innovative Value Towards a Sustainable Society, pp. 828–831. Springer, Netherland (2011)
5. Inoue, M., Nahm, Y.-E., Okawa, S., Ishikawa, H.: Design Support System by Combination of 3D-CAD and CAE with Preference Set-based Design Method. Concurrent Engineering: Research and Applications 18(1), 41–53 (2010)
6. Inoue, M., Nahm, Y.-E., Tanaka, K., Ishikawa, H.: Collaborative Engineering among Designers with Different Preferences: Application of the Preference Set-Based Design to the Design Problem of an Automotive Front-Side Frame. Concurrent Engineering: Research and Applications 21(4), 252–267 (2013)
7. Murakami, T., Inoue, M., Nahm, Y.-E., Ishikawa, H.: An Upgrade Design Method for Environmental Issues Based on the Concept of Set-Based Design. In: Matsumoto, M., Umeda, Y., Fukushige, S. (eds.) Design for Innovative Value Towards a Sustainable Society, pp. 500–505. Springer, Netherland (2011)

Integration of Design Intent during the Product Lifecycle Management

Min-Jung Yoo, Jumyung Um, Ian Stroud, Soumaya El Kadiri, and Dimitris Kiritsis

Laboratory of Computer-Aided Design and Production,
EPFL – Ecole polytechnique fédérale de Lausanne, Switzerland
{min-jung.yoo,jumyung.um,ian.stroud,soumaya.elkadiri,
dimitris.kiritsis}@epfl.ch

Abstract. There has been significant achievement in integrating product data during the whole lifecycle phases with shared common ontologies while taking advantage of intelligent retrieval mechanisms. In order to support integrated decision making on product redesign or maintenance operations, we should solve a challenging issue: 'how the product lifecycle management (PLM) stores and retrieves the know-how and the knowledge of an organization concerning manufactured products'. This paper describes the extension of a previously developed PLM Semantic Ontology Model toward integration with design intent. The proposed approach uses OWL2 to represent product lifecycle data and design knowledge. The approach was applied to the redesign of a car door part for laser welding. Our work demonstrates how to retrieve design intent as a specific type of knowledge data in the context of design decisions. Such an approach can ultimately contribute to reducing design time, making knowledge transfer clear and thus improving the quality of designed products.

Keywords: product lifecycle, semantic ontology, design intent, knowledge, know-how, OWL, Protégé, QLM.

1 Introduction and Motivation

The closed-loop product lifecycle management (PLM) system focuses on tracking and managing the information of the whole product lifecycle, with possible feedback on information to product lifecycle phases. It provides opportunities to reduce the inefficiency of lifecycle operations and improve competitiveness (Kiritsis 2013). Thanks to the advent of hardware and software related to product identification technologies, e.g., radio frequency identification (RFID) technology, closed-loop PLM has been recently highlighted as a tool for companies to enhance the performance of their business models. However, the information on PLM has primarily dealt with some predefined physical product data, i.e., material characteristics of designed products and their usage information. Knowledge data concerning the design of products has not been dealt with sufficiently in depth in currently available PLM approaches. Within the range of our knowledge, there are very few research results which handle the design knowledge coming from the product design

S. Fukuda et al. (Eds.): PLM 2014, IFIP AICT 442, pp. 101–110, 2014.

phases or redesign phases. The impact of design changes on the other manufacturing information has not been sufficiently studied, so there is a lack of experience in this area.

The management of companies' intangible assets and intellectual capital has long been a key issue in the domain of business and management science. Some parts of product data should be shared with the other intangible assets of a company. Product design requires intensive communication between designers and production engineers. In a general case, only the geometry and numerical data remain in the company's database once a product shape has been determined. This entails the loss of information about why this design was determined and what designers intended during redesign. The design is defined as this-is-the-way-we-do-things in the company. Lost knowledge, however, is critical information when introducing new manufacturing technology or new composite materials.

For the reasons mentioned above, domain professionals have already acknowledged the importance of representing and sharing product data during the different phases of the product lifecycle. There has been significant achievement in integrating product data from beginning of life (BOL), to the middle of life (MOL), until its end of life (EOL), especially using shared common ontologies and intelligent retrieval mechanisms (Matsokis and Kiritsis 2011). PLM has specific objectives in each phase of the lifecycle: During the BOL, the improvement of product design and production quality is the main concerns; During the MOL, improving reliability, availability, and maintainability of products is the most interesting issue; In the EOL, optimizing EOL products' recovery operations is one of the most challenging issues.

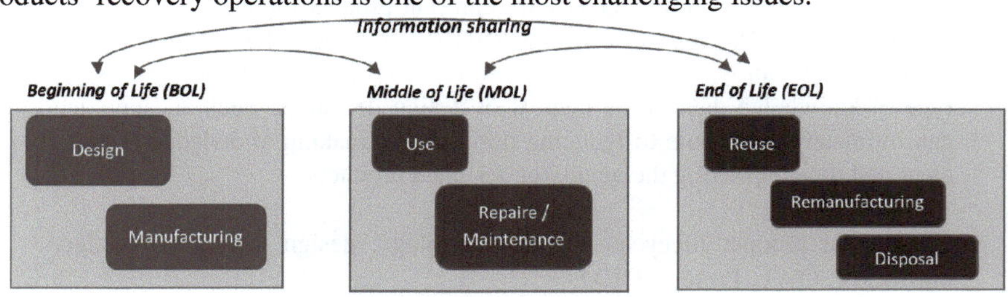

Fig. 1. Product lifecycle phase and data sharing

Turning to the research on representing know-how and knowledge, we can find some literature about approaches using meta-data and history-based models in design activities of BOL. At the end of the 1970s and early 1980s Kjellberg proposed having a 'description of origin' associated with geometric elements (Kjellberg 1983). After the publication of standard for product data exchange, Pratt mentioned the necessity to capture the intention of the designer which can get lost during product changes (Pratt and Anderson 2001). Mun defined 'design intent' and proposed macro files for saving the modelling commands with the parametric approach, which was standardized by ISO 10303 (Mun et al. 2003). Han also realized a macro-parametric method in commercial CAD systems (Han 2010). Through the efforts of these researchers, the fundamental of capturing design intents is possible. In the context of aircraft manufacture, Price tried to maintain intent by redesigning the parameters of frames related to joining processes in (Price et al. 2013).

This paper discusses new concepts for capturing general knowledge and shows how to share it during the real redesign process of an automotive door assembly line. Such integration will play an important role during decision making across different divisions including decisions about product redesign or maintenance operations.

From now on the paper is organized as follows. Section 2 presents a global concept of extended PLM Semantic Ontology Model (SOM) based on our previous work (Matsokis A. and Kiritsis D. 2011). Section 3 is devoted to the introduction of our case study: a car part manufacturing example focusing on its design data and parameters in use. Then in Section 4, we will show how the model presented in Section 2 is adapted to the case study, in terms of data popularization and query proposition for knowledge retrieval. Finally, Section 5 gives a short summary of our work and its impact.

2 Product-Lifecycle Data Management with Knowledge Management

2.1 Semantic Model

Ontology-based approaches to semantic modelling of product lifecycle management were one of the main outcomes from the European project PROMISE (Promise 2009). The PROMISE approach manages information and knowledge generated during the product lifecycle which are then linked with decision support systems and data transformation software. Their implementation demonstrated that the use of ontology makes it possible to reuse the PLM model increasing interoperability between different PLM phases. Currently the results are being submitted to Open Group Open Platform 3 (OpenPlatform3) in order to get the status of approved standard, which is one of the main activities of the QLM workgroup (Quantum Lifecycle Management – *see* QLM)

Fig. 1 illustrates the different phases of product lifecycle in general. The products' beginning of life (BOL) phase can be further divided into two categories of activity: i) The design of products, ii) the manufacturing of products. In PROMISE, the management of BOL data was mainly considered based upon the fact that a product has already been designed (Fig.2). As a result, the model describes well some details on the physical product, their composition and manufacturing information, however, still missing the capability of describing knowledge related with design activity of BOL.

Subsequently, our work focused on the extension and integration of Beginning of life (BOL) product data, putting special emphasis on the Design Phase BOL (corresponding to the upper-left part of Fig.1). Given that "Personal_Resource (the role of Human Actor)", "Material Resource" and "Physical Product" are already defined in PLM SOM, the new concepts in the extend semantic model include (Fig. 3):

1. Integration of the concept (i.e., ontology class) of "Knowledge Data" and "Knowledge Resource"
2. Definition of the "Competence" concept
3. Integration of the concept of "Service" which is on the hub of four other concepts, i.e., "Competence", "Knowledge", "Material Resource", and "Actor"

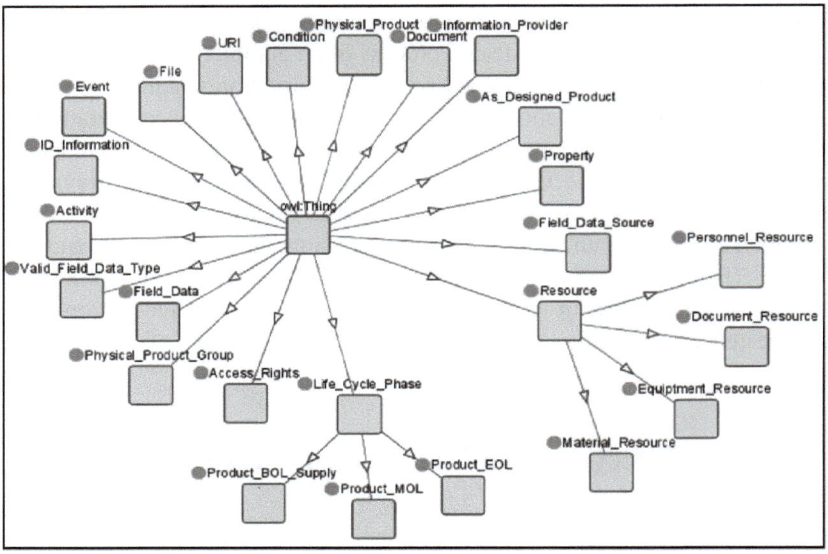

Fig. 2. PROMISE Product Data and Knowledge Management (PDKM) Semantic Object Model (SOM)

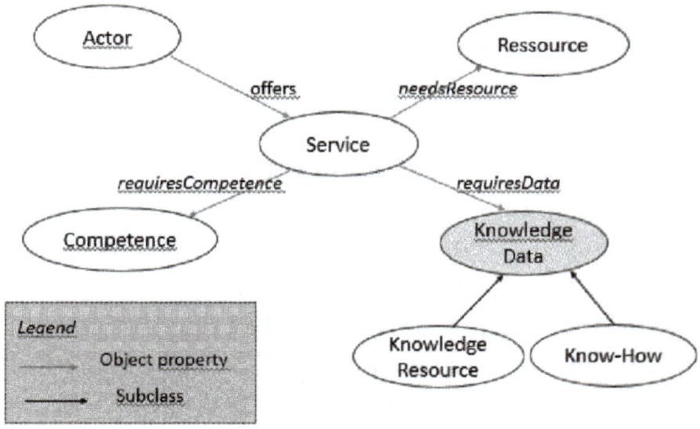

Fig. 3. Extended model of PLM SOM – High-level concept

The service concept represents general business activities offered by a human actor, a team or an organization. In that context, "Competence" is an important intangible asset for achieving the required service by a distinctive actor. Competence can be reinterpreted as being capable of doing some activities; capable of managing some situations; capable of using a tool or an application. Knowledge Data has two sub-concept definitions: i) Knowledge Resource, and ii) Know-How.

The Know-how class represents the company's information on cumulative, lifelong experience and activities which are related with the tangible and intangible product creation and improvement. Different to the technical knowledge on physical products, Know-How data may contain even some negative experience and resulting outcomes. From the point of a company's competence development, such kind of know-now management is important for the purpose of studying past cases and use it for "learning from experience". Therefore the following two points have driven this research direction: i) how to integrate an industry's intangible assets which are related to the product PLM data; and, ii) how to reuse them.

For that purpose, the model extension has been achieved being based on the high-level semantic model presented in Fig. 3. The resulting model was then further specialized in order to be suitable for an industrial design case: the welding assembly line of the car door frame (Fig. 4). Here we use the words 'class' and 'concept' as mutually interchangeable (similar) terms, which are the object class definition in Protégé (Protégé).

1. The class of Design_Parameter is created for the purpose of modelling some important parameters which are considered through design decision making.
2. Design_Process_Activiy class is defined as a subclass of existing Activity concept.
3. Computer_Aided_Tool is further specialized containing several subclasses: CAD_tool, CAM_tool, Specific_Software.
4. In this extended model, another product information in design phase is added, i.e., Design_InProgress, for the purpose of associating data which can either be produced or referenced during the product design phase. Consequently, the classes which indicate product lifecycle phases are also distinguished while representing more specialized product lifecycle phases, i.e., Product_BOL_Design and Product_BOL_Supply.
5. The Design_Intent class is newly created as a subclass of Know_How. Another subclass of Know_How, Consumer_Intent plays a similar role from the customer sides and internal service designe teams, which will not be detailed in this paper.
6. The existing class Physical_Resource is specialized providing three sub-classes: i) Environmental_Asset which represents information such as buildings, workshops; ii) Equipement; iii) Materials.

2.2 Model Description

The above-presented semantic model was built and tested using the Protégé-OWL ontology tool. Since its creation, OWL-DL(Description Logic) was used for the purpose of describing classes and individuals included in PLM PDKM SOM. OWL-DL was initially developed to provide the maximum expressiveness in tandem with guaranteeing both computational completeness (all conclusions are guaranteed to be computable) and decidability (all computations will finish in finite time). OWL-DL includes all OWL language constructs (such as transitive properties, which allow more of the semantics of sequences to be represented explicitly than in RDF or OWL lite) and it allows modelling at multiple levels of abstraction (and thus, sequences of classes can be characterized by their general or more specific properties).

In PROMISE SOM, there are already more than 70 object property definitions which relate different concepts and individuals. Some of them are given below as an example:

- isDesigned: in order to relate a physical product to its design details;
- hasDefined: as an inverse relation of isDesigned, that is to say, from a designed product to a physical product;

- Life_Cycle_Phase2Activity: which links the life cycle phase of a product to its activity details;
- Life_Cycle_Phase2Physical_Product: similarly to Life_Cycle_Phase2Activity, this property allows to retrieve the physical product of a given life cycle phase;
- Equipment_Resource2Property: for the purpose of searching the property of a given equipment resource, and so on.

For the purpose of complementing the existing object properties, we have newly created some supplementary relationships. Some key elements are given below.

- Contains_DesignedPart: this object property helps, based on a given types of physical product, retrieve the information of a designed product part.
- Defines: this object property is added in order to get the evaluation criteria of a given resource characteristic. The material characteristics are retrievable by giving a certain design intent category with the help of 'DesignResource_Concerns' (see below).
- DesignResource_Concerns: thie property links a particular design intent type to all related resources. Such an information is important for the purpose of retrieving a part of physical product information which were designed according to a certain design intent type.
- Design_Concerns: this property links a particular design intent type to a physical product for the purpose of retrieving information on past experience. With the help of this object property, we can answer to the questions as 'which products are designed as a result of design intent type xxx?'
- Refers2_Parameters: in order to search the KPI parameters which are related with a give design intent and to find further information such as equipment and material resources.

3 Case Study

An example of the importance of explicit design intent can be illustrated using the example of a car door and its use in the Remote Laser Welding project RLW Navigator. The RLW Navigator project studies laser welding, in particular in the car industry and uses the welding of a car door as an example.

Laser welding is an alternative to spot welding and offers several benefits over the traditional technology. However, it is not easy to realise all the benefits because current practice is built into the design at an early stage. In addition, the car door is a complex product for which commercial time pressures preclude rationalisation of the design process. However, without such rationalisation it is difficult to change process elements and hence take advantage of new technological advances. The car door example and its handling in the RLW project can be illustrated in Fig. 4.

The input for the modification task is a CAD file which lacks design intent information. As for many other applications the design intent has to be supplied through human interaction or semi-automatic feature recognition. The relevant features are those which can be modified for laser welding, in this case the flanges. The flange redesign tool is illustrated in Fig. 5. The flanges are classified, resized and reintroduced into the design to make the final CAD model.

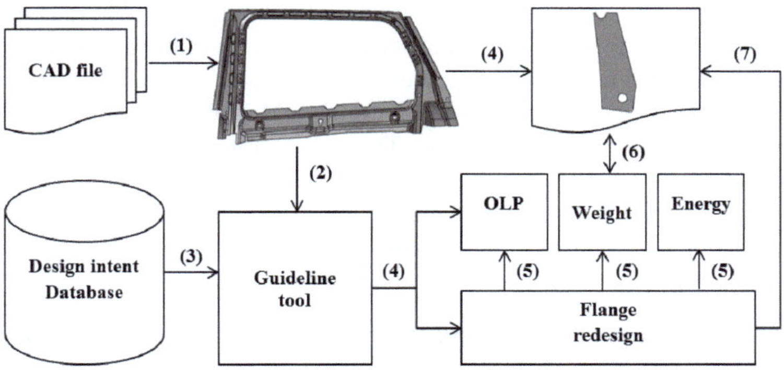

Fig. 4. Operation procedure of guideline

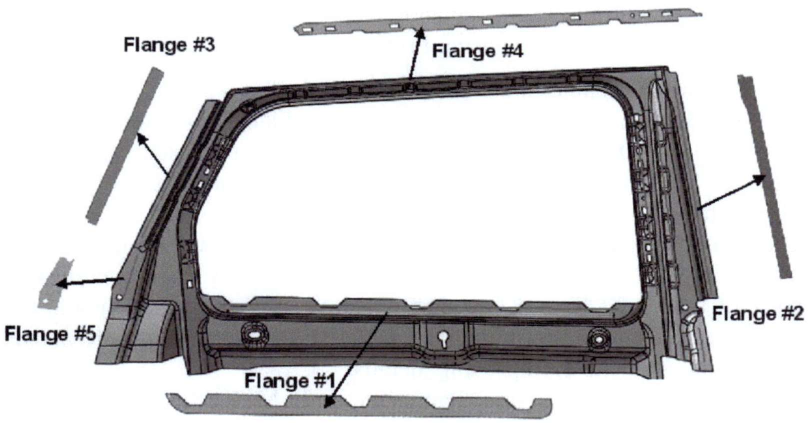

Fig. 5. Flange classification

In terms of design intent, this work is hindered both by the lack of special CAD tools and the integration of manufacturing information into the design at an early phase. Logically there should be a shaping phase to determine the part to be made and then a manufacturing phase to realise the shape, making appropriate modifications to the original shape to accommodate the manufacturing decisions. The realisation decision has various implications for manufacturing. For example, if the door is to be made as a solid frame with overlaid panels then this would be recorded as a decision, the door frame shape extracted from the overall shape and the door panels designed. A different decision about the manufacturing method would start from this point.

Current practice involves making the door out of pressed sheet metal. This involves creating a sheet metal frame which is done by splitting the door shape into parts, pressing them and then welding them together. Another consequence of this decision is that the hinge part needs to be reinforced because the rest of the door has to be made from thin material for weight reasons which is too weak for normal use. Other elements, such as a strengthening bar, are also added for different reasons. All these decisions need to be recorded and structured in order to be able to cope with future developments and avoid becoming locked into an inefficient production cycle. The flanges are added to the design as a consequence of the decision to split the door shape. The flange shapes depend on the join line and it would be logical to have an automatic tool to create the flange shape. This would also mean that the shape can be classified automatically as a flange rather than identified manually later. The use of advanced application tools to provide high-level information about complex shapes is an important step in recording design intent.

4 Instantiation of the Semantic Model for the Purpose of Data Popularization

The following individuals (i.e., instances of classes) are created in order to associate required field data with the PLM Semantic Ontology Model. Fig. 6 shows a part of individuals created and visualized using Protégé:

1. The five parts of flanges are modeled as five distinctive individuals of the Complex_Physical_Product, e.g., Flange1, Flange2, Flange3, Flange4, and Flange5.
2. Individuals of Design_Parameter class is created and linked : Efficiency, Energy_Use, Welding_Reduction, Processing_Time, Quality, Environmental_factor.
3. The individual elements of Design_Process_Activity have been created according to the general concept described by Nigel Cross, (Engineering design methods, Cross 2008): Clarifying_objective, Establishing_function, Setting_Requirement, Determining_characteristics, Generating_alternative, and Evaluating_alternative, Improving_details.
4. While using the existing class "Parameter" in PLM SOM, Designe_Parameter is associated.

Afterward, we verified the model using "Pellet" reasoner (Protégé). As a proof of concept of the case study, we used the DL Query and SPARQL Query tabs supported by Protégé, while looking for answers to the following queries:

- Which types of design intent were used in the past?
- Which design intent variables (primitives) are primarily considered for each type of design decision?
- Which design intent types are used for the purpose of "Flange design", for example?
- Which physical products are related with a given type of design intent? And in what PLM cycle (BOL, MOL, EOL) is the product currently?
- Considering a given material resource, which design intent is associated with it? This question is particularly important for the purpose of knowing the impact on the material resources and equipment in the case of choosing a certain design intent among several options.

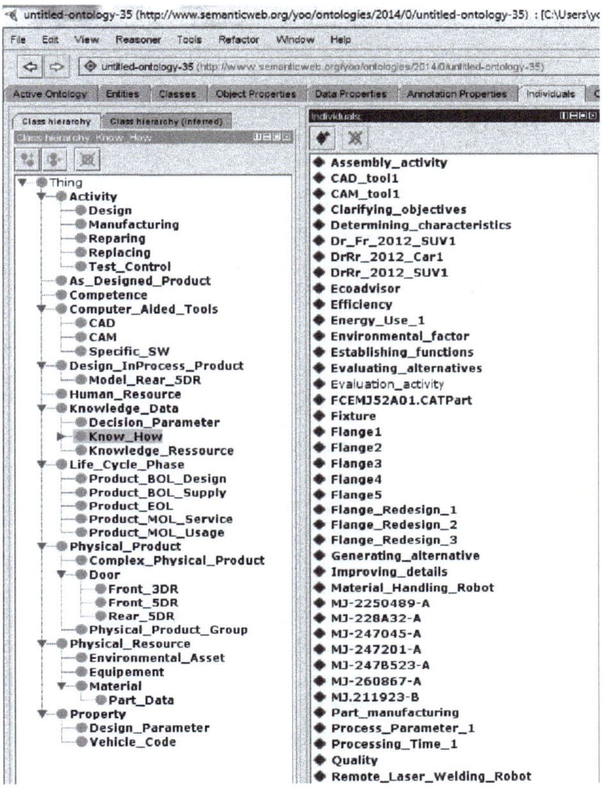

Fig. 6. Extended PLM Semantic Object Model – Classes in Protégé (Protégé)

5 Concluding Remarks

The purpose of the work presented in this paper is to demonstrate how to extend and improve previously developed ontology for product lifecycle management with the design intent know-how data within a semantically understandable concepts and relationships. The benefits from such integration are clear:

1. The relationship between a) Design Decision data (i.e., design intent) and b) Designed Product data (manufacturing details determined through some design intent and design decision.) during the whole cycle of PLM is visible and traceable.
2. We can predict which parameters or manufacturing processes are important whenever new design is proposed, and which tools were used for evaluating previous design. It means how to use the know-how and how to collaborate with related persons.
3. Supposing that individuals of human resources shall be provided according to the defined ontology, we shall be able to find as well who are the persons related to the decision of each part design or manufacturing process, which means who has the know-how.

Our work demonstrates suitable ontology model as well as the way of retrieving a particular type of know-how (i.e., design intent) in the context of current design decisions. Such an approach can ultimately contribute to reducing design time, making knowledge transfer clear and thus improving the quality of designed products.

Acknowledgement. The work on the PLM Semantic Ontology Model and its extension was partly funded by the LinkedDesign (FP7-2011-NMP-ICT-FoF-284613). The work on the flange tool described in the case study was funded by the Resilient Automotive Factories (FP7-2011-NMP-ICT-FoF-285051).

References

(Cross 2008) Cross, N.: Engineering design methods: strategies for product design, 4th edn. Wiley, Chichester (2008)

(Han 2010) Han, S.: Macro-parametric: an approach for the history-based parametrics. International Journal of Product Lifecycle Management 4(4), 321–325 (2010)

(Kiritsis 2013) Kiritsis, D.: Semantic technologies for engineering asset life cycle management. International Journal of Production Research 51(23-24), 7345–7371 (2013)

(Kjellberg 1983) Kjellberg, T.A., Stroud, I.A., Wingard, L.O.: GPM Volume module in CAM-I perspective. CAM-I solid modelling, Stockholm, Sweden (1983)

(Matsokis and Kiritsis 2011) Matsokis, A., Kiritsis, D.: An ontology-based implementation on a robotic assembly line for supporting lifecycle data management. In: Paper presented at the Sixth World Congress on Engineering Asset Management, Cincinnati, OH, October 3-5 (2011)

(Mun et al. 2003) Mun, D., Han, S., Kim, J., Oh, Y.: A set of standard modeling commands for the history-based parametric approach. Computer Aided-Design 35(13), 1171–1179 (2003)

(OpenPlatform3) Open Group Open Platform3 white paper, https://www2.opengroup.org/ogsys/catalog/w147 (last access on June 9, 2014)

(Pratt and Anderson 2001) Pratt, M.J., Anderson, B.D.: A shape modelling applications programming interface for the STEP standard. Computer Aided-Design 33(7), 531–543 (2001)

(Price et al. 2013) Price, M.A., Robinson, T.T., Soban, D., Murphy, M.A., Armstrong, C.G., McConnell, R., Roy, R.: Maintaining design intent for aircraft manufacture. CIRP Annual - Manufacturing Technology 62(1), 99–102 (2013)

(PROMISE 2009) PROMISE. Research Deliverable 9.2 (2009), information available on http://www.promise.no/downloadfile.php?i=69adc1e107f7f7d035d7baf04342e1ca

(Protégé) http://protegewiki.stanford.edu/wiki/Main_Page

(QLM) Open Group Quantum Lifecycle Management work group, information available on: http://www.opengroup.org/getinvolved/workgroups/qlm (last access on June 9, 2014)

A Short Portable PLM Course

Joel Sauza Bedolla[1], Javier Martinez Gomez[1,2], and Paolo Chiabert[1]

[1] Politecnico di Torino, C.so Duca degli Abruzzi 24, Torino 10129, Italy
{joel.sauza,paolo.chiabert}@polito.it
[2] Universidad Industrial de Santander, Calle 9 Cra.27, Bucaramanga, Colombia
javimar@uis.edu.co

Abstract. This paper presents the modern education principles of a short PLM course designed to be deployed all over the world in universities that do not have a PDM software. The main objective of this course is to present the advantages of using a PLM strategy during the Product Development Process. A case study is used to present and explore different process areas of a product lifecycle within a collaborative environment. Students are required to perform tasks and develop a technical solution. Special attention is devoted to the information exchange using an open source PDM system.

1 Introduction

The new economy demands that today's engineers are able to work in a distributed, interdisciplinary, problem-based, and technology-enhanced environment [1]. The growing interest in PLM in the industries has demanded college education to impart engineering students the necessary skills for collaborative design in a distributed environment [2]. In other terms, industry is requiring a new profile of students able to understand the PLM principles and to be trained in the tools that industry uses.

The purpose of engineering education is to provide the learning required by students to become successful engineers—technical expertise, social awareness, and oriented towards innovation [3]. The big issue for universities is which topics to include and how to teach them.

In the last years, Politecnico di Torino has been asked to assist other universities and technical institutes in the deployment of PLM courses. Specially, it was explicitly required to use the PDM software during the lectures. This situation had lead us to search for a PLM course that could be deployed all over the world using a PDM instrument.

Nowadays, there is no standard for defining the necessary skills and capabilities for a PLM expert and therefore it is impossible to define the educational path for new engineers. In this chaos, every university has decided to apply its own strategy: IT oriented, CAD oriented, PLM Project Management, user (data creators, reviewers or consumers) or super user (administrator). The first challenge was to define an original PLM course that covers different areas of a product lifecycle without being partial to one area.

Usually, the PDM software requires a server and client installation that requires time and technical skills. This condition makes almost impossible to use the tool outside the

S. Fukuda et al. (Eds.): PLM 2014, IFIP AICT 442, pp. 111–120, 2014.

network where the installation was made. In literature there are some examples of curriculum development of PLM courses or PLM projects with information exchange between different teams [4-6]. In these examples, the university which organizes the course is the owner of the PDM system and the course was executed with groups that work inside the network of the university. Instead, Segonds et al [7] develop a project using Dropbox as PDM for a collaborative project between two universities. This solution solves the installation problem but Dropbox cannot manage the configuration and change management process necessary to work in a PLM environment. The second challenge was to find a PDM solution that could be easily installed, managed and reachable from the outside of the university network.

This article presents an original short PLM course focused in the development of a new product (section 2). The exercise covers different process areas (section 3) and its integration (section 4) using an open source PDM. The course deployment and results are discussed in section 4 and 5 respectively. Finally, conclusions are stated in section 6.

2 Case Study

The sliding door trolley (Fig. 1) is a key component of commercial and garage doors and gates since it links the gate framework to the surrounding structure. The trolley runs on a monorail which is fixed to the wall. It should be designed and constructed in such a way as to prevent it from falling down, collapsing or derailment during normal operation or in case of contact with stationary obstacles.

Fig. 1. Sliding door trolley

3 Process Areas

During the development of the exercise there are a series of processes with similar goals which are grouped in Process Areas (PA). A PA is a cluster of related practices in an area that, when implemented collectively, satisfies a set of goals considered important for making improvement in that area [8].

Requirements Management (RM)

The purpose of this PA is to manage the requirements of the project's products and product components and to identify inconsistencies between those requirements and the project's plans and work products [9].

Project Management (PM)

Project Management is the application of knowledge, skills, tools and techniques to project activities in order to meet or exceed stakeholder needs and expectations from a project [10].

Quality Planning (QP)

Quality planning is part of quality management focused on setting quality objectives and specifying necessary operational processes and related resources to fulfil the quality objectives[11]. One of the most significant methods to assure quality is the Failure Mode and Effects Analysis (FMEA). FMEA is an analytical methodology used to ensure that potential problems have been considered and addressed throughout the product and process development phases [12].

Product Design (PD)

Product design is to conceive the idea for some artifact or system and to express that idea in an embodiable form [13].

Process Design (PrD)

Process design is to conceive the looks, arrangement and workings of something before it is constructed [14].

Configuration and Change Management (CCM)

Configuration is a management activity that applies technical and administrative direction over the life cycle of a product, its configuration items, and related product configuration information [15]. It is composed by four basic functions: identification, configuration control, status accounting and audit. The Institute of Configuration Management [16] has defined a closed-loop change process used to release new information and to change information already released. This loop is formed by a Problem Report (PR), Engineering Change Request (ECR) and Engineering Change Notice (ECN). A PR form is used to report a problem, where it occurred and the steps which led to its occurrence. An ECR form is used to request changes and initiate reviews that will result in a proper disposition. An ECN form is used to implement approved ECRs and provide the authority to upgrade and release associated documents.

4 Integration

Information technology, by the way of collecting, sharing and gathering data, exchanging information, optimising process through package software, is becoming one of the key developments and success for collaboration strategies [17]. The integration of the process areas was achieved by using the open source PDM software Aras Innovator [18]. Aras has been successfully used in different universities [19,20]

Innovator's solution suite constitutes of a full-featured engineering business solution supporting engineering and manufacturing processes throughout the plant and the extended supply chain [21]. Aras takes advantage of HTTP/HTTPS, XML, and SOAP protocols to deliver its functionality through a standard web browser (Internet explorer).

The server installation resides at Politecnico di Torino and is reachable from the outside. Even though Aras does not need a client installation, a small client configuration is mandatory. It consists of setting up some browser security issues.

All modules used in the development of the exercise come along with the standard version of Aras Innovator 9.3. The only exception is the Requirements Management module that was developed by a third party and delivered as an add-on to the software.

The only customizations made to the software were:

- Requirements classification
- Requirements sequence number
- Part sequence number
- Document sequence number

Fig. 2 presents an overview of the exercise. It covers the Imagination and Definition phases of a product lifecycle and includes the PAs described previously. PM and the CCM play in parallel to the other process areas. Further description of the graph will be given in the next sections.

Before starting, a training on the PDM software is essential. It is supposed that the attendees are new in the use of this instrument so in the first part of the course, the students receive the credentials to enter the system and a general overview of the most used applications.

The collaboration is achieved by using a project structure that permits information access to all team members. Projects inside Aras Innovator use a Work Breakdown Structures (WBS), which allows users to break down the project into manageable phases, activities and tasks. Each activity is identified uniquely and it can be associated to a deliverable, start and due date, assignee, and role. It is also possible to define predecessors or other constraints.

A project template (see Fig. 3) has been used to develop the new product. The template was previously prepared and filled with the information and dates of the course.

During the development of the exercise students use and learn almost all functions of PLM systems: versioning, vaulting, searching strategies, multi BOM management (eBOM and mBOM), concurrent engineering, workflow management and part reusing.

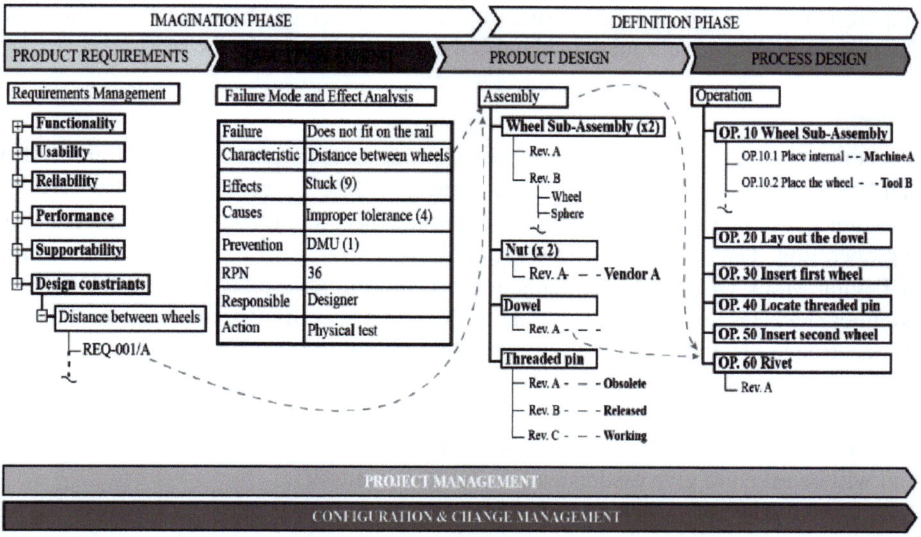

Fig. 2. Exercise overview

N	Project Tree	Predecessor	Plan Duration	Plan Hours	Attach Required	Attach Type	Lead Role	Required
	New Product				☐			
	Phase 0 - Requirements				☐			
1	Understand customer needs		1		☑	Document	Manager	☑
2	Define Product Requirements	1	1		☑	Document	Manager	☑
3	Validate Product Requirements	2	1		☑	Document	Manager	☑
4	Requirements end		0		☐			☐
	Phase 1 - Quality Planning				☐			
5	Select DFMEA team	4	1		☑	Document	Quality	☑
6	Perform DFMEA analysis	5	1		☑	Document	Quality	☑
7	Follow-up actions	6	1		☑	Document	Quality	☑
8	Quality end		0		☐			☐
	Phase 2 - Product Development				☐			
9	Create BOM	6	1		☑	Document	Design	☑
10	CAD Modeling	9	1		☑	Document	Design	☑
11	Material Specification	10,9	1		☑	Document	Quality	☑
12	Technical drawings	9,10,11	1		☑	Document	Design	☑
13	Product Assembly	10,12	1		☑	Document	Design	☑
14	Product development end	10,13,12,11,9	0		☐			☐
	Phase 3 - Process Development				☐			
15	Define component operations	14,8	1		☑	Document	Process	☑
16	Define assembly sequence	15	1		☑	Document	Process	☑
17	Process end		0		☐			☐

Fig. 3. Project Template

Phase 0

The kick off for the exercise is the list of requirements for the product. The requirement list was established by the role of Requirement Analyst (RA) which is an expert of the product. The RA has to understand customer needs and to translate this into product requirements. Finally, he has to validate them. Students are not involved in the requirements definition, instead they are asked to consider these requirements and to satisfy them. Requirements were classified according to FURPS+ [22].

For the sake of brevity, only one requirement is presented here that is going to continue for the rest of the phases as an example. Referring to the design constraint (Fig. 2) "the distance between the wheels", it can be deduce that it is a critical requirement since the distance assures the correct assembly between the trolley and the monorail. This requirement is identified and managed by the CCM.

Phase 1

The Quality Manager is asked to form a group and to perform a Design FMEA (DFMEA) using the integrated FMEA matrix. In Fig. 2, the failure mode "Trolley does not fit on the rail" is analysed. As a consequence, the trolley may impair the sliding operation. The cause of such failure could be an improper tolerancing of the parts. A Digital Mock-Up (DMU) is planned to prevent the failure. Then, the Risk Priority Number (RPN) is calculated according to the effect severity (9), the cause probability of occurrence (4) and the probability to detect the failure (1). The RPN helps to classify and rank the failure modes.

The most important thing is that once the FMEA is performed, an action is assigned to a role. The designer who has been commissioned will receive a notification and will be asked to give evidence of completing the task.

A product characteristic (distance between wheels) is created. This characteristic is managed by the CCM and must be considered during the product design. Aras links the FMEA characteristic to the product configuration by adding a tab in the BOM. Links can be made at assembly or part level.

The DFMEA lifecycle has a particular way of being conducted. It is created as draft and it remains in that state until the phase of product design is closed. The DFMEA can be released only after receiving the completion of all taken actions.

Phase 2

During the product Design, the Design leader creates the BOM of the product and assigns the design of the parts to other team members. Team members create the 3D models of the parts and deliver the technical drawings. The material selection is a task assigned to the quality team. Finally, the team leader performs the product assembly.

While performing this tasks, designers must take into account the product requirements and characteristics that have been established in previous phases. For example, the distance between the wheels requirement and characteristic are linked to the assembly level of the product. This distance can be obtained after all parts are assembled. Also, the designer must answer to the task assigned in the DFMEA.

By linking requirements, characteristics and DFMEA actions, the designer is lowering the risk level of committing a mistake. After completing the required actions, the DFMEA table will be updated adding two more rows, the action taken and a new RPN (which is expected to be lower).

During the product design, the single part is responsibility of the designer in charge and he performs a manual releasing. Instead, the assembly, due to its importance, is submitted to an ECN for its releasing.

Phase 3

The Process leader assigns the analysis of a part to different team members. Every team member develops the necessary operations to produce the part. During this development, the process designer has to link the part to the process and to consider all necessary resources (tools, machines, work areas, etc.).

Process leader is responsible of the operations definitions of the final assembly. He is also responsible for taking into account the product requirements and characteristics that are influenced by the process. For example, Op. 60 (see Fig. 2) is the final operation made to the assembly; by riveting a dowel, the trolley gets its final shape. This operations is the one that produces the desired distance between wheels. It is also possible to perform a Process FMEA and to establish a quality control plan of the operations.

All items of the process development must be managed according to CCM. Single part production are manual released while the final assembly is controlled by an ECN. Phase 3 ends up the project. The products is considered to be successfully produced and it reaches the market.

Phase 4

A client complaint is reported and managed with a PR automatic workflow. The change specialist evaluates the problem and asks for technical expert opinion. If the problem is accepted, it is then taken to an ECR.

The change board team evaluates the problem and looks for a technical solution. For example (Fig. 4), a change in the dimensions of the client's rail will cause a change to the requirement associated to the distance between the wheels. In the same way, the new requirement version will produce a change to the product, and the it will cause a process change. Finally, an ECN must be performed to inform all stakeholders that the change has been achieved.

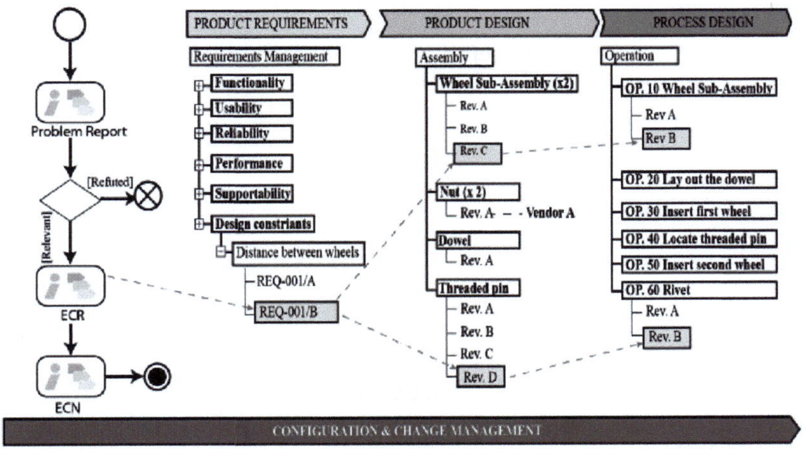

Fig. 4. Change Management

5 Deployment

The course has been deployed several times in different universities (Ss. Cyril and Methodius University in Skopje, FYROM; University of Novi Sad, Serbia; Arts et Mètiers ParisTech, France) and technical institutes (ITIS OMAR Novara, Italy). The course can be limited to a demonstration of the tool or expanded to a practical exercise. The number of hours employed vary according to this constraint.

The most complete experience (in terms of project achievement, number of students involved and number of hours dedicated) has been reached in June 2013 at University Federico II of Naples. Results and conclusions refer to this last experience.18 professional master level students from different backgrounds (electrical, mechanical, industrial and system engineering) participated in the 27 hours course. Students were assigned to different teams according to their preferences: 2 Project Managers, 4 Quality Engineers, 4 Product Designers, 4 Process Designers and 2 Change Specialists. The course was given in 6 days in sessions of 3 and 6 hours.

The connection to the PDM worked correctly and students accessed without problems. The performed activities were fairly clear and team leaders gave evidence of the completion of the tasks on time.

6 Results

At the end of the course an anonymous questionnaire (Likert scale) was used for measuring student perception. The more relevant (positive and negative) aspects are listed below.

Positive Aspects

Overall, the course achieved its objectives satisfactorily (Fig. 5a) and the contents of the course were considered original by the majority of students (Fig. 5b). The teaching method and material given were highly appreciated.

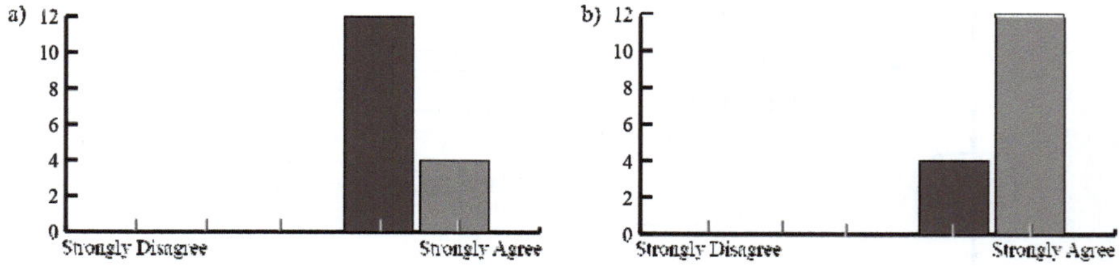

Fig. 5. a)Course contents are original. b) The course achieved its objectives.

Negative Aspects

Up to version 9.3, Aras worked exclusively on Internet Explorer (IE) using a .NET security framework. This situation limited the use of computers with Windows operating system. However, version 10 of Aras has been recently released and it does not require the .NET security framework and therefore it will be possible to connect also with Firefox on Windows and OSx.

During the days before the course, IE passed from version 9 to 10. This update caused a delay during client configuration. Though, from 17 computers, only one presented problems that were solved in the same day.

Moreover, Aras presents some usability errors (i.e. the insert row tab is missing while creating an FMEA) that made impossible some operations and influenced negatively student perception (see Fig. 6). In order to connect to the server, a non-restricted WIFI or LAN is compulsory. Other software (i.e CAD software) needed during the development of the course must be installed and licensed in the students computers.

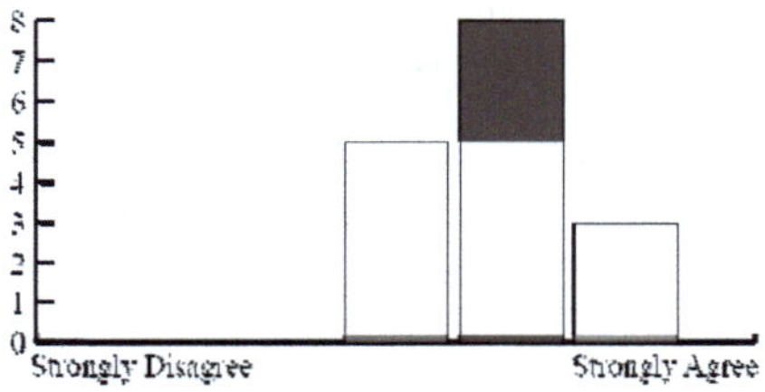

Fig. 6. I used the system (Aras innovator) without difficulty

7 Conclusions

This paper presents an original PLM course that covers different phases of a product lifecycle integrated in an open source PDM. This course includes the development of a new product within a collaborative environment.

Students are exposed to the complexity of managing product information through different process areas (product requirements, quality management, product and process design, project management, and configuration and change management). The course encourages the integration of product information, processes and people, and it is not oriented to a single technological area. A project structure is used to consent information access to all team members while they develop a technical solution.

The use of a web based open source PDM eliminates the need of a client/server installation and facilitates its use outside the network where the tool was installed. Despite some technological and usability problems, the system performs well.

From experience gained by organizing the course in different institutions, it is found that this course can be deployed all over the world. It is our belief that other universities can take this paper as a model to develop PLM courses exploiting the advantages of open source PDM or similar solutions.

References

1. Peng, X., Lough, K.G., Dow, B.: Teaching collaborative engineering design in a distributed environment through experiential learning. In: American Society for Engineering Education, Austin, TX (2009)
2. Peng, X., Leu, M., Niu, Q.: Integration of Collaborative Engineering Design Using Teamcenter Community in Mechanical Engineering Curricula. In: Tomovic, M., Wang, S. (eds.) Product Realization, pp. 1–19. Springer US (2009), doi:10.1007/978-0-387-09482-3_11
3. Crawley, E.F., Malmqvist, J., Östlund, S., Brodeur, D.R.: Rethinking Engineering Education: The CDIO Approach. Springer (2007)
4. Chang, Y.-H., Miller, C.L.: PLM curriculum development: Using an industry-sponsored project to teach manufacturing simulation in a multidisciplinary environment. Journal of Manufacturing Systems 24, 171–177 (2005), doi:http://dx.doi.org/10.1016/S0278-6125(06)80005-1
5. Sauza Bedolla, J., Ricci, F., Martinez Gomez, J., Chiabert, P.: A Tool to Support PLM Teaching in Universities. In: Bernard, A., Rivest, L., Dutta, D. (eds.) PLM 2013. IFIP AICT, vol. 409, pp. 510–519. Springer, Heidelberg (2013), doi:10.1007/978-3-642-41501-2_51
6. Sanin_Perez, P.: A PLM implementation in a design project course of Product Design EAFIT (2010)
7. Segonds, F., Maranzana, N., Rose, B., Caillaud, E.: Educational practices for collaborative distributed design of an innovative eco-designed product. In: International Conference on Engineering and Product Design Education, Antwerp, Belgium (2012)
8. Chrissis, M.B., Konrad, M.D., Shrum, S.: CMMI for Development: Guidelines for Process Integration and Product Improvement, 3rd edn. SEI Series in Software Engineering (2011)
9. CMMI for Development, Version 1.3, Carnegie Mellon (2010)
10. Project Management Institute, A Guide to the Project Management Body of Knowledge, 5th edn. (2013)
11. ISO 9000:2005 Quality management systems — Fundamentals and vocabulary (2005)
12. AIAG, Potential Failure Mode and effects Analysis (FMEA). 4th edn. (2008)
13. Ontwerpen FI. DELFT Design guide (2010)
14. Slack, N., Chambers, S., Johnston, R., Betts, A.: Operations and process management. Pearson (2006)
15. ISO 10007:2003 Quality management systems — Guidelines for configuration management (2003)
16. CMII. CMII Standard for Integrated Process Excellence and Configuration Management (2013)
17. Neubert, G., Ouzrout, Y., Bouras, A.: Collaboration and integration through information technologies in supply chains. International Journal of Technology Management 28(2), 259–273 (2004)
18. Aras, Aras Innovator (2014), http://www.aras.com/
19. Pérez, P.S.: A "PLM" implementation in a design project course of product design engineering program. EAFIT University (2010)
20. Morenton, P.: Rialto CATIA V5 integration for Aras Innovator (2009), http://www.aras.com/plm-newsletters/ViewNewsletter.aspx?ID=BF67A29929C946B882C45F7EAD7891B5
21. CIMData, How PLM is Being Applied to Support Today's Dynamic Enterprises (2006)
22. Grady, R.B.: Practical Software Metrics for Project Management and Process Improvement. Prentice-Hall (1992)

Product Lifecycle Management in Education: Key to Innovation in Engineering and Technology

Priyanka Gandhi

[1] Sr. PLM Consultant, USA
[2] Independent Researcher
priyankagandhi9@gmail.com

Abstract. Product Lifecycle Management in Education is the key to innovation and success in organizations in the engineering and technology sector. This paper illustrates that incorporation of PLM training in coursework and education of best practices, processes and solutions at educational institutions as well as organizations helps leverage the intellectual assets of an organization and turn them into deliverable assets. PLM education and training imparts vision, technical expertise and solutions to improve productivity and efficiency in the fields of engineering, business, operations and supply chain in different industries such as OEMs their suppliers, retail, pharmacy and apparel industry etc. PLM training and applications of core methods, tools and processes achieve major cost savings and resource sharing between different business segments besides advancing the innovation in engineering and technology.

Keywords: PLM, Education, Efficiency, Supply Chain, OEMs, Tools and Processes, Training, Productivity, Innovation, Design Engineering.

1 Introduction

Product Lifecycle Management has become one of the fastest growing technology solutions in the last twenty years in engineering organizations. PLM has gained its popularity and established its scope in engineering, manufacturing, retail, apparel, pharmacy and various other industries. It has become imperative to educate employees of OEMs (Original Equipment Manufacturers) and the suppliers in the use of Product Lifecycle Management tools and processes. Usually the product development team and its members prior to the implementation of PLM methodologies lack the vision and empowerment to avoid wasteful PLM implementation procedures and err along the lifecycle of product development, thereby under-utilizing the "PLM potential" for a %100 successful outcome[1].

Product Lifecycle Management education and training to experienced engineers and even recent graduates can help in producing better product development expertise, improvised skill and tool knowledge to carry out efficient design, technical competence to manage a large product base, industrial applicability to improve customer satisfaction and overall better engineering solutions to maintain and run existing processes seamlessly in the real world. Usually suppliers of engineering product/parts and services spend a humongous amount of resources in outsourcing the training and certification endeavors to OEMs or other suppliers

S. Fukuda et al. (Eds.): PLM 2014, IFIP AICT 442, pp. 121–128, 2014.

to educate and certify their engineering workforce to gain the technological knowledge to excel in application of PLM solutions to their product lifecycles [2].

Many companies have therefore realized the added value brought about by PLM Education in cost saving strategies to leverage the quality and productivity of their Product development Lifecycle. One of the essential components of Product Lifecycle Management is the knowledge of PLM tools and their functionality that forms the "Software area of the PLM" [1]. The application of PLM knowledge to specific industries like Industrial, Aerospace, Automotive, Retail or Pharmaceutical requires the knowledge of software tools along with the ability to translate PLM vision and strategy to good design practices and philosophies. Thus application based PLM training involving case studies from experts of the specific industry, industry specific lessons learnt, knowledge of the known wasteful processes, all form an application based approach in PLM training and coaching [7].

Organizations using PLM technology are actively seeking PLM Education and training for their workforce thus driving PLM Education to schools and institutions to lay stress on their need for improving productivity and eliminating engineering design downtime. Utilizing PLM- efficient systems to drive productivity and resource sharing between isolated business segments that don't interact with each other and are relatively closed niche has become one of the most important goals along with core functional areas such as engineering design and product development. Karina Kogan, President of Business Management Systems at Vertex believes that PLM education is core to the success of PLM implementation in any industry. She further goes on to saying that, Vertex encourages fresh graduates and students right out of college to work in the fields of PLM and that they are even willing to go a step further beyond and install their tools and products at educational institutions so that they can be trained in fields of PLM before starting out work [5].

Sue Welch, the CEO at Tradestone Software, states that she is very interested in capturing fresh talent as well as educating them on the real-world applications of PLM in the direction to succeed as future PLM leaders of the retail industry. Laura McCann, who is the CEO at Zweave, has been able to launch the first academic PLM project that supports PLM education in the retail and fashion industry. This enables the students to get the PLM knowledge and industrial experience at a much affordable cost. Gerber technology has provided free software to educational institutions for about 40 years now, so as to produce talented PLM consultants that are well versed in the PLM technology [1]. The V.P. of Vertical Market Strategy at PTC, Kathleen Mitford says that, PTC has always pioneered PLM education at the university levels and has provided the PTC software solutions to the academic institutions for learning and development purposes. Lenny Weiss, the V.P. of sales and marketing at Yunique Solutions, says that Yunique has provided access to their PLM tools and processes to the students at FIT (Fashion Institute of Technology) to provide PLM training to the student fraternity in the retail and fashion industry. Phillippe Ribera, the PLM development manager at Lectra, states that they target over 680 fashion and design institutions to impart PLM education. Over 70 schools have implemented coursework and training on PLM technology solutions and design technology developed by Lectra in their curriculum in order to produce well trained PLM graduates for the retail and fashion industry [1].The Vice President of R&D at Visual 2000 International, Charles Benoualid, states that he has always championed the give and take philosophy on PLM in Education. The give and take model allows him to supply free PLM software and technology for training purposes to students at universities to teach them about real life PLM technology solutions and in return the highly learned scholars in design and production with advanced degrees end up providing real solutions to customers across the globe. There are a few companies which are still thinking and giving consideration to the PLM in education perspective but are yet to adopt it. Lawson and Porine spA are a few to name [1].

2 PLM Training at Educational Institutions and Universities

2.1 PLM Education at Purdue University

Purdue University has developed a detailed Research and Development Program to foster the Product Lifecycle Management subject as a philosophy and as a tool that will serve as an important building block in producing successful industry leaders in this area of technology [7]. The PLM center of excellence at Purdue is a collaboration of the colleges of engineering, science and management, that have come together to conceive a "one stop" PLM educational research and training center to the academia and industries [1]. Purdue aims at propagating through this institute the best industry standards in PLM tools and technology by partnering with the PLM giants in business and merging them with the PLM educational community. The goals of this Research and Development center at Purdue is to advance the Product Lifecycle Management Tools and approaches by leveraging the existing PLM solutions from the tech-industry [11].

Purdue University understands the value and significance of PLM as a technology and as a management discipline in today's day and age of technological innovation. The benefits of Product Lifecycle Management as comprehended at Purdue are multiple; from better visualization and management of product data management to increasing the productivity and quality of the end product, it truly understands the potential of PLM and its unrealized scope [1].Purdue professes that PLM brings about streamlined product development at reduced costs through the different lifecycle stages of the product evolution from inception, execution to maturity in engineering design, manufacturing as well as maintenance disciplines. Encouraging PLM in Education Industry is the fundamental goal of the PLM R&D center at Purdue. Purdue University aims to establish s t rategic r elatio n sh ip s w i t h key organizations with a PLM focus through this media [1]. Purdue hopes to surface the advancements in PLM technology from time to time and propagate the PLM tools and training in the academia t o produce future leaders. It also aims at producing better PLM career prospects and seek funding for developing the PLM R&D Initiative. Purdue also has a vision of bringing brand new organizations on board with PLM tools and technology and encouraging more and more educational institutions to incorporate PLM coursework in their curriculum [1].

2.2 PLM Education at Michigan Technological University

The PHD program in Mechanical Engineering at Michigan Technological University (MTU) has Product Lifecycle Management as one of its main focus areas under the mechanical engineering umbrella. The PHD program at MTU is one of its kind research intensive programs that foster PLM as one of the research areas of course work and dissertation. The Graduate ranking of the Doctoral Program is 48th across US according to America's best college rankings. The Undergraduate degree program in Mechanical Engineering is ranked 22nd across US according to the Americas best college rankings. MTU is a pioneer institution that has about 7000 students enrolled in graduate and undergraduate degree programs. There are about 130 programs in arts, sciences, engineering, and several other subjects at MTU [1].

In order to obtain the undergraduate d egree at MTU, the students need to do a senior design capstone project that tests their design knowledge. In a group of 4 to 6 students they participate in this design challenge which is believed to be more of a first job for them rather than their last class. Michigan Technological University is one of the Major Customers of Siemens that is the creator of Unigraphics their signature PLM tool and solution. Students learn Unigraphics (NX) in their undergraduate degree program when they start out and use their design skills along with the PLM software tool knowledge to propose innovative design solutions and their CAD Design skills [1].

A typical example of a senior capstone design project was a case study with whirlpool dryers that ended up resulting in a 11 cents/ unit saving adding up to $ 1.85 million savings for the company annually [Fig 1]. There was an option to use Pro-E as the CAD tool but the Unigraphics tool's CAM option was more suitable and familiar for the senior design team. The systems noise level requirement was also taken into consideration and there were two options developed but it was demonstrated that one of the option that couldn't meet the systems noise requirements was rejected and the other option which met or exceeded the systems noise level requirements was chosen which led to savings of 11 cents per unit and $1.85 million annually [10].

PACE is the "Partners for the Advancement of Collaborative Engineering Education" Program that links several institutions academically including the Michigan Technological University for the development of PLM solutions that cater to the automotive OEMs . Several key team players of the Automotive Industry participate in judging the PACE endeavor like GM, Siemens, HP, Oracle, etc. PACE fosters the goals of PLM to provide Product Lifecycle Management as an integrated engineering solution from conceptualizing, product development, marketing, distribution, maintenance and ultimately disposition and recycling of the product, if necessary [7].

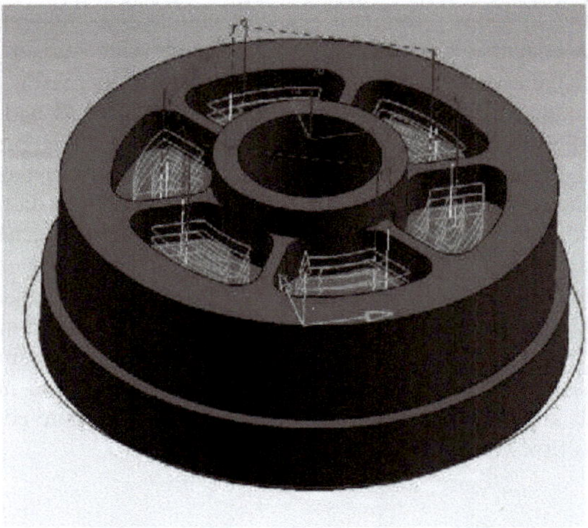

Fig. 1. Whirlpool Dryer Senior Design Capstone Project at Michigan Technological University. A dryer designed by MTU students that led whirlpool to alter its design and bring about savings worth $1.85 million dollars is shown above.

Michigan Technological University teaches a program on engineering modeling and design course the ENG1102 where eight students participate annually in the PACE design competition showcasing innovative design solutions to a panel of judges appointed by the MTU. The criteria for the selection of the best design project includes, form, fit, function of the design and the presentation and feasibility of the design. Examples of PACE winning team projects include a robotic vehicle and projects utilizing the alternative energy sources like solar and wind energy [9].

2.3 PLM Education at Oakland University

The center for Product Lifecycle Management at Oakland University in Michigan is one of its kind institutes that inculcate the important lessons of PLM implementation in the form of coursework offerings. Oakland University has developed a center for PLM Education that will touch upon the three areas of Product Development, PLM (Product Lifecycle Management), ERP (Enterprise Resource Planning) and MES (Manufacturing Execution Systems) in order to keep the jobs within the state of Michigan itself [Fig 2] [8].

The goals of the Academic Center of Excellence for PLM at Oakland University can be summarized into the following five points [Fig 3]:

1. To act as the main point of origination of Leadership Strategies for Development of the PLM Workforce.
2. Collaborate the academic center for PLM with Local K-12 schools and community colleges.
3. To help in the development of virtual manufacturing labs.
4. To help in the IT maintenance of the PLM centers for various academic institutions and schools.
5. Provide Educational Development of PLM, ERP and MES areas by including coursework in PLM in the existing Masters in Engineering and Management programs.

Fig. 2. Functional Areas of I.T. Enterprise Architecture. The figure shows the three integrated areas of Product Lifecycle Management, Enterprise Resource planning, and Manufacturing Execution Systems [6].

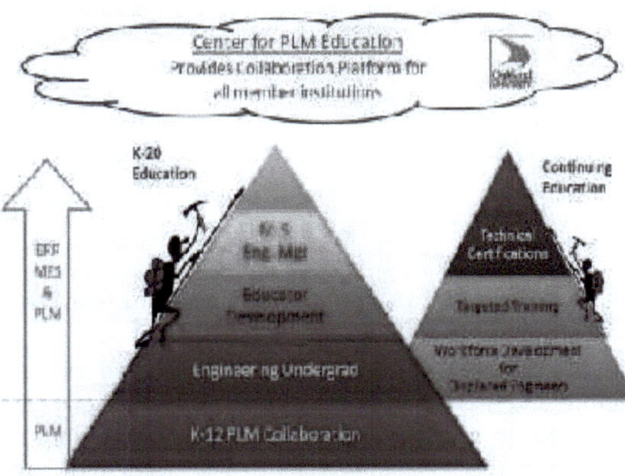

Fig. 3. Academic Center for PLM at Oakland University. This figure shows the breakdown of integrated areas of PLM.

The academic center of PLM development at Oakland University realized that Product Lifecycle Management (PLM) consists of the following steps, also summarized in Fig 4 [11].

1. Recognition of the market/ niche of the product.
2. Design of the products based on the business requirements.
3. Analysis of the performance criteria of the product
4. Manufacturing of the Product.
5. Customer Satisfaction and Product Support through its Lifecycle.
6. Reducing the impact of the product on the environment thus easing the recycling and disposition process.

The academic institutions in Michigan are striving hard to develop the PLM skills in their students and while doing so they face the challenge of lack of I.T. infrastructure to provide them with the necessary tools and processes. A collaborative online approach that provides them the necessary tool infrastructure and support along with the course curriculum is thus needed [1].

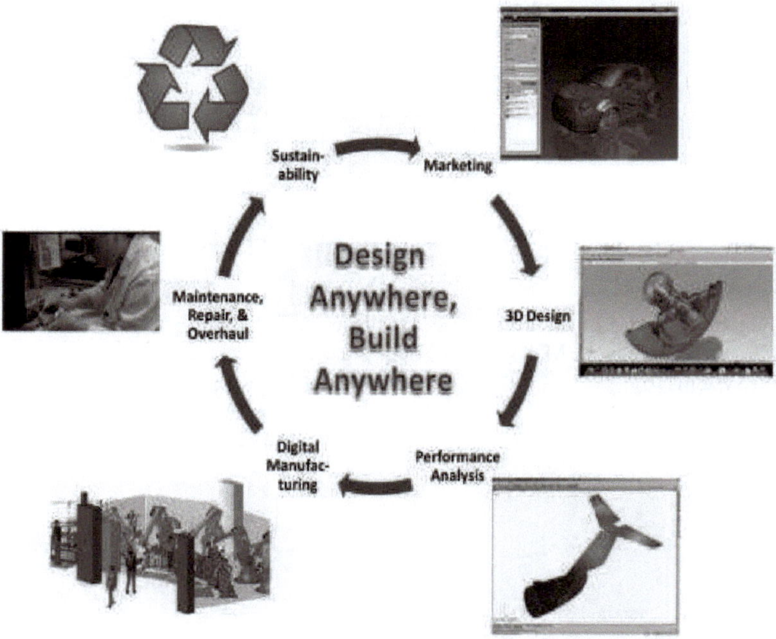

Fig. 4. Stages of PLM. This figure shows the different stages of Product lifecycle management.

The academic center has relationships with essential PLM vendors that can help provide the necessary IT infrastructure and the non-member academic institutions can in turn partner with this academic center in order to reap the benefits of their accessibility to the PLM tools and technology made available at this academic center. The academic center is also aiming at providing software tools installation and IT support to the member schools and services as the IT hub that all the member institutions can go to with license installation issues and tool support requirements [1].The academic center also aims at including PLM course offerings especially in the technology track courses like the masters in engineering management program to include the PL/ERP/MES courses. The academic center also aims at starting virtual manufacturing labs where the member institutions can access the software tools necessary to simulate manufacturing environments to test the feasibility of their product design. Virtual labs are better than physical labs since they do not need the full scale IT infrastructure to function [7]. As schools always face the lack of funds and staff to maintain and run the individual labs, the virtual labs help them to train their students in manufacturing domain of the PLM without the need to set up an actual lab [3]. The goals of the academic center are clearly also in line with the vision of President Obama who envisions that America is in need of smarter engineering and manufacturing solutions that create products and jobs within America versus outsourcing them to Asia or Europe. For the overall success of technology and innovation in USA, it's imperative to bring technology learning in schools and at the academic level [2].

3 Strategic Partnerships between Academic Institutions and Organizations to foster PLM

One example of a significant relationship between academic institutions and Organizations in the fields of PLM is the example of Siemens and Oakland University located in Rochester, Michigan. Siemens has provided Oakland University approximately $ 12 million in software licenses and products that will directly benefit the students in becoming future PLM leaders. Siemens has always propagated that it will support Oakland University in producing smart graduates that are well versed in PLM design and implementation methodology. In order to encourage and support Oakland University's PLM center's initiative, Siemens has come forth and provided the access to software licenses particularly the Technomatix Robcad Software amounting to $ 11,846,850. This software will enable in design, validation as well as automation of the manufacturing processes [1].

This is a pure example of academic institutions partnering with organizations to foster PLM education in Research and Development. Professor Robert Van Til from the department of Industrial and Systems Engineering Department vouches for the contribution of Siemens PLM software in establishing Oakland University as a premier PLM R& D center. Oakland University believes that this software along with other software licenses and products supplied by Siemens helps greatly in producing educated PLM graduates and helps promote the quality of the academic program significantly. Tom Hoffman, marketing director at Siemens PLM software for manufacturing processes believes that Siemens has been and will continue to be a major contributor to the academic wealth and knowledge bank in the field of PLM at academic institutions like Oakland. Organizations like Siemens have contributed significantly in turning South East Michigan as a major hub of PLM Engineering Services. Siemens feels privileged to be a supporter of the "STEM" programs offered at Oakland University. In return the students from Oakland University contribute to the lean manufacturing processes through these robotic software licenses [11]. Siemens has a distinct interest in donating and giving back to the community through its "GO PLM" initiative. The director of "GO PLM" initiative, Hula King says that they want to continue to provide PLM licenses and software to Oakland University to encourage the R&D Center to grow, as these software tools are not available readily and only used by multinational companies across the globe. This is a huge advantage to the academic development. Professor Robert Van also states that Siemens support further extends to training and support in the usage of their software and products to their academic community [7].

Dassault Systems is the world leader in PLM tools and technology like ENOVIA, DELMIA and SIMULIA. Dassault Systems and Oakland University have also partnered in coming up with a short 4 weeks post graduate course in PLM at the Academic Center for PLM research and development. This course has been developed with the collaboration of the School of Engineering and Computer Sciences (SECS) that integrates both engineering and business expertise. The main goal of this partnership was to retain the workforce within Michigan and to further the PLM endeavor as well [7]. Displacement of worked due to involuntary job loss was a common phenomenon in 2009 due to recession and to avoid the displacement of engineering workforce this step was taken[5].

Roy Smolky of DELMIA Academic Relations Program from Dassault believes that this program is the right step in the direction of retaining workforce within Michigan State itself as well as spreading the importance of the PLM subject matter expertise to produce future PLM leaders. The students during the course will be learning in detail the Dassault System DELMIA suite of tools for digital manufacturing and production and after completion of the course they will be administered to take the DELMIA proficiency certification exam. Professor Robert Van feels that this course is different from conventional professional courses as it is more hands on in training provided by Dassault Systems in the tools which will definitely experience double digit growth in the next 5 years [4].

Acknowledgments. Purdue Center of R&D for PLM, Oakland Center for PLM, MTU Center for PLM, Whirlpool, Dassault Systems.

References

1. Stark, J.: Product Lifecycle Management, 21st Century Paradigm for Product Realization, 2nd edn. Springer
2. Xu, X.W., Liu, T.: A Web-Enabled PDM System in a Collaborative Design Environment. Robotics and Computer-Integrated Manufacturing 19, 315–328 (2003)
3. Understanding Product Lifecycle Management, Datamation Limited (2002)
4. Grieves, M.: Product Lifecycle Management. McGraw Hill (2006)
5. Ameri, F., Dutta, D.: Product Lifecycle Management: Closing the Knowledge Loops. Computer Aided Design & Applications 2(5), 577–590 (2005)
6. Schuh, G., Rozenfeld, H., Assmus, D., Zancul, E.: By Process oriented framework to support PLM implementation. Science Direct, Computers in Industry 59, 210–218 (2008) (available online August 21, 2007)
7. Gandhi, P.: Configuration Management and PLM. International Journal of Engineering Research and Technology 2(6) (April 2013)
8. The Center for PLM Education at Oakland University, Patrick Hillberg, Ph.D
9. `http://plmjim.blogspot.com/2012/03/plm-education-is-key-to-innovation-and.html?m=1`
10. `http://www.whichplm.com/news/do-you-support-plm-in-education.html`
11. Gandhi, P.: Product Lifecycle Management Importance and Approach. International Journal of Applied Information Systems 5(6), 28–30 (2013)

Knowledge Management: A Cross Sectorial Comparison of Wind Generation and Naval Engineering

Gary Ford[1,*], Joel Igba[1], Chris McMahon[1], Kazem Alemzadeh[1], Chris Rowley[2], and Keld Henningsen[3]

[1] University of Bristol, UK
[2] Babcock International, UK
[3] Vestas, Sweden
cegnf@bristol.ac.uk

Abstract. Offshore wind farms and naval vessels are examples of complex systems. A number of differences exist, e.g. the first is an exemplar of a developing technology, the second a technology having been developed and enhanced over centuries. Never the less a number of similarities exist, e.g. the development of responsive systems in physically demanding environments. Each of the technologies adheres to a prescribed product lifecycle, e.g. "ISO 15288, Systems and software engineering -- System life cycle processes", whereby each phase has distinct information and knowledge requirements. Furthermore, the adoption of a structured lifecycle ensures each technology considers the complete lifecycle and its integration within a potential system of systems. This cross sectoral study will review in-service knowledge management in two different fields of engineering, firstly Offshore Wind Generation which is a complex infrastructure system and secondly Royal Navy vessels which are complex marine engineering systems.

Keywords: Knowledge Management, Offshore Wind Farm, Naval.

1 Introduction

This paper details a comparison of Knowledge Management (KM) in two distinct engineering domains, i.e. offshore Wind Farms (WF) and marine engineering in the Royal Navy (RN). Each domain may be viewed as a system of systems, i.e. whose system elements are themselves systems; typically these entail large scale inter-disciplinary problems with multiple, heterogeneous, distributed systems [1]. The KM issues are particular to each technology, however, a number of similarities and differences are seen to exist. The approach taken is as follows. After outlining key characteristics KM the paper examines each domain and summarises and compares a number of issues during in-service.

---

* Corresponding author.

S. Fukuda et al. (Eds.): PLM 2014, IFIP AICT 442, pp. 129–138, 2014.

2 Knowledge Management

The Knowledge is a relatively simple word; indeed the Oxford English Dictionary defines knowledge as "awareness or familiarity gained by experience" [2]. Within an enterprise, knowledge may be seen as the cumulative data/information acquired and developed, both tacit, written and recorded. The function of preventing its loss/corruption and thus obviating the time, experience and effort required to recreate may be seen as Information Management (IM). KM encompasses IM but also extends the capability and value of information by providing a Knowledge Lifecycle [3].

Charles Dickens in "A Tale of Two Cities" declares, "It was the best of times, it was the worst of times" [4]; KM may be viewed similarly. The "best of times" is reflected in the capability of hardware and software technology, whereas, "the worst of times" is illustrated by the lack of structure, accessibility, volume, etc. and potential unknown value of a strategic resource.

According to Wong et al. [5], there are four key activities in KM – creation, mapping, retrieval and reuse of knowledge. Other authors such as Goh and McMahon [6] may describe these activities as a process of knowledge capture (collection), feedback and reuse. With respect to the challenges in KM, there is not a very clear boundary which distinguishes the challenges faced in each activity of KM. However, with the advancement in information technology, one can easily know what the challenges are and where they lie. For instance, McMahon and Ball [7] stated:

> "We are constrained now not by the ability to capture but by our ability to retain, organise and interpret the information (and to some extent by our ability not to be overwhelmed by the quantity of data that we can capture)".

This implies that with the amount of data we can capture now, much effort is also needed to ensure knowledge feedback and reuse, suggesting that data has no value if it is not used for a purpose [8]. Furthermore, information reuse only occurs when it has been assimilated and used in new applications, producing useful insights and knowledge [6], for example – using in-service knowledge for new product development.

3 Offshore Wind Power

The gradual shift in trend from onshore to offshore wind power, which has largely been due to social and political reasons [9], has resulted in the steady growth of the offshore wind sector. However, the offshore wind sector is still in its nascent state, hence lots of new ideas and concepts needed to cope with the hostile marine environment keep emerging [9]. Examples of such new concepts can be seen in the evolution of offshore wind turbine foundation structures [10] and the pre-assembly of parts of the turbine on floating vessels while ashore before shipping to the offshore environment to install.

Offshore WFs are complex engineering systems which harness the energy from wind to generate electrical power. The nature of this complexity is not only defined by the number and interactions of systems that comprise the WF, e.g. electromechanical, structural, control, etc. It is also defined by the considerable number of inputs from nearly every field of engineering and many of the natural and even social sciences [11]. The WF itself is made up of individual wind turbines which are all interconnected to the grid. Furthermore, the extended supply chain related to the transportation, installation and operations & maintenance of WFs [11], which are heavily influenced by the weather and sea conditions [9,12], also contribute to the complexities of offshore wind power life cycle management. Other complexities result from the broad mix of stakeholders involved throughout the life cycle of offshore wind. Of interest in this paper are the issues relating to knowledge and information management during the in-service stage, which arise as a result of these complexities.

4 Naval Engineering

Unlike offshore wind power the RN has existed since the reign of King Henry VIII (1491 ~ 1547) and his development of a "Navy Royal". The design and configuration of a naval vessel is intended to provide a "sustained" capability as described in the Concept of Operations, e.g. air defence, humanitarian relief.

Capability requirements may be conflicting and competing, e.g. stable and maneuverable platform, capable of operating from the arctic to the tropics, fuel efficient but able to sustain 30+ knots, deck space for weapons and sensors but clear for replenishment at sea, etc. KM is utilised at the earliest stages of the lifecycle, whereby previous experience and designs are included / excluded. Indeed a modern naval vessel will encompass more than 100 integrated hard systems [13], linked electrical, hydraulically, mechanically, etc. Furthermore, the complexity of modern naval vessels dramatically skews the comparative cost of systems and hull,

> In the United Kingdom, systems represent the biggest percentage of the price of a warship – 70% compared to 30% for the hull. This is in stark contrast to commercial vessels, where almost the reverse is true, i.e. 20% systems, 80% hull [14].

Preventive maintenance is undertaken to sustain the capability of the vessel: the RN utilise Reliability Centred Maintenance (RCM). The methodology was selected following a review of failures in a Type 23 Frigate and comparing them with the Age-Reliability Patterns developed by Nowlan and Heap [15]. The results indicated within the naval domain only 7% of failures may be attributed to "wear" (Pattern A to C) whilst 93% were "random" (Pattern D to F) (Figure 1). It should be noted KM is incorporated at the early stages of formulating the maintenance package to ensure "lessons learnt" are incorporated.

Similar to offshore wind power, a broad mix of stakeholders are involved throughout the life cycle of a naval vessel, e.g. RN, Ministry of Defence (MOD), Babcock, BAe. Issues related to KM during the in-service stage will be reviewed.

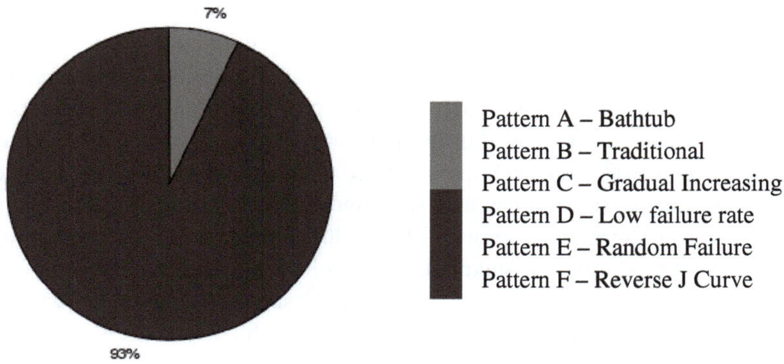

Fig. 1. Distribution of failures – Type 23 Frigate [16]

5 Current State-Of-The-Art in Knowledge Management and Challenges

Ford et al. [17] previously identified that the major challenges the wind industry face in life cycle KM are observed during the in-service stage. However, to build upon this and expand further, a brief review of the state-of-the-art of in-service KM in the offshore wind sector would be done. This would provide some context to the issues and challenges during in-service KM specific to offshore WFs.

Previous authors would agree that majority of the challenges experienced during the in-service stage of offshore wind turbines arise as a result of the harshness and unpredictability of the offshore environment. Furthermore, typical offshore WFs are sited at remote locations at distances from the shore ranging from about 5km to more than 50km [10]. Hence, be it transportation and logistics, or operations and maintenance, weather effects are a major source of uncertainty whilst in-service. This has prompted the need for extensive forecasting, planning and scheduling of tasks and activities, in a flexible manner so as to avoid delays caused by weather and sea conditions. Specific to KM, due to the remoteness of offshore WF's, the industry's state-of-the-art are remote monitoring and control through condition monitoring systems (CMS) and supervisory control and data acquisition (SCADA) systems. SCADA systems were primarily installed in wind turbines to measure operational and environmental conditions, such as wind speed, ambient temperature and temperature/pressure sub-systems in the turbine [18]. On the other hand, CMS are used to monitor parameters such as vibrations, acoustic emissions, and oil particle counts, to name a few. These two remote monitoring techniques produce large quantities of data collected either as 10 minute averages or even every 10 seconds. Apart from the remote monitoring data acquisition systems, other manual or human assisted techniques exist for documenting in-service records. These include: service or work orders, inspection reports and maintenance, repair and overhaul reports. Unlike the automated remote CMS and SCADA techniques, knowledge captured through these means are only obtained on an interval basis, depending on how frequent such service or maintenance actions are required.

1.) KM Challenges in Remote Monitoring Techniques:
One of the main issues with remote monitoring is linked to the size of data generated. Having huge data collected from a large number of turbines poses challenges in analysing and interpreting the data. Fast growing databases from remote monitoring of offshore WF's require advanced signal processing techniques and data mining to extract the most useful information [19]. However, such data are not without noise and can result in generating poor models [20]. It is also difficult to convincingly interpret and convey the results of analysis obtained from remote monitoring to wind farm managers and specialists [20].

Finally, there are concerns about the reliability and accuracy of the sensors that acquire the data [18], for instance, if the sensors are not installed properly and in the right location, the data collected might be erroneous. Hence a lot of effort is needed in the design and development stage in specifying remote monitoring technologies and their installation and operation.

2.) KM Challenges in Manual Techniques:
The primary challenge with capturing manual data is the issue with physical access to the WFs. Harsh weather conditions make it almost impossible to even attempt to capture maintenance records from inspections and other maintenance tasks in the turbine. For example, WFs which are just a few kilometers offshore have been previously known to have experienced months with over 20 unworkable days.

When service personnel eventual have access to the turbines there is then the inability to complete maintenance records within the turbine due to safety concerns and space limitations [17]. Hence, technicians who keep record of maintenance activities and inspections may have to result to other means like taking photographs and then completing the reports after leaving the turbine. The time lag between when the inspection is done to when reports are produced depends on the technician and is difficult to control. There is also the possibility of data being diluted and of poor quality between the time the maintenance task is done and when the report is made, since the technician may forget a few details even in the presence of pictures.

Furthermore, since the periods of access to the turbine is largely dependent on the weather and hence not predetermined, there is a risk of inconsistency in the periods between data capture. Hence the accuracy of captured maintenance data heavily depends on the selection of a suitable observation window [9]. For example, maintenance visits should be planned and periodic, giving consistency to findings, i.e. monthly, quarterly, yearly or a period defined by the age or condition of the turbine. However, this is very difficult to achieve for offshore WFs, hence giving difficulty in collating records to make suitable judgments about the service history of the turbines. As maintenance reports are largely a mix of hand written or typed spread sheets, there is always the risk of typographical and spelling errors [9].

A naval vessel will encounter similar issues with respect to the harshness and unpredictability of the marine environment; however, unlike a static WF a vessel whilst in transit may experience large variations in temperature, humidity and movement, i.e. heave, sway and surge in addition to shock and vibration. Unlike a WF, RN vessels have onboard operators and maintainers, however, base support, spares and tools may be thousands of km away [21] or not available due to operational constraints. For example, a Vanguard class submarine will remain submerged for 3 months with no contact or support but none-the-less required to provide 100% availability and capability throughout each patrol.

The RCM process formulates a maintenance regime which enables a maintainer to perform maintenance and ascertain the material state. Data created and utilised by maintainers includes, engineering logs, vibration data, oil samples, running hours, etc. The onboard operational maintenance data is typically objective and structured, e.g. diesel engine hours run. However, if a vessel encounters a defect that impacts the operational capability, assessment by naval command will often necessitate a subjective assessment of potentially unstructured and aggregated data.

6 Summary

It seems that offshore WF's largely rely on remote monitoring for obtaining information about the operational and performance data. Remote access provides the possibility of controlling wind turbines in multiple WFs from a central remote location. Another advantage not immediately apparent is the ability to optimise power production from the wind farm by matching operating and environmental conditions with wind turbine controls. One example of this, is the pitch control [10,18,22] of each individual blades to adapting blade angle to wind conditions so as to provide the optimum power output and noise levels. Even though state-of-the-art remote monitoring techniques are capable of providing useful measures of the condition of the major systems that constitute the WF, WF operators and technical specialists still rely on the information that are collected manually through human effort. The visual inspections, images and measurements taken manually, provide more explicit details about the nature of wear and tear in the turbines.

Given that WF operators need to rely on both sources of knowledge for life cycle management, it will also be useful to identify some common issues affecting both techniques. Some of the general issues with KM in offshore wind include:

- Inconsistency in data file formats: A typical modern WF would have at least a combination of 10-Minute average SCADA data, fault/alarm logs, service orders and O&M contractor reports [23]. Service and O&M reports, unlike SCADA, are a mixture of spreadsheets and hand written reports. As a consequence, a lot of effort is needed in filtering and preprocessing these disparate sources in order to aggregate them for suitable analysis. This poses a challenge of data reuse when seeking to combine data from multiple sources in order to make inferential judgments from it. It also increases the lead time to decision making as more time and effort is consumed in harmonising the information contained in different data sources. Experience by previous research have shown that a substantial effort is needed to connect these different sources [23].

- Organisational (institutional) barriers exist with respect to ownership of failure data of the wind turbine components. For example during the warranty period operators have general information of the number of failures and the general types, but may not have information of their root causes [24].
- Missing or incomplete information is very likely to occur in maintenance records, due to the weather and location effects interrupting scheduled service or inspections.

In-Service KM in the naval domain may be considered to exist in two distinct spheres, i.e. onboard and onshore. The onboard data and knowledge may be considered "tactical", i.e. single vessel, local, immediate, single stakeholder, whereas onshore has a "strategic" focus, i.e. aggregation of multiple vessels / systems, remote, latent, long term planning, multiple stakeholders. The "Common knowledge" relates to the interface and interaction of onboard and onshore knowledge

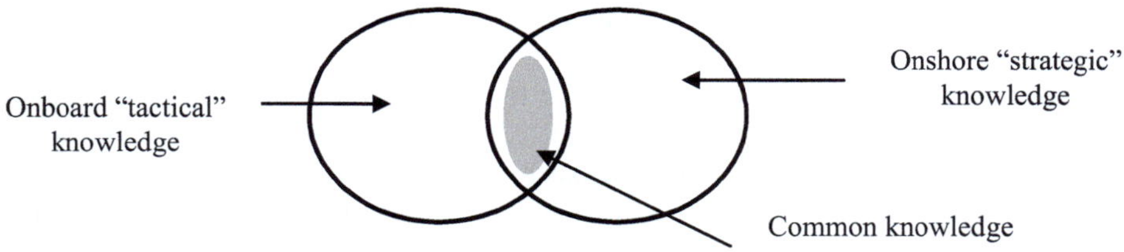

Fig. 2. Onboard/onshore knowledge spheres

The onboard management, maintenance information flow and KM is extremely hierarchical, e.g. junior operator/maintainer → senior maintainer → junior officer → Marine Engineering Officer (MEO). The MEO and staff have an enduring responsibility for "the good material order and maximum availability of all equipment and systems within its responsibility, in order to maintain the seagoing and fighting capability of the ship" [25]. Objective information originates from discrete systems and is collected by junior operators/maintainers which is collated, processed, aggregated and analysed by senior staff often requiring a subjective assessment of numerous information sources and influences both internal and external. The combination of structured / unstructured and objective / subjective information may be seen to exist as a matrix (Table 1), i.e.

Table 1. Information matrix

	Objective	**Subjective**
Unstructured	*Sector 1*	*Sector 2* Complex / complicated
Structured	*Sector 3* Simple, e.g. hours run	*Sector 4*

As information passes up the management hierarchy, e.g. typically originating in Sector 3, a broader perspective and higher level of KM function may be seen to exist as it passes to Sector 2. Whereupon the MEO may be expected to fuse numerous information sources / controls / enablers, deliberate and decide upon a course of action. Onboard, a large number of knowledge sources exist, e.g. Standard Operating Procedures (SOP), Books of Reference (BR), work books, tacit knowledge. Reflecting upon the principles of KM detailed by Wong *et al* [5], the onboard KM process is established, controlled and structured.

The onshore KM and associated stakeholder activity is dependant upon the function / role of the vessel, e.g. Upkeep (deep maintenance), Tasking (operational deployment). The KM activity of assessing the material state of a Tasking vessel and hence its operational capability is primarily the monitoring of Operational Defects, i.e. defects that may degrade the capability of the vessel – as contained within the "Common knowledge". The KM assessment is highly subjective and is frequently dependant upon the tacit knowledge of RN personnel within the context of the mission. The onshore KM of a Tasking vessel may be seen to exist extensively in Sector 2.

Prior to Upkeep, stakeholders responsible for deep maintenance will be dependant upon information that is highly subjective, e.g. diesel generator #1 is a bit noisy. However, a key KM function during Upkeep is the generation of detailed objective and structured information (Sector 3), e.g. survey reports, defects. The formulation of such information facilitates logical decision making, e.g. if valve leaking then replace. It also enables searching and comparison with previous records to enable reuse of existing knowledge.

Onshore, an even greater knowledge bases exists, e.g. design documentation, test spec's, original equipment manufacturer, SOP's, BR's, work books, tacit knowledge. Once more, reflecting upon the principles of KM detailed by Wong *et al* [5], the onshore KM process is also established, controlled and structured.

7 Conclusion

The KM process within the naval engineering domain is "mature", having been developed and refined over considerable time, whereas wind generation has yet to refine its procedures. The issues identified by wind generation, i.e. (i) inconsistency in data file formats and (ii) missing or incomplete information, also exist in the naval domain. However, they are not as prevalent as there is a single customer, i.e. MOD, instead of multiple. Furthermore, the issue of "organisational (institutional) barriers" is markedly less given the support of surface ships is undertaken by a Surface Ship Support Alliance. Consequently, all members of the alliance work together in support of the RN rather than in competition. Finally, the maturity of the naval engineering process and artefact is a key factor in minimising the issues compared with wind generation.

Acknowledgments. The work reported was supported by the Bristol/Bath Industrial Doctorate Centre in Systems, funded by EPSRC grant EP/G037353/1.

References

1. INCOSE, Systems Engineering Handbook. A Guide for System Life Cycle Processes and Activities. Ver. 3.2 INCOSE, San Diego, CA (January 2010)
2. OED. The Concise Oxford Dictionary of Current English. Clarendon Press. Oxford (1990)
3. Ammar-Khodja, S., Bernard, A.: An Overview on Knowledge Management. Springer eBooks (2008)
4. Dickens, C.: A Tale of Two Cities, Reprint edition. William Pub., Collins (1859) (April 1, 2010)
5. Wong, S., Crowder, R., Wills, G., Shadbolt, N.: Informing preliminary design by incorporating service knowledge, 1–12 (August 2007), http://eprints.ecs.soton.ac.uk/14234 (retrieved)
6. Goh, Y., McMahon, C.: Improving reuse of in-service information capture and feedback. Journal of Manufacturing Technology (2009), doi:10.1108/17410380910961028
7. McMahon, C., Ball, A.: Information Systems Challenges for through-life Engineering. Procedia CIRP 11, 1–7 (2013), doi:10.1016/j.procir,07.071
8. Markeset, T., Kumar, U.: Integration of RAMS and risk analysis in product design and development work processes A case study (2005), doi:10.1108/13552510310503240
9. Hameed, Z., Vatn, J., Heggset, J.: Challenges in the reliability and maintainability data collection for offshore wind turbines. Renewable Energy 36(8), 2154–2165 (2011), doi:10.1016/j.renene, 01.008
10. Berkhout.V., Faulstich, S., Görg, P., Kühn, P., Linke, K., Lyding, P., Stark, E.: Wind Energy Report Germany, Kassel (2012)
11. Dykes, K., Meadows, R., Felker, F., Graf, P.: Applications of systems engineering to the research, design, and development of wind energy systems (2011), http://www.nrel.gov/docs/fy12osti/52616.pdf (retrieved)
12. Igba, J., Alemzadeh, K., Anyanwu-Ebo, I., Gibbons, P., Friis, J.: A Systems Approach Towards Reliability-Centred Maintenance (RCM) of Wind Turbines. Procedia Computer Science, 00, (2013), http://www.sciencedirect.com/science/article/pii/S1877050913000860 (retrieved)
13. SIA, The Collins Class (2013), http://www.submarineinstitute.com/submarines-in-australia/The-Collins-Class.html (accessed: January 20, 2013)
14. Choi, T.: The Costs of 21st Century Shipbuilding: Lessons for Canada from the Littoral Combat Ship Program. Canadian Naval Review 8(4) (Winter 2013)
15. Nowlan, F.S., Heap, H.F.: Reliability Centered Maintenance, p. 46 (1978)
16. MTI. Maritime Technical Instructions (Maritime domain supplement to Defence Standard 00-45), Version 2.1 (June 2010)
17. Ford, G., Bartley, T., Igba, J., Turner, A., McMahon, C.: Product Life Cycle Data Management: A Cross-Sectoral Review. In: Bernard, A., Rivest, L., Dutta, D. (eds.) PLM 2013. IFIP AICT, vol. 409, pp. 58–67. Springer, Heidelberg (2013), http://link.springer.com/chapter/10.1007/978-3-642-41501-2_7
18. Yang, W., Tavner, P., Crabtree, C., Feng, Y., Qiu, Y.: Wind turbine condition monitoring: technical and commercial challenges. Wind Energy (2012), doi:10.1002/we

19. Nie, M., Wang, L.: Review of Condition Monitoring and Fault Diagnosis Technologies for Wind Turbine Gearbox. Procedia CIRP, 11(Cm), 287–290 (2013), doi:10.1016/j.procir, 07.018
20. Feng, Y., Qiu, Y., Crabtree, C., Long, H., Tavner, P.: Use of SCADA and CMS signals for failure detection and diagnosis of a wind turbine gearbox. EWEA (2011), `http://proceedings.ewea.org/annual2011/allfiles2/572_EWEA2011presentation.pdf` (retrieved)
21. Roulston-Eldridge, J.: HMS Illustrious Port Outer Gas Generator Exchange The Last Mount of Olympus at Sea? The Naval Engineer (Spring 2014)
22. Feng, Y., Qiu, Y., Crabtree, C., Long, H., Tavner, P.: Monitoring wind turbine gearboxes. Wind Energy (2012), doi:10.1002/we
23. Wilkinson, A.M., Hendriks, B., Spinato, F., Gomez, E., Bulacio, H., Tavner, P., Long, H.: Methodology and Results of the Reliawind Reliability Field Study. In: European Wind Energy Conference (EWEC 2010) (2010)
24. Walford, C.: Wind turbine reliability: understanding and minimizing wind turbine operation and maintenance costs. Sandia National Laboratories (2006), `http://www.preservethegoldencrescent.com/pdf/windturbinereliability.pdf` (retrieved)
25. BR 2013. BR – Marine Engineering Department Standing Orders (August 2013)

Information Resources for the Identification of Complex Asset Condition: A Naval Engineering Case Study

Gary Ford[1,*], Chris McMahon[1], and Chris Rowley[2]

[1] University of Bristol, UK
[2] Babcock International, UK
cegnf@bristol.ac.uk

Abstract. This paper describes the research in identifying the key data elements that are indicative of the material state of a naval vessel. Naval vessels are long lived complex artefacts, containing in excess of 100 integrated "hard" systems. The systems may be configured to provide a variety of prescribed capabilities and associated command objective. However, the "hard" systems will not fully integrate or function in a cohesive manner without the interaction of "soft" socio-technical systems (e.g. maintenance teams, operators); the two are interdependent and reliant. The In-Service phase will contribute 70% of the artefact's through-life costs and may comprise an operating period of more than 25 years. The data generated and utilised within each mode will reflect the operational and technical requirements of the numerous stakeholders and the functional state of the vessel.

Keywords: Lifecycle, Maintenance, Naval, Data.

1 Introduction

There is extensive interest today in how we may use information technologies to improve our capability to judge the condition of complex engineered assets such as buildings, energy, transportation and infrastructure systems [1,2]. In particular there is interest in exploiting the information collected during the design, manufacture, maintenance and operation of such systems. This paper is concerned with an example of such a complex engineered asset – naval ships – and with exploiting the information collected during their operation and maintenance for identification of their state.

Royal Navy (RN) surface ships and submarines are a compilation of complex systems, i.e. "integrated set of elements, subsystems, or assemblies that accomplish a defined objective" [3]. A warship / submarine will contain in excess of 100 integrated "hard" systems which are linked structurally, mechanically, electrically, hydraulically, pneumatically and electronically [4]. Warfare demands a constant change in offensive and defensive capability, and, in addition to its offensive and defensive capability a warship must also be capable of providing, "humanitarian assistance and disaster relief operations to relieve human suffering" [5] - e.g. the assistance of HMS Daring and HMS Illustrious in the Philippines following Typhoon Haiyan [6,7].

The United Kingdom's Ministry of Defence (MoD) utilise a systems lifecycle model known as CADMID. The 6 CADMID stages are Concept, Assessment,

---

* Corresponding author.

S. Fukuda et al. (Eds.): PLM 2014, IFIP AICT 442, pp. 139–148, 2014.

Demonstration, Manufacture, In-Service and Disposal [8]. A high degree of commonality exists between the stages specified in ISO 15288 (Systems and Software Engineering – System Life Cycle Processes) and CADMID (table 1).) During its life a vessel should experience a linear progression through each stage of the lifecycle.

Table 1. ISO 15288 / MoD CADMID Lifecycle

ISO-15288						
Concept		Development	Production	Utilisation	Support	Retirement
C		D	P	U	S	R
C	A	D	M	I		D
Concept	Assessment	Demonstration	Manufacture	In-Service		Disposal
MoD - CADMID						

In 2009 a Surface Ship Support Alliance (SSSA) was formed between the MoD, Babcock and BAE Systems, the intention being to "to reduce costs and increase availability" for surface ships. The SSSA introduced a "risk and reward" incentive, linking expenditure and availability, savings to be shared between all members of the alliance. The MoD remains the platform duty holder, with responsibility for the vessel. The formation of a Class Output Management (COM) team as part of the SSSA is intended to provide an industry, rather than a MoD led organisation with respect to planning and execution of maintenance.

Within the CADMID In-Service stage, a naval vessel will cycle through 3 discrete phases (Figure 1), i.e. Tasking, Upkeep and Regeneration.

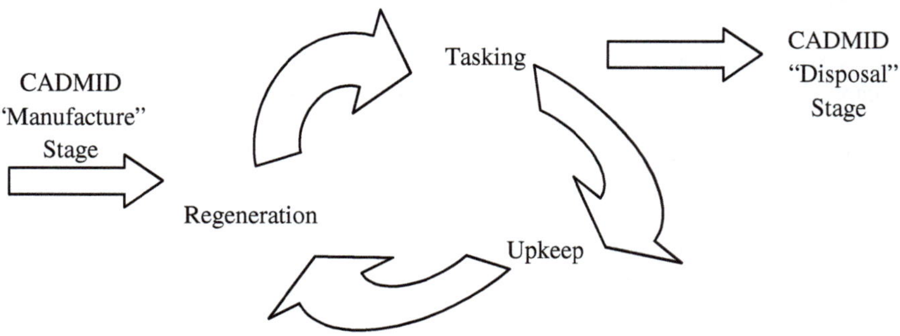

Fig. 1. Cyclical phase of naval vessels

Tasking is the phase during which a vessel is under Navy Command Authority and thus available for or undertaking operational tasks. The upkeep phase is when a vessel is subject to major maintenance work, typically including docking periods, Regeneration involves the timely activation, in full or in part, of existing force structures and infrastructure, including the restoration of manning, equipment and stocks to designated levels. The data generated and utilised within each mode will reflect the operational and technical requirements of the numerous stakeholders and the functional state of the vessel, as the examples in Table 2 illustrate. A naval vessel will complete numerous Tasking, Upkeep and Regeneration cycles, e.g. HMS Edinburgh was "In-Service" for 27 years [9].

Table 2. Stakeholder and objective as a consequence of cyclical phase

Phase	Stakeholder	Objective	Information Interaction
Upkeep	Maintenance organisation	Filter hydraulic system to remove particulates	Provide test results
	Ship staff	Observe filtration process	Validate results
Tasking	Maintenance organisation	Liaise with OEM as technical authority	Provide technical advice as requested
	Ship staff	Ensure availability of hydraulic system	Request technical support

In addition to the information available to ascertain the material state of a system varying with the cyclical phase, stakeholder and objective, the validity and life of information will also fluctuate, e.g.

- Engineering logs ~ primarily generated and exploited during Tasking and Regeneration phase
- Pre-Upkeep Maintenance Assessment (PUMA) reports ~ generated during Tasking phase but exploited for Upkeep
- Unit Maintenance Management System (UMMS) ~ generated and exploited throughout all phases.

This paper details an investigation into the key data sources that may be used to determine the material state during each operational phase. The data sources were identified from a series of recorded semi-structured interviews conducted at the interviewees' offices. All interviewees (In-Service stakeholders) were highly experienced MoD, RN, Babcock and system supplier personnel, divided in the key phases as follows:

- Tasking: Fleet Operations Maintenance Officer (FOMO), Ship staff
- Upkeep: COM team, Babcock Project Managers
- Regeneration: Force Generating Authority, Flag Officer Sea Training, Maritime Capability Trials and Assessment
- Support: Defence Equipment and Support (DE&S) Spares, Finance, Chilled Water System Supplier

The "Support" organisations are a component of "In-Service" lifecycle, consequently they were interviewed to assess their "enabling" and "control" influence during the cyclical phase of an RN vessel.

The objective of the interviews was to ascertain the Inputs, Controls, Mechanisms and Outputs within each functional cyclical phase (process), with a view to then exploring (in later research) how engineering experts make a judgement about asset state based on the information sources. In the remaining sections of this paper the key data sources generated at each phase will be explored and then a brief evaluation of their characteristics and their potential as a source of asset condition will be presented.

2 Key Data within Each Cyclical Phase

This section provides an overview of the processes and key data in each cyclical phase.

Tasking: Initiation of the Tasking phase and hence completion of any previous Regeneration phase is receipt of the "Ready for Ops" signal (see below). An operational vessel, although under the command of Commander Maritime Operations (COMOPS) must also operate as an autonomous safe seaworthy vessel under the direction of the captain. The Marine Engineering Officer (MEO) as department head is accountable for, "the good material order and maximum availability of all equipment and systems within its responsibility, in order to maintain the seagoing and fighting capability of the ship" [10].

Within the Tasking phase, two distinct information pathways detailing and assessing the material state may be seen to exist, i.e.

Internal data that is generated and utilised solely within the vessel. The internal reporting and assessment of the material state will typically comprise multiple "stove pipe" sources, e.g. hand written engineering logs, vibration records, oil sampling, UMMS. The information will be used by the MEO to facilitate the "maximum availability of all equipment and systems", as well as enabling the vessel to fight the *internal* battle, i.e. the preparation, training, management and rectification of action damage and systems failure, in effect enabling the vessel to continue to execute the *external* battle, e.g. engage air / surface / sub-surface combatants.

The internal information sources will typically be objective, e.g. temperature, pressure, vibration, failure, etc. trend analysis being limited to the vessel. Data is invariably current, given the source is contained within the vessel, however, the urgency of assessing the data / information or subsequent action will be dependent upon the "command aim", i.e. the mission objective. Consequently there may be a concentration of focus upon a singular system at the expense of more general analysis or maintenance. System failures that degrade the operational capability of a vessel are reported to naval command as Operational Defects (OpDef's). However, operational constraints may prohibit the vessel from seeking technical support or guidance from FOMO, e.g. submarines on submerged patrol, consequently the vessel is highly dependant upon the accuracy and currency of onboard documentation, configuration management and the knowledge / experience / training of maintainers. Furthermore, a solitary vessel may be unaware of deficiencies / performance issues affecting a system common to a class. Figure 2 illustrates the commonality of maritime systems in RN vessels

External data generated, analysed and (potentially) aggregated within the vessel before transmission to FOMO for interpretation, execution and provision of assistance. Typically, FOMO will assess OpDef signals and capability reports received from the vessel to assess the material state and subsequent impact upon capability / availability. The data available to FOMO is primarily a latent abstraction of the primary data source potentially containing a mix of objective and subjective data. The FOMO organisation will apply their extensive tacit knowledge to formulate a predominantly subjective assessment of the data and will advise command regarding the material state of vessel and any potential risk to capability in the context of the command aim.

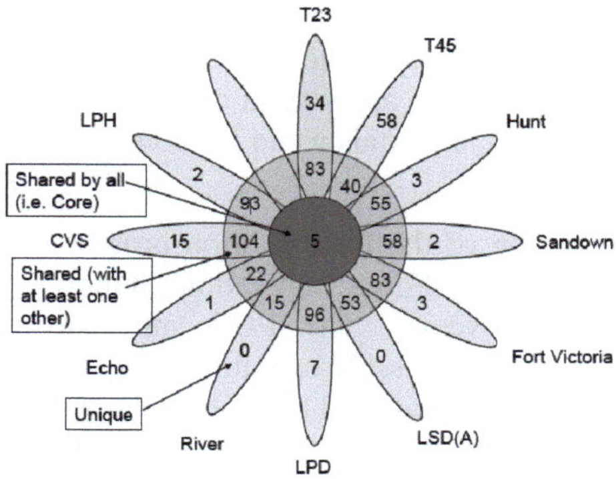

Fig. 2. RN Common Maritime Systems [11]

In addition to advising command, a key function of FOMO is to liaise with DE&S "desk officers" for the provision of support and stores. Where stores / equipment are not available from store, FOMO may initiate a 'stores robbery', i.e. the removal of items from other vessels, initially from those within DE&S control, e.g. HMS Duncan – "Early in build, one of our gas turbines was removed for [HMS] Daring after hers was damaged" [12]. If equipment / systems are not available from non-operational vessels, equipment will be taken from operational vessels. The potential impact upon condition assessment is that "new" equipment may have actually encountered considerable usage / load / shock / vibration and a maintenance regime that is possibly unknown to the final user.

Upkeep: The planning and preparation for the Upkeep of a naval vessel starts during the Tasking phase. Initial milestones / stages associated with the instigation and formulation of the work package are detailed in BR8593 [13].

The work package is a composite of numerous maintenance activities contained within UMMS, survey reports including statutory inspections "Lloyds Register class inspections", Work Requisition Forms, OpDefs, etc. The work package will often reflect the impact of operating the vessel in an environment at the limit of its design specification, e.g. high ambient temperatures as experienced in tropical regions. In addition to maintenance activities the work package will include Alterations & Additions, i.e. enhancements to a vessel's capability, life extensions, statutory modifications.

Pre-Upkeep surveys are often undertaken by the maintenance contractor, e.g. Babcock, supported by the Original Equipment Manufacturer (OEM), to provide a detailed material assessment of systems and equipment. The surveys are perceived as a datum with respect to defining the scope of the work package and potential variations. In addition to surveys conducted by the maintenance contractor BR1313 [14] specifies a requirement to undertake various pre-Upkeep inspections, e.g. resulting in PUMA reports.

A considerable number of surveys (structural and system) are undertaken early in the Upkeep phase, these are reviewed in detail at a Hull & Structural Assessment meeting where the initial work package is reviewed and potentially enhanced by means of Variation Orders.

The Upkeep phase will generate a considerable volume of documents including test specifications, Lloyds surveys, etc. however, the Material State Portfolio (MSP) created by the COM is an objective assessment of the vessel's state upon completion. The document details the work undertaken and the condition of the vessel and is a key data source.

Regeneration: The initiation of the Regeneration process is the receipt of a Force Generation Order (FGO) by the Force Generation Authority (FGA), specifying the required capability of the vessel. The FGO may be perceived as a "User Requirement" with respect to a vessels operational capability. Upon receipt of the FGO a meeting is held with ship staff and the FGA, whereupon deficiencies and areas of concern are identified given the planned objective and the potential impact upon hard and soft systems. Typically the ship will utilise the Manpower, Equipment, Training and Sustainability (METS) construct for reporting

The FGA will formulate the specific regeneration requirements of a vessel including any specialist Military Task Equipment (MTE). MTE, are equipments required for directed military tasks but which do not exist in sufficient numbers to fit to all platforms at all times, consequently, potentially resulting in a lack of familiarity regarding maintenance.

The FGA will subsequently liaise with Flag Officer Sea Training (FOST) to formulate the specific program of regeneration and systems necessitating particular assessment. It is the responsibility of FOST to generate the vessel to the capability specified by the FGA who, "own the regeneration process". The testing and validation of systems will reflect the planned deployment, including physical environment and potential threats, e.g. deployment East of Suez: prioritisation of chilled water cooling systems, davits for boarding.

It should be noted, a vessel may be generated with a specific capability but may subsequently be re-tasked potentially without the requisite capability: Naval Command will subsequently "manage" the associated risk.

In addition to the operational assessment the RN Maritime Capability Trials and Assessment (MCTA) organisation assess mechanical and weapons systems by means of Harbour Acceptance Trials, Sea Acceptance Trials, Ship Performance Assessment's (SPA) and Operational Capability Confidence Check's (OCCC). Detailed objective reports are provided by MCTA to the vessel detailing where standards have been achieved, partially achieved or not achieved.

Completion of Regeneration is marked by a "Final Signal" and a "Ready for Ops" signal that will detail within the METS pillars what is outstanding to generate as specified in the FGO and any associated risks to operational capability when in theatre, e.g. chilled water system. This will raise awareness within FOMO such that any subsequent OpDefs pertaining to highlighted equipment / systems may impact capability.

3 Review

Information: The information sources are diverse, ranging from very detailed objective records of temperature and pressure etc. to latent subjective assessments derived from numerous sources. Stakeholders will attribute characteristics / properties both to their own requirements and the individual data sources. Information characteristics may include:

- Accessibility – location, security, ownership, cost, media
- Process and uncertainty characteristics – fuzziness, randomness, incompleteness [15]
- Granularity – abstraction, aggregation
- Media – paper, digital, standard, propriety
- Validity – range, precision, accuracy
- Volume – growth rate, initial

A review of the information sources identifies a number of key sources that are exploited to ascertain the material state in all phases, i.e.

- OpDef's – defects that impact / reduce the operational capability, updated and interrogated constantly, i.e. identify maintenance / upgrades, performance, operational constraints
- UMMS – the system not only schedules preventive maintenance and will identify outstanding maintenance but is also a repository of persistent defects
- Stores – analysis of material usage provides information regarding persistent defects, i.e. Comprehensive Royal Naval Inventory Systems Project

The information sources identified as key during Tasking are the engineering and condition based maintenance logs. The sources are generated and analysed locally (onboard) and offer a high level of data granularity but provide poor accessibility due to the format, i.e. paper based. The Fuel and Lubrication Consumption (FLUBCON) report provides a record of engine and lubrication usage, analysis will indicate increased usage which may be indicative of increased wear.

During Upkeep the information is primarily objective and detailed, the numerous system and structure survey reports provide considerable detail when aggregated, however, this requires manual processing. Similarly the MSP is a reliable document, however, its creation is a manual process drawing together numerous digital and non-digital data sources, furthermore, it only provides a perspective for a given point in time.

The assessments undertaken by MCTA during Regeneration, i.e. SPA and OCCC are detailed assessments of the material state, which combined with the "Ready for Ops" signal provides a reflective assessment of issues.

Each information source will provide a perspective of the material state to each of the stakeholders, e.g. UMMS provide ship staff information regarding scheduled maintenance as well as a repository for defects. The MEO will be particularly interested in maintenance that is outstanding. The COM may interrogate UMMS to review persistent defects and potential assistance from the OEM.

Artefact Information: The distinctive "concept of operations" and design of naval vessels necessitates and creates a range of data that is not comparable with similar size commercial vessels. Although a number of systems may be similar to commercial vessels, the manner of operation within a naval vessel is not, e.g. "crash stop" a chilled water system to simulate action damage. A number of systems are unique thus minimising the opportunity for comparison. Comparing RN vessels with other naval forces highlights a high degree of similarity with respect to policies, procedures and data collected, e.g. engineering logs, vibration monitoring. The variation being the terminology, e.g. the US Navy refer to an operational defect (OpDef) as a CASREP - Casualty Report.

4 A Proposed Use Of Maintenance Data – "The Main Thing is, We Need to Deliver Capability" [16]

During Upkeep, substantial preventive and corrective maintenance is undertaken in addition to enhancing a vessels capability, e.g. HMS Ocean's Upkeep (2012-2014) ~ £65 million, 15 months planned duration that will including over 60 upgrades [17, 18].

The Upkeep work package will encompass numerous sources; however, key to developing the work package is an assessment of the material state prior to "Upkeep", i.e. Tasking. Information sources containing data indicative of the material state during Tasking are,

- OpDef's: Contains defects that degrade the operational capability of the vessel, the data is transmitted to a central repository
- SPA: Undertaken by an external authority during Tasking, identifying where standards have not been achieved
- UMMS: Contains details of preventive and corrective maintenance, however, the utilisation of the system is not consistent, furthermore, data is recorded onboard with periodic uploads to a central repository

RN vessels support UK maritime doctrine, i.e. the "ability to project power at sea and from the sea to influence the behaviour of people or the course of events" [5]. Consequently, a defect that degrades "capability" may potentially endanger and negate the *raison d'etre* of the vessel. The OpDef system records all defects that degrade capability and therefore must be perceived as a key information source and indicator of a vessels "capability" material state. The value of the SPA is the assessment is undertaken by an external authority and will identify ME and WE deficiencies necessitating rectification. In this instance UMMS is discounted as a consequence of the latency of the data and the variations in usage and management.

The OpDef system contains structured objective and subjective data which includes information detailing the "loss of operational capability", associated defect(s), the Effect category and associated Repair Indicator, the Operational Repair Plan and the rationale that prevented the defect being cleared [19].

Analysis of operational defects and SPA's across multiple platforms by Upkeep planners will not only reflect the value perceived by FOMO & DE&S but also provide a real time indication of single and re-occurring system defects / deficiencies and their resolution (Figure 3). The information will not only highlight systems of concern and hence the risk of future failure, forewarn of potential future maintenance activities but also identify systems necessitating detailed pre-Upkeep survey. Further analysis of OpDef's, SPA's and Hull & System surveys may highlight deficiencies in the provision of onboard spares and maintenance, thus providing a feedback loop with respect to through-life maintenance.

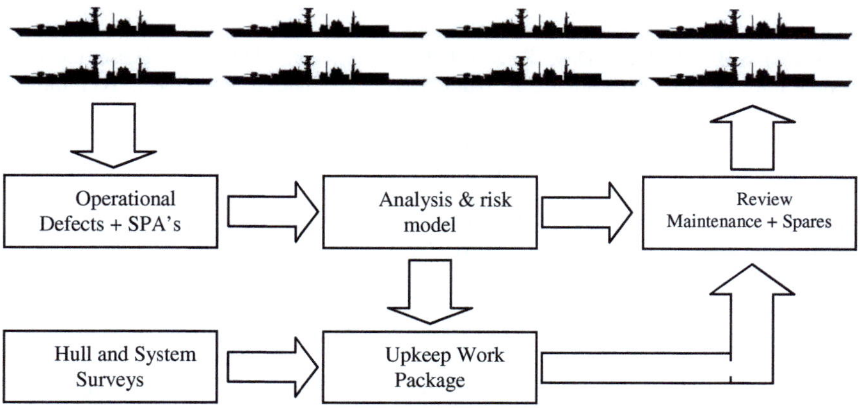

Fig. 3. Proposed Use of Maintenance Data

Currently SPA's and OpDef's are analysed in isolation by RN and DE&S staff but not systematically by Upkeep planners, the proposed change would utilise and combine existing data in a manner not currently undertaken. Furthermore, a risk model of potential defects would enable Upkeep planners to plan the availability of resources and purchase spares.

5 Conclusion

A range of issues have been identified as a consequence of this research, i.e.

- The lack of integration of the multifarious data sources is the initial conclusion; however, this reflects the development of dicrete functionality, e.g. UMMS, SPA, OpDefs
- The usage and interpretation of information for purposes it was not intended, e.g. FLUBCON records hours run and lubrication usage, the extrapolation of usage, wear and maintenance was potentially not considered as the report does not record environmental issues that may influence any conclusions.
- The remote operation and potential isolation of RN vessels is an issue not normally encountered in civilian / commercial industry. A Trident submarine with a complement of 135 will undertake a 3 month patrol without contact or re-supply whereas the International Space Station is in constant contact and receives supplies typically each month [20].

The proposed use of maintenance data detailed above is an initial step in improving vessel capability and reducing Upkeep costs by the early assessment of material state.

Further consideration with respect to the development of a "black box" capable of logging and retaining condition data will provide the potential for system prognostics.

Acknowledgments. The work reported was supported by the Bristol/Bath Industrial Doctorate Centre in Systems, funded by EPSRC grant EP/G037353/1.

References

1. Costello, S.B., Chapman, D.N., Rogers, C.D.F., Metje, N.: Underground asset location and condition assessment technologies. Tunnelling and Underground Space Technology 22, 524–542 (2007)
2. Ollier, B.D.: Intelligent Infrastructure The Business Challenge. Railway Condition Monitoring. In: The Institution of Engineering and Technology International Conference (2006)
3. INCOSE, Systems Engineering Handbook. A Guide for System Life Cycle Processes and Activities. Ver. 3.2 INCOSE, San Diego, CA (January 2010)
4. The Collins Class, `http://www.submarineinstitute.com/submarines-in-australia/The-Collins-Class.html` (accessed: January 20, 2013)
5. Joint Doctrine Publication 0-10 British Maritime Doctrine, Swindon, Wiltshire: Ministry of Defence (August 2011)
6. Britain will deploy a Royal Navy warship and RAF military transport aircraft to help people devastated by Typhoon Haiyan, `https://www.gov.uk/government/news/hms-daring-deployment-to-boost-uk-response-to-philippines-typhoon` (accessed November 13, 2013)
7. HMS Illustrious picks up stores for Philippines aid, `https://www.gov.uk/government/news/hms-illustrious-picks-up-stores-for-philippines-aid` (accessed December 1, 2013)
8. The CADMID Lifecycle, `https://www.aof.mod.uk/aofcontent/strategic/guide/lifecycles/sg_cadmid.htm?zoom_highlight=cadmid` (accessed: November 10, 2013)
9. HMS Edinburgh `http://www.royalnavy.mod.uk/The-Fleet/Ships/Decommissioned-Units/Type-42-Destroyers/HMS-Edinburgh` (accessed: January 20, 2014)
10. BR – Marine Engineering Department Standing Orders (August 2013)
11. Hyde, S.: Systems Engineering in Defence Procurement: A SEIG & Maritime Combat Systems Perspective (2012), `http://www.incoseonline.org.uk/Documents/Bristol/BLG_10_10_2012_Presentation.pdf` (accessed: September 10, 2013)
12. Henderson, S., Game, P.: Beating Last Ship Syndrome Delivering HMS Duncan. A Ship's Staff Perspective. The Naval Engineer (Winter 2012, 2013)
13. BR8593, 2012. BR 8593(12) Procedures For Compiling And Processing Work Packages For Upkeep Periods In Surface Ships (July 2012)
14. BR 1313 - Maintenance Managemen. In: Surface Ships. Issue 5 (March 2011)
15. Blockley, D.: The Importance of Being Process. Civil Engineering and Environmental Systems 27(3), 189–199 (2010)
16. Lt Cdr. Royal Navy (December 4, 2013)
17. £65 million contract to refit HMS Ocean, `https://www.gov.uk/government/news/65m-contract-to-refit-royal-navys-largest-warship-secures-hundreds-of-uk-jobs` (accessed: June 20, 2014]
18. Key milestone in major upkeep programme, as HMS Ocean undocks, `http://www.babcockinternational.com/media-centre/key-milestone-in-major-upkeep-programme,-as-ocean-undocks/?alttemplate=MobileNewsItem` (accessed: June 22, 2014)
19. BR OpDef Signals – Detailed Instructions
20. NASA, International Space Station. Vehicle Arrivals and Departures (2014), `http://www.nasa.gov/mission_pages/station/structure/resupply.html` (accessed: January 20, 2013)

A Requirements Evaluation Method for Ships to Maximize Operational Value under Uncertainty

Kazuo Hiekata[1] and Bryan Moser[2]

[1] Graduate School of Frontier Sciences, The University of Tokyo, Japan
[2] Engineering Systems Division, M.I.T. and Global Project Design, USA
hiekata@k.u-tokyo.ac.jp, bry@mit.edu

Abstract. Requirements defined by shipping firms play a role as the communication interface of product information between these firms and shipbuilders, and the product design is optimized based on the requirements. Ship service life is about 30 years, during which original requirements may lose some relevance. In this paper we explore the introduction of uncertainty and flexibility into requirements so that ships are designed optimally not only for a single given technical condition but for a range of possible operational scenarios, including shifts in the economic environment for shipping firms.

1 Introduction

1.1 Background

Shipping firms design their business plans and define the requirements for vessels to be newly acquired. The requirements include essential performance and constraints depending on planned routes and their forecasted demand. Therefore the characteristics of the vessels will be optimized for the specific requirements based on the shipping firm's strategy. Shipbuilders then proceed with basic design work to satisfy these requirements and constraints such as cost, delivery, performance and other dependencies.

From a shipping firm's point of view, the basis to measure performance of vessels will be different from the shipbuilders'. At the delivery of vessels, shipbuilders and shipping firms must find some common criteria for evaluation. Today, key performance characteristics are evaluated under standard protocols. Classification societies check the structural performance and the propulsive performance as evaluated in sea trials. During these propulsive performance evaluations, the protocol for sea trial considers only calm sea conditions, even though actual operation might occur across a large variation of sea conditions. Nominally, a shipbuilder can optimize the design of a vessel for calm seas at a given service speed, and the ship might demonstrate good performance in severe weather.

Recently shipping operations are in need of better fuel consumption rate and reduction of greenhouse gas (GHG) emissions. For example, the "10 Mode Performance Index for Ships [1]" was developed to evaluate the decreases in service speed at a

S. Fukuda et al. (Eds.): PLM 2014, IFIP AICT 442, pp. 149–158, 2014.

given power rating for the predefined sea conditions. The development and deployment of this kind of index may expose the performance of vessels in various conditions which were not explored in the trials held at calm seas.

As mentioned above, requirements defined by shipping firms play a role as the communication interface of product information between these firms and shipbuilders, and the product design is optimized based on the requirements. Ship service life is about 30 years, during which original requirements may lose some relevance. In this paper we explore the introduction of uncertainty and flexibility into requirements so that ships are designed optimally not only for a single given technical condition but for a range of possible operational scenarios, including shifts in the economic environment for shipping firms.

1.2 Objective

This research proposes the requirements evaluation method to maximize the benefit of ships in the operation. The key idea is to consider the changes in economic conditions in addition to the optimization for a given design requirement.

2 Proposed Method

2.1 Overview

The performance in fuel consumption rate is governed by the resistance of the ship hull in operation. Generally the resistance by the sea water increases for larger service speed as shown in Figure 1. Froude Number (F_n) is defined as the ratio of a characteristic velocity to a gravitational wave velocity and Reynolds number (R_n) is defined as the ratio of inertial forces to viscous forces. The design service speed is defined by ship owners to fit the planned route for the vessel and the design of the vessels is optimized for the service condition, therefore the main engine and propeller demonstrate optimal performance at the condition.

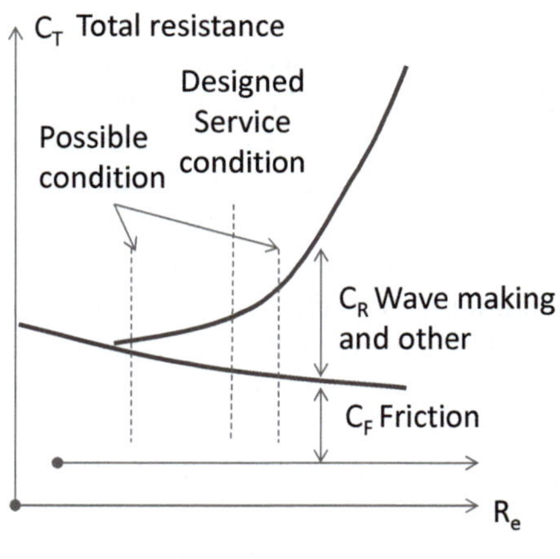

Fig. 1. Resistance of ship at various conditions

Though the fuel consumption rate is optimized at the given speed, the shipping firms will operate their ships at faster or slower speed to maximize the profit or minimize the loss in uncertain future economic situations during the service life of the vessels.

The proposed method calculates the performance at designed service conditions and possible various conditions to support the evaluation of requirements definition.

2.2 Fuel Consumption Model

The fuel consumption is the outcome of the interactions of the main engine, the propeller and the hull. The characteristics of these factors are nonlinear and the design of the plant is usually optimized for reducing the fuel consumption rate at the service speed which is assumed to be most likely at the acquisition. The fuel consumption model is based on the systematized ship design theory such as [2].

The ship hull is the major source of the resistance. Wave, viscous and viscous pressure resistances gives large effects on the performance. The total resistance of the ship hull will be calculated by the results of towing tank tests. The total resistance will be separated to friction and residual resistances . The friction has significant impact on slow vessels and the residual on the faster. Each type of resistance will be calculated as non-dimensional coefficients depending on Froude number and Reynolds number. The Froude number are about 0.15 for slow vessels such as tankers and about 0.27 for the faster such as container ships. The resistance is usually described as EHP (Effective Horse Power) at any ship speeds.

The output of the main engine is given by the rotation speed and the torque delivered from the shaft. BHP(Brake Horse Power) indicates the power generated by the main engine. Engines generally have their optimal load in the specific fuel consumption per output. A typical example is shown in Figure 2. Detailed behavior of the engine may be found in [3]. The power generated by the main engine will be transferred to the propeller with a certain amount of losses.

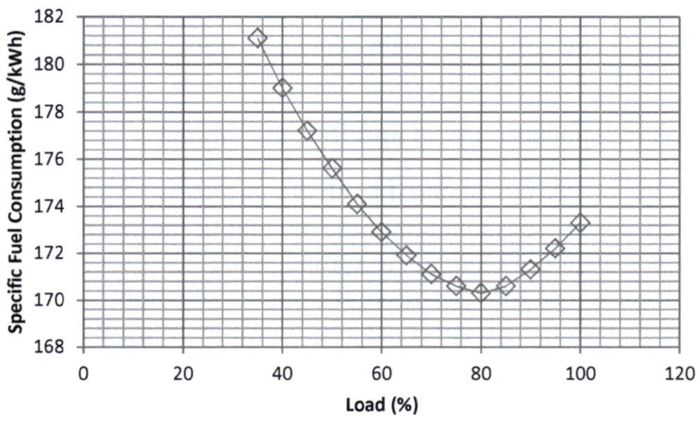

Fig. 2. Load and efficiency of a main engine

Finally, propellers will give the thrust to the ship hull through the use of the torque delivered from the shaft. The condition of the propeller in operation must be defined to calculate the performance of propellers. The performance of propellers is normally described like a graph shown in Figure 3. J is advanced coefficient and given by the following equation. V_A is advanced velocity into the propeller, K_T is thrust coefficient given by open water test and K_Q is propeller torque coefficient. Ship designers usually try to maximize the propeller efficiency η_0.

$$J = \frac{V_A}{nD}$$

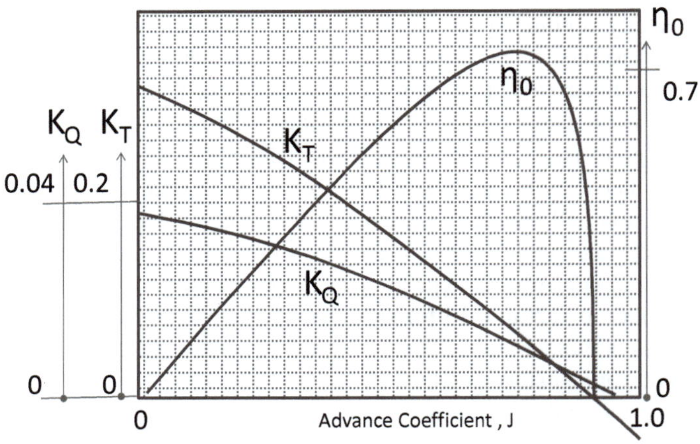

Fig. 3. Characteristics of a propeller

The service speed is defined in the requirement for a specific vessel, and then the propeller and the main engine will be configured. The design process will be iterated to improve the design of the vessel. The efficiency of ships is optimized at the specified service speed. The fuel consumption rate for other service speed can be calculated based on the characteristics of main engine, propeller and hull.

2.3 Marine Transportation Cost and Revenue Model

The forecast of the oil price is required to predict the ship service speed for maximizing the profit rate per oil consumption or the amount of the profit. The historical data of the oil price is shown in Figure 4. According to the fluctuation of the oil price, the vessels should be designed for varieties of the market situation.

The shipping market for oil tankers are described by using Worldscale flat rate issued by Worldscale association (LONDON) limited and Worldscale association (NYC) inc. The flat rate is defined as a tariff based on standard tankers in USD/metric ton for each shipping route. For example, the route from Ras Tannurah, Saudi Arabia to Chiba, Japan has the flat rate. The negotiations in shipping market are based on this Worldscale flat rate, and the rate for a specific route will be defined as the rate in

Worldscale. If the rate for the route from Ras Tannurah, Saudi Arabia to Chiba, Japan is 50 percent (WS50) and the flat rate (WS100) is 20 USD/metric ton, the freight will be 10 USD/metric ton, 50 percent of flat rate. The flat rates for all the routes in the world are published on January 1 and July 1 every year. As Worldscale flat rate is calculated based on the oil price, it has strong correlation with the oil price, so the flat rate can be calculated by given oil price. The historical data is shown in Figure 5.

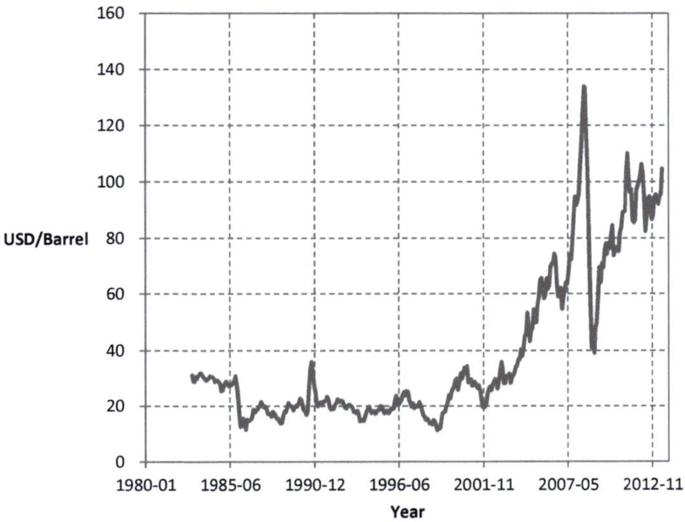

Fig. 4. Spot Oil Price West Texas Intermediate [4]

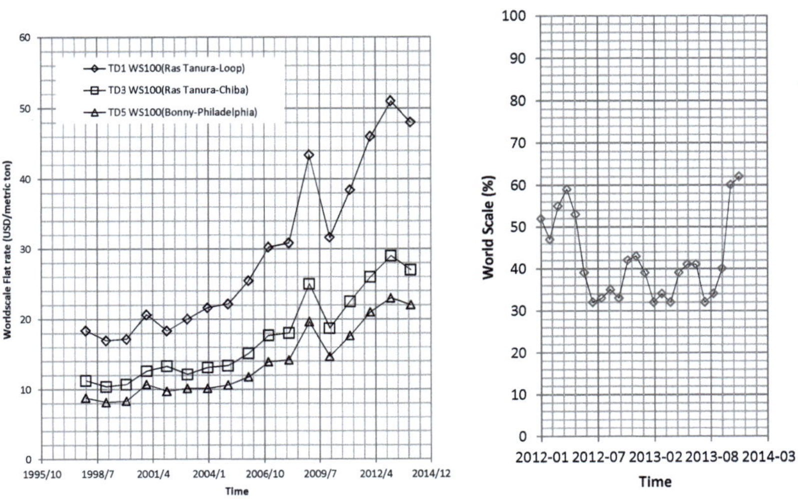

Fig. 5. Worldscale Flat Rate [5][6] and Worldscale Rate from Arabian Gulf to Japan [7]

If a route is given, revenue the amount of and fuel consumption can be estimated by the fuel consumption model described in 2.2. The fuel cost can be calculated by the fuel consumption is if the oil price is given. The revenue can be calculated if the duration of a round trip is given by defining the service speed. Finally the cost and the revenue will tell the gross margin of a designed vessel.

2.4 Simulation

If a profile of a ship is given, the ship performance including the fuel oil consumption rate can be calculated. The round trip date for a voyage can be estimated by the ship speed, so the basic revenue of a ship can be calculated based on the Worldscale rate. The general flow diagram is shown in Figure 6.

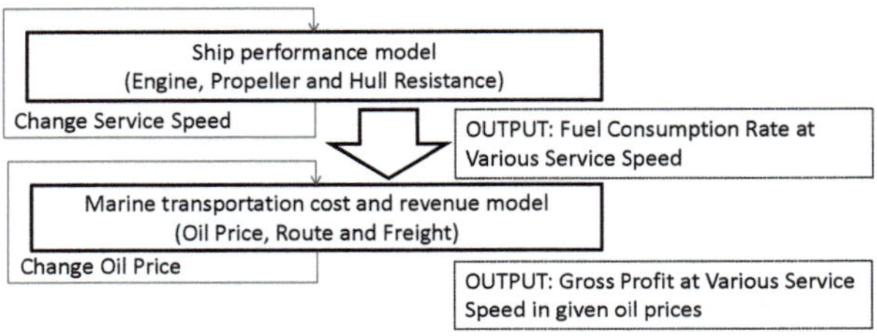

Fig. 6. General flow diagram of simulation

3 Case Study

This case study focuses on the requirement definition of tankers. The case illustrate potential for the improvement in terms of economic value to explore design requirement though configurations of the main engine, propellers, ship hulls and other components are optimized for a certain condition.

3.1 Route and Ship

In the case study, a route from Arabian Gulf to Japan is selected for detailed calculation. Basic information is shown in Table 1.

Table 1. Route overview

Origin and destination	From Ras Tanura (Arabian Gulf:AG), Saudi Arabia to Chiba, Japan via Strait of Malacca
Main Cargo	Crude oil
Distance (one way)	6,590 (mile)

Table 2. Principal particulars of the ship (based on [8])

Length overall (Loa) [m]	333
Length between perpendiculars (Lbp) [m]	324
Breadth moulded (Bmld) [m]	60
Depth moulded (Dmld) [m]	29
Draft [m]	20.529(m)
Deadweight [metric ton]	300,610
Gross Tonnage [G/T]	159,960
Displacement [metric ton]	341,610
Light weight [metric ton]	41,000
Block coefficient [non dimensional]	0.835
Maximum Continuous Output	27,160kw 74.0 rpm
Normal Output	23,090kw 70.1rpm
Maximum velocity at sea trial	16.74 knots
Service Speed at Normal Output	15.7 knots
Diameter of propeller	10(m)
Fuel consumption rate	97.1 (t/day)

Table 3. Specific fuel consumption of main engine (calculated on Man Diesel & Turbo SE web page)

Load(%)	SFOC(g/kWh)	Load(%)	SFOC(g/kWh)	Load(%)	SFOC(g/kWh)
100	173.3	75	170.6	50	175.6
95	172.2	70	171.1	45	177.2
90	171.3	65	171.9	40	179
85	170.6	60	172.9	35	181.1
80	170.3	55	174.1		

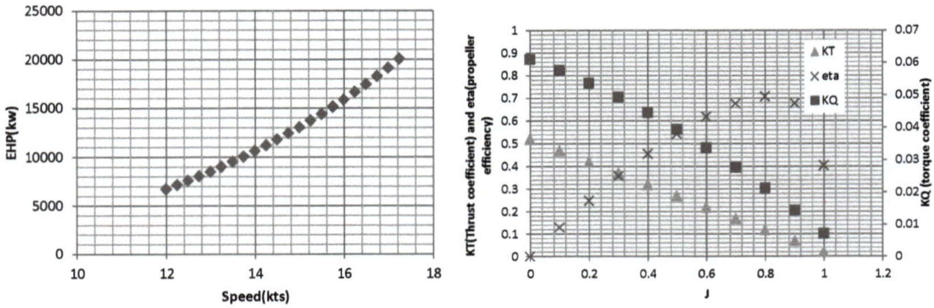

Fig. 7. Performance of Ship Hull (left) and Propeller (right)

In addition to the route, an average ship design model is also defined as shown in Table 2. This is a typical principal particulars referring to several ship design provided by shipyards and ship owners such as [8]. The specific oil consumption rate for the main engine is assumed based on the calculation provided by Man Diesel & Turbo SE web page. The performance of the ship hull and the propeller is assumed as shown in Figure 7. Load is the ratio of actual output to maximum continuous output of the main engine. The data is not actual data though the assumption is based on several design data.

3.2 Results

The calculation results of the gross margin which is subtraction of revenue and cost, and the fuel oil consumption rate given by the ship performance model.

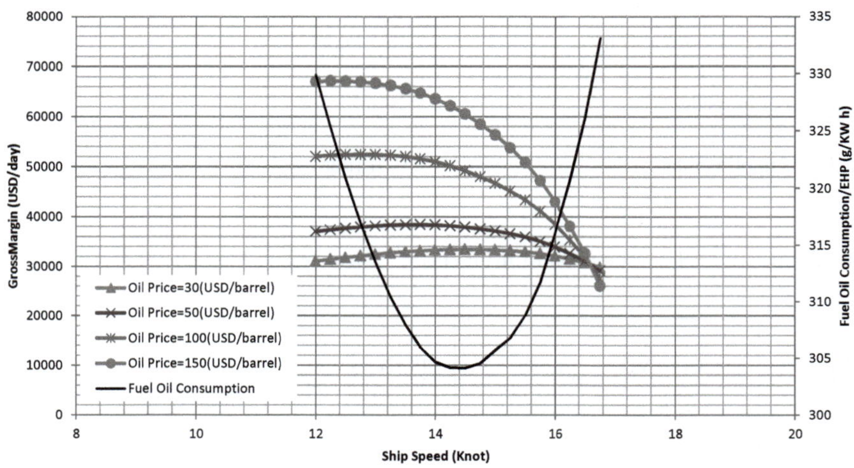

Fig. 8. Ship performance in terms of economic and technological evaluation

The revenue goes up by increasing the ship speed as the duration for a round trip of a voyage is getting smaller. The cost is getting higher because of the nonlinear increase of the resistance of ship hull shown as EHP. The results are shown as lines with markers in Figure 8. In this simulation, the Worldscale flat rate is projected by the oil price and the Worldscale rate for the route is fixed to WS45.

In terms of the fuel consumption rate, the main engine and the propeller have an optimal condition for operations. Ship design is usually optimized for the condition. This performance from the technological point of view is shown as a solid line in Figure 8.

The peak performance in terms of the technological perspective is found at around design service speed; however the optimal speed for the gross margin moves as the oil price changes. The oil price goes up and the optimal speed for maximizing the gross margin will getting smaller.

4 Discussion

The results are reasonable and explain the current marine transportation situation. The oil price is getting higher these years and slow steaming is widely deployed to decrease the cost of shipping firms. The design of ships still has to focus on the optimization in terms of the technological performance. It can be suggested that ship design should have a certain level of consideration for the economic performance to respond the uncertainties such as oil price and market in the future. This kind of idea is proposed by de Nufville [9].

Specifically, this research focuses on the evaluation of service speed and the performance with limited collected data. The detailed ship and market model and more data are required to obtain accurate simulation results.

5 Conclusion

A requirements evaluation method to maximize the benefit of ships in the operation is proposed and applied to a tanker traveling between Arabian Gulf and Japan. The simulation results based on the proposed method show that the optimal conditions are different in terms of economic and technological perspective. This research suggests ship design should consider the maximization against the uncertainties in economic situation because of the length of the service life.

References

1. Tsujimoto, M., Sasaki, N., Fujiwara, T., Ueno, M., Ushui, N., Kado, M., Nomura, D., Takagi, K.: A Calculation Method of 10 mode Index for Ships. Journal of the Japan Society of Naval Architects and Ocean Engineers 10, 97–104 (2009)
2. Gillmer, T.C., Johnson, B.: Introduction to Naval Architecture, U.S. Navy (1982)
3. Sanguri, M.: How to Use Main Engine Performance Curve for Economical Fuel Consumption on Ships? (August 16, 2012), `http://www.marineinsight.com/marine/marine-news/headline/how-to-use-main-engine-performance-curve-for-economical-fuel-consumption-on-ships/` (January 20, 2014)

4. Federal Reserve Bank of St. Louis, Crude Oil Prices: West Texas Intermediate (WTI) - Cushing, Oklahoma (MCOILWTICO) (February 20, 2014), http://research.stlouisfed.org/fred2/series/MCOILWTICO (February 28, 2014)
5. McQuilling Services, LLC, No 21 – 2013 Worldscale Flat Rate Forecast, Tankers (2012)
6. McQuilling Services, LLC., No 11 – 2012 Flat Rate Forecast, Tankers (2011)
7. MOL, Market Data (February 2014), http://www.mol.co.jp/ir-e/data_e/market_e.html (February 28, 2014)
8. IHI, Press release (July 2003), http://www.ihi.co.jp/ihi/press/2003/2003-7-08/index.html (February 28, 2014)
9. de Neufville, R., Scholtes, S.: Flexibility in Engineering Design. MIT Press (August 2011)

Using the Product Lifecycle Management Systems to Improve Maintenance, Repair and Overhaul Practices: The Case of Aeronautical Industry

Alejandro Romero[1] and Darli Rodrigues Vieira[2]

[1] Université du Québec à Montréal (UQAM), Management Project Chair, Canada
romero-torres.alejandro@uqam.ca
[2] Université du Québec à Trois-Rivières (UQTR),
Research Chair in Management of Aeronautical projects, Canada
darli.vieira@uqtr.ca

Abstract. Airlines companies trust in MRO facilities for extending lifespan of their assets to ensure the availability of transportation services. Nevertheless, MRO services are complex because they involve several processes whose performance depends on the design and manufacturing of products while airlines require the best-cost efficiency, quality and safety. Product lifecycle management (PLM) could improve the productivity and quality of MRO since it enables the collaborative creation, management, dissemination, use, maintenance and repair of products and its operational process information across the entire life of products from market concept to product retirement. However, it seems that PLM and MRO relationship in the aeronautical industry has been studied very sparsely in the literature. This paper attempts to gain a better understanding of the influence of product life management system in MRO services. The objectives of this study are twofold: 1) to identify MRO provider's requirements concerning PLM systems, and 2) to assess how PLM system could be improved to better support MRO services.

Keywords: Maintenance, repair, overhaul, aeronautical, product lifecycle management.

1 Introduction

The aeronautical sector including aircraft construction, aircraft parts supply or maintenance, repair and overhaul (MRO) service is today one of the most dynamic industries in the world. This industry creates enormous amounts of economic activity and fiscal benefits for several countries. AeroStrategy assessed that the global aerospace industry will be worth 1,200 billion dollars by 2014 [1]. Specifically, the defense sector will represent 71.8% of the market while the commercial aviation will contribute the remaining 28.2% [2]. The aerospace industry is closely linked to the continuous innovation and development of new technologies, new materials and new procedures, contributing in a significant manner to the economic and social development of countries.

The actual number of aircrafts in the air and the significant increase of new production, order backlog for Airbus and Boeing was approximately 9055 aircrafts in 2012

S. Fukuda et al. (Eds.): PLM 2014, IFIP AICT 442, pp. 159–168, 2014.

(Flight Global, 2013), have increased the importance of MRO services in this industry. For instance, U.S. airlines operate a mixed fleet of aircraft comprised of primarily older planes (60 % of their inventory). It was estimated that a large percentage of these old aircraft will be due for heavy checks or overhauls [4]. The increase in capacity of commercial and military sector, along with greater aircraft utilization, will lead to increased maintenance and safety demands, creating new challenges for the MRO industry [5]. In fact, MRO providers create the capability to support the functioning of the aeronautical machines, extending their lifespan and ensuring transportation services.

MRO services are complex since they involve several processes whose performance depends on the design and manufacturing of products while airlines require the best-cost efficiency, quality and safety. MRO entities ensure the maintenance of a variety of aircraft systems, components and parts, which requires investments in infrastructure, compliance with government regulations and updating of technical staff. Product lifecycle management (PLM) could improve the productivity and quality of MRO. Indeed, it enables the collaborative creation, management, dissemination, use, maintenance and repair of products and its operational process information across the entire life of products from market concept to product retirement. However, it seems that PLM and MRO has not been studied sufficiently in the literature [6]. Therefore, this paper attempts to gain a better understanding of the influence of maintenance repair and overhaul requirements on the product life management strategies in the aeronautical industry.

The objectives of this paper are twofold: 1) to identify MRO provider's requirements concerning PLM systems, and 2) to assess how PLM system could be improved to better support MRO services. The paper is structured as follows. The next section briefly presents a review of the literature. The third section outlines the methodological strategy. The fourth one examines the main PLM strategies to strengthen MRO services. The paper concludes with a discussion on the suitability of PLM in MRO.

2 Literature Review

2.1 Aeronautical Industry

The aerospace industry can be divided into two large sectors delimited by the operating range of products. The aeronautics sector is responsible for aircrafts operating within the earth's atmosphere and the astronautics is for products that may operate outside the atmosphere [7]. MRO services are necessary in both sectors, but MRO providers for aeronautical product are not equipped to provide the same service for astronautics products. Aeronautical sector include both military and commercial aircrafts [7]. All these sub-sectors share similar functional structure but focus on different markets and products (see figure 1).

Some products use the same technological platform irrespective of whether they were developed for military purposes or for commercial transport of passengers and freight [8]. Nevertheless, most aircrafts require special procurement procedures, certifications and specific technological features [9]. For instance, the interiors of the executive and civil aircraft have a high degree of customization and advanced materials, which will be used later in commercial aviation.

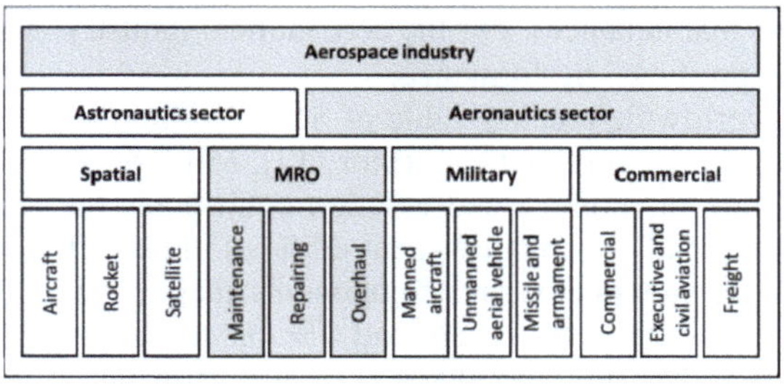

Fig. 1. Aerospatiale industry structure (based on [2])

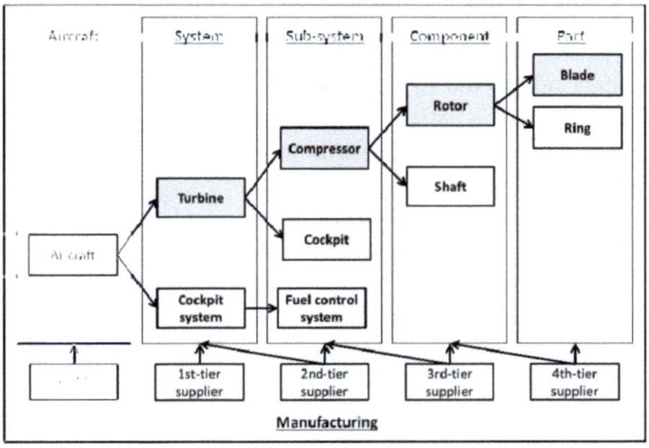

Fig. 2. Aircraft product and manufacturing structure (based on [10])

The structure of the commercial aviation industry is frequently compared to the automobile industry; however there are substantial differences in the level of demand certifications and standards, quality, safety, security, time to market, volume parts and life of the cycle product [11]. To better understand the differences between both industries, it's crucial to describe how aircraft products are structured. The largest unit is the aircraft, which is defined as a complete and operational unit. The aircraft is segmented into systems, covering key functions of the aircraft such as the turbine whose function is to provide the power for the lifting of the craft in the air [10]. Further, systems can contain subsystems or components depending upon their complexity. In the above example, a subsystem of the turbine is the compressor which has the function of compressing the air prior to mixing it with the fuel in the combustion chamber [10]. The turbine has several components such as the rotor and shaft. The rotor compresses the air to gradually reduce its size and the shaft spins the rotor [10]. Finally, these components are composed of several parts such as rotor blades (see figure 2).

2.2 Maintenance, Repair and Overhaul (MRO)

MRO is the set of activities designed to allow aircrafts to operate safety, efficiently and respecting aviation regulations. MRO services involve the repair of any mechanical, electrical, electronic, hydraulic component (unscheduled maintenance, faults detection and repairs). They also include the execution of routine activities that keep the components in working condition (scheduled maintenance) or that simply prevent failures (preventive maintenance). For the aeronautical industry, MRO is the basis for adding value to the products' performance.

MRO services worldwide reach a value of $149.2 billion by 2013 and are equivalent to 35% of sales in the aeronautical sector [12]. Military sector represents 70% of the total market while the commercial aviation contributes the remaining 30% [13]. For instance, commercial companies spent 35% of their MRO budget on turbine maintenance, 23% on subsystems and components maintenance, 20% on line maintenance, 15% on aero-structures repair and 7% on modifications [13]. The global MRO market has 300-400 suppliers, located in all continents. It is estimated that the global market for MRO services will have long-term growth rate of 3.3%, representing by 2019 a total expenditure of $ 183 billion dollars [14]. MRO service will be the fastest growing segment of the aerospace industry.

MRO facilities principally offer three services: maintenance, repair and overhaul. ***Maintenance*** corresponds to the review, cleaning, lubrication and replacement of minor parts of the aircraft. It's often programmed to be undertaken after a certain amount flight hours (every day for line maintenance or every month for minor maintenance) [15]. ***Repair*** refers to the mechanical reprocess for serious failures discovered during maintenance. Finally, ***overhaul*** corresponds to the complete review of the aircraft which is executed when aircraft has completed 4000 and 5000 flight hours. The objective is to check thoroughly every system, component and tool of the aircraft and meet the condition standards of quality required for all the components. Overhaul also includes the incorporation of new technologies or systems [16].

MRO providers offer different type of check services, namely A, B, C and D [17, 18]. An "A" check is performed approximately every 500-800 flight hours. It is usually done overnight at the airport. The recurrence of this service varies by aircraft type, the cycle count (one cycle consists of one takeoff and one landing), or the number of hours in air since last service. A "B" check is executed approximately every 3 or 6 months. It usually lasts for 1 to 3 days in a hangar. "B" check recurrence depends on the same factors as that of an "A" check. A "C" check happens approximately every 15 to 21 months or a certain number of flying hours. This service is more extensive than a "B" check. Almost the entire aircraft is inspected keeping it out of service until this check is completed at the maintenance site. The space required for the execution of the service is also higher. It requires the hangar and a maintenance base equipped with set of workshops. The average completion time is usually 1-2 weeks. Recurrence depends on flying hours, but specifically on the manufacturer's recommendations. A "D" check, also known as Heavy Maintenance Visit (HMV), is the most demanding of MRO services. This check is performed approximately every 5 or 6 years. Almost all the aircraft is disarmed for inspection and repair purposes. It can last for 3 weeks to 2 months depending on the service provider, its resources, and the general condition of the aircraft. A Boeing 747 for instance requires the participation of 100 technicians for executing a "D" check to the aircraft parts, executing tests and ensuring the necessary installations [16].

2.3 Product Lifecycle Management (PLM) for MRO Services

In the aeronautical industry, PLM aims principally to manage the aircraft-product definition with respect to the functioning of its relative subsystems (see figure 2), from their conception to their final disposal. PLM systems by inclusion of functionalities such as requirement management, data management, digital visualization and configuration management, allow for sharing product information throughout the product value chain. Furthermore, PLM allows for synchronizing nomenclatures resulting from different lifecycle phases namely design, manufacture, assembly and service.

Technology advancements could bring important benefits to improve MRO services. For instance, MRO facilities are looking for ways to streamline their maintenance operations through automation by way of informational technology. Advances in computer technology especially in the area of information technology have made the MRO procedures highly technical [19]. They can benefit from pervasive advantages of technology such as electronic manuals and electronic information which eliminates the need to deal with high volumes of paper to obtain needed maintenance information

Adopted years ago by different industries, PLM system could bring information about the aircraft components and pieces to the actors participating in the lifecycle of aircrafts. PLM systems are developed and adopted to gather all the relevant information that affects a product throughout its life, from concept through retirement (including its maintenance and repair) and managing the communication of that information to facilitate product and process improvement [20]. PLM capture principally information of the activities conducted during design engineering such as computer-aided design applications, 3D modeling and simulation or Bill of Material [21]. Specification data regarding component parts, materials, tools and other attributes is defined in these systems. Information improving MRO services are also integrated into PLM platforms such as process flows, work instructions and inspection criteria [17]. The resulting documentation contains every detail about the product and process definition.

The benefits of extending PLM to production can be realized quickly with manufacturing operations software tightly integrated to a manufacturer's PLM system, such as enterprise resource planning (ERP) customer relationship management, management of supply chain (SCM) and design applications (CAD) [21]. Supported by PLM, Aircraft manufacturers could improve their ability to enforce as-planned execution results with fewer mistakes, integrate engineering data facilitating faster decision making and communicate manufacturing data to engineering and providers [20, 22].

However, data contained in PLM applications often does not encompass the complete lifecycle of the product. Several authors in the literature stated that PLM improves the collaboration from design to manufacturing procedures but it must extend their benefits to the MRO services and final disposal [6, 17]. Further, PLM must capture and spread information into two directions: from supply chain upstream to downstream and vice versa. Lee et co-authors [6] studied the adoption of PLM tools by an MRO provider. They identified that PLM could establish a more comprehensive relation between customers, suppliers and business partners since MRO providers could get manufacturing information easily to provide the right MRO services. In turn, MRO facilities could register maintenance and repair information into PLM tools to share it to manufacturers and airlines for product improvement purpose [6]. Yu and Gulliver [17] conclude that PLM could provide accurate information to MRO providers to ensure quality and to reduce service cost.

3 Methodology

We executed an exploratory study based on a content analysis. Our goal is to answer to the following research questions: What are the main stakes for MRO providers?

Which are the benefits of integrating PLM systems into MRO services? How do MRO providers use PLM systems? How could PLM systems be improved? The executed content analysis is based on public information about PLM uses and MRO requirements. We identified several documents such as research papers, academic documents, white papers, industrial documents and news. Data were coded and classified based on the current topics: such as needs of MRO providers for its functioning, benefits of PLM in aeronautical section, information required by MRO's and PLM implementation. Table 1 shows the distribution of information collected in function of the above classification. Based on these classifications, we analyzed MRO needs and PLM capacities for aeronautical industry to identify the main benefits of integrating PLM systems into MRO procedures. Some limitations were also identified by analyzing MRO information requirement and current PLM applications. No relevant information were found from available PLM implementations documents.

Table 1. Classifications of collected data

Type of documents	Research papers	Academic documents	White papers	Industrial documents	News	Total
MRO needs	2	2	3	5	10	22
Current PLM benefits	8	6	5	2	6	27
MRO information requirements	2	2	1	2	3	10
PLM implementation	3	1	0	0	0	4
Total	15	11	9	9	19	63

Preliminary results were then validated by an expert on product lifecycle management in the aeronautical industry, by senior specialists from two aircraft manufacturing companies and by one senior specialist representing an MRO provider. Experts gave interesting insights that support research results.

4 Preliminary Results

4.1 PLM Opportunities for MRO

As shown in the literature and validated by the specialists, MRO services are complex for several reasons:

First, they must deal with a big variety of systems and sub-systems that have different maintenance procedures. Aircraft are sophisticated products since they are made up of thousands of components that come from a long supply chain and whose cycle life is measured in decades. To illustrate this, Airbus A300 was launched in 1969, he entered in service in 1974 and the last aircraft was delivered in July 2007. Apart from their long periods of production, aircrafts have long periods of use and consequently long periods of maintenance. For instance, the A380 underwent fatigue testing for 25 years of use. A quarter of the Airbus aircraft currently in service has exceeded its usage life of 20 years. These very long periods of service and production involve inevitably changes to the supply chain and changes to the system design. As mentioned by a specialist from an aircraft constructor, "during the prolonged life cycle of aircrafts, the customer requirements could evolve resulting in several product versions that differ from original design". PLM systems could capture this dynamic data and provide accurate information to MRO providers. In case of any version update, MRO provider could receive the instructions to upgrade systems and ensure that aircrafts in used respect requirements and specification of original manufacturers.

Second, MRO procedures depend deeply upon the production structure of aircrafts. Production comprises 5 levels (see figure 1): the first level is occupied by the main contractors, also called original equipment manufacturers (i.e. Airbus, Boeing, Embraer or Bombardier), that are responsible for designing and assembling aircrafts [23]. The first-tier supplier is in charge of assembling primary system and manufacture main components [24]. The second-tier supplier is responsible for sub-assembling primary systems and its components [24]. The third-tier supplier is in charge of manufacturing components. Finally, forth-tier supplier is responsible for producing simple components and parts [24]. For MRO services, providers must ensure the compatibility of their procedures with the recommendations provided by OEM manufactures, suppliers from all tiers, and airlines companies. They also require highly specialized aircraft expertise, a field that is constantly evolving and where specialties are changing over time. Following the above design-manufacturing structure, PLM systems could integrate the product information and the structure of their manufacturing. Indeed, OEM and systems providers integrate product information into a same platform for product assembly purposes. Using an effective PLM solution, MRO could get access to this integrated information and then communicate easily with the appropriate owner of products in case of any technical or specification problem.

Third, MRO demands are centered on safety and quality which are necessary to ensure airplanes are free from factors that may lead to injury or loss. Nevertheless, literature shows that MRO service could frequently fail. For instance, Aircraft maintenance and inspection errors have contributed to anywhere from 9 to 23 percent of airline accidents [25]. As described by a specialist participating in this study, the most common aviation maintenance problems include engine shutdowns, structural design problems, defective plane parts and flight employee negligence. Apart from high quality requirement, MRO solutions providers are also under pressure from commercial airlines for reducing costs. An estimated 20 to 30 percent of engine shutdowns are caused by maintenance errors, resulting in flight delays that could cost as much as $10,000 per hour [26]. The increasing pressures to maintain a highly competitive advantage in the aviation industry have dramatically changed perceptions from tradition models of the past. Therefore, MRO provider could use a PLM system to share the information produced during maintenance and repair procedures. As in original production, material and process data will need to be collected to document MRO procedures. This electronic record ensures operations are approved in sequence; replacement materials meet specifications and tasks are performed by authorized MRO providers. In order to reduce time and cost of MRO services, several lean strategies are adopted such as 5S process or Kaizen. PLM system could support the integration of these strategies. Indeed, it enables the identification of pieces using nomenclatures or codes. This identification system enables a better control of important volume of pieces. Therefore, MRO providers could decrease time spent on searching parts and finding their related information.

Finally, technology innovations not only bring opportunities to improve MRO services, they could increase the complexity of specifications and conditions for maintenance and repair. For instance, technological advancements in avionics systems require MRO providers to continuously provide up-to-date training to keep up with newer avionic platforms. Due to this increasing use of technology, more time is spent to repair aircraft systems. As mentioned by several specialists, sharing the same PLM solution with aircraft constructors and their suppliers could decrease the time to repair and improve knowledge. Extending PLM to maintenance can incorporate work instructions that are delivered in 3D just like during the manufacturing process. MRO workers could interact with the model to quickly and thoroughly understand the exact issue and solution. Original designs and historical maintenance data recorded in the as-built history can be viewed and compared.

4.2 PLM Limits for MRO

Some of the participants of this study pointed to the actual limits of PLM solution that could explain why this system is not totally used by MRO providers. The first limit described is that actual PLM solutions meet the needs of engineers and only extend up to the point where a product is built. For MRO providers looking for knowledge of the life cycle beyond design through production of aircraft parts and subsystems, the information is limited and don't meet MRO needs. Specialists participating into this study stated that current systems don't encourage collaboration between engineering, manufacturing, the supply network and MRO service. Actually, they hinder continuous improvement efforts. Another specialist examining the MRO documents observed that the information available electronically is astronomical. He suggested a better aggregation of information to allow MRO providers to have all the information they need to complete a repair anywhere and anytime, from any location.

Apart from sharing information, MRO providers, airlines, OEM and systems providers must use PLM to improve their relative processes. Critical information is collected and could be used to better understand the procedures and need of aircraft lifecycle partners. OEM and aircraft system providers should focus on MRO stakes in order to improve the design of their products and, therefore, make easier their maintenance and repairing. For instance, they could identify that disassembly of systems is a complex process for MRO providers. Therefore, they could add as design requirement that aircraft systems could easily be disassembled. Some participants suggested that PLM system could enable this type of analyses to change design strategies to make it easier for MRO's to provide services.

5 Conclusion

PLM system allows MRO providers to decrease the complexity of their activities since it enables sharing and collecting information about aircraft systems. This information could be used to improve the control of all the aircraft components, to obtain a better knowledge of pieces requirements and updates but also it contribute to improve

MRO quality and decrease time and cost. Beside these benefits, PLM systems are not completely used by MRO entities because they are not totally compatible with maintenance and repair processes and because the actual available information don't meet MRO requirement. It seems that even if PLM solutions become more sophisticated, aeronautical supply chain actors tend not to share their information. Improving PLM system to meet MRO needs could have several opportunities for MRO providers and commercial airlines. But, OEM and aircraft system providers could also get benefits. For instance, OEM could increase their revenues if they ensure that their products need less costly and timely MRO services [6]. To accomplish this objective, aircraft lifecycle actors must invest in improving their collaboration across their business wall. They should coordinate their efforts from design and manufacturing to MRO procedures. Indeed, PLM could make easier this task.

This paper presented an exploratory study that enables to have better understanding of the actual position of PLM in MRO services. This represents the first step for a grounded theory. Different data was collected from the content analysis and from specialist's validations and was coded into two main classifications: PLM benefits and limits. Further research will focus on analyzing how designers and manufacturers in aeronautical industry include into their activities the needs of their partners to improve the last phases of the product lifecycle, namely maintenance services provided by MRO's, recycling and final disposal.

Acknowledgements. The authors would like to thank the two anonymous reviewers for their valuable and insightful comments and suggestions.

References

1. Deloitte, LLP Global Aerospace & Defense Industry Financial Performance Study (2013), http://www2.deloitte.com/content/dam/Deloitte/global/Documents/Manufacturing/gx_AD_industryperformancestudy_june2013.pdf
2. Aerostrategy. Aerospace Globalization 2.0: Implications for Canada's Aerospace Industry, Discussion paper (2009) http://www.aiac.ca/uploadedFiles/Resources_and_Publications/Reference Docu-ments/The%20Implications%20Of%20Globalization%202%200%20For%20Canadian%20Aerospace(2).pdf
3. Flightglobal, Aircraft finance 2013, special report (2013), http://www.flightglobal.com/airspace/media/..pdf/../aircraft-finance-2013.pdf
4. Team SAI and back Aviation, Maintenance, Repair and Overhaul (MRO) world market forecast (2006), http://backavaition.com/MRO
5. Jackman, F.: MRO market up modestly as efficiencies take hold. Overhaul & Maintenance 12 (4), 43–50
6. Lee, S.G., Ma, Y.-S., Timm, G.L.: Product lifecycle management in aviation maintenance, repair and overhaul. Computers in Industry 59(2), 296–303 (2008)
7. Alternatives, C. Competitive Alternatives – Highlights, KPMG (2012), http://www.competitivealternatives.com/industries/CA2012_indprofile_aerospace.pdf
8. Anand, S.: Domestic use of unmanned aircraft systems: an evaluation of policy constraints and the role of industry consensus standards. ASTM Standardization News 35(9), 30 (2007)

9. Moir, I., Seabridge, A.: Aircraft systems: mechanical, electrical and avionics subsystems integration (21) (2008), http://Wiley.com
10. Kozakiewicz, A., Kowalski, M.: Unstable operation of the turbine aircraft engine. Journal of Theoretical and Applied Mechanics 51(3), 719–727 (2013)
11. Rossetti, C.L., Choi, T.Y.: Supply management under high goal incongruence: An empirical examination of disintermediation in the aerospace supply chain. Decision Sciences 39(3), 507–540 (2008)
12. Lombardo, D.: Study: 2013 World MRO Market Worth $49.2B, AIN Online (2013), http://www.ainonline.com/aviation-news/ainmxreports/2013-05-15/study-2013-world-mromarket-worth-492b
13. Michaels, K.: Air transport MRO Outlook, implications of high fuel prices. Aerostrategy management consulting (2011), http://www.aviationweek.com/events/html/mro11/MRO%20US%20-%204.12%20-%20230pm%20-%20D129%20-%20Michaels%20(for%20electronic%20distribution).pdf
14. Market research, The Commercial Aircraft Maintenance, Repair and Overhaul (MRO) Market 2012-2022. Market research report (2012), http://www.reportlinker.com/p0591746/The-Commercial-Aircraft-Maintenance-Repair-and-Overhaul-MRO-Market.html
15. Al-Kaabi, H., Potter, A., Naim, M.: An outsourcing decision model for airlines' MRO activities. Journal of Quality in Maintenance Engineering 13(3), 217–227 (2007)
16. Dixon, M.: The maintenance costs of aging aircraft: Insights from commercial aviation, vol. 486. RAND Corporation (2006)
17. Yu, J., Gulliver, S., Tang, Y., Ke, L.: New advances in aircraft MRO services: Data mining enhancement. In: 2011 Fourth International Workshop on Advanced Computational Intelligence (IWACI), pp. 199–204 (2011)
18. Zhilkin, O.N., Lopatkin, R.V.: Aircraft maintenance repair and overhaul market in Russia–challenges and opportunities of the high-tech industry in Russia. Readings Book, 1316 (2013)
19. United States Department of Labor, Aircraft and avionics equipment mechanics and service technicians (2006), http://www.bls.gov/oco/ocos179.htm
20. Dimitri, V.A.N., Eynard, B., Troussier, N., Belkadi, F., Roucoules, L., Ducellier, G.: Integrated Design and PLM Applications in Aeronautics Product Development. In: The 19th CIRP Design Conference-Competitive Design (2009)
21. Rashid, M.A., Riaz, Z., Turan, E., Haskilic, V., Sunje, A., Khan, N.: Smart factory: E-business perspective of enhanced ERP in aircraft manufacturing industry. In: Technology Management for Emerging Technologies (PICMET), 2012 Proceedings of PICMET 2012, pp. 3262–3275. IEEE (2012)
22. Cantamessa, M., Montagna, F., Neirotti, P.: Understanding the organizational impact of PLM systems: evidence from an aerospace company. International Journal of Operations & Production Management 32(2), 191–215 (2012)
23. Pritchard, D., MacPherson, A.: Boeing's diffusion of commercial aircraft design and manufacturing technology to Japan: Surrendering the US aircraft industry for foreign financial support (2009)
24. Doran, D.: Rethinking the supply chain: an automotive perspective. Supply Chain Management: An International Journal 9(1), 102–109 (2004)
25. Aviation Attorneys, Network newsroom (2006), http://www.avaitionattorneynetwork.com
26. Tegtmeier, L.A.: Training not immune from market, technology forces shaping industry. Overhaul and Maintenance (2002)

Integrating Eco-design and PLM in the Aviation Completion Industry: A Case Study

Natalia Moreira[1], Daoud Aït-Kadi[2], Darli Rodrigues Vieira[3], Alejandro Romero[3], Luis Antonio de Santa-Eulalia[4], and Yi Wang[1]

[1] Univertisy of Manchester, United Kingdom
[2] Université Laval, Canada
[3] Université du Québec à Trois-Rivières (UQTR), Research Chair in Management of Aeronautical projects, Canada
[4] Université de Sherbrooke, Canada
natalia.moreira@postgrad.manchester.ac.uk, daoud.aitkadi@gmc.ulaval.ca, {darli.vieira,romeroto}@uqtr.ca, l.santa-eulalia@usherbrooke.ca, yi.wang-2@manchester.ac.uk

Abstract. Aviation represents 12% of the CO2 emissions from all transport sources in the world. These pollutants are even stronger in their impact because they are released at high altitudes. Therefore, aeronautical companies have adopted the eco-design and PLM perspective to integrate the environmental concerns into the development of their products. PLM permits to include the environmental matters into every phase of the development process, not forgetting traditional arguments such as function, costs, production and aesthetics. Research regarding ecologically concerned textiles in aviation completion industry is not available in literature, especially those regarding its whole lifecycle and supply chain. Therefore, this paper aims to analyse this unexplored concern by assessing the integration of eco-design and PLM perspective for the use of textile materials in this industry sector. Through a case study, the research team explored the completion function of a north-American company in general and, specifically, the use of textile materials for internal completion of the aircraft. Even though representing 1% of the total weight of the aircraft, textiles represent an important factor in the composition of an airplane and the fact that it is being thought off as another recyclable and not disposable part of it should mean a shift in the perception of its growing importance in the development of the plane as a whole.

Keywords: Green aviation, project lifecycle management, eco-design, product development, completion.

1 Introduction

Aviation, term used to define the design, development, production, operation, and use of aircraft represents 12% of the CO2 emissions from all transport sources in the world [1]. This industry sector emits large volumes of CO2 each year, and whilst only being 2% of overall global production it still amounts to an additional

S. Fukuda et al. (Eds.): PLM 2014, IFIP AICT 442, pp. 169–180, 2014.

670 million tonnes in a year. That volume has doubled since 1990 and is predicted to more than double again by 2025 [2]. Pollutants from aviation are even stronger in their impact because they are released at high altitudes [3]. Scientists predict in different research that the total warming impact of aviation's emissions can be multiplied anywhere between 1.9 and 2.7 times, or even more in some scenarios, to estimate their true impact [4].

Besides the concern with the development of new products, there are a growing number of companies interested in guaranteeing the ecological contribution of aviation companies. There is a clear interest in increasing their responsibility, what can also be seen in publications such as Egri and Ralston [5] where they analyse the considerable increase in interest on corporate ecological responsibility as an academic topic as well as a competitive tool for international business. In this context, the Eco-design concept emerged as a trendy concept, integrating the environmental demands to the development of new products [6]. Integrated into the designer's practices and tools, eco-design provides more space for innovation and creativity within the industrial environment. Thus being a new opportunity for differentiation and a future competitive factor [7].

Coming from a gap in the literature on the development of green aircraft completion textiles, the main contribution of this paper is to investigate how products development process can be used to improve the production and acceptance of ecological textile systems for the aeronautic completion industry and decrease its ecological footprint from the PLM (Product Lifecycle Management) perspective. The article is organized into four sections. Starting with a literature review about eco-design and its relation with the product life management, the section 3 describes the methodological strategy and the case study chosen in this research. Finally, the section 4 and 5 expose respectively the main results and the conclusions.

2 Literature Review

2.1 Eco-Design in the Completion Industry

Eco design is defined as a proactive environmental management approach that integrates environmental issues into the product development and their related processes [8]. Within the product development process, the eco-design represents the inclusion of environmental matter into every phase of the development process, not forgetting traditional arguments such as function, costs, production, aesthetics, etc. [6]. Such a change means to evaluate the used materials, the environmental performance during the fabrication, maintenance, logistics, reutilization, dismantling, re-manufacturing, recycling and final disposal [9]. When it comes to the ecological performance of a product or a service, there is not much to do once the product is released into the market (and when there is it usually originates an extremely high cost), that is why this aspect of the development has to be considered and a high influence from the initial phases of the process [10].

Morelli [11] explains that a more ecological approach towards products development is a challenge as it not only represents the creation of a new product, but also the reorganization of already (or not) existing elements throughout the supply chain according to new needs and values. In addition, for the development of an "eco-product" the cultural and social values are equivalent to people and technologies [12], adding more complexity to the development process.

In the aeronautic industry textile materials can be found in the exterior structures, technical and fibrous composite materials applied to the fuselage, coating and internal items of the aircraft, as well as for special uniforms, parachutes, balloons, etc. Authors such as Dexter [13] and Suarez et al. [14] have already published a wide range of material regarding textile composites and its use in the exterior structure of the airplane. They believe that it is important to emphasize that designers who work with the performance of textiles in the aeronautic industry must develop further and try to standardize more, thus ensuring repeatability and structural integrity, needing considerable insight into the processing methodology to adequately define the part (through modelling tools), design the tooling and be confident in the end-product performance.

From the most sophisticated system to the less complex component, aeronautic pieces could get several benefits from ecodesign. Vezzoli and Manzini [12] claim that even low impact products may require clean technologies, but it demands for secure new design capacities, promoting sustainable consumption and behaviour. This is clearly the case of textiles for the aircraft completion. It was noticed that there is almost no academic research on textiles applied in the aeronautic industry, especially on what regards refurbishment, completion and its ecological aspects, what led to a need to research information not only in academic publication but also through a wide number of companies and white-papers in order to understand the development and disposal of textile material in the aviation industry.

2.2 Product Lifecycle Management (PLM)

UNEP [14] conceptualised PLM as tool permitting to achieve sustainable development and study the ecological impact of product throughout their lifecycle. PLM vision has been adopted by the eco-design to improve the conceptualisation of the new product and their relative processes. PLM was developed as a business activity of managing, in the most effective way, a company's products all the way across their lifecycles; from the very first idea for a product all the way through until it's retired and disposed of [16]. It is considered, by Abramovici and Sieg [17], to be the conversion of a combination of a multitude of acronyms: Product Data Management (PDM), Collaborative Product development (cPDM), Collaborative Product Commerce (CPC), Product Knowledge Management, etc.

PLM provides benefits throughout the product lifecycle (see Table 1). The main concept behind it is how to integrate people, processes, business systems and information in an efficient manner [18]. For Stark [16] examples include getting products to market faster in the Beginning-of-Life, providing better support for their use during the Middle-of-Life, and managing their End-of-Life better.

Table 1. Benefits provided by PLM implementation in companies [16]

Area	Benefit
Financial performance	increase revenue with earlier market introduction; reduce product development costs
Time Reduction	reduce project overrun time; reduce engineering change time
Quality Improvement	reduce manufacturing process defects; reduce the number of returns; reduce the number of customer complaints
Business Improvement	increase the innovation rate; increase the part reuse factor; increase product traceability; ensure 100% configuration conformity

On the other hand, Schuh et al. [19] states that, besides its clear advantages, PLM has serious limitation as the difficulty of implementing PLM in some industries due to its high complexity, what tends to lead to a very specific focus in particular aspects of it (such as for instance the supply chain), without the necessary holistic approach to the whole life-cycle and its underlying processes.

On an environmental perspective, with particular interest in the completion industry, PLM will play a key role in addressing all these positive and negative issues because it provides the opportunity to get control of products across their lifecycles. The problems it addresses, and the ideas for their solution, aren't new. Over the years, population growth, lack of disposal sites, and scarce natural resources have led to all sorts of reduction, reutilisation, recycling and recovery programs.

2.3 Research Gap

Research regarding ecologically concerned textiles is not available in the visited literature, especially those regarding its whole lifecycle and supply chain. We believe that it is, on one hand, due to privacy issue, and on the other, due to a known lack of interest in this line of textile products, also seen as superfluous by many (see case study later). This paper was built from this literature gap and criticism, the absence of interaction between the researched methodologies and the textile industry, for their potential to add interesting insights to each other.

The Product-Service Systems (PSS) [20] and the Systemic Design [21] propose to switch the production-consumption activities into a production-consumption system which would reduce the effects of all stages of life cycle throughout the whole supply chain. Thus, the relationship between supplier and buyer would not end with the moment of purchase, but perpetuates over time [22]. Within this scenario, PLM's five main phases: Imagine, Define, Realise, Use/Support, and Retire/Dispose [16], can then be used to assist the development team as it is supposed to manage a well-structured and valuable product portfolio. By doing so, it can help maximizing project's financial return, managing and providing control and visibility over products throughout the lifecycle, as well as feedback about products from customers, product & field engineers and the market, above all, enabling collaborative work between supply chain partners and customers, thus unifying the whole concept behind sustainable development.

In order to guide the empirical part of this study, we employed a clear and objective approach that takes into account three aspects: the literature on traditional development of products in aviation, the development of green products using PLM-based methodologies and the existing literature available on aviation.

First, the literature about the development of products is immense and focuses on the different existing approaches to the development of new products but Literature on aviation eco-design is quite limited. It provides a broad overview of the history, current situation and forecasts of the aviation industry as a whole, also evidencing a great level of concern with the industries' carbon emissions, not ignoring its environmental and social impacts. It does, oppositely, completely disregards the development and improvements being implemented by the industry, only providing forecasts of what is being intended, especially when considering green completion.

This analysis then suggests the importance of the combinations of the missing factors examined in the literature review: a comparison between traditional and environmental development of products using the supply chain viewpoint as a strategic differential; a combination of the theoretical and practical aspects of the development process; and the study of the state-of-the-art of the development of green completion, aiming to also involve the supply chain, the final consumers and local communities.

3 Methodology

3.1 Methodological Approach

To better respond to the gaps found during the literature review it was decided to develop a case study [23] as it is the preferred methodology when studying in-depth a contemporary problem. This was considered the best alternative to deal with different sorts of evidence: visits, interviews, artefacts, and observations.

During the literature review, in order to evaluate the current situation of the matter researched, many data about companies and manufacturers have been found. Such material was considered complementary to the theoretical information gathered. Considering companies environmental management, governments increasing concern regarding pollution and ecological disturbances, as well as the particular way used by each company to develop their products, the companies were scanned and highlighted. Thus, to properly assess the priorities to be analysed in the case study it was decided to develop a comparing, broader, conceptual framework using the best practices of the methodologies discussed during the literature review.

3.2 Designing the Case Study

The case study was executed into the North-American context for a period of six months. Ten Canadian and U.S. companies were chosen for a first screening according to their proximity to the Green Aircraft Completion subject. From them, one, named in this paper as 'the Company' due to privacy issues, was chosen for being the most suitable for the research, for providing a broader view of the whole supply chain and, finally, for being a highly environmentally forwarded business. Indeed, the Company not only deals with refurbishment and completion activities, but also with the production of new aircrafts and the development of both products through partnerships with companies around the globe. This company has adapted an environmental focus which shapes the future of its technological innovations. Environmental challenges are therefore being addressed by the Company from a global perspective using a four pillars approach (see table 1).

Table 2. Environmental focus of the studied organisation

Organisation	Environmental pillars	
The Company	Technology	New aircraft designs, new lightweight materials, new engine advances
	Operations	Improved operational practices, more efficient flight procedures, weight reduction measures
	Infrastructure	More efficient air traffic management and airport infrastructure
	Economic measures	Consistency in addressing and assessing noise and emissions within the industry, incentives supportive of environmental sustainability

The case study focuses on the completion function of the Company in general and, specifically, on the use of textile materials for internal completion of the aircraft. Completion function is crucial for the Company because it permits to personalise products in function of customers' needs. The completion team establishes a strong relationship with them to identify their requirements and adding more value to the final product. The Company estimates that a customized aircraft could increase it value by 50 to 100 million dollars. Textile materials could also add value to the aircraft. The company propose several types of textile products for aircraft walls, carpets, seats and sofas. These textiles have different characteristics, such as resistance, safety issues, cleaning characteristics, composition (natural sources), among others.

During our visits, three main representatives of the company were interviewed: two engineers (the Interior Completions Manager – ICM and the Interior Completion Engineer – ICE) and a designer in charge of stylist and sales of the completion centre (DSSCC). These participants were chosen either for their connection to the completion as a department (ICM), for the contact with suppliers (ICE) or for being the link between the company and the final consumer (DSSCC), as well as for their academic backgrounds.

These three participants provided us interesting insights of the product lifecycle for textile materials and the actual efforts to include the green perspective into aircraft completion. For instance, they enable to identify the different phases of the textile lifecycle for aircraft completion (production, transportation, setting up, completion, dismantling and disposal or recycling) and the organisations involved for each phase (see the right hand-side of the Figure 1).

4 Results

4.1 Green Initiatives

Empirical evidence highlights that the Company has included the ecological perspective into its strategies for ensuring its "neutral emission commitment". In its 2011 Market forecast, the Company claims that it environmental focus was based on building on a strong track record of technological innovation and, in addition, it has formally committed to a future of carbon-neutral growth and increased environmental sustainability. These statements, during the visit were proved to be true, but the Company's greatest concern is the fuel consumption of the aircrafts. As the consumption is directly related to the weight of the aircraft, development companies and suppliers are more concerned with decreasing the weight of the airplane parts, than the composition or production techniques. This disregards the intense usage of highly pollutant composites in the aircraft structure, and a minimal concern with different development techniques on the used fabrics and textiles components (which represent around 1% of the total weight).

In addition, it is interesting to highlight that the social aspects of the Company and its ecologically forwarded initiatives are also visible throughout its mission. One of them is to enable and motivate its workers to buy and sells carbon credits during their trips with the company's aircrafts; the company also encourages its employees to suggest environmental improvements through projects, which might be implemented. Being then a company interested in the well-being and environmental development not only of its consumers but also its personnel.

On what regards the development of green products in the aircraft's industry, it is clear that there is an entrance gap in which the conceptual framework can be inserted and from where the eco-development can grow and expand, initially using few suppliers and eventually growing, constantly ensuring the participation of the final consumer in the development as an essential stakeholder. Indeed, the company has established a strict control for choosing suppliers and materials that could consolidate its strategic goals. Suppliers and their products are screened by an external consultancy company to guarantee aviation authority certification and product quality. Due to carbon neutral commitment of the aviation industry, most of the suppliers seem to be interested in supplying green products but actual efforts are limited. The company also focuses on the consumer's vision. The customer becomes an important stakeholder of the aircraft design process and its participation for defining ecological initiative is crucial for ensuring product profitability.

As the company holds an ISO1400, it has a great concern with the disposal of its trims and leftovers. However, this concern only regards the company if the remains are created within the company's propriety. In order to guarantee the accordance to the ISO rules, the company hires the disposal services of a third party. Therefore, the Company is not directly connected to the disposal or aware of its destination and eventual uses.

Table 3. General Green Aircraft Completion (GAC) topics discussed during the interviews

Topic	Points discussed	Answer similarities	Parallel with eco-design and PLM perspectives	Highlights
Demand	Number of GAC per year; price difference; offer of colours, materials, textures, etc.	None of the interviewees believe there is an interest coming from consumers to acquire GAC in their planes	It is in this matter that the framework could provide important improvement measures as it aims to use the final consumer as an asset of the development, thus creating a product consumer-oriented	Lack of interest from consumers
Consumer's acceptance	Sales manager believe the main problem for consumers to accept GAC in their jets is the fact that they don't consider it an improvement in their completion, they consider it a poor/no value adding investment	In order to satisfy the company's neutral carbon emission commitment, they say that the Company try as much as possible to convince costumer of the qualities and improvements offered by this line of products	With the creation of a product that answers to consumer-oriented criteria the level of acceptance and persuasion should raise as a response to a product oriented to those who actually need to be convinced of its quality, advantages and features	Doubts about the quality of GAC products have to discussed with clients and final consumers
Disposal	Recycling processes by for this sort of materials; What happens with the trims of the upholstery which is not used for the refurbishing; how can the 3 main sorts of materials used in a completion (leathers, carpets, wood and natural fibres) be reused or recycled	The company uses a third-party to dispose the left-over material, however all the interviewees agree that, due to the high-end characteristic of the materials they are ordered by quantity, an amount very close to the actual need, what, in the end, leaves few leftovers to be sent to this third-party partner	Essential aspect of the eco-development the disposal gains a new level of importance and its characteristics change as the supplier will have to consider its recyclability or 'compostability' and the producer will aim to provide end-of-life services	Possibility of a new system for the disposed material internally in the company
Importance of green completion in aviation as a whole	How GAC is better for aviation: through the decrease of the aircraft's total weight; by the reduction of waste produced; through the diminution of the use and emission of chemicals; better marketing; decrease the company's footprint; reduce carbon emission; etc.	For the interviewees (specially the completion manager) percentage of weight GAC accounts for is minimal, however it still represents an improvement in the aircraft as a whole	When dealing with the framework, the importance of every feature in the aircrafts raises size and the responsibilities are shared, therefore, even if representing one per cent of the total weight of the aircraft, it can increases the environmental value of the aircraft as a whole	It does not account for great changes in aviation as a whole but is an improvement nevertheless. In addition, textiles are in direct contact with costumers, what can in future be an important element of as customers become more aware and demanding
Usage of textile left-overs in different projects	Start a handicraft atelier or cooperative within the company's community	Once again the interviewees were not very faithful on the possibility of implementing some activity which would use the left-over materials	The completion manager believes this might be a possibility in some of the plants which already have programmed with the local community	Investment in projects within the companies' community can contribute to its targets connected to sustainability

4.2 Eco-Design for the Aircraft Completion

In order to better identify and discuss the results of the interviews, the Table 3 was organized highlighting the similarities on the interviewees' arguments, the main points discussed. According to this table, the interest of the industry and practicality of the conceptual framework are in harmony as they exist in the same level. However, it also led to an important initial finding: the lack of interest coming from the final user towards green completion. Even though, there is a strong trend towards this practice and that suppliers are constantly increasing the availability of ecologically sound product, its request and acceptance is minimum, reaching only 2% of the requests (mainly by environmental companies or young trend followers).

Since development risks are shared between the company and its suppliers, they are already working together and dealing with the environmental problems, as summarized in Figure 1. However, so far they do not fully satisfy the whole cycle of PLM as it does not yet integrate completely the end-of-life stages of the development. On the other hand, the company's suppliers had been working mainly with two concepts when dealing with textiles: its decompostability and production (to ensure recyclability and rapidly renewal - produced of an organic source and be 100% decomposed within a 10-year or shorter cycle).

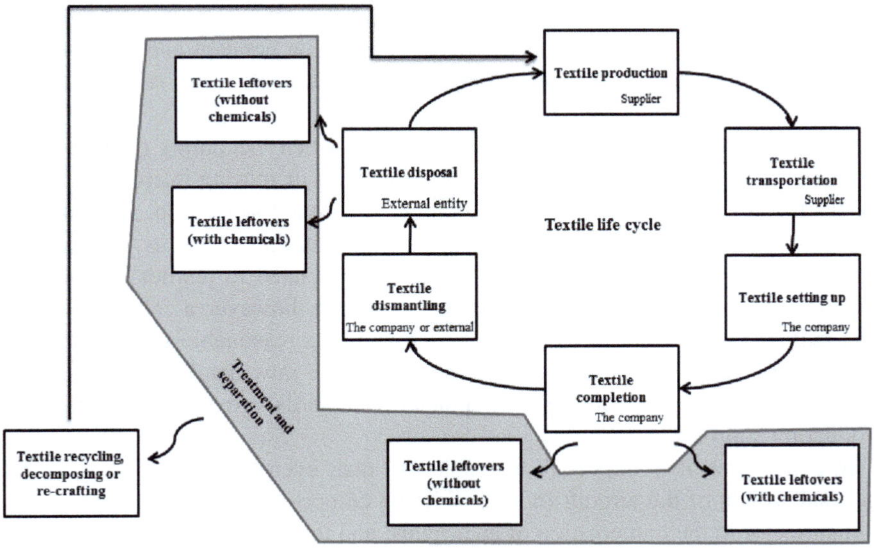

Fig. 1. Ideal PLM cycle for textiles used in the completion process

Regarding this matter, Lee et al. [24] highlights that the ideal PLM approach should be able to manage inspections and maintenance records throughout the product life spam, but these elements are not included so far in the model.

5 Conclusions

Aiming to decrease their carbon footprints, adapt to regulations or to lean towards a neutral carbon emission industry, the aviation industry is investing largely in the improvement of a large number of aspects in its assembly, one of them being the use of ecologically sustainable textiles. Even though the aeronautic industry is currently one of the biggest pollutants worldwide, its concern in becoming green is mainly a response to directives and environmental regulations than an answer to consumer's interests and demands.

Elaborated from the need to better understand and to identify the development and ecologic requirements of the aeronautic industry this research was developed to understand the use of fabrics in the aeronautic industry and possible applicable improvements. Thusly the presented article served to provide an initial idea of what was being considered 'eco' in Aviation, what could be done for it to be more ecologically forwarded and the main ecological objectives of the industry, as well as its consumer's behaviour.

Quality is not yet associated to GAC in this sector as the consumers tend to demand opulence rather than sustainability. Consumers played a very important role in the quest for the use and implementation of ecologic methodologies and products in the aviation industry, even though they seem to be working as a barrier to the introductions and diffusion of the green aircraft completion concept and fundaments, the industry believes that will change once they become an active stakeholder of the process.

The most important aspect seen for the industry when 'becoming green' is directed to a need to emit less carbon dioxide. Along with an increasing interest coming from the textile suppliers to produce more ecologic solutions for aviation, not only regarding weight (and fuel consumption) but also the materials used, its recyclability or clean disposal. Most of the problems currently associated to textiles used inside the aircraft have a chemical and highly pollutant source, however a solution or suitable alternatives do not seem to have yet been found in a reasonable price and in accordance to the supply and demand expectative. But the raw material or the fabrics before the finishing phase are leaning gradually towards 'greener' development and production approaches.

In conclusion, it is important to emphasise that, even though representing 1% of the total weight of the aircraft (not considering composites), textiles represent an important factor in the composition of an airplane and the fact that it is being thought off as another recyclable and not disposable part of it should mean a shift in the perception of its growing importance in the development of the plane as a whole. Especially when considering the fact that this industry is the biggest adopter of PLM [24], and that PLM represents an important production shift for aviation and can be a key asset towards a more sustainable industry.

References

1. A.T.A.G., Facts and figures. ATAG, Air Transport Action Group, Geneva – Switzerland (2012)
2. McCollum, D., Gould, G., Greene, D.: Greenhouse Gas Emissions from Aviation and Marine Transportation: Mitigation Potential and Policies. In: Change, P.C.o.G.C (Ed.), California - U.S.A., p. 56 (2009)
3. Keynes, J.M.: Characteristics of the airline industry. In: The Airline Industry: Challenges in the 21st Century, pp. 13–44. Springer, Heidelberg (2009)
4. GreenAviation, Humans need to fly. Green Aviation International Ltd. (2011)
5. Egri, C., Ralston, D.: Corporate responsibility: A review of international management research from 1998 to 2007. Journal of International Management 14, 319–339 (2008)
6. Darnall, N., Henriques, I., Sadorsky, P.: Do environmental management systems improve business performance in an international setting? Journal of International Management 14, 364–376 (2008)
7. Riopel, D., Chouinard, M., Marcotte, S., Aït-Kadi, D.: Ingénierie et gestion de la logistique inverse. Hermès – Lavoisier, Paris – France (2011)
8. Pigosso, D.C.A., Zanette, E.T., Filho, A.G., Ometto, A.R., Rozenfeld, H.: Ecodesign methods focused on remanufacturing. J. Clean. Prod. 18, 21–31 (2010)
9. Rozenfeld, H., Forcellini, F., Amaral, D., Toledo, J., Silva, S., Alliprandini, D., Scalice, R.: Gestão de desenvolvimento de produtos: uma referência para a melhoria do processo. Saraiva, Sao Paulo – Brazil (2006)
10. Dewulf, W., Willems, B., Duflou, J.: Estimating the environmental profile of early design concepts. Innovation in Life Cycle Engineering and Sustainable Development, 321–334 (2006)
11. Morelli, N.: Product-service systems: a perspective shift for designers. Design Studies 24, 73–99 (2003)
12. Vezzoli, C., Manzini, E.: Design for environmental sustainability. Springer, London (2009)
13. Dexter, H.B.: Development of Textile Reinforced Composites for Aircraft Structures. In: 4th International Symposium for Textile Composites Kyoto Institute of Technology, Kyoto, Japan (1998)
14. Suarez, J.A., Buttitta, C., Flanagan, G., DeSilva, T., Egensteiner, W., Bruno, J., Mahon, J., Rutkowski, C., Collins, R., Fidnarckis, R., Clarke, S., Michel, R.: Novel composites for wings and fuselageapplications: textile Reinforced Composites and Design Guidelines. NASA contractor report, Hampton, United States of America (1996)
15. U.N.E.P., Lifecycle management: How business uses it to decrease footprint, create opportunities and make values chain more sustainable. White paper (2009), Consulted from: http://www.unep.fr/shared/publications/pdf/DTIx1208xPA-LifeCycleApproach-Howbusinessusesit.pdf
16. Stark, J.: Product Lifecycle Management: 21st century paradigm product realisation. Springer, London (2011)
17. Abramovici, M., Sieg, O.: Status and development of product lifecycle management systems. In: Proceedings of IPPD 2002. Wroclaw, Poland (2002)
18. Zheng, L., McMahon, C., Li, L., Ding, L., Jamshidi, J.: Key characteristics management in product lifecycle management: a survey of methodologies and practices. Proceedings of the Institution of Mechanical Engineers, Part B: Journal of Engineering Manufacture 222, 989–1008 (2008)

19. Morelli, N.: Product-service systems, a perspective shift for designers: A case study: the design of a telecentre. Des. Stud. 24, 73–99 (2003)
20. Schuh, G., Rozenfeld, H., Assmus, D., Zancul, E.: Process oriented framework to support PLM implementation. Computers in Industry 59, 210–218 (2007)
21. Bistagnino, L.: Systemic Design: designing the productive and environmental sustainability. Slow Food Editore, Torino – Italy (2011)
22. Manzini, E., Vezzoli, C.: Product-Service Systems and Sustainability: Opportunities for sustainable solutions. UNEP, Paris - France, p. 18 (2003)
23. Yin, R.: Case Study Research: Design and Methods. Sage, United States of America (2009)
24. Lee, S., Ma, Y., Thimm, G., Verstraeten, J.: Product lifecycle management in aviation maintenance, repair and overhaul. Computers in Industry 59, 296–303 (2007)

Decomposition Analysis Resolution Process (DAR) of Systems Engineering Applied to Development of Countermeasure on Leakage of Engine Head-Gasket

Satoshi Ohkawa[1], Hidekazu Nishimura[2], and Yoshiaki Ohkami[2]

[1] SDM Lab., Graduate School of System Design and Management, Keio University, Japan
[2] Graduate School of System Design and Management, Keio University, Japan
ohkawakmt@gmail.com

Abstract. This paper reviews a countermeasure development of leakage from coolant seals of head-gaskets in a diesel engine applying the Decomposition Analysis and Resolution Process (DAR). We can find complexity arising from some causes of leakage even in a simple square-ring rubber seal. The major causes are (1) large displacement around a head-gasket generated by the combustion, (2) seal distortion at a high compression, (3) seal rubber degradation induced by coolant microorganism deterioration, (4) uncontrolled seal production and (5) unsuitable rubber composition. Through our DAR, we can resolve the complexity of the leakage and can clarify all the cause positions and their relationships. We can confirm that an improved silicone rubber seal, which has a higher fatigue strength, an excellent acid-resistance and a uniform contact property, is the correct resolution. This paper also shows development of a hydrogenated nitrile rubber seal as a permanent measure, which can extend the Middle of Life (MOL) of Product Lifecycle Management (PLM) of the industrial diesel engine production.

Keywords: DAR, PLM, MOL, engine, head-gasket, coolant, seal, leakage.

1 Introduction

The purpose of this paper is to describe importance of the DAR for resolving a problem of parts: head-gasket (antifreeze) coolant leakage. This paper also shows that the Middle of Life (MOL) of Product Lifecycle Management (PLM) [1] for an industrial diesel engine can be extended by a permanent measure, which is derived from the countermeasure development. A long-term MOL is required, because an industrial diesel engine is generally manufactured during 10-20 years like capital goods [2]. Extending the MOL of the engine production period leads to increase revenue, to reduce all the engine related costs and to obtain customers confidence.

Although a coolant seal is only a simple square-ring part, the leakage process has complexity. Fig. 1a) shows the configuration of the engine head-gasket and coolant seals. Coolant and oil galleries both in a cylinder block and cylinder heads are connected with each seal of the head-gasket. The head-gasket is a steel plane plate. The previous coolant seals adopted the same silicone rubber: Rubber-P, as those of oil

S. Fukuda et al. (Eds.): PLM 2014, IFIP AICT 442, pp. 181–192, 2014.

seals. Within a year from its production, newly developed high-output diesel engines caused the coolant leakage from the head-gasket in the field. After dismantling all cylinder heads, unusual seal cracks were found as shown in Fig. 1b). Although the oil seals adapt the same Rubber-P, and have similar dimensions as those of coolant seals, the oil seals never caused oil leakage or a crack in the field. The cause of coolant leakage seemed to have complexity. Therefore, we have conducted thorough DAR for analyzing the complexity and for confirming appropriateness of the countermeasure.

Technical reports on this issue have published by the author as a transaction paper [3] of the Society of Automotive Engineers (SAE) and as a paper of Japanese technical magazine [4].

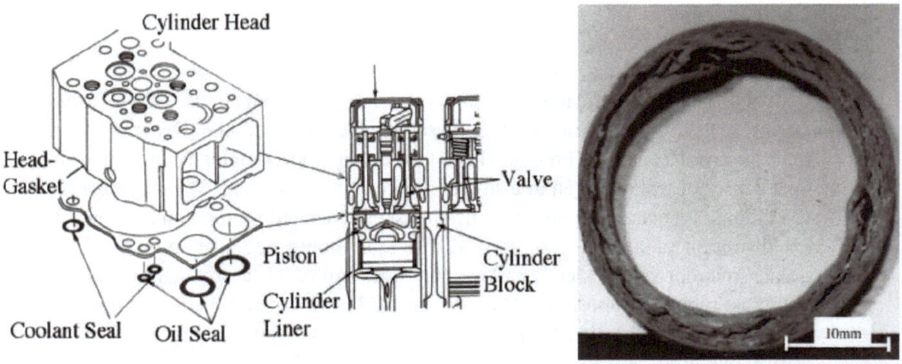

a) Schema of Engine Head-Gasket and Coolant Seals b) Unusual Coolant Seal Crack

Fig. 1. Schema of Engine Head-gasket and Unusual Crack of Coolant Seal (Ohkawa S. et al. 1994 [4])

2 Approved baseline Requirements, CONOPS and DAR

Approved baseline requirements of the countermeasure are to develop a replaceable improved seal as soon as possible and to clarify the leakage mechanism. For agile repairing in the field, the engine-side modification like a cylinder head change was prohibited.

The CONOPSs of the coolant seal are to use from -50ºC to +110ºC, to have oil-compatibility and to keep 10,000 hours seal life. The CONOPSs limit rubber type only to a silicone rubber.

Fig. 2 summarizes all the critical issues of the coolant leakage as the DAR [5]. Every critical issue is discussed in the following sections from the top of the system to the bottom of material composition.

2.1 Methodology

To clarify the complexity of the unusual seal crack mechanism, we have conducted thorough investigations using following methodologies:

- Measurement of engine head-gasket temperature and distortion
- Observation/measurement of seal mechanical behavior and the seal rubber strength and microscopic observation of seal fracture
- Chemical analysis and microscopic observation of deteriorated seal rubber and deteriorated coolant both on biological and chemical effects
- Process check of seal manufacturer (quality control)
- Chemical and instrumental analyses of rubber composition.

All the methodologies are consistent with all the critical issues and heading titles from 2.2 to 2.6.

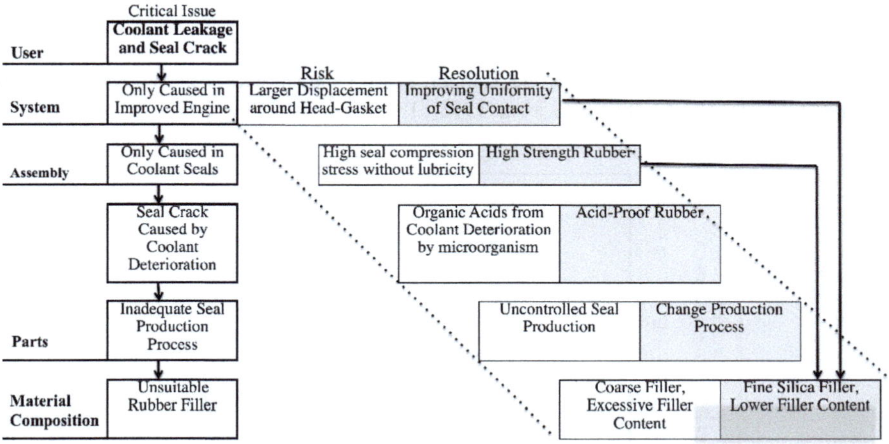

Fig. 2. Critical Issues of Coolant Seal Leakage

2.2 Leakage only Caused in High-Output Engine

It became clear that a larger distortion generates around the head-gasket by increasing engine output. Since the head-gasket temperature is preserved below the same 120 ºC as that of the previous engine at coolant seal positions, the seal temperature has no relation with the leakage.

Therefore, we investigated uniformity of seal contact at a higher compression condition. Fig. 3 shows a visual observation of seal contact condition on the engine cylinder block. A front square-ring seal: previous Rubber-P, generates air-bubbles on the square-ring surface because of seal distortion. Contrarily, a rear square-ring seal; candidate Rubber-S, does not cause air-bubble.

Fig. 4 shows upper limits of compression ratio up to the generation of unequal pressure distribution. The beginning of seal distortion was measured using a pressure measurement film. The Rubber-P has the lowest property on contact uniformity and causes distortion only at 28% compression. Since the seal compression range in the head-gasket is 20-40%, the Rubber-P and a Rubber-A (COTS) seals cause unequal contact in the head-gasket.

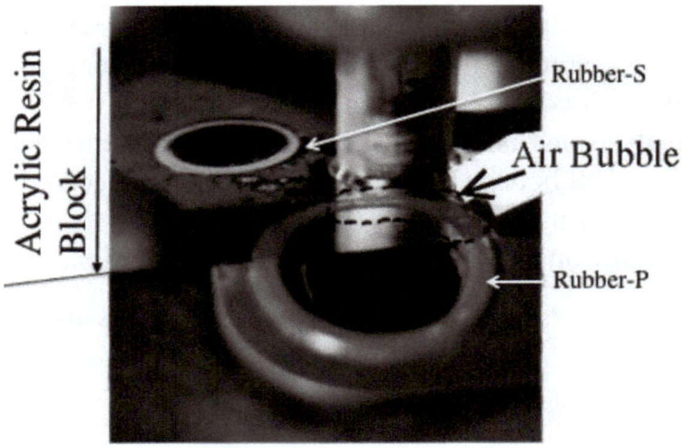

Fig. 3. Visual Observation of Silicone Rubber Seals Contact with Acrylic Resign Block: Simulated Cylinder Head (Ohkawa S. et al. 1993[4])

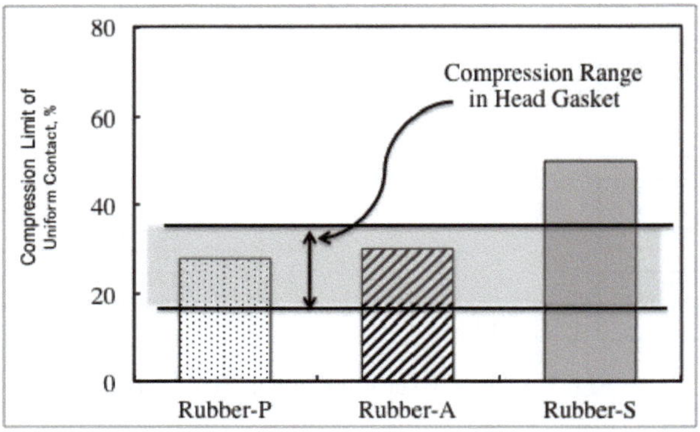

Fig. 4. Upper Limit of Compression Ratio for Keeping Uniform Contact

The candidate Rubber-S can keep uniformity of seal contact in the head-gasket.

2.3 Leakage Caused Only in Coolant Seal

In our measurement, a viscosity of a typical ethylene-glycol coolant is only 3-4% value of that of an engine oil at 80ºC. Therefore a coolant can easily leak from even in a narrow gap and has no lubricity. On the other hand, an engine oil can not pass through the gap and can lubricate seal surface. Lack of seal surface lubrication induces a high compression stress [6].

From our seal fracture observation, we clarified that the unusual seal crack is fatigue damage. Fig. 5 shows the results of seal compression fracture test on the Rubber-P, candidate Rubber-S and COTS's silicone rubbers (A to D). It is clear that the silica filler content has a relationship with the facture strength. Although the Rubber-Ps show lower facture compression ratios, the values are higher than the maximum compression ratio in the head-gasket. Therefore a seal fatigue test was planned as a verification test to reproduce the unusual crack. The Rubber-S and COTS Rubber-A show the highest fracture strength.

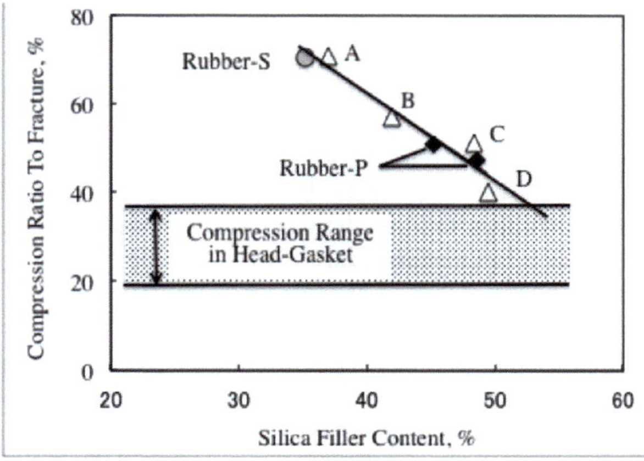

Fig. 5. Compression Fracture Test Results (ts: Seal thickness, tg: Head-gasket thickness) (Ohkawa S. et al. 1993[3]

2.4 Seal Crack Caused by Coolant Deterioration

In an emergency-use generator engine, the previous Rubber-P caused coolant leak and cracks after only 18 operating hours. The generator engine had long-term stoppages. The used coolant smelled of mold; microorganism. The rubber polymer was severely decomposed by organic acids. Table 1 shows the analytical data of used coolants in the generator engine and in a reference marine engine. Despite of short operating hours, the generator coolant contains excessive organic acids comparing with that of the marine engine. From these facts, it can be estimated that the organic acids were generated from a microbial degradation of ethylene-glycol. Tsuneki T. [7] indicates that bacteria propagate in a ethylene-glycol solution under 20% concentration. The concentration of the ethylene-glycol coolant in the generator engine was 15% by poor maintenance.

By immersion tests in an organic acid solution, we found that the candidate Rubber-S, which adopted an acid-proof polymer, shows lower degradation than that of Rubber-P. Dynamic sealing tests of acid immersed seals are planned for a verification test.

Table 1. Chemical Analysis of Organic Acids in Used Coolants

	Emergency Generator Engine 18 hrs (2 years)	Marine Engine 2,100 hrs (2 years)
Total Acid Ion, ppm	607	109

2.5 Inadequate Seal Production Process

Since a manufacturing failure of seals was also considered as a cause of unusual seal cracks, we conducted process check to the seal manufacturer. We found that the seals were manufactured in the 3rd sub-contractor and they did not conduct any quality control on rubber cure conditions (Fig. 6). Therefore, an engine quality assurance division soon changed this situation and ordered the seal supplier to conduct strict quality control of the seal production.

Despite the serious potential risk on previous seal quality, we could not find any seal quality problem in all the stock seals. The estimated potential risk is to cause the crack by lowering the rubber fatigue strength. We came to the conclusion that the process is not the cause of the unusual crack.

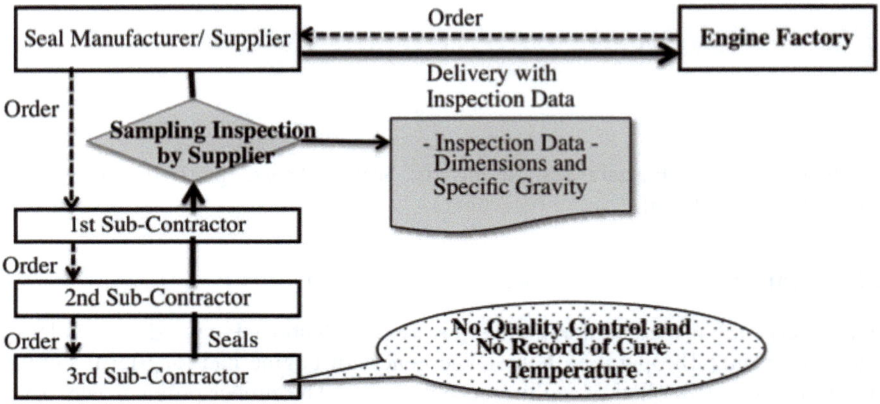

Fig. 6. Previous Seal Production Process

2.6 Unsuitable Rubber Filler

Fig. 7 shows filler photos of scanning electron microscope (SEM) in the silicone rubbers. The non-uniform contact property of the Rubber-P can be generated by a coarse filler. On the contrary, a fine silica filler of the Rubber-S can keep uniform contact as mentioned above. In addition, the Rubber-A, which contains 30% coarse filler has the highest fracture strength but causes distortion at a low compression. This indicates that the coarse filler mainly causes seal distortion and a high filler content causes strength reduction.

Therefore, it became clear that a quality control on both the filler size and the filler content are important for preventing coolant leakage.

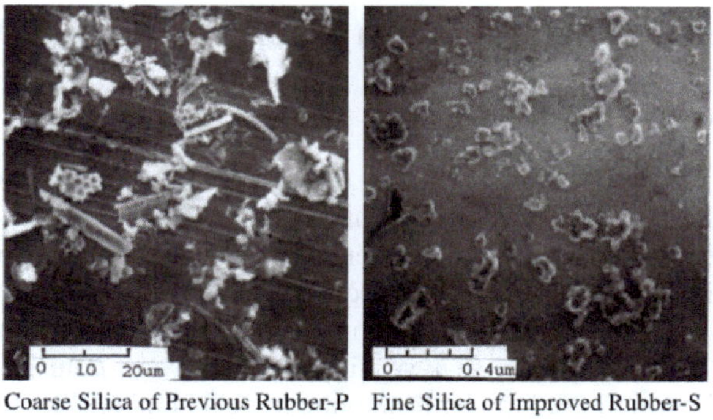

Fig. 7. SEM Photos of Fillers in Rubber-P and Rubber-S (Ohkawa S. et al. 1993 [3])

2.7 Estimated Mechanism of Coolant Leakage by DAR

Through the DAR, we can estimate the coolant leakage mechanism as shown in Fig. 8. The leakage initially occurs the seal distortion, which is caused by coarse filler, and then the seal crack generates by rubber compression fatigue from excessive filler content. Since the type and the content of silicone filler in the silicone rubbers mainly affect the coolant leakage, adoption of the candidate Rubber-S, which contains smaller volume of fine silica filler, becomes the best suitable resolution for improvement. The rubber degradation by the microorganism is a rare case. Other possible crack cause is by the lack of quality control of the seal production. Although a common leakage cause is seal permanent deformation, there is no permanent deformation problem of the coolant seal in the field.

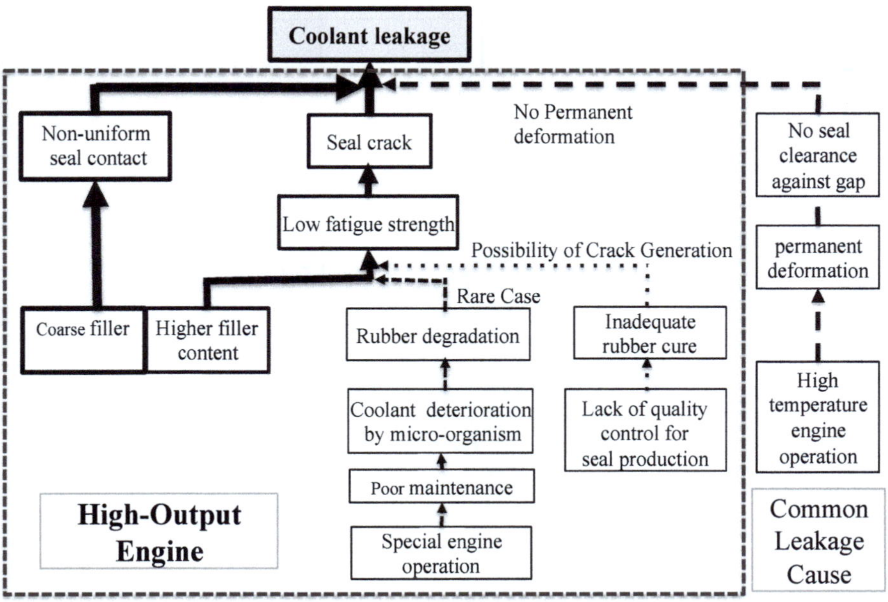

Fig. 8. Estimated Mechanism of Coolant Leakage

3 Verification And Validation Resolution Process (Var)

3.1 Methodology of VAR

Table 2 shows verification and validation (hatched parts) of the improved Rubber-S. The test methodologies are head-gasket unit tests by a newly developed tester, engine bench tests and field survey of modified engines, which adopted improved Rubber-S seals. Since agile countermeasure was requested, thorough validation: field survey, was conducted as soon as the verification was completed. To simulate the actual engine coolant seal conditions, seal verification tests were conducted by the head-gasket seal tester, which used the high-output engine assembly. Fig. 9 shows the tester schema. A cyclic hydraulic pressure is applied to a piston cavity. The cyclic pressure, which simulates engine firing, re-produces the largest displacement around the head-gasket in the engine tests. To adjust seal compression ratios, some head-gaskets having different thickness are used in every test.

Table 2. Verification and Validation Plan

No.	Critical Issues	Items for Countermeasure	Verification and Validation(hatched cell) Plan		
			Head Gasket Seal Tester	Engine Bench Test	Countermeasure and Field Survey
1	Only caused in improved engine	Improving uniformity of seal		✓	✓
2	Only caused in coolant seals	Adoption of high strength rubber	✓	✓	✓
3	Seal crack caused by coolant deterioration	Acid-proof rubber (Rubber-S)	✓	✓	✓
4	Inadequate seal production process	Change of seal production process			✓
5	Unsuitable rubber composition	Fine silica filler (Rubber-S)	✓	✓	

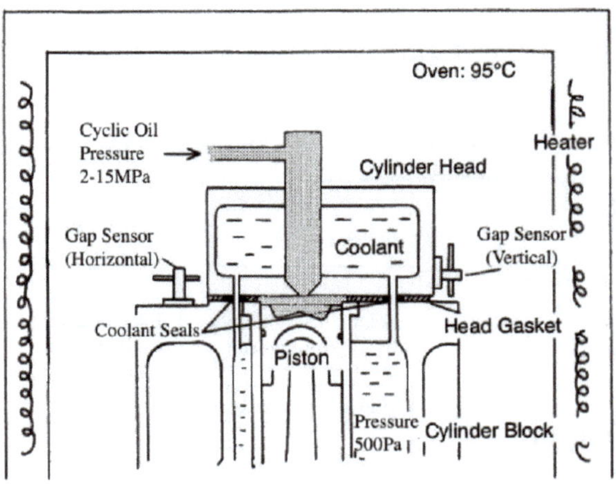

Fig. 9. Head-Gasket Seal Tester (S. Ohkawa et al. 1993 [3])

3.2 Verification Using Head-Gasket Seal Tester

Fatigue Test of Seals to Verify Seal Strength of Improved RUBBER-S. The unusual seal crack could be reproduced by this tester as shown in Fig. 10. The fatigue curves, drawn by the crack generation, were also obtained. The previous Rubber-P and the improved Rubber-S clearly shows different fatigue lives. The fatigue life of the Rubber-S is 10 times longer than that of the Rubber-P at the same compression.

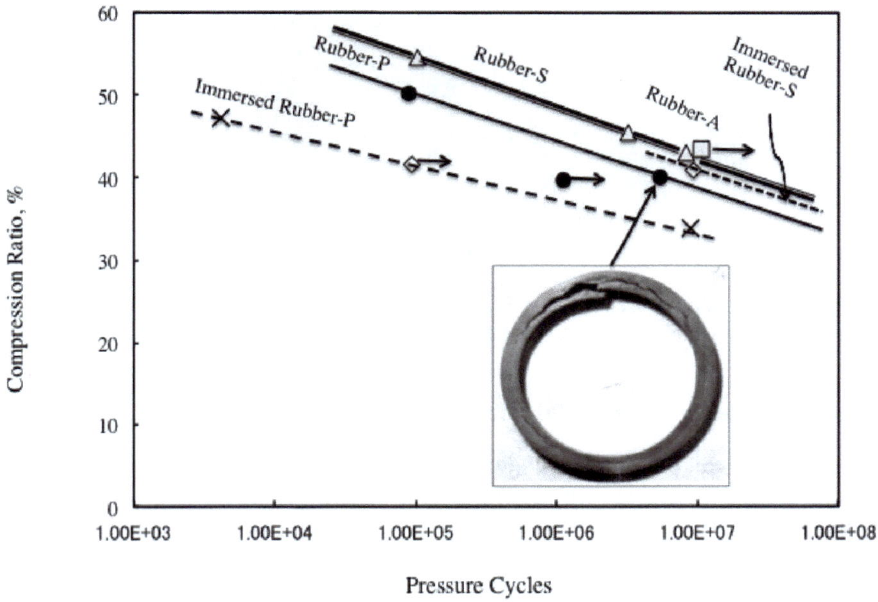

Fig. 10. Seal Fatigue Curves Obtained by Head-Gasket Seal Tester

Fatigue Test of Acid Immersed Seals to Verify Effectiveness of Acid-Resistant Polymer. After both Rubber-P and Rubber-S were immersed in an organic acid solution, the fatigue tests were conducted (Fig.10). The Rubber-P shows a large drop of decrease of the fatigue life. The fatigue life reduction of the immersed Rubber-S is small due to adoption of the acid-proof polymer. Therefore the fatigue life of the Rubber-S is about 100 times longer than that of the Rubber-P.

3.3 Verification Engine Bench Tests

Engine Tests to Verify the Improved Rubber-S Durability. By the 19 times engine tests from 50 - 2,000 hours, the previous Rubber-P seal have caused 5 times coolant leakages in the 10 tests at 100 - 2,000 hours, but the improved Rubber-S seals have never experienced leakage and crack in the 9 times tests from 50 - 2,000 hours. From the compression set data, it was confirmed that the Rubber-S has enough reserve to keep 10,000 hours life.

Verification of Coolant Leakage Mechanism on Seal Distortion. On the bench engine test of the Rubber-P, we found that the coolant often leaks without seal cracking. To verify the leakage mechanism, the engine head was frozen with dry ice as soon as the leakage was detected. The cylinder head was removed and the leak was inspected using an ultraviolet rays as shown in Fig. 11. The leakage is detected clearly by the ultraviolet rays. The leaked seal did not generate any crack. Therefore it was proved that a leakage factor of the Rubber-P is unequal pressure distribution.

Fig. 11. Detected Coolant Leakage on Engine Bench Test Right: Detected Coolant (arrow mark) Left: Leaked Seal (arrow mark) (S. Ohkawa et al. 1993 [3])

3.4 Countermeasure and Field Survey

The coolant seals of all kinds of engine were exchanged to the improved Rubber-S seal. All the engines, which caused coolant leakage in the field, were dismantled and were exchanged to the improved seals. As the results, the field coolant leakage problem is not reported in the field.

4 Permanent Measure of Coolant Seal

All the high-output engines should be used for a longer period of time than U.S. final off-road emission regulation of 2014 [8] as shown in Fig.12. In order to obtain the longer MOL of the high-output engine production, the engine should withstand 5 times improvements/modifications for the emission regulations. Therefore a high-output engine, which attached exhaust emission reduction devices, was tested. As the result, the improved Rubber-S reduced the compression ratio down to 0%, and we have developed a further improved hydrogenated nitrile rubber [9, 10]: Rubber-T seal according to the DAR and the VAR as a permanent measure. Although a hydrogenated nitrile rubber shows shorter life than that of a silicone rubber in the air, we have found that a Rubber-T in the coolant extends its life 10 times longer than that of the Rubber-S. The timing of the permanent measure adoption is in the beginning of the MOL.

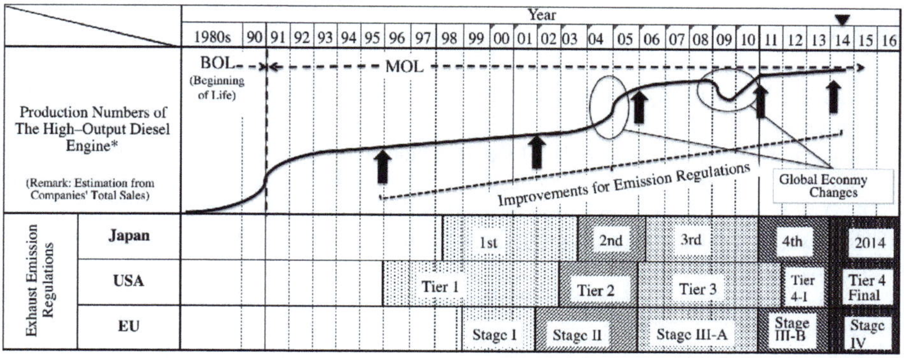

Fig. 12. MOL of the high output diesel engine and world off-road exhaust emission regulations [8]

Table 3 shows accelerated high temperature test results using the head-gasket seal tester. The previous Rubber-P seal caused cracks. Although the improved Rubber-S seal did not cause any crack, its compression ratio reduced down to less than a lower limit. The Rubber-T could endure in this test and showed the highest compression ratio. However, we had to change the lower temperature range of the CONOPS from -50ºC to -30ºC because of poor low temperature property of the Rubber-T. We kept the Rubber-S as a specialized seal for cold weather regions.

Table 3. High Temperature (155℃) Test Results using Head-Gasket Seal Tester (Ohkawa S. et al. 1994 [4])

	Rubber-P	Rubber-S	Rubber-T	Remark
Test Cycles	4.7×10^6	1.2×10^7		
Compression Ratio, %	1 (NG)	<1 (NG)	10 (OK)	Lower Limit: 5
Seal Condition			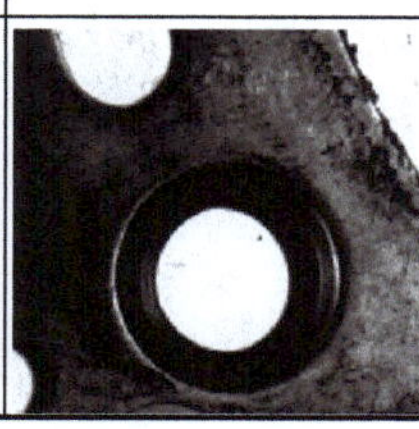	

5 Conclusion

Using the DAR of the system engineering, we can resolve the complexity composed of major causes and can clarify all the cause positions and relationships by analyzing the countermeasure of coolant leakage. We can confirm that the improved Rubber-S is the most appropriate countermeasure resolution and the Rubber-T is the best permanent measure resolution for the off-road emission regulations. The permanent measure resolution can extend the MOL of the high-output engine production and can withstand 5 times improvements/modifications for the emission regulations. Also we can recognize an importance to conduct thorough DAR even in the LCI and further down to the material composition.

References

1. Stark, J.: Product Lifecycle Management: 21st Century Paradigm for Product Realization. Springer, Berlin (2011)
2. Saaksvuori, A., Immonen: Product Lifecycle Management, p. 4. Springer, Berlin (2002)
3. Ohkawa, S., Iwakata, K., Kawashima, Y.: Coolant Seal Elastomer for Diesel Engine Head Gasket. Society of Automotive Engineers (SAE) Paper 932375 (1993)
4. Ohkawa, S., Iwakata, K.: Coolant Seal for Engine Head Gasket. Valqua Review 38(2), 1–9 (1994)
5. Forsberg, K., et al.: Visualizing Project Management, pp. 240–246. Wiley, New York (2005)
6. Kaneko, H.: The Applied Rubber– Physics - 20 Lectures. Sanseido, p. 127 (1978)
7. Tsuneki, T., Motizuki, F.: Corrosion and Examples of Countermeasure, pp. 359–363. Kaibundo, Tokyo (1985)
8. Japan Society of Tribology, Lubrication of Industrial Vehicles, Yokendo, Tokyo, p. 10 (2012)
9. Keller, R.W.: FKM and HSN Material for Diesel Engine Cylinder Liner Seals. SAE Paper 910967 (1991)
10. Farinella, B.H., et al.: Long-Term Serviceability of Elastomers in Modern Engine Coolants. American Society of Testing Materials STP 1335, 142–180 (1999)

Introduction to a Model for Life Cycle Optimisation of Industrial Equipment

Daniele Cerri[1], Valerio Contaldo[1], Marco Taisch[1], Sergio Terzi[2]

[1] Politecnico di Milano, Department of Management, Economics and Industrial Engineering
Piazza Leonardo da Vinci, 20133, Milano, Italy
daniele.cerri@polimi.it valerio.contaldo@mail.polimi.it
marco.taisch@polimi.it
[2] Università degli Studi di Bergamo, Department of Engineering, Viale Marconi 5, 24044, Dalmine (Bergamo), Italy
sergio.terzi@unibg.it

Abstract. In this evolving context, to pursue a Life Cycle approach, realizing green products / system at the less cost of ownership, can be a strategic key for Advanced Countries companies to compete and survive in the global market. Aim of this paper is to present a model for Life Cycle Optimisation, considering both economic and environmental dimensions. At the end of the paper a first applica- tion of this model will be presented.

Keywords: Life Cycle Assessment, LCA, Life Cycle Costing, LCC, Life Cycle Optimisation, Life Cycle Simulation.

1 Introduction

During the last years, the operating context of global companies has been dramatically changed due to several reasons, often mutually related.

Firstly, globalization pushed the industrial companies of Advanced Countries (European, American and Japanese) to face the ones of emerging countries (BRICS) in a "flat" world [1], where global competitors start from the same line. In this context, Advanced Countries companies are forced to face the low cost pressure of emerging countries.

At the same time, also the customers' behaviour changed. Global customers demand for personalized solutions [2] at the lowest total cost of ownership, more reliable systems, less polluting equipment, less consuming plants / facilities, greener products, etc.

Environmental consciousness is more and more felt, also due to the imposition of regulations and normative. In fact, national and international institutions are strictly regulating the environment, like Kyoto protocol or the tons of EU Direc- tives.

In this evolving context, to pursue a life cycle approach, considering both economic and environmental dimensions, and realizing green products / systems at the less cost of ownership, can be a strategic key for Advanced Countries compa- nies to compete and survive in the global market.

Designers and system engineers are the main involved actors to pursue a life cycle approach, due to their influence on product life cycle costs and environmental

S. Fukuda et al. (Eds.): PLM 2014, IFIP AICT 442, pp. 193–200, 2014.

impacts. Different studies like [3], [4], [5] and [6] estimates how designers, during the design phase, fix about 65%-85% of the total costs. The same consideration, about product life cycle environmental impacts, is reported in [7].

The aim of this paper is to propose a first model to support designers and system engineers in the creation and identification of best life cycle oriented concept. The paper is so organized: in Section 2 a brief state of the art of Life Cycle Optimisation will be presented. In Section 3 the conceptual framework of the model will be explained, while in Section 4 first results are reported. Finally, in the Section 5, conclusions will end the paper.

2 State of the Art

To pursue a Life Cycle approach, in terms of costs and environmental impacts, it is necessary to study and depth two methodologies: Life Cycle Costing (LCC) and Life Cycle Assessment (LCA). Both the methodologies are well known in literature, being developed by the 60s.

Life Cycle Costs are described as "cradle-to-grave" costs summarized as an economic model of evaluating alternatives for equipment and projects [8]. [9] defined LCC as the total cost of acquiring and utilizing a system over its entire life span, in other words LCC is the total cost of procurement and ownership. More detailed definitions are proposed by [10] – Life cycle cost is the total cost of ownership of machinery and equipment, including its cost of acquisition, operation, maintenance, conversion, and/or decommission – and [11] – LCC are summations of cost estimates from inception to disposal for both equipment and projects as determined by an analytical study and estimate of total costs experienced in annual time increments during the project life with consideration for the time value of money.

Life Cycle Assessment is described as a technique to assess environmental impacts associated with all the stages of a product's life from-cradle-to-grave [12]. [13] instead stated LCA as a methodological framework for estimating and assessing the environmental impacts attributable to the life cycle of a product.

The LCA process is a systematic, phased approach and consists of four components: goal definition and scoping, inventory analysis, impact assessment and interpretation. This process is described in the standard "ISO 14040 Environmental Management - Life Cycle Assessment - Principles and Framework" [14].

The above described methodologies allow only an evaluation / estimation of costs and environmental impacts along the product lifecycle, comparing few alternatives. Therefore, to be more effective in the product development, it is necessary to explore a huge number of alternatives – if it is possible all the ones –, in order to find the best solution. The idea is to apply something similar to Set Based Concurrent Engineering (SBCE), exploring and testing several concepts in parallel. The results of the alternatives are presented in different forms like trade-off curves, checklist, etc., in order to support the decision [15] [16].

To pursue this approach, LCC and LCA methodologies are not sufficient. Therefore it is necessary to support them, applying methods and techniques so as to explore the different alternatives, evaluating costs, environmental impacts and technical performances along the whole life cycle.

Analysing the literature, two main areas are identified: optimisation and simulation. Within our group, two works try to explore these areas. In [17], 79 contributions from the last 15 years (39 related to LCC methodology and 40 related to LCA methodology) are analysed, in order to find which types of optimisation method are used and if costs and environmental impacts were together optimised, or at least both considered. In [18] authors analysed the state of the so called Life Cycle Simulation (LCS). 43 contributions from the last 15 years are analysed, in order to classify the field.

From these analyses some gaps / discordances came to light. In literature, optimisation methods are applied in few contributions, while the majority used simply the life cycle methodologies for an evaluation, using in some cases software (mainly applied to LCA). Moreover, using a multi-objective optimisation there is not a unique solution, obviously, but a set of optimal solutions, due to the trade-offs incurred between the different objectives. Therefore the decision makers have to choose the best solution for their customers within a set of optimal solutions.

In simulation area, instead, there are several discordances in the definition of lifecycle boundaries and which should be the inputs and outputs of the simulation. Moreover, different tools are used to perform a simulation of the product life cycle, from spread-sheets, mathematical software, and programming languages to specialist computational packages. Found these gaps / discordances, the objective of the paper is to define a model for Life Cycle Optimisation, considering the literature analysed. In the next section the Conceptual Framework behind Life Cycle Optimisation model will be presented.

3 Conceptual Framework of Life Cycle Optimisation

In the light of the deficiencies / discordances shown in the previous section, the aim of the paper is to show the develop of an integrated, structured and robust model, completed by methods and tools, to support designers and system engineering during the concept phase, in order to create and identify the optimal life cycle oriented concept, in terms of economic and environmental dimensions. The conceptual framework of the model is reported in this Section (see Fig. 1).

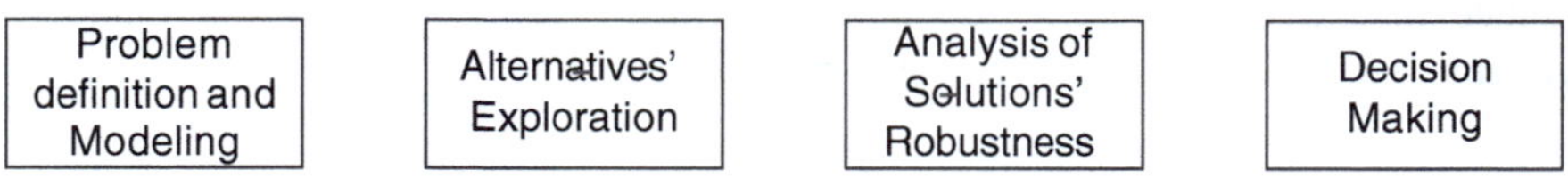

Fig. 1. Conceptual Framework of Life Cycle Optimisation model

The framework is composed of four main blocks. In the first one, *"Problem definition and Modeling"*, the problem will be defined, in order to determine which costs, environmental impacts and performances take into account. This allows understanding which data and information are necessary to model the problem. The output of this block is all the possible concepts.

In the second one, *"Alternatives' Exploration"*, methods or techniques will be applied, in order to narrow the initial number of concepts, selecting a set of optimal ones. As previously discussed, the most used optimisation method is genetic algorithm, that is very fitting with multi-objective problems, like the minimization of costs and environmental impacts generated along the product life cycle.

In the third one, *"Analysis of Solutions' Robustness"*, methods or techniques will be used, in order to evaluate the robustness of the solutions changing some parameters. Analysing the literature, a method like Life Cycle Simulation or Sensitivity Analysis could be useful for the purpose. The output will be a set of optimal and robust concepts.

Finally, in the last block, *"Decision Making"*, methods or techniques will be applied, in order to choose the more appropriate life cycle oriented concept for the customers. Having a multi-objective problem, the output at the end of the third block will be a set of optimal concepts. To weight the objectives, satisfying customer's requirements and needs, allow finding the more appropriate life cycle oriented concept for itself. Methods like Multi-Criteria Decision Making (MCDM) are effective to return the best concept.

In the next Section a first application of the model will be shown.

4 First Application

The conceptual framework developed and described in the previous section has been applied to a real case study: we have performed the Life Cycle Optimisation of an engine assembly line.

A. Problem Definition

In particular, we have considered a fraction of the line composed by five stations. As shown in Fig.2, each station forming the analysed assembly line has been actually provided with a set of available alternatives: we have considered 16 station alternatives (2 alternatives for the first station, 4 alternatives for the second station, and so on, where "aut", "saut" and "man" stand for automatic, semi-automatic and manual, respectively), but the set of available alternatives to be evaluated during the optimisation can be easily extended. Taking up the definitions of *Cartesian product* and *cardinality*, since the line is formed by 5 stations and the number of alternatives each station is provided with is known, the number of available line alternatives can be evaluated as follows:

$$|S_1 \times S_2 \times S_3 \times S_4 \times S_5| = |2 \times 4 \times 2 \times 4 \times 4| = 256$$

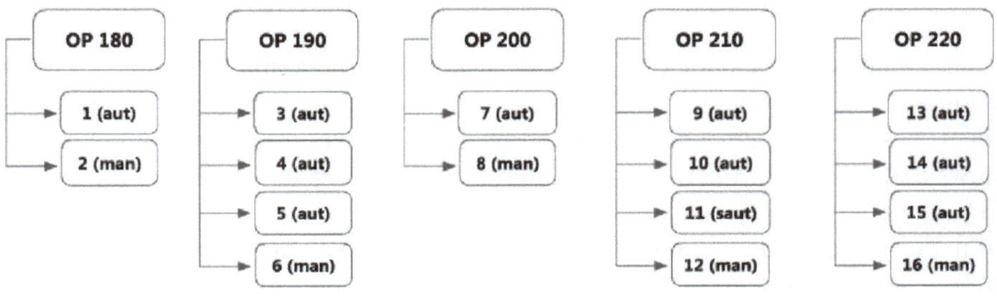

Fig. 2. Station code and corresponding station alternatives

B. Alternatives' Exploration and Analysis of Solutions' Robustness

The aim of the analysis has been finding the optimal line configuration or line alternative. From an economical point of view, the "optimal" line configuration is the one that minimizes life cycle costs; therefore we have performed a single-objective optimisation:

$$\min LCC_{tot} = \min \sum_{s=1}^{5} LCC_s$$

where LCCs represents the lifecycle cost of s-th station that forms the line analysed. Being a single-objective problem, in this particular case the *Decision Mak- ing* block has not been implemented. Moreover, *Alternatives' Exploration* and *Analysis of Solutions' Robustness* have been realized in one single step, combining simulation and optimisation. In particular, in the proposed model the life cycle behaviour of a station is simulated by means of Discrete Event Simulation (DES). Therefore, allowing the user to replicate the station model an arbitrary number of times, it is possible to create the model of any industrial equipment (e.g. an assembly line or a production line) and simulate its costs and environmental impacts from a life cycle perspective. Optimisation by means of genetic algorithm is also implemented to identify the values of each station's input parameters which permit to minimize a suitable objective function: processing simulation outputs in an iterative way, the optimisation method eventually finds the "optimal" line configuration. Adopting simulation-based optimisation allows to get significant information during the early design stages: simulation permits to cover the whole life cycle perspective, while optimisation ensures that final results — in terms of input parameters — denote the selection of best elements (with regard to some criteria specified in the objective function) from some set of available alternatives. The implementation of this model is realized taking advantage of the potentialities provided by MATLAB® and Simulink®: in such a way it is possible to make use of one single software tool — Simulink is integrated with MATLAB — to com- bine optimisation with simulation.

In Fig. 3 the outward appearance of the "station block" is presented, i.e. the Simulink block that implements the simulation of the life cycle behaviour of a manufacturing plant's station. In the right side of the block it is possible to recog- nize the output ports that allow extracting the signals generated within the block. In such a way these output signals are made available for visualization and post- processing analysis. Particular attention has been paid to realize an in depth mod- elling of the station's maintainability, since at equipment and system level main- tainability has a great influence on reliability and availability; it is thus an im- portant parameter in the optimisation of availability and life cycle costs.

C. Results

In Fig. 4 results are presented. The first graph of Fig. 4 shows the convergence of the genetic algorithm to the optimal solution; the algorithm stopped according to the

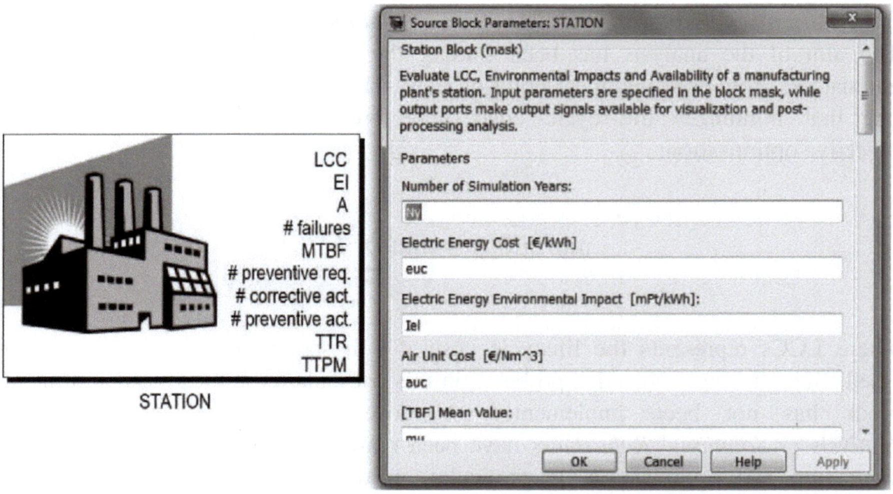

Fig. 3. Station block and its mask: SimEvents® block of industrial equipment's station.

selected stopping condition, i.e. on the basis of the evaluation of the weighted average relative change in the fitness function value. The second graph provides the vector entries of the individual with the best fitness function value, i.e. the number of the selected alternative of each station forming the line. Even if these results refer to the optimal solution from an economical perspective, the value of its environmental impacts has been kept under control, so as to satisfy environmental requirements too.

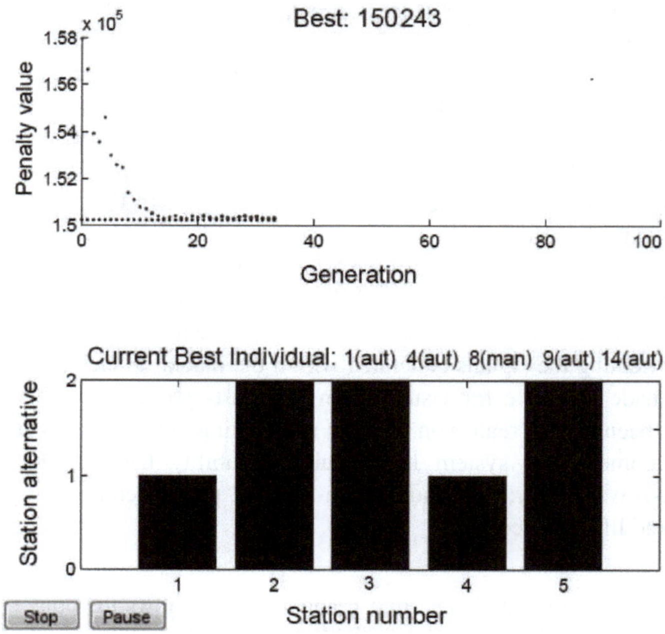

Fig. 4. Results

Results have been validated and the model has been regarded as an interesting support tool during the early stages of the detailed design.

5 Conclusions

In this paper the aim is to present a model for Life Cycle Optimisation of indus- trial equipment. Introduction (Section 1) points out the context where Advanced Countries companies operate, highlighting how to pursue a Life Cycle approach can be a strategic key to compete and survive in the global market. Moreover, the main actors involved in Life Cycle approach are identified in designers and system engineers.

Analysing state of the art about life cycle methodologies (Section 2), two main methodologies are identified: Life Cycle Costing and Life Cycle Assessment. However, these methodologies are not sufficient to explore a huge numbers of alternatives. The idea is to apply something similar Set Based Concurrent Engi- neering, exploring different concepts in parallel. To pursue this approach it is nec- essary to support LCC and LCA, applying methods and techniques so as to ex- plore the different alternatives, evaluating costs, environmental impacts and tech- nical performances along the whole life cycle. In literature two main areas are identified: optimisation and simulation. Analysing these areas, gaps/discordances came out.

In the light of these deficiencies, a conceptual framework of Life Cycle Opti- misation model is presented (Section 3), and in Section 4 a first application is shown.

Designers and system engineers of the first application have appreciated this model, because it allows them a fast exploration of a huge number of concepts.

However, further analyses are necessary to improve the proposed model. First of all, a more accurate literature analysis is necessary, in order to define all the existing methods / techniques, to classify them and to select the more appropriate one for the model.

Finally, a new application cases will be searched, to test in depth and to make the most general possible the model proposed. In particular, a comparison between an application case in B2B (Business-to-business) market and another one in B2C (Business-to-customer) market could be really interesting, in order to understand if a different approach in Life Cycle Optimisation exists.

Acknowledgments. This work was partly funded by the European Commission through the Linked Design Project (FoF-ICT-2011.7.4: Digital factories: Manufacturing design and product lifecycle management, http://www.linkeddesign.eu/). The authors wish to acknowledge their gratitude and appreciation to the rest of the project partners for their contributions during the development of various ideas and concepts presented in this paper.

References

1. Friedman, T.: The World Is Flat: A Brief History of the Twenty-First Century. Farrar, Straus and Giroux (2005)
2. McCarthy, I.P.: Special issue editorial: the what, why and how of mass customization. Production Planning & Control 25(4) (2004)
3. Munro, A.S.: Let's roast engineering sacred cows. Machine Design 67(3) (1995)
4. Romm, J.J.: Lean and Clean Management: How to Boost Profits and Productivity by Reducing Pollution. Kodansha International, New York (1994)
5. Dowlatshahi, S.: The role of logistics in concurrent engineering. Journal of Production Economics 44 (1996)
6. Blanchard, B.S.: Design To Cost, Life-Cycle Cost. In: 1991 Tutorial Notes Annual Reliability and Maintainability Symposium, available from Evans Associates, 804 Vickers Avenue, Durham, NC 27701 (1991)
7. Rebitzer, G., Ekvall, T., Frischknecht, R., Hunkeler, D., Norris, G., Rydberg, T., Schmidt, W.P., Suh, S., Weidema, B.P., Pennington, D.W.: Life cycle assessment Part 1: Framework, goal and scope definition, inventory analysis, and applications. Environment International 30(5) (2004)
8. Barringer, H.P.: A Life Cycle Cost Summary. In: ICOMS (2003)
9. Elmakis, D., Lisnianski, A.: Life cycle cost analysis: Actual problem in industrial management. Journal of Business Economics and Management 7, 5–8 (2006)
10. Society of Automotive Engineers (SAE) (1999): Reliability and Maintainability: Guideline for Manufacturing Machinery and Equipment. M-110.2, Warrendale, PA (1999)
11. Landers, R.R.: Product Assurance Dictionary. Marlton Publishers, 169 Vista Drive, Marlton, NJ 08053 (1996)
12. Scientific Applications International Corporation (SAIC): "Life Cycle Assessment: Principles and Practice". Technical Report (2006)
13. Rebitzer, G., Ekvall, T., Frischknecht, R., Hunkeler, D., Norris, G., Rydberg, T., Schmidt, W.P., Suh, S., Weidema, B.P., Pennington, D.W.: Life cycle assessment Part 1: Framework, goal and scope definition, inventory analysis, and applications. Environment International 30(5) (2004)
14. ISO (1997): ISO 14040 Environmental Management - Life Cycle Assessment - Principles and Framework
15. Sobek, D.K., Ward, A.C., Liker, J.K.: Toyota's Principles of Set - Based Concurrent Engineering. Sloan Management Review 40 (1999)
16. Ward, A.C., Shook, J.K., Sobek, D.K.: Lean Product and Process Development. The Lean Enterprise Institute, Cambridge, Massachusetts (2007)
17. Cerri, D., Taisch, M., Terzi, S.: Multi-Objective Optimization of Product Life-Cycle Costs and Environmental Impacts. In: Emmanouilidis, C., Taisch, M., Kiritsis, D. (eds.) Advances in Production Management Systems. IFIP AICT, vol. 397, pp. 391–396. Springer, Heidelberg (2013)
18. Garetti, M., Rosa, P., Terzi, S.: Life Cycle Simulation for the design of Product–Service Systems. Computers in Industry 63 (2012)

Integration of Environmental Assessment in a PLM Context: A Case Study in Luxury Industry

Djamel Yousnadj[1], Guillaume Jouanne[2], Nicolas Maranzana[1], Frédéric Segonds[1], Carole Bouchard[1], and Améziane Aoussat[1]

[1] Arts et Metiers ParisTech, LCPI, 151 bd de l'Hôpital, 75013 Paris, France
{djamel.yousnadj,nicolas.maranzana,frederic.segonds, carole.bouchard, ameziane.aoussat}@ensam.eu
[2] EVEA, 35 rue de Crucy, 44000 Nantes, France
g.jouanne@evea-conseil.com

Abstract. Nowadays, the environment becomes a major issue in our society. It gives rise to regulations, market demand and stakeholder's pressure which are concerning companies. These latter have to reduce the negative impact of their new product by eco-design and adopting a continuous improvement for their existing product portfolio. To do so, environmental assessment system is needed. Life Cycle Assessment (LCA) is the most known and recognized. However, this method is complex, requires significant resources and a large amount of accurate data. We propose a methodology to connect a simplified LCA tool with PLM system and ERP to evaluate an entire product portfolio at any time. This will allow design teams to consider the environmental issues in early design phase and gives the companies a global vision of their product portfolio. This methodology is experimented with packaging products of luxury brand, using the Teamcenter PLM system and a Simplified LCA Tool.

Keywords: Simplified LCA, Product portfolio assessment, Eco-design, PLM.

1 Introduction

Nowadays, the environment becomes a major issue in our society [1-3]. Governments are key drivers for environmental and sustainable management practices. They may coerce actions trough regulations, and use fines and trade barriers. Companies have also to deal with Non-Governmental Organizations requirements, or risk a loss in their brand value and a negative impact on global marketing and production strategies [4]. But the central objective of a company to remain competitive is fulfilling customer needs, which are increasingly directed toward the social and environmental performance of a product [4]. These different stakeholders ask companies for environmental certificates such as ISO 14001 [5], FSC[1] while products have to be developed quicker since the market requests new ones frequently [4].

[1] *Forest Stewardship Council*: sustainable label for wood-based products, www.fsc.org

S. Fukuda et al. (Eds.): PLM 2014, IFIP AICT 442, pp. 201–212, 2014.

In this context companies have to develop not only competitive products but to make them also more respectful to the environment [6]. They have to reduce the negative impact of their new product by eco-design and adopting a continuous improvement for their existing product portfolio. To do so, environmental assessment system is needed and Life Cycle Assessment (LCA) is the most known and recognized. However, this method is complex, requires significant resources and large amount of accurate data. Numerous researches propose Simplified Life Cycle Assessment (SLCA) tools which streamline the data collection. This make it more usable at the early stages of design with reliable results [7-9]. When companies need to establish carbon footprint report, eco-labels on their products or engaging continuous improvement actions, they first need a reliable environmental assessment of the whole product portfolio. However, it still requires important resources and data for big companies' portfolio, even by using SLCA.

In this paper, we propose a methodology to connect a SLCA tool with PLM and ERP systems. This will help to evaluate the entire product portfolio (existing and developing product) of luxury industry at any time.

After this introduction, the second section presents a brief review on eco-design tools and environmental PLM Systems. Section 3 proposes a methodology to connect SLCA tool to PLM/ERP system. This proposal is experimented in section 4, and further works and perspectives will be presented in section 5.

2 From Eco-design Tool to Environmental PLM System

2.1 Eco-design Tools

Eco-design is a methodology for designing products and services, which considers in particular the reduction of their environmental impact throughout their complete lifecycle, "from cradle to grave", without compromising other criteria like function, quality, cost and appearance. Several eco-design approaches have been studied and many tools and methods exist [10-11]. However their industrial use is still limited [12]. Some classifications exist but we took Janin's one which identifies two main categories of eco-design tools: Environmental assessment ones, and improvement ones that help designers to find eco-design solutions [13]. In this paper, we will focus our study on the assessment tool that we will connect to PLM system. They enable the comparison of the existing products, or a product against a norm, a recommendation, or even legislation. They also allow the identification of the weakest points of the product to find a path towards improvement [10]. Two main categories may be distinguished: qualitative and quantitative assessment tool.

Qualitative Assessment Tools. These qualitative tools, such as checklist and guidelines/rules, are the easiest to use and are among the most prevalent tools in the industry, especially in SME. Checklist is a set of items used for quick assessing a product from the environmental perspective over its entire life cycle [10, 19, 20] as "are toxic materials used in the product?". Guidelines/rules can enhance the design process and ensure that the most important environmental issues and impacts are addressed. The most famous are the ten golden rules which are a highly generic guidelines adapted for product development process [16]. The enterprises can also develop more concrete and specific guidelines in relation to their own specific product development context [15]. These tools are developed particularly for the early stages of the product design. They can also be considered as "improvement tool" as they propose a way to reduce the environmental impact by focusing on one item [14]. However, challenge remains when trade-offs exists between different life cycle stages or different environment impact categories [14]. The proper use of these tools requires extensive experience and knowledge. Compared with quantitative tools, qualitative ones are more subjective.

Quantitative Assessment Tools. Many tools exist to evaluate the environmental impacts associated to product lifecycle but Life Cycle Assessment (LCA) is the most popular and recognized [2, 9]. It provides quantitative data on product environmental impact along its complete lifecycle: from the extraction and production of material to the end-of-life. Known as the most mature tool for eco-design [15], it has been formalized in the ISO series 14040 and implemented in various software tool [15]. LCA is divided into four phases: first, the goal and scope of the product assessment are defined as well as, the context, the boundaries and the environmental indicators. Then, Life Cycle Inventory (LCI) comprises the compilation and quantification of the input (energy, material) and output flows (emissions, wastes), for all the processes related to the lifecycle of the product under investigation. In the impact assessment phase, these flows are converted into ecological effects such as global warming potential, abiotic depletion, human toxicity and finally compared with the objective.

LCA represents an assessment and comparison tool for existing products [9, 13]. It assists decision-makers in industry by identifying opportunities for improving the environmental performance of a product and can also help governments and non-government organizations by the implementation of eco-labeling [6]. However, it is complex and requires expertise and it's also both time and resource consuming due the large amount of accurate data needed to perform it [7, 9]. We identified three LCA limits and some propositions to overcome them:

- **LCA is not applicable in the early stages of design**

Many existing tools based on LCA fail because they do not focus on design, but instead, they are set to a strategic management or a retrospective analysis of existing products [17]. A complete LCA can only be correctly used for a completely defined product where data about lifecycle are available and accurate. This data collection is also time-consuming. So LCA cannot be properly used in the early stages of design phases where many alternatives are studied and product lifecycle data are incomplete. To enable early application as well as to improve overall use of LCA within design, less complex and data demanding, Simplified Life Cycle Assessment (SLCA) have been developed [9, 13, 23]. The simplification is related to data reduction either by excluding a lifecycle stage (use or end of life) and/or by reducing the complexity of the Life Cycle Inventory [7]. Then, it could be a source of error if it is not well parameterized or used by non-experts. So SLCA lowers the level of consensus among the scientific community because reducing the data inputs increases the level of uncertainty [6]. However, some method exist to manage the data quality of the inventory such as Pedigree Matrices [25, 26] which allow an easy identification of the inventory weaknesses. It is then possible to improve its quality by directly working on these data. SLCA estimates the environmental impacts of design alternatives according to product characteristics such as the type of material or the weight. Thus, SLCA method reduces the time necessary to run the LCA [9, 24] and makes it usable in design process to evaluate different alternatives.

- **LCA do not lead to eco-designed solutions**

LCA needs expertise especially to define the scope of the study or the relevant environmental indicators, and review their reliability. Designers have some difficulties to interpret the environmental results and to identify the product improvement areas [22]. This can be due to the lack of correlation between the environmental impacts and the product designer parameters such as material or manufacturing process [23]. If designers cannot use the method or interpret its results, the product cannot be eco-designed. Thus, it's important to create tools for non-expert users. That will to provide indicators which help designer to identify what product characteristics are the source of an impact in order to lead to eco-designed solutions. Then, human oriented interface is recommended [6]. The result indicators should be structured and flexible in a way to obtain easily selective, relative, absolute and environmental information linked to product characteristics.

- **LCA is not adapted for a global corporate vision**

When companies need to establish carbon footprint report that includes its product, eco-labels on their products or engaging continuous improvement actions [24], they first need a reliable environmental assessment of the whole product portfolio. But, LCA is both time and resources consuming and thus not usable for global portfolio assessment. The central problem for sustainable business alignment is to analyze, to optimize and to communicate on product portfolio with the least effort [6]. It is then necessary to find a way to perform global environmental assessments with limited resources at an acceptable quality level [24]. The intelligent use of existing digital databases as PLM, ERP systems, design tools and a good supplier relationship may streamline the data collection to obtain explicit and tacit environmental knowledge [5, 13]. The table 1 compares LCA and SLCA on selected criteria.

Table 1. Comparative between LCA and SLCA

Criteria	LCA	SLCA
Usable in early design phases	-	+
Lead to eco-design solutions	-	+
Results reliability	+	0
Global portfolio assessment	-	0

SLCA seems to be a good compromise to overcome most of LCA limits. The main challenges are to reduce complexity of product and portfolio data collection (inputs) and the indicators comprehension (outputs), while maintaining the main features and accuracy of a complete LCA. Then, it is important to study:

- Inputs: what type of information is required and how this could be collected.
- Outputs: what kind of results should be produced to help designers and how to manage their accuracy?

One way to simplify data collection is to connect SLCA with design tool as CAD or PLM system where product characteristics are included. Connection with ERP will then provide a global vision of the product portfolio.

2.2 Connecting PLM to Environmental Assessment Tool

The results of industrial surveys identified CAD Geometric models as data reference, CAD, PLM and PDM systems as the most used tools during the design phase [9]. PLM is an approach in which processes are as important as data, or even more [25]. Thus, many authors agree that PLM is the key concept for the establishment of eco-design processes [4-6, 14, 27, 28]. The opportunity to influence a product's sustainable characteristics is prevalent in the design phase. The connection between PLM/CAD and sustainability might provide useful insights to a sustainable new product development approach [4]. This connection should be bi-directional [4, 23]. PLM supplies the necessary data for an LCA, which then ensures and evaluates the environmental character of a product. Different interoperability approaches have been studied to connect environmental with design tools. These can be defined following three distinct points of view [28]: integration, unification and federation. System structure will be easier to evolve on a federative way than on an integrative one, if one of the tools have to change [23]. This connection between environmental and design tools is one of the emerging challenges that design software companies, like Dassault Systèmes, have to face [29]. Here below are described existing software with their main functionalities and limits:

- **Module in CAD tool: Sustainability in Solidworks by Dassault Systèmes [29]**

It's an SLCA module integrated into CAD Solidworks. The user can choose the material and the main process so the tool will calculate environmental indicators. However, it's often criticized because of its low accuracy [16, 22]. Morbidoni et al. proved its weakness comparing its results with those of a specialized tool [8].

- **Information transfer PLM (SmarTeam) – Environmental tool (EIME) [3]**

Compared to CAD, various relevant information can be extracted and imported from PLM into LCA software (mass, material, process, location…) [9]. It's also flexible since PLM data transfer can be customized according to the product context. However, only few studies explain how to customize and formalize the necessary information for accurate LCA [23] and it doesn't include global reporting.

- **PLM / CAD / ERP / environment platform: Environmental Data Workbench**

It is an integrative platform based on central standard model that connects design (PLM, CAD), ERP and environmental tools [21, 29]. It is able to create global corporate report such as material compliance or carbon footprint as well as "product environmental profiles". However, the environmental data are decontextualized since the link between environmental results and design parameters is lost.

- **Knowledge transformation between design and environmental tool**

This solution proposed by Rio et al. [23] is a federative system with flexible data exchange (knowledge transformation) between design and environmental tools used during the design process. It also keeps the link between design and environmental parameters. However, the formalization of the necessary information for reliable evaluation has not been studied.

2.3 Existing Solutions Limits

A synthesis of existing solutions based on the criteria defined in paragraph 2.1. is presented in Table 2.

Table 2. Comparative between different existing solutions

Criteria/System	Solidworks Sustainability	Smarteam EIME	EDW	Knowledge Transformation
Usable in early design phase	+	+	+	+
Lead to eco-designed solutions	+	+	-	+
Results reliability	-	0	+	0
Global portfolio assessment	-	-	+	+

However none of these tools or methods gives a reliable and time efficient product portfolio assessment.

Existing models prove the relevance of connecting SLCA with PLM system for eco-design and product portfolio assessment when connected with ERP system. However, few studies discussed the customization of the PLM which take into account the reliability of results, which also have to be usable by designer to lead to eco-designed solutions. In the following, we propose a methodology to customize PLM and connect it with SLCA tool and ERP system for (1) An environmental assessment in the early stages of design process. (2) Meaningful results without weighting on product design time: this will lead to trade-offs between reliability of SLCA results and the information that the design team has to provide. (3) Ensure that environmental factors remains manageable and environmental potentials for a product can be identified and influenced early. (4) A time efficient product portfolio assessment and reporting.

3 Proposed Methodology and Architecture

In order to connect PLM with SLCA tools and ERP system, we propose a four steps methodology (Figure 1).

- **Planning**

According to the environmental strategy of the company, the objectives of the assessment are established such as carbon footprint reduction or product labeling. This will define the scope of the assessment, the relevant environmental indicators and their level of accuracy, as well as the methodology to calculate them. A preliminary analysis of existing database and tools containing product lifecycle information (transport, sales, markets…) is recommended. Applying a complete LCA on some products could help to determine the relevant lifecycle stages. The system operators (users, administrators…) and system development team are defined. According to the objectives and the available data, the assessment scope can consider a part of the product portfolio and limit the lifecycle stages included. This planning step is an important input of the system design.

- **Definition of required elements**

For reliable results without compromising product design time, the level of information required is defined. It has to limit the amount of additional data that designers provide. The indicators depend on the objective and strategy. The results must be structured in a way to be usable by designers and decision makers. Uncertainty indicators can be used for decision-making. These results have to be duplicated and stored in the PLM as report to avoid computing time for global assessment.

- **System specifications and development**

Once inputs and outputs are outlined, this step defines the functional and technical specifications of different parts, modules and interfaces of the PLM system.

- **Deployment of the eco-design**

Creation of the tool is not sufficient. Relevant KPI, involvement of all design team and adapting the design process are also important to lead to eco-design.
A synthesis of this methodology is presented in Figure 1.

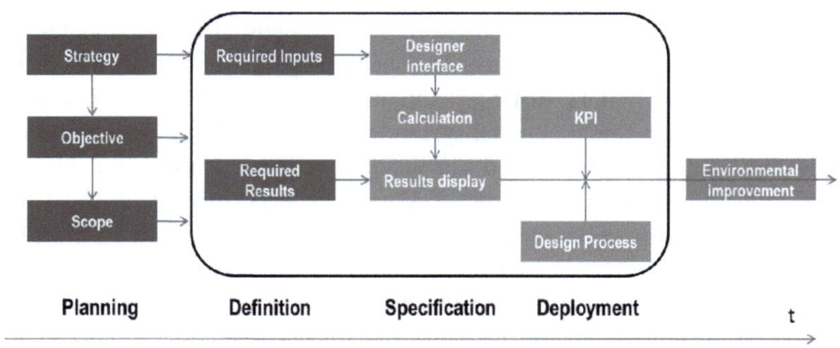

Fig. 1. Proposed methodology

The architecture resulting of the methodology deployment in an industrial luxury industry is an environmental assessment system able to deal with information already available in the PLM. We present it in the Figure 2. This architecture is based on three pillars: ERP, PLM and environmental expert tool. It can provide, thanks to SLCA module included in PLM, an environmental assessment at the early stages (filled arrow) or global assessment and reporting when connected with an ERP (empty arrow).

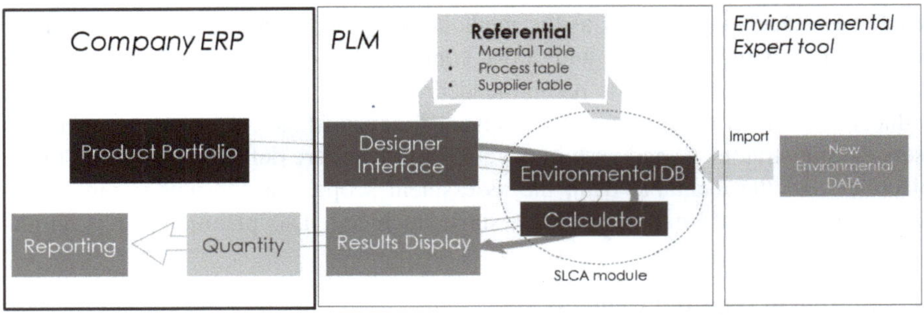

Fig. 2. Architecture to connect SLCA with PLM and ERP System

4 Case Study

The methodology, previously described has been deployed in the context of packaging development in a luxury brand. This company is implementing Teamcenter PLM system of Siemens and the SLCA is a part of it. It should be underlined that Siemens integrates for the first time environmental assessment in their PLM system. This method has been conducted until the specification phase (Figure 1).

4.1 Planning

First, the aim of this integration is determined according to company's strategy. This will help the company to achieve different goals such as: Allowing new product eco-design by providing "usable" and reliable environmental assessment results at the early stages of the design process; answering to a potential environmental labeling program in discussion in the French and European scope, carbon footprint calculation, material compliance (REACH, RoHS…) and allowing a global vision of product portfolio to enhance improvement actions; system operators (users, administrators…) and system development team are defined to consider user's needs as well as IT and environmental constrains. Three complete LCA have been performed on three products and show that packaging is the main contributor on the selected indicators and helped to choose the relevant lifecycle stages. Regarding the scope, the products portfolio covers all the samples, tests, gifts and sales products. Only the packaging is taken into account and the formula is not yet included. This is about 1.600 references and more than 12.000 different parts. The lifecycle stages covered by the assessment are: Material extraction, manufacturing process, transports and end-of-life. The use phase and conditioning are not included since the formula is not yet considered.

4.2 Definition of Required Elements

Some representative products are selected to run Life Cycle Assessment: typology, manufacturing technologies and suppliers. These analyses helped to define how the results should be presented to be usable. Besides, lifecycle inventories have been performed for each product to identify the environmental hotspot.

Required Results. The environmental indicators should be adapted to objectives that companies have to fulfill such as carbon footprint or product labeling. As consequence, the environmental assessment needs to be connected directly (or indirectly) to the ERP in order to link individual product impact with the sales quantities (information not available in the PLM). At least three different environmental indicators need to be calculated for the product labeling a*biotic depletion*, *water consumption* and *global warming potential*. This latter indicator must be calculated in two different ways: the first for the product environmental labeling and the second for carbon footprint. These results will help designers to find areas of improvement for eco-design. So, the interface needs to give a strong detail of the origin of the environmental impact: component, lifecycle stage and the most important sources of impacts as well as total results with uncertainty indicators for decision-making. It is semi-quantitative to avoid computing time and rely on Pedigree matrices [25-26].

Required Inputs for Relevant LCA. In order to define the relevant level of information and data collection required, we perform different studies. The company has chosen to create a specific SLCA tool to perform their studies and use it pending the PLM development. All these assessments allow drawing some rules and defining data that need to be taken into account in order to have a relevant result. These data, as material weight, was not already completely included in the PLM. Discussions in system development team leads to find the best way to integrate them without compromising data collection time, for example:

The Part Weight. The detailed weights were not capitalized by the design team while it is really important to evaluate environmental impact of manufactured parts. It has been added in the design interface for each element. This data could not be extracted automatically from other company's tools, so designer will enter it manually as CAD tools are not used internally.

Country Where the Part is Processed. Accurate evaluations need the electricity mix: The impact of producing 1 Kwh which varies according to the country. We decided to get it indirectly from "supplier reference table" where the country will be informed. So the evaluation will be more precise without any consequence on the designer interface where only plant name will be selected.

4.3 System Specifications and Development

According to the input/output and the objective, the functional and technical specifications of the system are created. Modules, interfaces, referential, databases, information flow, calculation algorithm and data management are specified in order to collect all relevant data to perform SLCA at different stages of design phase. Validation is necessary on a case study before the launching for software development. The experimentation is currently in this phase. Once the software is ready it will have to be tested before the integration in real work environment.

5 Conclusion and Perspectives

This article proposes a methodology and an associated architecture to connect PLM, SLCA and ERP in order to eco-design new products and get easily a product portfolio assessment. The necessary data for accurate results have been identified through several LCA studies on representative products. A qualitative indicator on reliability results has been set. The system results keep the link between the environmental impact and their sources from products characteristics in order to identify improvement areas. This methodology has been conducted as part of a project to implement Teamcenter PLM system in a luxury company for packaging products. This is a first time Siemens integrates environmental assessment in their system. It's currently in the specification phase and will be soon integrated. Other environmental tool will be considered as packaging recyclability indicators and specific guidelines-checklist. A further work could compare the results of the proposed evaluation system with complete LCA in order to find improvements. This methodology could also be enriched by including new functionalities to improve data collection by connecting CAD tools, web platform to collect data from suppliers and different design tools.

References

1. Van Hemel, C., Cramer, J.: Barriers and stimuli for ecodesign in SMEs. Journal of Cleaner Production 10, 439–453 (2002)
2. Le Pochat, S., Bertoluci, G., Froelich, D.: Integrating ecodesign by conducting changes in SMEs. Journal of Cleaner Production 15(7), 671–680 (2007)
3. Mathieux, F., Brissaud, D., Zwolinski, P.: Product ecodesign and materials: current status and future prospects. In: 1st International seminar on Society & Materials, pp. 6–7 (March 2007)
4. Gmelin, H., Seuring, S.: Determinants of a sustainable new product development. Journal of Cleaner Production 69, 1–9 (2014)
5. International Organization for Standardization, "ISO 14001 - Environmental management systems: Requirements with guidance for use" (2004)
6. Eigner, M., Faißt, K., Keßler, A., Schäfer, P.: A Concept For An Intuitive And Interactive Fully Plm-Integrated Eco-Efficiency Assessment In Real-Time. In: International Conference on Engineering Design (ICED 2013) (2013)
7. Morbidoni, A., Recchioni, M., Otto, H., Mandorli, F.: Enabling an efficient SLCA by interfacing selected PLM LCI parameters. Tools and Methods of Competitive Engineering (TMCE) (2010)
8. Morbidoni, A., Favi, C., Germani, M.: CAD-Integrated LCA Tool: Comparison with dedicated LCA Software and Guidelines for the Improvement (2011)

9. Mathieux, F., Roucoules, L.: Connecting CAD and PLM systems with ecodesign software: Current experiences and future opportunities. In: International Conference on Engineering Design (ICED 2007) (2007)
10. Trela, M., Omhover, J., Aoussat, A.: Integration of EcoDesign in the early steps of the innovation process. International Journal of Environmental Technology and Management (2012)
11. Rio, M.: Improving Design to Environment Modeling knowledge transformations within product designers and environmental engineers activities (2012)
12. Lindahl, M.: Engineering designers' experience of design for environment methods and tools – Requirement definitions from an interview study. Journal of Cleaner Production 14(5), 487–496 (2006)
13. Janin, M.: Ecodesign approach in company – A stake: building a coherence between tools and design process. PhD Thesis, Arts et Métiers ParisTech (2000)
14. Ramani, K., Ramanujan, D., Bernstein, W.Z., Zhao, F., Sutherland, J., Handwerker, C., Choi, J.-K., Kim, H., Thurston, D.: Integrated Sustainable Life Cycle Design: A Review. Journal of Mechanical Design 132(9) (2010)
15. Favi, C.: Toward eco-design: an integrated lifecycle engineering system to develop sustainable mechatronic products and services, Università Politecnica delle Marche Scuola (2013)
16. Luttropp, C., Lagerstedt, J.: EcoDesign and The Ten Golden Rules: generic advice for merging environmental aspects into product development. Journal of Cleaner Production 14(15-16), 1396–1408 (2006)
17. Morbidoni, A., Favi, C., Mandorli, F., Germani, M.: Environmental Evaluation From Cradle To Grave With Cad-Integrated Lca Tools. Acta Technica Corviniensis, 109–115 (2012)
18. Hochschorner, E., Finnveden, G.: Evaluation of Two Simplified Life Cycle Assessment Methods. The International Journal of Life Cycle Assessment 8(3), 119–128 (2003)
19. Cluzel, F., Yannou, B., Leroy, Y., Millet, D.: Towards Parametric Environmental Profiles of Complex Industrial Systems in Preliminary Design Stage. In: 37th Design Automation Conference, pp. 241–250 (2011)
20. Leroy, Y.: Development of a methodology to reliable environmental decisions from life cycle assessment based on analysis and management of uncertainty on inventory data, PhD Thesis, Arts et Métiers ParisTech (2009)
21. Rio, M.: At the interface of engineering and environmental analysis: federation for proactive eco-design. PhD Thesis, Université de Technologie de Troyes (2012)
22. Millet, D.: Intégrationde l'environnement en conception: l'entreprise et le développement durable Integration of environment in design process: Company and sustainability, Hermès Sciences (2003)
23. Rio, M., Reyes, T., Roucoules, L.: Toward proactive (eco)design process: modeling information transformations among designers activities. Journal of Cleaner Production 39, 105–116 (2013)
24. Cluzel, F.: Eco-design implementation for complex industrial systems Mise en œuvre de l'éco-conception pour des systèmes industriels complexes. PhD Thesis, Ecole Centrale Paris (2012)
25. Segonds, F., Maranzana, N., Véron, P., Aoussat, A.: Collaborative Reverse Engineering Design Experiment Using PLM Solutions. International Journal of Engineering Education 27(5), 1037–1045 (2011)

26. Dufrene, M., Zwolinski, P., Brissaud, D.: An engineering platform to support a practical integrated eco-design methodology. CIRP Annals - Manufacturing Technology 62(1), 131–134 (2013)
27. Bey, N., Hauschild, M.Z., McAloone, T.C.: Drivers and barriers for implementation of environmental strategies in manufacturing companies. CIRP Annals - Manufacturing Technology 62(1), 43–46 (2013)
28. Segonds, F., Iraqi-Houssaini, M., Roucoules, L., Véron, P., Aoussat, A.: The use of early design tools in engineering processes: a comparative case study. International Journal of Design and Innovation Research 5(3), 61–76 (2010)
29. Theret, J.-P., Evrard, D., Mathieux, F.: Integrating CAD, PLM and LCA: new concepts, data model, architecture & integration proposals. In: EnviroInfo 2011: Innovations in Sharing Environmental Observations and Information (2011)

Escalation of Software Project Outsourcing: A Multiple Case Study

Hsin-Hui Lin[1] and Wen-Liang Wang[2]

[1] Department of Information Management, National Sun Yat-sen University, Kaohsiung, Taiwan
hhlin@mis.nsysu.edu.tw
[2] Kaohsiung Chung-Cheng Industrial High School, Taiwan
wwlccvs@hotmail.com

Abstract. Project escalation is the phenomenon of continuously devoting resources into a seriously delayed and troublesome project. This study focuses on project outsourcing in which both client and vendor may lead to the result of escalation. As both parties may take a position of termination or continuation of the project, four escalation types were studied. In each escalation type, two cases were studied through in-depth interview. Using content analysis, determinants of escalations were identified. In the case of low intention of continuation by the vendor, but high intention of continuation by the client, credible deterrence resulted in project escalation. In the case of high intention of continuation by the vendor, but low intention of continuation by the client, credible commitment resulted in project escalation. This study provides lessons learned from eight escalation cases to avoid ineffective investment in time and money.

Keywords: Escalation, Information System Project, Outsourcing, Credible Deterrence, Credible Commitment.

1 Introduction

Any project has a predefined budget, a schedule, and a set of goals. Project escalation is the situation where more and more resources are invested into a delayed and troublesome project [17, 19]. Regardless of the additional investment, these escalated projects eventually fail or their goals are not entirely met. Staw and Ross (1987) proposed a framework of four dimensions, including project factors, psychological factors, social factors, and organizational factors, to explain the phenomenon of project escalation. Previous research in escalation focused on in-house project, however, in today's competitive environment, outsourcing has become a common practice. These outsourced projects saw a higher percentage of project failure, often demonstrating a more complicated escalation effect. This complexity involves the vendor characteristics, the client characteristics, the contract terms, and the relationship between the two stakeholders.

S. Fukuda et al. (Eds.): PLM 2014, IFIP AICT 442, pp. 213–224, 2014.

As project runs into serious delay, both the client and vendor may choose to terminate or to continue by devoting more resources into the project. During the negotiation process, client who holds the money often has stronger bargaining power. However, the vendor is the one that has control over crucial project technology. Because of this, the objectives and strategies of both parties may be quite different. Considerations of long term relationship, company image, and strategic system development lead to continuation, while short term profit, lack of value in relationship, low transition cost, or working with mature technology often lead to termination of a project. In this paper, four scenarios (client/vendor × continuation/termination) were studied to determine the considerations of each party and the true reasons behind escalation.

2 Literature Background

2.1 Project Escalation

The escalation determinants can be explained using the framework of project factors, psychological factors, social factors, and organizational factors proposed by Staw and Ross (1987). This topic has been discussed by many authors.

(1) Project factors include low salvage value, high closing costs, long term benefit, and benefit of project completion [4, 5]. Other situations include the development of a complementary set of core competencies [22] or regarding the problem as temporary and solvable [6].
(2) Psychological factors include responsibility of the project manager, determination for success, and avoidance of punishment. The classic example is project manager's self-justifying their decision [7].
(3) Social factors include the social value of turning a defeat into victory, keeping one's promise, over commitment [20], and the habit of carrying on till the end [2, 4, 5].
(4) Organizational factors include the lack of control mechanism [18], conformance to organizational policy, and the disproportional influence by vocal leaders [8, 9, 10].

From a theoretical point of view, Keil et al. (2000a) explained the complex in-house escalation phenomena using self-justification theory, prospect theory, agency theory, and avoidance theory.

2.2 Software Outsourcing

Outsourcing is a way to acquire technology, to reduce cost, to share workload, and to achieve strategic goals. The client wishes to achieve these goals by leveraging external resources and maximizing cost effectiveness [11, 12, 13, 14]. To obtain these benefits, it is necessary to build an effective project control system, vendor selection mechanism, contract management system, and risk management system. The vendor wishes to utilize its technical skill, to gain experiences, and to make profit. Similarly, the vendor has to build up competitive technology, project management ability, risk management system, and customer relationship [15] to obtain these benefits.

The requirements of software project are often vaguely defined or prone to change. Therefore, staying on schedule and quality control become difficult to the developers. These characteristics all contribute to project escalation [24].

3 Research Steps and Method

The process of this study included four steps. In the first step, a pilot study was conducted. In the second step, eight cases were selected based on the results from the pilot study. In the third step, interviews and data collection were conducted. Data analysis is the final step.

3.1 Step 1: Pilot Case Study

First, a pilot case study was conducted to obtain the following objectives:

1. To clarify the definition of escalation for outsourced project.
2. To understand the situation, attitude, and major decisions of the client and vendor during project escalation.
3. To modify the escalation determinants from literature review and to develop guidelines for interview questions.

The pilot case was originally a one year project. This project ultimately lasted three years before being terminated. Based on literature review and our learning from this pilot case, the following criteria were set to help define an escalated project:

1. Serious overrun in schedule or budget.
2. The client has detected serious problems with its vendor and vice versa.
3. Termination has been proposed by at least one party.
4. Additional resources have been devoted to the project.

3.2 Step 2: Cases Selection

Based on the method of pattern matching in case study [27], four scenarios (2x2; client/vendor x continuation/termination) were defined. Each scenario yielded two escalation cases resulting in a total of eight cases. The set of criteria defined in step 1 were used to select the eight cases for further study. The eight cases cover all four scenarios and represent a variety of industry to reduce sampling bias. The basic information of these eight cases is summarized in Table 1.

Table 1. Surnrnary of the eight infornation system outsourcing cases

Case	Industry/System	Schedule	Project situation
	Rubber/ERP system	Plan: l.Syrs Actual: 2.5yrs Final: terrninated	• Client is a leading rubber rnanufacturing company. • Vendor expected to enter the new rnarket but clid not have sufficient domain knowledge. • Client proposed to terminate the project due to serious delay. • Vendor proposed to continue the project without extra charge.
2	Gas/GIS system	Plan:4yrs Actual:8yrs ter- Final: rninated	• Vendor expected to enter GIS rnarket and build up experiences. • The vendor's project manager was the key technical person yet busy with two projects. • The client changed three presidents during that period. • Both parties did not have good project control.
3	Hospital/MIS system	Plan: lyr Actual:4yrs Final: closed	• Vendor expected to enter the hospital infor-rnation system market. • Client was not familiar with the new devel-oprnent platform. • Two project rnanagers resigned due to pressure from project delay.. • Top management of client side clid not notice the problerns until too late.
4	Insurance/ Transaction system	Plan: 3 months Actual: 1.5yrs Final: closed	• Vendor prornised a compressed schedule of 3 months but did not have enough people to work on the project. • Personnel change in client side caused delay in requirernents analysis.
5	Banking/Asset rnan-agement system	Plan: lyr Actual:4yrs Final: closed	• Frequent change of contact person. • Changes of acceptance criteria. • Client bas strong bargaining power. • Vendor had to conform to client's requests.
6	Electronics/ Manufacturing system	Plan: l.Syrs Actual: 5yrs Final: closed	• Pioneer project for both client and vendor. • Vendor had financial problem due to long developrnent tirne. • Client is a leading company in that industry. • Vendor cares about company irnage.

Table 1. *(Continued)*

Case	Industry/System	Schedule	Project situation
7	Steel/ERP system	Plan: 1.5yrs Actual: 2.5yrs Final: closed	• Client and vendor are business unit of the same business group. • Rely on top management communication rather than contract. • Only finish part of the original requirements. • Long term cooperation to finish the incomplete requirements.
8	Government/ Property management	Plan: 1.5yrs Actual: 1yr and 8 months Final: closed	• Government unit had a firm deadline of system completion. Vendor did not have the experience of deploying large scale information system of 265 sites. • Vendor had to complete the project under tight schedule and budget. • Vendor devoted significant amount of extra cost to finish the project. • Company image and future business opportunities are important considerations of the vendor.

3.3 Step 3: Data Collection

For each case, a semi-structured interview was conducted. The interviewees included top management and project manager of both the client and vendor. The interview questions were developed to include project factors, psychological factors, social factors, and organizational factors. The specific questions were modified to take into account of learning from literatures and our pilot case study. The interviews were recorded, transcribed, and verified later for assurance. In addition to the interview data, project documents, meeting records, and e-mails were also collected for analysis. Data triangulation technique which validates the consistency and correctness of data through cross verification of multiple sources was used [26].

Along the timeline, there are some major events associated with project escalation. These major events include initial contract agreement, observation of serious problems, proposals of termination, negotiation, major decisions, and final resolutions. Data of these major events were collected through interview and documents.

3.4 Step 4: Data Analysis

Using coding and categorization, the raw data was grouped into escalation determinants. The importance of a determinant is rated as low (L) if it's mentioned once, rated as medium (M) if it's mentioned twice, and rated as high (H) if it's mentioned three times or more. The grouping is listed in Tables 2-5.

Table 2. Escalation determinants of project factor

Determinant/case	1	2	3	4	5	6	7	8
Vendor: low salvage value	L	L	L	L	H	H	H	H
Vendor: high termination cost (contract penalty)	H	L	H	H	H	M	L	L
Vendor: long term benefit if the project is finished	H	H	H	M	M	M	H	H
Vendor: alternative solutions	N	N	N	N	N	N	Y	Y
Vendor: sunk cost	H	H	H	H	H	H	L	L
Vendor: experiences learned from the project	H	H	H	M	L	L	L	L
Client: high transaction cost	M	M	H	M	M	H	H	H
Client: high agency cost	M	M	M	M	H	M	H	H

Table 3. Escalation determinants of psychological factor

Determinant/case	1	2	3	4	5	6	7	8
Vendor: risk aversion attitude	M	M	M	M	M	L	L	M
Vendor: decision biases	H	H	H	M	L	L	L	M
Vendor: loss aversion attitude	H	H	H	M	H	L	L	L
Vendor: over commitment	H	H	H	M	H	L	M	M
Client: responsibility for project success	H	M	H	M	H	H	M	H

Table 4. Escalation determinants of social factor

Determinant/case	1	2	3	4	5	6	7	8
Vendor: importance of company image	H	H	H	M	H	H	H	H
Vendor: challenge from other vendors	H	H	M	M	M	M	H	H
Vendor: experiences of previous success	H	H	H	M	H	H	H	H

Table 5. Escalation determinants of organizational factor

Determinant/case	1	2	3	4	5	6	7	8
Vendor: poor project control	L	L	M	M	L	H	H	M
Vendor: comply with company policy	H	H	H	M	L	L	L	M
Vendor: top management support	H	H	H	M	L	L	L	M
Client: poor project control	L	L	L	L	L	M	M	L
Client: need of project completion	L	L	H	M	H	H	H	H
Client: importance of the project	L	L	H	M	M	H	H	H

The results in Tables 2-5 are further summarized into Table 6.

Table 6. Escalation determinants of outsourcd project

	client	vendor
Project factors	• high transaction cost • high agency cost	• low salvage value • high termination cost • long term benefit • sunk cost • experiences learned from the project
Psychological factors	• responsibility for project success	• risk aversion attitude • decision biases • loss aversion attitude • over commitment
Social factors	n/a	• importance of company image • challenge from other vendors • experiences of previous success
Organizational factors	• poor project control • need of project completion • importance of the project	• top management support • comply with company policy • poor project control

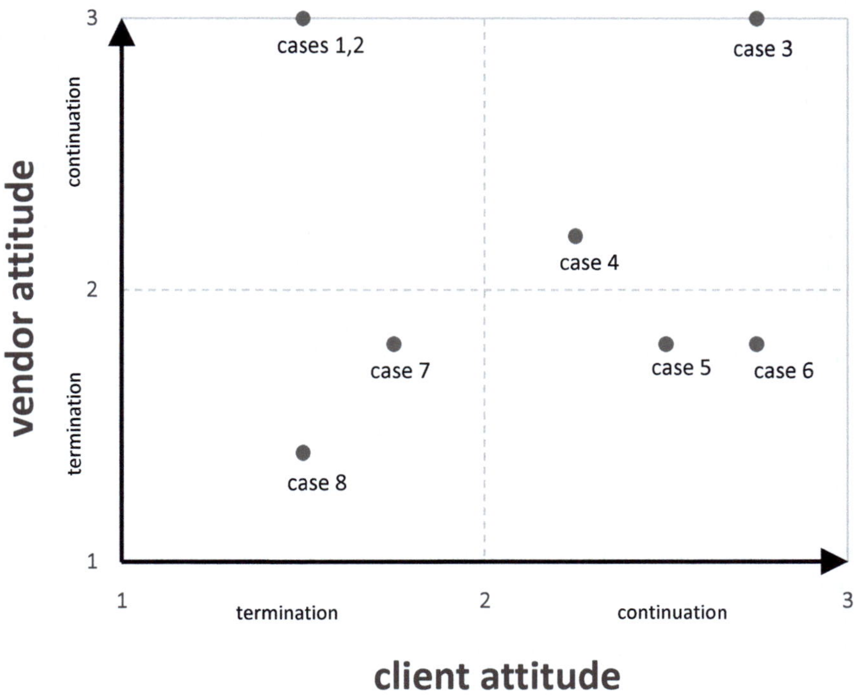

Fig. 1. The attitude of client vs. vendor

Factors related to the attitude of escalation were retrieved from Tables 2-5. The escalation index is calculated by averaging the rating of related determinants. The rating of (H, M, L) is translated into (3, 2, 1). The two-dimensional index represents (client escalation score, vendor escalation score). The final escalation indexes of the 8 cases are (1.5, 3), (1.5, 3), (2.75, 3), (2.25, 2.2), (2.5, 1.8), (2.75, 1.8), (1.75, 1.8), and (1.5, 1.4) and shown in Figure 1.

In cases 1 and 2, the vendors wanted to continue and were committed to devoting resources into a delayed project. In both cases, the vendors cared very much about their company image, wanted to build experiences, and expected the project benefits to be long-tern. They also had support from top management and their actions were aligned with company policy. In both cases, however, the client preferred to termination as the project was not critical to their business. The chairman of the vendor in case 1 showed strong determination to support the project. "To develop this market, we have invested large amount of money and efforts. Shall the project be terminated, all of our investment will vanish." He said, "I promise to fully support the project team and to add experienced people from our headquarters without extra charge." The president of the client side in case 1 was willing to give this vendor a chance after seeing their commitment to complete the project. "We understand that the vendor have absorbed a large amount of extra cost sending people from their headquarters to support this project. We may not be able to find a better vendor at this moment." Interview data shows that credible commitment is a key cause of escalation in cases 1 and 2. This escalation situation is labeled as the commitment type.

In cases 3 and 4, both the client and vendor were willing to continue and devoted resources into the project. For the client, the project was critical to the company and changing vendor would incur high cost. The vendor's considerations were similar to those observed in cases 1 and 2. For an escalation situation like this, where both parties made a common choice based on their best interest, this escalation situation is labeled as the equilibrium type.

In cases 5 and 6, clients preferred to continue the project while vendors preferred to terminate. For the clients, the project was important enough that board of director showed special concerns. Their management team was consequently pressured to finish the project. For the vendors, however, termination bared little risk and continuation would have led to moderate benefits. Regardless, in each case, the vendors were still forced into continuing the project. "Security and reliability are so important to the banking industry. They maintain a long term relationship with information systems providers. They only do business with vendors they think they can trust." said an upper management in case 5. The vendor of case 6 recalls "The client is a world class semiconductor manufacturer. They have a strong legal department, so even though the requirements are not clearly defined in the contract, terminating the project and going through the legal process would not be wise." These are evidences that credible deterrence is the key factor causing cases 5 and 6 to escalate. Therefore, this escalation situation is labeled the deterrence type.

In cases 7 and 8, both the client and vendor sought termination. On the vendor side, the sunk cost and termination cost were low. In these cases, conflicts were resolved through top management, which diluted the responsibility of the project managers. Although schedule was delayed and only part of project was completed, both parties decided to close the project and solve the problem at a later time. This escalation situation is labeled the cooperation type.

Figure 2 shows four types of escalation observed in this study and how credible commitment of the vendor and credible deterrence of the client lead to project escalation.

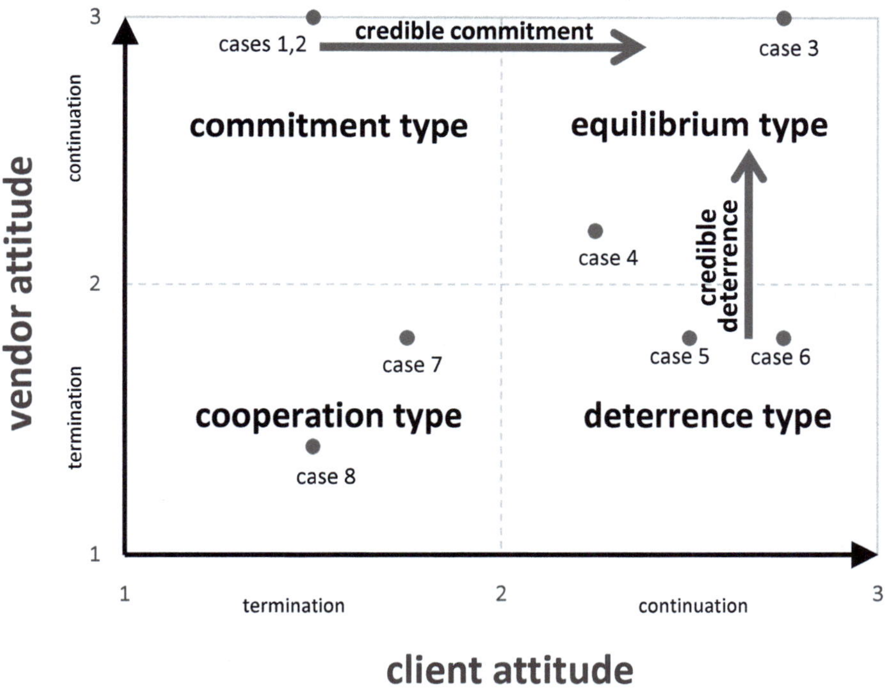

Fig. 2. Attitude change toward escalation

4 Discussions and Suggestions

The commitment type escalation resulted mainly from an over-commitment by the vendor. Long-term benefit and market potential were the major considerations to continue on with the project. The vendor underestimated the complexity of the project and did not have sufficient domain knowledge. This proves that commitment alone cannot guarantee the success of a project. As shown in data analysis, lack of control mechanism is a common problem for both the client and vendor. Continuing the project without improving project management does not help completion.

In the equilibrium type escalation, both stakeholders decided to continue with the project. The client bears the responsibility of project success, while the vendor fears the large amounts of penalty and damage to their image as a result of termination. This is similar to the prisoner's dilemma in game theory [25]. Both parties choose the alternative in their best interest but ends up with a poor result. In this situation, the loss of termination is immediate, but will be smaller than the loss of continuation.

In the deterrence type escalation, the clients are leading company in the industry with strong bargaining power. In this situation, vendors tend to comply with the requests of the client. However, if vendor do not have sufficient domain knowledge and technology know-how, delaying the problem will only incur higher cost for both parties. The client must consider the opportunity cost of project failure as deterrence alone cannot help the completion of a project.

In the cooperation type escalation, the client and vendor maintained a cooperative relationship and the project was either reassigned into phases or reduced [21, 23]. The unfinished parts were delayed but could be completed in the future.

Escalation wastes time and money. Through our learning from this study, suggestions are made to avoid escalation or to reduce the damage. For vendors, trying to enter a new market, starting out by working on the projects with a leading company is often costly and risky. First off, an imbalance in bargaining power often throws these projects into a rabbit hole. Taking a joint development approach or cooperative relationship can reduce risk. Secondly, being overly optimistic about the potential market often results in over-commitment. Always evaluate a potential market based on solid market research. Thirdly, project opportunities must be evaluated not only based on technology and cost, but also with a risk management point of view. Inexperienced users, frequent change to requirements, frequent change to the contact person, and changes to the client policy are all risks to be evaluated and managed.

For client, evaluation of continuation or termination should be based on long-term benefit rather than short-term problem solving. With the fear of taking an immediate loss and the trouble of restarting a project, continuation may seem like an easy solution. However, if the underlining problems are not solved, the project will fail eventually. Furthermore, a monitoring system for outsourced project must be built. Poor project control is one of the most common problems observed in this study. Lastly, deterrence has a negative effect on escalation. It leads to vendor hiding the problems and client overlooking them. In summary, a cooperative attitude and ample communication between the client and its vendor can avoid ineffective measures and reduce losses.

References

1. Staw, B.M., Ross, J.: Knowing When to Pull the Plug. Harvard Business Review 65(2), 68–74 (1987)
2. Newman, M., Sabherwal, R.: Determinants of Commitment to Information Systems Development: A Longitudinal Investigation. MIS Quarterly 20(1), 23–54 (1996)
3. Staw, B.M.: The Escalation of Commitment to a Course of Action. Academy of Management Review 6, 577–587 (1981)

4. Ross, J., Staw, B.M.: Organizational Escalation and Exit: Lessons from the Shoreham Nuclear Plant. Academy of Management Journal 36(4), 701–732 (1993)
5. Keil, M.: Pulling the Plug: Software Project Management and the Problem of Project Escalation. MIS Quarterly 19(4), 421–447 (1995)
6. Keil, M., Tan, B.C.Y., Wei, K.K., Saarinen, T., Tuunainen, V., Wassenaar, A.: A Cross-Cultural Study on Escalation of Commitment Behavior in Software Projects. MIS Quarterly 24(3), 299–324 (2000b)
7. Brockner, J.: The Escalation of Commitment to a Failing Course of Action: Toward Theoretical Progress. Academy of Management Review 17, 39–61 (1992)
8. Kirby, S.L., Davis, M.A.: A Study of Escalating Commitment in Principal-Agent Relationships: Effects of Monitoring and Personal Responsibility. Journal of Applied Psychology 83(2), 206–217 (1998)
9. Keil, M., Rai, A., Mann, J.E.C., Zhang, P.: Why Software Projects Escalate: The Important of Project Management Constructs. IEEE Transactions on Engineering Management 50(3), 251–261 (2003)
10. Fombrun, C., Shanley, M.: What's in a Name? Reputation Building and Corporate Strategy. Academy of Management Journal 33(2), 233–258 (1990)
11. Ang, S., Cummings, L.L.: Strategic Response to Institutional Influences on Information Systems Outsourcing. Organization Science 8(3), 235–256 (1997)
12. Ang, S., Straub, D.: Production and Transaction Economies and IS Outsourcing: A Study of the U.S. Banking Industry. MIS Quarterly 22(4), 535–552 (1998)
13. Loh, L., Venkatraman, N.: Determinants of Information Technology Outsourcing: A Cross-Sectional Analysis. Journal of Management Information Systems 9(1), 7–24 (1992)
14. Slaughter, S., Ang, S.: Employment Outsourcing in Information Systems. Communications of the ACM 39(7), 47–54 (1996)
15. Currie, W.L., Willcocks, L.P.: Analyzing Four Types of IT Sourcing Decisions in the Context of Scale, Client/Supplier Interdependency and Risk Mitigation. Information Systems Journal 8, 119–143 (1998)
16. Keil, M., Mann, J., Rai, A.: Why Software Projects Escalate: An Empirical Analysis and Test of Four Theoretical Models. MIS Quarterly 24(4), 631–665 (2000a)
17. Keil, M., Montealegre, R.: Cutting Your Losses: Extricating Your Organization When a Big Project Goes Awry. Sloan Management Review 41(3), 86–95 (2000)
18. Keil, M., Depledge, G., Rai, A.: Escalation: The Role of Problem Recognition and Cognitive Bias. Decision Sciences 38(3), 391–421 (2007)
19. Lee, J.S., Keil, M., Kasi, V.: The Effect of an Initial Budget and Schedule Goal on Software Project Escalation. Journal of Management Information Systems 29(1), 53–78 (2012)
20. Jani, A.: Escalation of Commitment in Troubled IT Projects: Influence of Project Risk Factors and Self-efficacy on the Perception of Risk and the Commitment to a Failing Project. International Journal of Project Management 29(7), 934–945 (2011)
21. Gefen, D., Wyss, S., Lichtenstein, Y.: Business Familiarity as Risk Mitigation in Software Development Outsourcing Contracts. MIS Quarterly 32(3), 531–551 (2008)
22. Levina, N., Ross, J.W.: From the Vendor's Perspective: Exploring the Value Proposition in Information Technology Outsourcing. MIS Quarterly 27(3), 331–364 (2003)
23. Heiskanena, A., Newmanb, M., Eklinc, M.: Control, Trust, Power, and the Dynamics of Information System Outsourcing Relationships: A Process Study of Contractual Software Development. The Journal of Strategic Information Systems 17(4), 268–286 (2008)

24. Sabherwal, R.: The Evolution of Coordination in Outsourced Software Development Projects: A Comparison of Client and Vendor Perspectives. Information and Organization 13, 153–202 (2003)
25. Elitzur, R., Wensley, A.: Game Theory as a Tool for Understanding Information Services Outsourcing. Journal of Information Technology 12(1), 45–60 (1997)
26. Merriam, S.B.: Qualitative Research in Practice. Jossey-Bass, San Francisco (2002)
27. Trochim, W.M.K.: Outcome Pattern Matching and Program Theory. Evaluation and Program Planning 12(4), 355–366 (1989)

Design Information Management for Product Sound Quality: Requirement Definition

Kazuko Yamagishi[1], Koichi Ohtomi[2], Kenichi Seki[2], and Hidekazu Nishimura[1]

[1] Graduate School of System Design and Management, Keio University, Japan
[2] SDM Lab, Graduate School of System Design and Management, Keio University, Japan
kaz-yamagishi@a6.keio.jp

Abstract. In a current design information management of consumer products, it is difficult to take into consideration of the sensory preference of users in requirements definition phase. Especially, sensory preference on sound of products might be different individually and depend on environment where the products are used. The engineering metrics are necessary to be connected to the sensory preference of users to design the right products to user preferences. In this paper we propose a process to manage design information considering product sound quality, and investigate a consistent description method using SysML (Systems Modeling Language) from requirement definition to engineering metrics setting. Picking up a camera as an example of consumer products we extract customer demands using the evaluation grid method according to the cases where the camera is used. By applying the DSM (Design Structure Matrix) clustering analysis to the results of the interview, we cluster the fundamental requirements relating functional and performance requirements which include sound quality. Also a stepwise refinement from the requirement definition to the architectural design is performed using SysML diagrams, and the appropriate engineering metrics are derived.

Keywords: sound quality, SysML, evaluation grid method, use case, DSM clustering analysis, Product Lifecycle Management.

1 Introduction

In recent years, the value of product sound quality is increasing, and many researches for sound design have been conducted. Ohtomi et al. (2008) considered that sound quality could add values to product. Yanagisawa et al. (2009) proposed a systematic approach which guides from the definition of requirements to functional and structural design in terms of product sound. Sound demands for product may vary depending on use cases, and it is difficult to set sound quality target which matches the customer needs. Thus, it is not easy to integrate the sensory preference such as sound as system requirements using the existing design-information management. Since the sound design process needs to carry over the sound demands to multiple

S. Fukuda et al. (Eds.): PLM 2014, IFIP AICT 442, pp. 225–235, 2014.

design domains, the common understanding of the sound-related design information among the engineers are essential.

In a recent study of product design processes, SysML (Systems Modeling Language) have been utilized as a common notation for the system model (Balmelli et al. 2007; Zhu et al. 2009; Seki et al. 2009). However, few studies using SysML manage the demands about sensory preference depending on use cases as far as authors know.

By using the evaluation grid method (Kelly, 1995), we have already drew out customer demands for digital cameras depending on their use cases (Yamagishi et al. 2013). In addition, we have proposed to extract requirement clusters by applying DSM (Design Structure Matrix) clustering analysis (Eppinger et al. 2012) to the result of the evaluation grid method test. Through these processes, the demands for the product and its sound demands have become clear, and finally we have set the subjective sound quality target according to each use case.

In this paper, we investigate the description method of a system model using SysML, which can clarify sound demands as system requirements and to carry over the design information to multiple design domains. First, in the process of requirement analysis, the functionality which a system provides, and its relationship with actors around the product are clarified by using use case diagram. To clarify the function of the system, we describe use cases using sequence diagram and extract the interaction between a system and actors. Then the requirement diagram, which associates the functional requirements and the sound demands, is created and further the functional requirements are associated with the requirement clusters obtained from the evaluation grid method test and DSM clustering analysis. The requirement diagram ensures traceability between demands for a camera as a product and the functional and performance requirements.

In the process of functional design, sequence diagram is used in order to clarify the function of emitting shutter sound. The components of the camera are defined in block diagram. Behavior of the system components relevant to the sound are clarified using the activity diagram. The physical engineering metrics are allocated to these components, and values of the engineering metrics of each components are defined using proper simulation models. Through the proposed process, subsequent structural design can be proceeded effectively using the engineering metrics to realize the product that satisfied sensory customer demands.

2 SysML Based Representation of Sound Design Information

2.1 Requirements Transfer Process

In order to integrate the sensory preference such as sound quality as system requirements as well as functional requirements, and carry them over multiple design domains, we propose requirements transfer process as shown in figure 1.

In conventional camera design, requirement analysis is conducted mainly focusing on functional requirements such as taking an image. In the proposed process of requirements analysis, first, a use case diagram is used to clarify the function of a product system and the relationship with other participants around the product. Then, next, multiple sequence diagrams describe interactions among actors for every use case, and they detail interaction including sound related events. Through a stepwise refinement in functional and structural design of this process, sound quality requirements are transferred to the appropriate engineering metrics.

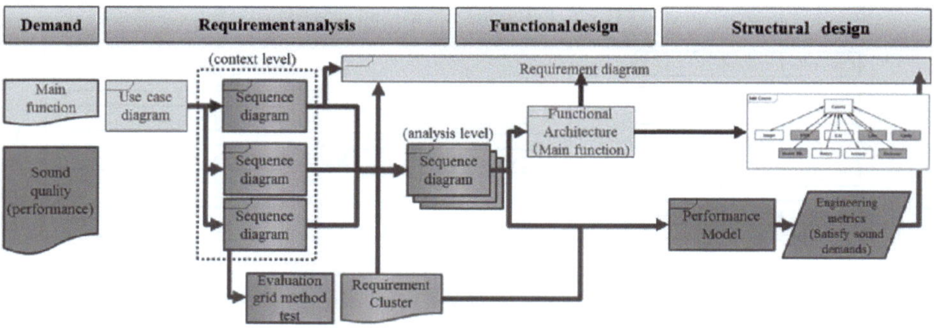

Fig. 1. Requirements transfer process

2.2 Clustering Analysis for Requirements Using the Evaluation Grid Method [7]

In order to capture demands for product which varies depending on situations, we carry out an evaluation test using the evaluation grid method that assumed use cases. Evaluation grid method is the personal interview method based on alternative constructivism and psychological theory by G.A. Kelly (1995). This methodology enables us to clarify recognition structure of value or attractiveness for the subject.

Figure 2 shows steps to extract requirement clusters from the test using the evaluation grid method. Following steps were taken: In STEP 1, we asked the participants about their preferred products and reasons. We determined the term that the participants used when comparing the products as 'Evaluation points'. 'Evaluation points' are the criteria used by the participants to assess the products' relative superiority, and thus can be interpreted as demands for product. Next, the participants were asked why the 'Evaluation points' inspired their choice. This rudder-up step was performed to lead higher demands. We determined the term used to describe the reason as 'Reasons (WHYs)'. Similarly, a rudder-down step was performed to lead concrete measures for each evaluation point. We determined the term used to describe the measures as 'Concrete measures (HOWs)'. In STEP 2, three requirements—evaluation points, reasons and concrete measures were assigned as items in the rows and columns of the DSM. The circular symbol (●) in the matrix represents the correlation between requirements in the rows and in the columns in DSM. The sound symbol (S) represents the requirement correlation in terms of sound. In STEP 3, to find the group of highly correlative requirements, the clustering analysis was used. From requirement clustering analysis, the requirements were interpreted in each cluster, and thus we can capture the structure of demands for product. When sound demands (S symbol) are included in a cluster, it indicates that realizing sound demands can satisfy demands for product of the cluster. The requirement diagram for a camera is created referring to this DSM clustering result.

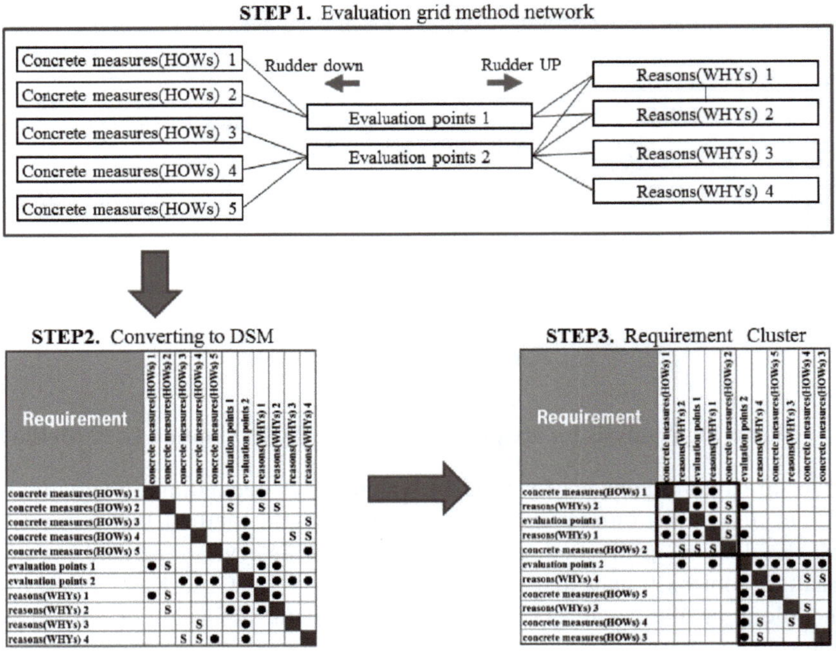

Fig. 2. DMM for requirement clusters

2.3 Functional and Structural Design for Performance Requirements

From the requirement clustering analysis, functional requirements to the system and sound demands are classified, and the structure of requirements becomes clear. To realize sound demands physically, a function of sound is examined. A sequence diagram is used to clarify the functions of emitting shutter sound. From the sequence diagram, interaction between each component relevant to sound such as vibration force and sound wave become clear. Next, the components of a camera which have connections with the function of sound, such as the shutter block and the cavity, are identified. To visualize and organize the physical energy flow about sound and vibration among these components, activity diagram is used. Thus, engineering metrics relevant to each component is derived. Since the sound demands for every use case is clear as a sound quality target, a product sound quality can be achieved by considering the shutter mechanism which realizes the desired engineering metrics by simulation.

3 Application to Camera Shutter Sound

3.1 Use Cases for a Camera

This section illustrates the application for the shutter sound design. As for the camera shutter sound is required for customers to know whether the product is functioning normally. However, the sound may be unnecessary in a quiet place. Customer demands for shutter sound of a camera may vary depending on use case. The use case diagram of 'taking photo' is shown in Fig. 3. From the viewpoint of sound design which considers the impact of shutter sound to other persons in a quiet place, it is necessary to think 'the surrounding people' who may hear shutter sound other than the user and subject people as an actor. About three camera use cases; record a photographic subject, take a photograph of landscape, and take a photograph at the quiet place, sequence diagrams describe interactions among actors and are shown in Fig. 4.

By describing use cases with sequence diagrams, it became clear how sound is concerned with actors associated with main function of a camera 'taking photograph' depending on each use case. Moreover, the visual contents for the evaluation grid method test could be decided according to above-mentioned investigations using use case and sequence diagrams, and the questionaries' contents about sound were also able to be prepared without shortage.

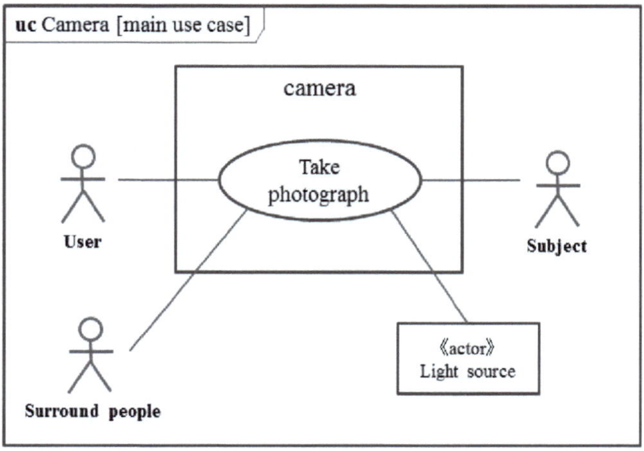

Fig. 3. Main use case of a camera

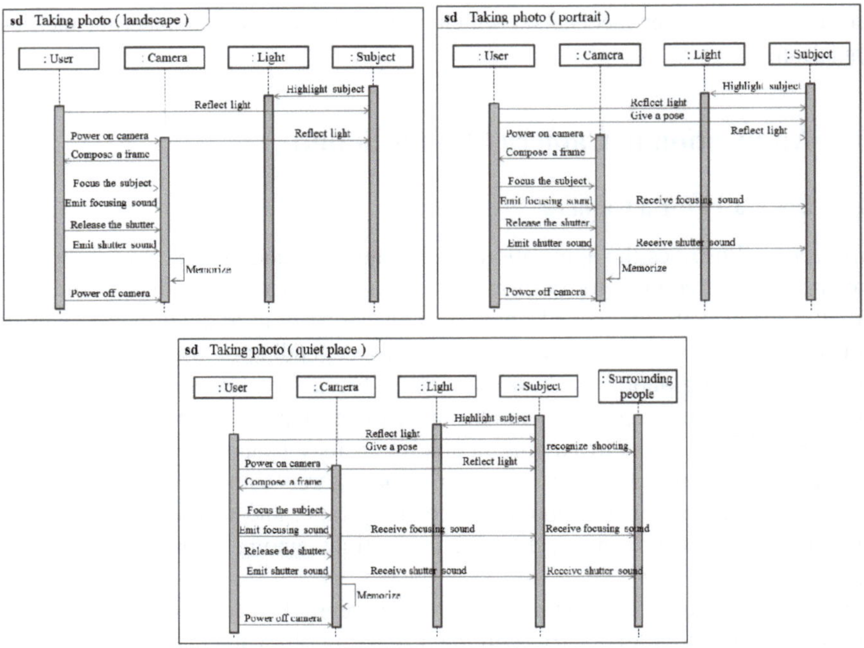

Fig. 4. Sequence diagram assuming use cases

3.2 The Requirement Analysis Using the Evaluation Grid Method for Camera

We conducted the evaluation test of camera using the evaluation grid method with about ten interviewees. The participants used five evaluation cameras with screen images, which assuming use cases decided by the method described in section 3.1 to determine customer demands depending on use cases. Specifically, to make them feel as if they are present in the scene, they operated all cameras freely in front of four types of video pictures by a 4K projector. The four scenes included an athletic meet, magnificent scenery, the bustle of the city and animals. We interviewed the participants about their preferred product and the reasons.

As shown Fig. 5, DSM data were constructed as described in section 2.2 using evaluation grid method. Through this process, close requirements were concentrated, making it easier to understand demands for product. Customer demands for the camera are clarified into the following six requirement clusters.

1) Pleased with clicking the shutter
2) Use the camera casually, fashionably
3) Enhance their cool look by possessing and operating the camera
4) Feeling of comfort in taking photos as will
5) Quiet sound that matches the scenes and circumstances
6) Regard the camera's functionalities to take photos as import

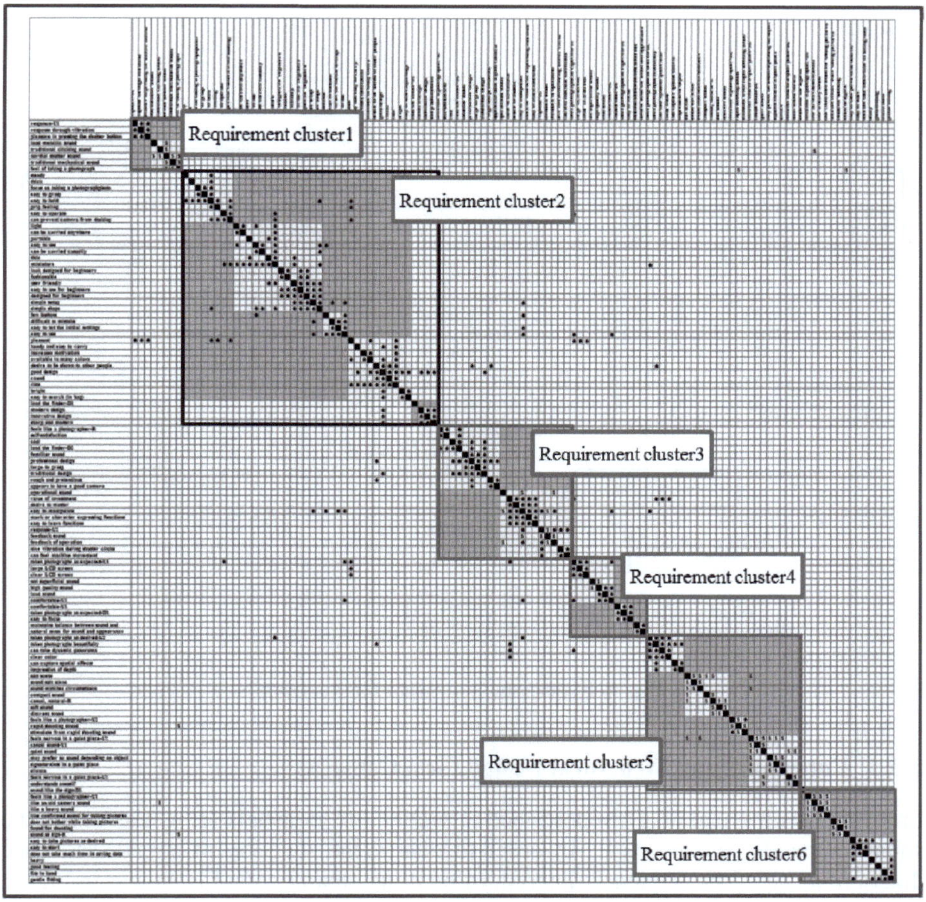

Fig. 5. DSM for Requirement cluster

First, we analysed system requirements focusing main function of a camera by drawing requirement diagram. And, the sound demands derived from the requirement clusters are added to the requirement diagram of a camera. The items which were highlighted gray were added after using the requirement clustering analysis. This resulted requirement diagram is shown in Fig. 6. For example, the demands about quiet sound which does not cause circumference problem is a requirement which did not come out unless we performed the evaluation grid method test. Thus, the demands which are not visible from usual requirement definition become clear from requirement clusters using evaluation grid method test. Furthermore, it revealed the relationship between the sound demands and demands for a camera. Therefore, We can trace demands for the camera are came out of which cluster and can know the sound to satisfy the demands from the cluster., and we can share the demand structure among the people in associated development organizations.

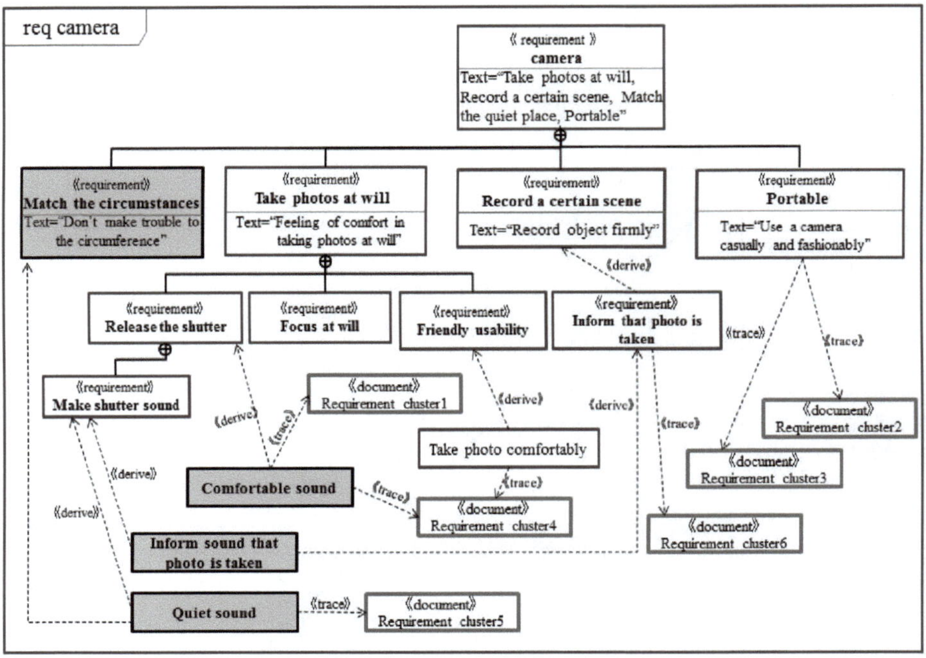

Fig. 6. Requirement diagram for a camera

3.3 Functional and Structural Design for a Camera

From the requirement diagram described in section 3.2, demands for a camera and the sound demands became clear. In order to clarify the function of sound, sequence diagram is used. The sequence diagram of emitting shutter sound is shown in Fig. 7. As shown in Fig. 7, interaction between each component relevant to sound such as vibration force and sound wave can be recognized during the shutter release behavior from the observation of sequence diagram.

Next, the block diagram of the camera components which realize the functions of a camera is shown in Fig. 8. The items which are highlighted gray are the components which have a connection with the function of sound. Activity diagram shown in Fig. 9 visualize the physical energy flow about sound and vibration among these components. Paying attention to a 'shutter block', 'Cavity', etc. which is the module structure relevant to sound, engineering metrics relevant to each module is derived.
Since the sound demands for every use case is clear as sound requirements, the demands can be realized by considering the performance requirements which are quantified as engineering metrics. The value of the engineering metrics is determined based on the sound quality targets assigned as system requirements. The relationship between engineering metrics and the structural and acoustic vibration mechanism relevant to shutter sound is shown in Fig. 10. The product sound quality can be achieved by designing the shutter structures with the engineering metrics.

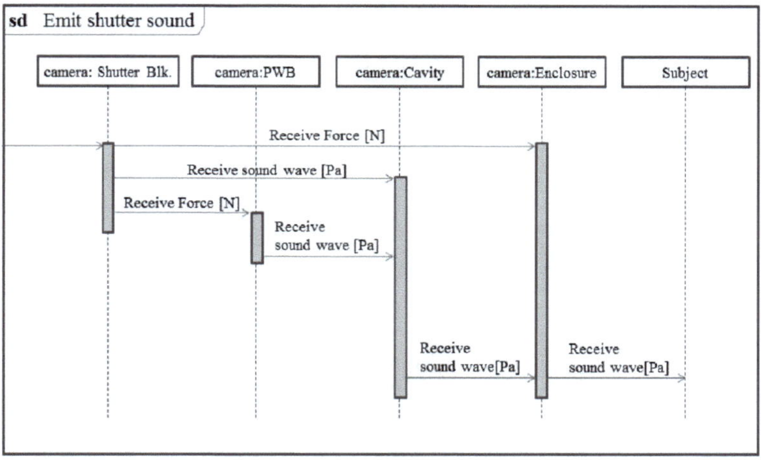

Fig. 7. Sequence diagram of 'Emit shutter sound'

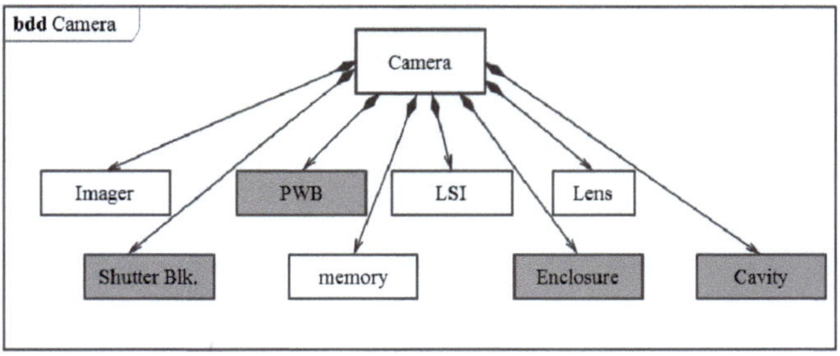

Fig. 8. Definition block diagram of a camera

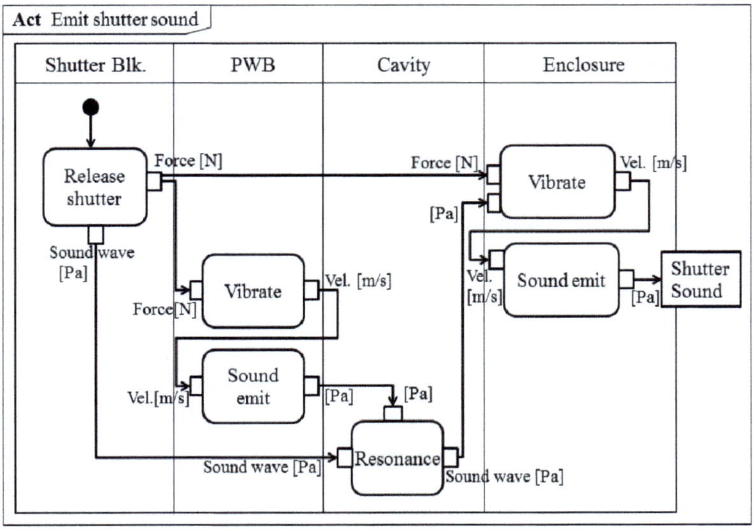

Fig. 9. Activity diagram of 'Emit shutter sound'

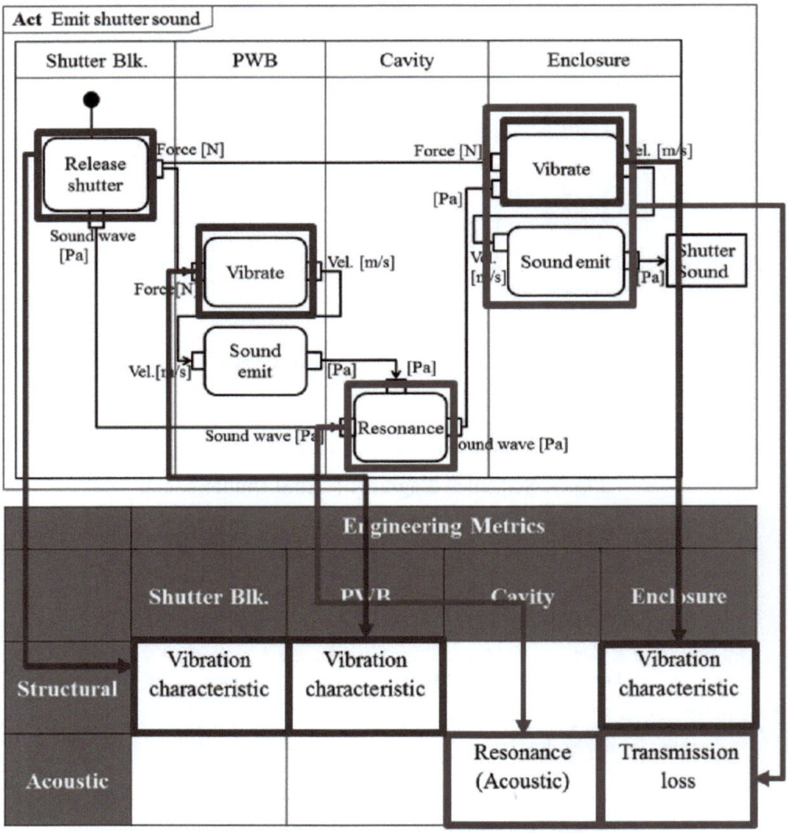

Fig. 10. Correlation of engineering metrics and components

4 Conclusion

In this paper, we propose a process to manage design information considering product sound quality. And we investigate the description method of a system model using SysML in order to clarify sound demands as system requirements and to carry over the design information about sound demands to different product development organizations. Sensory preference on sound of products might be different individually and depend on environment where the products are used. Therefore, based on the use case investigations, the customer demands were explored thoroughly by the evaluation grid method. DSM clustering was performed to the result of the evaluation grid method test, and the requirement cluster was extracted. Through the requirement clustering analysis, it is possible to set sound target depending on use cases. Then the requirement diagram, which associates the functional requirements and the sound demands, is created and further the functional requirements are associated with the requirement clusters obtained from the evaluation grid method test and DSM clustering analysis. Thus, the demands which are not visible from usual requirement definition become clear. And the requirement diagram ensures traceability between demands for a camera as a product and the functional and performance requirements.

In order to realize sound demands physically, a function of sound was examined. A sequence diagram is used in order to clarify the function of emitting shutter sound, and identify the interactions among component relevant to sound. To visualize and organize the physical energy flow about sound and vibration, activity diagram was used. Thus, engineering metrics relevant to each component were derived and stored as performance requirements. Through a stepwise refinement in functional and structural design, sound quality requirements are transferred to the appropriate engineering metrics. This process can help design teams to realize successful product that satisfied sensory customer demands.

The developed SysML system model considering product sound quality can be used in the test phase of the product at manufacturing sites. This sound design process is helpful for design teams in terms of product lifecycle management.

References

1. Balmelli, L.: An Overview of the Systems Modeling Language for Products and Systems Development. The Journal of Object Technology 6(6), 149–177 (2007)
2. Eppinger, S., Browning, T.: Design Structure Matrix Methods and Applications. The MIT Press (2012)
3. Kelly, G.A.: The psychology of Personal Constructs, vols. 1 and 2. Norton, New York (1995)
4. Ohtomi, K.: Design of Worth for Consumer Product Development. In: Special issue Of Japanese Society for the Science of Design 2009, pp. 31–38 (2009)
5. Ohtomi, K., Hosaka, R.: Design for Product Sound Quality. In: INTER-NISE and NOISE-CON Congress and Conference Proceedings. Institute of Noise Control Engineering 2008, pp. 2257–2264 (2008)
6. Seki, K., Nishimura, H., Ishii, K., Balmelli, L.: Thermal/Acoustic trade-off design for Consumer Electronics in a distributed design environment. The International Council on Systems Engineering (INCOSE 2009) (2009), 0723.pdf
7. Yamagishi, K., Ohtomi, K., Seki, K., Nishimura, H.: The Sound design process using the use-case driven requirement and functional modelling. The Japan Society of Mechanical Engineers Annual Meeting 2013 (2013) (in Japanese)
8. Yanagisawa, H., Kataoka, A., Murakami, T., Ohtomi, K., Hosaka, R.: Extraction of latent emotional factors by analyzing human sensitivity towards unexplored design: Application to product sound design. In: Proceedings of the 17th International Conference on Engineering Design (ICED 2009), vol. 7 (2009)
9. Zhu, S., Nishimura, H., Balmelli, L.: System Integration of Motorcycle Driving Stability Control Using SysML. In: Proceedings of 3rd Asia-Pacific Conference on Systems Engineering, pp. 1–10 (2009)

Thermal Management of Software Changes in Product Lifecycle of Consumer Electronics

Yoshio Muraoka[1], Kenichi Seki[2], and Hidekazu Nishimura[1]

[1] Graduate School of System Design and Management, Keio University, Japan
[2] SDM Research Institute, Keio University, Japan

Abstract. Because the power consumption of consumer electronic products varies according to processor execution, which depends on software, thermal risk may be increased by software changes, including software updates or the installation of new applications, even after hardware development has been completed. In this paper, we first introduce a typical system-level thermal simulation model, coupling the activities within modules related to software, electrical parts, and mechanical structure. Then, we investigate a case study of thermal management in both the development and maintenance phases of the product lifecycle. Reusing the simulation model, the thermal risk of software changes that may cause an enormous number of variations can be efficiently evaluated.

Keywords: Product lifecycle management, Thermal design, SysML, Software change, Electronic products, Embedded system, System level, Simulation, Collab- orative design, Low-temperature burn injury.

1 Introduction

1.1 Thermal Design of Electronic Products

Because of the demand for small and fast processing speeds, thermal design has become increasingly difficult in the development of consumer electronic products such as smartphones, tablets, and video game consoles. Although technology for power reduction and heat spreading has been continually developed, product temperatures have become high during operations. For example, handling content-rich applications such as video games and shooting high definition video cause high temperature rise (Consumer Reports 2012, Qualcomm 2012), and this becomes a major issue for product quality. Temperatures exceeding the optimum operating temperature range of a component may damage the product. Moreover, high enclosure temperatures induce low-temperature burn injuries if the user touches the product. Fig. 1 shows a diagram of an electronic product that has several layers of modules. In the modules, the semiconductors within the electrical parts dissipate heat based on the software. Because mechanical structures spread heat, the objects targeting in thermal design include all the modules shown in the figure.

S. Fukuda et al. (Eds.): PLM 2014, IFIP AICT 442, pp. 237–246, 2014.

Because many features of electronic products are flexibly implemented by software, product complexity increases (Siemens 2012). Product variation now occurs mostly after purchase by the installation of software, including applications and new operation system (OS) (Kuusela 2012). The number of available Android application has already reached one million, and the Android OS is updated several times a year at least (Google 2013).

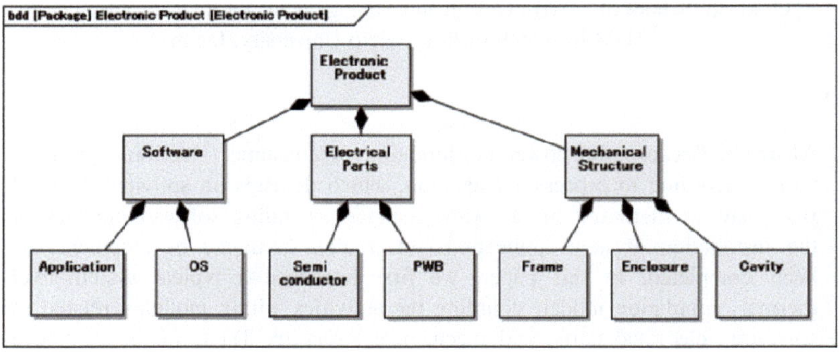

Fig. 1. Diagram of modules in an electronic product

Fig. 2 shows an example of the product lifecycle of electronic product. After product planning is authorized, the product system is designed, verifying that the planned system can meet the requirements. For example, temperatures must not exceed the target for product quality. In a design approach for systems engineering, architecture design initiates in the concept phase of the lifecycle. An outline of the system is then checked in detail, decomposing elements into physical speci- fications. In general, software, electrical parts and mechanical structure are devel- oped by different engineering teams. These modules are developed in parallel; however verification is necessary to ensure that the functions of system work to satisfy the requirements. For thermal verification, thermal simulation is often used besides temperature measurement, especially when the modules are being developed. Before mass production, the designed modules are integrated into physical prototypes. Quality Assurance (QA) tests are conducted, and modules that fail these tests are improved during further development. Verification must be performed at the correct time, considering that modules vary in the level of pro- gress during their developments. In addition, software also changes in the mainte- nance phase, i.e., after hardware development is complete. As cited above, product variation now occurs mostly after distribution. In this study, a simulation model is used to verify the architecture design during development. Further, the simulation model is also used for maintenance during the product lifecycle.

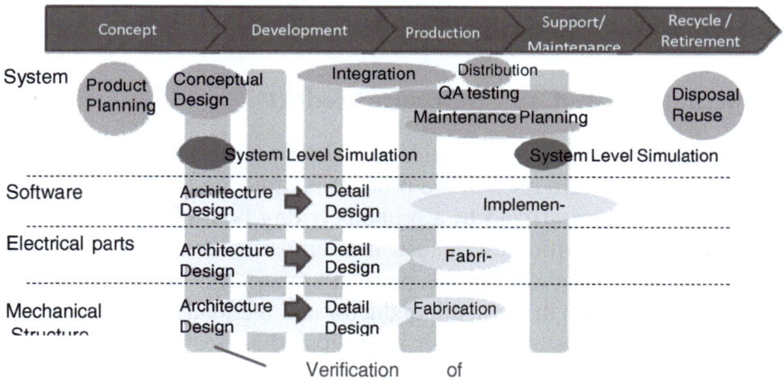

Fig. 2. Example of the product lifecycle of electronics product

1.2 System-Level Design Approach

As a collaborative design to prevent thermal problems, this study proposes a system-level simulation for the system consisting of different engineering domains. The system-level design approach is also known as a model-driven development method. To achieve a coordinated design within multi-disciplinary design teams, Balmelli (2007) proposed model-driven systems development using systems modeling language (SysML). This approach adopts operational, functional, and physical viewpoints to separately address different engineering concerns, while maintaining an integrated representation of the underlying design.

For the collaborative design of consumer electronics, Seki et al. (2011a) investigated a module-based design approach using SysML. Their study used initial target values (ITVs) as tentative boundary conditions for assigning different design sites and refined them during product development. This approach reduced inconsistent performance of the modules that resulted from a lack of communication between design sites and the work iterations required to correct such inconsistencies when applying ITVs to independent module design. In addition, Seki et al. (2011b) proposed a thermal design approach on the basis of the design structure matrix (DSM) to systematically assign ITVs. In the study, ITVs were created between module designs of hardware, pertaining to electrical parts and mechanical structures, particularly those including cavities.

By assigning ITVs to software modules, Muraoka et al. (2013a) investigated a system-level thermal simulation model. While the temperature that causes low-temperature burn injuries is quantified, thermal risk is evaluated based on the calculated temperature. A simulation model for resolving conflicting user requirements was developed by changing the design parameters. In addition, Muraoka et al. (2013b) applied this approach to develop design specifications with regard to a software change. ITVs were used to prepare alternative scenarios as countermeasures. These approaches were aimed at developing design specifications in the development phase. In this study, a system-level thermal model is used during verification of both the development and maintenance phases in the lifecycle. We also investigate a case study to improve the verification workflow.

2 System-Level Thermal Model

2.1 Temperature Rise of An Electronics Product

This study investigates the temperature rise of a simple electronic product. The mechanism by which the temperature rises in the product is illustrated in Fig. 3. Electrical parts such as semiconductors are affixed to a printed-writing board (PWB) that is fixed to a mechanical structure. Activities that cause the tempera- ture to rise are also shown. Semiconductors are activated during the product's operation (a1). During the device's operation, software executes in the semiconductor and the load is processed at a specific frequency. Because, the consumed power is dissipated as heat, we consider that heat is generated by operations within the semiconductor (a2). This generated heat is then transmitted to the surface (a3). Temperature increases in electronic products create various problems such as parts failure, system defects, and burn injuries to the user. As electronic products reduce in size, while their capabilities increase, surface temperature rises related to burn injuries become an urgent concern (Roy 2012). Moritz and Henriques (1947) investigated low-temperature burn injuries on human and pigskin. They established that the minimum temperature that caused burns over a six-hour contact period was 44 °C. Contact temperatures sufficient to cause a burn injury are plotted as a function of time in Fig. 4. During a short usage period, the temperature rise during operation probably will not cause a burn injury. However, at a temperature as low as 44 °C, users may not regard the device as uncomfortably hot and may unconsciously continue to operate or hold the heated product. In the following thermal design case, the maximum temperature limit depends on the required usage time. Here, we ignore the temperature rise time because this is considerably shorter than the required usage time.

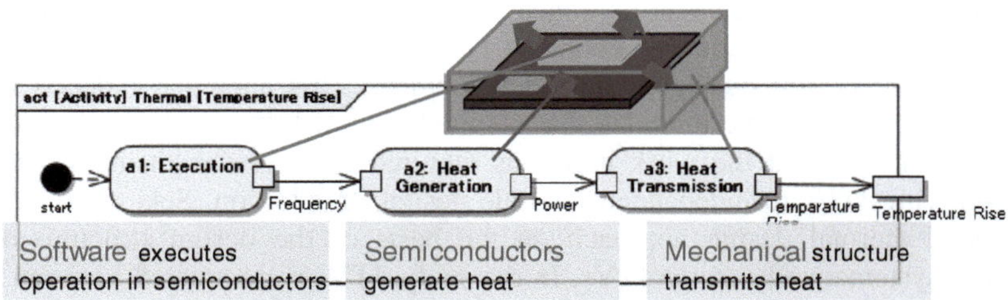

Fig. 3. Temperature rise in an electronic product

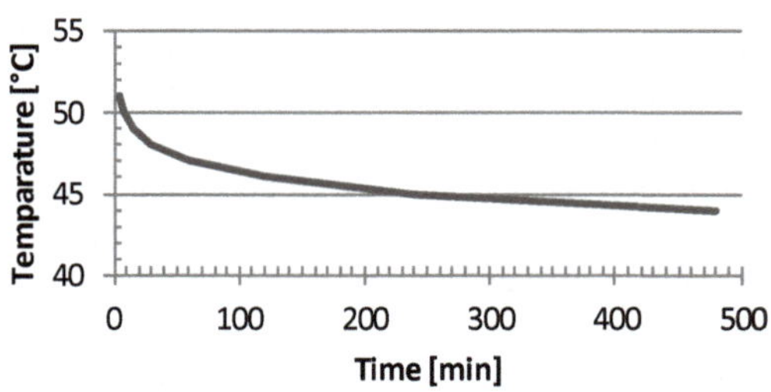

Fig. 4. Temperature that causes a low- temperature burn injury as a function of contact time (Adapted from Moritz 1947)

2.2 System-Level Simulation Model

In this section, the temperature rise is modeled on the internal variables of the module design and ITVs, which constitute boundary conditions between modules. We describe each activity shown in Fig. 3, and its numerical calculation. The first activity is load assignment, which sets the frequency, F, of the semiconductor. The software should be designed to optimally operate at the specified processing fre- quency. The second activity involves heat generation. Power, P, is calculated us- ing Equation (1) that includes internal variables, namely the physical semiconduc- tor capacitance, C, voltage, V, and frequency, F, assigned by the software.

$$P = C \cdot F \cdot V^2 + P_{charge} + P_{static} \quad (1)$$

This equation is simplified and based on the switching power dissipation of the CMOS (Chandrakasan et al. 1992). It also assumes that semiconductors are fully activated at the specified frequency. P_{charge} is power consumption caused by voltage conversion loss during charging. P_{static} is the power consumption of the product, assumed static; i.e., it excludes the dynamic power required by the processor and charging, but includes power consumption of other components such as a power management IC and display.

The final activity concerns heat transmission. Heat transmission in a cross-sectional view of the product is shown in Fig. 5. Heat is generated at the boundary between the top and bottom parts, and it is dispatched to ambient air from both the top and bottom surfaces. This heat transmission can be described using thermal network analysis, a commonly used method for estimating the temperature rise in a simplified system (Hatakeyama 2010, Muraoka 2013).

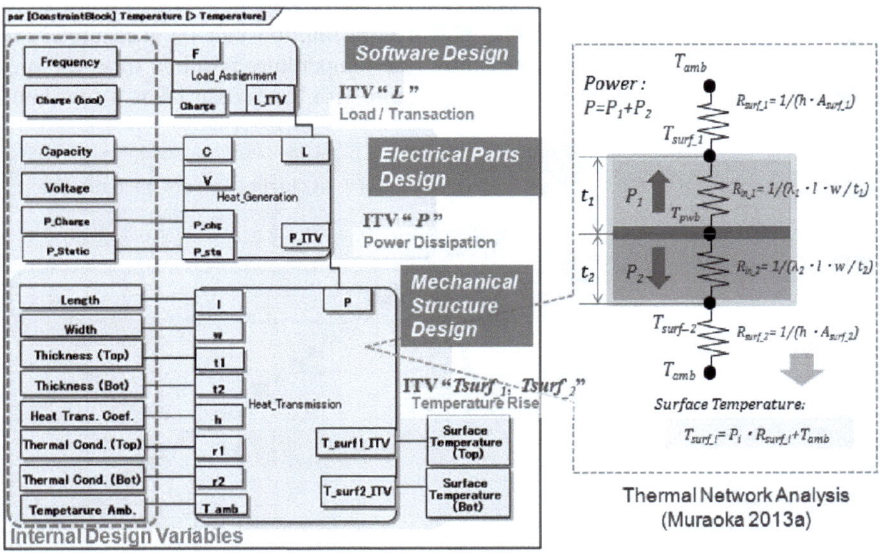

Fig. 5. Parametric model to simulate the temperature rise

In SysML, a parametric diagram is used to simulate and evaluate whether the constraints are satisfied. The calculation process of surface temperatures, T_{surf_1} and T_{surf_2}, using internal design variables is shown in the figure. The internal design variables are assigned to values in the modules. These values are used to calculate the ITVs transmitted between activities. In the diagram, three constraint properties are related to each module design and activity. Each constraint property is described by an algorithm that computes the related equations stated above. The ITVs influence the module designs. Each module is designed to satisfy a target ITV using the internal design variables.

3 Case Study

3.1 System-Level Design Approach in Development and Maintenance

In the design process shown in the DSM of Fig. 6, we introduce a system-level design approach using ITVs. In the early stage of the product development phase, system-level thermal simulation is applied to develop a product design specification (Muraoka et al, 2013b). ITVs are calculated to satisfy the requirements. Module design then starts to utilize the assigned ITVs.

Even after hardware development is complete, software changes often occur in the maintenance phase. Fig. 7 describes the verification process using a system-level thermal model. After the outline of the software change is seen in maintenance planning, thermal risk can be estimated using calculated ITVs. The effect of the software change for the ITVs can be presupposed as a change in processor frequency considering the load of task execution. Other power estimation techniques can also be used. It has been studied in different approaches such as bytecode profiling (Hao 2012) and modeling of component behavior for various applications (Zhang 2010). If the software prototype is available, power consumption can be measured using the hardware developed. Because measuring the temperature requires time for preparation and data sampling during the temperature rise, one case takes a few hours,

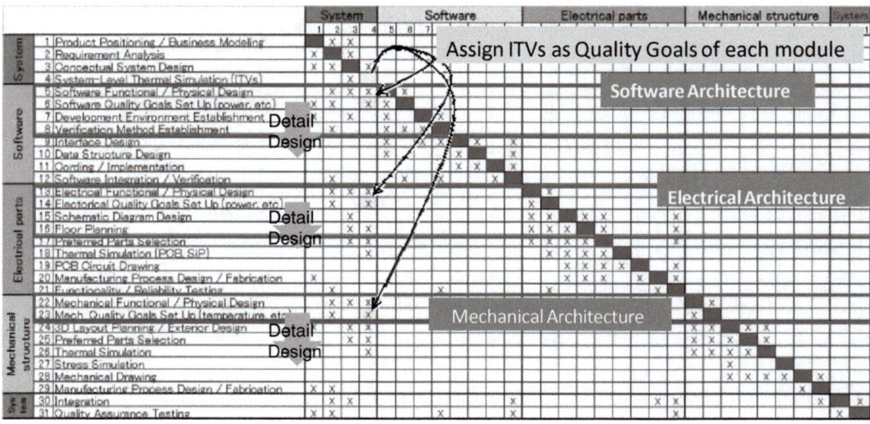

Fig. 6. Design structure matrix (DSM) in the development phase

in general. Therefore, the verification time and effort can be saved by estimating the temperature using system-level simulation to filter the level of thermal risk. System-level simulation is based on simple and fast calculations. The number of measurements is limited only for critical cases. The simulation model can be the same as that used in the development phase or updated for a more accurate simulation approximating the developed system.

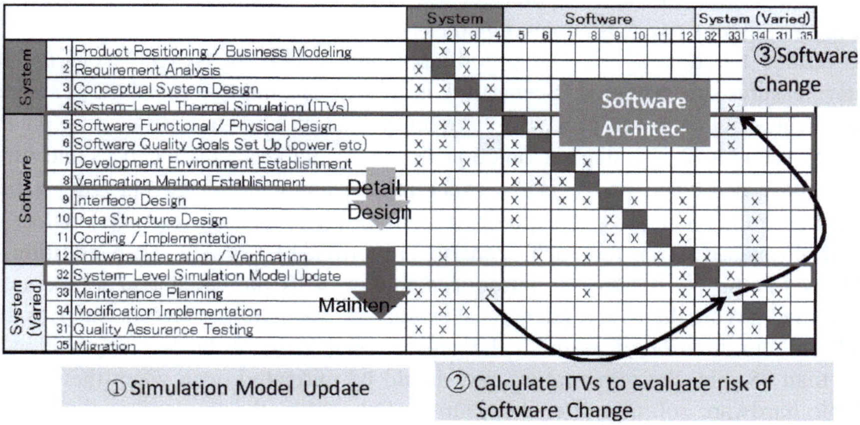

Fig. 7. Design structure matrix (DSM) in the maintenance phase

3.2 System-Level Simulation

As a case study, we developed the design specification of electronic products to satisfy a target temperature. To prevent a burn injury, the surface temperature should be below 44 °C (Moritz 1947). Table 1 provides the initial design parameters for small size electronic products. The top part of the product consists of various components such as a display and speaker, as well as an air gap for assembly tolerance. The bottom part consists of hardware such as PWB, semi-conductors, and a battery. Table 1 also provides the calculated ITVs for a certain application and battery

Table 1. Initial design parameters and ITVs in development phase

Software	F	0.9 GHz
Electrical Parts	C	0.4 μF
	V	2 V
	P_{charge}, P_{static}	0.4, 0.9 (W)
Mechanical Structure	l, w, t_1, t_2	120, 60, 5, 5 (mm)
	h	11 W/(°C·m^2)
	λ_1, λ_2	0.1, 2 W/(°C·m)
Environment	T_{amb}	25 °C
ITVs	F	0.9 GHz
	P	2.74W
	T_{surf_1}, T_{surf_2}	34.6, 43.1 (°C)

charging. For this condition, the temperature is below the target 44 °C. Then, each module design can start to satisfy the ITVs.

During maintenance planning, thermal risk for a new software application is studied. As shown in Table 2, the new application requires a higher processor frequency to execute more tasks, and the ITV, *F*, rises to 1.2 GHz from 0.9 GHz. Because the power consumed by the processor is increased, the surface temperature exceeds the target 44 °C, temperature which causes a low temperature burn by touching for 98 min, as approximated by the temperature curve in Fig. 4.

To reduce the thermal risk in a new application, two alternative scenarios for countermeasures are prepared. Scenario 1 is a software improvement that executes the application at a lower processor frequency, optimizing task processing in the software. Scenario 2 is a disable function that is available to use at the same time. The use case described above is for executing an application and charging a battery. By disabling charging, the power consumption of voltage conversion loss is reduced. Proposed ITVs for each scenario are provided in table 2. In addition, a workflow for this verification is introduced in Fig. 8. If the calculated temperature exceeds the target, then thermal risk is evaluated, considering factors such as the probability and duration of usage. If the general usage time of the new application is longer than 98 min, the temperature rise should be mitigated even when there is no available hardware solution after distribution. Otherwise, the implementation of the application should be stopped at the point of QA. However, although the two countermeasure scenarios in Table 2 reduce temperatures, the temperature in scenario 1 still exceeds the target. If it is very rare to use this application for more than 204 min, thermal risk can be considered to be much reduced by this counter-measure. Scenario 1 requires a software improvement effort, and still has some risk for prolonged usage. Scenario 2 is inconvenient for users. It may result in running out of battery power, which disables all the features of the product. Using system-level simulation, a number of scenarios can be proposed and the most practical solution can be chosen at different points.

Table 2. ITVs developed in the maintenance phase

		New App	Scenario 1	Scenario 2
Countermeasure		-	Execute at a lower frequency	Disable charging
Simulation result	ITV *F*	1200 MHz	1100 MHz	1200 MHz
	P	3.22 W	3.06 W	2.82 W
	T_{surf_1}, T_{surf_2}	36.3, 46.3 (°C)	35.7, 45.2 (°C)	34.8, 43.6 (°C)
	Allowable usage time	98 min	204 min	>480 min

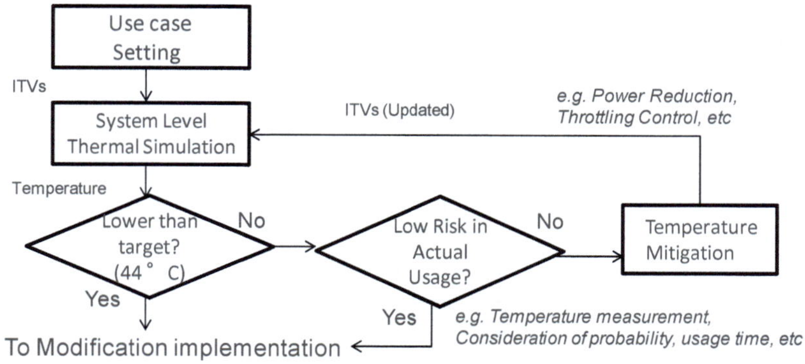

Fig. 8. Verification workflow

4 Conclusions

This study introduces a verification approach for electronic products in both the development and maintenance phases of the product lifecycle. In system-level simulations, ITVs are calculated as boundary conditions within module designs, which comprise software, electrical parts, and mechanical structures. We investigate the use of a thermal simulation model based on SysML. The effect of software changes is evaluated as thermal risk with a quantified temperature that caus- es low-temperature burn injuries. As a case study, we also investigate a verification workflow. Using the simulation model, countermeasures are proposed in the event that thermal risk is increased. By estimating the risk in advance, a number of measurements can be limited. This system-level approach makes efficient verification beneficial, especially for large numbers of product variations that are caused by software changes in the maintenance phase.

References

Balmelli, L.: An Overview of the Systems Modeling Language for Products and Systems Development. J. Object Technology 6(6), 149–177 (2007)

Chandrakasan, A., Sheng, A., Brodersen, W.: Low-power CMOS digital design. IEEE J. Solid-State Circuits 27(4), 473–484 (1992)

Consumer Reports, Our test finds new iPad hits 116 degrees while running games (2012), `http://news.consumerreports.org/electronics/2012/03/our-test-finds-new-ipad-hits-116-degrees-while-running-games.html` (accessed February 17, 2014)

Qualcomm, Snapdragon S4 Thermal Comparison and Butter Benchmark (2012), `http://www.qualcomm.com/media/videos/snapdragon-s4-thermal-comparison-and-butter-benchmark` (accessed February 17, 2014)

Siemens, Role of PLM in the Software Lifecycle. White Paper (2012), http://m.plm.automation.siemens.com/en_us/Images/15825_tcm1224-75783.pdf (accessed February 17, 2014)

Kuusela, J.: How variation changes when an embedded product ceases to be embedded? In: WICSA/ECSA, Companion Volume, p. 147 (2012)

Google. In: Google Press Event, San Francisco (July 24, 2013)

Hatakeyama, T., Ishizuka, M., Nakagawa, S.: Estimation of maximum temperature in 3D-integrated package by thermal network method. In: Electronics Packaging Technology Conference (EPTC), p. 68 (2010)

Hao, S., Ding, L., Halfond, W.G.J., Govindan, R.: Estimating android applications' CPU energy usage via bytecode profiling. In: Green and Sustainable Software (GREENS) (2012), doi:10.1109/GREENS.2012.6224263

Moritz, A., Henriques, F.: Studies of Thermal Injury: II. The Relative Importance of Time and Surface Temperature in the Causation of Cutaneous Burns. Am. J. Pathology 23, 695–720 (1947)

Muraoka, Y., Seki, K., Nishimura, H.: A system level thermal design approach of elec- tronics products to resolve conflicting user requirements. In: Asia-Pacific Council on Systems Engineering 2013 (ACPOSEC 2013), Yokohama (September 2013a)

Muraoka, Y., Seki, K., Nishimura, H.: A System-Level Thermal Design Specification Development of Electronic Products Considering Software Changes. In: International Conference on Engineering Design 2013 (ICED 2013), Seoul, (August 2013b)

Roy, S.: An Equation for Estimating the Maximum Allowable Surface Temperatures of Electronic Equipment. In: 2011 27th Annual IEEE Semiconductor Thermal Measurement and Management Symposium (SEMI-THERM), p. 54 (2011)

Seki, K., Nishimura, H., Zhu, S., Balmelli, L.: A Parametric Design Framework to Sup- port Structural and Functional Modeling of Complex Consumer Electronics Products. In: International Conference on Engineering Design 2011(ICED 2011), p. 282 (2011a)

Seki, K., Nishimura, H.: A module-based thermal design approach for distributed product development. Research in Engineering Design 22(4), 279–295 (2011b)

Zhang, L., Tiwana, B., Qian, Z., et al.: Accurate online power estimation and automatic battery behavior based power model generation for smartphones. In: CODES/ISSS '10 Proceedings of the eighth IEEE/ACM/IFIP International Conference on Hard- ware/Software Codesign and System Synthesis, p. 105 (2010), doi:10.1145/1878961.1878982

A Study for Building a Comprehensive PLM System Based on Utilizing the Japanese Strength of Industry

Akio Kamoshita[1] and Hiroyuki Kumagai[2]

[1] Digital Process Ltd., Japan
[2] Fujitsu Ltd., Japan
akamoshijp@gmail.com

Abstract. Keeping "the Japanese Strength" in digitizing the process of product development is important for the Japanese industry to survive in the intensifying global competition of market. This paper researches about the way of building a comprehensive PLM system based on "the Engineering Process Integrated Architecture (EPIA)" to realize it by taking up actual cases. The system, based on integrated database, consistently integrates the whole process of product planning, development and design, manufacturing preparation, production, purchasing, sales, service and maintenance, and it enables the mutual cooperation of the information of PLM/SCM/CRM.

Keywords: Product Development Process, 3D Digitization, Design and Manufacturing, Product Design Architecture, Organizational Capability, Process Optimization, Product Globalization, CAD, CAE, PDM, BOM, PLM.

1 Introduction

Keeping "the Japanese Strength" in digitizing the process of product development is important when a PLM system is built. If you look at the characteristics of product development in terms of "product architecture", "manufacturing organizational capability" and "design and manufacturing process", it is necessary to connect them based on the "digital data standards" in the PLM system construction. Among them, the strength of Japan, in particular, is in a tight connection with the "manufacturing organizational capability" and "design and manufacturing process", and it has a feature that allows for flexible system operation. (Fig.1) [1], [2]

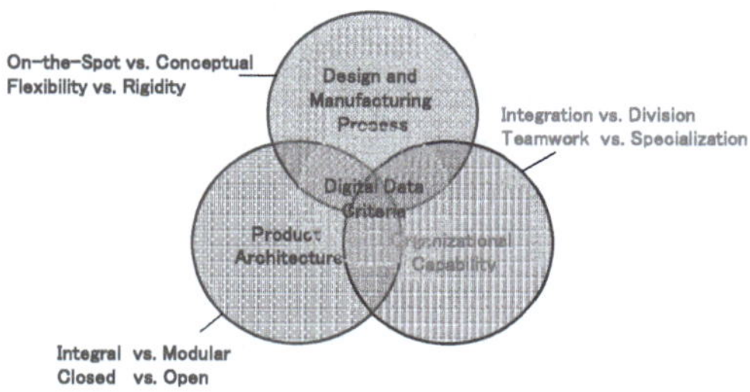

Fig. 1. Characteristics of the product development

In this paper, based on taking up actual cases, we study a comprehensive PLM system construction which integrates consistently the whole process of product planning, development and

S. Fukuda et al. (Eds.): PLM 2014, IFIP AICT 442, pp. 247–256, 2014.

design, production preparation, production, procurement, sales, service and maintenance. The system will become important in the future, in the digitization of the produc! development process to utilize the Japanese strength of industry, in the intensifying global competition market.

2 Development History of the PLM System

2.1 To a Mutual Cooperation System from a Individual System

PLM systems that support the actual business of product development was first constructed in the individual work of each department. Then, it has been built consistently, from the design and development work of the upstream process, in turn manufacturing arrangements, production process, etc. Among these, the system is constructed as to allow cooperation between departments adjacent individually.

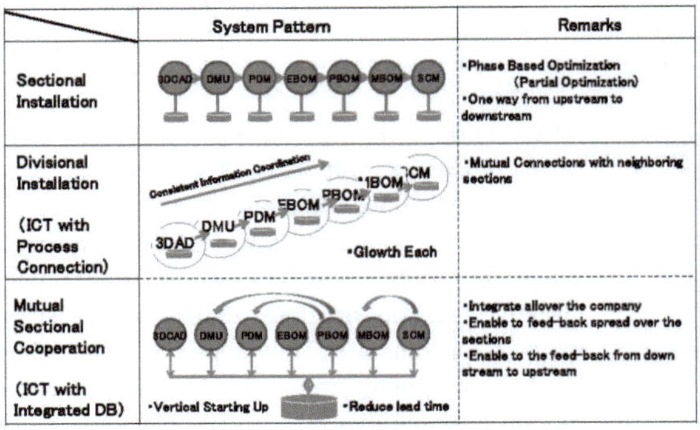

Fig. 2. Growth history of PLM system

Al present, by globalization of manufacturing industry, localized production and purchasing has progressed, the needs to send the local information to upstream process is increasing. To respond to such needs, there has been seen such a case for feeding back information to the upstream process from the downstream process, by building a system of mutual cooperation between business, based on an integrated database. (Fig.2).

2.2 Design Concept of the Cooperative System

In the intensifying competitive global market, to take advantage of the strengths of product development of Japan, the spiral cooperation in the design development and manufacture is the key, that is made of not only a top-down approach from the upstream process of Western thought but also made of a bottom-up approach from the production site of Japan. In

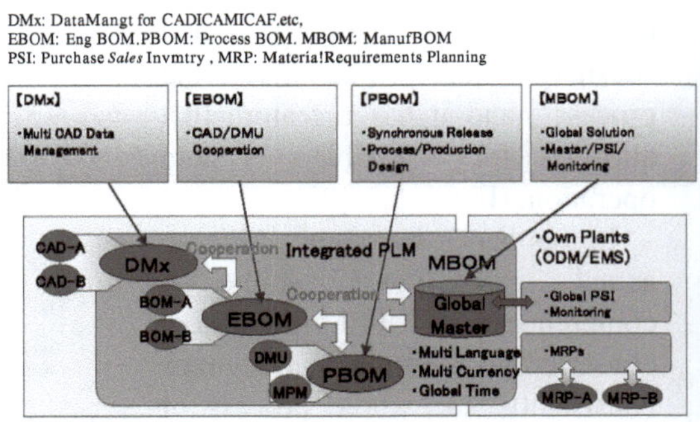

Fig. 3. Architecture of integrated PLM system

order to strengthen it, in the digital development of the Japanese manufacturing industry in the future, it should be aimed at to build a PLM system by an architecture that enables the consistent conjunction of information with assembly process BOM and manufacturing BOM in the downstream process along with the control of CAD, PDM and design BOM in the upstream process. (Fig.3)[3]

3 Expansion into a Comprehensive PLM System

3.1 The Concept of a Comprehensive PLM System

Up to the previous section, a desirable PLM system has been shown from the globalization point of manufacturing preparation, production and procurement process. In the future, the system construction which hold the entire life cycle of a product as consistent process becomes important for promoting the "manufacturing innovation". The system includes not only the current process of design development, manufacturing preparation, production and procurement, but also the upstream process of the product planning, and the downstream process of sales, service and maintenance. A design concept in this system building, "Engineering Process Integrated Architecture (EPIA)" is shown in FIG 4.[2]

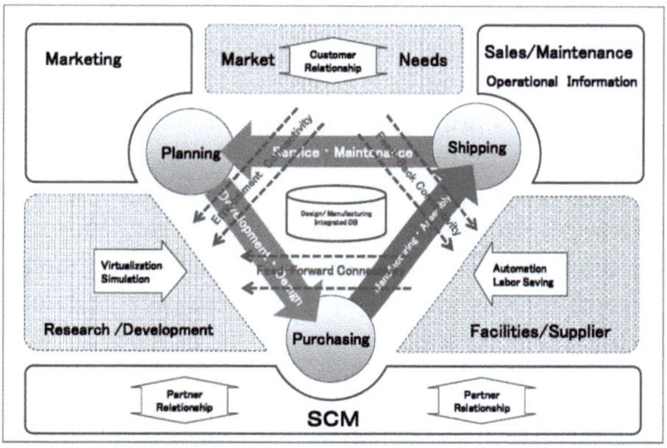

Fig. 4. Engineering Process Integrated Architecture

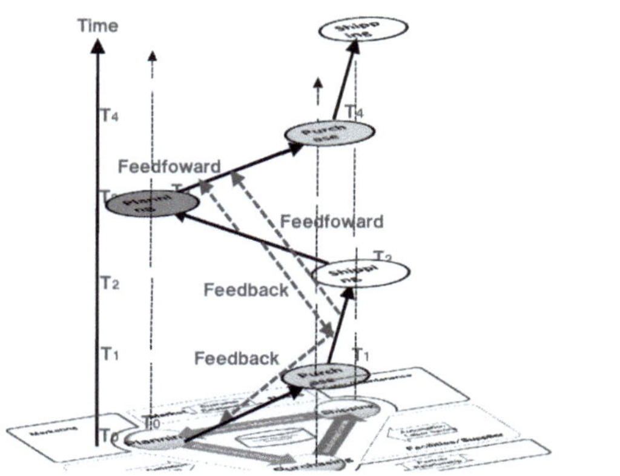

Fig. 5. Process Axes & Data linking of Each Process Axis

The representation put the time axis within each process axis is shown in Fig.5. In each process axes, depending on the progress of each process, data related to the product is stored and updated in the integrated database. Further, the data linkage performed by each arrow between each process axes is also performed through the integrated DB. The data is feed-forward between the virtual process and the real process, and feed-back as the same. Similarly, the data is feed-forward between virtual process and field process, and feed-back as the same. In order to perform the close communication between organizations involved in each process, the Japanese "manufacturing organizational capability" is easily allow this data linkage. The following describes the concept by which in turn take up the actual cases.

3.2 Cooperation with the Manufacturing Site Information and Planning and Design Information (Data Linkage between the Virtual Process and the Real Process)

By using a digital mock-up, feed-forward and feed-back to the design by the production site information are performed by the design study of interference gap and operability etc. and by the productivity study of assembly and maintenance operation and the like. Further, by using a simulation, a similar function is performed by the performance study of design strength and heat resistance and so on.

In the product development of Japanese companies, this has been done through the teamwork of people at manufacturing sites and design, by sharing information with the drawings. Now, it came to be organized as (simultaneous) concurrent engineering, information cooperation by the system is carried out.

In recent years, the case that production site and design site is separated geographically is increasing. Originally, innovation of the product is realized based on awareness by trial and error in the site of production, by devising a new knowledge through teamwork of design and production. In terms of taking advantage of the strengths of Japan, cases such as the following are desirable.

3.2.1 A Case of the Automotive Industry

Toyota Motor Corporation says that new products and new technology are born from Japan with strong manufacturing site, high technology and a high-performance material. Therefore, competitive edge is in the domestic plant. In order to deploy the car of high quality into the factory of the world, to enhance the technology to produce low-cost in a short period of time, it is necessary to strengthen the mother plant in Japan (Iwate Prefecture, etc.). To do so, to carry out business as minimum, it is required domestic production of 3 million units in the maintenance of the pyramid structure of the domestic business.

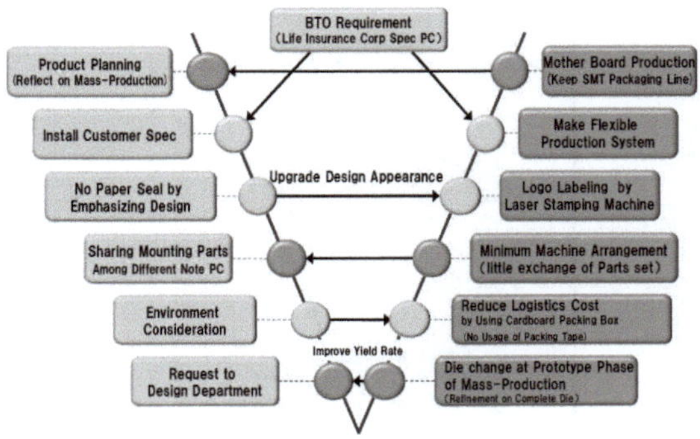

Fig. 6. Synergic Effects of Development and Manufacturing Dept

3.2.2 A Case of Electrical Precision Industry

In the production of notebook / Tablet PC, in order to suppress the domestic labor costs, Fujitsu limited promote automation (robotic) of the assembly process. Thereby, synergy to co-exist manufacturing and production operations, and design and development is prioritized. (Fig.6)

3.2.3 A Case of Heavy Machinery Industry

The characteristic of production and development system of Komatsu is coexistence of production and development department at all plants. Thereby a strong cooperation of both sectors is promoted. The key components that give a competitive advantage to competitors are developed and manufactured only in Japan. There is a mother plant in Japan in each product group, child factory carries out the production and development in a place close to the market. As a result, the building-cost and product quality, product development that meets the market needs are carried out.

3.3 Sophisticated Use of Information in Planning and Design of Upstream Process (Data Linkage between the Virtual Process and Field Process)

3.3.1 Sophisticated product planning method

In recent years, with the progress of globalization, the need of information required in the planning stage of product development is increasing to include production, purchasing and marketing from those around the product so far, i.e. where to buy, where to make, where to sell, where to make money, how to maintain? In this respect, feed-forward and feed-back of information of market and services and maintenance to the design and marketing has become more important. The following is one of the advanced cases of product planning.

3.3.1.1 A Case of Automotive Industry

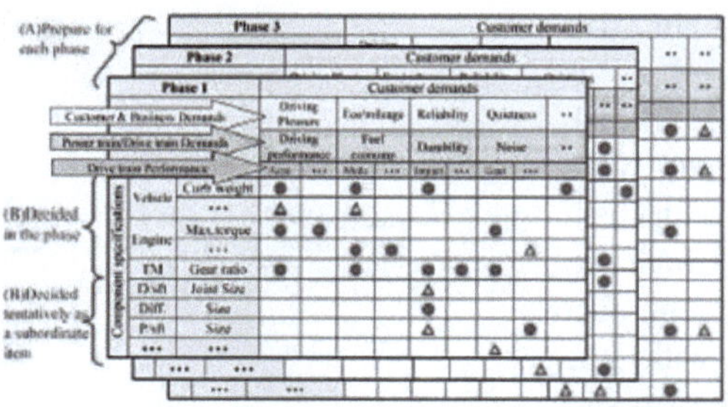

Figure 5. Simplified product architecture matrix (Image)
(A) Prepare a matrix linked to the development phases.
(B)Focus on key specifications and tentatively define the sub-set of items.

Quoted from reference[4]

Fig. 7. Method of Defining Product architecture for Each Dev. Phase

A method for determining the procedure of product development incorporating tacit knowledge from the upstream planning

Technique to clarify the optimal product development logic has been developed by

Nissan Motor Co., Ltd. The complexity of the product architecture is assessed multilaterally by architecture analysis from the upstream planning stage to downstream stage. And, implicit knowledge (know-how) of the design process that veteran designers have is transformed to explicit knowledge.[4]

As shown in Fig.7, the matrix of performance items and specification items (QFD matrix) that make up product architecture is prepared in size in accordance with the purpose of each development phase. In each phase, to determine the order in which they evaluate the degree of influence performance, specifications, and decide by priority of having a large impact. At this time, an efficient procedure is obtained by sorting of logical priority, and also by weaving know-how that is based on past experience. A consensus of the decision-making of each phase including especially difficult upstream processes is facilitated while incorporating the implicit intellectual approach of Japan.

3.3.1.2 A Case of Electrical Precision Industry

White Home Electric Appliances for Emerging Countries

In the Panasonic Corporation, volume segment products in the global, are positioned as strategic products in order to capture the emerging countries, and are classified into three categories. One is "leading global V" products intended to be sold to wealthy emerging countries, the value-added products that are popular in Japan and other developed countries. The second is products that fight head-to-head with other companies in the main battlefield of the global. Using a common base model, expand in multiple countries, it aims to increase market share in each country. The third is products developed by the idea of local market, in order to capture the middle layer of emerging countries.

Currently, Lifestyle Research Centers and equivalent organization are established in five countries, that is China, India, Brazil, Germany, and Vietnam. A mechanism has been built to create a product equipped with the functionality required for different countries by visiting to the country site actually to investigate the actual use.

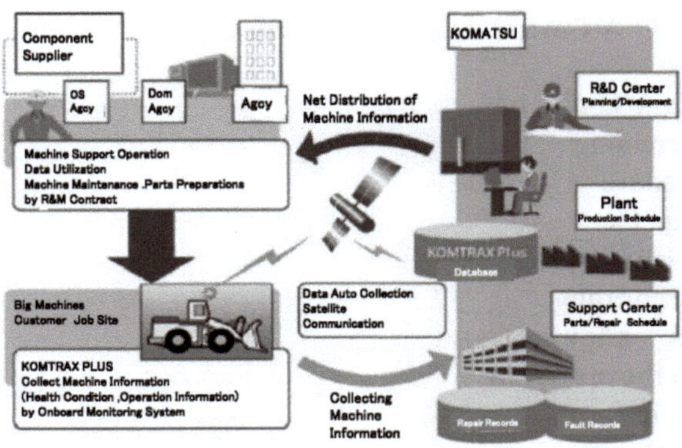

Fig. 8. Corresponding to the Market by Utilizing Field Information

3.3.2 Collaboration with Field Information

3.3.2.1 A Case of Heavy Machinery Industry

Meanwhile, In Komatsu Ltd., there is the case to enhance the more competitiveness of the product by utilizing market information, service and maintenance information, when the product is used in the market. By having a guideline of component replacement and maintenance time through the grasp of the actual usage in the market, they take advantage of the collaboration with production and parts procurement, and improve the quality of attractiveness by reflecting on the design specifications during product planning. (Fig.8)[5]

4 Manufacturing Organization Capability of Japan to Support the Comprehensive PLM System Construction

Here, the Japanese "manufacturing organizational capability" will be discussed. By performing a close communication between organizations, it allows in product development in Japan, the tight linkage of data between processes.

4.1 Characteristics of Design Information Management in Japan

An overview of the differences of Japanese-style and Western-type is shown in Fig.9 regarding the management method of design information in product development.

In the Western method, the information that is determined by the design is deployed by top-down in one direction to each relevant departments of the next step. In contrast, in the method of Japan, the information which is determined by the design, and is received feedback from each department, is deployed as the information that has been refined mutually in both directions.

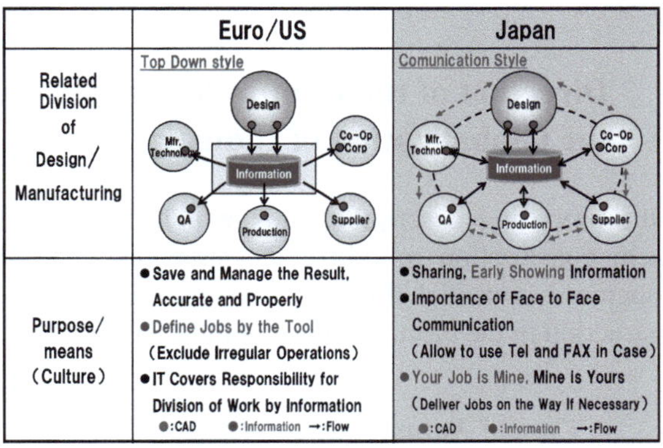

Fig. 9. Feature Comparison of Design Information Management

As shown in this figure, the management method of Japan has good compatibility with such as product development involving many technical elements, and especially with integrated products that require close cooperation of the data It is because it works by compromise, while allowing the ambiguity, and incorporating the diverse opinions of many stakeholders including the manufacturing site.

4.2 Characteristics of Organizational Culture of Japan

And also regarding the organizational culture, an overview of the differences of Japanese-type and Western-type is shown in Fig.10.

As shown in the table, it has the characteristics focusing on more bottom-up consensus in team play than personal top-down leadership. Hence, as mentioned above, tight linkage of data for managing the product development information is done naturally.

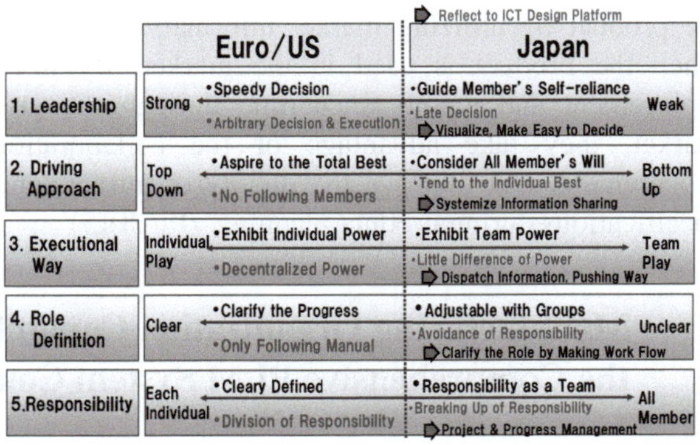

Fig. 10. Characteristics Comparison of Organizational Culture

Such as shown above, the characteristics of the Japanese "product development organizational capability" is considered to be intended to support the comprehensive PLM system construction. It should be noted that, at the time of comprehensive PLM construction, improving the weaknesses by emphasizing consensus is required, while following the strengths of Japan that has been demonstrated so far. For this purpose, the measures indicated by the arrow in Figure, is desirable to be reflected in the ICT design platform.

5 Direction of the Comprehensive PLM System Construction in the Globalization of Industry

In the preceding description, in the industrial globalization, comprehensive PLM system construction to utilize the strengths of product development of Japanese companies is essential. Here, a direction of it is shown based on actual cases of PLM construction in the electric precision industry and the automotive industry in Japan.

5.1 A Case of Automotive Industry

In the automotive industry, according to the vertically integrated production structure, an industry pyramid is created in each region, and the core functionality of development and manufacturing, is located in Japan. The Planning, development and design by the OEM at the pyramid top is done in cooperation with other countries and Japan headquarters, and Teir1 below also has cooperation with local site and head office.

In this case, with respect to PLM tool, it is necessary to use a system of the same type as the OEM, or to use a system that does not have a problem on data distribution. Feedback to the design of information from production preparation, procurement and production is carried out in each layer of the Tier; a smooth cooperation with the Japanese headquarters of each layer is one of the most important issues.

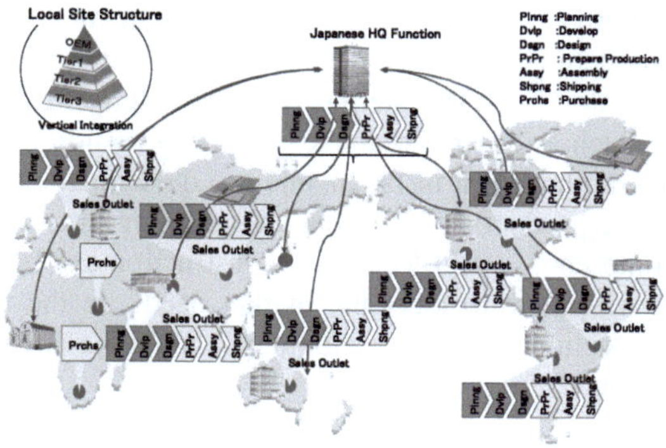

Fig. 11. Globalization Style of Automobile Industry

Hereafter, along with the development of the modular design of an automobile, global procurement of general-purpose products is carried out. For the PLM tool, a product of an open architecture having a higher degree of freedom increases the more importance in the product development of each company.

5.2 A Case of Electrical Precision Industry

Unlike the automobile, there is no pyramid structure of Tier; there is a horizontal specialization structure in which headquarters make procurement of general-purpose goods. The core functionality of development and manufacturing is located in Japan. Although production bases are deployed globally, the sourcing is concentrated in Japan headquarters. In that sense, in response to the globalization of product markets, production bases are located globally, planning and development functions does not moved, and each research site is placed in each market. (Fig.12).

In this case, PLM tool is a separate product for each part of each company. If necessary, assembly products manufacturer make design consideration by preparing data of the components for their own system. Feedback to the design of information from production preparation, procurement, and production is needed to be carried out direct and quickly to the headquarters. But the size of the spatial-temporal distance is increasing the difficulty of cooperation.

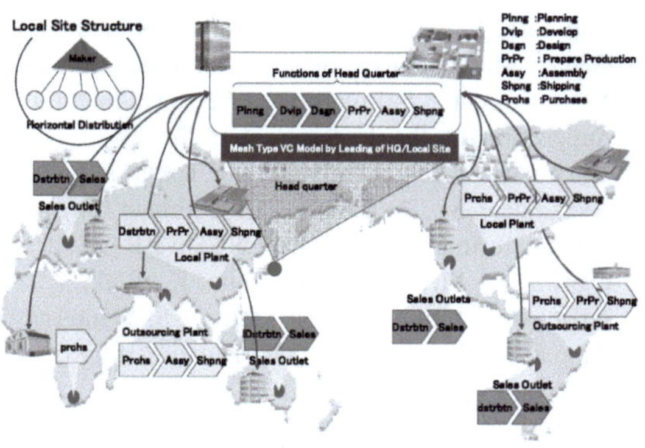

Fig. 12. Globalization Style of Elec./Prec. Industry

Future, since production bases movement, and speed up needs of procurement and production information F / B, the domestic production by returning to Japan is also considered. PLM system is required to have flexibility against such base movement.

Such as described above, electric precision industry and automotive industry place the mother plant in Japan, and has developed globally, while retaining the technology of the product development and grasping the local market needs. The direction of the comprehensive PLM system construction can be understood for carrying out product development to meet the market needs, in the two-way information cooperation of production site and development and taking advantage of the product development of Japan.

6 Conclusion

In this paper, for the sake of global expansion of Japanese industry, as a mechanism of information utilization to take advantage of the product development of Japan, a comprehensive PLM system based on a system architecture named as "Engineering Process Integrated Architecture(EPIA) is discussed by taking up the actual cases. The system, based on the integrated data base, consistently integrates the whole process of product planning, development and design, manufacturing preparation, production, purchasing, sales, service and maintenance. And also it enables the mutual cooperation of the information of PLM/SCM/CRM.

When the manufacturing industry of Japan performs the process reform to build a system based on this idea, it is possible to perform global deployment by leveraging the strengths of product development in Japan, drawing a line from the global expansion of Western industry.

References

1. Fujimoto, T.: Tokyo University of 21st Century COE Manufacturing Management Research Center: Manufacturing business administration, Kobunsha (2007)
2. Youngwon, P., Fujimoto, T., Abe, T.: Integral Type of Manufacturing and IT system-Suggestion of the framework of the IT utilization to bring competition predominance. University of Tokyo University of Tokyo 2010-MMRC-302 (2010)
3. Nakamura, M., Watanabe, I.: Ultimate form of the global production to extend the manufacturing power in Japan Nikkei BP (2011)
4. Ogawa, Y., Miyoshi, H., Iwashita, K., Park, Y., Abe, T.: Drivetrain System Design Based on an Architecture Analysis Method. SAE International 2013-01-0968 (2013)
5. Komatsu website, company information, service solution: Use of ICT(2013), `http://www.komatsu.co.jp/Company/profile/product_supports/`
6. Kamoshita, A., Kumagai, H.: A Study of the Design/Manufacturing Characteristics of Products And of an Integrated Architecture of the Engineering Process In Building the PLM System. In: Asian Conference on Design and Digital Engineering 2012 (ACDDE2012), proceedings No. 100011 (2012)

PLM Reference Model for Integrated Idea and Innovation Management

Manuel Löwer and Jan Erik Heller

Institute for Engineering Design (ikt), RWTH Aachen University, Germany
loewer@ikt.rwth-aachen.de

Abstract. The authors present their research results and practical experience regarding implementations of PLM systems in a set of companies. In detail, the very early stages of product planning and innovation management are considered. As most of today's enterprises already operate PDMS (Product Data Management Systems), excellent foundations for a company-spanning idea and innovation management exist. An extensive analysis showed that idea management – if established – uses autonomous databases and data models which are not merged into or consistent with already existing PLM models. Potential is scattered due to disruptions in the information flow. Mostly, marketing and strategic groups have no direct access to relevant development and service data and thus lack customer feedback and stimuli for new strategic product ideas. Furthermore, strategic, technological and market boundaries have not been modelled yet to allow for an efficient handling of « postponed » ideas. The authors developed an extended data model in combination with a reference process model for innovation and idea management. Strategic data comparable to business intelligence information is consolidated with regular PLM information offering advanced opportunities and efficiency for innovation management. The paper also features an implementation of the introduced reference data and process models in a state of the art PLM system. Additionally, the approach serves as a guideline for SMEs and enables the set-up of professional innovation and idea management including presets for workflows, model attributes and open innovation functionalities.

Keywords: Integrated Product Lifecycle Management (PLM), Innovation and Idea Management, Product Planning and PLM, PLM Reference Model.

1 Introduction

In today's increasingly fast changing markets, enterprises are constantly forced to come up with fresh ideas and new products in order to remain competitive. In other words, they are forced to innovate. However, the term « innovation » has been one of the most used words during the last years when it comes to strategic product development. But innovation is more than the actual invention since it needs to match economic conditions and requires a successful market launch. Several approaches exist to transform ideas into products, subsumed as innovation management. Even

S. Fukuda et al. (Eds.): PLM 2014, IFIP AICT 442, pp. 257–266, 2014.

though innovation management is implemented by larger enterprises on business process levels, a sustainable integration of reasonable data, information and processes has not been realized. Moreover, SMEs typically lack the financial resources to set up explicit staff positions and introduce broad and comprehensive approaches.

Product lifecycle management offers all means to provide that integrated platform. Per definition, PLM covers all phases of products' lifecycles from ideas to their disposal [1, 2]. From the authors' perspective, this common understanding of PLM has its limitations since the phase « zero » is improperly addressed. Hence, information about circumstances which led to the initiation of a focused idea development are not recorded and associated with the future product. Affected data mainly includes external or internal needs and strategic considerations which are subject to change rapidly. In addition, it usually needs a large number of ideas for the successful launch of a single product (Fig. 1). This does not necessarily mean that most of the withdrawn ideas in the process have no economic potential.

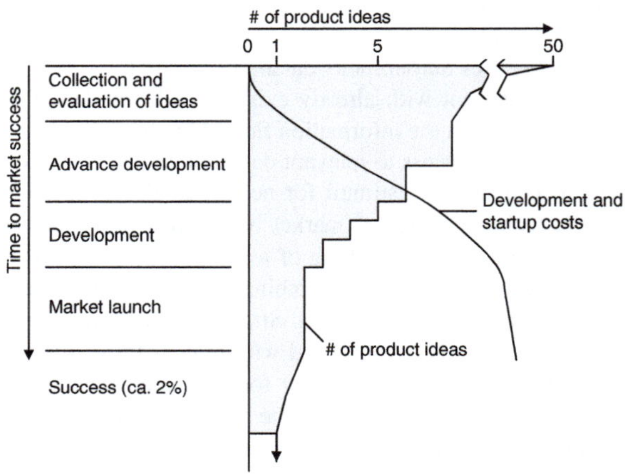

Fig. 1. Reduction of ideas along the innovation process [3]

There is actually a large number of different reasons for not following ideas in a specific innovation cycle, ranging from insufficient company knowledge for needed production technology to currently non-economical commodity prices or even political influences such as punitive tariff duties. Studies show that most of the ideas which are transferred into commercial products originate from the development departments (Fig. 2). Since these divisions are historically constraint to document their work for further processing, engineering or product data management (PDM), in the majority of companies is implemented with the most advanced technical means in terms of process and data management. Thus, the technical availability of such systems can be exploited and broadened to the innovation and idea management affected departments of the company.

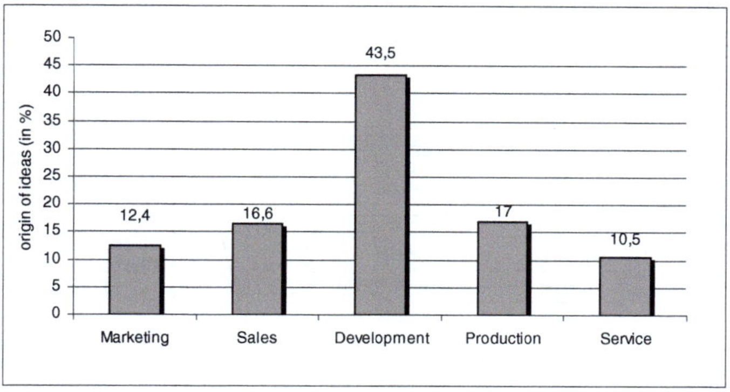

Fig. 2. The origin of product ideas [4]

2 The Process of Idea and Innovation Management

The buzzword innovation is frequently misinterpreted as the invention itself. In 1934 Schumpeter already emphasized that innovation describes the transformation of an invention or at least enhancements of existing products into a commercial application for a company [5]. One of the characteristics of this innovation is a so called degree of novelty, which can be subjective or objective and applies to products, services or processes [6]. Regardless of the type of innovation, the driver and catalyst commonly is the acquisition of market shares or the sustainment of the actual position [7, 8]. Hence, innovation cannot be seen as a nonrecurring, singular activity but rather as a periodic and complex business process which demands for a profound workflow suitable for the particular company. Within such a framework, the innovation management addresses and affects the three different layers: normative, strategic and operational ones (Fig. 3). The normative management sets the boundaries and restrictions for the definition of the innovation management on the strategic layer leading to the innovation targets and a structured innovation program.

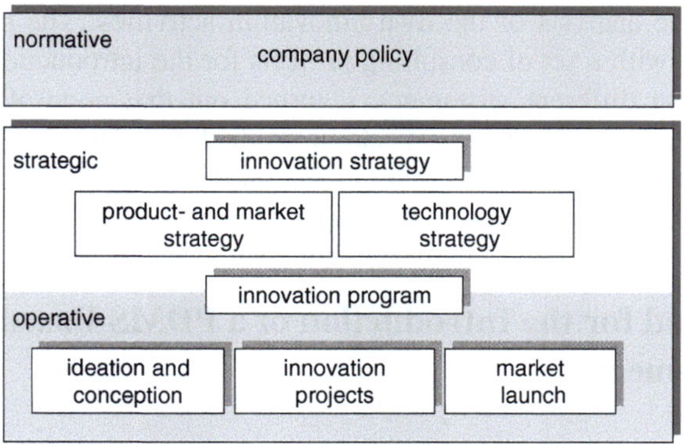

Fig. 3. The framework of innovation management [on the basis of 9,10]

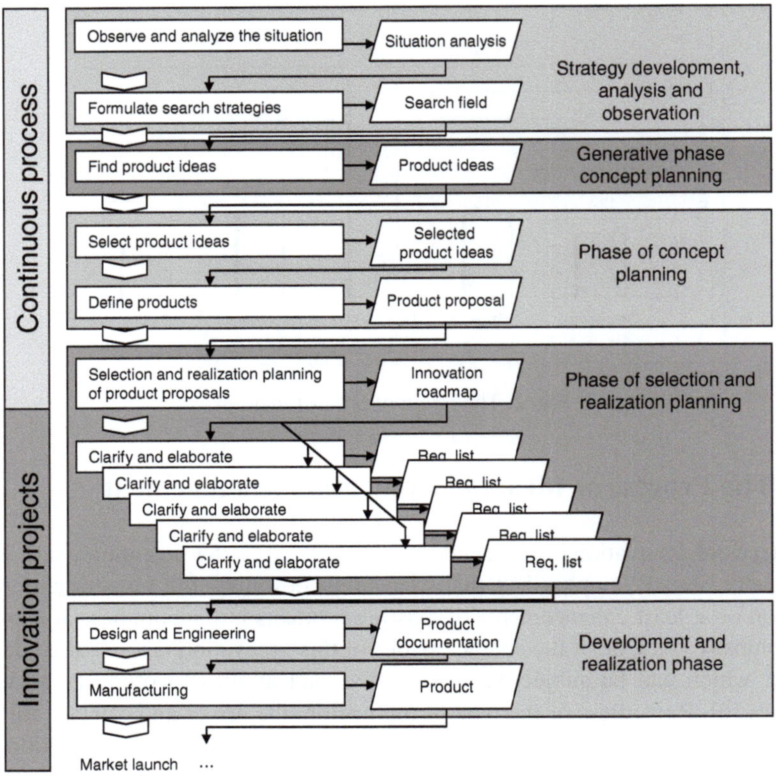

Fig. 4. The process of innovation management

This program is then systematically operationalized with ideation and conceptualization following e.g. the generic process of product planning as provided by VDI2220 and can also be realized within innovation projects also incorporating tools and methods of industrial design. As part of the undertaken research, different innovation processes have been evaluated and basic proceeding was setup (Fig. 4). It should serve as a landmark for the analysis of the own innovation activities. The research has been conducted in line with a set of consulting projects for the introduction and implementation of PDMS at different customers. It turned out that none of them had rather defined nor implemented strategic aspects of product planning. Due to this, the need for a method to introduce a PDM based innovation management arose. This method is presented in the following section of this paper.

3 A Method for the Introduction of a PDMS Based Innovation Management

The innovation process is a sequence of deductive acquisition and processing of information. In each step a concretion using different methods and models is achieved.

Compared to common technical parameters, strategic and normative boundaries are often of descriptive character, not quantifiable and hardly reducible to a single attribute. This complicates the extension of standard PLM data models and an evaluation of prospective costs and efforts in comparison to the anticipated benefit is highly recommended. The developed method (Fig. 5) is divided into three main phases and entails different evaluation milestones to ensure an effective controlling.

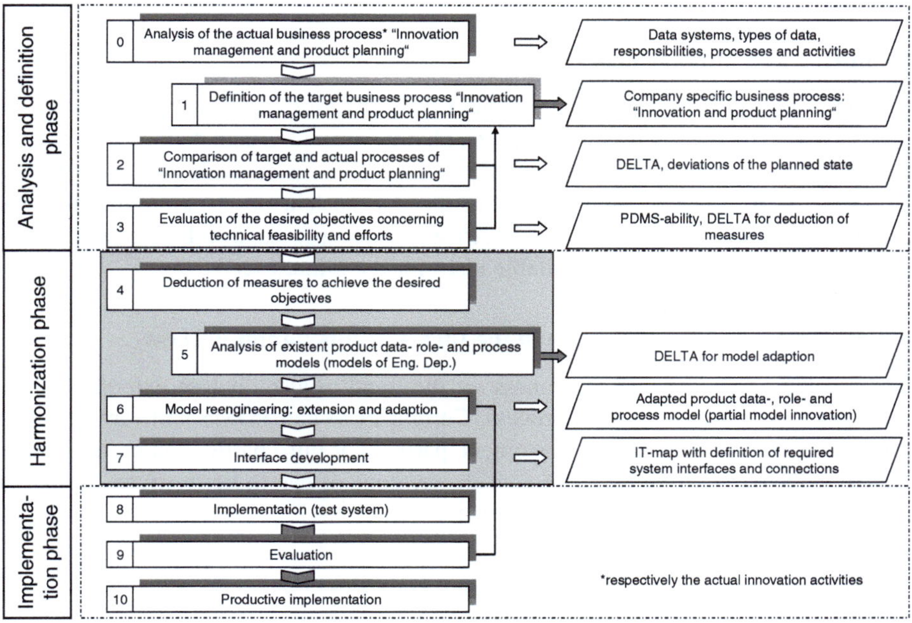

Fig. 5. Method to introduce a PDM based innovation management

The first phase (analysis and definition) closes with a conclusion about the company's needs and ability to deploy a PDM based innovation and idea management, the resulting efforts and the technical feasibility. Within the second phase, measures to achieve the intended state are taken. In most cases this requires a noticeable reengineering of product data, process and role models, assuming that PLM-supporting systems or respectively PDMS are already implemented for a restricted group of users. The third phase starts with the implementation of key functionalities on a test system, followed by different evaluation scenarios. Throughout this whole process the so called Capability Scorecard (CSC) is used that allows for the transition of a PLM strategy into operational activities and a quantifiable assessment of the achievement of objectives [11]. Once the testing has proved positive an implementation in the productive system and roll out can be pursued.

The use of IT systems to support business processes implies the understanding that these systems are not intended to substitute or directly control employees. Acceptance and the success of a later deployment strongly depend on the proper communication of what the clear benefits are for the involved parties in their daily routine. In addition, implementing every sub process as a workflow will lead to getting the implementation efforts out of hand and the project to fail.

3.1 Support of the Continuous Innovation Process

The following subsection gives an overview of requirements for the IT-based innovation planning and the key objectives.

Capturing and Management of Ideas

Per definition, ideas have a higher degree of abstraction compared to product concepts. Textual descriptions of ideas are an obvious way to articulate their content and to make them explicitly available. However, a system based evaluation, selection or clustering is not directly made possible through such a description. Additionally, characteristics and criteria such as classification schemes have to be realized to ease the search and identification of suitable ideas for the future user.

Simple Access and Participation in the Idea and Innovation Process

Globalization and customer awareness set the trend to also enclose external sources and resources in the innovation process. Current PLM and PDMS software generally offers web technologies so that customers, partners or third parties can easily be integrated. Depending on the level of confidence, content has to be restricted trough an advanced role model and rights management.

Monitoring and Evaluation of Innovation Activities

The association of ideas available in the database to innovation projects and created products should provide a traceable realization rate. Not only the outcome but also the actual status of an idea or project as well as a report of current activities for a specific search field, a business unit or braches should be available in real-time. Financial incentives for top innovation performers or significant sources for good ideas, which can be identified by the system, can be implemented. Integrated project management functionalities provide controlling mechanisms and inform about the innovation costs.

3.2 Support of Innovation Projects

As already stated, there can be different initiations for innovation projects. One is the continuous observation of the market or main competitors. Another one can be a specific planned activity or technology push. For both (and additional) cases, a process template has to be defined, providing a suitable framework to guide the user. Beyond project specific data, information from product planning and monitoring of later lifecycle phases has to accessible.

4 PDMS Centred Innovation Management

The aspects of PDMS for the usage in the area of idea and innovation management can thus be divided into the core functionalities of innovation planning and controlling, project management and execution as well as idea-, concept- and data management. The different sub functionalities are also depicted in Fig. 6. Data- process- and role model serve as the backbone and ensure the integrated PLM approach. These models should be a digital mirror of the company in terms of its innovation activities and associated data and organizational structures. For those who do not have an established and documented process, the authors set up a process model as a maximum template which covers all relevant activities of innovation planning. The structure allows for a direct utilization for the three business models listed above. To unambiguously describe each process element, several parameters have to be included: process id, superordinate process (e.g. business process), predecessor and successor process, input (data, kind of data, format, location and association to predecessor processes), output, involved parties (groups, roles), responsible instances (process owner and authorized for changes), media and tools needed for the transformation of input to output.

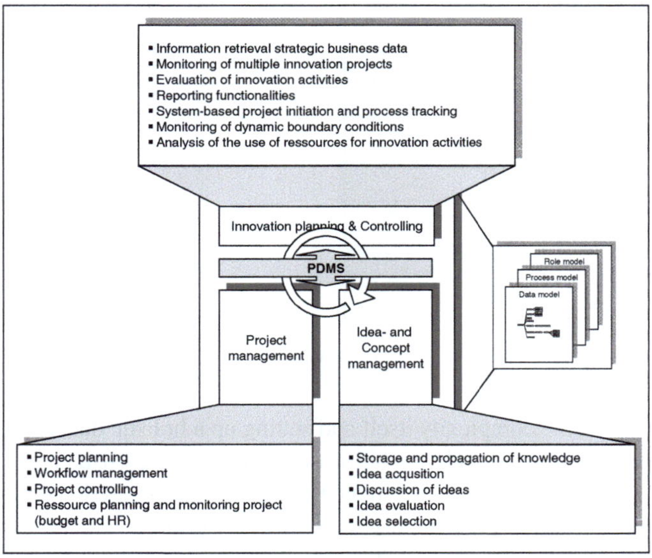

Fig. 6. PDMS centred innovation management [12]

Referring to the product data model the different data objects, their dependencies and attributes have to be analysed. In order to model a PDMS data object also the object lifecycles have to be considered. In addition, the object can contain different objects itself as part of the object master record. These objects can conclusively own attributes. In the previous section of this contribution, it has been emphasized that ideas and the management of ideas is crucial for successful innovation.

Thus, the data model for the object "idea" to be implemented in a PDMS is described for clarification (Fig. 7). To comprehensively describe an idea and to make it sustainably available in a PDMS, the authors identified the need for integrating different elements: an idea description, a sketch, note/comments, discussion forum and evaluations. For the idea object, these documents or fields constitute the major record. The idea description should be covered as a document to allow for versioning and idea adaption in later phases. This document in turn owns a large number of attributes, and also has different lifecycle stages, the document lifecycles.

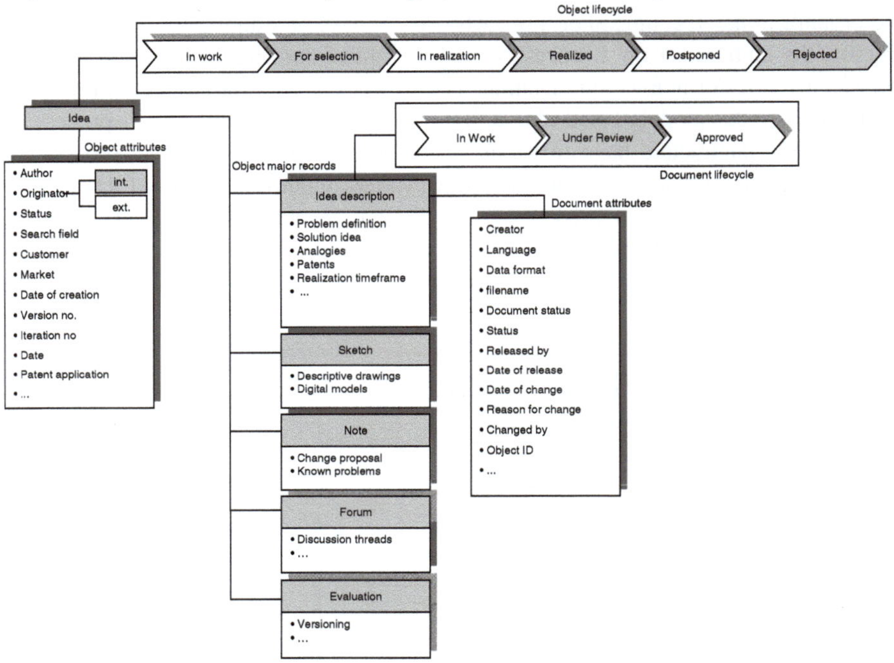

Fig. 7. Data object "idea"

It is obvious, that the complexity itself and setting up a holistic data and process model can overstrain the resources and capabilities of SMEs, as they usually do not have according staff positions. Therefore the created templates can be used and efforts can drastically be reduced. Anyway, it is highly recommended to involve experienced third parties to act as consultants from the early beginning and to focus on the project objectives.

5 Prototypic Implementation

The last step of the proposed method is the implementation in the given IT system of the company. For the evaluation of the developed innovation process, role and data models and implementation has been performed using PTC Windchill 9.1 with its modules PartsLink and ProjectLink and an Oracle 11g1 data base. Decision for this PDMS has been taken due to its completely web centred approach which does not need a client installation, hence also fulfils the requirement of open innovation needs.

Besides the different objects, their states and the associated processes, method sheets have been implemented in the "library context" which give additional information about appropriate methods to be used in each of the innovation phases (e.g. method 635, pest-analysis, ...). The processes themselves have been implemented as (partly) automated workflows to guide the user and ensure a consistent data basis. Fig. 8 depicts the different operations of idea management which are supported by the PDMS.

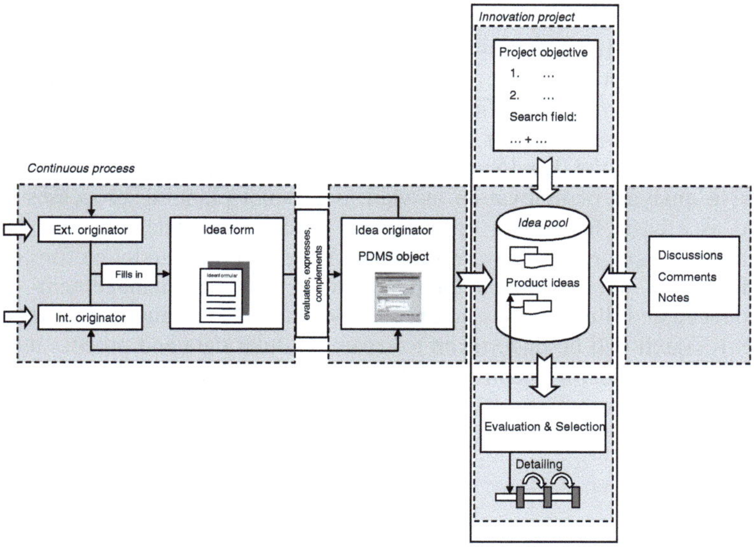

Fig. 8. Process of PDMS idea management

The best practice experience with customers for innovation projects led to the implementation of a project template consisting of all required milestones, activities and deliverables. Not only the project members' workload on the organizational level is reduced by using this predefined template but also the controlling and outcome of different innovation project has shown to be better comparable and evaluable.

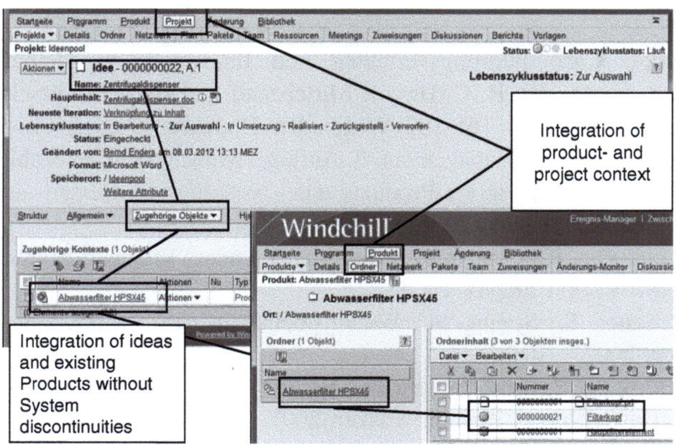

Fig. 9. Windchill implementation for idea and innovation management

A screenshot of the system implementation is depicted in Fig. 9. Following the PLM approach, it is possible to link ideas (Windchill project context) with existing products (Windchill product context). In case the idea relates to a product improvement which has been initiated by service evaluation or warranty cases, the idea can directly be linked to these reports and thus close the information loop.

6 Conclusion and Outlook

This contribution outlined that although PLM has become one of the key aspects in today's business, a lot of further potential has not been unlocked yet. Innovation and idea management have not sufficiently been comprised in an integrated PLM approach to close the gap between strategic considerations prior to the early stages of product planning and the development phases. In order to overcome these drawbacks, an extensive analysis of innovation as well as product planning processes has been conducted as a basis for setting up a generic process and data model to be implemented in PLM supporting software systems. A method and guideline for companies how to determine and implement their innovation and idea management needs has been introduced and illustrated by an exemplary setup in a commercial system.

Further research will be undertaken to create modular data and process models and to provide industry sector specific bundles as an out of the box solution to further decrease the implementation efforts of companies. Besides, the company specific analysis and objective definition will still remain necessary and meaningful.

References

1. Eigner, M; Stelzer, R. Product Lifecycle Management - Ein Leitfaden für Product Development und Life Cycle Management, 2nd Ed. Berlin; Heidelberg: Springer, 2009.
2. Feldhusen, J. et al.: Development of methods to support the implementation of a PDMS. In: Innovation Life Cycle Engineering and Sustainable Development. Dordrecht: Springer, 2006.
3. Ehrlenspiel, K. Integrierte Produktentwicklung. München; Wien: Carl Hanser, 2003.
4. Pelzer, W. Methodik zur Identifizierung und Nutzung strategischer Technologiepotentiale. Aachen: Shaker, 1999.
5. Schumpeter, J. Theorie der wirtschaftlichen Entwicklung; Eine Untersuchung über Unternehmergewinn, Kapital, Kredit, Zins und den Konjunkturzyklus. Berlin: Duncker & Humblot, 1934.
6. Meiler, Rudolf Carl: Führungsverhalten und Innovation in kleinen und mittleren Unternehmen. In: Meiler, R. C.(Hrsg.): Mittelstand und Betriebswirtschaft: Beiträge aus Wissenschaft und Praxis. p. 165-182. Wiesbaden: Deutscher Universitäts-Verlag, 1999.
7. Hauschildt, J. Innovationsmanagement, 3. Auflage. München: Franz Vahlen, 2004.
8. Brezing, A. Planung innovativer Produkte unter Nutzung von Design- und Ingenieurdienstleistungen. Aachen: Shaker, 2006.
9. Bleicher, Knut: Das Konzept integriertes Management: Visionen-Missionen-Programme. Frankfurt; New York: Campus, 1999.
10. Völker, R.; Sauer, S.; Simon, M.: Wissensmanagement im Innovationsprozess. Heidelberg: Physica, 2007.
11. Gebhardt, Boris N. B. Abschätzung der Produktdatenmanagement-Systemfähigkeit produzierender Unternehmen. Aachen: Shaker, 2007.
12. Löwer, M. PDM basierte Innovationsplanung im Rahmen eines durchgängigen Product Lifecycle Managements. Aachen, Shaker, 2012.

Unification of Multiple Models for Complex System Development

Nesrine Ben Beldi[1,2], Lionel Roucoules[1], François Malburet[1], Tomasz Krysinski[2], and Pierre Gauthier[2]

[1] Arts et Métiers ParisTech, CNRS, LSIS, 2 cours des Arts et Métiers, 13617 Aix en Provence, France
[2] PSA Peugeot Citroen, Innovation powertrain project, 18 rue des fauvelles 92250 La Garenne Colombes, France
nesrine.benbeldi@mpsa.com, nesrine.benbeldi@ensam.eu

Abstract. In the design of automotive product, the constant evolution of customer requirements and international regulations leads to new considerations of the sys- tem design process. The authors propose a modeling approach for complex system design based on the coupling of collaborative models and heterogeneous experts' (i.e. authoring) models used for product behavior assessment. The approach aims at modeling a system at different systemic and temporal levels in the design process and allows a flexible navigation with the possibility of changing or adding models in the design space. The purpose behind the use of this approach is to lead to an optimal design solution in the context of innovative design for complex system.

Keywords: Mechanical system design, Model Driven Architecture (MDA), design system process, data modelling.

1 Introduction

Automotive industry market is witnessing a continuous expansion which is changing from a local to a global one. Nowadays, car manufacturers are finding themselves forced to assure the requirements of an international market that needs to be satisfied, taking into account new regulations in terms of cars' pollutant emissions. This expansion has led automotive designer to innovate and make an evolution in their designed products. Consequently, in order to realize that, they have to consider their product design process in another way in order to take into account these new design requirements and constraints.

Concepts of design process and complex system modeling are presented in the second section of the communication. A particular focus towards their applications in the automotive field is given in order to set forth the design methods applied and modeling tools used.

The third section, introduces the different models for system design found in the scientific literature. Our focus is done towards the interaction of all those models

S. Fukuda et al. (Eds.): PLM 2014, IFIP AICT 442, pp. 267–276, 2014.

used in a design process and how they are linked together. The issue of design data transfer between one model to another according to the level of the granular decomposition of the system is discussed highlighting the interoperability between models in complex system modeling for design purpose.

Section fourth proposes the unification models approach based on a mediator structure. Such approach allows a dynamic navigation in the design environment between expert's (i.e. authoring) models at different granular levels of the system decomposition. Design constraints are taking into account from the beginning of the modeling and evolve simultaneously by the evolution of the model itself.

The proposed Information Technology (IT) system is also presented and discussed with respect to interoperable performances.

The fifth s ection, illustrates this proposal by presenting its application on a mechanical system. The aim is to evaluate the pertinence of the modeling approach proposed in order to optimize the design of complex system in a context of innovative design.

Conclusion and recommendations for further work are therefore presented.

2 Complex System Design Process and Modeling

Automotive products are considered as complex systems, since their design requires an effort of understanding relationships among knowledge [1] of several scientific domains: mechanics, hydraulics, electronics and automatics, mathematics, Information Technologies, etc. The multi-physic aspect for such systems implies the involvement of multiple experts according to the knowledge required. Indeed, each experts has its own representation (i.e. model) of the system; each model being different than the others. Each model is therefore created for a specific use and product assessment (functional analysis, CAD, CAE, CAM, etc.).

As presented in [2], in a groovy design approach where system specifications are known through previous experimentations, design activities are considered as a simultaneous and/or sequential concatenation of expert knowledge to find "best" values of an already-defined-product breakdown and already identified product parameters. On the other hand, innovative design approach involves new knowledge considering the systemconfiguration since the design activity is to find new solutions (i.e. alternatives) in the design solution space. The innovative alter natives can be found either in the functional, conceptual, embodiment or detail design phases of the whole design process [3].

During the design process, the impact of each expert is therefore considered as a constant loop leading to the augmentation of the amount of product data dealt with (scientific knowledge, design constraints, system specifications, models data, physical principle, etc.) [4]. Such expert's specification depicts a function in the design process and is translated according to the concept of ***Knowledge-Intensive-Engineering*** [5] by technological attributes. In this amount of design alternatives, the final decision making is done according to performances assessments.

Nevertheless, this assessment has to take into account both local and global system performances based on multiple-perspective criteria.

One of the greatest challenges in this context related to complex system design is therefore to get to a complete mastery of the evaluation and the control of the relationships existing between all of the defined product's models taking into account their various specifications.

3 Overview of the State of the Arts with Respect to Product Meta-Models Used in Innovative Complex System Design

3.1 Product Meta-Models Over the Whole Product Life Cycle

According to [6], building a model is an iterative procedure. It starts with the identification of essential features of inherent mechanisms of a dynamic system to be designed. In a step by step refinement of the understanding of a dynamic physical system, different forms of representation are used.

When processing a design problem, according to Pahl & Beitz's phases, four major aspects have to be taken into consideration for the system definition: The system functional description, the concepts selection, the embodiment of the system architecture (i.e. product breakdown) and the detailed parameters definition.

Functional description of a system can be done through models such as "Func- tional Block Diagram" [7] or "FAST Diagram" [8], etc. Those models are made in order to define the functional behavior of the system in terms of required perfo r- mance. That enables the determination of first possible configurations for the technical solution that represent *the system concept selection.* These models are complementary to systems engineering activities and they represent the first level of system modeling leading to fix its operational concept [9].

In order to evaluate the *energetic aspect of a system*, representation models can also be used, and their exploration leads often to the establishment of the system control system strategy. Bond Graph models falls precisely within this context. This language of modeling consists in representing the energetic flows transfer between system components and sub components, bringing up the relations of cause and effect existing between each part of the system in order to systematically construct the mathematical models that will be used for system control.

Finally, current design practices use a lot of models in the detailed design phase to model *form features* (ex. CAD model) and assess the numerous multi-physics *product's behaviors* (ex. Finite Element Analysis models). A lot of authoring applications currently exist in commercial or academics solutions.

3.2 Meta-Models for Collaborative Relationships Definition, Information Classification and Retrieval

The previous section has presented meta-models related to specific design phase. Those meta-models are generally defined by specific individual designer.

Another level of meta-model is also used to define relationships among all those design phase (function, concepts, detailed design) and product assessment (man u- facturing, structural analysis…) and to classify all the information (i.e. knowledge) in order to be retrieved (i.e. knowledge management) . The scientific literature gives plenty of Meta-Model proposals that all treat those two levels of concepts (knowledge modelling and knowledge relationships): Core Product Model [10] (CPM), FBS [11], MOKA model [12], PPO model [13], KC model [14].

3.3 Discussion on the State of the Arts towards the Scientific and IT Proposal

Since many meta-models have been proposed in commercial or scientific solutions, it appears idealist for us to find only one (i.e. integrated model) that could be the "best" one and that could gather all the conceptual fundaments. Many standards have also been proposed for many years but none has been accepted as universal so far (cf. STEP, SYML, PLCS… [15]).

Therefore, authors argue that the current issue is then not to battle about which model fit the best anymore. It would be a wrong approach. As discussed in [16], authors argue that it is better to go toward a flexible approach that should be a h ybrid one based on federative and unified approach (cf. figure 1): federative approach goals at linking straight one meta-model to another one (concepts of A are linked to concepts of B), unified approach goals at linking one meta-model to others via a mediator. A mediator can be one of the meta-model presented in 3.2. In a recursive mode, one mediator can be federated to another one. That approach goes toward a more adaptive way of modeling since concepts (seen as a meta-model) can be added or removed over the time and depending on the industrial design context. The "best model structure" is therefore the one set according to each design situation. This paper is focused on "unified meta-modeling". Federative approach can be found in [16].

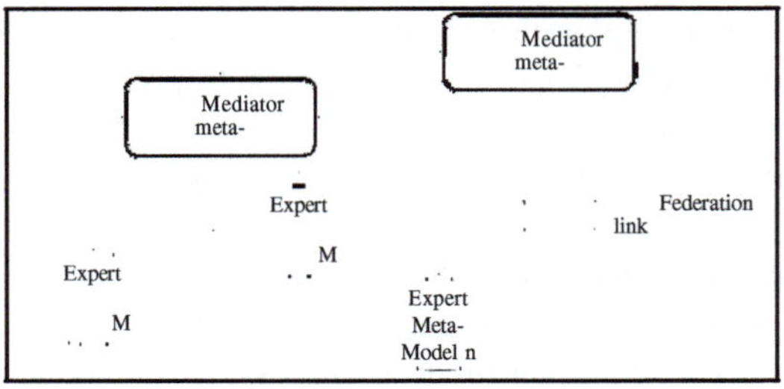

Fig. 1. Hybrid Federative and Unified approach

In the following section, authors propose a modeling approach based on the concept of Model Driven Engineering [17] which allows a flexible navigation with the possibility of changing or add models in the design space. This approach allows the coupling of unified collaborative meta-models and heterogeneous experts' (i.e. authoring) meta-models used for system behavior assessment.

4 Proposal: Model Driven Engineering Approach for Complex System Modeling

As previously introduced, numerous models have to be set during the design phase. To treat the design of complex systems authors use a classification based on three main axes (cf. figure 2):

- Product life cycle mainly restricted of design phases as defined in [3]
- System granularity as mentioned in system engineering concepts
- Structure/Control chain axis of the dynamic system in order to link Multiple-perspective modeling in both structural and control domains.

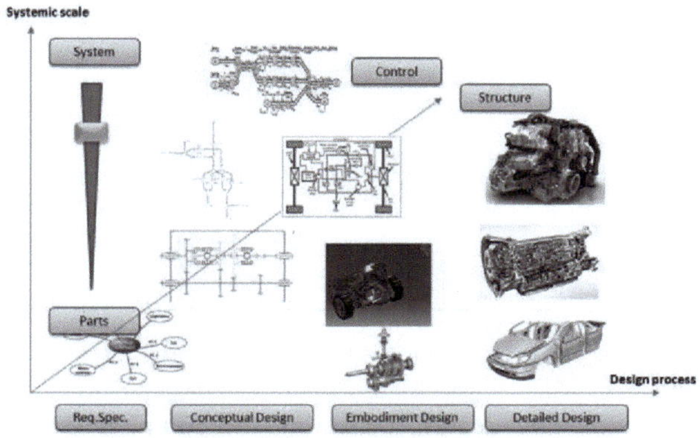

Fig. 2. Three axes for complex system modeling

4.1 Mediator Meta-Model for Unification Approach

While modeling a complex system, multiple views representing the evolution of the system and its components during the design process can appear depending on the complexity of the system itself and the number of performance required. Those views go from a macroscopic representation of a general functional view of the system to a specific technological or geometrical view of a sub component of it. In order to represent that aspect while modeling a complex system, experts use multiple-view models to separate concerns during the design process and to control system evolution at different levels from functional aspects to deployment and verification. The concepts of this modeling are issued from works done by [13] in order to optimize the gathering of system information and formalization of the e x- isting relations between it. These concepts have been updated and are given in figure 3:

- *Component* that represents the used objects to describe the system. This description can be done at different granular and multiple-views levels.
- *Interface* defines the part of one component allowing it to be in a relation with another one.
- *Relations* in order to formalize the existing relations between components through Interface.

- Each of the above concepts is inherited from the virtual classes *Modeled Entity* in order to construct the global mediator model. Each Modeled Entity is de- fined by *Attribute*.

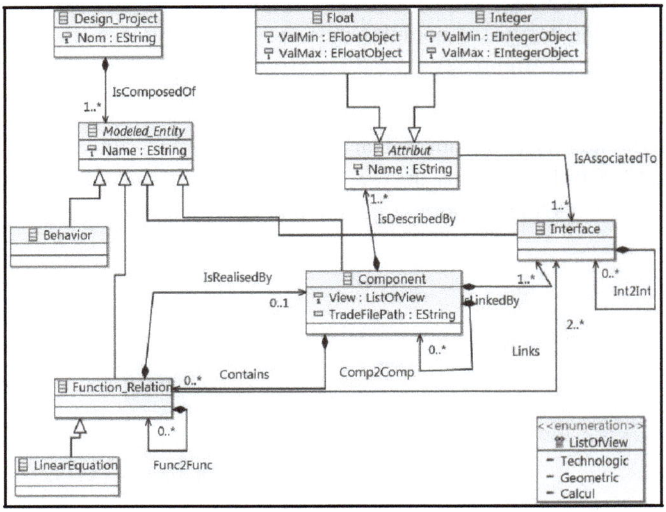

Fig. 3. Current mediator meta-model

In a context of innovative design, mastering the complete evolution of a complex system as for its components and sub components, is a work that is build and done through the evolution of the design process itself. Experts' models are constructed upon specific design constraints in order to validate a specific performance at each level of the system decomposition. And they evolve in a dynamic way during the design process. Thereby, experts can be brought to add and/or suppress some models or design constraints at some level during the design process.

The author proposes to work on a certain level of system modeling in order to cre- ate flexible and dynamic information exchange between design experts during a design process. This can be done through a representation of the existing mathematical and/or physical relations between the parameters of each expert's model at different systemic level of the system, insured through a constraint propagator.

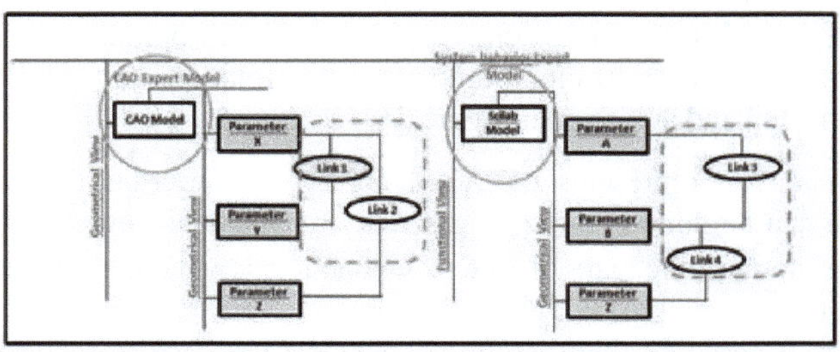

Fig. 4. Multi-views Decomposition of the system based on mediator model given on Figure 3

The concept of multiple views that is used in this approach represents the different part of the product breakdown and the set of parameters that are shared among experts. That is the main role of a mediator model. (cf. figure 4).

Expert models can be found at different levels in system decomposition. A part from views related to the global system; components, sub components and sub -sub components can have also views related to the expertise used for their design and their own performance to validate (manufacturing, multi-physics simulation, CAD…). And by that, expert models can be found at different systemic level and can have a local use (validate a component performance) and/or a global use (validate a component function and its interaction with other components) (cf. figure 4). Thus, authors show that it is possible to create a flexible navigation process between each model and another based on the modeling of the existing relations between the specific parameters of each models and by that the design constraints used to build each model and design the system. Relations manage both break- down relationships (i.e. system engineering relations) and parameters relationships to be used in a local or global constraints solving problem to insure coherency among designers' knowledge. For instance, during the design of a mechanical system the CAD expert can decides to review a technical constraint that he has considered at the beginning of modeling and that is no more suitable at this stage of system design (cf. figure 4, Link1). This reconsideration automatically leads him to readjust the value that he has chosen before for the different parameters in order to integrate this constraint and also to make sure that the other constraints of his model are still respected. But by doing that, he is also changing the common parameter (parameter Z) that exists between his CAD model and the Scilab model of the system behavior expert. This parameter is going to influence the results given by the Scilab model through its relations with other parameters specific to Scilab model (parameter A, B), and of course the constraints considered by the system behavior expert while building hid functional model to validate his desired performance. This change is transferred to the system behavior expert by a notification alert appearing in the functional model. This transfer is ensured through the mediator meta-model that contains all the relations between the existing parameters that are common in both models.

4.2 Infrastructure of the Information System

As far as Information technologies are concerned, and in coherency with modeling approaches presented in the previous section, authors argue that one unique integrated software solution is an idealist solution. Industrial and modeling context are indeed evolving very often over the time. IT system has therefore to be flexible (i.e. agile). The infrastructure that has been developed is therefore based on many layers (cf. figure 5) implemented into the Eclipse Modelling Framework (EMF):

- Authoring applications (i.e. expert model) used by design experts.
- Unification layer that manage the relationships. This layer allows the navigation among the entire three axes space of data (cf. figure 2).
- External CSP solution that keeps the coherency among relationships.

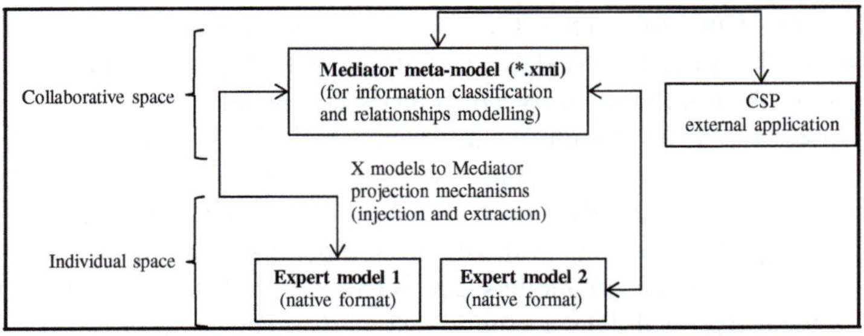

Fig. 5. Layers of the developed IT infrastructure implemented in EMF

As far as the design context is defined, adequate authoring application can be plugged or unplugged to the unification layer. This plug function is based on Meta-model projection [16] that allows easy way to use the "best" application for the current situation.

5 Illustration of the Approach through the Modeling of Mechanical Coupling System for Hybrid Transmission

In order to validate the modeling approach, a case study of hybrid transmission system is considered in the context of innovative powertrain project (cf. figure 6).The geometrical view is done through CAD modeling tools and the functional view is achieved through Scilab tool. Each one of the models is built by an expert in order to select the "best" architecture for the system allowing validating the fixed performance that is CO2 emission for a driving cycle.

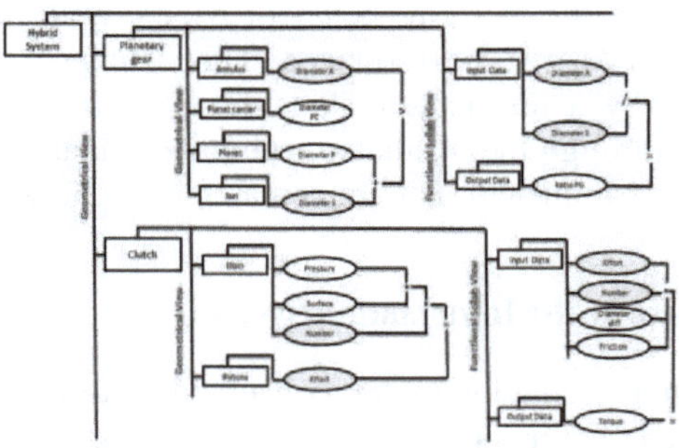

Fig. 6. Multi views modeling for hybrid system

The multi view model is constructed in parallel to the design of the system allowing mastering at different levels the relations between the different parameters. And from that base, the mediator model is constructed taking into account these relations and a navigation between one model to another and one view to another (i.e. navigation between geometrical view and functional scilab view). This model integrate the possible changes, adds and retrieves that can occur on the different parameter of each model and allow the propagation of its related information to other models.

6 Conclusion and Recommendations for Further Work

In order to support the design of complex system in innovative design context, the authors propose to model and optimize the design process through a unification approach by allowing the navigation product models based on a three axes design framework. This navigation can be done through a model driven architecture concept based on a mediator meta-model that takes into account the existing relations between product breakdown and parameters of each model. This provides a new approach in order to support data exchange and to accelerate time consuming tasks. This approach is more flexible since it is based on one meta models and agile IT solution that can be modified or changed according to the modifications occurring on experts' models and design environment.

The illustration of this approach is done through a hybrid powertrain system for its prototype design. The implementation of this proposal in EMF (Eclipse Modelling Framework) is in progress. A possible further work will be to test the approach for the design of the series version of the hybrid powertrain system and to define performance indicators allowing optimizing the process design and the system architecture.

References

1. Suh, N.P.: Applications of Axiomatic Design, Integration of process Knowledge into Design Support. Kluwer Academic Publishers (1999) ISBN 0-7923-5655-1
2. Frey, E., Gomes, S., Yan, X.T.: Numeric chaining of design process In- formation for mechatronic products. In: Mechatronics Conference, Zurich (2010)
3. Pahl, G., Beitz, W.: Engineering Design: A Systematic Approach, 2nd edn. Springer, London (1996)
4. Roucoules, L., Lafon, P., et al.: Knowledge intensive approach towards multiple product modelling and geometry. In: CIRP Design Seminar, Alberta, Ca (2006)
5. Tomiyama, T.: A design process model that unifies general design theory and empirical findings. In: Design Engineering Technical Conferences – ASME 95, Boston, USA (1995)
6. Borutzky, W.: Bond Graph Methodology: Development and analysis of multidisciplinary dynamic system models. Springer, London (2010)
7. AFNOR, Recommandation pour obtenir et assurer la qualité en concep- tion, norme X50-127 (1988)
8. Bytheway, C.: FAST Creativity & Innovation. J.Ross Publishing (2007) ISBN1-932159-66-5
9. Luzeaux, D., Ruault, J.R.: l'Ingénierie système, AFNOR edition (2013)
10. Sudarsan, R., Fenves, S.J., Sriram, R.D., Wang, F.: A product infor- mation modelling framework for product lifecycle management. Computer- Aided Design 37, 1399–1411 (2005)

11. Gero, J.S.: Design prototypes: a knowledge representation schema for design. AI Magazine 11(4), 26–36 (1990)
12. Stokes, M.: Managing engineering knowledge: MOKA methodology for knowledge based engineering applications. MOKA Consortium (2001)
13. Noël, F., Roucoules, L.: The PPO design model with respect to digital enterprise technologies among product life cycle. International Journal of Computer Integrated Manufacturing 21(2), 139–145 (2007), doi:10.1080/09511920701607782
14. Badin, J.: Using the Knowledge Configuration Model (KCModel) to manage configurated knowledge for upstream phases of the design Process. Editorial Manager(tm) for International Journal on Interactive Design and Manufacturing (IJIDeM) (2011)
15. Rachuri, S., Subrahmanian, E., Bouras, A., Fenves, S., Foufou, S., Sriram, R.: Information sharing and exchange in the context of product lifecycle management: Role of standards. Computer-Aided Design 40(7), 789–800 (2008)
16. Medhi, I., Mathias, K., Lionel, R.: Model-based (Mechanical) Product Design. In: Models Conference, New Zealand (2011)
17. Bézivin, J.: Model Driven Engineering: An Emerging Technical Space. In: Lämmel, R., Saraiva, J., Visser, J. (eds.) GTTSE 2005. LNCS, vol. 4143, pp. 36–64. Springer, Heidelberg (2006)

Performance Indicators for Configuration Management

Tanja Minzenmay, Maximilian Zeiss, Masoud Niknam, and Jivka Ovtcharova

IMI, Karlsruhe Institute of Technology, Karlsruhe, Germany
{tanjaminzenmay,zeiss.maximilian}@gmail.com
{masoud.niknam,jivka.ovtcharova}@kit.edu

Abstract. Configuration Management (CM) with its aim to ensure functional and physical consistency between the product requirements and the reality during the whole lifecycle is becoming more and more important, since the awareness of the resulting advantages rises in many companies. The Institute for Information Management in Engineering at Karlsruhe Institute of Technology has developed a maturity model to evaluate the CM maturity for different organizations on the basis of different CM dimensions. The following paper enhances the capability of this model by developing performance indicators, which are aimed at measuring the quality of implemented CM activities as a supplement to their extent of application, which was measured before. Such indicators have been developed based on an extensive state-of-the-art analysis and were validated and refurbished through interviews with industrial experts.

Keywords: Configuration Management, Product Lifecycle Management, Performance Measurement, Maturity Model.

1 Introduction

Configuration Management (CM) can be seen as a coordinated framework of activities to manage and control configurations [1, 2]. Due to the primary aim of keeping consistency between what needs to be there, what is actually there and what we say is there [3], CM provides several benefits. Many researchers confirm that CM exerts positive effects on product quality, product lifecycle costs and therefore on the ability to compete in an environment with growing complexity [3, 4, 5]. Niknam & Ovtcharova [6] have developed a CM maturity assessment framework which enables the organizations to investigate their CM maturity with respect to the extent of CM application throughout the organization. However, for a higher framework capability, concrete measurements are needed to assess the CM quality. Many organizations are already measuring their overall performance by using performance indicators (PIs), which usually control important business units or the organization as a whole[7]. Well known examples are the Return on Investment (ROI) or the amount spent on research and development. In order to ascertain organizations performance and success in high levels, the performance of every discipline shall be investigated by utilization of detailed PIs. Thus, the aim of this paper is to develop and present PIs for Configuration

S. Fukuda et al. (Eds.): PLM 2014, IFIP AICT 442, pp. 277–286, 2014.

Management based on the critical success factors and dimensions in the CM Maturity Model [6].

The remainder of this paper is structured as follows. In section 2, the CM Maturity Model of [6] is briefly presented. Later, a general introduction to performance indicators is given. The research methodology is described in section 4 and in section 5 the PIs developed by the authors are introduced. Finally, section 6 gives a conclusion and outlook of future work.

2 Configuration Management Maturity Model

Since maturity models available do not cover CM in detail, Niknam & Ovtcharova [6] have developed the Configuration Management Maturity Model (CM^3). They define five primary dimensions of CM, which influence the level of success for an organization's application of CM discipline. These five dimensions are Strategy & Performance, Processes, Information Technology, Organization & Value-stream as well as Knowledge & Support. Furthermore, they have created sub-dimensions or critical success factors, describing particular activities and attributes of the each primary dimension which needs to be considered for implementation and establishment of an effective CM discipline. (Figure 1)

Strategy& Performance	Processes	Information Technology	Organization& Value-Stream	Knowledge& Support
CM Strategic Objective and Policy	Clear processes	High level of visualization and user-friendliness	Suitable CM Organization Structure with Respect to Organization Complexity and CM Needs	Standard CM Terminology and Knowledge Support Accessible by Stakeholders
Deployment of CM Strategy in Different Organization Levels	Standard processes	Integration of CM-Tool with other IT-Systems	Defined Roles and Responsibilities for CM Personnel	Regular CM-Related Training Activities
Communication of the Deployed Strategy to Stakeholders	Process ownership, maintenance and update based on feedbacks	Supporting the CM-Functionalities	Cross-Functional Collaboration among Different Stakeholders for CM Purposes	Accessibility and Promotion of Latest Standards, Lessons Learned, Best Practices and Benchmarks
KPIs for Performance Measurement	Stakeholder access to processes	Solid IT-Tools all over the Organization for all Lifecycle Phases	Consideration of Suppliers and Subcontractors in CM Activities	Support and Empowerment of CM Discipline by Top Management
Regular Measurement and Update of KPIs	Process customizability for different scenarios	Authorization Capabilities for different CM activities	Involvement of Key Stakeholders in Major Configuration Changes	Communication of CM Benefits to Stakeholders by Top Management

Fig. 1. CM Maturity Model sub-dimensions

For assessing the current CM maturity of various industries and validating the developed critical success factors, Niknam & Ovtcharova [8] have done a cross-industry survey using the CM^3 model. The results illustrate a high potential for improvement in CM with respect to its penetration level in the organization.

3 Measurement by Performance Indicators

In this paper, as outlined in the Introduction, the assessment framework of CM^3 is enhanced by the development of performance indicators. These performance indicators shall measure the application quality of each sub-dimension. Therefore, only the quality of CM-activities concerning the given sub-dimensions is the point of interest, and not "well-known" measures which focus on the overall performance of a company or different organizational units, as for example Return On Investment. Quality in the context of the indicators refers to the question: “How ‘good’ is activity A performed?”.

Performance measurement in general is used for monitoring and improving performance. Klingebiel [7] highlights that no matter how the performance measurement system looks like, three main perceptions are important:

1. You cannot manage what you cannot measure
2. What gets measured gets done
3. Measurement influences behavior

The three perceptions can be transferred to the context of this paper, since the aim is to manage the improvement of CM.

4 Research Methodology

In order to get a first list of possible PIs for the different sub-dimensions, a broad literature analysis was done. Based on this first collection, the authors conducted semi-structured interviews with industry experts to both validate the indicators and adjust them with respect to their feasibility of application, data availability and importance. The interviews have been done with four experts, coming from automotive and aerospace industry, from plant engineering industry as well as engineering consulting. Summarized about 7 hours of interview time have been done. As a result of the interviews some of the indicators have been approved without any further remarks, some have been supplemented for a better understanding, and a few have been excluded because of doubts about the general significance.

5 Performance Indicators

The authors propose the following performance indicators. They are presented in the following format in 3 columns.

Performance Indicators:	Initial source:	Expert Comments:
% - percentage	[ ] : Reference	V : validated
# - number/amount of	A : Authors’ proposal	U : updated
Ø - average	I : Interview	E : emerged
		- : Not sure

Strategy& Performance

CM Strategic Objective and Policy: For successful CM, objectives and policy should be available and be adapted to the corporate strategy		
- % to which CM strategic objectives are derived from overall strategy: the CM strategy needs to fit to the company's overall goals to support their achievement	[9] [10]	V
- Actual frequency / target frequency of updating CM objectives: CM objectives need to be rechecked regularly to be adapted to new corporate goals	[9] [11]	U
- % to which CM policy & objectives are covering all main CM activities in the organization: proper policy and objectives should cover all important subjects to avoid confusion and constitute a guideline	[12] [13]	V
Deployment of CM Strategy in Different Organization Levels: CM strategy needs to be deployed to all levels to provide adapted objectives for all teams		
- % of deployed goals, which can be clearly linked to a higher CM objective	[10] [14] [15]	V
- # CM units having a mission statement that clearly defines their objectives and mission: it is important that all organizational units know what they need to do to achieve main CM objectives	[I]	E
Communication of the Deployed Strategy to Stakeholders: To be able to support CM objectives and policy guidelines, the strategy has to be communicated to the stakeholders		
- # of strategic deviations associated to communication: communication quality can be assessed by conducting audits.	[16]	U
- % employees who can explain the CM strategy and what it means in terms of their daily work: if employees know how their work contributes to CM success the communication has worked properly	[16]	V
- Effectiveness of policy implementation: the policy should not only be mentioned on a document but it should be understood and applied in the operative business	[14] [15]	V
KPIs for Performance Measurement: The fulfillment of objectives needs to be measured with Key Performance Indicators		
- Quality of data available for KPI results (sufficient quantity, completeness): if the database for the KPI application is not sufficient, then the KPI results won't be reliable	[17] [18] [19]	V
- # of KPIs: an organization should always focus on a limited number of KPIs to keep the focus	[18]	-
- % KPIs linked to strategic objectives and critical success factors:	[20]	V
- % KPIs from which an action plan can directly be started in case outcoming results are bad: KPIs should always point out success and drawbacks	[18]	-
- Frequency of KPI reviewing and improvement: the usefulness of a KPIs should be checked regularly	[18]	U

Regular Measurement of KPIs: KPIs needs to be measured regularly		
- Frequency of measurement and reporting: depending on the focus the measurement needs to take place constantly and results be reported	[18] [17]	V

Processes

Clear processes for different org. units, projects and lifecycle phases: Processes should be defined, transparent, controllable, effective, efficient, straightforward, robust and at a right level of detail.		
- # questions/requests about processes due to a lack of understanding: clear processes should be defined in a comprehensible way	[21]	U
- % cases where the result of the process is constructive in a way that predefined objectives are achieved	[21, 22]	U
Standard processes: Standard CM processes like configuration identification, baselining, product structure management, change evaluation –control & implementation, status accounting and configuration audits.		
- ∅ time to approve Engineering Changes	[17, 23, 24]	V
- ∅ costs per change	[17, 23, 24]	V
- # non-confirmative configurations at the final product: all standard processes are trying to prevent these deviations	[I]	E
- Frequency of reports and audits	[23]	V
- # deviations to make a "fast" design change: this kind of deviation should be totally avoided	[17]	-
Process ownership, maintenance and update based on feedbacks: A specific person is responsible for a process - processes are maintained, updated and improved - feedback among the employees is encouraged and maybe rewarded.		
- ∅ benefit per feedback: if possible to measure financial	[A]	V
- Frequency of feedbacks: more reasonable if combined with the benefit	[21, 22]	U
- % of processes with a specific and active process owner, who is responsible for process audit and the interfaces with adjacent processes	[21]	U
Stakeholder access to processes: Access of stakeholders to process information must be defined and managed in an efficient way.		
- ∅ Time until process information can be found by the stakeholder	[A]	V
- % of satisfied stakeholders regarding accessing process information	[25, 26]	U
Process customizability for various scenarios: Processes should be able to handle different requirements in a continuously changing working environment.		
- Availability of shortcuts: increases the efficiency for less complex scenarios (also called fast tracks)	[21]	V
- # scenarios which cannot be covered by the company's processes: this can be minimized by very robust or flexible processes – some industrial sectors need very flexible processes others very robust ones	[I]	E

Information Technology

High level of visualization and user-friendliness: IT-tools should be easy to handle and operate as well as being capable of providing all the information needed. The user should like the usage of these tools and recognize the benefits easily.		
- Ø time a user needs to complete a specific task: this standard tasks must be executed with the IT-system	[27]	V
- IT-happiness-score: measuring the satisfaction level of stakeholders with the CM IT system	[27]	V
- Meaningful and intuitive wording is used for the user interface and wrong data typed in by the user is avoided	[28, 29, 30, 26]	-
Integration of CM-Tool with other IT-Systems		
- % time spent on finding CM-information in the IT system out of overall time spent on CM-activities: if many IT-systems must be accessed, systems are not integrated efficiently	[A]	V
Supporting the CM-Functionalities		
- # processes developed based on given IT-systems: should be minimized because the IT-systems must be specified by CM needs and processes and not the other way around	[A]	V
- % CM-activities supported by IT	[23, 24]	V
Solid IT-Tools all over the Organization for all Lifecycle Phases		
- # cases during the product lifecycle where the format of information needs to be changed because of different IT-tools or databases	[23]	V
- Frequency of data backups	[32]	V
Authorization Capabilities for different CM activities		
- # access rights following logical, transparent and comprehensible rules which are defined by the company	[33, 34]	V
- Ø loss due to wrong authorization	[A]	-

Organization & Value Stream

Suitable CM Organization Structure with Respect to Organization Complexity and CM Needs		
- # of CM employees / product complexity: if there are different product programs with different variants and the amount of products are high, more contributions are necessary	[9] [35]	U
- CM integration / organization complexity: for managing high complexity a high degree of integration, defined as communication, control and coordination, is necessary	[35]	V

Defined Roles and Responsibilities for CM Personnel: all required roles need to be defined clearly and the responsibility needs to be distributed to individuals		
- # escalations caused by unclear responsibilities (difficult to measure, could be also assess in audits): if responsibilities are unclear misunderstandings will occur which can end in escalations	[9] [5]	V
- % roles which are clearly defined and documented	[A]	E
Cross-Functional Collaboration among Different Stakeholders for CM Purposes: CM is a cross-functional discipline, which is why the collaboration between functions is required by CM's very nature		
- % of process target achievement for each value chain element: an effective cross-functional collaboration between stakeholders along the value chain will enable every chain element to achieve its goals corresponding to CM activities	[A]	E
- Cycle time per changes involving the value-chain: if collaboration works well, such changes should be able to get passed through fast	[A]	E
- # revisions for change changes involving the value-chain: if collaboration works well revisions should not be necessary	[A]	E
Consideration of Suppliers and Subcontractors in CM Activities: suppliers need to be integrated in CM activities to ensure the CM targets for sourced parts		
- # non-conformities resulted from lack of value-chain involvement: if the exchange of information about changed specifications, requirements etc. does not work well, non-conformities can occur	[9] [24]	U
- # of non-conformities (opposite perspective): if the contractor does not deliver what has been specified, non-conformities can occur	[13] [5]	U
Involvement of Key Stakeholders in Major Configuration Changes:		
- # of complains after changes were implemented (internal or external)	[5] [13]	V
- # of review cycles needed for changed implementation: if all stakeholders are involved from the beginning, changes can be defined in detail and implemented without any more changes to the change	[A]	E

Knowledge and Support

Standard CM Terminology and Knowledge Support Accessible by Stakeholders		
- Frequency of updating the provided information: ensuring actuality of information	[19] [36]	V
- Ø time to find the needed information: ensures a convenient access to knowledge	[36] [19]	V
- # of audit findings illustrating insufficient knowledge of the employees in CM	[A]	E

Regular CM-Related Training Activities: Employees need to be prepared for CM tasks by trainings to ensure the quality of the task execution		
- % of CM activities for which training is available - ∅ amount of training taken by each employee associated with CM - # of obligated trainings for each role: if the training is necessary to fulfill a role/ tasks it is a sign for a high quality of the training	[17] [24] [24] [17] [A]	V V E
Accessibility and Promotion of Latest Standards, Lessons Learned, Best Practices and Benchmarks		
- % of projects for which CM lessons learned is recorded and accessible by future stakeholders - % coverage of CM activities by standards and benchmark documents accessible to corporate search engines: - % of lessons learned used in future projects	[19] [19] [9]	V V U
Support and Empowerment of CM Discipline by Top Management: To ensure the fulfillment and acceptance of CM, management support is necessary		
- % of management attending CM meetings: - Frequency of management demands for CM reports: indicates that management's attention to CM	[A] [A]	E E
Communication of CM Benefits to Stakeholders by Top Management: For motivation and acceptance of CM it is necessary that the benefits are communicated to all stakeholders		
- Frequency of promoting CM as an influential discipline by Top Management	[37]	-

6 Outlook

In this paper, performance indicators for the sub-dimensions of the Configuration Management Maturity Model have been introduced. The developed PIs extend the model's functionality and enable the assessment of not only the implementation extent of CM in the target organization, but also the quality of this implementation. The PIs so far are identified on the basis of literature review and expert interviews. A necessary further step is to apply the PIs in a case organization to find out the feasibility measuring them. The trade-off between the importance and measurement feasibility shall be identified and a more applicable list of KPIs shall be developed. Moreover, to enable an assessment and identifying various maturity levels, an extensive cross-industry assessment is required to understand various available ranges for each PI. After defining the levels the next step would be to define activities which support organizations in achieving the next maturity level.

References

[1] BS ISO 10007. Quality management systems: Guidelines for configuration management, British standards (2003)
[2] (IAQG), International Aerospace Quality Group, Supply chain management handbook, chapter 11 (2012), http://www.sae.org/iaqg/publications/ (accessed December 2013)
[3] International Atomic Energy Agency (IAEA) Report Series, Application Of Configuration Managemen. In: Nuclear Power Plants (2010)
[4] Rouse, W., Sage, A.: Handbook of Systems Engineering and Management, pp. 267–289. Jon Wiley & Sons (2011)
[5] Dvir, D., Lipovetsky, S., Shenhar, A., Tishler, A.: In search of project classification: a non-universal approach to project success factors. Research Policy 27 (1998)
[6] Niknam, M., Bonnal, P., Ovtcharova, J.: Configuration Management Maturity in Scientific Facilities. International Journal of Advanced Robotics, Special issue on Robotics and Systems Engineering in Scientific Facilities (2013)
[7] Klingebiel, N.: Performance measurement-systeme. Das Wirtschaftsstudium 26(7) (1997)
[8] Niknam, M., Ovtcharova, J.: Towards Higher Configuration Management Maturity. In: Bernard, A., Rivest, L., Dutta, D. (eds.) PLM 2013. IFIP AICT, vol. 409, pp. 396–405. Springer, Heidelberg (2013)
[9] Hass, A.M.J.: Configuration Management principles and practice. Addison-Wesley, Boston (2003)
[10] Robbins, S., De Cenzo, D., Coulter, M.: Fundamentals of management. Pearson, Boston (2013)
[11] Rohm, H.: Is There Any Strateg. In: your Strategic Plan, Balanced Scrorecard Institute, Strategy Management Group (pub.), Cary, North Carolina (2008), http://balancedscorecard.org/Portals/0/PDF/IsThereAnyStrategyInYourStrategicPlanWeb.pdf (assessed on January 11, 2014)
[12] Ulrich, H.: Unternehmungspolitik. Gesammelte Schriften Band 2, 11 (2001)
[13] Department of Defense, MIL-HDBK-61-A(SE) (2001)
[14] CMS Policy for Configuration Management, (2012) Centers for Medicare and Mediacaid Services, https://www.cms.gov/Research-Statistics-Data-and-Sytems/CMS-Information-Technolgy/SystemLifecycleFramework/downloads/cmpolicy.pdf (accessed on March 04, 2014)
[15] Martin, J.: Information Engineering. A triology, Book II, pp. 70–95. Prentice Hall, Englewood Cliffs (1990)
[16] Barret, D.: Change Communication: using strategic employee communication to facilitate major changes. Corporate Communications: an International Journal, 219–231 (2002)
[17] Watts, F.B.: Configuration Management Metrics. Elsevier Inc. (2009)
[18] Eckerson, W.: Performance Dashboards: Measuring, monitoring and managing your business, pp. 197–212. John Wiley, Hoboken (2006)
[19] Maier, R.: Knowledge Management Systems. In: Information and Communication Technologies for Knowledge Management, vol. 248, pp. 110–111. Springer, Berlin (2004)
[20] Parmenter, D.: Key Performance Indicators: Developing, Implementing and Using Winning KPIs, 2nd edn., pp. 1–10. John Wiley, Hoboken (2007)
[21] Fischermanns, G.: Praxishandbuch Prozessmanagement. Verlag Dr. Götz Schmidt, Gießen (2009)

[22] Becker, T.: Prozesse in Produktion und Supply Chain optimieren. Springer (2008)
[23] Lyon, D.D.: Practical CM, Best Configuration Management Practices. Butterworth-Heinemann (1999)
[24] Watts, F.B.: Engineering Documentation Control Handbook. William Andrew Inc. (2008)
[25] Bourne, L.: Stakeholder Relationship Management. Gower Publishing (2009)
[26] ISO 9241-12, Presentation of information (2011)
[27] Nielson, J.: Usability Engineering. Academic Press, San Diego (1993)
[28] Heinecke, A.M.: Mensch-Computer-Interaktion. Springer (2012)
[29] Plaisant, B.S.A.C.: Designing the User Interface. Pearson Education Inc. (2010)
[30] Schneiderman, B.: The eyes have it: A task by data type taxonomy for information visualizations, Institute for Systems Research University of Maryland (1996)
[31] Vaupel, J., Birkhölzer, T.: IT-Architekturen. VDE Verlag (2003)
[32] Patton, P.C., Jayaswal, B.K.: Design for Trustworthy Software. Pearson Education Inc. (2007)
[33] Benantar, M.: Access Control Systems. Springer (2006)
[34] Lampson, B.W.: Protection. In: Proceedings of the 5th Princeton Conference on Information Sciences and Systems (1971)
[35] Baccarini, D.: The concept of project complexity - a review. International Journal of Project Management, 201–204 (1996)
[36] Lehner, F.: Wissensmanagement: Grundlagen, Methoden und technische Unterstützung, 3rd edn. Hanser, Wien (2009)
[37] Doppler, K.: Unternehmenswandel gegen Widerstände, Change Management mit den Menschen. Campus Verlag, Frankfurt am Main (2011)

System Lifecycle Management: Initial Approach for a Sustainable Product Development Process Based on Methods of Model Based Systems Engineering

Martin Eigner, Thomas Dickopf, Hristo Apostolov, Patrick Schaefer, Karl-Gerhard Faißt, and Alexander Keßler

Institute for Virtual Product Engineering, University of Kaiserslautern, Germany
thomas.dickopf@mv.uni-kl.de

Abstract. Modeling today's products means modeling interdisciplinary 'product systems' integrating various authoring systems with the technical-administrative product structure and the related processes. Achieving sustainability of the stated product systems, yields new artifacts, expanding the area to be considered and impedes traceability. This paper introduces System Lifecycle Management as key concept. Along with an approach based on methods of Model Based Systems Engineering the outlined problems are solved on an exemplary sustainable development process. The paper defines a framework for modeling the product system in the early development phases, which accompanies system design considering sustainability aspects in a prospective view. To demonstrate the proposed method, the paper focuses on expanding existing modeling constructs by relevant behavior elements capturing semantic links and information. First analyses and capabilities of the approach are presented in a case study of a wheeled excavator.

Keywords: System Lifecycle Management, Model Based Systems Engineering, Sustainability, Traceability.

1 Introduction

Contemporary technological products are multi-disciplinary systems developed by multiple engineering disciplines. The risen requirements on these systems led to a complexity explosion, especially with regard to the information flow within the product development process [1]. As a result of new upcoming legislation focusing on sustainability, complexity is increasing furthermore [2]. But, in parallel to the challenges arising, great opportunities are also evolving for manufacturing companies to make their contribution to the sustainability paradigm and to gain advantage over their competitors through ecologically, economically and socially motivated system and process innovations [3] [4]. A multi-disciplinary system development requires a rethinking of common methods, processes, IT solutions and organizational forms as known in product development today. To cope with complexity and to assure

S. Fukuda et al. (Eds.): PLM 2014, IFIP AICT 442, pp. 287–300, 2014.

fulfillment of new requirements, traceability throughout the entire system lifecycle is needed. Today, traceability in a Product Lifecycle Management [1] [5] solution manifests itself only in relations defined between product requirements and elements of the bill of material.

This paper considers System Lifecycle Management [6] as a key concept for the definition of engineering design processes. Model Based Systems Engineering [6] [7], as essential part of the System Lifecycle Management concept, is a multi-disciplinary engineering paradigm to guide the design process in the early phases and to achieve traceability [8]. In this paper a new approach for a comprehensive system description based on an extended V-Model [9] is presented. It constitutes a promising new instrument for functional system description assisting to achieve a multi-disciplinary system development taking into account the environmental aspect of sustainability. The model builds on work of the ERMA research project [10], which aims at proactive estimation of the eco-performance of future concepts of wheeled excavators.

2 Motivation and Objective

In the field of construction equipment, with well-established, mechanical, hydraulic, hybrid and electronic solutions, the need of eco-design will raise significantly because of further increase of energy costs, stricter energetic requirements and growing competitive pressure. The prospective view within ERMA [10] requires analysis of the wheeled excavator and the application of Life Cycle Assessment [11] [12] in a proactive manner supporting the product development.

Table 1. Key Drivers of Environmental Impact

Lifecycle Phase	Environmental Impact Parameter
Production	Raw Material Extraction
	Manufacturing Processes
Operation	Usage, Maintenance, Energy Consumption
	Replacement of Spare Parts and Fluids
Recycling	Recycling, Disposal,
	Includes all Waste from Maintenance

Extensive concepts and new structures, such as innovative and integrated technical solutions for increasing the total energy efficiency, are needed [13]. New requirements on the product's sustainability and eco-performance as well as the demand for high flexibility lead to complex product systems which contain mechanic, hydraulic, electric and even hybrid subsystems [14]. Systems like the investigated wheeled excavator are characterized by a large number of constituent parts, complex processes and, referring to the lifecycle, a dominance of the usage phase due to high energy consumption throughout a long lifecycle [15] [16]. The overall effect of energy and resource reduction through new technical concepts is often hard to predict, especially in the case of multi-disciplinary systems. To quantify these predictions is even harder. This leads to the need for a comprehensive system solution [17].

The results shown in *figure 1* are based on an exemplary product structure, related manufacturing, transportation and distribution processes as well as an assumption for the usage phase. Regarding the lifecycle of a commercial vehicle, more than 90% of the greenhouse gas emissions are resulting from energy consumption out of the usage phase.

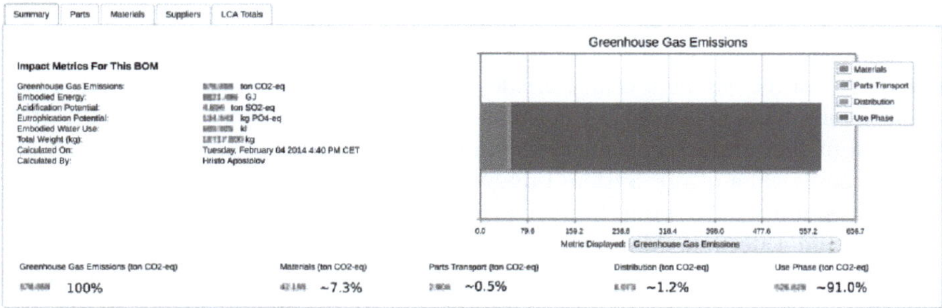

Fig. 1. Environmental Impact (Example: Greenhouse Gas Emission) Regarding the Lifecycle of a Commercial Vehicle (adapted from [18])

The paper is limited to the consideration of the usage phase as main driver of the environmental impact. It deals with the outlined problem of an early system description based on a dynamic view referring to specific behavior artifacts using the example of greenhouse gas emissions. Challenges for a sustainable development process are:

(a) Multi-disciplinary View on Complex Product Systems:
Current development processes of complex mechatronic products are heavily influenced by multiple disciplines like mechanic, electronic and informatics as well as dependencies between information elements and engineered system parts. System specification, modeling and first simulations are still discipline-specific.

(b) Lifecycle View on Complex Product Systems:
Beside the assessment of the used materials based on the product structure, a comprehensive consideration of all related processes, starting from raw material extraction to the end-of-life activities as well as all supporting processes like transportation, are of central importance in regard to sustainability.

An approach based on methods of Model Based Systems Engineering can help to improve traceability within complex multi-disciplinary systems throughout multiple lifecycle phases and thereby to identify key areas to be targeted by an exemplary case scenario of the sustainable development process of a product system.

3 Related Work

To enable an early system description, the new concept of System Lifecycle Management, with a proposed extension on the V-Model within, is a promising new instrument for functional description of a product system. In order to introduce an approach for exemplary sustainable product development process, the theses that are described in this paper build upon the previous work on sustainability assessment [2] [3] [19] [20] [21] [22] [23] [24] and research on the topic of Model Based Systems

Engineering performed at the Institute for Virtual Product Engineering (University of Kaiserslautern, Germany) [8] [25] [26] [27].

3.1 System Lifecycle Management

Up to 80% of the essential characteristics of each system are determined in the early phase of its development [1]. Decisions made here are fundamental for the entire lifecycle of the product system. Revising the system or changing processes in later phases causes great effort. System Lifecycle Management represents a concept rather than a monolithic IT system. Similar to Product Lifecycle Management [3] [5] [20] [23], System Lifecycle Management [6] [29] is an integrated, information-driven concept to improve the performance of a product system over the entire lifecycle. It achieves efficiency by using a shared information core system that helps engineers to efficiently manage complexity in the lifecycle of the product system from first definition of requirements to end-of-life activities. Thus, the concept does not provide innovative systems but can contribute to engineering at administrative level *(see figure 2)* by providing the right information at the right time in the right context.

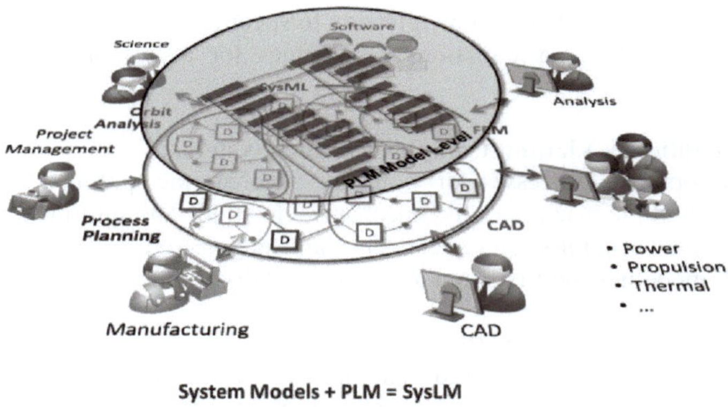

Fig. 2. Two-Layer-Model of System Lifecycle Management (adapted from [6] and [7])

Definition. System Lifecycle Management (SysLM) is a general information management solution extending today's Product Lifecycle Management to the early phase and all disciplines including services. The concept is based on the direct or indirect (via TDM[1]) integration of various authoring systems along the system lifecycle with the technical-administrative backbone for system or product models and processes. All development phases and the resulting models (R,F,L,P, …[2]) of the system's lifecycle are included and connected to achieve traceability.

---

[1] Team Data Management (TDM): Authoring tool-close (local) management system for a development team, regardless of the PLM backbone.

[2] Requirement, Function, Logical System Element, Physical Part, etc. (R, F, L, P, …): Defines information artifacts out of system or product model within the development process.

As an exemplary extension to Product Lifecycle Management in regard to eco-design and sustainability [1] [3] [30] [31] [32], System Lifecycle Management can help to improve the environmental and sustainability performance of a product system by achieving traceability with regard to the material flow, starting from extraction of raw materials, processing, production, manufacturing, storage, transport, usage and disposal. In addition, requirements traceability is realized over the entire development process. Within, the concept of Model Based Systems Engineering provides methods to guide the cross-disciplinary, virtual product development process and to achieve the required traceability.

3.2 Model Based Systems Engineering

Model Based Systems Engineering (MBSE) is a multi-disciplinary engineering paradigm propagating the use of models instead of documents to support analysis, specification, design and verification of the system being developed [33]. Systems Engineering as such, comprises technical but also management processes to generate a balanced system solution in regard to various stakeholder needs and to reduce risks that can hinder the success of a project [34]. In the case of sustainability, this could be an early consideration of the usage phase. In the study introduced in this paper, by using models instead of documents, a discipline-neutral view of the system specification is created. The resulting coherent system model helps to understand and to overview the complexity of the developed system and, moreover, it simplifies the communication in a multi-disciplinary development team. Interdependencies between individual system components are managed; the system is kept consistent to the specification and satisfies all defined requirements. In this context, requirements traceability can be archived over the entire development process. In previous work done at the Institute for Virtual Product Engineering [25] [26], a methodical guideline for the use of the Model Based Systems Engineering paradigm has been developed and conceptually realized by extending the V-Model from [9].

With regard to the V-Model, the extended version *(see figure 3)* enables a model-based and structured system description on the left wing of the 'V' in the early design phases. The systemization on the left wing of the V-Model is used to describe the three levels of specification, first simulation and discipline-specific modeling. Parallel to these overlapping levels, the information artifacts or model elements are differentiated in requirements (R), functions (F), logical solution elements (L) and physical parts (P), which are modeled in authoring tools and languages.

Through semantic links between different model elements, as well as between elements of the same type, traceability could be ensured from a 'horizontal' and 'vertical' point of view. 'Vertical' traceability is to be guaranteed by linking system elements hierarchically above different system levels. The allocation links between different model types (R-F-L-P) permit 'horizontal' traceability over the different system specification stages [25]. New in this context is the consideration of behavior (B) within the system development. The behavior of the system and the user's behavior have high impact on the regarded eco-performance.

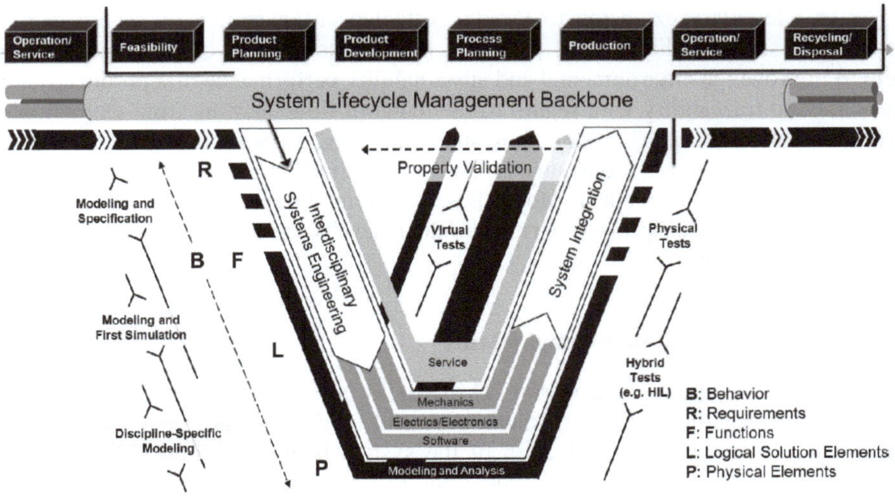

Fig. 3. Extended V-Model for Multi-Disciplinary Product Development (based on VDI 2206 [9], adapted from [25][26])

System models are created by application of the Systems Modeling Language (SysML). In addition, a specific data scheme describes and defines these elements as well as the semantic links between them. Furthermore, it allows integrating and managing the information in a System Lifecycle Management (SysLM) backbone.

4 Approach

Several solutions for sustainability assessment of product systems have been developed [21] [23] [35] [36] but the subject is still not solved satisfactory. None of these solutions considers both of the introduced challenges in one joint and integrated approach. Following, an initial approach for an exemplary sustainable product development process based on methods of Model Based Systems Engineering is introduced.

4.1 Methodology to Include Behavior in the Early Development Phases

The V-Model from VDI 2206 [8] defines a systematic methodology for developing mechatronic systems, but it is not addressing all aspects of model-based design. This gap between requirements engineering and the intellectual model of the product system has been closed by research [6] [7] [25] [26] within the RFLP-approach and the three layers of modeling and specification, specification and first simulation as well as discipline specific modeling on the left wing of the V-Model. However, the V-Model is not suited to model and maintain behavior such as the usage phase of a product system. An approach for the extension of the V-Model is depicted in *figure 3*.

The following steps describe the procedure of modeling behavior in the early design phases:

Step 1 - Identification of Key Drivers Following the RFLP Approach

In the first step the occurring gap between requirements and physical parts has to be closed. The outcoming traceability of structural elements along RFLP helps to identify the key drivers at an early level of development.

Step 2 - Specification of Behavior Artifacts in the Early Phase

Corresponding to the 'horizontal' traceability of structural elements in step 1, a 'horizontal' traceability of behavioral artifacts has to be specified, which allows a quantitative consideration of behavior from an abstract view at requirements level to a concrete description on the level of logical elements. Thereby, the identified key drivers from step 1 could be observed in the context of their main functions.

Step 3 - Analysis of Behavior Artifacts in the Early Phase

For a first calculation and simulation of system's behaviors in the early phases of development, it is needful to generate an analysis context which describes the subset of elements that are needed as well as their relationships through constraints and properties.

Step 4 - Requirement Traceability, Verification and Validation

Based on the previous steps, with the help of specific simulation and calculation tools the developed system model has to be verified and validated against the requirements. The procedure takes place in iterative loops.

Step 5 - Interpretation and Visualization of the Results

In this step, the interpretation and visualization of the results are carried out. Concrete recommendations for decisions have to be derived from it.

4.2 Case Study: Modeling Behavior in an Exemplary System Model

The specification of the system, modeled by structure elements in the early phase is too coarse for a detailed assessment which can support the engineering eco-design. It is important to take the usage phase into account already in the early design phase and to provide traceability between the requirements of the product *(see figure 4: R-level)* and the product's physical elements *(see figure 4: P-level)*. Based on an abstract example for the modification of an environmental constraint, it will be shown how it is possible and helpful to consider the requirements derived from the usage phase of a working machine, or a similar product, already in the early phases of development by using Model Based Systems Engineering.

Problem Description. The greenhouse gas emission for a working machine, e.g. in Japan, should be lowered to a maximum average value of 1.000 t CO_2-eq. (based on the results of *figure 1* in our example we limit the accruement of the greenhouse gas emission only on the usage phase).

Step 1 – Identification of Key Drivers Following the RFLP Approach

At the example of changed requirement on the allowed average CO_2-equivalent emissions of the machine, the traceability provided by the presented approach will help to identify the engine, for example, as a key driver at the logical system level. *Figure 4* describes the context schematically.

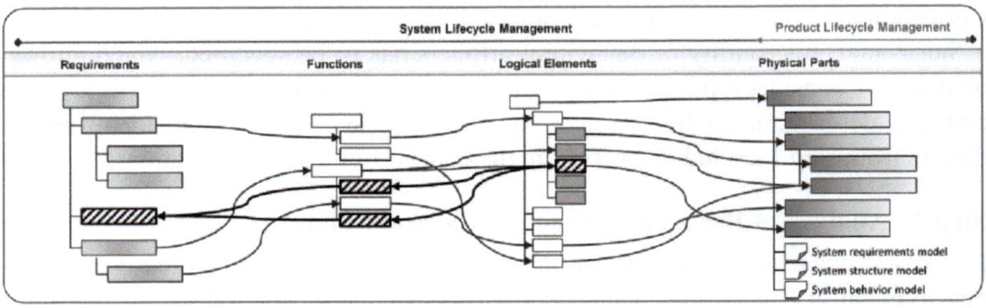

Fig. 4. Schematic Representation of the Identification of Key Drivers through Traceability along RFLP (adapted from [25])

Step 2 - Specification of Behavior Artifacts in the Early Phase

Since the engine as an assembly is not of big importance for the environmental impact, rather a quantitative consideration of working behavior, energy consumption and thereof resulting emissions has to be taken as a basis. The mainly used functionalities have to be modeled at the beginning of the specification and to be considered referring to the design of the machine for specific markets.

The Systems Modeling Language (SysML) allows describing these major functions in an abstract way with the help of the use case diagram. It illustrate how the system is used to achieve the goals, set by its users, and with which elements it interacts during operation. These could be people, other systems or the environment [33]. Based on the example of the wheeled excavator *(see chapter 2),* the lower right part of *figure 5* shows the main use case scenarios according to a test method for energy consumption of hydraulic excavators [37], here modeled in SysML. One possible way to define these use case scenarios in SysML is to associate them with activities in a block context including relevant properties as parameter elements [38].

Activities in SysML describe behaviors performed by specific parts of a system or their components over the entire lifecycle [33]. The relations between different model elements *(see figure 5)* in the system are described through allocation relationships. In regard to the further use of the defined parameter properties, it is important to differentiate their types in the SysML model. The parameter properties might be based on a specification (such as a limitation through a requirement) or on a prediction (such as results from simulations or conclusions from field data).

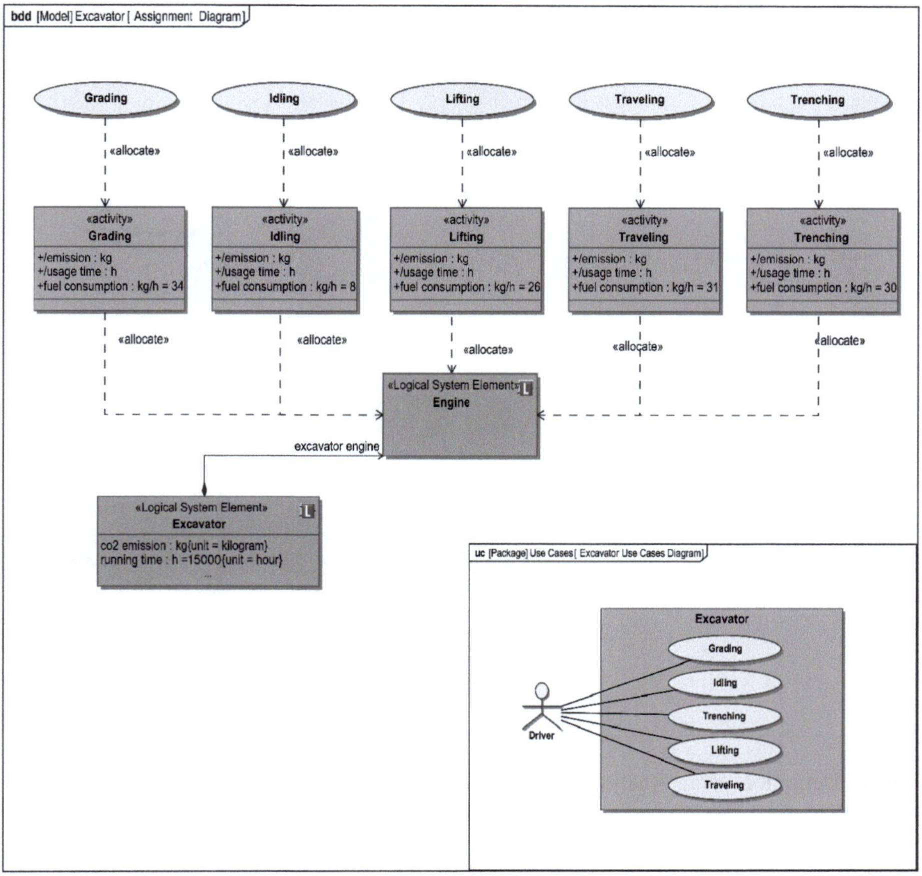

Fig. 5. Setting of Use Cases and their Parameters Referring to Logical Solution Elements

Within the considered situation of usage cycles of a wheeled excavator, a running time of 15.000 hours is supposed to be a specification property as well as a new limitation rate for a greenhouse gas emission lower than 1.000 t CO_2-eq. A prediction property is represented in this case by the simulated value.

Step 3 - Analysis of Behavior Artifacts in the Early Phase

To simulate or calculate the emission values of the different use cases or, respectively, the emission of the whole wheeled excavator in regard to its usage, SysML allows generating a first specification of a simulation through different diagrams. With the help of a block definition diagram it is possible to determine the context of an analysis *(see figure 6).* Blocks of the system which are utilized in this context are linked to the analysis block by associations. These blocks provide the parameters that are used for the analysis and a placeholder for prediction properties which represent the outcoming results. The current calculation is described by different constraints. These constraints are connected to the analysis context element through a composite association.

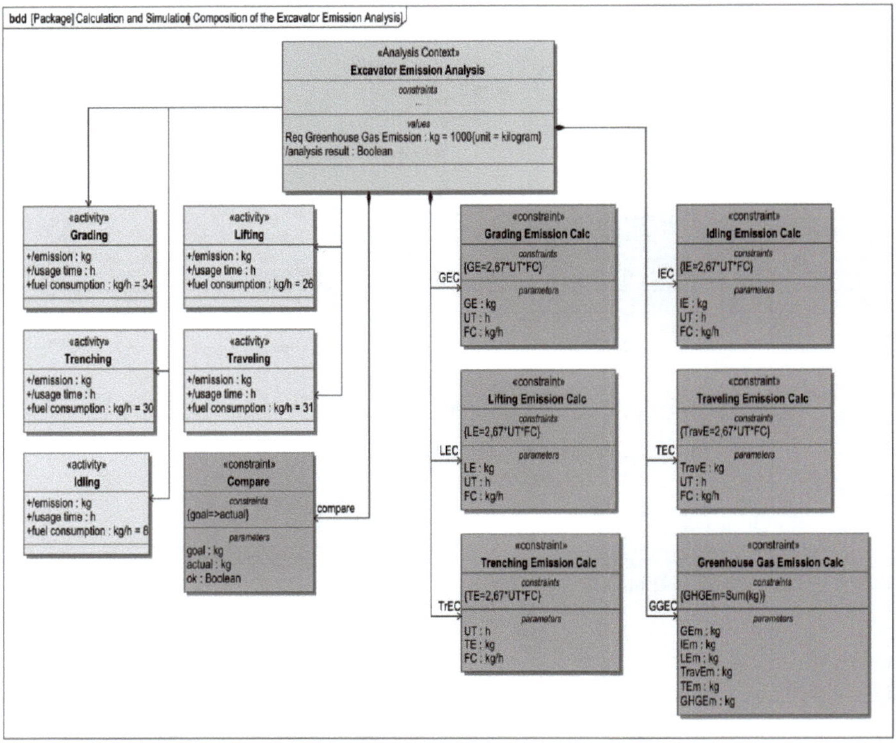

Fig. 6. Definition of an Analysis Context for the Greenhouse Gas Emission of a Wheeled Excavator

With the help of the SysML parametric diagram the relationship between the different model elements of the analysis context can be described through their parameters and specified constraints [38]. *Figure 7* clarifies the mathematical progression for the calculation of the greenhouse gas emissions of the whole wheeled excavator, as well as separately for the different use case scenarios. Additionally the constraint block 'compare' checks if the current value satisfies the given requirement. Based on the information of this diagram and the structural system description, test cases can be generated and executed by specific calculation and simulation tools.

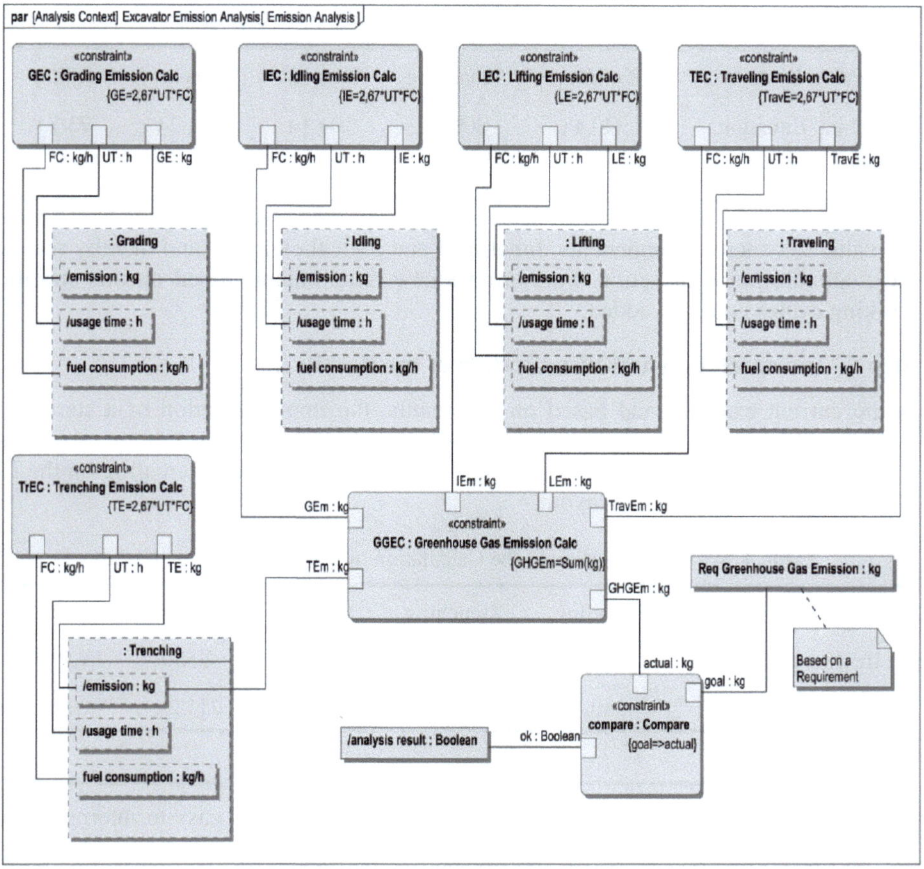

Fig. 7. Parameter Relations for the Analysis of Greenhouse Gas Emission

Step 4 - Requirement Traceability, Verification and Validation

In the current example, a need for action on the system's L-level can result from the changed requirement on the average CO_2-eq. emissions and the engine has been tracked down as main driver of the impact. Considering the machine's behavior over its lifetime *(see table 2)* assuming the following localized working-cycle distribution:

Table 2. Exemplary Working Cycle Distribution of an Excavator (according to [37])

Working Cycle	Grading	Trenching	Lifting	Traveling	Idling
Percent of life time	25%	25%	10%	17%	23%
Fuel consumption, kg/h	34	30	26	31	8

Arising from a machine lifetime of 15.000 hours of operating service the following values for greenhouse gas emission as shown in *table 3* are the results of this calculation.

Table 3. Results from the Calculation in Different Working Cycles

Working Cycle	Grading	Trenching	Lifting	Traveling	Idling
CO2-eq. Emission	340,4 t	300,4 t	104,1 t	211,2 t	73,7 t
Total			1029,3 t		

In regard to the result and with the help of the SysML model it is possible to trace the value to concrete components, functional and logical elements and thereby realize most suitable fields of action. Furthermore new requirements based on this specific working cycles could be added.

Step 5 - Interpretation and Visualization of the Results

In the current example and based on the results, the implementation of a start-stop system for a reduction of the time spent in idling would improve the system as well as optimizing the drive train. Otherwise alternative concepts could be creating on the F-level to improve the systems layout.

Table 4. Variation referring to the Calculation in Different Working Cycles

Working Cycle	Grading	Trenching	Lifting	Traveling	Idling
Life time in hours	3.750	3.750	1.500	2.550	1.050
CO2-eq. Emission	340,4 t	300,4 t	104,1 t	211,2 t	22,4 t
Total			978,5 t		

Last but not least, this information has to be visualized in an easy to interpret way and supplied to decision-makers. An appropriate integration of the proposed behavior artifacts and of a general behavior description into the System Lifecycle Management backbone is part of further research.

5 Conclusion and Outlook

Modeling a complex product system requires the integration of various authoring systems and the product structure with related processes. Following this way, full traceability can be achieved. The paper introduced System Lifecycle Management as key concept integrating the introduced two layers. The proposed approach which is based on methods of Model Based Systems Engineering addresses exemplarily one specific outlined problem of a sustainable development process of a product system. The paper reuses and adapts existing modeling constructs for capturing relevant behavior artifacts at the example of the usage phase of a wheeled excavator. Semantic links are formalized between early definition phase and first prediction in form of constraint blocks regarding sustainable product development. For the future, the implementation of the introduced approach will be provided within a System Lifecycle Management backbone. To give the user the capability to trace the impact of design decisions easily, an intuitive and graphically rich user interface will be implemented on top of the System Lifecycle Management backbone.

Acknowledgments. The authors would like to acknowledge funding from the German Bundesministerium für Bildung und Forschung attended by PTKA for research of mecPro^2 and from Stiftung Rheinland-Pfalz für Innovation for research of ERMA. The authors would like to thank Torsten Gilz and Radoslav Zafirov for their contribution and research on the topic of Model Based Systems Engineering, for their input and assistance.

References

1. Eigner, M., Stelzer, R.: Product Lifecycle Management - Ein Leitfaden für Product Development und Life Cycle Management, 2nd edn. Springer, Heidelberg (2009)
2. Azevedo, K., Bras, B., Doshi, S., Guldberg, T.: Modeling Sustainability of Complex Systems - a Multi-Scale Framework using SysML. In: Proc. of the ASME 2009 Int. Design Engineering Technical Conference, San Diego, USA, pp. 1437–1448 (2009)
3. Bras, B.: Incorporating Environmental Issues in Product Realization. United Nations Industry and Environment 20(1-2), 7–13 (2009)
4. Barreto, L.V., Anderson, H., Anglin, A., Tomovic, C.: Product Lifecycle Management in Support of Green Manufacturing – Addressing the Challenges of Global Climate Change. Int. J. of Manufacturing Technology and Management 19(3/4), 294–305 (2010)
5. Stark, J.: Product Lifecycle Management – 21st Century Paradigm for Product Realisation. Springer, London (2011)
6. Eigner, M.: Modellbasierte Virtuelle Produktentwicklung auf einer Plattform für System Lifecycle Management. In: Sendler, U. (ed.) Industrie 4.0 - Beherrschung der indus-triellen Komplexität mit SysLM, pp. 91–110. Springer, Heidelberg (2013)
7. Paredis, C.: Why Model-Based Systems Engineering? - Benefits and Payoffs. In: 4th PLM Future Tagung, Mannheim (2012)
8. Eigner, M., Roubanov, D., Zafirov, R. (eds.): Modellbasierte Virtuelle Produktentwicklung. Springer, Heidelberg (to be published, 2014)
9. VDI 2206: Design Methodology for Mechatronic Systems. Beuth, Berlin (2004)
10. Eigner, M., Schäfer, P.D., Apostolov, H.: Leveraging Product Development for a Sustainable Future: Energy and Resource Efficiency in Lifecycle Analysis. In: Abramovici, M., Stark, R. (eds.) Smart Product Engineering. LNPE, vol. 5, pp. 725–734. Springer, Heidelberg (2013)
11. ISO 14040: Environmental Management - Life Cycle Assessment: Principles and Framework. Beuth, Berlin (2006)
12. Kloepffer, W., Grahl, B.: Oekobilanz (LCA) – Ein Leitfaden für Ausbildung und Beruf. Wiley-Vch, Weinheim (2009)
13. Finzel, R., Jaehne, H., Helduser, S.: Energieeffiziente Antriebssysteme mobiler Arbeitsmaschinen. In: Proc. of 4th Fachtagung Baumaschinentechnik, Dresden (2009)
14. Schindler, C., Eigner, M., Scholler, C., Schaefer, P.: Eco-Efficiency Analysis for Hydraulic and Hybrid Concepts for Mobile Working Machines. In: Proc. of the 13th Scandinavian International Conference on Fluid Power, Linkoeping (2013)
15. Pickel, P., Eigner, M.: Life Cycle Assessment (LCA) and its Importance for the Agriculture Sector. In: Proc. of the 23rd Annual Meeting of the Club of Bologna, Bologna (2012)
16. Kwak, M., Kim, H.: Exploring Opportunities to Improve Life Cycle Environmental Performance of a Complex Product. In: Abramovici, M., Stark, R. (eds.) Smart Product Engineering. Lecture Notes in Production Engineering, vol. 5, pp. 735–744. Springer, Heidelberg (2013)
17. Bras, B.: Sustainability and Product Life Cycle Management - Issues and Challenges. Int. J. Product Lifecycle Management 4(1/2/3), 23–48 (2009)

18. Eigner, M., Schaefer, P., Apostolov, H.: Improving the Life Cycle Eco Performance of a Wheeled Excavator - in the context of ERMA. In: Proc. of the 3rd Commercial Vehicle Technology Symposium, pp. 244–253. Shaker, Aachen (2014)
19. Kloepffer, W.: Life Cycle Based Methods for Sustainable Product Development. Int. J. Life Cycle Assessment 8(3), 157–159 (2003)
20. Grieves, M.: Product Lifecycle Management – Driving the Next Generation of Lean Thinking. McGraw-Hill, New York (2006)
21. Romaniw, Y., Bras, B., Guldberg, T.: An Activity Based Approach to Sustainability Assessments. In: Proc. of the ASME 2009 Int. Design Engineering Technical Conference, San Diego, pp. 1131–1139 (2009)
22. Ciceri, N., Garetti, M., Terzi, S.: Product Lifecycle Management Approach for Sustainability. In: Proc. of the 19th CIRP Design Conference, Cranfield, pp. 147–154 (2009)
23. Terzi, S., Bouras, A., Dutta, D., Garetti, M., Kiritsis, D.: Product Lifecycle Management – from its History to its New Role. Int. J. PLM 4(4), 360–389 (2010)
24. Eigner, M., von Hauff, M., Schaefer, P.: Sustainable Product Lifecycle Management. In: Hesselbach, J., Herrmann, C. (eds.) Glocalized Solutions for Sustainability in Manufacturing, pp. 501–506. Springer, Heidelberg (2011)
25. Eigner, M., Gilz, T., Zafirov, R.: Proposal for Functional Product Description as Part of PLM Solution in Interdisciplinary Product Development. In: Proc. of the Design Society International Design Conference 2012, Dubrovnik, pp. 1667–1676 (2012)
26. Eigner, M., Gilz, T., Zafirov, R.: Systems Engineering VPE Data Schema - PDM Integration of a Functional Product Description Model in SysML. In: Proc. of the 13th International Conference Mechatronics 2012, Trauner, Linz, pp. 651–657 (2012)
27. Gilz, T.: PLM Integrated Interdisciplinary System Models in the Conceptual Design Phase based on Model-Based Systems Engineering, University of Kaiserslautern, Kaiserslautern (to be published, 2014)
28. Liu, W., Zeng, Y., Maletz, M., Brisson, D.: Product Lifecycle Management – A Review. In: Proc. of the ASME Int. Design Engineering Technical Conference, San Diego (2009)
29. Sendler, U. (ed.): Industrie 4.0 - Beherrschung der industriellen Komplexität mit SysLM. 1, pp. 1–20. Springer, Heidelberg (2013)
30. Moeller, A., Rolf, A.: Eco Product Lifecycle Management. In: Proc. of the 2nd International Symposium on Environmentally Conscious Design and Inverse Manufacturing, Tokyo, pp. 739–744 (2001)
31. Abele, A., Feickert, S., Kuhrke, D., Clesle, F.: Environmental Product Lifecycle Management – Customizing the Enterprise Specific Manufacturing Processes. In: Proc. of the 13th CIRP Int. Conference on Life Cycle Engineering, Leuven, pp. 651–656 (2006)
32. Feickert, S.: Oekologisches Product Lifecycle Management – Ein Integrationskonzept der oekologischen Produktbilanzierung in betrieblichen ERP-Systemen. Shaker, Aachen (2007)
33. Friedenthal, S., Moore, A., Steiner, R.: A Practial Guide to SysML – The Systems Modeling Language. Morgan Kaufmann Pub., London (2009)
34. Haskins, C.: Systems Engineering Handbook – A Guide for System Life Cycle Processes and Activities, San Diego (2011)
35. Ramani, K., Ramanujan, D., Bernstein, W., Zhao, F., Sutherland, J., Handwerker, C., Choi, J., Kim, H., Thurston, D.: Integrated Sustainable Life Cycle Design – A Review. Int. J. Mechanical Design 132(9), 1–15 (2010)
36. Lindow, K., Woll, R., Stark, R.: A Conceptual Framework for Sustainable Engineering Design. In: Proc. of the 19th CIRP Int. Conf. on Life Cycle Engineering, Berkeley, pp. 197–202 (2012)
37. JCMAS H020: Japan Construction Mechanization Association. Earth-Moving Machinery Test Methods for Energy Consumption of Hydraulic Excavators. JCMAS H020 (2010)
38. Delligatti, L.: SysML Distilled – A Brief Guide to the Systems Modeling Language. Addison-Wesley, New York (2013)

Interoperability Framework for Supporting Information-Based Assistance in the Factory

Mohamed Anis Dhuieb, Farouk Belkadi, Florent Laroche, and Alain Bernard

L'UNAM Université, IRCCYN, Ecole Centrale de Nantes,
1 rue de la Noë, 44300 Nantes, France
mohamed-anis.dhuieb@irccyn.ec-nantes.fr

Abstract. The aim of this paper is to propose new interoperability solution, based on Info-Engine framework and web services technology to support data exchange and extraction from PLM system, specially the Windchill tool. This solution will be implemented as a connector module of more generic framework, named Digital Factory Assistant (DFA). The DFA framework aims to provide factory workers by a set of knowledge and information based decision support to improve their activity performance.

Keywords: Product Lifecycle Management, Interoperability, Knowledge and Data extraction, Windchill.

1 Introduction

Visions about the factory of the future affirm that future production lines will be characterized by learning capability and decisions support in all stages of the process chains involved. The aim of such propositions is to achieve higher manufacturing outputs by integrating knowledge-based modules into the engineering systems concerned in the factory. Despite the evolution of digital tools in the factory, the role of the human being in the whole product lifecycle development remains a key factor to be continuously improved by means of several actions of training and assistance. For this, one of the main challenges in today's production systems is to provide factory actors with robust tools helping them to perform more efficiently their daily activities and to enhance their reactivity in front of critical working situations.

The proposal of this paper is developed as a part of the ARTUR project that aims to deal with the topic of worker assistance through the development of the "Digital Factory Assistant" (DFA). By means of this assistant, the operator will benefit from an omnipresent support along the manufacturing process. The DFA restitutes knowledge from distributed sources and relies on different ways of interaction with the user in order to provide him relevant information and decision supports.

Different knowledge sources can be considered in the factory, such as Product Lifecycle management system (PLM), CAx tools (Computer aided Design/ Manufacturing/engineering CAD/CAE/CAM…), material flows, process chains, and simulation data. The basic idea of the DFA concept is to allow each person being able

S. Fukuda et al. (Eds.): PLM 2014, IFIP AICT 442, pp. 301–310, 2014.

to respond on any given situation, mainly thanks to high-speed simulation and performance evaluation models and methods. For that need, an interoperability framework is proposed, aiming to support information extraction and knowledge routing in the factory.

The next section of the paper describes the idea behind the ARTUR project and the proposed Digital Factory Assistant framework. In the third section, we made a state of the art about the interoperability issue within recent research works and in PLM context. The fourth section describes the proposed framework of the PLM connector and then, the last section includes some perspectives of the current work.

2 The Concept of "Digital Factory Assistant"

In a production system, the worker may be faced with critical working situations that require an efficient reaction by making the right decision in the right time. As it is described in the introduction, the aim of the DFA is to support the factory workers to react in front of difficult tasks by providing them the right information and knowledge using advanced methods and technologies supporting information visualization and manufacturing process simulation.

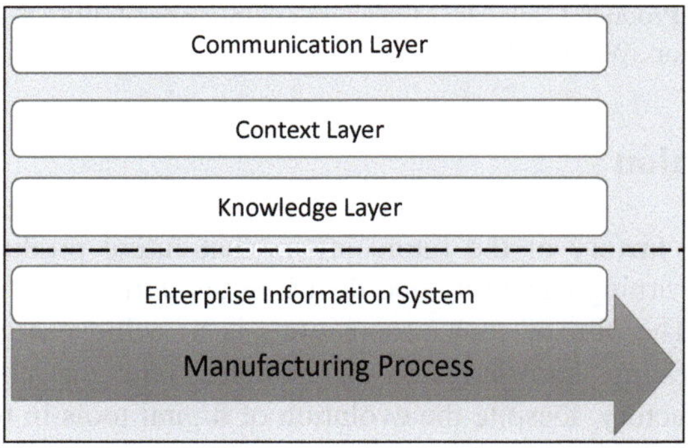

Fig. 1. Conceptual architecture of the Digital Factory Assistant

As shown in figure 1, the generic conceptual architecture of the DFA is composed of three main layers:

- Communication layer: the communication layer deals with the human machine interactions and the problem of information and knowledge representation. Virtual technologies are used to propose a better restitution of the information. This layer implements also advanced simulation interfaces connected to the manufacturing process simulation module, to guarantee a better understanding and control of the process. Thanks to this simulation interface, the user can manipulate some parameters of the manufacturing process and observe the outcome of the simulated process before committing on the real working situation.

- Context layer: the context layer is an integration of the working situation [1]. This layer is related to the human-machine level, where contextual information related to user's working situation can be acquired. The proposal of this assistant is based on context awareness issue [2]. Context-aware systems have the particularity of anticipating the user's needs in a particular situation and act proactively to provide appropriate assistance [3]. Contextual information can be acquired from real working situation and part of it may be extracted from the manufacturing enterprise information system.
- Knowledge layer: The role of this layer is to introduce a new way of definition, representation, and exploration of knowledge in the factory. The main idea is to provide worker by useful knowledge according to a multi-level structure, in which each level represents the completeness degree of knowledge [4]. The workers performance will be measured before and after using the DFA in daily activities and in front of difficult tasks in order to evaluate their improvement using the DFA.

Regarding the functional architecture of the DFA (figure 2), several interaction modes are preconized to provide data and knowledge capitalization and reuse. The first category of interactions concerns the communication between the user and the treatment module of the digital assistant throughout augmented reality and virtual reality interfaces. According to this interaction, user input his request and the DFA provide user useful assistance regarding his request, his profile and his working situation. The second category of interaction concerns data exchange between the DFA and other existing enterprise information systems through specific connectors. The third category of interactions, between the treatment module, solution finding and knowledge base, aims to perform knowledge reuse purposes. The last category supports the purpose of knowledge capitalization from both experts and external simulation software.

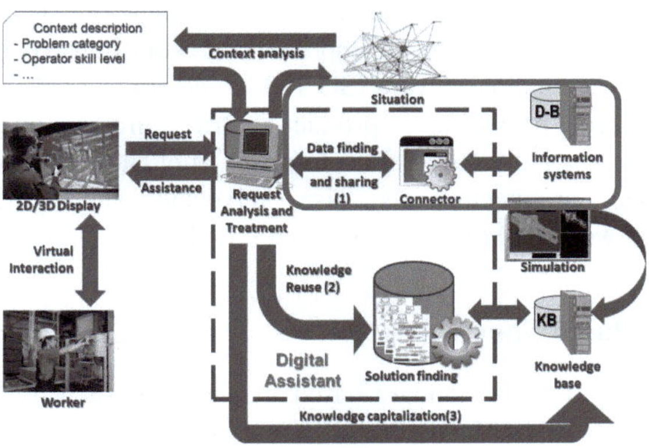

Fig. 2. Functional architecture of the digital factory assistant

To perform data exchange and extraction actions, interoperability mechanisms are required as fundamental capacities of the connector module, for each kind of information system to be connected. This paper deals with the interoperability issue and focus on the definition of a technical solution in order to support interoperability with PLM System and particularly, the Windchill PLM solution.

Before presenting the detailed architecture of the interoperability solution, the following section presents an overview of related works in the field of interoperability in PLM context.

3 Interoperability with PLM Systems: A State of the Art

Generally, three scopes of interoperability are distinguished with different terms and definitions. For instance: 1) the Conceptual interoperability that concerns the definition of concepts and semantic supporting the communication between data and knowledge models; 2) the Organizational interoperability, which focuses on the connection between processes and 3) the technical interoperability that deals with technological issues to support data exchange between software applications.

In PLM domain, three major approaches are currently used to support the interoperability and data exchange between Computer Aided applications (CAX) (X such as Design, simulation, etc.) and between CAX and data management systems.

3.1 Ontology and Web Semantic Technologies

The first category uses the ontology and Web Semantic technologies to achieve the data mapping between heterogeneous software at the conceptual level. Several studies implementing different approaches to product design have been conducted on Ontology, as standard for data exchange between design and other engineering activities in collaborative tasks [5]. In PLM field, [6] have proposed the ONTO-PLM framework, as a common core model to provide an interoperability solution between product data (encapsulated in PLM) and enterprise applications that will manage them such as ERP, CAD and MES. The conceptual framework consists in conceptualizing of existing standards, principally were ISO 10303 and IEC 62264, related to product technical data modeling providing a ''product-centric'' information model to concepts that can be processed by several enterprise applications. Model driven and Knowledge based architecture is also advocate supporting the semantic interoperability between PLM systems and other applications [7].

3.2 Standard-Based Approaches

The second category uses a standard-based mechanism, such as XML (eXtensible Markup Language), to guarantee the semantic translation between heterogeneous models [8]. For instance, in the ATHENA project, process standards (ISO15288, CMII) and product standards (STEP: STandard for the Exchange of Product model data. Ex: AP214, 233, 209, 239) have been studied [9]. IGES (Initial Graphics Exchange Specifications) and DXF (Drawing Exchange Format) standards are also used to manage the geometric data of the product [10].

In PLM field, the PLCS (Product LifeCycle Support) correspond to the STEP AP239 standard realized by the International Standard Organization in 2005 [11] to offer a generic framework for the integration, exchange and management of technical data necessary for the support of a complex product and its evolution along its whole lifecycle. Based on this standard, [12] have proposed an interoperability framework to perform data mapping between ERP and PLM.

3.3 API Standards and Web Services

The last category uses dynamic interfaces, based on API Standards (Application Programming Interface) and web services technologies, to guarantee the communication between software [13]. In this kind of interoperability mechanism, software integration is fulfilled through the web services to support the distribution of heterogeneous information between members of a project team. In PLM field, "OMG PLM Enablers" based on middleware technologies and "PLM Services" are Web technologies developed to support communication between PLM systems and between PLM and other CAX applications [14].

The specification of the PLM Services 1.0 defines a Platform Independent Model (PIM) for Product Lifecycle Management Services. This specification defines a Platform Specific Model (PSM) applicable to a Web services implementation defined by a WSDL specification, with a SOAP binding, and an XML schema specification [15]. For instance, in [16], an XML-based neutral file is defined by referring to PLM services for the building of PLM integrator as software that can exchange product, process and resource information between commercial PLM systems. The PLM integrator consists of the XML adapter and the PLM adapter to extract PPR (Product Process Resources) information from a commercial PLM system.

PLM Services standard is used in another work by [17] to support data exchange between two different PLM systems via Internet; an implementation is fulfilled to support interoperability between two commercial PLM solutions: SmartPLM and DynaPLM. In this architecture, the product data inside the PLM system is translated to PLM Services reference server by the data transfer module. The data transfer module captures the PLM system data by using APIs and translates it into the format which PLM Services reference implementation can read and visualize. Any permitted XPDI client of PLM Services from the remote side can access the translated PLM data in the PLM Services server.

The work developed in this paper can be included in the last category of interoperability approaches. The aim is to develop a technical framework exploiting the features of the Info*Engine framework provided by PTC and the SOA standards.

4 PLM Connector Framework

Windchill, developed by PTC (Parametric Technology Corporation), is a PLM system offering to users a large variety of tools to support different aspects of their collaborative development projects and data and document management. Regarding the growing interest in interoperability, PTC has embraced Open Standards, such as Service Oriented Architecture (SOA), as its strategy for supporting integration between the PLM and other IT applications. For this need, Windchill, exposes functionality for purposes of integration through a standards-compliant Web Services framework populated with an extensive library of prebuilt services.

4.1 Info*Engine® Architecture

Windchill integration with other enterprise's applications requires the use of low-level APIs and complex application adapters. Support new integration scenarios is a labour task and requires strong developpment skills. For this need, Windchill Info*Engine server provides mechanisms for retrieving and manipulating the data that users or custom applications want to view or receive from the PLM Server.

As shown in figure 3, the proposed architecture is based on Info*Engine Java 2 Enterprise Edition (J2EE) that is an implementation of J2EE Connector Architecture (JCA). JCA was designed to supply standard implementation for interaction between J2EE application servers and enterprise information systems (EIS).

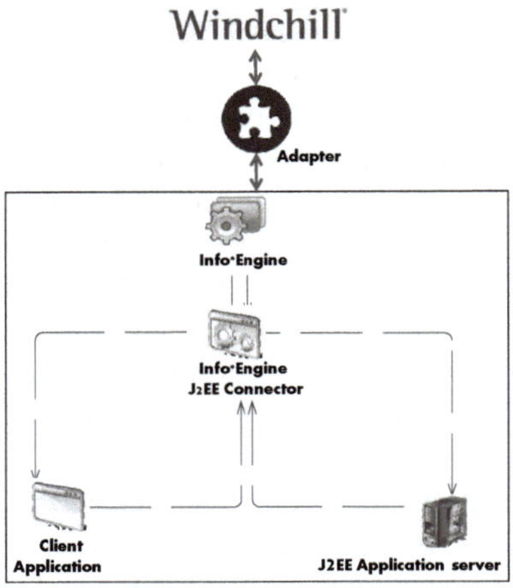

Fig. 3. The info*Engine based architecture

The Info*Engine J2EE connector uses SOAP protocol to allow communication between Info*Engine and the two modules of the interoperability application. For instance, J2EE application server and associated client application are developed as an integrated solution for the interoperability purpose.

The client application is deployed on Oracle 11g application server. By means of this client application, the user can perform different interoperability actions like creating/deleting an object in the Windchill server or even adding a link between a part and a document. The J2EE application server support the interperetation and execution of actions prescripted by the client application. Otherwise, Info*Engine is directly interfaced with Windchill application by means of the Native Adapters component. The implementation of the proposed solution is achieved by a set of interactions between the different components of Info*Engine framework and those of the interoperability client application.

As it is shown in figure 4, the client application communicates directly with the Info*Engine SOAP Servlet that catch and process SOAP requests and send in the same protocol the required information to the client application. For this need, the SOAP servelt invokes tasks execution on the SAK (Service Access Kit), which is an API facilitating the development of Java applications using of Info*Engine functions and features.

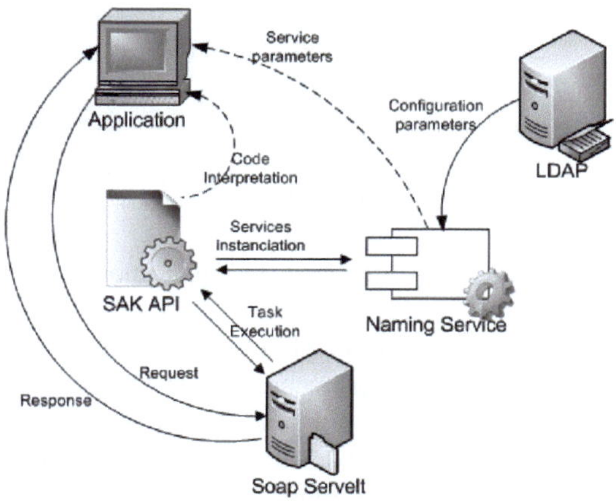

Fig. 4. Internal and external interactions in the proposed framework

During task execution, SAK interacts with the naming service in order to instantiate the required services. With the Naming Service, SAK can identify in the LDAP directory all network addresses and configuration properties. In the meantime, the client application has a direct connection to the SAK and the naming services to extract the services parameters and code interpretation respectively, which are required for the definition of the Webservice request.

4.2 Interactions Process

Based on the technical architecture presented above, a webservices based application is developed. Figure 5 illustrates the interactions schema between the user, the interoperability client application and Windchill, throughout the Info*Engine framwork.

After the user identification by entering his Windchill login and password, the client application receives from Windchill a list of different objects that are associated to the user role in the database.

At the right of the interface, a set of authorized actions are proposed to the user to perform on the Windchill server throughout the Info*Engine based framework. For instance, the user can obtain more details about the selected object, check out, modify or delete this object or also, creates link with other Windchill objects.

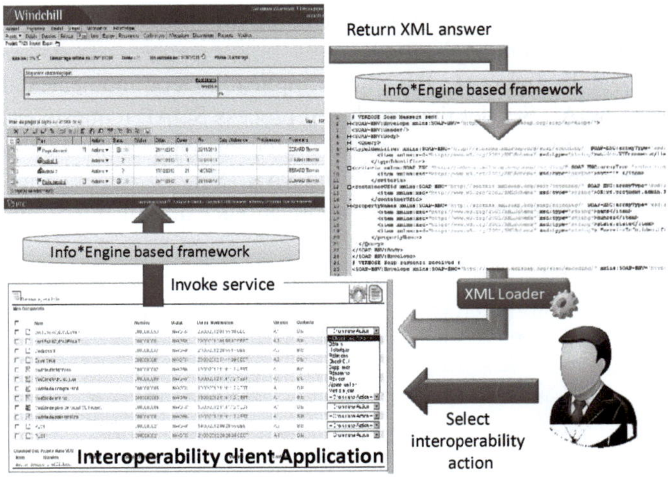

Fig. 5. Webservice-based application

When the user validates his action, the client application invoke the corresponding service(s) on the info*engine framework according to the general interaction schema presented in figure 5. Then, the Windchill send the answer in a predefined XML file to the info*Engine framework. It will be a list of information about the selected object, a validation message about the modification or deleting a specific object or also a notification of a denied action.

5 Conclusion and Future Work

Windchill is one of the most popular PLM software, which proposes robust solutions to support communication with external information systems. The purpose of this paper is first to prospect the interoperability mechanisms offered by PTC editor as a solution to interoperability issue.

Then, a new interoperability framework is proposed as a web-service based solution using the capacities embedded on the Windchill Info*Engine mechanisms and J2EE application technology.

The first results of the interoperability tests performed on the proposed framework illustrate a high level of reactivity to different requests. The main advantages of the proposed architecture is that it offer a large possibilities to pilot the communication with Windchill server through an external third-party application while ensuring a coherence with internal mechanisms of Windchill, since it exploits directly the internal components of Windchill.

This framework is a first step for the development of an integrated connector for Windchill server. The main utility of this connector is to handle process and product knowledge to be integrated in a virtual decision support system. Further work will aim at the definition of robust loader tool to support the interpretation of Windchill responses by the treatment module of the Digital Factory Assistant.

Acknowledgements. This work is financed by the region of Pays de la Loire (France). The research project involves four teams from Ecole Centrale de Nantes (IS3P and PsyCoTec teams from IRCCyN laboratory, GEM, and CERMA), and one virtual Reality applications integrator CLARTE. Particular thanks are addressed to the industrial partner, for accepting the validation of this scientific proposal.

References

1. Hasan, R., Bernard, A., Ciccotelli, J., Martin, P.: Integrating safety into the design process: elements and concepts relative to the working situation. Safety Science 41(2-3), 155–179 (2003)
2. Schmidt, A.: Context-Aware Computing: Context-Awareness, Context-Aware User Interfaces, and Implicit Interaction, 2nd edn. The Encyclopedia of Human-Computer Interaction (2013)
3. Laroche, F., Bordeu, F., Bernard, A., Chinesta, F.: Towards the factory of future An integrated approach of material-processes-information-human being. In: Proceedings of the 2012 Virtual Reality International Conference, p. 13. ACM (2012)
4. Dhuieb, M.A., Laroche, F., Bernard, A.: Toward a cognitive based approach for knowledge structuring. In: 2013 IEEE 4th International Conference on Cognitive InfoCommunications (CogInfoCom), pp. 407–412. IEEE (December 2013)
5. Bellatreche, L., Xuan, D.N., Pierra, G., Dehainsala, H.: Contribution of Ontology-based Data Modeling to Automatic Integration of Electronic Catalogues within Engineering Databases. Computers in Industry 57(8-9), 711–724 (2006)
6. Panetto, H., Dassisti, M., Tursi, A.: ONTO-PLM: Product-driven ONTOlogy for Product Data Management interoperability within manufacturing process environment. Advanced Engineering Informatics 26, 334–348 (2012)
7. Bermell-Garcia, P., Fan, I.S., Murton, A.: Towards the semantic interoperability between KBE and PLM systems. In: International Conference on Engineering Design, cite des Sciences et l'industrie, Paris, France, August 28–31 (2007)
8. Chen, D., Vernadat, F.: Standards on enterprise integration and engineering: A state of the art. International Journal of Computer Integrated Manufacturing 17(3), 235–253 (2004)
9. Ruggaber, R.: ATHENA - Advanced Technologies for Interoperability of Heterogeneous Enterprise Networks and their Application. In: International Conference on Interoperability of Enterprise Software and Applications, Geneva, Switzerland, February 23-25 (2005)
10. Choi, G.H., Mun, D., Han, S.: Exchange of CAD Part Models Based on the Macro-Parametric Approach. International Journal of CAD/CAM 2(1), 13–21 (2002)
11. Rosen, J.: Federated through life-cycle support. In: 1st Nordic Conference on PLM, NordPLM 2006, Göteborg, Sweden, January, 25-26 (2006)
12. Paviot, T., Cheutet, V., Lamouri, S.: A PLCS framework for PLM/ERP interoperability. International Journal of Product Lifecycle Management 5(2/3/4), 295–313 (2011)
13. Song, H., Roucoules, L., Eynard, B., Lafon, P.: Interoperability between Cooperative Design Modeller and a CAD System: Software Integration versus Data Exchange. International Journal for Manufacturing Science & Production 7(2), 139–149 (2006)
14. Wang, Y., Ge, J., Shao, J., Han, S.: Research on Web Service-based Interoperability of Heterogeneous PLM Systems. In: International Conference on Measuring Technology and Mechatronic Automation, Hunan, China, April 11–12 (2009)

15. Lukas, U., Nowacki, S.: High Level Integration based on the PLM Services Standard. In: ProSTEP iViP Science Days 2005, September 28-29, pp. 50–61. Cross-Domain Engineering, Darmstadt (2005)
16. Choi, S.S., Yoon, T.H., Noh, S.D.: XML-based neutral file and PLM integrator for PPR information exchange between heterogeneous PLM systems. International Journal of Computer Integrated Manufacturing 23(3), 216–228 (2010)
17. Gunpinar, E., Han, S.: Interfacing heterogeneous PLM systems using the PLM Services. Advanced Engineering Informatics 22, 307–316 (2008)

A Socio-technical Approach to Managing Material Flow in the Indonesian Fertiliser Industry

Issa D. Utami[1,2], Raymond J. Holt[1], and Alison McKay[1]

[1] School of Mechanical Engineering, University of Leeds, United Kingdom
[2] Department of Industrial Engineering, Universitas Trunojoyo, Indonesia
mnidu@leeds.ac.uk

Abstract. The Indonesian fertiliser industry is a significant contributor to the national economy. Given the need to distribute its products to customers on the 17,000 islands making up availability of ports are major factors in managing fertiliser product lifecycles. However, managing the flow of material around a port is a complex process, affected by a range of socio-technical factors. This paper proposes a conceptual model of supply network processes and their relationships to infrastructures such as ports based on a socio-technical systems analysis of material flow. Results from an application of the model to explore how changes to a port is operated affect material flow. These results were used to inform the development of an agent based simulation model to support decision makers in investigating the effects of their decisions in considering the impact of potential management interventions on the flow of materials within the port. The conceptual and simulation models are illustrated using a case study taken from a port in the Indonesian fertiliser industry.

Keywords: material flow, socio-technical system, agent based simulation modelling, Indonesian fertiliser industry.

1 Introduction

Balancing infrastructure availability is a substantial issue when managing industrial product lifecycles. Benefits will not be accrued from the excess if the availability of the infrastructure is over and above that required. On the other hand, if there is inadequate key infrastructure availability, this can cause delays in operation or even failure in process [1]. Supply network is important element of product life cycle management approach. This is because the process of managing the distribution of the product is a preventive action to maintain the product's lifetime [2]. Considering the role of infrastructure in supply networks is essential to developing decision-making tools that result in more resilient supply networks. Fertilizer is a type of chemical product which distribution process must be maintained to prevent product damage and maintain lifetime of the product [2]. In global product distribution systems such as the Indonesian fertiliser industry, physical infrastructure, such as ports are important as these affect the supply network's performance. Inefficiencies in loading or unloading of material in ports cause negative which have a detrimental impact through the product lifecycle, from production process to consumer satisfaction [3]. For this reason, port availability needs to be managed in order to

S. Fukuda et al. (Eds.): PLM 2014, IFIP AICT 442, pp. 311–322, 2014.

maintain continuity and increase performance of key supply networks processes such as logistics operations and manufacturing. This paper argues that the effectiveness of material flow in ports is critical in life cycle management processes. This paper proposes a conceptual model and an agent-based simulation modelling approach that was used to introduce people movement and interaction in scenarios of technology and infrastructure changes. A case study from the Indonesian fertiliser industry was used to specify and evaluate the model.

The paper begins with a review of literature on system thinking and socio-technical systems in decision-making design in Section 2. Conceptual framework to optimise decision making is presented in Section 3. The methodology used in this research is explained in Section 4. Section 5 describes the case study and an application of agent based simulation modelling using the framework to the case study. Finally, Section 6 discusses the key outcomes of the research.

2 System Thinking Approach in System Design

System thinking is an approach to analyse the component of systems and their environment comprehensively in order to conduct conceptual models based on reality. Since systems are composed of sub systems, co-ordination within the sub-systems helps to improve system performance. Supply networks are complex systems. Complexity in the system can be reduced by considering the system to be composed of smaller, manageable sub-systems interacting among themselves.

2.1 Socio-technical Systems in Decision Making Design

Parallel consideration of social and technical issues is needed in system design to deliver optimal whole system performance including people, processes and technology [4]. The idea of socio-technical systems was designed in response to theoretical and practical problems of working conditions in industry. The concept of the socio-technical system was established to focus on interrelationship between humans and machines in order to increase efficiency by considering the technical and the social conditions of work [5]. Challenger and Clegg [6] propose a socio-technical frameworks that identifies six components in an organization, namely: goals, people, culture, process and procedures, buildings and infrastructure, and technologies, as shown in figure 1. This framework supports the establishment or operation of the systems, which focuses on social and technical as important factors [6].

In recent years, socio-technical systems approaches have been applied to a range of complex systems. However, complex socio-technical systems are difficult to analyse. Stanton and Bessell [7] developes Cognitive Work Analysis that offers an integrated way of analyzing complex systems in multiple interpretations. The effects of knowledge sharing, training, team coordination and human interactions have been an interesting focus of research into the socio-technical approach. Siemieniuch and Sinclair [8] propose the socio-technical approach as an effective way to entrain information communication technology as global drivers. In human interdisciplinary interaction, McGowan et al. [9] suggest that socio-technical approaches might be critical need in interaction of humans and organization in interdisciplinary systems.

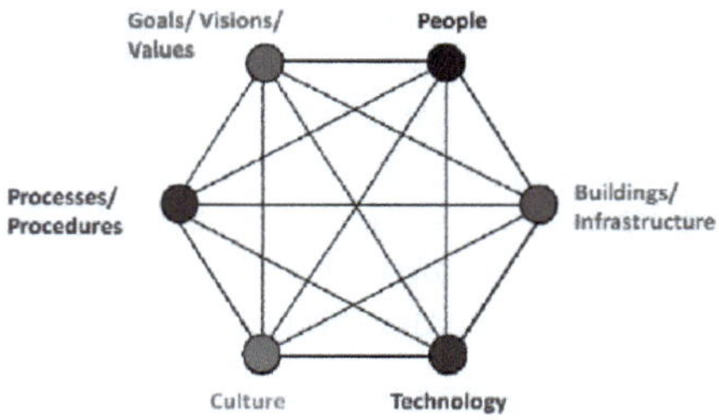

Fig. 1. A socio-technical system framework, Challenger and Clegg (2011)

2.2 Enterprise Engineering Framework

Enterprise engineering framework aids the supply networks to represent alignment between the industry and networks element. Table 1 describes component of the enterprise engineering framework. The framework contains three steps: Define, Develop, and Deploy, and contains three aspects: Purpose, Agency, and Product and Services [10]. Enterprise operating systems are socio-technical system. By visualizing the structure of the supply network strategy, the improvement process can be conducted. Enterprise engineering framework is flexible and can be applied in industries based on their purposes.

Table 1. Enterprise engineering framework (McKay et al., 2009)

	Define	**Develop**	**Deploy**
Purpose	*Mission definition strategy*	*Action programmes*	*Direction*
Agency	*Enterprise architecture*	*Enterprise operating system*	*Operation*
Products and services	*Product & service architecture*	*Product & services*	*Solutions*

There are some applications of the enterprise engineering framework. For instance: the application of the enterprises engineering framework in the aerospace sector to improve a questionnaire in identifying requirement for interface between quality of system and strategy [10]. Another application of the enterprise engineering framework was in the Malaysian palm oil industry, where the framework was used to build a holistic view of enterprise operating system in different sustainability needs [11].

2.3 Agent Based Modelling in Supporting the Decision Making Process

Agent based simulation has been applied in studies which consider the effect of human roles and behaviour on system performance and decision-making. For example, Siebers et al. [12] report an application of agent based simulation on assessing the effect of human resources management practices on customer satisfaction through observing changes in customer behaviour in a service-oriented organization. Crowder et al. [13] proposes an agent based modelling framework to facilitate the decision making process in managing the impacts of team composition and working process in product development.

In this paper an agent based simulation approach was used to help to visualise material flow management and determine the influence of variable changes in the material flow system of the port on the duration of the loading process and percentage of berth occupancy ratio.

3 Conceptual Framework

This paper proposed a conceptual framework adopted from the Enterprise Engineering Framework [10] to contextualize the different aspects of the research.

The conceptual framework is summarised in Table 2 and described here:

1. Define the purpose

The first step is to define the purpose of building tools or prototypes based on problems that exist in the system.

2. Define the agency

The second step is to define the systems or organisation of research focus, for example: individual, organisation, industry or departments.

3. Define the outcome of product or service

The third step is to define outcomes that would be generated to resolve the existing problems in the system. The outcome could be a prototype, an approach, and strategy or decision support system.

4. Develop the tools or prototype

The fourth step is to determine how to make the outcome or prototype in step 3, for instance; by employing simulation modeling.

5. Applying the tools to the system

Tools or prototype developed to be applied in the system in order to obtain result and optimise solution.

Table 2. Conceptual framework to optimise decision making

	Define	**Develop**	**Deploy**
Purpose	Define the purpose		
Agency	Define the agency	Develop the tool or prototype	
Products and services	Define the outcome of product or service		Applying the tool to the system

4 Methodology

This paper applies case study approach as methodology to investigate and observe phenomenon in depth and within real life in material flow system. The case study approach allows researcher to retain holistic and meaningful characteristics of real life events [14]. This paper states a proposition that the performance relies on material flow system can be optimise by balancing social and technical factors in the system. The unit of analysis of this paper is the material flow system in Indonesian fertiliser supply networks. A semi-structured questionnaire was developed as a tool for data collection in the case study and supported with historical data.

5 Case Study: The Indonesian Fertiliser Industry

The Indonesian fertiliser industry was chosen as the case study due to the contribution of the industry to the Indonesian economy and the complexity of material flow in supply networks such as this that are influenced by government regulation. This study focused on a port that is owned by the Indonesian fertiliser industry. Most of the processes in the distribution of raw materials and products on the system supply network are dependent on material flow through the port. For this reason, if problems occur in the process of material flow at this port, the performance of the entire supply network is affected. Data collection was carried out in the Indonesian fertiliser using semi-structured questionaires. The participants were key people who had tasks and responsibilities in material flow and supply network management.

This paper presents a new application of the socio-technical system approach by applying it to a material flow system in the context of broader supply network system. Identification of key elements in the material flow system used the six perspectives Challenger and Clegg framework:

a. Goal: to ensure the efficient flow of material through the port;
b. Procedure: standard operating procedures for material flow;
c. People: people in material flow;
d. Culture: administrative and production management process cycles;
e. Infrastructure: finished product warehouse and port loading area
f. Technology: trucks as facilities for product distribution

The result of the conceptual model in this paper is expected to assist decision makers to determine the number and combination of elements in order to measure loading time of products and measure berth occupancy ratio in the port.

The implementation of the conceptual framework in section 3 into the case study is summarised in Table 3and described as follow:

1. Define the purpose

As the focus of this research is on the influence of socio-technical changes, this study applies the IDEF-3 method [15] to visualise product and process flows in order to better understand decision makers' perspectives. It can be seen from Figure 2 that raw material from suppliers is processed in three stages of chemical processing. Quality control activities are applied at the end of the process, before fertiliser is packed and distributed. Meanwhile, risk assessment is implemented in activities in the departments. Brainstorming with participants concluded that the greatest risk in the product life cycle was the process of distributing of the products from warehouses to loading process on ship in the port area, as described in figure 3. Material flow from the trucks to the ships is often delayed; this affects the berth occupancy ratio (measured as percentage) at the port. Currently the fertiliser industry has set a target of berth occupancy ratio at 70%. If the percentage of berth occupancy ratio is more than set target, this will cause loss to the company because the company has to pay larger demurrage costs.

2. Define the agency

The agency of this paper is a fertiliser industry supply network, especially the departments involved in the flow of fertiliser material, ie: the Sales Department, and Risk Assessment Department and the Ports Department.
The fertiliser industry distributes products to consumers (farmers) based on government policy. The amount of fertiliser demand, delivery schedules, buffer stock and the amount of fertiliser to be shipped are dependent on government regulations that have been established in the earlier years. Thus, the industry applies a special delivery schedule that has been established by the Sales Departments; they are The Sales Department Region I which distributed fertiliser to Java and Bali islands; and The Sales Department Region II which distributed fertiliser to the other islands (ie: Kalimantan, Sumatra, Sulawesi, Nusa Tenggara and Papua) product. A further-result of brainstorming with participants indicated that the greatest problem in material flow was maintaining operators' performance in the unloading process of product from trucks into ships in the port area.

3. Define the outcome of product or service

An outcome reported in this paper is a prototype simulation model that is expected to help the decision maker in optimizing the process flow of material through the supply networks. By applying a socio-technical systems approach and the enterprise engineering framework, the research assist participants to determine the optimum value of variables in the supply network system to measure the loading time and the berth occupancy ratio. An agent based simulation modelling was to be applied in this study.

4. Develop the tools or prototype

This paper applies agent-based model software to build models of material flow analysis. The product-handling operators are important agents in the material flow of the supply network. Therefore, their movements in processing loading or unloading were analysed. This research designed the agent based modelling by using Netlogo 5.0.4 to visualise operators' movement in handling the product from the trucks to the ships in the port.

5. Applying the tools to the case study

The case study is represented using simulation model by using historical data on material flow system in the fertiliser industry supply network. Historical data from the fertiliser industry was used as input to the simulation model. Table 4 shows input variable names and values used in the agent-based model and Figure 4 shows a dynamic modeller of variables.

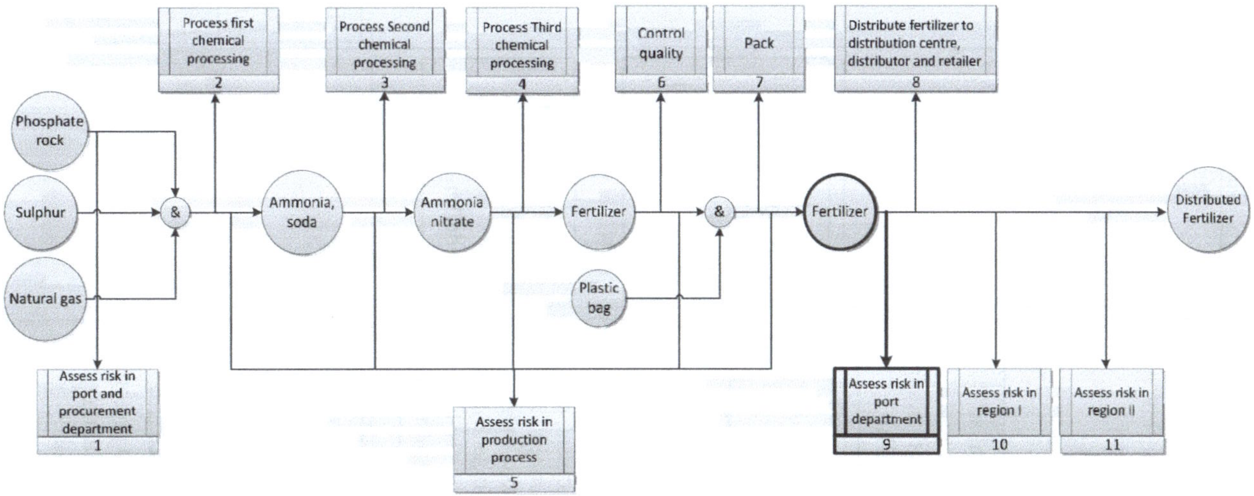

Fig. 2. IDEF3 the fertiliser product and process flow and the focus of this paper was in process 9

Table 3. A Conceptual frameworks for managing material flow in supply networks

	Define	Develop	Deploy
Purpose	How to manage material flow in the supply networks ↓ 1 To visualise product and process flows by using IDEF3		
Agency	The supply networks departments ↓↑ 2 To analyse the coordination between sales department, port departments and risk assessment department and to identify the biggest risk in material flow	To build conceptual and simulation modelling for managing material flow ↓ 4 To apply system dynamic and Agent based modelling	
Products and Services	Information availability for decision making process ↓ 3 To build prototype of simulation model for optimising material flow		How should the model be used for decision making? ↓ 5 To implement the model by using historical data from the fertiliser industry

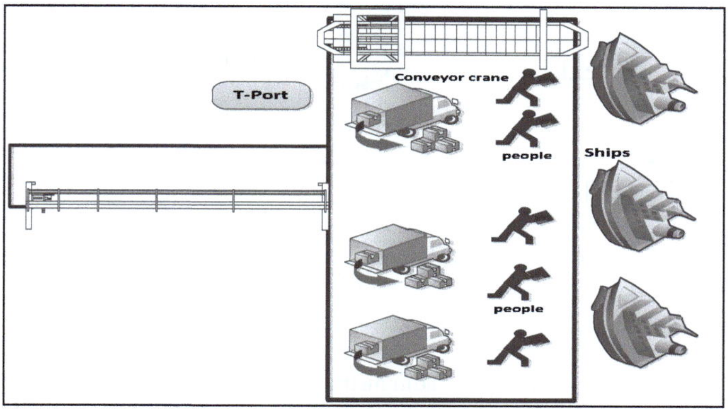

Fig. 3. Material flow in the Fertiliser Industry port

Table 4. Variables and code of the agent based model

Code / slider	Value
Number-of-trucks	represent number of truck used, scale: 0 to 1000 (units)
Number-of-operators	represent number of people scale: 0 to 100 (person)
Number-of-stocks	represent number of products distributed, scale: 0 to 100000 (tons)
Number-of-ships	represent number of ships docked in the port, scale: 0 to 50 (units)
Number-of-warehouses	represent number of warehouses used, scale: 0 to 5 (units)
Number-of-departments	represent number of departments, scale: 0 to 30 (units)
Number-of-board_directors	represent number of decision makers, scale: 0 to 3 (person)

Flow of processes on system modeller was arranged based on flow of information and reporting procedure on the material flow process in the case study. A process was represented by a variable. For instance, administration time represents the process of reporting and recording the amount of products that will be distributed from warehouses to the trucks. This model assumed that the administration time was twenty four hours. This variable was inserted as an input in length of reporting process in reporting cycle. The Model assists decision makers to visualize flow of information and material on the system by analysing the calculation of time on each variable.

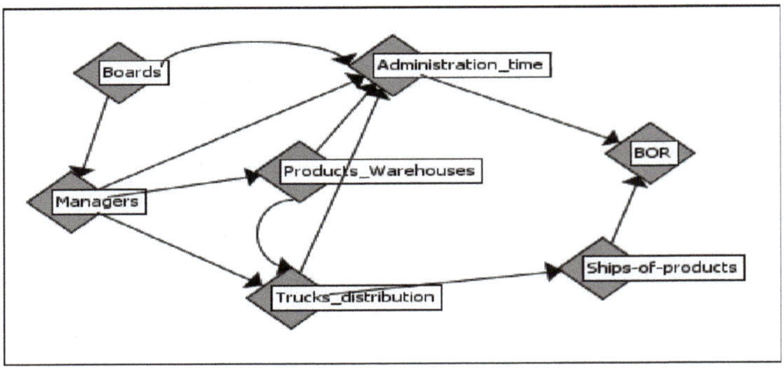

Fig. 4. Material flow system cycle: administration and report process of material flow

Figure 5 shows the interface of the agent based model developed for material flow optimization. Sliders at the interface of the model can be changed as the user desires. For example: the number of operators can be changed from zero to fifty or more. Sliders on the interface are used to set the values of the input variables. For example: the number of operator can be changed from zero to fifty or more. The graph shows result of running simulation model for loading time, number of operators, length of administration time, and of the berth occupancy ratio against an x-axis that represents time using Netlogo ticks. Face validation [16] was used to validate the conceptual and the simulation models. In the validation activities, people in the system were asked to review the model. In addition, the researcher conducted experiments using scenarios that change variables in simulation modelling. An experiment was carried out to investigate the influence of variables changing to the loading time and the berth occupancy ratio.

The output of the simulation model in Table 5 shows the number of operators, the length of material flow process and the percentage of berth occupancy ratio in five scenarios. Decision makers can use the output to determine the standard time of the loading process in order to achieve targets for the berth occupancy ratios. For instance, scenario one describes the berth occupancy ratio at 98.76%. The percentage will be occurred if decision makers employ fifteen operators in material flow and decide to use five trucks to transport fertiliser from three warehouses in the fertiliser industry to the port. As a result, administration time is 260 minutes and loading time is 531.60 minutes. On the other hand, in the second scenario, the berth occupancy ratio at 72.55% could be achieved if the material flow used 20 operators, 7 trucks and distributed fertiliser from one warehouses with administration process in 200 minutes. By using those variables, loading time in port would be in 401.05 minutes. This two scenarios show that the decision makers should add number of operators in order to decrease the berth occupancy ratio. However, as a further result of simulation model, scenario five shows a different significant effect of variable changes on the berth occupancy ratio. The berth occupancy ratio was declined from 98.76% in scenario one to 80.50% in the scenario five. This percentage can be accomplished by employing 15 people and using six trucks and the decision makers should transport the fertiliser from two warehouses in order to minimize administration time and result in the same length of loading time with scenario one. Thus, scenario five is the best scenario to obtain the optimum value of variables and minimise the berth occupancy ratio. The results of the scenarios were used to inform the decision-makers in investigating the effects of their decisions in considering the impact of potential variable changes on the flow of materials within the port and achieve optimum percentage of berth occupancy ratio.

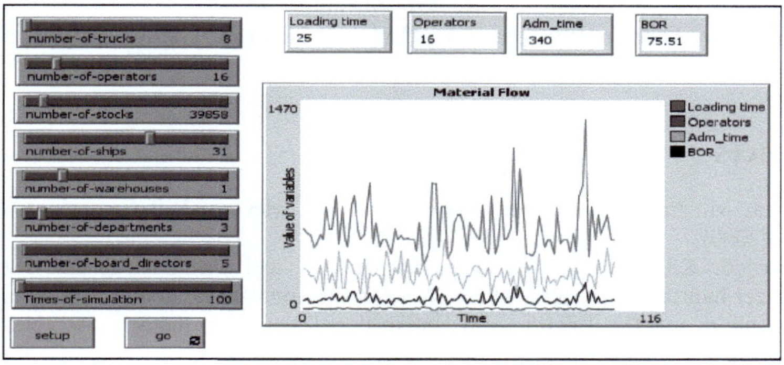

Fig. 5. The interface of simulation model

Table 5. The output of simulation model in five scenarios

Fertiliser	Trucks	Ware-houses	Depart-ments	Board Directors	Loading Time	Opera-tors	Adm-time	BOR
39696	5	3	3	2	531.60	15	260	98.76
40065	7	1	1	1	401.05	20	200	72.55
39747	10	4	6	1	664.42	12	420	94.20
40032	6	2	1	1	499.85	16	200	80.64
39999	6	2	1	2	531.15	15	220	80.50

6 Conclusions

Managing material flow by applying socio-technical perspectives has initiated a new opportunity for research in product life cycle management. This paper presents a conceptual framework that considers human and technical factors in order to assist decision makers in managing material flow. An Indonesian fertiliser industry supply networks has been presented as a case study to apply the conceptual framework. Result from the case study analysis indicated that an inappropriate loading process in the material handling flow reduced the effectiveness of the loading process at the port. This tardiness resulted in a significant impact on the berth occupancy ratio of the port and delays in supply networks flow. An agent based simulation model was used to visualise and evaluate the material flow system based on the real data from the case study. The output of the simulation model showed the effect of variables in the material flow system on berth occupancy ratio of the port. The model can assist decision makers to optimize variables in the material flow system in order to reduce loading time and determine the percentage of berth occupancy ratio of the port. The standard time for the loading process, as the output of the simulation model can be used as information to determine and reduce target of loading time and number of operators to accomplish the material flow process. In addition, this model aids decision makers in assessing and predicting material flow performance in their supply networks by changing the value of variables in the simulation model.

Acknowledgment. This research was carried out at The University of Leeds in the Institute for Design, Robotics and Optimisation and was supported by a PhD fellowship from Directorate General of Higher Education, The Ministry of Education of Republic of Indonesia.

References

[1] Grieves, M.: Product Lifecycle Management. The McGraw-Hill Companies, Inc., New York (2006)
[2] Isherwood, K.F.: Mineral Fertilizer Distribution and the Environment International Fertilizer Industry Association United Nations Environment Programme. Mineral Fertilizer Distribution and the Environment, International Fertilizer Industry Association, Paris (March 2000)
[3] Utami, I.D., Holt, R.J., McKay, A.: The resilience assessment of supply networks: A case study from the Indonesian Fertilizer Industry. In: Proceeding of Sustainable Design and Manufacturing, Cardiff, United Kingdom, April 28-30 (2014)
[4] Ropohl, G.: Philosophy of socio-technical systems. Phil. & Tech. 4(3), 59–71 (1999)
[5] Clegg, C.W.: Sociotechnical principles for system design. Appl. Ergon. 31(5), 463–477 (2000)
[6] Challenger, R., Clegg, C.W.: Systems perspective Crowd disasters: a socio-technical systems perspective. In: Contemporary Social Science, pp. 37–41 (2011)
[7] Stanton, N., Bessell, K.: How a submarine returns to periscope depth: analysing complex socio-technical systems using Cognitive Work Analysis. Appl. Ergon. 45(1), 110–125 (2014)
[8] Siemieniuch, C.E., Sinclair, M.: Extending systems ergonomics thinking to accommodate the socio-technical issues of Systems of Systems. Appl. Ergon. 45(1), 85–98 (2014)
[9] McGowan, A.R., Daly, S., Baker, W., Papalambros, P., Seifert, C.: A Socio-Technical Perspective on Interdisciplinary Interactions During the Development of Complex Engineered Systems. Procedia Comput. Sci. 16, 1142–1151 (2013)
[10] McKay, A., Kundu, S., Pennington, A.D.: Supply Networks: an approach to designing an extended enterprise. In: International Conference on Product Lifecycle Management (2009)
[11] Choong, C.G., McKay, A.: Sustainability in the Malaysian palm oil industry. Journal of Cleaner Production (2013)
[12] Siebers, P.O., Aickelin, U., Celia, H., Clegg, C.W.: Towards the development of a simulator for investigating the impact of people management practices on retail performance. J. Simul. 5(4), 247–265 (2010)
[13] Crowder, R.M., Robinson, M., Hughes, H.P.N., Sim, Y.W.: The Development of an Agent-Based Modeling Framework for Simulating Engineering Team Work. IEEE Trans. Syst. Man, Cybern. - Part A Syst. Humans 42(6), 1425–1439 (2012)
[14] Yin, R.K.: Case study research: Design and methods, 4th edn. (2009)
[15] Li, Q., Ying, C.: Modeling and Analysis of Enterprise and Information Systems: from requirements to realization. Higher education Press, Springer, Beijing (2009)
[16] Sargent, R.G.: Verification and Validation of simulation Models. In: Johansson, S., Jain, J., Montoya-Torres, J. (eds.) Proceedings of the 2010 Winter Simulation Conference, pp. 166–183 (2010)

PLM Serious Game Approach Available Both for Change Management and Knowledge Assessment

P. Pernelle[1], T. Carron[2,*], S. Elkadiri[1], A. Bissay[1], and J.-C. Marty[3]

[1] University of Lyon 1- UCBL – DISP, Lyon, France
philippe.pernelle@univ-lyon1.fr
[2] Sorbonne Universites, UPMC Univ Paris 6, LIP6,
UMR 7606 & University of Savoie Chambery, France
thibault.carron@lip6.fr
[3] Université de Lyon, CNRS
Université Lyon 1, LIRIS, UMR 5205, 69622, France

Abstract. Minimizing the reluctance of actors in change management is a well-known and key issue that can be resolved thanks to a serious game approach during the upstream PLM deployment phase. If our initial choices have already allowed us to validate the relevance of a serious game for change management process, we found that the participants, who were familiar with the area of technology in question, have systematically initiated a high level discussion about the models used in the PLM. We thus tried to take into account these unexpected observation results to also address the downstream phase concerning knowledge identification and assessment. Indeed, the capitalization of industrial knowledge is an important issue for enterprises who wish to master the development and the innovative element of their product. A substantial amount of knowledge extraction methods has the drawback to require expensive work by KM experts. We witnessed that besides this, it is necessary to evaluate both knowledge and knowledge use. In this article, we present the two uses synthesized in a same Serious Game Environment. From an identification methodology based on an analysis under a PLM (Product Lifecycle Management) deployment, we developed and experimented a Serious Game platform to both minimize the reluctance of actors and validate the identification work of KM experts.

1 Introduction

The deployment of a PLM project is an opportunity for companies, even for SMEs/SMIs, to reconsider their work methods. It involves a formalization of the processes currently in place. The MPPI method (fig.1) is based on this observation and offers a combined approach to take into account capitalization of know-how during stages of PLM project discussions. This approach is called combined because it combines three different objectives (deployment methodology, change management and knowledge capitalization approach). The first part of this paper will present the

* Corresponding author.

S. Fukuda et al. (Eds.): PLM 2014, IFIP AICT 442, pp. 323–332, 2014.

methodology MPPI (Methodology for PLM Project Implementation) that is a global approach for coupling a deployment methodology (implementation of a new information system) and a phase for integrating knowledge (company specific configuration). Thanks to our previous works on PLM system deployment, we acknowledged that this phase is particularly favorable to identify tacit knowledge. Nevertheless, these method presents some drawbacks in terms of cost and attractiveness. We decided then to bare on recent educational trends where playful approaches are supporting learning content.

The second part of this article focuses thus on the integration of the use of gaming techniques inside the MPPI method. In this part, we will characterize the gamification of industrial processes as well as the emergence of new usages and some specific scenarios to facilitate change management and knowledge integration in two particular and relevant steps of the method.

The third section will describe the serious game platform designed for supporting this integration method. This section is then illustrated by the way of a real case study concerning a project of coupling between a PLM platform and a Serious Game environment.

The last part will focus on results and feedback concerning the experiments that have been set up.

2 Methodology for PLM Project Implementation

The companies which deploy a PLM system wish to reduce the development cycle to promote innovation. For the implementation of a PLM system, these companies must analyze their information and processes. It seems interesting to take advantage of this revision of information system to make explicit the crucial knowledge in order to manage it more efficiently. Through MPPI method, we want to integrate and capitalize on the knowledge generated by a process in a PLM system.

2.1 Description of the Approach

The following figure (Fig.1) schematizes the approach proposed in MPPI [2] [3]. Thus, MPPI is structured around two processes: the process of draft (pre-project) and deployment process. We can note that the accompanying and adaptation process must be considered as a transversal subprocess included in the first two.

The overall approach MPPI exhibits a comprehensive process implementation modeling of an information system focused on the product. A specific part concerning the deployment process is called MPPI-KI (for Knowledge-Integration). MPPI-KI approach can be divided into two cycles. In the first cycle (Identify, Modeling, Use, Evaluate), the goal is to characterize the global model of the information system called "PPO model" (Product / Process / Organization). In the second cycle (outer circle), the objective is then the integration of a specifically "knowledge perspective".

As for the PPO model cycle, this integration is performed through 4 steps: Identify, Modeling, Use and Evaluate. In this article, we are interested in the problems that concern the first two stages. Thus, the identification step consists in characterizing from the PPO model, the activities which contain knowledge. From these activities (built from business processes), the knowledge expert makes explicit the elements of the data model that are knowledge-containing and enriches this model with the necessary attributes. Subsequently, the modeling phase will consist in completing the PPO model enriched by the business rules that formalizes this knowledge. The advantage of this approach is to facilitate this expertise by mapping relevant areas from the viewpoint of business processes.

2.2 Discussion

As explained before, these steps are difficult, expensive to exploit and do not resolve the problem of reluctance of the users. In this article, our main proposal concerns the use of a serious game for specific stages of MPPI approach. From our experience and in the context of our work, the use of a serious game is suitable for two aspects of the MPPI method. The first aspect concerns the transversal process of change management, the second aspect relates to the stages of evaluation of the MPPI-KI process.

In the next section, we will then focus on the integration of gaming concepts into the MPPI method.

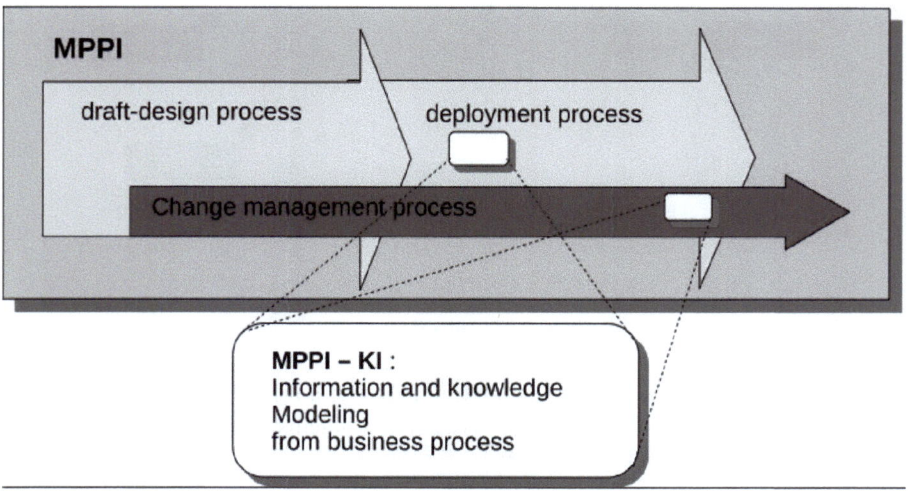

Fig. 1. Principles of the MPPI method

3 Gamifying a PLM Method

3.1 Gamification of Industrial Context

In the context of change management within MPPI, we used a gamification approach [6] for industrial processes. In this approach, the game designer must choose some specific target characteristics of the platform (e.g. what has to be learnt) [5].

From the previous example (section 2.2), we initiated gamification process with the following choices:

- A contemporary and realistic world, quite close of the real enterprise (with the complete modeling of a production building of the enterprise).
- A first linear scenario, multi-user : every player has the same scenario. Being together simultaneously in the same "virtual world" strengthens the feeling of immersion and the user's motivation (implicit competition, possibility of exchanging messages, etc.).
- Another, nonlinear scenario, multi-user, multi-role, collaborative: in this context, the game actions are not necessarily predetermined. Players may have different roles and must work together to continue to advance.

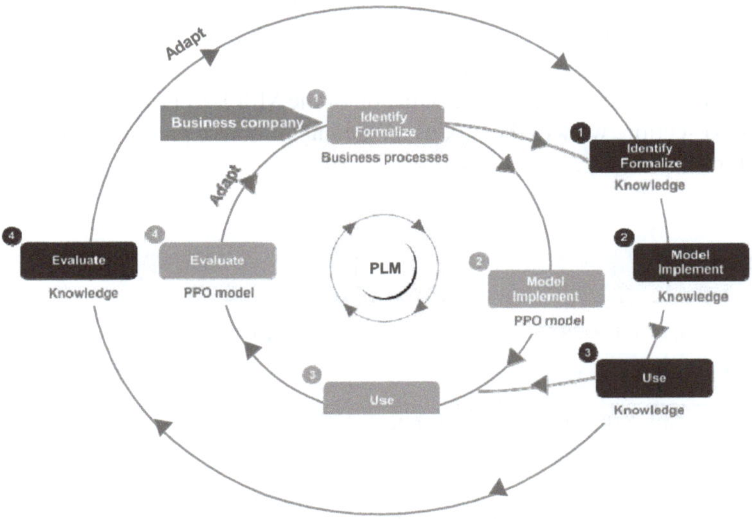

Fig. 2. Steps in the MPPI-KI method

As we will see now, our main assumption is to use a role play approach where the user with her/his avatar is faced with practical problems of her/his everyday work (see below screenshots in Fig. 4 and 3).

3.2 Change Management Process

Indeed, the change management (identified in the MPPI method as a transversal process) is a sensitive issue at the origin of many failures. The causes of these problems are diverse (system malfunctions, poor ergonomics, ...). But they are often due to the reluctance of actors to use a new information system. The real cause of these rejections is relatively conventional: Users are forced to change from an informal environment to a formal one (their personal information becomes collective). It is thus important to make the user experiment effectively the gain brought by the new system.

Finally, the analysis of these results underscores the need to conduct a policy of change management that clearly explains the constraints of the system and the overall gain for the company and each of its actors. As it was defined, this approach is based on scenarios designed for including connections with the PLM system, as well as metaphors to introduce the game concepts concerning business process.

We thus experimented several scenarios for change management [7]. The following figure shows an example of scenario around the RFQ[1] process. In these scenarios, the players must perform both game activities and business activities without then with a PLM system to better understand the benefits of these systems.

For example, the part without a PLM system exhibits the difficulty to retrieve a correct product reference at the right moment, at the right place. As everybody knows, a company with services, protocols, agents is always evolving and there is a gap between theory and practice.

3.3 Knowledge Use and Evaluation Step

Concerning the second step, the final approach is similar but the cause is different. It is well-known that it is difficult to extract tacit expert knowledge from the workers. We faced the same problems when exploiting the method or even conceiving the serious game. Nevertheless each serious game is finished with a debriefing discussion in order to better incorporate the acquired knowledge and surprisingly, we observed that the experts have naturally exposed their reticences or doubts concerning the models they found in the game during such a discussion with the others.

We decided then to adapt our scenarios in order to actively promote the identification and validation of knowledge. Our proposal is to provide additional context that allows the player to explicitly validate his skills about the domain. We have established a dual strategy to answer this question : on the one hand, we added some quests specifically dedicated to the knowledge use; on the other hand, we have added new artifacts in the game.

This new game context is characterized by new indicators, an annotation tool and the ability to learn new skills (Fig. 3):

- The new *K-quests* are game activities (or industrial activities in PLM) concerning knowledge or result from an acquaintance. A K-quest can be individual or collective.
- The *K-indicators* that may be individual (or collective) ones, represent the level of expertise of the player (or group of players). This indicator is viewable by the player and the value of its skill level is affected by some particular game actions including the use of the annotation tool.
- The *K-annotation tool* is an artifact that the player can use in some situations (interaction with NPC[2], object, ...). Annotation is a simple marking (grading system equivalent to "i like") or a marking type description (with additional text). The use of this tool automatically modifies the previous indicator.

---

[1] Request For Quotation.

[2] Non Playable Character.

- New *K-skills* explicitly characterize the actors (or groups of actors) whose expertise level indicator is considered relevant at the end of the scenario.

In order to be able to evaluate dynamically the concept acquisition, the whole system is traced: the business system and the serious game environment as we will see later. This allow us to assess the skills and the expertise level.

Skills and Expertise Level

Traces collection aims to be able and provide indicators and also to calculate the user model of each player. This user model characterizes the whole user skills. We define a user model simply from a declarative manner as the following set:

$$UM_p = \{(p, skill_i)/p = player, skill_i = (field, value)i > 0\} \tag{1}$$

The user model is used to calculate, for each player, a set of characteristics acquired during the game. In our case, game activities, activities within the PLM and annotations will provide traces needed to calculate the user model of each player.

The user model skills have two uses: On one hand, it allows to obtain game artifacts that increase player motivation; on the other hand, it identifies motivated people and those who are able to validate a specific knowledge. The definition of K-skill can be seen as a motivating factor, but it should help especially characterized objectively the actors expertise according to activities that have been traced in the game.

Finally, it is the combined use of these tools (K-Quest, K-Annotation, K-Indicator, K-Skill) which allows us to define a global scenario of knowledge validation. All these scenarios have been experimented several times in real situations with a specific serious game environment that will be described in the following sections.

4 A Serious Game Use for MPPI Enactment

4.1 A Generic Serious Game Platform : Learning Adventure

Learning Adventure (L.A.) is a generic Serious Game based on a role-play approach [1, 8]. The players (students or teachers), possibly represented by their own avatars, can move through the environment, performing a sequence of sub activities in order to acquire knowledge. This environment is generic in the sense that the teacher can adapt the environment before the session by setting pre-requisites between sub activities and by providing different resources (documents, videos, quizzes) linked to the course. The collaboration takes place in L.A. by constituting groups of users. The NonPlayableCharacters (NPCs) give objectives to the members of a group and provide them with access to collaborative tools. As said before, we have modeled a company building from the actual architectural plans in order to ensure the players' immersion. Indeed, it is easier for them to find the different locations (e.g. coffee room, secretary's office) in the game if they are situated in the same places as in the real building. A compass to help players reach a specific place is however available in the game (see the upper right circle in Fig. 4). Moreover, the fact that the users understand that this game or formation is specifically dedicated to them is a great factor of motivation.

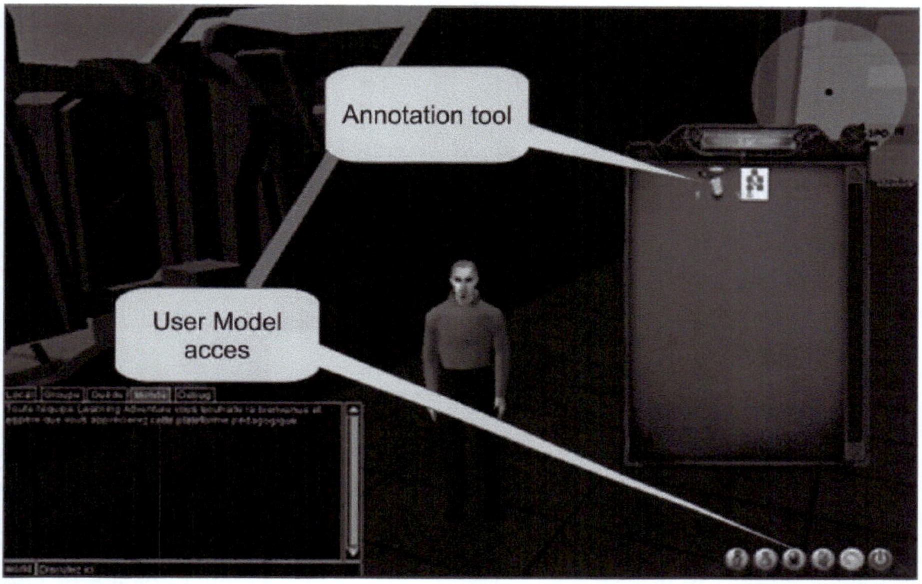

Fig. 3. Additional device for knowledge

As mentioned in the previous section, in the game environment we also get a lot of trace left by the users in order to adapt the system.

4.2 Traces Analysis and Indicators

The implemented system uses all significant traces: game traces (interactions, movement, etc.) and activity traces within the PLM system (document consultation, creation, etc.). The aim of these traces is to improve the user monitoring for individual actions but also and especially during interactions and group actions. Annotation traces will complement game traces and activity traces. The interest of these annotation traces is twofold: on the one hand, they are used to validate PLM data and business rules that were identified as holder of knowledge by expert. On the other hand, they can implicitly define an "organizational mapping" of knowledge. Here, the meaning of mapping concerns actors' identification with a level of professional expertise in relation to the formalized knowledge.

In the previous example, relevant traces for the expert analysis are:

- Moves and passed time in interaction with the NPC that informs the mini-quest.
- Dialogues (with "chat" = instant messaging) between the players during this period

- Consultations within the PLM system on the data related to the injection speed
- Players' responses to the proposal
- Number of annotation by player and their descriptions

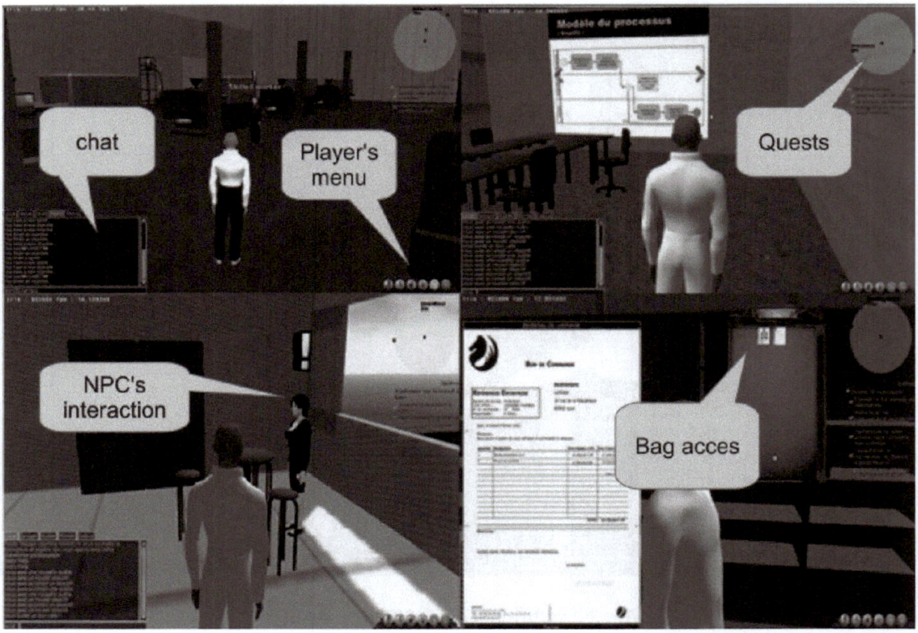

Fig. 4. The Learning Adventure Serious Game Environment

They are used by the trainer to validate with the business expert, the relevance of formalized knowledge and the actors identified as mastering this knowledge.

Aggregating different indicators allows us to define a K-indicator. This K-indicator is a visual element of motivation for the players.

Concerning the experiments, the system is now used in education for several years (more than 500 people) but there are each year some slight evolutions in order to improve the system or to adapt to a changing context (sessions with industrial experts for example). In the following section, we will describe the general conditions of experiments in formation context and give some feedback concerning the user acceptation of the system.

5 Conditions of Experiments and Results

Experiments have taken place in general training programs (master's degrees) as well as in a further training course for interested professionals. All experiments were conducted in the same experimental context. During the experiments, all groups of people were present with a teacher and an external observer. Concerning the social presence perception [4], players were oriented one behind the other, limiting mutual eye contact, in a row of four students. Each student accessed the virtual environment through her/his workstation and had a personal (adapted) view on the world. They were explicitly allowed to communicate through the chat tool provided with the system and were warned that they would be observed and filmed concerning the use of the system.

We did two types of experiment. The first one dealt with students who had a basic level of knowledge concerning PLM (for change management). This experiment took place in a PLM training module for the Institute of Technology in Lyon. This training module is an introductory module lasting 15 hours with second year students. These students did not know the PLM but had skills in mechanical engineering. 254 students from 18 to 21 years old were split into 20 practical work groups. 10 groups started the module by playing the game scenario, without any theoretical lesson. The other ten groups did have two hours of theoretical training on PLM before their experiment in order to evaluate the benefit of the learning game session. All the experiments took place in the same room belonging to AIP-Primeca (Regional Engineering platform organization).

The second experiment was carried out with students who had no knowledge on PLM (For knowledge evaluation). This experiment took place with a group of students preparing a master's degree in the PLM domain. Each student involved in this one-year program works part-time for his/her company (one week at the university, three weeks in his/her company). The experiment took place on the last day of the first week at the university. At this time, the students had attended theoretical lessons and practical classes concerning another PLM system than the one included in the Serious Game Scenario. The students were aged from 24 to 50 years old. They had all chosen this training program for new opportunities and jobs offered in this domain. The initial skills of the students were diverse (computer science, electrical engineering, industrial engineering).

Thanks to traces and indicators, correct actions were automatically rewarded with the relevant skill level up. Concerning these experiments, two evaluation methods were chosen:

- Quantitative, thanks to collaborative indicators elaborated with traces left by the users when collaborating,
- Qualitative, with live questions at the end of the session and explicit feedback from the teacher/PLM expert.

We can observe :

- 90 % of the participants have identified the features and goals of the systems and 40 % would have recommended them to their manager (3% before using the game).
- The number of student requests for collaborative projects has been multiplied by two. In the second experiment, the sequence of the game session has had no measurable impact on student achievement.
- The work on the knowledge validation has implicitly validated 70% of structural models defined in the PLM system.

6 Conclusion

In this article, we explained that we tried to couple a methodology for PLM integration and a serious game in order to facilitate the change management and the knowledge capitalization. From our point of view, the results are satisfying. Indeed, these approaches are very attractive thanks to their novelty and thus reinforce the motivation of the users. The immersion is also used to help the users to exhibit tacit or expert knowledge more easily. Some drawbacks remains: some parts concerning the game elaboration are always costly in time and expensive in code/design development. The sessions are limited to around 20 persons at the same time for the moment. Nevertheless, some reuse possibilities are more and more evident when we are elaborating new scenarios indicating a certain maturity for the approach. The PLM domain is also evolving and for future work, we are studying the possibilities of extension given by Service Lifecycle Management (SLM) or Knowledge Lifecycle Management (KLM),

References

1. Baptista, R., Vaz de Carvalho, C.: Funchal 500 years: Learning through role play games. In: Proceedings of ECGBL 2008, Barcelona, Spain (2008)
2. Bissay, A., Lefebvre, A., Pernelle, P., Bouras, A.: Deployment methodology of is. In: SIG-PLM Workshop (IFIP WG 5.7), Lausanne, Suisse (2008)
3. Bissay, A., Lefebvre, A., Pernelle, P., Bouras, A.: Integration of business processes and performance indicators in a plm. In: International Conference on Advances in Production Management Systems (APMS 2008), Espoo, Finlande (2008)
4. De Kort, Y.A.W., Ijsselsteijn, W.A.: People, places, and play: Player experience in a socio-spatial context. Comput. Entertain. 6(2), 18:1–18:11 (2008), `http://doi.acm.org/10.1145/1371216.1371221`, doi:10.1145/1371216.1371221
5. Galarneau, L., Zibit, M.: Online Game for 21st Century Skills. In: Games and Simulations in Online Learning: Research and Development Frameworks, pp. 59–88. Information Science Publishing, Hersey (2007)
6. Mayer, I.S.: The gaming of policy and the politics of gaming: A review. Simulation and Gaming 40, 825–862 (2009)
7. Pernelle, P., Marty, J., Carron, T.: Serious gaming: A new way to introduce product lifecycle management. In: L.U., et al. (eds.) IEEE Workshop on Learning Technology for Education in Cloud 7th International Conference on Knowledge Management in Organizations, pp. 89–100. Springer (2012)
8. Yu, T.W.: Learning in the virtual world: the pedagogical potentials of massively multiplayer online role playing games. International Education Studies 2(1) (2009)

PLM Maturity Evaluation and Prediction Based on a Maturity Assessment and Fuzzy Sets Theory

Haiqing Zhang[1], Aicha Sekhari[1], Yacine Ouzrout[1], and Abdelaziz Bouras[1,2]

[1] DISP laboratory, University Lumière Lyon 2, France,
160 Bd de l'Université 69676 Bron Cedex
[2] Computer Science Department - Qatar University, ictQATAR, Box. 2731, Doha, Qatar
haizhang@mail.univ-lyon2.fr
{yacine.ouzrout,aicha.sekhari}@univ-lyon2.fr
abdelaziz.bouras@qu.edu.qa

Abstract. Companies adopt PLM maturity models to evaluate PLM implementation and recognize relative positions in PLM selection to better harness PLM benefits. However, the majority traditional PLM maturity models are relative time-consuming and energy-consuming. This work focuses on proposing a fuzzy extended PCMA (**P**LM **C**omponents **M**aturity **A**ssessment) maturity model to brightly evaluate the gradual process of PLM maturity accompaniment with time changes, which aims to reduce the efforts spent on maturity evaluation. The proposed PCMA uses triangular fuzzy elements to express maturity levels that can solve vague and complexity issues in PLM evaluation. The proposed fuzzy PCMA is tested by two Chinese firms. The first evaluation uses PCMA maturity model to obtain the maturity levels for a Chengdu company in 2010. The PLM maturity for this company from 2011 to 2013 is conducted by the fuzzy extended PCMA maturity model through inputting the KPIs' value. Fuzzy extended PCMA is also used to predict the maturity level for a Shanghai company. A comparison of the results obtained by fuzzy extended PCMA model and the real-life situation verify the effectiveness of the proposed model.

Keywords: PLM maturity model, Triangular fuzzy elements, Key performance indicators, PLM maturity evaluation, PLM components maturity assessment (PCMA).

1 Introduction

Product Lifecycle Management (PLM) manages a company's product from its early conception stages to the final disposal stages. PLM drives cost reductions, facilitates reducing lead time, and improves product quality [1, 13]. To pave the way toward obtaining the true benefits of PLM, the users should have a clear understanding of PLM definition, PLM components, PLM functionalities, and the relative position of PLM implementation. To address full PLM functionalities, Vengugopalan et al.'s work [2] decomposes the functionalities of PLM into four major dimensions based on the TIFO Framework (TechnoWare, InfoWare, FunctionWare, and OrgaWare). Vengugopalan et al.'s work focuses on the functionalities in beginning of life phase and middle of

S. Fukuda et al. (Eds.): PLM 2014, IFIP AICT 442, pp. 333–344, 2014.

life phase. The functionalities in the end of life phase, in terms of: DFE (Design for Environment), TRIZ (Theory of Inventive Problem Resolution), and LCA (Life Cycle Assessment), need to be integrated and collaborated with PLM to satisfy performance requirements. Thus zhang et al. [3-4] extends the TIFO framework into TIFOS framework by adding a new dimension called SustainWare in consideration of sustainability.

Several basic components construct PLM functionalities. Stark et al. [5] state that PLM is a holistic approach and PLM contains nine PLM components, which consist of products, data, applications, processes, people, work methods, and equipment. Abramovici et al. [6] define five PLM levels, and each PLM level has several concrete PLM components that can have interdependencies with other components. Fifteen different types of PLM components in TIFOS framework is collected and described by zhang et al.[3], which include techniques & practices, PLM software & applications, strategy & supervision, quality management, business management, maintenance management, BOM management, PDM, financial management, people, distributed collaboration management, workflow & process management, eco-friendly & innovation, life cycle assessment, and green conception. This work will adopt these fifteen PLM components to analyze PLM implementation.

Many companies start to enlarge investment of PLM to reap PLM benefits. Decision-makers have yet to clarify PLM adoption and implementation, because of PLM being large and complex. Measuring PLM components adoption, running condition, and maturity situation, can reflex implementation of PLM and provide guidelines for decision-makers in a company. This work aims to solve the following research questions:

1. *How companies can* ***self-evaluate*** *a PLM implemented situation and* ***recognize the gradual process*** *of PLM adaptation in present and future years?*
2. *How to guide companies to* ***automatically evaluate a PLM implemented situation based on the existing value*** *instead of setting new values for exhausted evaluation criteria to measure maturity level every year?*

To solve the two questions we study literature works as well as experimental research. In literature studies, PLM maturity models [1, 7-12] identify different maturity growth stages that can evaluate PLM adoption; but these maturity models are still weaker to aid companies in self-evaluation PLM and to recognize the gradual process of PLM accompaniment through time changes. Most of the PLM maturity models define several maturity levels and describe the differences between each level by using linguistic terms. The linguistic terms have a feature of uncertainty and vagueness, which makes the decision-makers, not able to input accurate values for each maturity level. The third research question is:

3. *How can companies* ***maximally keep and express decision-makers' intentions,*** *while evaluating PLM implementation by using PLM maturity models?*

A fuzzy extended PCMA maturity model is proposed to be able to resolve these research questions. This model is used to evaluate and predict the gradual process of PLM maturity by using the first year's evaluation results and the KPIs values to reduce the efforts spent on PLM evaluation. The proposed maturity model is examined by a structured survey. The experimental research is conducted to validate the survey and the fuzzy extended PCMA maturity model. The survey was conducted in two Chinese firms in 2013. The work is structured as follows: section 2 gives the literature view of PLM maturity models and fuzzy sets theory; section 3 describes the running mechanism of PCMA maturity model; section 4 proposes a fuzzy extended PCMA maturity model to automatically evaluate PLM maturity; section 5 examines the proposed fuzzy extended PCMA by two case studies; section 6 concludes our work.

2 State of the Art

2.1 PLM Maturity Models

PLM maturity models provide guidelines to PLM implementation for any given company. CMMI (Capability Maturity Model Integration) [7-9] has the potential to significantly improve the organization's profitability, because it has the abilities to evaluate an organization's maturity and process area capability. CMMI defines multiple process areas, and provides the goals for each level of implementation. Yet it has not proposed **a roadmap to implementation or identification of key process improvement areas**. A company usually needs to prepare lots of documents to suit CMMI assessment in China. These prepared documents are specially used for one-time assessments. Strategies have not been given to analyze the weaker items obtained from the assessments, which makes the companies cannot receive the true benefits of maturity assessments. Besides the whole assessment process is quite time-consuming and energy-consuming. Stark [1] proposes a PDM (product data management) maturity model with four stages of evaluation, and defines the activities that a company needs to carry out at each stage. Batenburg [10] develops a PLM framework to assess and guide PLM implementations for organizations in terms of five dimensions: Strategy and policy, Monitoring and control, Organisation and processes, People and culture, and Information technology. Henk and Kees [11] apply Batenburg model in 20 companies to analyze PLM implementation of these companies. Sääksvuori Model [12] determines the maturity of a large international corporation for a corporate-wide PLM development program and develops business and PLM related issues. Yet, it should be mentioned that most of these maturity models are qualitative analysis, which cannot give a satisfactory impression of companies' relative position, and cannot solve research questions mentioned in introduction.

2.2 Applying Fuzzy Sets Theory to Describe Maturity Levels

Maturity models adopt linguistic terms to express the content of maturity levels. The linguistic terms have to be changed into numbers to make the maturity results easier understand. Crisp numbers cannot precisely express maturity results due to complex and vague features of linguistic terms. Fuzzy set theory is proposed by Zadeh [14] and this theory is a revolutionary way of solving the vagueness issues. Fuzzy sets theory allows objects to exist in more than one set. The membership function is proposed to demonstrate how much degree of an element belongs in a set, which means that the associated membership function of an object is multivalued. Fuzzy triangular elements and the corresponding membership function of fuzzy sets theory is used to express performance evaluation of maturity levels, because the advantages of fuzzy triangular numbers in fuzzy sets [15].

3 The Running Mechanism of PCMA Maturity Model

The goal of PCMA maturity model is to measure and monitor PLM dimensions. Key performance indicators (KPIs) are used to help define concrete actions in evaluation [16-17]. PCMA provides a holistic assessment for PLM dimensions based on a comprehensive set of KPIs in each maturity level. These KPIs are defined by the authors in collaboration with representatives from partner companies. We derive five dimensions based on TIFOS framework which are called 'TechnoWare', 'InforWare', 'FunctionWare', 'orgaWare' and 'SustainWare'. Fifteen PLM components are proposed based on the five dimensions. The maturity level of each PLM component is explained by linguistic terms in PCMA maturity model. This work determines the corresponding KPIs for each maturity level in PCMA and calculates the final maturity score based on these KPIs.

An example of outcome of PLM maturity evaluation is shown in Table 1. The evaluation concerns a PLM dimension called 'FunctionWare' in TIFOS framework. Five maturity levels are defined, based on 'standard' scale in PLMIG [19] and CMMI scale [7-9]. The maturity score on each KPI is represented by a black rectangle. The maturity level of this dimension of the company is determined by the average score of all related KPIs. The relative weights among each KPI will be discussed in the future.

Table 1. PLM components and corresponding key performance indicators

PLM dimensions	PCMA maturity	KPIs	Levels				
			Ad-hoc	*Repeatable*	*Defined*	*managed*	*Optimized*
D1: TechnoWare	The detail explanation of maturity levels for each component	D1_K1: %of new products		■			
		D1_K2: Produce accurate products			■		
		D1_K3: Running cycle time				■	
		D1_K4: Installation Planning costs			■		
		D1_K5: Clear Product Innovation Strategy					■

Several components consist of 'FunctionWare' dimension. Product data management (PDM) is a set of functionalities which can fulfill the practical activities and provide technology solutions. Therefore, PDM is considered as one component of 'FunctionWare'. The maturity levels and maturity level contents for PDM are shown in table 2. We outline part of the KPIs for the 'PDM' based on three categories in terms of 'cost', 'time', and 'quality' in Table 2. More categories including 'complexity' and 'distributivity' will be studied in the future. Maturity levels, indicators for PDM maturity, and KPIs have numerous mapping relationships in Table 2. Similarly, we can obtain the maturity score of every PLM dimension.

Table 2. PCMA Maturity Level and Corresponding Content

<table>
<tr><th>Maturity Levels</th><th>PCMA maturity level content for PDM component</th><th>KPIs</th></tr>
<tr><td>1 ad-hoc</td><td>• The activity of product data management is done with expediency
• Nobody is responsible for product data management
• Documentation is at the lowest point to satisfy operational needs
• PDM system and the corresponding processes have deficiencies</td><td rowspan="5">Cost
1. Average Data storage cost
2. Average Document using frequency per day
3. Average Document finding time-to-cost
4. Average using cost per document
Time
1. Acceptance necessary time:
2. Average number of training hours per employee
3. Average time for data change version
4. Average time for data creation
Quality
1. Data Accuracy Ratio
2. Data Duplication Ratio
3. Potential same data (data cleaning)</td></tr>
<tr><td>2 Repeatable</td><td>• The activity is defined and managed, but it is repetitious
• Documentation and record is carefully studied
• Mutual actions are finished in processes and departments
• PDM systems are involved and used in the proper places.
• No effort has been made to consider about recycling</td></tr>
<tr><td>3 Defined</td><td>• The activity is formalized and supported by sta ndards
• Documentation and record is studied and shared
• Personal actions and mutual actions are carried out efficiently
• PDM systems are easily implemented
• Environmental awareness occurs</td></tr>
<tr><td>4 managed</td><td>• Activities run smoothly
• PDM systems cooperate with other enterprise systems
• The products run efficiently and are effective
• Progressively eliminates errors and failures</td></tr>
<tr><td>5 optimized</td><td>• The activity runs optimally
• PDM system helps company make improved decisions
• Best practices and innovative ideas are documented, archived and concretely re-used.
• Research and Development service continuously improve the products</td></tr>
</table>

A survey is conducted to obtain the values of KPIs. Four KPIs from cost category are selected, a detail description for each KPI is given, and the related questions are proposed to deduce the value of the KPIs in Table 3.

Table 3. Maturity description of PDM and the corresponding key performance indicators

KPIs	Description	Questions
1. Average Data storage cost	Measure of all data storage/ number of documents (categories)	How much you pay for information storage (including hardware and software)?
		How many documents you have to manage?
		How much memory you need to manage information? (GB)
2. Average Document using frequency per day	Number of document using frequency/ number of all documents using frequency	How many documents you used more than 30 minutes per day?
3. Average Document finding time-to-cost	How many time it takes for users to find it in seconds/minutes	How long you spend to find the documents you use every day?
4. Average using cost per document	Average cost for printing and creating the pdf per document	How much you spend to use these documents (including printing, creating the .pdf, ...)

4 Fuzzy Extended PCMA Maturity Model

Fuzzy sets is adapted to address PLM maturity levels to better express decision-makers' intentions in PLM maturity evaluation. Five out of nine level fundamental scales of judgments are described via the triangular fuzzy numbers to express the relative difference among maturity levels in Table 4. The triangular fuzzy numbers is made up of a triple of numbers (L, M, U), including the medium value (M) of the membership function μ(x), the lower (L) and the upper (U) bounds which limit the range of the maturity evaluation.

Table 4. PCMA maturity levels and the corresponding fuzzy scale

Maturity levels	*Ad-hoc*			*Repeatable*			*Defined*			*managed*			*optimized*		
Fuzzy Scale	*L*	*M*	*U*	*L*	*M*	*U*	*L*	*M*	*U*	*L*	*M*	*U*	*L*	*M*	*U*
	0	*0.1*	*0.3*	*0.1*	*0.3*	*0.5*	*0.3*	*0.5*	*0.7*	*0.5*	*0.7*	*0.9*	0.7	0.9	1

PCMA maturity model in section 3 is used to do the first evaluation. The companies need to spend time, costs and human resources to evaluate PLM. To answer the first and the second research questions, a strategy should be proposed to help companies to predict the gradual process of PLM in the following years to reduce the amount of efforts that spend on evaluation PLM. A real case is analyzed for a swimming industry in China. The maturity situation of PDM in 2010 is gotten by PCMA and the values of KPIs from 2011to 2013 is obtained from the company, which is shown in Table 5.

Table 5. Primary data of KPIs and initial maturity level

KPIs	2013	2012	2011	2010	Maturity Level (2010)
1. Average Data management cost	3.0-4.0 (range)	2.8-4.2 (range)	8.0-10.0 (range)	35-40 (range)	*Defined* [0.3,0.5,0.7]
2. Average Document using frequency per day	10	7	5	2	*Repeatable* [0.1,0.3,0.5]
3. Average Document finding time-to-cost	*managed*	*managed*	*managed*	*managed*	*managed* [0.5,0.7,0.9]
4. Average using cost per document	10 RMB	40/7RMB	6 RMB	5 RMB	*Defined* [0.3,0.5,0.7]

A fuzzy extended PCMA maturity model is proposed to calculate the maturity levels from 2011 to 2013 by adopting the data in Table 5. Set $C\_K_i^{j-year}$ is the i KPI (K_i) in the j year (K^{j_year}) for a specific category(C); let $C\_M_i^{j-year}$ represents the maturity value (M_i) of the i KPI in the j year (M^{j_year}) for a specific category(C). Then the ratio between two maturity levels in two selected years (j year and x year) can be gotten from the ratio of the j year to the x year for the same KPI. The formula to get the maturity level in x year is shown in the following:

$$\frac{C\_M_i^{x-year}}{C\_M_i^{j-year}} = f(k_i)\bullet\frac{C\_K_i^{x-year}}{C\_K_i^{j-year}} \tag{1}$$

To be more precise, the formula (1) can be replaced by formula (2):

$$C\_M_i^{x-year} = f(k_i)\bullet\frac{C\_K_i^{x-year}}{C\_K_i^{j-year}}\bullet C\_M_i^{j-year} \tag{2}$$

This formula represents the maturity level in the x year that can be deduced from the maturity level in the j year. The ratio between the j year and the x year for the i KPI in C category determines the changing trend and the varying degree of the maturity level in j year.

"f(k_i)" is the coefficient and the signal that express the influence degree of the changing value and the changing range. The value of f(k_i) is given based on the real-life problem. For instance, we select the first KPI value in 2010 and 2013 in Table 5. The maturity level in 2013 for the first KPI in cost category is calculated by formula (2) in the following:

$$Cost\_M_1^{(2013)\_year} = f(k_i)\bullet\frac{Cost\_K_1^{(2013)\_year}}{Cost\_K_1^{(2010)\_year}}\bullet Cost\_M_1^{(2013)\_year} = f(k_1)\bullet\frac{[3,4]}{[35,40]}\bullet[0.3,0.5,0.7] \tag{3}$$

The sign $f(k_i)$ shows that formula (3) need to do numerical calculation and the value of $f(k_i)$ equals to 1 in this case based on the information given by the company. Then the way to obtain the maturity level is arithmetic operation. The average data management cost range is from 3 to 4 in 2013, the lowest value in formula (3) is the lowest value of the range: (3/40)*0.3=0.06; the middle value is the average value of the possible middle numbers: (((3/35+3/40)+(4/35+4/40))*0.5)/4=0.046875; the upper value is the largest value of the range: 4/35*0.7=0.08. Then formula (3) is changed into formula (4), which indicates the maturity level is '*Ad-hoc*' in 2013.

$$Cost\_M_1^{(2013)\_year} = 1\bullet[0.0225,\ 0.046875,\ 0.08] = [0.0225,\ 0.046875,\ 0.08] \tag{4}$$

The second example is the second KPI value in 2010 and 2013 in Table 5. The maturity level in 2013 for the second KPI in cost category is calculated by formula (2) in the following:

$$Cost\_M_2^{(2013)\_year} = f(k_i)\bullet\frac{Cost\_K_2^{(2013)\_year}}{Cost\_K_2^{(2010)\_year}}\bullet Cost\_M_2^{(2013)\_year} = f(k_2)\bullet\frac{10}{2}\bullet[0.1,0.3,0.5] \tag{5}$$

The sign $f(k_i)$ shows that formula (5) needs to do range calculation. Every increase 'four' of 'Average Document using frequency per day' from the year 2010, then the maturity level will go to the next higher level based on the information from the company. The extent of changing the maturity level in formula (5) is calculated in formula (6):

$$f(k_2)\bullet\frac{10}{2} = (10-2)/4 = 2 \tag{6}$$

The maturity in 2013 is increased two times of 'four', then it go to the second higher maturity level: [0.5,0.7,0.9]. The maturity levels for the cost category in four KPIs from 2011 to 2013 are calculated by formula (2). The maturity level of cost for each year is the average value of the maturity value in total KPIs.

5 Case Studies

This section concerns two parts: using fuzzy extended PCMA maturity model to predict maturity scores in different years; studying the effectiveness of the proposed fuzzy extended PCMA maturity model by comparing the predict maturity scores with maturity model evaluation scores. Experimental data and important information have been collected by interviewing the managers of two Chinese companies.

The first case study is related to a swimming industry in Chengdu (China) studied from 2010 to 2013.We calculate the final maturity score per each category including cost, time, quality, safety, defects, infrastructure, and profitability. The results can be seen in the radar chart (left figure 1) showing the level of achievement for each category. The maturity level for each category is combined by three parts: lower value (blue line), middle value (green line), and upper value (red line). For instance, the maturity value of cost in 2010 is: (0.3, 0.4, 0.7), which is read from blue line, green line, and red line respectively. The overall product data management maturity (right figure 1) can be obtained by the signed distance defuzzification method [18] that calculating the average score of the lower value, middle value, and upper value.

To examine the effectiveness of fuzzy extended PCMA maturity model, we evaluate maturity level for product data management in seven categories by using PCMA maturity model (right figure 2) and compare with the results which have been gotten from the proposed fuzzy extended PCMA model (left figure 2). The comparing results show that the maturity levels for two models are the same. More data is studied to evaluate the maturity levels of this company; similarly, results of maturity level in 2012 and 2013can be obtained by the proposed model. The maturity evaluation shows that the introduced software and hardware in 2010 is getting out-of-date. The average time consuming and the quality of PDM is decreasing year by year; this company starts needing more energy to organize the documents in 2013, because of the safety of PDM is decreasing and the defects of PDM is increasing. The maturity analysis reveals that this company should improve PDM or introduce new PDM to satisfy the requirements of document management.

The second case study is to predict the maturity level in a company in which the industry control field is located in Shanghai, China. This company bought Aopeng PDM in 2007, the expected lifespan of this software is 10 years. But the company has to invest new software to satisfy the new requirements after five years later. Therefore, the company bought Windchill at 2012, in which using permission is two years, which means the company needs to make a decision of which software should be invested in 2014. The general maturity level (Figure 3) shows that the new introduced PDM is acceptable in 2013 except the 'quality category' is relatively lower than the other categories.

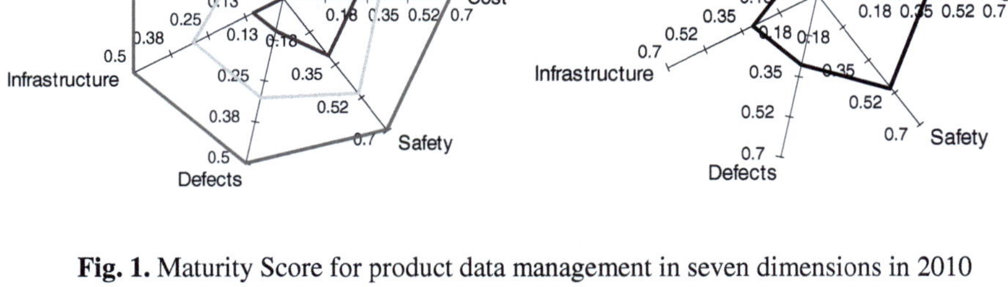

Fig. 1. Maturity Score for product data management in seven dimensions in 2010

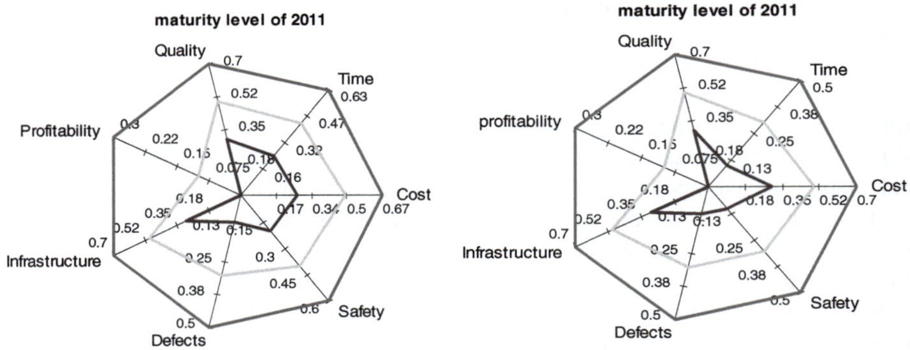

Fig. 2. Maturity levels comparison for fuzzy extended PCMA maturity model and PCMA maturity model in 2011

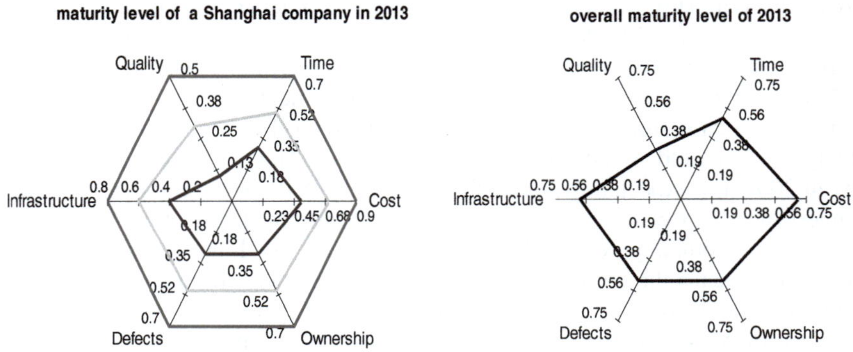

Fig. 3. Maturity Score for product data management in seven dimensions in 2013 for a Shanghai company

6 Conclusion and Future Work

This work analyzes PLM components that can fulfill PLM functionalities. To better handle PLM implementation, a PCMA maturity model is used to evaluate the maturity of PLM components. PCMA maturity model first gives the maturity level, then proposes the detail description of each maturity level, and collects the corresponding KPIs based on the content of each maturity level; finally obtaining the values of KPIs through a survey. A fuzzy extended PCMA maturity model is proposed to reduce the energy that spends on maturity evaluation. This model builds the relationship between the ratio for a pair of maturity levels and the ratio for the corresponding KPIs in two selected years in formula 2. A coefficient in formula 2 can determine how to get the changing degree and changing range for an unknown maturity level. The comparison results show that the proposed model can be used in real-life cases and can efficiently reduce the use of human resources, time, and expense in maturity evaluation.

The restriction of the proposed model is that the selected years must be in the same stage of the company. The results of the proposed model should be recalculated when the company has significant decisions changes. The future work will use more realistic data to examine the effectiveness of the proposed fuzzy extended PCMA maturity model. The realistic data that extracted from social media are diversity and complexity. Therefore, strategies will be given to demystify Big Data based on data structures (structured data, semi-structured data and non-structured data) that enhancing the credibility of the proposed PLM maturity model.

References

1. Stark, J.: Product Lifecycle Management – 21st Century Paradigm for Product Realization. Decision Engineering Series. Springer, Berlin (2005)
2. Vengugopalan, S.R., et al.: Application of AHP for PLM Tools Selection. Product Lifecycle Management: Fostering the culture of innovation. PLM-SP4, 111–125 (2008)
3. Zhang, H., Ouzrout, Y., Bouras, A., Mazza, A., Savino, M.M.: PLM components selection based on a maturity assessment and AHP methodology. In: Bernard, A., Rivest, L., Dutta, D. (eds.) PLM 2013. IFIP AICT, vol. 409, pp. 439–448. Springer, Heidelberg (2013)
4. Zhang, H., Ouzrout, Y., Bouras, A., Della Selva, V., Savino, M.M.: Selection of product lifecycle management components based on AHP methodologies. In: 2013 International Conference on Advanced Logistics and Transport (ICALT), pp. 523–528 (2013)
5. Stark, J.: Product Lifecycle Management. In: Product Lifecycle Management, pp. 1–16. Springer London, London (2011)
6. Abramovici, M., et al.: Decision Support Framework for PLM Harmonization Projects within Industrial Companies. In: Product Lifecycle Management. Towards Knowledge-Rich Enterprises, pp. 535–546. Springer (2012)
7. Alfaraj, H.M., Qin, S.: Operationalising CMMI: integrating CMMI and CoBIT perspective. Journal of Engineering, Design and Technology 9, 323–335 (2011)
8. Team, C.P.: CMMI for Development. Version 1.3 (CMU/SEI-2010-TR-033). Software Engineering Institute, Carnegie Mellon University (2010)
9. Chrissis, M.B., Konrad, M., Shrum, S.: CMMI for Development®: Guidelines for Process Integration and Product Improvement. Part of the SEI Series in Software Engineering series. Addison-Wesley Professional (March 10, 2011)
10. Batenburg, R., Helms, R.W., Versendaal, J.: PLM roadmap: stepwise PLM implementation based on the concepts of maturity and alignment. International Journal of Product Lifecycle Management 1, 333–351 (2006)
11. Pels, H.J., Simons, K.: PLM maturity assessment. In: The 14th International Conference on Concurrent Enterprising: Concurrent Innovation: a New Wave of Innovation in Collaborative Networks, Lisbon, Portugal, pp. 23–25 (June 2008)
12. Sääksvuori, A., Immonen, A.: Product lifecycle management (electronic resource). Springer (2008)
13. Stark, J.: Product Lifecycle Management. In: Product Lifecycle Management, Decision Engineering, pp. 1–16. Springer, London (2011)
14. Zadeh, L.A.: Outline of a new approach to the analysis of complex systems and decision processes. IEEE Transactions on Systems, Man and Cybernetics (1), 28–44 (1973)
15. Zhang, H., Sekhari, A., Ouzrout, Y., Bouras, A.: Optimal Inconsistency Repairing of Pairwise Comparison Matrices Using Integrated Linear Programming and Eigenvector Methods. Journal of Mathematical Problems in Engineering (in press, 2014)

16. Rohloff, M.: Case study and maturity model for business process management implementation. In: Dayal, U., Eder, J., Koehler, J., Reijers, H.A. (eds.) BPM 2009. LNCS, vol. 5701, pp. 128–142. Springer, Heidelberg (2009)
17. Wetzstein, B., Ma, Z., Leymann, F.: Towards Measuring Key Performance Indicators of Semantic Business Processes. In: Abramowicz, W., Fensel, D. (eds.) Business Information Systems. LNBIP, vol. 7, pp. 227–238. Springer, Heidelberg (2008)
18. Chou, S.-Y., Chang, Y.-H., Shen, C.-Y.: A fuzzy simple additive weighting system under group decision-making for facility location selection with objective/subjective attributes. European Journal of Operational Research 189, 132–145 (2008)
19. PLMIG. 'PLM Maturity Reference Manual (Version 1.0)', PLM Interest Group, 50 pages (March 19, 2007)

Towards an Enhancement of Relationships Browsing in Mature PLM Systems

Marianne Allanic[1,2,3], Thierry Brial[3], Alexandre Durupt[1], Marc Joliot[2], Philippe Boutinaud[3], and Benoit Eynard[1]

[1] Université de Technologie de Compiègne, Department of Mechanical Systems Engineering, CNRS UMR 7337 Roberval, 60200 Compiègne, France
[2] UMR5296 GIN CNRS CEA Universitéde Bordeaux, 33000 Bordeaux, France
[3] CADeSIS, 37 rue Adam Ledoux, Bat. B, 92400 Courbevoie, France
marianne.allanic@utc.fr
http://www.plm-conference.org

Abstract. Product Lifecycle Management (PLM) domain is at a key point in its development: its concepts and technologies are mature. PLM systems not only manage documents but information associated to a product along its lifecycle, such as Bills-Of-Material (BOM) or require- ments at different levels of granularity. All the dependencies between concepts lead to complex relationships from which it is not easy to get a coherent overview. The purpose of the paper is to know whether PLM systems are able to deal relationships complexity. Two case studies – one form manufacturing industry and the other one from a new application domain of PLM, Bio-Medical Imaging - are developed in the paper. They show that hierarchical browsing of existing PLM systems is not suitable to manage relationships complexity and must evolve to graph browsing.

Keywords: Product Lifecycle Management (PLM), Heterogeneous Data, Information Visualisation, Graph Theory, Bio-Medical Imaging (BMI).

1 Introduction

Product Lifecycle Management (PLM) began to emerge in the late 1980s as an integrated approach for the design management of products developed by automotive and aerospace industries [11]. The complexity of products in these domains, as well as the increasing competition caused by global markets, posed the need for a better product management system [12]. To stay competitive by reducing product lifecycle duration, the main concern was to provide the right information in the right context at the right time among the global flow of information and throughout the lifecycle of the product [3].

PLM can be defined as a "product centric - lifecycle-oriented business model, [...] in which product data are shared among actors, processes and organizations in the

S. Fukuda et al. (Eds.): PLM 2014, IFIP AICT 442, pp. 345–354, 2014.

different stages of the product lifecycle" [19]. PLM integrates modelling, engineering, manufacturing and project management software into one collaborative platform [12]. When PLM concepts matured from Product Data Management (PDM), manufacturing companies evolved from managing documents to the management of enterprise concepts. Indeed, users at different stages along the product lifecycle need to access to different information, and PLM systems manage product data at many levels of granularity. Some of them are Bill Of Material (BOM) which describes assemblies and parts that constitute the product, engineering BOM (eBOM) which decomposes the product as it is designed, and manufacturing BOM (mBOM) as it is built. The relationships that link the product information levels are of major importance to be able to manage in a consistent way all the phases of the product lifecycle and to enable collaboration between the different teams.

PDM systems were initially designed to manage Computer Aided Design (CAD) files, thus PLM systems were developed mostly around this type of data in the context of manufacturing industry. However, more and more works address other domains, such as Computer Aided Engineering (CAE), Mechatronics, Architecture Engineering and Construction (AEC), Services and Bio-Medical Imaging (BMI). These domains are multidisciplinary and handle heterogeneous data linked by complex relationships inside which it is not easy to browse. The specific needs coming from new application domains of PLM have been overlooked so far, but the whole PLM community could benefit from them.

Because the complexity of data relationships is growing in manufacturing industry and new application domains of PLM, it is important to study relationships management in PLM systems so as to improve their understanding and analysis. Current data visualisation and relationships browsing in PLM sys- tems are presented in the paper. Then two case studies are developed. They were chosen to show two current challenges of applications of PLM. The first case study deals with the migration from one PLM system to another inside the manufacturing company ACME[1]. The second case study focuses on specific needs of a new application domain of PLM: neuroimaging. A discussion about the conclusions from the two case studies ends the paper.

2 Visualisation and Browsing in Mature PLM Systems

2.1 PLM Data Models

PLM is a mature technology known to increase productivity, maximise product value and reduce cost in organisations [17]. Object-oriented approach was shown to be adequate to model and integrate product, process and resource data through UML diagrams [8]. The Core Product Model (CPM), which defined form, function and behaviour of a product, has been extended [9] and enables the design of product

---

[1] ACME is a French company designing and manufacturing thermal systems. The name is modified, as the authorisation of the company to use their name in the paper is under approval.

information-modelling framework to support the full range of PLM requirements [18]. Data organisation models in PLM systems are now well-tried.

Three phases define PLM: the design and manufacturing phase is the Beginning- of-life (BOL), the distribution and use phase is the Middle-of-life (MOL), and the retired phase is the End-of-life (EOL) [10]. Only the BOL phase -with few exceptions - is managed in PLM systems, as most of the research work focuses on this phase. However, many teams need to collaborate and interact during the BOL phase. So they require to access to different levels of information that have to be properly connected, for instance requirement specifications, design or manufacturing.

2.2 Product Modelling in PLM Systems

Important information about a product is stored in product representation or modelling. In manufacturing companies, product modelling is mostly composed of Computer-Aided Design (CAD) models, but these last are heavy, application dependent and focus on one information level. Some lightweight product modelling, on which Ding et al. [7] made a survey, support users at different stages of the product lifecycle in rapidly browsing, retrieving and manipulating product information across platforms. They constitute interesting exchange formats. Examples of CAD lightweight modelling available in PLM systems are U3D, JT format and XML-based formats (X3D, 3D XML and PLMXML). However these product modelling only address one degree of information complexity for a product. Some works address the design of a multi viewpoints framework [5, 6] with semantics and relationships management, but they do not indicate how to visually read and understand the relationships complexity.

2.3 Interface and Browsing in Current PLM Systems

The interfaces of PLM systems have not been studied by the PLM research community up to now, although they are widely and daily used. It is nothing to say that PLM software interfaces are overall not ergonomic nor intuitive. Compa- nies spend too much time and money in training their employees on information systems, PLM not being an exception. The main critics on the interface are the number of sub-windows and the profusion of menus and icons. Product data instances are presented under the shape of a list and only one level of product information can be displayed at a time. Besides, the interface vocabulary is too manufacturing-industry oriented, which limits the extensibility of PLM systems to other domains.

Rich client installed as a standalone application on local device is widespread among the PLM systems. However, web-based clients are little by little becoming a unavoidable evolution of PLM systems in manufacturing industry in order to access data everywhere and on new mediums such as tablets. The main purpose of web-based clients is to enable easy browsing and retrieval of data, but their interface is not suitable enough. Some interesting PLM web clients have been developed recently - for instance web ARAS system or new Teamcenter 10 active workspace client -, but they still propose an overloaded interface.

Therefore the study of two case studies is proposed to decide whether:

1. The interfaces of PLM systems both comply with the requirements of manufacturing industry and of a new application domain of PLM, such as Bio-Medical Imaging,
2. The PLM research community should address more work on PLM interfaces.

3 Case Study 1: Migration of ACME PLM System

Manufacturing companies are now mostly equipped with PLM systems, and because of information management strategies or costs, they decide to change their PLM system more and more frequently. Therefore, new issues come out such as data consistency in source PLM systems and data import in target PLM systems. In this section, the migration of ACME PLM system is developed to highlight the need for relationships management and visualisation.

3.1 Context and Data to Migrate

In 2011, ACME decided to migrate its Windchill PLM system to Teamcenter PLM system. The CAD software Pro/E remained the same after the migration, so there was no conversion operation. A PLM system handles two distinct types of data: metadata which are stored in a relational database, and data files which are stored in the vault, a securised file system accessible only through PLM. Relationships between data files and metadata are described in the PLM system. In the case of ACME migration, data files are drawings and 3D CAD assemblies. An Extract Transform Load (ETL) type of implementation was set up for the migration. Indeed, Windchill and Teamcenter do not have the same concepts and data models, so an intermediate migration platform is needed to transform the data. The migration platform is composed of a temporary data files storage and a Graph DataBase (GDB), Neo4J. PLMXQuery tool [16] is used to populate the migration platform, which constitutes the Extract phase of ETL. Through XQuery language, the metadata are converted into PLMXML language [14] and the data files are represented with their dependencies in a ASCII instruction file. Finally, during the load phase of ETL, the target Teamcenter platform is populated thanks to PLMXML Import Tool for the metadata and IPEM tool for the data files.

A GDB was chosen to store temporarily the metadata, because a PLM system can be seen as a set of unique objects having a set of attributes (key or value) and being linked together by typed relationships. A graph corresponds as well to this definition, as it is composed of nodes and edges having attributes. Moreover, it is easy to populate a GDB through standard formats. A screenshot of an item extracted from Windchill and displayed in Neo4J is shown in figure 1.

3.2 Issues during the Migration

CAD files are by nature tricky data: when they are opened by appropriate CAD software, some CAD files require other dependent CAD files to be opened. This means that these dependency relationships are described somewhere in the CAD files, but must also be described in the PLM systems. When a user asks the PLM system to open a CAD file locally, the target CAD file and all dependant CAD files are downloaded from the vault. The relationships dependency must be taken in account during the migration, as data files with dependencies can only be migrated after the dependent files. Thus, the imports have to be scheduled in the right order.

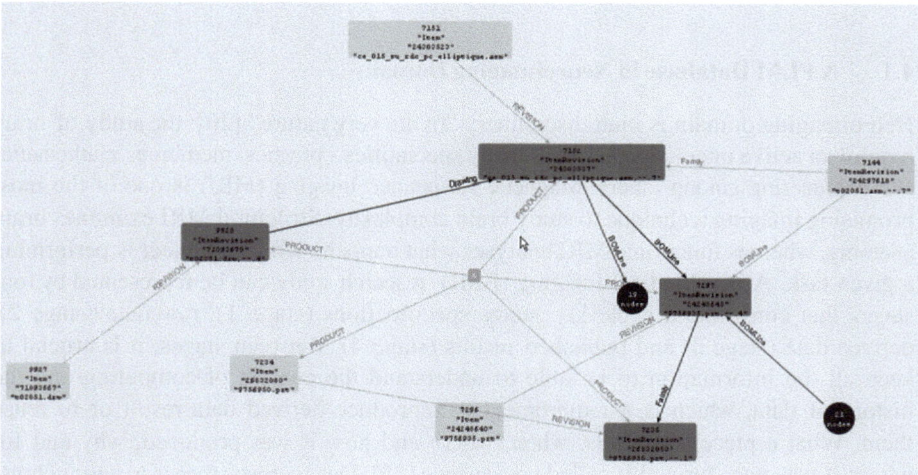

Fig. 1. Screenshot in Neo4J of an item extracted from Windchill with relationships to its revisions, drawing, relatives (family items) and BOM components

Many errors occurred during the migration, due to wrong referencing between objects: obsolete instances, missing references between CAD files and between templates and drawings, dependency cycles. These issues were a real burden during the migration process which lasted for one year instead of the few months planned initially, because the initial data had to be "cleaned". An algorithm - called Kdeep - was designed to analyse referencing errors on the GDB. It is able to locate when the errors occurred in time, and to solve automatically these issues. This algorithm was applied on the Neo4J database. Once the Kdeep algorithm had passed through the whole database, there were still some errors due to inconsistency of complex relationships, and they had to be solved by hand.

The main lesson from the migration is the unexpected number of wrong referencing of the relationships between the levels of granularity in PLM systems. The ACME company was not aware that these issues were existing in its PLM system. Obviously, it is difficult to analyse dependencies and identify referencing problems between objects in a PLM system. Besides, the Neo4J GDB used for the migration turned out to be useful to do the job. Indeed, algorithms can be easily computed on graphs to retrieve statistics and apply display filters for a better understanding of the relationships between graph nodes. Some of the errors could not have been solved out without a visual representation of the dependencies.

4 Case Study 2: Management of GIN Research Studies

A growing number of domains outside manufacturing industry are implementing PLM systems. Most of these domains handle heterogeneous data with complex relationships, which require to browse, retrieve and visualise information efficiently. Browsing needs of neuroimaging domain are developed in this section.

4.1 A PLM Database in Neuroimaging Domain

Neuroimaging domain is multidisciplinary "by its very nature" [20]: the study of brain require an active interaction between many specialities - physics, medicine, mathematics and engineering among others. Magnetic Resonance Imaging (MRI) is one of the most promising imaging technique to study brain complexity. Structural MRI examines brain anatomy, whereas functional MRI analyses what happens while a subject is performing a given task. A Bio-Medical Imaging (BMI) research study can be represented by four stages that constitute a cycle [1]: study specifications (stage 1), raw data (stage 2), derived data (stage 3) and published results (stage 4). Between stages, it is crucial to keep all the information to be able to understand the context of computing and the history of data, which is a requirement to reproduce derived data result or to reuse them. What a piece of data is, when, where and how it was produced, why and for whom it was per- formed is called provenance [15]. Due to costs, trends to huge cohorts of subjects and growing complexity of analyses, neuroimaging researchers must collaborate and share data between disciplines and laboratories [21], which are similar issues than the one of manufacturing industry.

PLM was proposed and shown to be relevant to manage efficiently neuroimag- ing heterogeneous data and to enable the conditions of sharing and reuse of data [2]. Since 2010, the GIN[2] has been using the GIN first Brain Imaging Laterality (BIL&GIN1) dataset, which is composed of 300 subjects - balanced by gender and handedness - and which was acquired between 2009 and 2011 [13]. In 2013 a PLM system – Teamcenter 9 – was installed at the GIN, populated with the BIL&GIN1 dataset.

4.2 Limits of PLM Systems Browsing

The figure 2 shows the two main ways of browsing information in Teamcenter – the concepts are similar in other PLM systems –: hierarchy view (descending) and impact

---

[2] Groupe d'Imagerie Neurofonctionnelle - Neurofunctional Imaging Research Group.

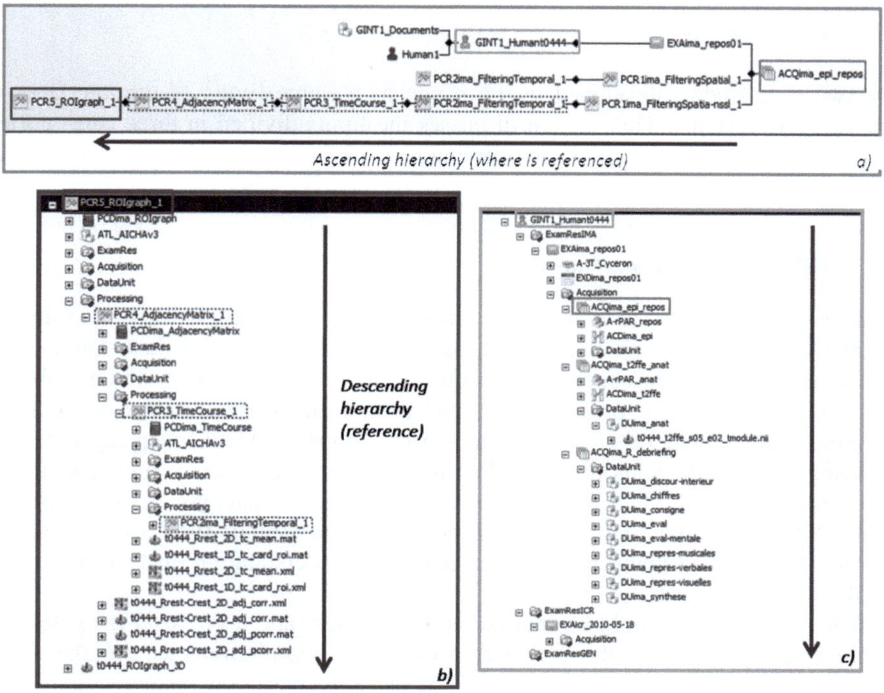

Fig. 2. Screenshots of Teamcenter rich client browsing interfaces. Impact analysis view shows that acquisition A€Qima_epi repos is referenced in a raw data branch and two processing sequence branches(a) Similar information in shown in hierarchy view from top - objects PCR_ROIgraph_1 (b) and GINT1 Humant0444 (c) through descending hierarchy.

analysis view (ascending). It is easy to see where an object has been used on close levels, as well as referencing sequences, with a limited number of relationships. However, users have to switch from one view to another to be able to navigate freely among objects relationships. Indeed, research work requires data exploration to build new hypotheses, but the PLM system allows no overall view of the complexity.

The feedback of the GIN researchers on the PLM system was good concerning the capacities of the system to manage neuroimaging data organisation. How- ever, they were very critical about the interface of the software (basic Teamcenter rich client display): there are too many menus, icons and sub-windows in the en- vironment. Besides, the actions of searching for information is not immediate. What they are looking for in terms of ergonomics is an over-simplified interface with few choices to make for each options, as well as a relationships full manage- ment (browsing, consistency checking, visual information retrieval. In addition, they express the will to handle the system almost without any training. In the end, the GIN researchers are reluctant to use the PLM database, even if they recognise that it is of great benefits for storing and sharing data and associated provenance.

5 Discussion

The two case studies developed in the paper show some limits of the interfaces of current PLM systems. This section discusses the limits divided in three cate- gories: query, analyse and browsing. Leads for future work are proposed at the end of each subsection.

5.1 Information Access: Query

In neuroimaging there is a trend for cross-domain analyses: imaging results are correlated with demographical, clinical, psychological and genetics data. There- fore, numerous joins between concepts are required for one single query, which make the search process complex. Indeed, to design customized queries, users have to know the exact data model organisation. From user's point of view, querying is textual browsing: the search fields that are filled in make the query engine browsing among data relationships. Without efficient retrieval capacities, a database is just a storage room. Apart from the limitation of users' daily data search, the lack of effective querying in PLM systems has an impact on the understanding of data provenance and therefore data reuse.

PLM data models should be transparent to the users and a proposal is to design a graphical query builder, with which users would be query-autonomous. Another future work would be semantic enrichment of PLM systems, based on ontology, and which handles the management of relationships between objects in a flexible way [4]. This would improve performances. Besides, managing PLM concept as a graph would facilitate search processes as well as query perfor- mances, thanks to graph theory algorithms.

5.2 Information Visualisation: Reading and Analyse

The way the information is displayed inside the space of the PLM systems win- dows is meaningless. Only one information level is displayed at a time, under the shape of a list. As a result, it is difficult to read and understand two information levels, especially because they do not require the same display format. PLM systems interfaces are not ergonomic nor intuitive, and companies spend significant time and money in training. If in the manufacturing industry world companies have to use a PLM system to stay competitive, other PLM application domains would be reluctant to use PLM systems because of their current interfaces, which is emphasised by the case study 2 of the paper. So it is of importance that the PLM community addresses the limits of PLM interfaces. Moreover, reducing users' training time on information systems would be obviously a competitive advantage for companies.

Some future work should address new ways of information display in data management systems, particularly focusing on multi viewpoints display. On figure 1, different levels of information are displayed in the Neo4J graph. The positive aspect is that it is easy to access to all the relationships between data and concepts, but the positive aspect is that all the edges look the same, and nothing distinguishes one level of information from the other, for instance CAD files view and product view. So multi viewpoints developments should take this remark into account.

5.3 Information Access and Visualisation: Browsing

The two case studies developed in the paper show that graphical relationships browsers in current PLM systems are not satisfactory. Ascending and descending data relationships hierarchy can only be browsed in two different windows, which prevent from consulting two product information levels at a time or from checking relationships consistency between information levels throughout product lifecycle. As shown in the case study 1, there exists no way to analyse references consistency in a PLM system, which implies a loss of information that could be important for the competitiveness of a company.

Therefore, a major concern in the upcoming works is to visualise data relationships by graphs in one single sub-window, in order to improve browsing and visualisation of every component of data provenance in PLM systems. Further researches should be conducted regarding the application of graph theory to the analysis of relationships in PLM systems.

6 Conclusion

Current PLM systems present limits, notably relationships browsing and analysis, as well as meaningful information visualisation. PLM community would gain to address the design of a simplified graphical user interface that presents multi viewpoints product information. Leads of future work include semantic enrichment and application of graph theory. It is time to make PLM systems evolve towards a more adequate relationships browsing and visualisation.

Acknowledgments. The authors wish to thank in particular the Association Nationale de la Recherche et de la Technologie (ANRT) for its financial support to their work (CIFRE 2012/0420).

The work presented in the paper is conducted within an ANR (Agence Nationale de la Recherche) founded project (n° ANR-13-CORD-0007) for thematic axis n°2 of the Contint 2013 Call for Proposal: from content to knowledge and big data.

References

1. Allanic, M., Durupt, A., Joliot, M., Eynard, B., Boutinaud, P.: Application of PLM for bio-medical imaging in neuroscience. In: Bernard, A., Rivest, L., Dutta, D. (eds.) PLM 2013. IFIP AICT, vol. 409, pp. 520–529. Springer, Heidelberg (2013)
2. Allanic, M., Durupt, A., Joliot, M., Eynard, B., Boutinaud, P.: Towards a data model for plm application in bio-medical imaging. In: 10th International Symposium on Tools and Methods of Competitive Engineering, TMCE 2014, Budapest, Hungaria, May 19-23 (2014)
3. Ameri, F., Dutta, D.: Product Lifecycle Management: Closing the Knowledge Loops. Computer-Aided Design & Application 2(5), 577–590 (2005)
4. Assouroko, I., Ducellier, G., Eynard, B., Boutinaud, P.: Semantic relationship based knowledge management and reuse in collaborative product development. In: Rivest, L., Bouras, A., Louhichi, B. (eds.) PLM 2012. IFIP AICT, vol. 388, pp. 1–13. Springer, Heidelberg (2012)

5. Davies, D., McMahon, C.A.: Multiple viewpoint design modelling through semantic markup. In: ASME 2006 International Design Engineering Technical Conferences and Computers and Information in Engineering Conference, pp. 561–571 (2006)
6. Demoly, F., Dutartre, O., Yan, X.-T., Eynard, B., Kiritsis, D., Gomes, S.: Product relationships management enabler for concurrent engineering and product lifecycle management. Computers in Industry 64(7), 833–848 (2013)
7. Ding, L., Ball, A., Matthews, J., McMahon, C.A., Patel, M.: Product representation in lightweight formats for product lifecycle management (PLM). In: 4th International Conference on Digital Enterprise Technology (2007)
8. Eynard, B., Gallet, T., Nowak, P., Roucoules, L.: UML based specifications of PDM product structure and workflow. Computers in Industry 55(3), 301–316 (2004)
9. Fenves, S.J., Foufou, S., Bock, C., Sriram, R.D.: CPM2: a core model for product data. Journal of Computing and Information Science in Engineering 8(1), 014501 (2008)
10. Kiritsis, D., Bufardi, A., Xirouchakis, P.: Research issues on product lifecycle management and information tracking using smart embedded systems. Advanced Engineering Informatics 17(3-4), 189–202 (2003)
11. Konstantinov, G.: Emerging standards for design management systems. In: Computer Standards Conference, 1988: Computer Standards Evolution: Impact and Imperatives, pp. 16–21. IEEE (1988)
12. Ming, X., Yan, J., Lu, W., Ma, D.: Technology solutions for collaborative product lifecycle management–status review and future trend. Concurrent Engineering 13(4), 311–319 (2005)
13. Petit, L., Crivello, F., Mellet, E., Jobard, G., Zago, L., Joliot, M., Mazoyer, B., Tzourio-Mazoyer, N.: BIL&GIN: a database for the study of hemispheric specialization. In: Proceedings of the 18th Annual Meeting of the Organization for Human Brain Mapping, Beijing, China (2012)
14. SDK and PLMXML. Plm xml schema functional description v6, (November 2005)
15. Simmhan, Y.L., Plale, B., Gannon, D.: A survey of data provenance in e-science. ACM Sigmod Record 34(3), 31–36 (2005)
16. Sriti, M.-F., Boutinaud, P.: PLMXQuery: Towards a standard PLM querying approach. In: Rivest, L., Bouras, A., Louhichi, B. (eds.) PLM 2012. IFIP AICT, vol. 388, pp. 379–388. Springer, Heidelberg (2012)
17. Stark, J.: Product lifecycle management: paradigm for 21st century product realization (2004)
18. Sudarsan, R., Fenves, S.J., Sriram, R.D., Wang, F.: A product information modeling framework for product lifecycle management. Computer-Aided Design 37(13), 1399–1411 (2005)
19. Terzi, S., Abdelaziz, B., Butta, B., Garetti, M., Kiritsis, D.: Product lifecycle management from its history to its new role. International Journal of Product Lifecycle Management 4(4), 360–389 (2010)
20. Van Horn, J.D., Grethe, J.S., Kostelec, P., Woodward, J.B., Aslam, J.A., Rus, D., Rockmore, D., Gazzaniga, M.S.: The functional magnetic resonance imag- ing data center (fmridc): the challenges and rewards of large–scale databasing of neuroimaging studies. Philosophical Transactions of the Royal Society of London. Series B: Biological Sciences 356(1412), 1323–1339 (2001)
21. Yarkoni, T., Poldrack, R.A., Van Essen, D.C., Wager, T.D.: Cognitive neuroscience 2.0: building a cumulative science of human brain function. Trends in Cognitive Sciences 14(11), 489–496 (2010)

Comparison Framework for PLM Maturity Models

Tom Stentzel, Masoud Niknam, and Jivka Ovtcharova

Institute for Information Management in Engineering, Karlsruhe Institute of Technology

Abstract. Throughout the recent years research about maturity models as well as their application possibilities has vastly increased in all sorts of organizations and institutions. The range of the topics they address has expanded as much as the way they can be structured and applied. One area, where the use of maturity models can have a great impact, is product lifecycle management (PLM). PLM is becoming more and more essential for companies as a way of staying competitive on any market due to enhanced understanding of complex processes and increased efficiency in the use of information throughout all stages of the lifecycle. In this regard, maturity models can be beneficial as methods to assess the organizations' product lifecycle processes, illustrate improvement opportunities and even customize a roadmap to exploit them. However, considering the complex application options of maturity models, it can be difficult to choose an appropriate model for a certain purpose. This paper will provide a comparison framework for maturity models in the PLM area. The collected attributes as well as their categorized comparison shall provide guidance in choosing the correct maturity model depending on the user requirements.

Keywords: maturity model, product lifecycle management (PLM), model comparison.

1 Introduction

Nowadays, companies and organizations consistently strive for improving their ongoing business to preserve their position in the market. In order to do that they need to maintain their competitive advantage by reducing their overall costs, being innovative with their products and services, and ensuring their customers' satisfaction with supreme quality. As stated by the Total Quality Management (TQM) principles taught by Shewhart, Juran, Deming and Humphrey, "The quality of a product is largely determined by the quality of the process that is used to develop and maintain it". Additionally to the quality of the utilized process, the choice of technology and people that provide the connection will guarantee a high level of quality throughout the entire company.

One way of pursuing the above-mentioned goals is to implement the use of maturity models. These models help to analyze the current state and the progress made over a period of time concerning processes or structures, assess their current level of maturity, identify strengths and weaknesses, and possibly propose improvement solutions. Also, the use of maturity models by itself will enhance the awareness of the

S. Fukuda et al. (Eds.): PLM 2014, IFIP AICT 442, pp. 355–364, 2014.

employees being assessed and this alone could have positive effects within the organization.

However, since there is a vast amount of maturity models to choose from, depending on the specific goal, the application domain, and several other criteria, how should someone know which one to choose? This paper will try to provide an answer to this question by examining existing maturity models based on specific criteria that have been collectively put into a comparison framework. A few attempts have already been made to structure these criteria and organize them in classification systems. However, the still increasing number of maturity models entails problems of retrievability and reusability, which this paper shall help to overcome. [8]

2 State-of-the-Art Analysis

To get a better understanding of the topic of maturity models and their influence on the PLM domain, this paper will briefly describe their evolution as well as their current, interrelated use.

2.1 Maturity Models

As mentioned above maturity models provide excellent support in assessing the maturity of an entire organization with the aim of improving the competitive advantage on dynamic markets. Starting off in 1987, the Software Engineering Institute (SEI) introduced the Capability Maturity Model (CMM), one of the first models to assess the maturity of processes and the predecessor of many-to-follow maturity models. [13] Following the official CMM version 1.0 in 1991, the CMM Integration was launched in 2002, which eventually lead to the most current CMMI version 1.3, released in 2010. Especially addressing software development, the SEI introduced the concept of having five maturity levels (initial, managed, defined, quantitatively managed, optimizing), indicating the process capabilities expected at a certain level. These process capabilities describe a range of expected results achieved by following the observed software process. Each level also contains a number of key process areas, regulating which goals to achieve according to a set of activities. These key process areas will mostly be considered as business dimensions in other models. Lastly, a detailed description of how to conduct improvement activities is covered in the key practices, which in concerning the CMMI are included in five common features. Some models use the CMMI structure as a reference frame, although many others choose a different approach, mostly due to specific domain requirements.

Since maturity models start to become more and more popular, many different variations in their development have been attempted. As stated by Fraser (2002), all maturity models shall include six basic components, which will be necessary for them to be well-structured: (1) a number of levels (typically three to six), (2) a descriptor for each level (such as the CMMI's differentiation between initial, repeatable, defined, managed, and optimizing processes), (3) a generic description or summary of the characteristics of each level as a whole, (4) a number of dimensions (such as the "process areas" in CMMI), (5) a number of elements or activities for each dimension, and (6) a description of each element or activity as it might be performed at each level of maturity. As stages (1) to (4) are usually met with ease, some models struggle with clear definitions for stages (5) and (6). Regarding those models the idea and fundamental structure is often well designed, but they lack detailed descriptions for the implementation and/or improvement activities, which leads to less appreciation by end users due to limited practicality.

As of today, research related to maturity models heavily focuses on the development, including basic descriptions, more detailed conceptualizations, and approaches with different scientific structuring methods, e.g. design-oriented research or Delphi studies. About a third of all researches concentrates on the application of maturity models, e.g. to specific domains, with the help of maturity assessments, or transferring this knowledge to other contexts. Only very few works conduct empirical studies or simulations, compare maturity models, or conclude model validations of some sort. This paper shall reduce this gap by providing a new concept for model comparison. [16]

2.2 Product Lifecycle Management

Similar to the term maturity there are various ways of defining the area of PLM. A widely-spread definition used by Stark (2005) states 'Product Lifecycle Management (PLM) is the activity of managing a company's products across the complete lifecycle, from the early stages of conception to the final disposal or recycling of the product.' PLM can rather be considered a concept than a system due to its focus on maintaining sustainable market advantage by addressing flexibility and innovation. [2] This concept can be considered as a combination of business rules, processes, methods, and guidelines including descriptions for the practical implementation. [11]

The concept of PLM is very powerful as mentioned benefits include shorter time-to-market, increased innovative ability and profits, fewer engineering changes late in the lifecycle, higher efficiency, and less product faults. [15] Other drivers for the use of PLM consider the demand of more complex products with regard to functionality and components, shorter product lifecycles, customization options because of higher demand standards, management of eventually more complex supply chains, as well as factoring in the increasing regulations concerning safety and environmental issues as mentioned by Batenburg *et al* [2].

Since the PLM concept addresses very common business goals that are pursued by different organizations Batenburg *et al* [2] also state that it has been used in various industries, including e.g. the automotive and transport sector, aerospace and defense, process industry, life sciences and heavy machinery. However, this versatility needs specific application adjustments with respect to the addressed domain and industry. One way to cope with these adjustments is the use of maturity models. They can either be used to assess the maturity of an organization with respect to their readiness to introduce the PLM concept or assess the maturity of an already implemented PLM system in regards to the efficiency of processes, structures, etc. Some of these models provide further guidelines and roadmaps for the improvement of specific gaps and aspects. However, it is always important to realize the strength and weaknesses of the available maturity models in the field and choose the most suitable with regard to the organizations' requirements.

3 Development of an Assessment Framework

As stated in Wendler's study [16], there is a significant lack of research in the area of maturity model validation, which by his means covers maturity model comparisons. Therefore, the aim here is to develop a comprehensive framework to facilitate a fair comparison of the models with respect to their different attributes. Although there have already been attempts to classify, categorize, compare, and evaluate maturity models, the intent of this paper is to develop a framework considering all important general aspects that could be relevant for a comparison on the base of explicit literature research analysis. The basic structure of the framework consists of three attribute dimensions, similar to the dimensions addressed by Mettler [7]: *general attributes, design attributes,* and *usage attributes*.

3.1 General Attributes Dimension

The *general attributes dimension* will cover two blocks of attributes. The first block will include the "basic information", which represents top level information that is necessary to get a simple distinction between all kinds of models. This includes the name of the model, the acronym (if existent), the primary source (where information was collected), the addressed topic, the origin (academic or practitioner-based), the year of publication, the granted access (free or charged), and the addressed audience (management- or technology-oriented). The second block "structure details" will go more into detail on aspects like the covered business dimensions and maturity levels as well as possible testing parameters.

3.2 Design Attributes Dimension

This dimension will focus on design related issues concerning the maturity models. That includes the main purpose of the model, which can be either *descriptive* (the application is a single point encounter with no intention of maturity improvement or analysing performance relationships), *prescriptive* (analyzing domain relationships in order to boost business performance and thus increase the business value, therefore identifying gaps and creating a road-map for improvement), or *comparative* (performing an industry-wide benchmark across different organizations to compare similar practices). [3] As mentioned by Mettler [7] the concept of maturity covers the focus of the model, including *process maturity* (to which extent a specific process is explicitly defined, managed, measured, controlled, and is effective), *object maturity* (to which extent a particular object like a software product, a company report or similar reaches a predefined level of sophistication), and *people capability* (to which extent the workforce is able to enable knowledge creation and enhance proficiency). Additionally, Kärkkäinen [5] introduced a fourth *customer* dimension (capability for management of all customer-related data, information and knowledge concerning the whole product lifecycle), which will be factored into the comparison. The composition shows that a model can either be concluded as a *maturity grid* (text descriptions for each activity at each maturity level with moderate complexity), a *Likert-like questionnaire or hybrids* (questions are statements of 'good practice' to score the relative performance; hybrids combine this with a maturity grid), or *something else* (e.g. the CMMI). [4] As for the chosen assessment approach, the model can either be *staged* (the model matures the organisation as a whole) or *continuous* (improves capability of specific processes within the organization). [14] Whether a model is designed to be *one-* or *multi-dimensional* (being adaptable to multiple domains) will be covered in the scope as well. The flexibility or rather adaptability of a model can either be represented as a change in its *form* (e.g. the underlying meta-model or model schema, the descriptions of the maturity levels or question items) or its *function* (e.g. how maturity is assessed). [8] Lastly, the reliability of the model will be addressed. When there is at least one testing available, it can be assumed that the model has been *verified.* Only until a model has been thoroughly tested and accepted by many practitioners it could be considered as *validated.*

3.3 Usage Attributes Dimension

The *usage attributes dimension* covers five attributes mainly concerning application issues. First off, the method of application is defined by either being done by a *self-assessment, a third-party assisted assessment*, or be concluded by *certified practitioners.* A variety of instruments is used for this application, including *document reviews, work groups,* and/or *questionnaires.* When self-assessing support for the application is needed. If there are any, this support could include *textual descriptions or handbooks,* or a *software assessment tool.* Since not all of the observed models *provide specific improvement guidelines* when trying to advance from one level to the next, this attribute shows importance to be covered. As for the practicality of evidence, *implicit improvement activities* for future development of the model as well as *explicit recommendations* are covered. Lastly, some models might need specific training for correct application. This training can range from *basic* to *extended,* depending on the level of detail and the desired purpose of use.

4 Results of the Assessment Framework

The comparison framework as described in Chapter 3 is applied to a variety of maturity models in the PLM area, including the PLM framework proposed by Batenburg *et al* [2], the Capability Maturity Model Integration (CMMI), Version 1.3, by the CMMI Institute [13, 14], the Configuration Management Maturity Model by Niknam *et al* [9], the EDEN Maturity Model by the BPM Maturity Model eden e.V. (all information translated from German) [1], the addition of a customer dimension of PLM maturity based on Batenburg's model by Kärkkäinen *et al* [5], the Knowledge Management Capability Assessment Model by Kulkarni *et al* [6], the PLM Maturity Reference Model by PLM Interest Group [10] the Product lifecycle management model by Saaksvuori *et al* [11], the PLM Maturity Model by Savino *et al* [12], and the PLM Components Maturity Assessment by Zhang *et al* [17]. The comparison is based on the available literature about the aforementioned models, which were found and reviewed by the authors in order to extract the categorized information with respect to the comparison framework's requirements.

The results of the *general attributes dimension* are listed in Table 1 below. Although the scope of their application might vary, all models are associated to the PLM domain. Most of the models are academically based, although some have a rather practitioner-based background. Seven of the ten described models are entirely free to access and for three of them some fees shall be paid for a granted access to assessment tools and extensive documentation or professional assistance in the application of the model. Although most of them have different termed business dimensions, similarities and correlations can be found. For example, Kärkkäinen's model proposes adding another dimension to the Batenburg model. Concerning the number of business dimensions, there is a vast variety of approaches to be found. Some models focus on only four to five dimensions, coping with the covered subject in a more general matter, while other models show up to 15 or 16 dimensions. In case of the Savino and Zhang models, they use the TIFO(S) framework for their coverage, which provides another layer of structure. The observed maturity levels range from four to six and, similar to the business dimensions, they have different labels. For more than half of the models testing is available and has been concluded in different industries. Concerning the CMMI, due to its popularity and widespread acceptance, there are two annual reports that cover the main status of their usage and the maturity of their clients.

The results of the *design attributes dimension* are listed in Table 2 below (unclear or unverified information in parentheses). All of the observed models present a minimum of "descriptive" purpose meaning that they can at least be used to assess the maturity of the organization or certain processes. Seven of them still provide certain prescriptive actions for improvement and only three provide options for benchmarking. Mostly all of them feature process, and more or less object and people maturity concepts, only few models can be considered to have covered the customer dimension. The composition spreads out very diverse throughout all attribute options, although the Likert-like questionnaires / hybrids and other concepts are used most of the time. Only two models are considered multi-dimensional, being able to be applied to almost any domain. Most models are in some way mutable, whether it is by adapting the form, function, or both. Many models feature at least a basic test, but only few models have concluded thorough testing, which might lead to consider them as being validated.

Table 1. General attributes dimension

General attributes dimension										
Attribute category	Model									
	Batenburg (1)	**CMMI** (2)	**CM3** (3)	**EDEN** (4)	**Kärkkäinen** (5)	**Kulkarni** (6)	**PLMIG** (7)	**Saaksvuori** (8)	**Savino** (9)	**Zhang** (10)
Name	PLM framework for the assessment and guidance of PLM implementations	Capability Maturity Model Integration, Version 1.3	Configuration Management Maturity Model	EDEN Maturity Model for BPM	Defining the Customer Dimension of PLM Maturity	Knowledge Management Capability Assessment Model	PLM Maturity Reference Model	Product lifecycle management	PLM Maturity Model	PLM Components Maturity Assessment
Acronym	-	CMMI-DEV, V1.3	CMP	EDEN	-	KCMA	-	-	-	PCMA
Primary source	[1]	[10]	[7]	[1]	[4]	[6]	[8]	[9]	[12]	[17]
Addressed topic	PLM	Process Improvement	Configuration Management	Process Management	PLM adoption	Knowledge Management	PLM	PDM/PLM	PLM implementation	PLM Components
Origin	Academic	Academic	Academic	(Academic) / Practitioner-based	Academic	Academic / Practitioner-based	Practitioner-based	Academic	Academic	Academic
Year of	2006	2010	2013	2009	2012	2004	2007	2004	2012	2013
Access	free	free (materials, books available) /charged (e.g. consultants)	free	charged	free	free	charged (access to materials, consultants)	free	free	free
Audience	both	both	management-oriented	management-oriented	both	both	management-oriented	both	technology-oriented	both
Business dimensions (BD)	1. Strategy & Policy 2. Management & Control 3. Organization & Processes 4. People & Culture 5. Information Technology	16 Key Process Areas including: 1. Configuration Management 2. Integrated Project Management 3. Measurement and Analysis 4. Project Planning 5. Risk Management 6.-16. [...]	1. Strategy & Performance 2. Process 3. Information Technology 4. Organization & Value-stream 5. Knowledge & Support	170 single criteria within: 1. Goals 2. Strategy 3. Methods 4. Organization 5. Measurement 6. Competencies 7. Communication 8. Documentation 9. IT	1. Strategy & Policy 2. Management & Control 3. Organization & Processes 4. People & Culture 5. Information technology 6. Customer Orientation	Knowledge Capability Areas (KCA): 1. Expertise 2. Lessons learned 3. Knowledge documents 4. Data	1. Data 2. People 3. Processes 4. Technology 5. Knowledge	1. Process 2. Structures 3. IT systems 4. PLM strategy 5. People in PLM change management	15 PLM Components within the 4 TIFO Areas: 1. Technoware-IT 2. Infoware 3. Functionware 4. Orgaware	15 PLM Components within the 5 TIFOS Areas: 1. Technoware-IT 2. Infoware 3. Functionware 4. Orgaware 5. Sustainware
Number of (BD)	5	16	5	9	6	4	5	5	15	15
Maturity levels (ML)	I. Ad Hoc II. Departmental III. Organizational IV. Inter-organizational	I. Initial II. Managed III. Defined IV. Quantitatively Managed V. Optimizing	I. Initial II. Managed III. Standard IV. Optimizing	0. Chaotic I. Rudimentally II. Advanced III. Consistent IV. Controlled V. Sustainable	I. Chaotic II. Conscientious III. Managed IV. Advanced V. Integration	0. Difficult / Not possible I. Possible II. Encouraged III. Enable / Practiced IV. Managed V. Continuously Improved	I. Ad-hoc II. Managed III. Defined IV. Quantitatively managed V. Optimized	I. Unstructured II. Repeatable but intuitive III. Defined IV. Managed and measurable V. Optimal	I. Lowest II. Low III. Medium IV. High V. Top	I. Ad-hoc II. Managed III. Defined IV. Quantitatively managed V. Optimized
Number of ML	4	5	4	6	5	6	5	5	5	5
Testing of the MM	Yes	Yes*	Yes	Yes	Not available	Yes	No access	Not available	Yes	Yes
Number of questions	40	-*	53	No access	-	145	-	-	Not available	Not available
Number of respondents	23	-*	67	No access	-	~750	-	-	~250	Not available
Basic features of the participants' organizations	A: Medium size (15-1000 employees) B: Large size (Over 1000 employees) - Equipment and transport companies (A:3/B:5) - ICT solution providers (A:1/B:5) - Product software companies (A:6/B:1) - Financial service (A:1/B:1)	*As one of the very few maturity models the CMMI has been tested on many occasions in different industries and organizations. The latest testing results found in the 'Maturity Profile Reports' of September 2013 stated around 6,000 concluded appraisals.	Distribution: - 72% in private sector - 28% in public sector Industry sectors: - aerospace (33%) - transportation (12%) - military, defence, government (12%) - automotive (11%) - IT (11%) - others (21%)	-	-	One leading manufacturing company in semiconductor industry - 2 Business Units - All knowledge workers Strong focus on model validation within the organization: - Translation validity - Criterion-Related Validity	-	-	SME's of electromechanical sectors based in southern Italy	Italian prefabrication company (one of the most important companies in the precast and construction field in southern center of Italy)

Table 2. Design attributes dimension

Capabilities / Cases	[16	[17	[18	[19	[20	[21	[22	[23	[24	[25	[26	[27	[28	[29	[30	[31	[32	[33	[34	[35	[36
Elimination of duplicated and inaccurate data through 3D modelling	!													!							
Analyse and simulate design to support preventive and reactive maintenance	!	!					**!**			**!**											
Life cycle costs and environmental analysis	!																	!			
4D as-built model containing construction process information			!																		
3D as-built model				!	!		**!**	!						!			!			!	
3D as-built model linked to estatutory/maintenance information						!								!	!		!		!		
3D linked to cleaning schedule							**!**														
3D linked to waste disposal schedule							**!**														
Maintenance linked to expenditure history							**!**														
Order/supply linked to inventory schedule							**!**							!	!		!		!	!	
Energy Simulation witin as-built								!													
Maintenance schedule									**!**	**!**				!	!	!					
Accurate as-built model											**!**									!	
Maintenance as-done record of event/problem description and solution												!	**!**						!	!	
Real-time, mobile resource location tracking													**!**								
Facility condition analysis																!					
Building Automation System																	**!**				
Travelling path of maintenance																					**!**

Implemented
Simulated

Table 3. Usage attributes dimension

Baseline Measure	[16]	[17]	[18]	[19]	[20]	[21]	[22]	[23]	[24]	[25]	[26]	[27]	[28]	[29]	[30]	[31]	[32]	[33]	[34]	[35]	[36]
Better customer service	!																				
Better decision-making	!	!						!		!	!						!	!			!
Better cost forescast		!					!								!						
Improved data consistency			!		!		!	!				!				!	!		!	!	
Better access to information				!								!							!	!	
Reduced response time					**!**																
Increased process efficiency						!								!							
Better planning							!								!	!					
Better AEC-FM Integration									!												
Reduction of maintenance failure											!										
Strealined processes											!						!		!	!	**!**
Improved tracking of inventory													!		!	!					
Reduction of reactive maintenance															!						
Reduced cost of operations															!	!					
Reduced time of operations																**!**		!			
Reduce effort of operations																					!

Implemented
Simulated

The results of the *usage attributes dimension* are listed in Table 3 below (unclear or unverified information in parentheses). Most of the models use a self-assessment as the application method. Certified practitioners are usually only available with models that are used by institutions or consultant agencies and that come with a charge. The instrument for application divides up quite evenly between all possible attributes, although the charged models tend to rather strive towards using work groups than only document reviews or questionnaires. An often used supporting tool for the application is a software assessment tool, which has been provided by five of the ten observed models. Also, the charged models seem to provide more support in general. About half of the models exhibit guidelines for specific improvement activities based on the achieved maturity level. Almost all of the models show regular implicit improvement activities. The adaption to the dynamically changing requirements is very relevant and important for future usage purposes. A downside of the charged models is the required training. Depending on the intensity and future plans of use the training can be more or less extended.

5 Conclusion

As illustrated in Wendler's study [16], only a fraction of the research in the field of maturity models strives into the direction of validation. With this paper we tried to provide a more comprehensive maturity model comparison framework based on general categories extracted from literature. The few past categorization and comparison approaches have thoroughly been analyzed to develop a framework that covers all the important attributes. The comparison result is aiming to not only reduce the search time for specific models, allow easier communication, identify differences and similarities, and thus enhance retrievability, but also provide a baseline of attributes needed for a high-quality development of future models. Thus, this framework can serve as a benchmark for future PLM maturity model developments.

However, since the comparison approach only covers a qualitative evaluation, a weighting system regarding individual preferences could be implemented to add further detail to the analysis and to be able to rate the models more precisely with respect to their intentioned application and organization needs. A possible approach on adding quantitative value to the comparison might be to use plus and minus values instead of checkmarks, which could eventually add up to show a preference of certain models in specific categories. Additionally, because the PLM area is generally becoming more important to companies and organizations, further research on "which models might also be suitable for this domain" (e.g. due to their mutability) should be concluded. Since in this paper only models with easy access and available documentation were covered, further research on models with limited access might provide an even more comprehensive overview.

References

[1] Allweyer, T., Knuppertz, T., Schnägelberger, S.: EDEN - Reifegradmodell 'Prozessorientierung in Unternehmen'. s.l.:BPM Maturity Model EDEN e.V (2009)
[2] Batenburg, R., Helms, R., Versendaal, J.: PLM roadmap: stepwise PLM implementation based on the concepts of maturity and alignment. Int. J. Product Lifecyle Management 1(4) (2006)
[3] de Bruin, T., Freeze, R., Kulkarni, U., Rosemann, M.: Understanding the Main Phases of Developing a Maturity Assessment Model. In: Australasian (ACIS): ACIS, Proceedings (2005)
[4] Fraser, P., Moultrie, J., Gregory, M.: The use of maturity models / grids as a tool in assessing product development capability, Centre for Technology Management, Institute for Manufacturing, University of Cambridge. IEEE (2002)

[5] Kärkkäinen, H., Pels, H.J., Silventoinen, A.: Defining the customer dimension of PLM maturity. In: Rivest, L., Bouras, A., Louhichi, B. (eds.) PLM 2012. IFIP AICT, vol. 388, pp. 623–634. Springer, Heidelberg (2012)

[6] Kulkarni, U., Freeze, R.: Development and Validation of a Knowledge Management Capability Assessment Model. In: s.l.:Twenty-Fifth International Conference on Information Systems (2004)

[7] Mettler, T.: A Design Sciene Research Perspective on Maturity Models in Information Systems. Institute of Information Management, St. Gallen (2009)

[8] Mettler, T., Rohner, P., Winter, R.: Towards a Classification of Maturity Models in Information Systems. Springer, Heidelberg (2010)

[9] Niknam, M., Ovtcharova, J.: Towards Higher Configuration Management Maturity. In: Bernard, A., Rivest, L., Dutta, D. (eds.) PLM 2013. IFIP AICT, vol. 409, pp. 396–405. Springer, Heidelberg (2013)

[10] PLM Interest Group (2014), PLM Interest Group, `http://www.plmig.com/` (accessed on March 2014)

[11] Saaksvuori, A., Immonen, A.: Product Lifecycle Management, 3rd edn. Hrsg. s.l. Springer, Heidelberg (2008)

[12] Savino, M.M., Mazza, A., Ouzrout, Y.: PLM Maturity Model: A Multi-Criteria Assessment in Southern Italy Companies. s.l.:International J. of Opers. and Quant. Management 18(3) (2012)

[13] Software Engineering Institute (SEI), Software Engineering Institute, Carnegie Mellon University (2014), `http://www.sei.cmu.edu/` (accessed on March 2014)

[14] Software Engineering Institute (SEI) & CMMI Product Team, CMMI for Development, Version 1.3. Carnegie Mellon University: s.n (2010)

[15] Stark, J.: Product Lifecycle Management: 21st Century Paradigm for Product Realization. Springer, Berlin (2005)

[16] Wendler, R.: The maturity of maturity model research: A systematic mapping study. Elsevier B.V., Technische Universität Dresden (2012)

[17] Zhang, H., Ouzrout, Y., Bouras, A., Mazza, A., Savino, M.M.: PLM Components Selection Based on a Maturity Assessment and AHP Methodology. In: Bernard, A., Rivest, L., Dutta, D. (eds.) PLM 2013. IFIP AICT, vol. 409, pp. 439–448. Springer, Heidelberg (2013)

How to Improve PLM Approach Efficiency Based on Knowledge Engineering, Knowledge Management and Semantic Web Technologies Domains?

Bernard Chabot, Philippe Gautreau, and Brice Sommacal*

PCO Innovation, Europarc, 1 place Berthe Morisot, 68900 Saint-Priest, France
{firstname.lastname}@pco-innovation.com

Abstract. The objective of this article is to show that SEAMLESS, a designed and developed method from PCO Innovation, allows improving PLM approach efficiency by proposing to set up a business/Information System referential. PLM, as a PLM solution, is a software which basically supports product conception and product industrialization business processes (and potentially other upstream and/or downstream business processes). The functional scope may be really wide and the various amounts of subjects are strongly connected to each other. A PLM approach (which seeks to establish a PLM solution in the organization) is basically composed of a program with several projects. Among all PLM approach activities; upstream activities (and specifically specification activities) are absolutely crucial. This kind of approach is, generally, lengthy and complex. Specification activities raise many challenges. They come from a functional positioning (whereas a business one is expected) of user's requirements and also from the deliverables documentary nature. Looking at what is a business/Information System referential; we observe that it has all the ingredients to avoid misunderstanding of user's needs and the nature of the document. SEAMLESS is an assisted method to modelize, capture and restitute (graphically and/or textually) the underlying knowledge domain delimitating a set of activities. SEAMLESS allows implementing any knowledge referential by using a generic approach as well as modular and reusable components. By applying SEAMLESS approach on PLM specification activities, we improve PLM approach efficiency.

Keyword: Product Lifecycle Management, Project and Program management, Knowledge management, Knowledge engineering, Semantic web, business referential, knowledge referential, Ontology, Knowledge base.

Foreword: In every section of this article, the PLM term used alone designates a PLM solution by default, meaning a technical solution in the field of computing, otherwise known as one (or many) software program(s) / software package(s) interacting together and acting as a single software solution.

---

* Corresponding author.

S. Fukuda et al. (Eds.): PLM 2014, IFIP AICT 442, pp. 365–376, 2014.

1 Introduction

As business consultants, we are solicited by our clients to help them set up a PLM solution in their company. Alongside this progress, most of the time, we encounter some behaviors (independently of their sectors) which prevent to run successfully our mission. That's why; we want to show how our SEAMLESS methodology allows improving PLM approach efficiency.

This article is divided into 4 complementary sections. The first section describes the general nature of the PLM approach (i.e. as a PLM solution) and the specificities of a PLM project. The second section describes how activities which contribute to the specification of a PLM are traditionally apprehended, as well as the pitfalls which are usually encountered and the factors which are at the origin of these pitfalls. The third section describes what a business/information system referential is and how it could solve pitfalls mentioned in the previous section. The fourth section describes SEAMLESS, an assisted semantic methodological approach which allows implementing this kind of referential.

2 The PLM and the PLM Approach

This section will be used to define exactly what a PLM is by identifying what the PLM is used for, what PLM speak about, how PLM works and finally what are the reasons for a company to acquire a PLM.

This prerequisite will strengthen the understanding of what a PLM project is and what the main activities in it are. It will also describe the recurring features of a PLM project and show how a PLM project is not really like other projects.

2.1 The PLM at a Glance

A PLM, as defined by a "PLM solution", is a software solution which generally comprises a PLM software package, is to an extent configured and/or "customized" and serves as the main component, as well as many other software applications which are more or less integrated with the main component. The ultimate purpose of a PLM is to support and coordinate every activity which is linked to every step in the lifecycles of products and/or services in a company: product innovation needs definition, design, industrialization, production, distribution and others, and in any other case (relative to the nature of the product): operation, maintenance and support, dismantling or even recycling. Depending on certain criteria (product nature, business model type, company strategy, etc.), this end goal will also encompass activities located upstream or downstream of the product lifecycle. A PLM solution will allow a company to design more products and/or design them quicker and/or design less costly products (Miller 2003).

Due to the nature of activities supported by PLM solutions, we may deduct that the major topics (in terms of area of interest) of a PLM are core business concepts used during design and industrialization activities. Other « Core » subjects can be found, such as products informations, but also other subjects which are more or less related to products such as customers, product component suppliers, product requirements, control, verification and product validation methods. These subjects have traditionally been portrayed, described and/or characterized in documents or office software format (Word, Excel, PowerPoint, etc.) such as briefs, functional and technical specifications, assembly nomenclature or mixing recipes, audit files, procedural file control plans, …

It can easily be said that the primary function of a PLM solution is to organize and to bind together the various concepts which are handled by the trades relative to differing views of the "Product". The most known views are:

- "As required" view (describing the uses and requirements for the future product),
- "As designed" view (describing the product's technical reference solution)
- "As to be built" view (describing a local industrial solution for the product)
- "As built" view (describing a real product which has already been built)
- "As maintained" view (describing a real product which has been modified)

It also covers configuration mechanisms and upholds the coherence of these different views, modification tracing, data access control (access rights) and the orchestration of the various tasks which handle these (responsibilities, workflow).

2.2 A PLM Project in Short

Since a PLM project must ultimately deliver a software application, this type of project is too often considered as an ordinary IT project. The apparent software nature of a PLM project is a trap which must not be fallen into. Even if the advent of a PLM solution in the application landscape represents an opportunity to rehabilitate and simplify (which is not trivial) by eliminating many established legacy programs, it is not an end in itself but rather an opportunity to restructure the company's technical craft. This is why a PLM project must be considered as being a project which is essentially related to the company's core business activity but with a software component to it.

As with any project, a PLM project potentially requires pure project management activities (like planning, resource allocation, budget fixing), project steering activities (like meetings with various committees) and project quality assurance activities (like project quality implementation plan, analysis and project risk analysis activities). As with any project which must ultimately deliver a computer-related solution, a PLM project may potentially require:

- Application specification activities (identification of project issues, determining the project perimeter, formalizing the needs of users, functional and technical specifications, etc.),
- Application construction activities (PLM software package parameterization, specific development and screen customization, associated application interfacing, etc.),
- Application deployment activities (existing software landscape integration, data recovery and interface preparation and execution, etc.),
- Activities regarding the migration of existing application data to the PLM (migrating data identification, preparation, consolidation, migration, etc.),

- Activities surrounding application decommissioning (in order to guarantee that the PLM will be used efficiently and effectively and that "legacy programs" will eventually be removed from the application landscape),
- Change management activities (adapted communication to several groups: project deciders and sponsors, project team members, key and end users, user training, administrator and user support activities, etc.).

Each one of these activities does not weigh on the success of the PLM project and its overall efficiency in the same manner (generally apprehended via the Scope / Schedule / Cost (Newell and Grashina 2004).

A PLM has several recurring features which are almost systematically found in every PLM project. The first recurring feature of a PLM project is its *transversality*, which is to say that the processes which are sustained by the future software application cross over many of the company's functional areas (e.g. marketing, R&D, engineering and design, purchasing, production, logistics) and also many technical subjects (whose list closely depends on the nature of the product which is offered by the company and covers a very large spectrum of components: mechanical, electrical, electronic, pneumatic, software, chemical, organic, living beings, etc.). This implies that the different core business participants in the company are capable of understanding each other and that the project team has the ability to make sure that they are coherent. The reason is that it is essential to identify and define the core business concepts which are handled through the activities in project perimeter. The second recurring feature of a PLM project is its major impact on the existing application landscape. This implies being able to precisely define which applications store and/or handle data within the project perimeter. The third recurring feature of a PLM project is its *timeframe*. It is generally acknowledged that a PLM project is one which is set over a length of time: many months or even many years are often required to deliver a complete PLM project (which is often organized into several projects). And of course, over this type of period, many kinds of changes are likely to appear (like changes in the company's organization, technological developments, and changes in the project's participants). This implies that the ability to express which needs must be fulfilled within the scope of a project by relying on invariable descriptions of the company's field of expertise is required. The fourth recurring feature of a PLM project is linked to the target application's nature as a software package. Nearly every PLM solution in the market is based on software packages which load a certain number of generic structures and/or mechanisms which must be configured in order to adapt them to the company's context. This implies ensuring that the selected generic elements (structural and/or functional) implementing each core business need are relevant. The reason is that this approach can be used to limit the immediate cost of specific development and the future costs of application maintenance.

Every previously cited feature confirms that a PLM project is first and foremost a company-related project. It is an "in depth" transformation project that affects how the company is run, and even if this transformation strongly affects the application landscape in the company, it's a transformation that must be steered by business and for business. It is also acknowledged that this type of project may become a structuring agent for an organization since, bearing the right tools, it forces the company to follow the rules and processes it has set out for itself.

As a result, a PLM approach is complex because it depends on many factors. In the next section, we will see that this complexity is also integrated into PLM specification activities.

3 The Traditional Approach and its Pitfalls

This section will describe, within the context of a PLM project, how PLM specification activities are traditionally apprehended, which classic pitfalls result from them and what their root causes are. In this section and later in the article, we focus exclusively on *PLM specifications activities* because all others activities depend on the produced informations from this step.

3.1 PLM Specifications Activities Positioning

The root cause comes from the fact that this kind of project is addressed from a *computing perspective*. In many cases, PLM software is selected in the earlier phase of the PLM project (even before user's needs are specified). It may also be justified by the fact that the organization already has a PLM solution in production and would like to change their solution (from minor version upgrade to editor's change). Evidence shows that more and more companies wish to drive PLM projects with an "Agile" method (of the "Scrum" type) as is the case for the development of functional components such as internet browsers.

Another root cause is when the starting point to capture user's need consists in describing the "as is" situation by focusing on the current practice on the one hand and the evolutions of these practices on the other hand (said "to be" situation). Therefore, the business processes description (which should describe what the business has to do) become the application processes description (e.g. how the business makes things). In others words, instead of capture what the business does (independently of the manner), we capture the way things are realized (or will be), whom realize them, and how they are realized (like resources, tools). It means that user's need capture is done at a procedure level (describe the way to make an activity) instead of at a process level (describe what has to be done). This doesn't allow the organization to take a step back regarding theirs original and genuine needs.

Capturing information at a level which is highly functional and settling for "as is" and "to be" practical descriptions often results in implementing current practices to the upcoming PLM solution, since the description of needs was never done in a way which was focused on what needed to be done (independently to the motivations for doing so and the means to do so). In the end, the company will not have benefitted from the new opportunity to lay flat its core business processes and to reflect on a new way of putting them into practice, in a way closer to best industrial practices and more compatible with the standards in the PLM software package, all of which is provided by the PLM project. We may also encounter that the various business stakeholders may have trouble to understand each other, because from a functional level, the real profession has been erased.

The capture is made from an applicative way whereas it should only be focused on the needs (push from PLM approach and/or selected PLM solution).

3.2 PLM Specifications Activities Deliverables

Specifications activities produce a huge amount of informations which describe business organization in the company, PLM program organization, potential business scope and the one covered by PLM program, existing practices (using legacies system), future practices (using PLM solution), business process “to be”, business concepts semantic model, logical data model and applicative cartography. This list is not exhaustive, but, what is important is that these deliverables are produced in corpus of document.

The necessary information to complete activities to specify the PLM solution (define the trade perimeter and the parceling of the project, formalizing user needs, depicting core business processes, specifying system functions, etc.) is almost exclusively managed with office document-type support tools (Word, Excel, PPT, Visio, etc.). Unfortunately, this approach implies that a large corpus of documents is created, with many different documents relating to the same topics (business usage cases, artefacts and business concepts, business roles, application, etc.), viewed under different perspectives (process, responsibility, access to information, etc.) and created by different participants in the project (sponsors, business experts, solution experts, etc.) who often use different jargons.

The fact remains that this body of documents rapidly swells in the project development phase and becomes increasingly difficult to maintain, always requiring greater effort to preserve overall coherence. The resulting pitfall is that an important burden is dragged throughout every phase in the project, which consequentially reduces the productiveness of the project team and increases the risk for error.

Table 1. Criteria to avoid pitfalls

Criteria	Description	Example
Accurate semantic	Don’t have the possibility to associate several terms to one concept (Roche 2011)	The same business concept may exist in the corpus of documents but named in different manners.
Translation	For each information, dispose of the translation in one or several languages	Each document has to be translated.
Coherence	Dispose of a consistent corpus of document	The same business concept could be implemented by 2 different applicative objects in the context of 2 projects
Completeness	Can list a specific kind of information	Difficult to list all business roles involved in all projects
Inference	Can easily deduce informations from a corpus of documents	Not possible to deduce inter project dependence from inter processes dependence

4 Business/Information System Referential

This section allows showing that a business/information system referential approach is well-suited to support PLM specification activities. Essentially by the fact that it allows to avoid a large majority of traditional effects linked to deliverables produced form.

4.1 What's a Business/Information System Referential?

A business/information system referential is a computer application which would allow storing all required elements representing deliverables contents (traditionally produced by PLM specification activities). It allows capturing elements from different levels such as business, functional and/or technical and the entire set of relations that we have to create in the aim of reconstitute the globality of information retrieved in traditional deliverables. The following table shows examples of *the type of elements* we could retrieved in a business/information system referential:

Table 2. Example of business/information system referential

Referential	Level	Type of element	Example
Business	Business	Business process	Design a product, Industrialize a product, Buy a component, etc.
		Business concept	Need, "As designed" product, "As to be built" product, etc.
		Business role	Designer, Industrializer, Buyer
		Semantic conceptual model	N/A
Information System	Functional	Logical object	Technical specification, purchase order, etc.
		Functional role	Technical specification writer, purchase order validator, etc.
		Logical data model	N/A
	Technical	Application	Team Center, SAP, MySQL, etc.
		Applicative object	TC.OT_DOC, TC.OT_PART, etc.
		Workflows	N/A

Note that what it is named here *a business/information system referential* (in the context of this article about PLM) could be renamed *enterprise referential* in the context of another approach such as Information system urbanization or enterprise architecture. In fact, if instead of taking in account PLM subsection of information system, we could considerate all the information systems of the company, we could execute a similar approach.

4.2 What are the Main Functionalities of a Business/Information System Referential?

First and foremost, a business/information system referential has a *model*. It means that elements can only be captured in accordance with this model. In other words, it's model duty to allow defining what type of element to capture in the model and what type of relationship to capture between elements. It is also due to this model that user's need specification could be more oriented to the business level

Then, a business/information system referential allows ensuring element *unicity* (independently of its type). In this manner, even if an element is used at several places in the referential, it's stored like a unique occurrence. For example, the same business role may occur in several business processes. The unicity of the information allows identifying that the business role is engaged into several business processes.

Finally, a business/information system referential allows allocating to a particular element *one or several labels* in one or several languages. In this manner, we are able to capture several designations for a same thing (as it is often observed in the same enterprise) and also in a multilingual way. For example, the same business concept is named differently by R&D and marketing team.

Furthermore, we are able to determine new informations (from existing informations) using *inference mechanism.* For example, interaction between projects is induced by interactions between processes

Also, knowledge referential can be considered like a structured database which can be requested to only extract some elements (depending on the context). For example, we may consider these extractions:

- Compact or detailed representation of business process (with or without interims informations)
- Provide adapted representation for each kind of actors in the different projects of a PLM program
- Publish representations for all actors (synthesis)

4.3 The Ins and Outs of Business/Information System Referential Approach

This kind of approach allows facilitating the communication (less ambiguity or misunderstanding) between various team's actors (program, projects, business), respecting the terminology of each party and find a common term for each thing, ensuring each specification element unicity, global consistency and informations exhaustivity, helping actors to apprehend – without minimizing it – the complexity of a PLM demarch and providing to all a view of the PLM specification (with not more, not fewer informations). However, this approach is time consuming and should be started as soon as the PLM approach is launched.

5 The Ins and Outs of SEAMLESS

5.1 What's SEAMLESS?

In a few words, *SEAMLESS* is *an assisted methodological semantic approach* to *modelize*, *capture* and *restitute* (graphical and/or textual formats) the knowledge domain supporting a range of bordering activities.

What it is called *knowledge domain* is all of the concepts and relationships underlying activities (independently of the type of these activities). SEAMLESS is an *approach* in the sense that it suggests a specific course of action to support its specific activities, in the instance of PLM specification activities within the context of a PLM project.

SEAMLESS is *methodological* in the sense that this approach is rooted in best practices which are stable, invariable and repeatable, which adds formality and rigor to each step within this approach.

SEAMLESS is *semantic*, in the sense that this methodological approach gives fundamental importance to specifying what it covers but also because one of the key components of this approach is the use of ontology (e.g. a formal semantic model with concepts).

SEAMLESS is *assisted*, in the sense that this methodological semantic approach could theoretically be implemented without any particular tool, but in practice relies on a software solution which is specifically adapted to sustain it.

It is a key point to note that SEAMLESS has been initially designed to be applied on a knowledge domain (even far away from PLM); and that's why, in the scope of this section, the primary interest will appear to be focused on SEAMLESS approach and then on the particular *application field*: "SEAMLESS applied to PLM specification activities".

5.2 SEAMLESS Fundamentals

SEAMLESS mission is to propose solutions which allow effectively equipping any controlled activity by PCO Innovation at an industrial level, quickly apprehending a new knowledge domain, capitalizing self-supporting semantic data (not about tools) and restituting all or some parts of knowledge domain by graphical and/or textual manner.

In the context of the missions (consulting or integration) of PCO Innovation, SEAMLESS allows properly understood communication by having the assurance to speak about the same thing (by the use of a semantic model), guarantying the coherence and description homogeneity of the scope (unicity informations), converging to the same terminology (differentiation between terms and concepts) (Roche 2011), describing as much relationships as necessary between different elements - semantic network (Sowa 1991) - and identifying all susceptible elements to have an interest for the current application field (exhaustively).

In order to achieve this, SEAMLESS designs, develops and deploys solutions which allow equipping activities of increasing knowledge, management and necessaries informations restitution to execute a mission. These solutions are respectful of knowledge management and engineering best practices, adaptable to context (because they are comprised of generic software components, re-usables), consistent to web semantic technologies, norms and standards and based on open-source tools (like Jena API and Protégé software).

SEAMLESS approach is an iterative approach which allow specifying knowledge domain model, building knowledge model-driven referential (eg. populate the knowledge base with respect to the specified model) and, then, exploiting them using pre-cabled requests which allow representing and visualizing all or some parts of the knowledge referential.

Methodologies used by SEAMLESS directly report to *knowledge engineering* and *management domains*. They allow specifying semantic model of knowledge domain (textually or graphically expressed as a semi-formal mode) and then *ontologies* (expressed as a formal mode – eg. OWL).

5.3 SEAMLESS Technologies

Tools used by SEAMLESS directly report to *semantic web technologies norms and standards domain* (Hebler, Fisher, Blace, Perez-Lopez and Dean 2009).

Note that, in the matter of equipment, SEAMLESS may be considerate as Excel. It means that it is a generic tool which allows supporting a huge amount of various *application fields*.

Globally, this is a computer solution only constituted of generic standard components (eg. no links with PLM, PLM project, PLM specification activities or even with enterprise architecture) which are customizable by using *ontology*. This kind of application is named *ontology driven application* (Kühne and Atkinson 2003).

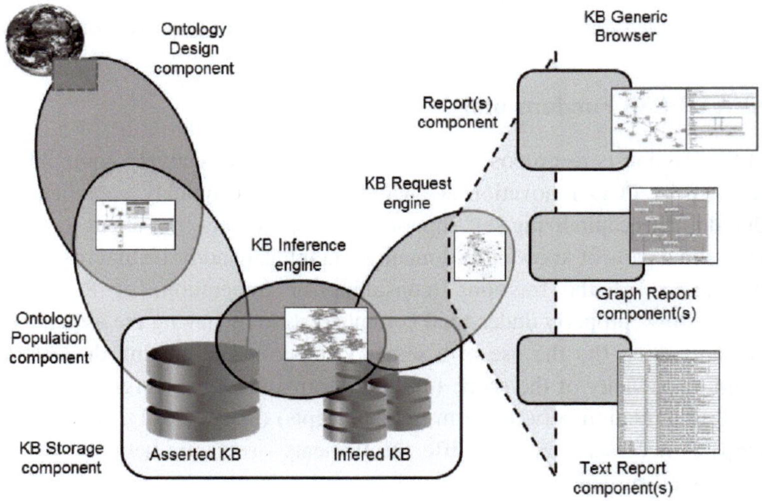

Fig. 1. SEAMLESS functional architecture

The principle of this kind of application is that the ontology is used to drive knowledge base population with individuals (and links between individuals), which allow to guarantee the fact that the knowledge base respect as a whole all the rules (typing rules, optionality, cardinality, etc.) defined in the ontology.

The generic components allow for example:

- Storing ontology, storing individuals, add, read, modify and delete individuals from the knowledge base.
- Requesting the knowledge base using SPARQL, infering new knowledge from existing knowledge using reasoner like Pellet (Sirin and Parsia 2004) or by creating new data with SPARQL, extracting informations about individuals
- Putting these informations in a good shape (graphical and/or textual reports). Note that we basically use MS Office Excel to visualize tabular data, and yEd for graphical data.
- Maintaining the knowledge base (save, export, import, back-up)

These different components are mainly used with an open-source license, but some of these are commercials. All remaining components are developed by PCO Innovation (like web applications, Protégé plug-ins).

6 Conclusion and Perspectives

We have shown that PLM projects are complex and business / information system referential could improve their efficiencies. The key component for reaching this goal is the ontology. Our current ontology is mainly focus on business concerns and information system concerns are just defined by a small set of core concepts. In the future, the ontology should be completed with more accurate concepts in order to cover a whole enterprise architecture scope : business, functional, logical & technical aspects.

Our SEAMLESS approach allows the knowledge base population thanks to an ontology-driven knowledge acquisition process. This is really an added value which allows to easily check the knowledge base coherency and/or completeness and also to produces text and/or graphical reports with a high quality level. But our acquisition module based on Protégé is not really suitable for end-user and not useful for collaborative knowledge acquisition. In the future, we could avoid those pitfalls thanks to a web interface for the knowledge acquisition process.

In short, one complete and relevant enterprise architecture ontology and an ontology-driven web interface for an ontology-driven acquisition process are the 2 mains perspectives for improving our global approach.

References

Allemang, D., Hendler, J.: Semantic Web for the Working Ontologist (2008)

Chappelet, J.-L., Glassey, O.: Comparaison de trois techniques de modélisation de processus: ADONIS, OSSAD et UML (2002)

Charbonnel, G., Dumas, P.: La Méthode OSSAD pour maîtriser les méthodologies de l'information, Tome 1 : principes (1990)

Guarino, N.: Concepts, Attributes, and Arbitrary Relations (1992)

Hebler, J., Fisher, M., Blace, R., Perez-Lopez, A., Dean, M.: Semantic Web Programming. Wiley (2009)

Kühne, T., Atkinson, C.: Model-driven development: a metamodeling foundation (2003)

Le Duigou, J.: Cadre de modélisation pour les systèmes PLM en entreprise étendue (2010)
Miller, E.: State of the PLM Industry. In: Proceedings of the CIMdata PLM – Conference, Dearborn, USA (2003)
Newell, M., Grashina, N.: Amacom, The Project Management Question and Answer Book (2004)
Partridge, C.: Businesss Object: Re-Engineering For Re-Use, 2nd edn (2005)
Praxème Institute, http://www.praxeme.org/index.php?n=Main.HomePage?userlang=en
Roche, C.: Terminologie conceptuelle versus Terminologie textuelle (2011)
Sirin, E., Parsia, B.: Pellet: An owl dl reasoner (2004)
Sommacal, B.: Outillage support à une méthodologie de cartographie sémantique (2013)
Sowa, J.: Principles of Semantic Networks (1991)
Tricot, C.: Cartographie Sémantique: Des connaissances à la carte (2006)
Vandenbussche, P.-Y., Charlet, J.: Méta-modèle général de description de ressources terminologiques et ontologiques (2009)

Future Product Development Cost Prediction Model for Integrated Lifecycle Assessment

Jan Erik Heller, Manuel Löwer, and Jörg Feldhusen

Institute for Engineering Design (ikt)
RWTH Aachen University, Germany
heller@ikt.rwth-aachen.de

Abstract. Beneficial for PLM implementation is the use of data from every product phase for optimising future goods. The objective is to decrease engineering efforts. In order to determine monetary efficiency and its influence on the product's lifecycle, it is essential to anticipate revenues and obtain information about expected costs. Most approaches focus on production expenses as they evoke the major share of costs. Development expenditures are not identifiable reliably. Existing methods premise the availability of accurate values as input. A new approach has been developed, that is based on requirements. Assuming that products with similar indicators cause similar development efforts, databases are set-up to allow for development cost prediction. The model was validated for civil aircraft. A retrospective analysis of existing aircraft and their requirements provided the necessary input. Approach and validation are presented and information about the software demonstrator that was integrated into a lifecycle assessment platform is given.

Keywords: Product Lifecycle Management, Development Process Efficiency, Sustainability Analysis, Lifecycle Tool.

1 Introduction

For new product development projects, it is essential to acquire information about potential revenues as well as anticipated costs in order to predict the economic feasibility of the prospective product. However, the determination of the development costs already at project start is not reliably possible in a grand number of cases. Too many and unquantifiable factors make a forecast inaccurate and lead to mostly unrealistic cost information. Often, predictions are also restricted to an indication of only the expected production and assembly costs neglecting the costs for the product development process and the operating design departments. Numerous methods are known that aim at the estimation of the efforts that are *defined by* engineering departments. FEKIS [1] or XKIS [2] may serve as examples. Admittedly, in many cases, production and assembly efforts exceed those for design and development [3]. Nevertheless, as a result of more and more contested market conditions because of globalisation, companies are increasingly forced to also cut their costs for design and development projects besides the reduction of the manufacturing costs [4]. Existing methods for the determination of the development costs are often designed to determine comparably

S. Fukuda et al. (Eds.): PLM 2014, IFIP AICT 442, pp. 377–386, 2014.

precise values. Therefore, they require correspondingly accurate input values. Some of them incorporate extrapolation techniques, which, for example, implement algorithms to predict the prospective costs based on the number of positions from the bill of materials. Others are based on the precise knowledge of specific parameters of the future product, such as precise masses of individual components. These approaches provide formulas for correlations between those values and the development costs. However, at the beginning of a development project neither the complete bill of materials is known nor are parts designed with their final shape and volume. Thus, the product is not yet sufficiently defined in order to provide the necessary input variables for the existing methods.

In order to still be able to obtain a forecast of the development costs at this stage, despite the prevailing stadium of indeterminateness, it is necessary to develop a method that only relies on few design parameters based on the requirements list.

2 Current Cost Estimation Methods and Tools

Methods for the cost estimation and the effort of product development projects that can be applied in early phases are hardly described in the course of conventional methodologies for systematic engineering design. Typical methods are based on estimates of the cost on the basis of experience from previous projects for the development of similar products. For example, it is common practice to estimate the number of necessary drawings and documents and to map them to a comparable number of so-called document square meters. With appropriate in-house experience for the time needed to create one square meter of documents, the actual effort can be concluded. However, this approach requires detailed knowledge of the product structure and in particular the number and type of components to be developed [5]. Thus, this approach is considered unsuitable for a prediction of the anticipated costs prior to or during the early stages of the development process.

Other approaches consider the number of positions from the bill of materials. This number is then used to correlate with company specific effort factors that allow for a prediction of the typical workload for a single position. Often, characteristic figures like engineering hours per position from the bill of materials are implemented. Similar with the previously presented approaches is the necessity to have knowledge about an elaborated bill of materials in order to be able to estimate accurate cost values.

The software business uses methods to estimate the effort that arises during the development phase itself since several decades. In general, a software product invokes design and development costs. Opposed to that, its actual production typically evokes only costs for the manufacturing of the data storage medium and the package. Boehm introduced the Constructive Cost Model (COCOMO) first in 1981 [6]. Since then it has been constantly extended. However, the idea and the core remain the same: it is based on a prediction of the effort that is estimated based on the physical size of the program. This is mostly implemented as the number of expected source lines of code. Besides that measure, Boehm has included another seventeen parameters that are required to be estimated before the approach can be used for effort prediction. Amongst others, characteristic figures describing the complexity of the product and the similarity with previous projects as well as indicators for the collaborative capabilities of the team are implemented [7]. A transformation of the COCOMO method to the needs of mechanical engineering design processes has already been undertaken by the author [8]. The seventeen factors of the COCOMO II model have been adapted to meet the specific needs of the discipline and combined into a total of seven parameters. For example, the degree of innovation in the sense of the expected novelty of the product is measurable both in software development and in conventional mechanical product development [9]. This parameter could directly be applied. However, some of the seventeen original parameters do not have a direct correspondent. Thus, additional factors like the distribution of the engineering team over several sites have been included. Although many of the required factors are known in advance or their determination often can be achieved regardless of the product to be developed, yet the knowledge of the *size* (which can be considered the counterpart of the source lines of code, for example the number of positions in the bill of materials) of the product is essential. Thus, this method also does not provide itself as useful to adequately predict the development costs in advance with the use of only the design parameters.

Other methods exist, that are specially designed to be used for commercial and military aircraft development. They are characteristically focussing on the determination of lifecycle costs of aircraft. In particular, development costs are addressed as well.

Cost estimation relationships are a typical tool to predict development costs. For example, Raymer suggests a formula for the estimation of necessary engineering hours. Parameters like the mass of the aircraft, the maximum speed and the overall size of the vehicle are used. With company-determined factors, the resulting engineering hours can then be converted to the expected efforts [10]. The drawback is that Raymer's equations are only valid for aircraft with vessel and wings made from aluminium. A simple adaption for current aircraft, being largely made from fibre reinforced plastics and metals, is unmanageable. Moreover, an adaption of the method for industrial sectors other than aerospace seems to be impossible without completely revising the formulas. Another approach that is presented by Raymer tries to anticipate development costs as a fraction of production expenses [10]. However, this approach requires that the costs of production are well known. Typically, assessments are only available towards the end or even only after the development phase so that a prediction of the development costs in the early stages is difficult.

Also specific to aircraft development is the model presented by Roskam. It determines the development costs as a function of weights of individual key components of the aircraft to be designed. For example, it is necessary to know the empty weight of the aircraft as well as individual weights for wheels, brakes, engines, batteries, aviation systems, climate control systems, fire extinguishment systems and the auxiliary power unit before a cost estimate can be conducted [11]. In general, these detailed weight distributions are not known at the beginning of a new development project. As not all products can be considered new product development projects, Raymer's prediction approach cannot be utilised for follow-up designs. He suggests a difficulty factor that has to be incorporated on company-specific discretion [11]. Existing approaches allow for a prediction of the effort for development projects. However, the different methods require precise input values that generally are not accessible prior to or during the early phase. As a consequence, their application is restricted to advanced phases of the development process.

3 Methodology for Product Development Cost Prediction

A new methodology that intends to enable the prediction of development costs has to be conceptualised in order to improve this unsatisfying situation. The methodology has to be usable with only basic design parameters as input values. Another requirement is that the cost prediction must be enabled already during or even prior to the early phases of development process.

3.1 Setup of the Methodology

The methodology is set up by two methods. The first of which is aiming at building up and qualifying a data model that is used to store and supply lifecycle data for the second one. This method is applied when an actual cost prediction is conducted. The second method requires a working and validated data model. Thus, the first method has to be successfully executed at least one time prior to the first prediction runs.

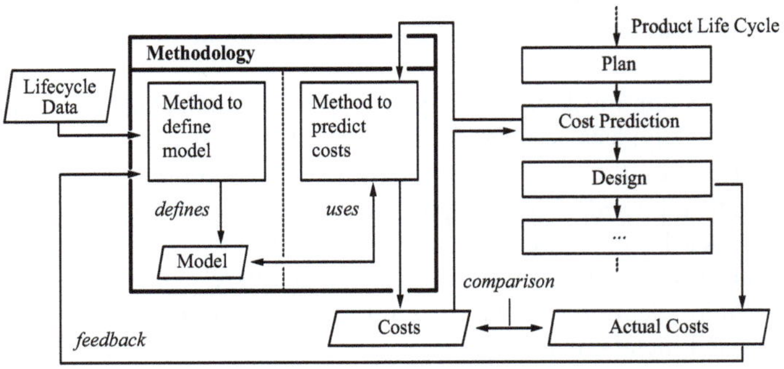

Fig. 1. Structure of the cost prediction methodology

An overview of the structure of the methodology is given in Fig. 1. On the right side the general procedure for a product development process embedded in the product lifecycle is displayed including the coupling point for the cost prediction methodology that is comprised of the two basic methods. Two hypotheses are introduced: the fundamental one postulates that products can be described by physical parameters, for example by their mass or their volume. Moreover, correlations can be deducted between these parameters and the factors that economically determine lifecycle phases (e.g. the development phase). In addition to that, a similarity condition is established postulating products with similar parameters will evoke similar costs. Typically, three different kinds of correlations can be distinguished: economies of scales, statistical models or equation-based mathematical relations [12]. The last one will be implemented here. The second hypothesis is that the cost of the development project depends on the year in which it is performed. Due to technological progress, it is inferable that the development of a product in a specific year evokes less effort, compared to the development of the same product if it had taken place some years earlier.

3.2 Method 1: Lifecycle Data Modelling

Before the second method for the cost prediction can be applied, it is essential to perform the lifecycle data modelling and set up the mathematical relationships between parameters and economic data. The steps that are necessary for this approach can be taken from Fig. 2.

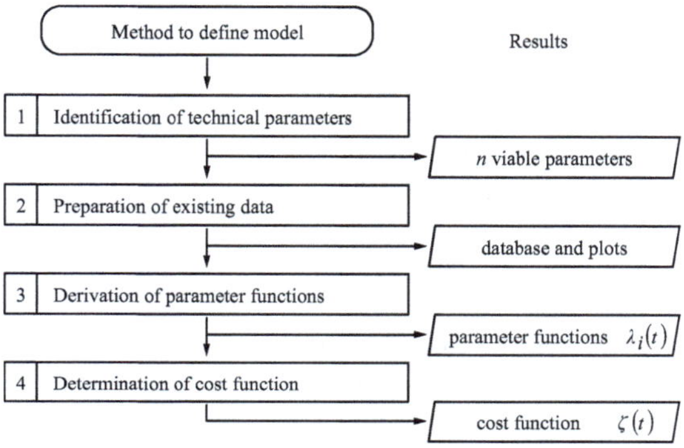

Fig. 2. Method for model qualification: steps and results

The identification of a set of suitable parameters forms the first step of the method. It is important to identify the parameters in a way that they unambiguously define the prospective product. In addition, the parameters must have a substantial influence on the development costs. The colour of a product is not as useful as the allowed mass. In most cases, colour does only have a low influence on the development costs.

Forming combinations of several single parameters is helpful in order to achieve indicators of a higher quality. Exemplarily, the length of the landing field that is necessary for an aircraft already is a good indicator for the effort. Vehicles that can operate with a short landing field generally are more difficult to develop. But, if the landing field length is divided by the maximum weight of the aircraft, the effect of the indicator is increased as it is more difficult to develop a vehicle that has a huge weight and operates with a short landing field length at the same time. Concluding, it is possible to choose any design parameter and any combination of them for the modelling step. However, the performance and the quality of the model are significantly increased with more meaningful parameters. The method analyses data ranging from lifecycles of already existing products and its predecessors in addition to data that is incorporated from similar competitor products. Thus, a sufficient amount of data has to be researched, estimated and prepared for the qualification of the model, before it is ready to be used by the second method. The second step of the method therefore addresses the preparation of data. The model has to be fed with characteristic values for the identified parameters from already conducted development projects. For all parameters that have been selected values have to be retrieved and put in context with temporal information, i.e. the year, in which the original development project has taken place. After that, the parameter functions $\lambda_i(t)$ can be established for every identified parameter in the third step. This is achieved with the help of parameter value charts. An example is given in Fig. 3. The mathematical function is conceived by entering all pairs of parameter values and the corresponding year into the chart. Then, the maxima or minima for a defined time period are computed depending on the industrial sector or the type of the product. The length of the period can be chosen individually based on the typical duration of development projects in the industrial sector under consideration.

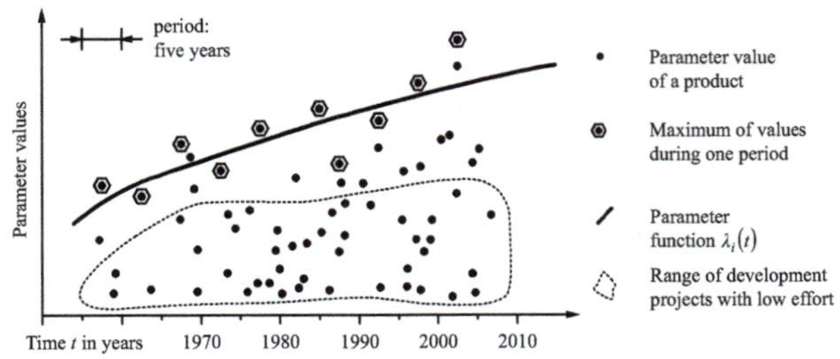

Fig. 3. Exemplary parameter value chart with parameter value function

For the example in Fig. 3, the maxima approach has been chosen. Thus, higher development costs are related to a higher parameter value. A line of best fit is derived and referred to as the parameter function λ. This parameter function can be interpreted as the average border of the technological progress of the respective parameters in the specific year in case enough and representative development projects are included in the chart. As a consequence, there are no other development projects surpassing this border significantly. For every identified parameter this step has to be performed. Finally, the fourth step serves to derive the mathematical representation of the development cost function. Similar to the parameter functions the cost function ζ is derived based on the same data. Likewise, a chart is conceived that contains all pairs of cost values and related years. A linear regression curve is estimated with the maxima. In order to allow for comparisons between the different results, all cost values have to be harmonised regarding inflation. The results of the first method are a number of parameter functions and the corresponding cost function with the according charts.

3.3 Method 2: Development Cost Prediction

After the successful execution of the first method, the model is qualified with lifecycle data of existing development projects. The second method which is used for the actual prediction of the effort for the development of future products can be performed. The required steps and the related results are given in Fig. 4. During the first step, the values of the design parameters for the new product have to be identified. These values are the key input for the method. The year in which the design project is undertaken is required as well. Typically, it is the current year. However, the method is capable of predicting effort for projects in the past as well as in the future, as long as the year value remains inside the specified system boundaries. The estimation of key figures based on the parameters is conducted in the second step. Key figures are implemented in order to investigate similarities between existing data points and the current development. The similarity indicators ξ_i are calculated dividing the value Λ_i of the design parameter by the value of the corresponding parameter value function λ_i at the defined time. Each key figure locates the prospective product in relation to a theoretical product that resides on the border of the technological progress at a given time t. An innovation number φ is calculated in the third step. In the current implementation, φ is determined by the arithmetical average of all key figures ξ_i.

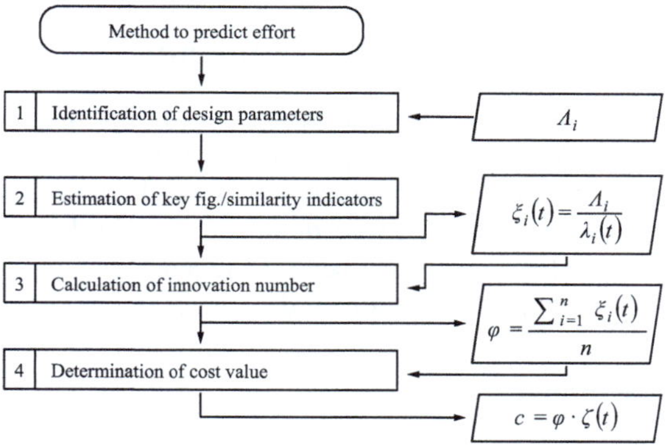

Fig. 4. Method for effort prediction: steps and results

However, it is possible to train the model with a weighted emphasis on specific indicators if this enables a model of higher quality. The decision to opt for a weighted mean has to be carried out within the first method. The weighted mean can be advantageous compared to the arithmetic mean, in case the identified design parameters are describing similar technological difficulties. In this case, the forming of groups of similarity indicators that are weakened by appropriate weighting factors can be beneficial in order to maintain a balanced representation of the prospective product. The fourth step of the method for the prediction of the effort is defined by the determination of the actual cost value for the prospective development project. By multiplying the dimensionless innovation number φ with the year-dependent value of the cost function of the model ζ, the cost value can be predicted.

3.4 Product Lifecycle Engineering Platform Integration

Typically, within engineering departments, the application of this methodology is not limited to a *prediction* of product development costs. Apparently, the majority of products for which the prediction has been performed will be realised after the design phase is completed. It is possible to then effectively determine the actual costs and compare them with the initially predicted costs. This brings with it two advantages: the feedback that is collected on this way can be used to verify if the model that has been set up with the first method is capable of reliable cost predictions. In addition to that, the feedback information can also be used to add new data points to the parameter value and cost charts aiming at a further refinement of the data base. With an increasing amount and extensiveness of interpolation points, the predictions gain accuracy. Fig. 1 also shows the established verification and feedback loops. When it is intended to permanently integrate this methodology in the product emergence process of a business it is necessary to continuously include new data points. Else the model would be out-of-date and thus unable to predict current project costs accurately.

A lifecycle assessment project whose goal was the investigation of the complete lifecycle of civil aircraft formed the framework for the methodology presented here [13]. In the course of the project, a lifecycle engineering platform has been implemented that allows for an assessment of different preliminary aircraft designs and their impacts on production, operation and end-of-life phases.

4 Civil Aircraft Design and Development

Section 3 presented a model for the cost prediction of future products with a surrounding methodology. A prototypical application of both model and methodology has been undertaken as a part of design processes for civil aircraft that have a capacity of more than 100 passengers. A software demonstrator has been conceptualised to support data handling and set up. It has been designed to interact with the lifecycle engineering and assessment platform addressed in the previous section.

4.1 Application Example

Conventionally, the key concept requirements in preliminary aircraft design are defined and referred to as TLAR (Top Level Aircraft Requirements) [14]. In general, the TLAR are defined prior to the beginning of the actual design and development phase. For aircraft that are available on the market at present, the parameters constituting the TLAR can be determined from literature and manuals of manufacturers. Thus, it can be made sure that a set of suitable data is available. In the application example, the design parameters that are used for the model in method 1 have been taken from the set of TLAR. However, an adequate set of design parameters had to be extracted from the list of all top level requirements.

Table 1. Overview of implemented parameter values and parameter functions

Parameter	Description	TLAR
λ_1, Λ_1 and ξ_1	Max. Takeoff Weight	MTOW
λ_2, Λ_2 and ξ_2	Max. Landing Weight / Landing Field Length	MLW / LFL
λ_3, Λ_3 and ξ_3	Number of seats · Range	Seats · R
λ_4, Λ_4 and ξ_4	Number of seats / Operating Weight Empty	Seats / OWE
λ_5, Λ_5 and ξ_5	Max. Payload · Range / Sea Level Static Thrust	Max. Payload · R / SLST

After that, each parameter and every group of parameters had to be tested regarding the applicability for the intended cost prediction. The parameters that have been chosen for the implementation are displayed in Tab. 1. An exemplary discussion demonstrates the impacts: the maximum take-off weight has a huge impact on the costs, as expected. But to only rely on this design parameter did not produce satisfying prediction results. Although key factors in the aerospace sector are masses, other parameters do have significant impact on the development costs as well. Thus, more parameters are necessary in order to express the technical feasibility by the parameter value functions. Other considered design parameters did not have significant or unambiguous impact on the development costs at all. The allowed noise emission of an aircraft has a notable effect on the design of the geometry of the wings and the engines. But with the available data no feasible parameter function could be conceived.

Eventually, five parameters have been identified which have a notable impact on development costs. Both single parameters and combinations of several values have been implemented in a software demonstrator. Fig. 5 displays the prototype that has been established with Excel. In addition, an xml interface was set up for the connection with the existing lifecycle assessment platform [15].

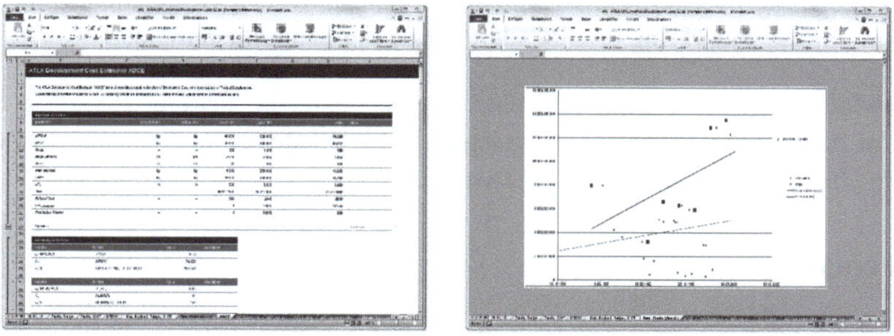

Fig. 5. Software demonstrator implementing the methodology with cost function chart

4.2 Discussion and Comparison

Actual aircraft development projects have been used for a verification of the method. The set of projects included in the verification process contained both projects being used for the model qualification and projects that have been left out on purpose. In our tests, the average deviation between predicted and actual costs was not exceeding 22 %. Thus, the initially postulated hypotheses can be considered true.

The advantages of the presented approach clearly can be found in the applicability during the early stages of the design process. Admittedly, the accuracy cannot be compared with actual cost calculation methods that are applied in later phases when cost defining components are already agreed upon and fixed. Nevertheless, in order to obtain a first impression of the expected efforts, the methodology has proven valuable. Its disadvantage is the dependency on the precisely established model that has to be complete in a sense of existing development project data. In addition, the model is sensitive regarding break through changes in the technological feasibility that would change the parameter value functions significantly. Comparison with existing methods is given in the second section of this paper. Similar approaches that address aircraft design can be found in [10, 11]. However, they cannot be easily adapted to the underlying boundary condition of this research that set out for only incorporating the top level requirements into the estimation.

5 Conclusion and Prospects

This paper introduced one approach to predict development efforts and expenses. The presented methodology relies only on a small number of technical requirements that are already defined at or before the start of the development project. Because of its structure which separates data model and prediction method, the methodology is applicable in many industrial sectors. Lifecycle assessment data from similar products is incorporated to allow for a prediction of the lifecycle impacts for future products. In order to validate the methodology, investigations for the civil aircraft sector have been presented. In addition to that, a software demonstrator that enables the integration of the predicted data into a lifecycle engineering platform has been addressed.

Further research will be conducted regarding the generalisation of its application. The investigations will include the research for suitable sets of design parameters being largely valid for other industrial sectors. Moreover, it is intended to extend the validation of the underlying methods with other application examples.

Acknowledgments. The authors would like to thank the Federal Republic of Germany for funding the project "Air Transport Vehicle Life Cycle Analysis" through the German Universities Excellence Initiative.

References

1. Wolfram, M.: Feature-basiertes Konstruieren und Kalkulieren. Hanser, München (1994)
2. Reischl, C.: Simul. von Produktkosten in der Entwicklungsphase. Diss. TU München (2001)
3. Ehrlenspiel, K., Kiewert, A., Lindemann, U.: Kostengünstig Entwickeln und Konstruieren: Kostenmanagement bei der integrierten Produktentwicklung. Springer, Berlin (2007)
4. Feldhusen, J., et al.: Methode zur Produktivitätsmessung für Entw. und Konstr. Konstruktion, pp. 49–54 (2002)
5. Hichert, R.: Praktische Ansätze zur Termin-, Kapazitäts- und Kostenplanung in Entwicklung u. Konstruktion. In: Moll, H.H. (ed.) RKW-Handbuch Forschung, Entw. Schmidt, Berlin (1976)
6. Boehm, B.: Software Engineering Economics. Prentice-Hall, Englewood Cliffs (1981)
7. Boehm, B., Abts, C., et al.: Software Cost Estimation with COCOMO II. Prentice Hall (2000)
8. Feldhusen, J., et al.: Progn. des Entwicklungsaufwands: Adaption des COCOMO Modells auf die Produktentwicklung. In: Brökel, K., et al. (eds.) Proceedings KT 2010. docupoint (2010)
9. Hauschild, J., Schlaak, T.: Zur Messung des Innovationsgrades neuartiger Produkte. Zeit-schrift für Betriebswirtschaft 71 (2001)
10. Raymer, D.: Aircraft Design: A Conceptual Approach, 4th edn. AIAA Education Series. American Institute of Aeronautics and Astronautics, Reston (2006)
11. Roskam, J.: Airplane Design: Airplane Cost Estimation, Ottawa, vol. 8 (1990)
12. Duverlie, P., Castelain, J.M.: Cost Estimation During Design Step. Parametric Method versus Case Based Reasoning Method. Intl. J. Adv. Manuf. Technol. (15), 895–906 (1999)
13. Franz, K., Ewert, A., et al.: Interdisziplinäre Bewertungsplattform zur Lebenszyklusanalyse im Flugzeugvorentwurf. In: Proceedings of DLRK 2013 Stuttgart (2013)
14. Franz, K., Hörnschemeyer, R., et al.: Life Cycle Engineering in Preliminary Aircraft Design. In: Dornfeld, D.A., Linke, B.S. (eds.) Leveraging Technology for a Sustainable World: Proc. of the 19th CIRP Conf. on Life Cycle Eng., pp. 473–478. Springer, Heidelberg (2012)
15. Risse, K., et al.: An Integrated Environment for Preliminary Aircraft Design and Optimization. In: 53rd AIAA/ASME/ASCE/AHS/ASC Conference (2012)

Product Data Management – Defining the Used Terms

Merja Huhtala, Mika Lohtander, and Juha Varis

Lappeenranta University of Technology, LUT School of Technology,
LUT Mechanical Engineering, Lappeenranta, Finland
{merja.huhtala,mika.lohtander,juha.varis}@lut.fi

Abstract. The Product Data Management (PDM) system and its associated terminology have changed over the years. Product Lifecycle Management (PLM) has become the predominant system and tends to overshadow PDM. However, PDM remains relevant and is a system commonly used by design engineers; mainly as a storage place for drawings and a place where drawings can be found for further editing.

To obtain full benefit from the PDM/PLM systems, precise definitions are required. Without such definitions, the systems cannot function as they should and they cannot be used optimally. Furthermore, shortcomings in definitions may lead to a situation where the engineering community is unaware of the kind of help the systems can offer.

The main focus of this conference paper is definition of some of the terms inherent to PDM/PLM systems and their data.

Keywords: Product Data Management, PDM, data, product data.

1 Introduction

Industrial production has increased over the years, especially in China. Competition on global markets is intense and this has led to a situation where companies try to reduce design and manufacturing costs by moving such activities to low-cost countries. Figure 1 presents data for a number of different countries and shows how their industrial production has increased over the last decade. When looking at the situation from Finland's point of view, it can be seen that production, as elsewhere in the Euro area, has not increased greatly. The trend in Finland seems to be to that production and design are being moved to low-cost countries; especially to China, Korea and India. [1]

Increasingly competitive markets are putting pressure on engineering work: designs have to be completed in relatively short time periods. Robinson [3] recently researched time usage in the work of design engineers. He compared the latest results with earlier findings and made a surprising observation: time usage of design engineers remains the same as 20 years earlier. Technical tools have developed and new tools have become available to facilitate the work of design engineers, but neverthe-

S. Fukuda et al. (Eds.): PLM 2014, IFIP AICT 442, pp. 387–396, 2014.

less most of design engineers' time is taken up with something other than technical work. Figure 2 presents how design engineers' time is allocated. [3]

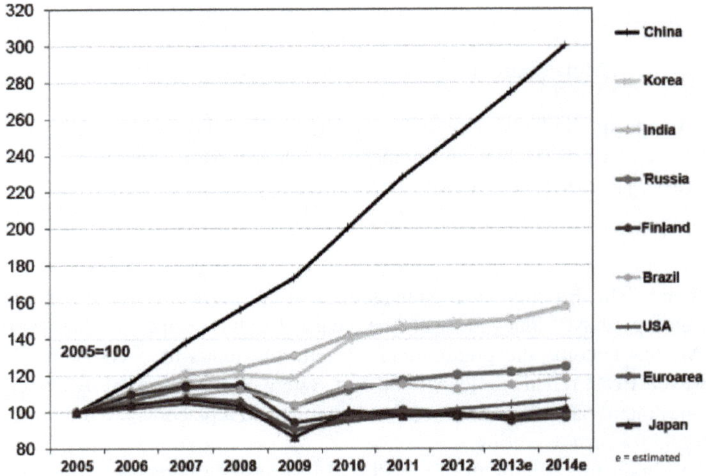

Fig. 1. Industrial production development in different countries [2]

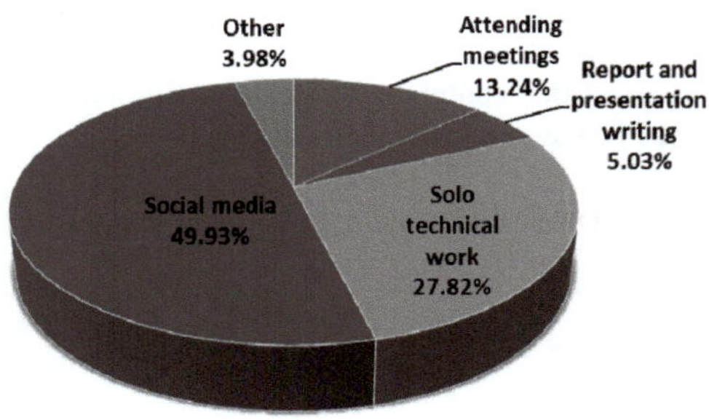

Fig. 2. Engineers' time consumptions [3]

The nature of modern markets and increased emphasis on product development means that companies can ill afford ineffective design practices, and effective data management is critically important. Product Data Management (PDM) is a system that can help companies remain competitive in rapidly changing markets and that can make engineers use time more effectively.

2 Method

This conference paper was written as part of the Finnish Metals and Engineering Competence Cluster (FIMECC)'s MANU P3 Product Knowledge Management in Global Networks (ProMaGNet) –project. During the ProMaGNet project interviews were done in different Finnish industrial companies. It was clearly noticed that the definition of PDM was different in every company: generally, PDM was handled either as separately PDM or as an element of Product Lifecycle Management (PLM). Often, PDM was seen only as a design engineering tool whereas PLM was seen as a lifecycle tool for the company as a whole. Without a clear definition of the terms, use of these two systems cannot be effective.

This paper is based on study of how to determine terms associated with PDM. The definitions are based on literature review and relevant standards. Three main standards [4-6] were found and used alongside information published in journal articles and books.

3 Introduction to PDM System

The Product Data Management system was created in the 1980s. Its main purpose was to help design engineers save time and get products faster to the production stage. In the first stages of PDM, it only served design engineers by being a storage place for drawings: drawings were easy to find and subsequent changes to drawings easier to handle. These features helped reduce engineering costs. In the 1990s most data became electronic and the PDM system spurred companies to realize the importance of data handling. [7-8] Concerns about product development and time usage of design engineers (Fig. 1 and Fig 2.) led to pressure to use the PDM system more effectively. However, the use of this system did not affect the time spent on technical work as much as it should have.

Documentation in industrial design should start from the very beginning of the design process. The Aberdeen Group [9] examined the point where companies' documentation is started. In most cases, documentation started when a product concept was initiated (60%) and when a conceptual product structure was developed (22%). However, some companies started the documentation after the BOM (Bill of Materials) was developed or finalized. It can be seen that companies have understood the significance of documentation; without documentation drawings may go missing, which may cause the design process to take more time. Mainly because designs are not final in the first draft, iterative changes to the drawings have to be possible. [9] In such iterative processes, the flexibility of the systems and subsystems is crucial for improved production and design. By utilizing the PDM system companies can make sure that designs are available to those who may need them; this is a stage of documentation flexibility. Workflow and product data can be managed more effectively. [10]

The amount of used product data in companies has grown in recent years; consequently, storage capacity has also increased. For example, in 2000 global disk storage per person (GDSP) was 472 MB and in 2008 it was over 400% greater, 2000 MB. [11] Production patterns have also changed: it is now common that products have many different variants. To handle these variants and associated changes to designs, it is crucial that data handling is fast. It is also important that the information is available for many years: many products are long-lasting and products may need spare parts and maintenance long after the original design was made. [10]

In light of developments in industrial production, design engineers' time usage, documentation starting point and disk storage, it is important that the PDM system works as it should. PDM has certain key functions, which are shown in Figure 3. If the system works as it should, the benefits accruing from the system are, according to [10] and [12-15]: the data can be better controlled; people have easy access to data; the latest versions of drawings are always available and change management thus easier to handle; all data are stored in one safe place; and the information is available in an easily accessible format (e. g. PDF) to whomever may need it.

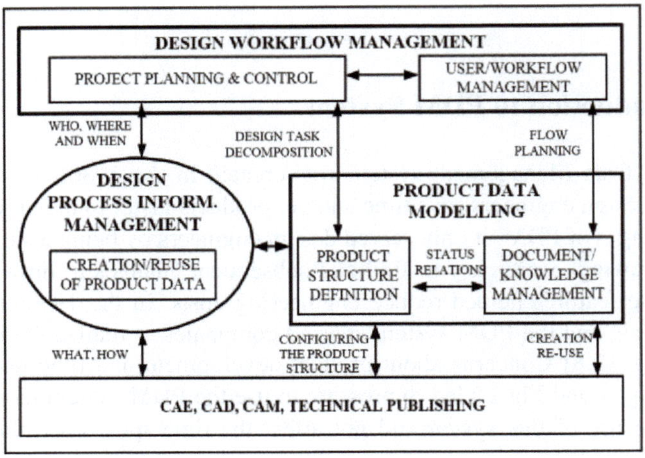

Fig. 3. Key functions of PDM [15]

All people in the company have to be aware of the PDM system, from those involved in manufacturing to top managers. For this reason, the PDM system has to be a part of the business strategy of the company. PDM may be an individual system but it has to be integrated with other systems, e.g. design software and software used on the manufacturing plant floor and in purchasing operations. PDM has to be able to link all the systems together [10] but before the actual integration and the purchase of a system it has to be clear what kind of system is going to be purchased and what are the definitions of the system and its related terms.

4 Definitions of Used Terms

In the authors' opinion the most important terms in the context of this discussion are: data, product data and product data management. Firstly, to make sure that the PDM system works as it should it has to be clear what PDM actually is and what it stands for. Secondly, if the terms data and product data are unclear, it may mean that information entered into the system is not valid. Clearly, without valid information it may not be possible to manufacture the part or product.

4.1 Data – The Definition

According to SFS-ISO standard 16792 [6] the definition for data is "information represented in a formal manner suitable for communication, interpretation or processing by human beings or computers". The terms *data* and *document* are normally used as synonyms. The definition for document, according to SFS-EN ISO standard 11442:en [5], is a "fixed and structured amount of information that can be managed and interchanged as a unit between users and systems".

Other sources define the term data differently and the definition of data can be different at different stages of the product, i.e. during different parts of its lifecycle. The prime function of data is to define the product: defined properties can be physical and/or functional properties. The data has informational value through its images and descriptions of its characteristics. The data can be lifecycle data: data between the starting point (of designing) and the end point (when the product is recycled). And the data can be handled as meta data, i.e. information about who has produced the data and where the data is located. [16]

Companies need information to enable operations, and companies' products include information that enables them to be manufactured. This information is data and includes, for example, information about the materials used and functionality of a product. Product data also include information about suppliers and vendors and should include information that has value for customers. Thus, the data comprise different types of information and this information together can be called master data. [17] It should be borne in mind that not only the product is important for the company, the data is also important. According to [18] the data should be treated like a product. When treating data as a product, Stark [10] claims: "The definition of the product does not have to be identical at all stages, but it does have to be consistent."

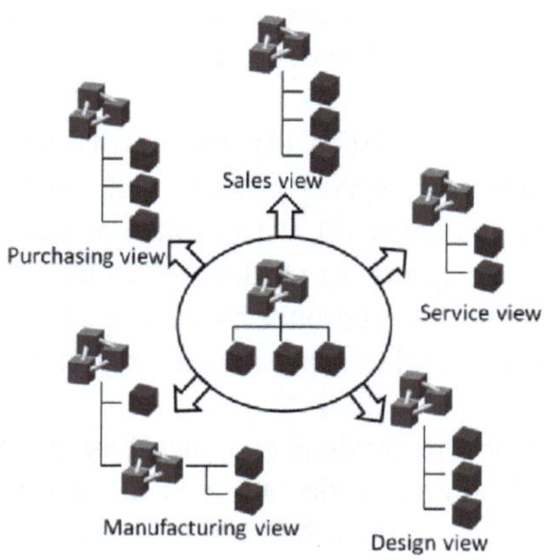

Fig. 4. Different points of view of the data (and the product) [19]

Although some standards attempt to define the term, there is no widely accepted definition of data that is considered valid throughout all areas of engineering and definitions given by design engineers, people involved in purchasing and those in manufacturing all differ. Not only do the individuals give different definitions, different design programs also handle and understand the word differently. [10] This situation is described in Figure 4; the different units in a company see the definition of data differently, which means that also the product is seen differently [19].

4.2 Product Data – The Definition

When starting to define the term *Product Data*, the product should first be defined. It can be seen from Figure 4 that the product can be seen differently in different departments within a company. Generally, the terms part and product are taken as meaning the same thing. But according to [20], these two terms are different, although related. A part is an already manufactured object or soon going to be manufactured. While a product is an object which has been already sold, or is going to be sold soon. However, standard SFS-EN ISO 10303-210:en [4] gives the definition for a part as: "a product with operational functionality that is expected to be used as a component of one or more assembled products".

According to Rueckel et al. [21], a product description can include: CAD-models, simulation models, FEM structures, calculation results, CAD-drawings, object list, task schedules, NC-programs, test plans, assembly instructions, QA-documents et cetera. By these different classifications the product can be fully described. It should be noticed that these are most common classifications and in every product all of these classifications may not exist. But the main key is that every product has to have some kind of information which describes the product so it can be identified and manufactured. [21]

The simplest definition for product data is given by Kropsu-Vehkapera [22]: product data is data that is related to the product. Product data can be divided to three different sectors: product description, lifecycle data and meta data. All these sectors are related to each other, e.g. lifecycle data does not exist if there is no description for the product. [22]

Standard SFS-EN ISO 10303-210:en [4] has its own definition for product data: "all data that is used to describe aspects of a product." But according to Stark [10]; "The term 'product data' includes all data related both to a product and to the processes that are used to design it, to produce it, to use it and to support it." This means that product data is not created only by designing engineers, all units that are somehow connected to the manufacturing and selling of the product create product data. [10]

Specifications depend on the product and therefore the product data depend on these specifications. The product includes not only the physical product itself but also the product specifications and product definition. These three aspects together create the product data. Process planning and materials are included in the data for the product definition, and data for the actual product describe the object physically (measurements) and from the point of view of the design process (e.g. the design date) [20] A product data model is needed to define the term product data. [23]

4.3 Product Data Management (PDM) – The definition

According to Burden [12]: "PDM is often defined differently by different industries and consequently it can be a rather difficult and elusive entity to grasp, implement, and measure." The main purpose of PDM is to handle product-related data, and this has led to a situation where the system can be given different names, such as Engineering Document Management, Technical Information Management etc. However, the system essentially concentrates on managing the data. The PDM system can be seen as a supporting tool for PLM. On the other hand, the PDM can be seen as a part of PLM. The reason why these two terms have become confused is not clear; from the point of view of some researchers, over the years PDM has grown to be PLM. [24-26]

Figure 5 illustrates how the PDM system is linked to PLM. It can be seen that PDM supports the PLM concept and without PDM the PLM system cannot work properly. [15] According to Könst et al. [11] the definition for PDM is "a business wide methodology and strategy which makes the appropriate product-related and process-related information accessible to the appropriate people at the appropriate stage in the product lifecycle."

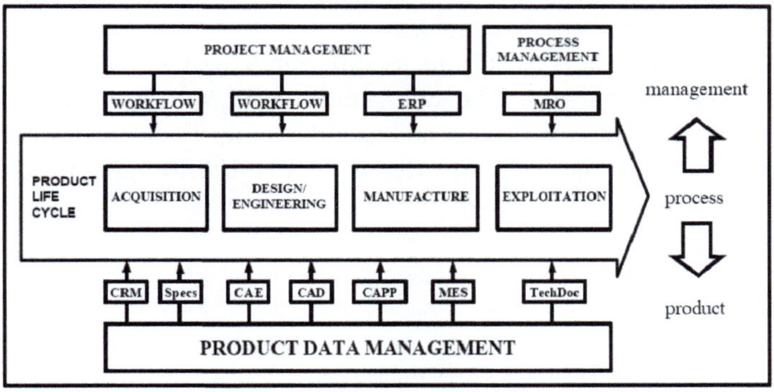

Fig. 5. Position of PDM system according to PLM [15]

The PDM system can also be seen as an individual system, as in Bergsjö et al. [27] and Chan and Yu [28]. Although the system is separate it still helps to organize co-operation between different units in the company. Although PDM is its own application, Stark [10] states that PDM is always part of PLM. PLM could not work without PDM and the main task of PDM is to manage information during the product lifecycle. At the same time, PDM improves productivity: workflow in the company can be fully controlled. [10]

As mentioned earlier, the data should be available to all who may need it. Integration between PDM systems and different CAD software makes this possible. Effective integration is the only way to fully control the information created. [21] Philpotts [29] points out that companies have many different kinds of management systems and claims that the PDM is a solution to integrate these systems together. All the information is in electronic format and safe in one place, and the data can be revised, used as a basis for new products, and viewed to get more information about the product. However, PDM is not just about handling data; PDM is a tool for communication and notification between system users. [29]

5 Conclusions

Based on the above discussion, the following conclusions can be drawn. Definitions for the terms vary greatly and depend on the source. Data can be handled as a product, but a common factor found in the literature is that it is important to handle data correctly within the company. Data is related to the product and products are parts that companies produce to get profit. Co-operation inside the company is crucial: the product should include data that is valid for each department such that they can all do their work on time and in an effective way. Data should thus not be from one point of view (e. g. from design engineers' point of view) alone: the main purpose of the data is to describe the product.

The system itself that handles the data is PDM. PDM, on the other hand, is the core of PLM. These two systems mainly occur together and which term should be used depends mainly on the lifecycle stage of the product. In the design stage engineers tend to use the PDM system, but after manufacturing of the product employees talk about PLM. However the main purpose of PDM/PLM is to store data and keep it available even for decades. The system should integrate all programs in the company, including those related with subcontractors.

The PDM/PLM system is used in many different ways and the system is different in every company. But to get full benefit from PDM/PLM, it is crucial that the terms are defined clearly: what is important and useful data for the company, what actually is product data, and last but not least, what is the PDM/PLM system and how should it be used.

References

1. The Federation of Finnish Technology Industries, `http://www.teknologiateollisuus.fi/file/7250/jpkv07af_Teollisuustuotannonkehitysvuosittain.pdf.html`
2. The Federation of Finnish Technology Industries, `http://www.teknologiateollisuus.fi/file/2764/Metallien_hintoja.pdf.html`
3. Robinson, M.A.: How design engineers spend their time: Job content and task satisfaction. Design Studies 33, 391–425 (2012)
4. SFS-EN ISO 10303-210:en: Industrial automation systems and integration. Product data representation and exchange. Part 210: Application protocol: Electronic assembly, interconnection, and packaging design (ISO 10303-210:2001). European Committee for Standardization (CEN), Brussels (2003)
5. SFS-EN ISO 11442:en: Technical product documentation- Document management (ISO 11442:2006). European Committee for Standardization (CEN), Brussels (2006)
6. SFS-ISO 16792: Technical product documentation - digital product definition data practices. Finnish Standards Association (SFS), Helsinki (2010)
7. Ahmed, Z., Gerhard, D.: Contributions of PDM Systems in Organizational Technical Data Management. In: The First IEEE International Conference on Computer, Control & Communication. IEEE Press (2007)

8. Borrmann, A., Schorr, M., Obergriesser, M., Ji, J., Wu, I.-C., Günthner, W., Euringer, T., Rank, E.: Using Product Data Management Systems for Civil Engineering Projects – Potentials and Obstacles. In: Caldas, C.H., O'Brien, W.J. (eds.) Proceedings of the 2009 ASCE International Workshop on Computing in Civil Engineering, EUROSPAN, London (2009)
9. The Aberdeen Group, http://www.plm.automation.siemens.com/zh_cn/Images/Aberdeen__Enabling_Product_Innovation__The_Roles_of_ERP_and_PLM_in_the_Product_Lifecycle_05-12-01_tcm78-4641.pdf
10. Stark, J.: Product Lifecycle Management – 21st Century Paradigm for Product Realisation. Springer-Verlag London Limited, USA (2005)
11. Könst, J.S., La Fontaine, J., Hoogeboom, M., Wilkinson, J.: Product Data Management – A Strategic Perspective. Maj Engineering Publishing, Netherland (2009)
12. Burden, R.: PDM: product data management: a guide to PLM: product lifecycle management. Resource Publishing (2003)
13. Liu, D.T., Xu, X.W.: A review of web-based product data management systems. Computers in Industry 44, 251–262 (2001)
14. Sendler, U., Wawer, V.: CAD and PDM: optimizing Processes by Integrating Them. Hanser Publications, München (2008)
15. Storga, M., Pavlic, D., Marjanovic, D.: Reducing design development cycle by data management within the design office. In: International Conference on Engineering Design, ICED 2001 (2001)
16. Saaksvuori, A., Immonen, A.: Product Lifecycle Management. Springer, Heidelberg (2005)
17. Loshin, D.: Master Data Management. Elsevier, United States (2009)
18. Wang, R.Y., Lee, Y.W., Pipino, L.L., Strong, D.M.: Manage Your Information as a Product. Sloan Management Review 39, 95–105 (1998)
19. Kemppainen, T., Kropsu-Vehkaperä, H., Haapasalo, H.: Introduction Product Data Ownership Network. University of Oulu: Research Reports in Department of Industrial Engineering and Management (2011)
20. McKay, A., Bloor, M.S., de Pennington, A.: A Framework for Product Data. IEEE Transactions on Knowledge and Data Engineering 8, 825–838 (1996)
21. Rueckel, V., Koch, A., Feldmann, K., Meerkamm, H.: Process Data Management for the Shortening of the Whole Product Creation Process. In: Shen, W.-m., Chao, K.-M., Lin, Z., Barthès, J.-P.A., James, A. (eds.) CSCWD 2005. LNCS, vol. 3865, pp. 616–625. Springer, Heidelberg (2006)
22. Kropsu-Vehkaperä, H.: Product structure and lifecycle management: A systematic literature review. In: Haapasalo, H., Kropsu-Vehkaperä, H. (eds.) The 3rd Nordic Innovation Research Conference - NIR 2008 – IEM Arctic Workshop. Oulu University press, Oulu (2009)
23. Lanz, M., Kallela, T., Järvenpää, E., Tuokko, R.: Ontologies as an Interface between Different Design Support Systems. In: Dimitrov, D.P., Mladenov, V., Jordanova, S., Mastorakis, N. (eds.) Proceedings of the 9th WSEAS International Conference on Neural Networks, Bulgaria, pp. 202–207 (2008)
24. Abramovici, M., Gerhard, D., Langenberg, L.: Application of PDM technology for Product Life Cycle Management. In: Krause, F.-L., Selinger, G. (eds.) Life Cycle Networks: Proceedings of the 4th CIRP International Seminar on Life Cycle Engineering, pp. 17–31. Springer, Berlin (1997)
25. COE, http://www.coe.org/newsnet/feb04/industry.cfm
26. Cao, H., Folan, P.: Product life cycle: the evolution of a paradigm and literature review from 1950-2009. Production Planning & Control 23, 641–662 (2012)

27. Bergsjö, D., Malmqvist, J., Ström, M.: Architectures for mechatronic product data integration in PLM systems. In: Marjanovic, D. (ed.) International Design Conference – Design, Croatia, pp. 1065–1076 (2006)
28. Chan, E., Yu, K.M.: A concurrency control model for PDM. Computers in Industry 58, 823–831 (2007)
29. Philpotts, M.: An introduction to the concepts, benefits and terminology of product data management. Industrial Management & Data Systems 96, 11–17 (1996)

Assessing the Role of Knowledge Management in the New Product Development Process: An Empirical Study

Romeo Bandinelli[1], Elisa d'Avolio[1], Monica Rossi[2], Sergio Terzi[3], and Rinaldo Rinaldi[1]

[1] Department of Industrial Engineering, University of Florence, Florence, Italy
{romeo.bandinelli,elisa.davolio,rinaldo.rinaldi}@unifi.it
[2] Department of Management Engineering, Politecnico di Milano, Milan, Italy
monica.rossi@polimi.it
[3] Department of Industrial Engineering, University of Bergamo, Bergamo, Italy
sergio.terzi@unibg.it

Abstract. The actual competitive context is stressing the importance of knowledge management (KM) enhancing organizational performance through the creation, sharing and reuse of knowledge.

The purpose of the present study is to empirically explore the role of KM in the enhancement of new product development (NPD) process within a set of companies with at least a R&D department located in Italy. The authors formulated a conceptual research model, including the relation between KM, NPD performance and strategies, that has been validated through statistical analyses. The outcomes confirm the positive relation between KM maturity and NPD performance in the Electrical sector. Moreover, the identification of Critical Success Factors (CSFs), is influenced by KM techniques adopted, revealing the impact of KM on NPD strategies. Finally the achievement of good NPD performances, such as the ease to fill out reports and projects, appears related to appropriate NPD strategies.

Keywords: Knowledge Management (KM), New Product Development (NPD), New Product Development performance, New Product Development strategies.

1 Introduction

Nowadays knowledge management (KM) is becoming a strategic resource to be challenging in the present competitive context. The increasing amount of data and information to manage in different industries has led to the fact that leveraging knowledge in an organization can sustain its long term-term competitive advantage [1].

Moreover, enterprises have to innovate their products in order to survive in this complex market, choosing appropriate new product development (NPD) strategies and measuring the performances. Reducing the time to develop new products and decreasing time-to-market constitute strategic business goals.

S. Fukuda et al. (Eds.): PLM 2014, IFIP AICT 442, pp. 397–406, 2014.

Knowledge management competencies are fundamental to innovation, enabling it to survive competitively and to grow [2]. The potential benefits of systematic knowledge diffusion and recombination are now acknowledged to render NPD more effective and efficient.

The purpose of the present study is to empirically explore the role of KM in the enhancement of NPD process within a set of companies having at least a R&D department located in Italy.

The paper is structured as follows: in the first section a literature review describing the general features of KM and its relationship to NPD is presented. Then, the authors have focused on the methodology adopted, designing a research model and formulating several hypotheses that have been tested through an empirical research, based on questionnaires distributed to different companies. In the following section, the authors have performed an item analysis to validate the internal consistency of the items in the research model and then other statistical analyses to verify the initial hypotheses and the positive correlation through the items. Finally, a discussion of the main results and conclusive remarks have been proposed.

2 Literature Review

This section provides a review of the existing literature, focusing on the knowledge management frameworks realized by several authors and the impact of KM on NPD process.

The main keywords have been inserted in the following databases: Google Scholar, Sciencedirect, Emeraldinsight, Ingenta connect, Scopus and IEEE. The paper found at this stage, have been read and their references highlighted, to make sure any relevant works not detected through original database search were included, and a decision about their inclusion was then made.

The definition of the term "knowledge" has represented, for many authors, the first step to introduce the theme of KM. In particular it has been distinguished from the terms "information" and "data". Data are considered as raw facts, information is regarded as an organized set of data, and knowledge is perceived as meaningful information [1]. According to [3], knowledge is personalized or subjective information related to facts, procedures, concepts, interpretations, ideas, observations and judgments. But, from an organizational viewpoint, it is also an organized combination of data, assimilated with a set of rules, procedures, and operations learnt through experience and practice [1]. Knowledge can be either tacit or explicit [4]: tacit knowledge refers to the knowledge that has a personal quality that makes it hard to articulate or communicate; in contrast, explicit knowledge refers to the codifiable component that can be disembodied and transmitted.

The purpose of knowledge management is to enhance organizational performance by explicitly designing and implementing tools, processes, systems, structures and cultures to improve the creation, sharing, and use of all types of knowledge that are critical for decision making [5].

Companies are beginning to implement information systems designed specifically to facilitate the codification, collection, integration, and dissemination of organizational knowledge, that are referred to as Knowledge Management Systems (KMS) [6].

2.1 The Relationship between KM and New Product Development

This first step of literature review has shown a lack of frameworks assessing the important role of KM in the NPD process, but a description of the relationship between the two processes exists.

Liu et al. [7] conduct a research on the correlation between the knowledge management method and new product development strategy performance. The intention to engage KM in new product development is to decrease the uncertainty in the course of new product development thought that knowledge management integration is dependent on a wider and trans-functional integration capability.

Therefore, the effectiveness of the knowledge management method plays an important role in new product development strategy. In fact the authors have found that the stronger the knowledge management method, the higher the new product development performance.

According to Pitt and MacVaugh [2], for organizations whose long-run competitive advantage and economic success is based on knowledge-intensive activities, effective NPD processes are crucial. The methods and practices of knowledge management significantly affect how the organization generates, stores, accesses, recombines and mobilises what it knows about NPD .

A knowledge strategy for NPD should accommodate and integrate human processes with technical processes in the complex socio-technical system that is NPD.

The challenge is to underpin the processes that are necessary for NPD by enabling information and knowledge flows that aid knowledge creation and recombination, via enhanced communication, both formal and informal. This holistic conception of knowledge management, if implemented effectively, can have a positive impact on the effectiveness of NPD processes.

A KMS supporting the NPD process has to capture informal, internal knowledge including externalization of tacit knowledge. To transfer tacit knowledge from individuals to a repository, Ramesh and Tiwana [8] suggest support for some form of community-based electronic discussion. A key feature of a KM support is its ability to capture and retrieve uncodified or tacit knowledge. Therefore, intelligent support for the capture, use, and maintenance of process knowledge appears to be essential for the NPD success.

3 Methodology

3.1 Purpose and Assumptions

The goal of the research is to adopt an empirical approach to analyse the influence of KM on the NPD process managed by a generic company.

The first section has represented an important background to introduce the issue of KM enhancing the NPD process. The set of reviewed papers has not been exhaustive for the purpose of the present study: the relationship between KM and NPD is basically discussed through dissertations and the existing frameworks are related to a specific concern. In order to fulfil this gap, the authors formulated a conceptual research model (Fig. 1), inspired to the one developed by Liu et al. [7], in which three main hypotheses, guiding the following results, have been highlighted:

H_1: The relationship between KM and NPD performance.

$H_{1\text{-}1}$: a stronger KM approach has a positive correlation with NPD performance.

$H_{1\text{-}2}$: the opportunity to manage formal, informal, internal and external knowledge and to update it frequently has a positive correlation with NPD performance.

$H_{1\text{-}3}$: the use of advanced KM techniques and tools has a positive correlation with NPD performance.

$H_{1\text{-}4}$: the use of proper KM software has a positive correlation with NPD performance.

H_2: the relationship between KM and NPD strategy.

$H_{2\text{-}1}$: a stronger KM approach has a positive correlation with NPD strategy.

$H_{2\text{-}2}$: the opportunity to manage formal, informal, internal and external knowledge and to update it frequently has a positive correlation with NPD strategy.

$H_{2\text{-}3}$: the use of advanced KM techniques and tools has a positive correlation with NPD strategy.

$H_{2\text{-}4}$: the use of proper KM software has a positive correlation with NPD strategy.

H_3: the relationship between NPD strategy and NPD performance.

$H_{3\text{-}1}$: the use of performance measurement sets will affect NPD performance.

$H_{3\text{-}2}$: the decision to improve the NPD process will affect NPD performance.

$H_{3\text{-}3}$: the importance of different CSFs will affect NPD performance.

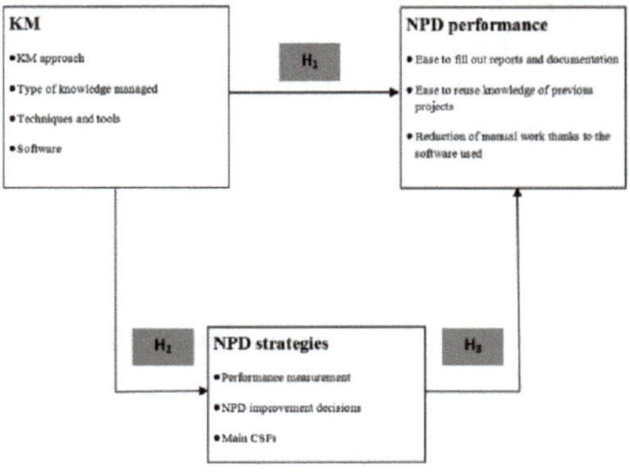

Fig. 1. The research model

3.2 Data Collection and Analysis

The empirical study has been carried out through the administration of a questionnaire, properly structured to test the hypotheses listed above. The questionnaire has been distributed to 103 companies with at least a R&D department located in Italy and it gave the authors the opportunity to investigate the three domains represented in Fig.1.

The domain of KM refers to the way KM is managed within the processes: knowledge capturing, packaging, distribution and reusing. The domain contains four measurement items:

1. the KM approach, which refers to the planned methods to manage knowledge in the NPD process;
2. the type of knowledge managed, that may be formal/informal and internal/external, and its update frequency;
3. techniques and tools, i.e. the way to capture, store, share and reuse design knowledge in the company (lessons learned documents, questionnaire/checklist, poster and visual management, Intranet, Wiki, PDM/PLM Systems);
4. software implemented to support KM in the NPD process.

The domain of NPD performance includes three measurement items:

1. the ease to fill out reports and documentation, that refers to a minimum time wasted by the designers in this process;
2. the ease to reuse knowledge of previous projects, that refers to a minimum time wasted in knowledge reusing;
3. reduction of manual work thanks to the software used;

Finally, the NPD strategies domain contains three measurement items:

1. Performance measurement, that describes if and how performance are measured within NPD process;
2. NPD improvement decisions, that refers to the eventuality of a strategic plan enhancing the NPD process;
3. Main CSFs, that describes the importance of CSFs (Return On Investment, costs related to life cycle costs, Time To Market, range of different products, level of customization, level of innovation, brand image and environmental sustainability) in NPD decisions;

The sample of companies that have answered to the questions includes different industries: industrial machinery and equipment, defence, automotive, industrial engineering, household electrical appliance, electric equipment, software and telecommunications, electronic equipment, fashion, chemicals and materials manufacturing. The subjects interviewed had full understanding of KM and NPD: in fact, in order to enhance the questionnaire validity, it has been administered to R&D and Information and Communication Technology (ICT) mangers and new product development directors. From January 2012 to April 2013a total of 103 complete questionnaires have been collected.

A structured questionnaire with closed questions has allowed the author to use quantitative and comparable scales, especially required in the verification of results. The outcomes presented in the following section have been provided by the statistic software Minitab 17. A first Item analysis has been used to assess how reliably multiple items in the survey measure the same construct. Then, in order to verify the hypotheses, t-test, multiple regression and other method for verification analysis have been performed.

4 Findings

The research model designed in Fig.1 has been validated through an Item analysis: it is a measure of internal consistency used to test the same skill or characteristic. The Cronbach coefficients for the three domains were calculated: each domain included several items, corresponding to questions within the survey. If Cronbach's alpha is low, then the items may not reliably measure a single construct. Typically, a value of 0.7 or higher is considered good.

The values in Table 1 are greater than the common benchmark of 0.7 and suggest that the items are measuring the same construct.

Table 1. The Item analysis for the research model

Domain	Items	Cronbach α
KM	KM approach	0,7302
	Type of knowledge managed	
	Technique and tools	
	Software	
NPD performance	Ease to fill out reports and documentation	0,7096
	Ease to reuse knowledge of previous projects	
	Reduction of manual work thanks to the software used	
NPD strategies	Performance measurement	0,7592
	NPD improvement decisions	
	CSFs	

This study has shown that the requirements for reliability have been satisfied so the items can be arranged as done in the research model.

Moreover, the relation between the three domains has been verified. A t-Test for KM, NPD performance and NPD strategies has been conducted, followed by a multiple regression analysis.

4.1 The t-Test Results

A t-Test has been performed in order to prove the validity of H_{1-1}-H_{1-4}, H_{2-1}-H_{2-4} and H_{3-1}-H_{3-3}. Samples are normally distributed and independent, so the t-Test can be used. If the p-value is below a specified level of significance of 0.05, the test's null hypothesis can be rejected and the differences between means are statistically significant.

All KM aspects, analysed in the detail, have a significant effect on the NPD performance because p-value is lower than the α-level. Therefore, the $H_{1\text{-}1}$-$H_{1\text{-}4}$ were proven valid.

The t-Test for KM and NPD strategies has shown greater problems of significance. In fact, not many KM aspects have shown significance on the NPD strategy according to low p-values. It seems that the use of several advanced KM techniques and software is related to the adopted NPD strategy.

Therefore, the strategies fixed by the companies interviewed, focused on the need to measure performances, to improve NPD and to identify CSFs, are not influenced by the type of knowledge managed. Only hypotheses $H_{2\text{-}3}$-$H_{2\text{-}4}$ were proven valid.

Finally, almost all new product development strategy aspects have shown significance on new product development performance. Only the relation between the use of performance measurement, as an NPD strategy, and the NPD performances does not show significance, due to its higher p-value. In particular, the decision to improve the NPD process and the identification of CSFs affect the performances achieved within the NPD. Therefore, hypotheses $H_{3\text{-}2}$-$H_{3\text{-}3}$ were proven valid.

4.2 The Multiple Regression Analysis

Multiple regression is an example of complex multivariate statistics that analyses the effects of two or more independent variables on the dependent variable. Parameters as R^2, adjusted R^2, and S (Standard Error of the regression) are measures of how well the model fits the data. R^2 is a statistic used to evaluate the fit of the model, i.e. the percentage of variation in the response that is explained by the model. R^2 adjusted is a modified R that has been adjusted for the number of terms in the model. S is measured in the units of the response variable and represents the standard distance that data values fall from the regression line. The better the equation predicts the response, the lower S is and the larger the R^2, the better the model fits the data.

In the present study, the multiple-regression analysis has provided some insights and challenges. In fact the outputs of Minitab about correlation and regression have shown that the model doesn't fit the data. Therefore the original data have been filtered basing on the sector the companies belong to, in order to understand if the organizational aspects are able to improve the analysis.

Four main sectors have been identified: the first includes Mechanics and Industrials, the second includes Electrical and household products, the third concerns Technology and telecommunications, and the fourth is devoted to Chemicals, food, textile and apparel.

The regression has been applied to analyse the relation between KM, NPD performance and NPD strategies, as previously stated in the research model. The relation between KM and NPD performance has been confirmed only by the companies belonging to the second sector.

The regression analysis based on the particular response "reduction of manual work thanks to the software used", has shown high R^2 values and a S lower than 2,5 revealing that the model is precise enough (Table 2). Nevertheless, just between the KM approach and the management of formal and external knowledge there is a strongly significant and positive relationship (underlined in grey), confirmed by a p-value lower than 0,05 (α level). The other variables appear to be not significantly related or negatively related.

The results shows that the adoption of software reducing manual work has a positive correlation with the maturity of KM, explained basically in the KM approach.

Table 2. The multiple-regression analysis for the KM method on the NPD performance "reduction of manual work thanks to the software used" (Sector 2)

Model one	**Term**	**Coefficient**	**Standard Error**	**T-Value**	**P-Value**
	Constant	6,78	1,94	3,49	0,004
KM approach	KM approach	0,478	0,170	2,81	0,016
Type of knowledge managed	Formal and internal knowledge managed	0,182	0,262	0,70	0,500
	Formal and external knowledge managed	0,381	0,182	2,09	0,058
Techniques and tools	Lessons learned documents	-0,083	0,140	-0,59	0,565
	Questionnaire/checklist	0,179	0,150	1,19	0,258
	Poster and visual management	0,027	0,130	0,21	0,841
	Intranet	0,084	0,122	0,69	0,503
	Wiki	0,134	0,231	0,58	0,573
	PDM/PLM Systems	0,134	0,109	1,23	0,243
Software:	Knowledge Based Engineering (KBE) and Design Automation	-0,573	0,163	-3,52	0,004
R^2	72,47%				
Adjusted R^2	42,65%				
S	1,47232				

Moving to the second hypothesis, the aim has been to find a positive relation between KM and NPD strategies. The sectors one, three and four have shown that the model based on the response "CSFs" fits the data. The management of formal and internal knowledge and several KM techniques and tools are positively related to a particular NPD strategy, that is the identification of CSFs. The other sectors analysed have confirmed the same relation, excluding additional linkages between other KM methods or other NPD strategies. Therefore the type of knowledge managed has a positive correlation with the strategy of identifying CSFs.

Finally, the third hypothesis based on the relationship between NPD strategy and NPD performance has been confirmed in the second and third sectors. Two models, based on two main responses, concerning the ease to fill out reports and documentation and the ease to reuse knowledge of previous projects, fit the data. Hence, the Technology and telecommunications sector, that identifies the range of different products as its main CSF, reveals also the interest to improve NPD performances.

Within the second sector, the response "ease to reuse knowledge of previous projects" has a significant and positive relationship with the NPD-oriented strategy and with the identification of CSFs related to innovation and sustainability.

5 Discussion and Conclusion

In the present study the role of KM in the improvement of NPD process has been analysed combining a literature review and an empirical research. The first methodology has allowed a comprehension of knowledge management, identifying its main processes and its relation with the new product development.

Literature review has triggered the formulation of three hypotheses, based on the relationships between KM, NPD performance and NPD strategies, as suggested by Liu et al. [7]. A research model has been designed, containing several items gathered from literature.

A survey has been proposed to enterprises with at least a R&D department located in Italy belonging to a wide range of industries, containing questions specifically defined to validate the research model. The set of data collected has been elaborated by a statistical software providing lots of interesting outcomes.

First of all, the internal consistency of the items in the research model has been confirmed through the item analysis. Then, the mentioned hypotheses have been tested through a t-Test and a multiple regression analysis. The latter has aimed to identify a positive relation between independent and dependent variables present in the model. The organizational aspects have been taken into account because the regression analysis has been conducted on the different sectors the companies belong to. Nevertheless, not all the hypotheses have been validated.

In the Electrical sector, a stronger KM approach and the opportunity to frequently manage formal knowledge has a positive correlation with the reduction of manual work in the NPD process. On the other hand, companies providing tools such as Product Data Management and Product Lifecycle Management (PDM/PLM) do not necessarily better perform in the NPD process.

In Mechanics, Technology, Chemical, Food and Fashion industries the regression analysis has shown that the frequent management of formal and internal knowledge and the KM tools, such as intranet and checklists, are positively related to the definition of CSFs, among the possible NPD strategies.

In the Electrical and also in the Technology and telecommunication industries, the definition of particular CSFs, including the range of different products, the level of innovation and the sustainability aspects, and the NPD improvement decisions are positively correlated to the achievement of NPD performances, such as the ease to fill out reports and to reuse knowledge.

Therefore, better NPD performances may be ensured through a mature KM approach and also through the definition of appropriate NPD strategies.

The paper provides valuable insights from the academic viewpoint, because of the use of different statistical analyses to validate or reject the initial hypotheses and also thanks to the overview of literature about KM. But the present study also underlines the impacts on enterprises belonging to different industries.

Especially in mechanical and technology sectors, enterprises need to acknowledge the importance of KM and its impact on performances and long-term strategies related to the NPD process in order to be challenging in the competitive context.

The present research may be improved through the collection of more questionnaires in order to enhance the consistency of the analysis. This way, probably the hypotheses that have been rejected could be accepted, according to a different behaviour of the variables.

Moreover, the research may be extended to other industries or focus on a particular one to assess the importance of KM in the NPD process. Other issues, such as the impact of KM on increasing innovation and sustainability should be examined.

References

1. Bhatt, G.D.: Knowledge management in organizations: examining the interaction between technologies, techniques, and people. Journal of Knowledge Management 5(1), 68–75 (2001)
2. Pitt, M., MacVaugh, J.: Knowledge management for new product Development. Journal of Knowledge Management 12(4), 101–116 (2008)
3. Alavi, M., Leidner, D.E.: Knowledge Management Systems: issues, challenges and benefits. Communications of the Association for Information System 1(7) (1999)
4. Hahn, J., Subramani, M.R.: A Framework of Knowledge Management Systems: issues and challenges for theory and practice. Knowledge Management Systems, 302–312 (2000)
5. De Long, D.W., Fahey, L.: Diagnosing Cultural Barriers to Knowledge Management. The Academy of Management Executive 14(4), 113–127 (2000)
6. McDermott, R.: Why Information Technology inspired but cannot deliver Knowledge Management. California Management Review 41(4), 103–117 (1999)
7. Liu, P.-L., Chen, W.-C., Tsai, C.-H.: An empirical study on the correlation between the knowledge management method and new product development strategy on product performance in Taiwan's industries. Technovation 25, 637–644 (2005)
8. Ramesh, B., Tiwana, A.: Supporting Collaborative Process Knowledge Management in New Product Development Teams. Decision Support Systems 27, 213–235 (1999)

A Study on Developing a Decision Support Agent for Project Management

Shinji Mochida

University of Marketing and Distribution Science, Japan
shinji_mochida@red.umds.ac.jp

Abstract. The term "business system" refers to the methods which use to manage their information or knowledge. All companies employ business systems during the development of new software, mechanical equipment or other projects. There are several stages in development projects. There are stages of planning, development, system examination, and upgrade. However, because business knowledge and system development knowledge are united in the systems engineer individual, and the final system image is designed in the engineer's mind, the knowledge earned in the project is not adapted to the next system development project. Business knowledge and system development knowledge are different. A unification of measures for value of these two types of information is needed to treat the information equally. Then, this paper aims to achieve the decision support agent. This decision support agent should have the function of evaluating the value of knowledge and supporting judgment through all stages of the project. Additionally, because the environment around the system development is always changing, a function to evaluate the importance of knowledge from the data stream is needed so that the decision support agent may acquire and interpreted information in real time.

Keywords: project management, knowledge, agent, prioritization.

1 Introduction

In business development projects, there are stages of planning, development, system examination, and upgrade. However, the person in charge of each these stages are different, and knowledge is not adapted to the next system development project. The uncertainty of scope, project duration and cost planning are repeated every time during development project due to knowledge shortages. These uncertainty causes schedule delays and cost overruns for the project [1][2]. One reason for cost overruns is that during the requirement assessment stages of a project, each project engineers' level of skill and experience is variable. This paper will use the term' subject ' to engineering staffs, engineers. Subjects may misunderstand the scope or requirements of the clients. Thus subjects do not know the best way to make the system at the early stage.The progress management is important and difficult work while the project is executed[3][4][5]. Generally in a business system development project, the feasible scope and the achievement method are designed after the subject investigates or

S. Fukuda et al. (Eds.): PLM 2014, IFIP AICT 442, pp. 407–416, 2014.

studies the business for systematization. Business knowledge and system development knowledge are united in the systems engineer individual, and the final system image is designed in individual subject's mind. Thus, if business knowledge and system development knowledge are treated in the same way and used at the early stage of the project, it becomes possible to plan the duration and cost of the project accurately. Sub-optimization is necessary to develop the productivity and reduce costs of projects. Developing the productivity is important to achieve the sub-optimization. Offering appropriate knowledge to the all subject at appropriate time is necessary to develop the productivity and reduce costs of developing business systems.

2 Previous Studies

The current research studies techniques for the accumulation of information that is distributed and exists in the computer system, and also implements knowledge mining using a high performance computer [6]. However, there is no research on unification of values to deal with different information, such as business knowledge and the system knowledge, etc. in the same way. Moreover, there is no research that analyzes, evaluates the data stream including environmental information from consecutive work, and acquires knowledge continuously during a project [7]. Many researchers are studying techniques for implementing knowledge mining from information that has already been acquired, not real time processing [8].

3 Productivity and Knowledge

This paper aims to achieve a software agent that collects effective business knowledge and system development knowledge in the business system development projects. Figure 1 shows software agent. First this research need to create the function of compiling knowledge in Figure 1 for the software agent [9][10]. This software agent should have a function to evaluate the value of information automatically and support subject's judgment in all stages of the project. These judgments will allow subject to decide which work to do at what time. This paper will refer to this software agent as “the decision support agent”. This decision support agent should is expected to accumulate, and maintain the knowledge acquired from all stages of the project, as well as to offer the knowledge to the all subject when necessary. When subjects engage in the project, it is thought that productivity increases as time spent on the project passes. This also assumes that productivity is low at the beginning of the work because necessary skills have not yet been developed and there is luck of detailed information necessary to start the work. We collected the productivity data from the computer system development project, and apply to the Weibull distribution. Thus we defined the model which is suitable for productivity curve in order to estimate productivity at specified time. The physical model and parameters are shown in Expression (1).If the productivity data collected from a computer system development project is substituted into Expression (1), then productivity at a certain time is obtained by f(t) as shown in Figure 2 at time:t, and Table 1 shows the parameters obtained from the screen design work in a past system development project. Figure 2 was created using the parameters obtained the system development project.

$$f(t) = K\left(1 - \exp(-(\frac{t+a}{\eta})^m)\right) + d \tag{1}$$

$K : final\ productivity$
$a : preparationdays$
$\eta : studyresistance$
$m : proficiency$
$d : workrepetition$

Table 1. Parameters gotten from the screen design work

K	a	η	m	d
1	9	13	2.4	0

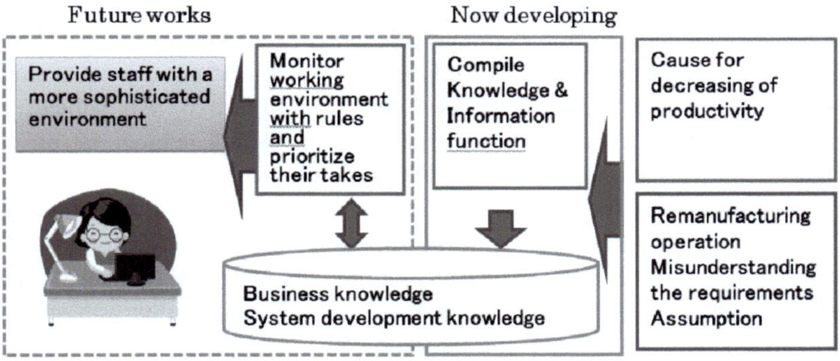

Fig. 1. Decision support agent software

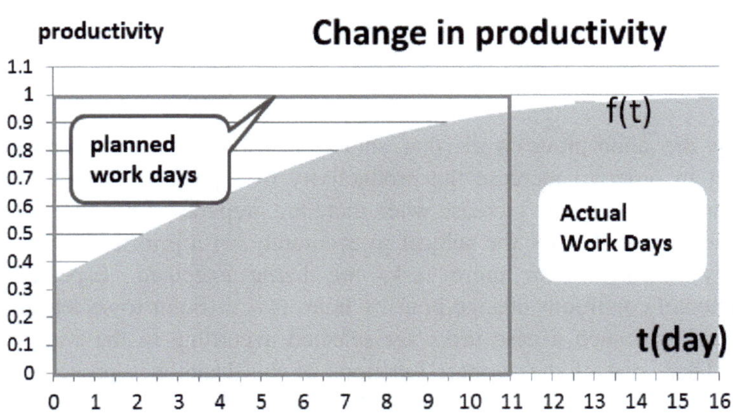

Fig. 2. Curve of productivity and actual work days

The area of square in Figure 2 shows the planned work days and graph shows actual work days. Figure 2 shows the difference of actual work days and planned work days. In this example, it was estimated that it would take 11 days to finish the part of the project, however 25 days were required. The number of actual work days shown Figure 2 as the area under the curve F(t) were integrated using F(t) and t(time). The number of calculated actual work days was 12.8 days, while estimated work days were 11 days. In this example, therefore, calculated actual work days are nearly equal to planned work days. If high productivity achieved, then work will finish according to the schedule. Preparation work is necessary to achieve the expected level of productivity. The productivity does not increase if there are mistakes in preparation. Mistakes in preparation are caused by lack of knowledge or appropriate preparation work not be done. It is necessary for all subjects to decide what they must do before beginning work. Then, this paper proposes a method to recognize the work launch date. The work launch date is the day when information gathering and a preliminary examination of the project is begun. Assigning a work launch date which allows all subject to complete appropriate preparation work in anticipation of the planned work start date is necessary in order to achieve high earlier in the work cycle and shorten the number of work days. Because it is inevitable that there many tasks to be completed simultaneously, for example; scheduled task, preparation task for the next task, and troubleshooting work, it is important for subject to judge what they should do during preparation work phase as follows in Figure 3. All subject needs to prioritize their tasks. Then the psychological value which subject set on each task effects how they prioritize their takes. The psychological value which subject set on each task is limited by the short-term memory and their actual understanding at each task. Then, the decision support agent should support the selection of the most important task to do at each specific time. During any task it is especially necessary to make time to prepare for the next scheduled task. Then, the decision support agent should understand each subject's working characteristic, their skill and their involvement in other tasks. Prioritization mistakes during the preparation work phase causes schedule delays and cost overruns in projects. Work efficiency during the entire project decreases because of mistakes in preparation.

4 Set the Work Priority Level

Selecting the appropriate work that should be done at any given time is very important in order to increase the productivity of a project. The efficiency of the subsequent work does not increase when there are preparation mistakes in the project. It becomes impossible for the subject to accurately set a priority level for each task accurately when two or more tasks are being executed. Especially, because environmental conditions change hour by hour, it is difficult to select an appropriate task. Usually in such a case tasks are selected according to the experience of the subject. Then, one of the support functions of the decision support agent is to set appropriate priority levels for each task. Awareness of the environmental condition is necessary in order to select the work accurately. Then, the task selection process was examined by the questionnaire which has some completion targets; today and tomorrow, the day after tomorrow and complete in one week. For example, the task which should be done by today is review of the plan. The task which should be done by tomorrow is creating the schedule of tasks. The task which should be done by the day after tomorrow is creating documents of tasks. The task which should be done one week after is checking the report of tasks. Figure 4 shows the result of the subject selection process when subjects are asked to choose which tasks they would begin working on during three time periods; today, tomorrow, the day after tomorrow. In the questionnaire subjects are asked to order three out of four tasks over three days(designated today, tomorrow and the day after tomorrow);by according to their first, second and third priorities. The task which subjects wants to begin previously has high priority. Figure 5 shows the results in a situation similar to Figure 4 when subjects are asked to choose which tasks they would begin working on during four time periods; today, tomorrow, the day after tomorrow, one week after. From the above results, the priority level of the tasks is set according to the time limit in logical in Figure 4. However, the priority level of tasks is not set according to the time limit in Figure 5. Figure 5 show that subjects do not always consider the time limit when prioritizing tasks over a longer range of time. Subjects are expected to select tasks according to the time limit, and not their individual skills. In actual working situations the prioritization of tasks would be left to the subject's individual skills. A Person's short-term memory is one reason why appropriate work cannot be selected. The short-term memory is maintained for only a few minutes. Because the time when subjects get the information about the tasks is different, prioritizing the tasks is not correctly evaluated in the subjects' minds. It is said that human can memorize only 10 pieces in a few seconds~[11][12]. There is a limitation in the number of tasks which a subject can prioritize within a specific time.

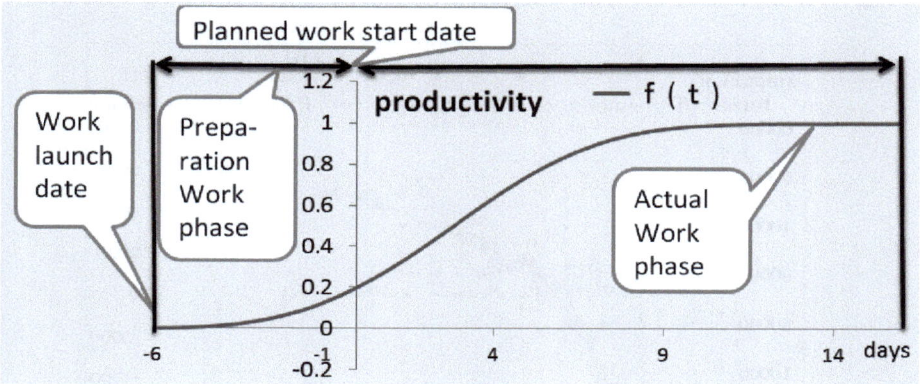

Fig. 3. Work start date and work launch date

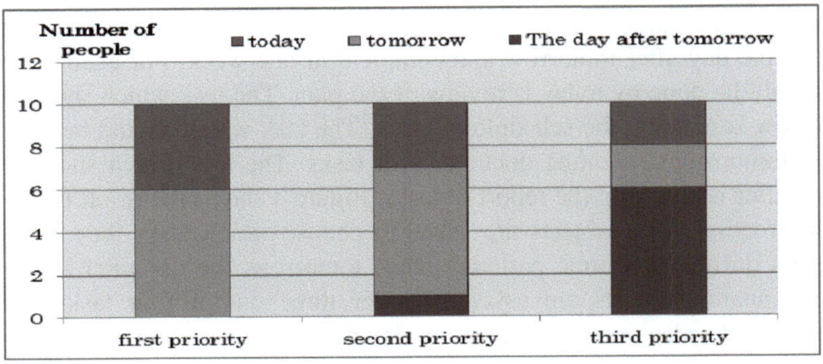

Fig. 4. Priority level of today, tomorrow, and the day after tomorrow's work

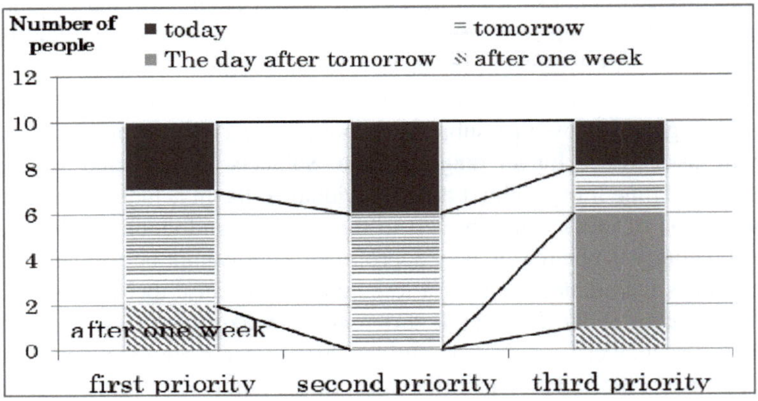

Fig. 5. Priority level of work after today, tomorrow, the day after tomorrow, and one week

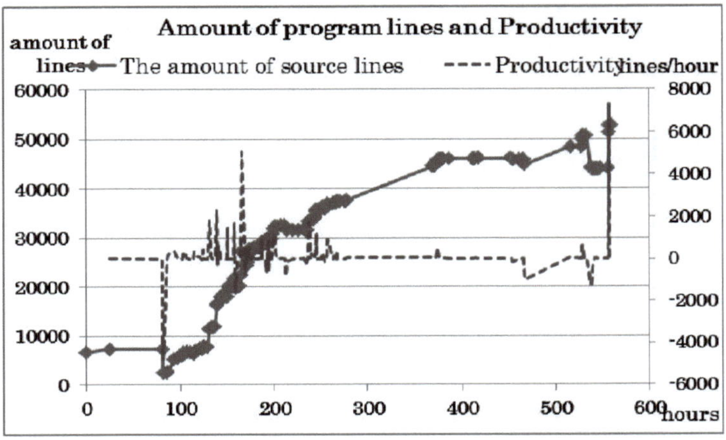

Fig. 6. Changes in productivity

Table 2. Reasons why productivity decreases

NO	Reason why productivity decreases
1	Insufficient time to revise work according to new specifications
2	Revision work to correct cording errors
3	Revisions in cording standards following review
4	Revisions in order to improve execution efficiency

5 Changes in Productivity

There are changes in productivity in the system development project as follows in Figure 6.Figure 6 shows productivity during the system development project. Productivity is measured according to increases or decreases in the number of lines of source code per an hour. The programming criteria of productivity which we have is 60 200 Line/day(Not include comments).The main reasons why productivity decreases are shown in table 2. From table 2, we can understand that it is necessary to clarify specifications and avoid violations of coding standards in order to improve productivity. Additionally, revisions in cording following review or specification changes are a one of the major causes of work delays. Offering appropriate knowledge is important to improve the productivity of staffs. Thus it is necessary to compile not only technical knowledge for programing but also knowledge for assessing of requirements of clients. One of functions to compile many kind of knowledge for decision support agent is creating. Additionally prioritizing tasks is vital to offering appropriate knowledge when it is needed. It is necessary to evaluate correctly the difficulty of their tasks according to their current working situation. Observation of the environmental conditions in real time is needed in order to evaluate the appropriate time when appropriate knowledge should be offered. It is necessary to be aware of the changes in the work situation to prioritize object's tasks. Productivity is changing every day. Prioritizing tasks appropriately is important to prevent cost overruns and delays in system development project.

6 Decision Support Agent

This paper aims to demonstrate the efficient of the decision support agent. This decision support agent should have the function to evaluate the value of knowledge and offer that knowledge to the subjects at the appropriate time. Additionally, the decision support agent should have the function to prioritize subjects' tasks in all stages of the project according to the environmental situation. Importantly, Figure 7 shows that subjects give the same level of priority to tasks both one week and one month in the future, thus leading to incorrect prioritization of their assigned tasks. Because subjects cannot effectively prioritize tasks further than one week in the future (see Figure 7), it is necessary to support subject's prioritization of tasks. Additionally, the decision support agent is needed to support prioritization of subjects' tasks when dealing with various kinds of interruptions. The decision support agent should also have the function of taking into account the subjects' work pat-terns as follows in Figure 8. Figure 8 shows a histogram of the self-reported level of concentrated for two subjects during a typical day of work on the system development project. Then, this paper proposes the decision support agent in Figure 1 .The decision support agent prioritizes their tasks according to the score obtained by the following Expression (2). Expression (2) shows the *f(x,t)*;function which calculates of prioritization of tasks according to their complexity. This *f(x,t)* is the most important function of Decision support agent. Because as tasks become more complex, the figures become larger. In this function smaller values indicate a higher priority. Simple task is needed a few knowledge. It is important that tasks can be done in order of it is easy to work and simple. This *f(x,t)* shows priority level of the task x at time t. *g(x,t)* shows the number of knowledge for completing the task at a specific time t. $h(x,t_1)$ shows proportion to have obtained knowledge for completing the task at time t. Table 3 shows the expected effect when the priority level of tasks are appropriately set by this function; f(x,t), and revision work is not generated. The productivity of the system development project is shown by the amount of increase in the amount of source code.

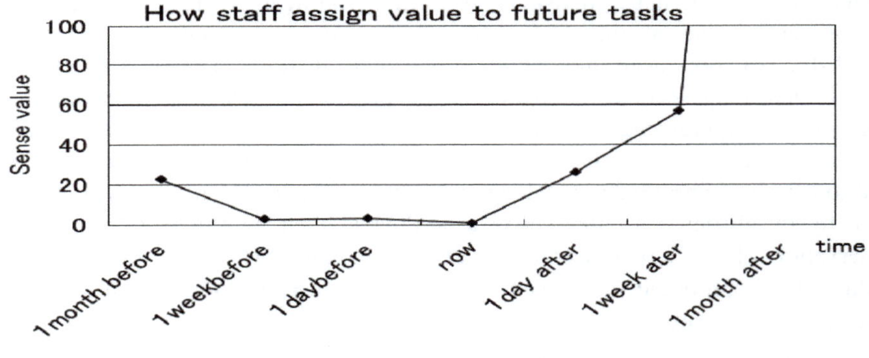

Fig. 7. Task priority values

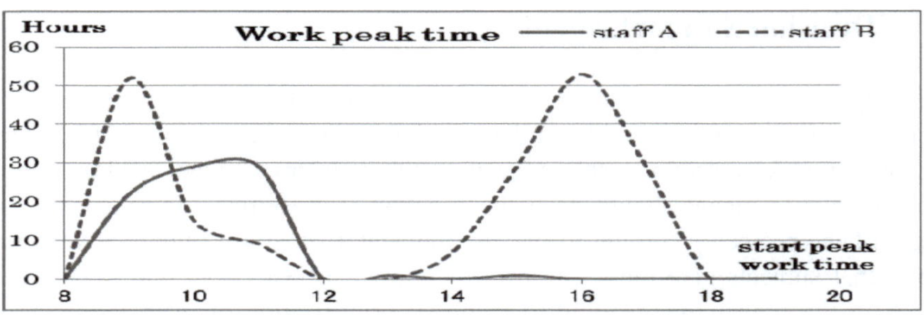

Fig. 8. Work patterns of subjects

$$f(x,t) = g(x,t)h(x,t) \tag{2}$$

Table 3. Expected effect

project name	L(lines)	D(lines)	H1 (hours)	H2 (hours)
A	44478	1348	964	28.9
B	52746	21505	1616	618
C	8589	91	973	10.7

L : The total number of lines written
D : The number of deleted lines
H1: Total working hours
H2: Working hours which could be saved if revision work is avoided.

7 Discussion

In this study the researcher gathered data from an actual information retrieval software project. In order to increase the productivity of software development, this study proposes a formal or explicit work lunch date be set. The work launch date is the day when information gathering and a preliminary examination of the project is begun. In the management of a project launch date, a preparation work phase will be added before the actual work phrase. In the preparation work phase it is necessary to achieve a required level of productivity for the scheduled work. During this preparation work phase, there are many tasks which must be done at specific times. For example; scheduled tasks, preparation for the next stage, and troubleshooting. It is important for subjects to prioritize when must begin each specific task. It is also necessary to schedule their task in detail during each week. Then, this study proposes a decision support agent which is able to prioritize objects' tasks according to the score generated by the function in Expression (2) and which offers subjects applicable knowledge. Additionally, this agent should take into account the subjects' work patterns as shown in Figure 8. Although in the function in Expression (2) the connection between tasks is not expressed. Future tasks should take into account the environmental information to prioritize the tasks appropriately and clarify the effect of the prioritizing function; $f(x,t)$.

8 Conclusion

Meeting budget, finishing on schedule, and maintaining high quality are all important in project management. Because project managers and engineers are usually working on multiple projects simultaneously, they must be able to make appropriately prioritized decisions in order to achieve these three goals. Then, this paper shows that it is effective to schedule a formal work launch date one week prior to the planned work start date, and to prioritize engineers' tasks appropriately. However, further research and study is needed to refine and improve the method of prioritizing engineers' tasks especially in the week before the planned work start date.

Acknowledgment. This work was supported by JSPS KAKENHI Grant Number 24500266.

References

[1] Rad, P.F., Itou, K.: Project Estimating Cost Management, Seisannsei syuxtupan (2004)
[2] Project Management Inst, A Guide to the Project Management Body of Knowledge: Official Japanese Translation (2009)
[3] Royer, P.S., Minemoto, N.: Project Risk Management, Seisannsei syuxtupan (2009)
[4] Rad, P.F., Kou, I.: Project Estimating and Cost Management, Seisannsei syuxtupan (2004)
[5] Jeffery Tyler, M.: Practical Project Evm: The Application of Earned Value Management to Project Management. Springer (2011)
[6] Rzepka, R., Ge, Y., Araki, K.: Common Sense from the Web? Naturalness of Everyday. Journal of Advanced Computational Intelligence and Intelligent Informatics 10(6), 868–875 (2006)
[7] Agrawal, R., Srikant, R.: Mining Sequential Patterns. In: Proc 1995 Int. Conf. on Data Engineering (ICDE 1995), pp. 3–14 (1995)
[8] Nakagawa, T., Matsumoto, Y.: Detecting Errors in Corpora Using SupportVector Machines. In: Proceedings of the 19th International Conference on Computational Linguistics(COLING 2002), Taipei, Taiwan, pp. 709–715 (2002)
[9] Mochida: Dynamic Knowledge Collection System Using,Web Technology. Journal of Biomedical Fuzzy Systems Association 5(1), 31–36 (2003)
[10] Mochida: Knowledge Mining for Project Management and Execu-tion. Journal of Advanced Computational Intelligence and Intelligent Informatics 15(4), 454–459 (2011)
[11] Lindsay, P.H., Norman, D.A., Nakamizo, S.: Human Information Processing Japanese Translation vol. 2, pp. 52–53. Saiensu-Sha Co.,Ltd (1989)
[12] Lindsay, P.H., Norman, D.A., Nakamizo, S.: Human Information Processing Japanese Translation vol. 3, pp. 111–113. Saiensu-Sha Co.,Ltd (1989)

Segregating Discourse Segments from Engineering Documents for Knowledge Acquisition

Madhusudanan N., B. Gurumoorthy, and Amaresh Chakrabarti

Virtual Reality Laboratory, Centre for Product Design and Manufacturing,
Indian Institute of Science, Bangalore – 560 012
{madhu,bgm,ac123}@cpdm.iisc.ernet.in

Abstract. The broader goal of the research being described here is to automatically acquire diagnostic knowledge from documents in the domain of manual and mechanical assembly of aircraft structures. These documents are treated as a discourse used by experts to communicate with others. It therefore becomes possible to use discourse analysis to enable machine understanding of the text. The research challenge addressed in the paper is to identify documents or sections of documents that are potential sources of knowledge. In a subsequent step, domain knowledge will be extracted from these segments. The segmentation task requires partitioning the document into relevant segments and understanding the context of each segment. In discourse analysis, the division of a discourse into various segments is achieved through certain indicative clauses called cue phrases that indicate changes in the discourse context. However, in formal documents such language may not be used. Hence the use of a domain specific ontology and an assembly process model is proposed to segregate chunks of the text based on a local context. Elements of the ontology/model, and their related terms serve as indicators of current context for a segment and changes in context between segments. Local contexts are aggregated for increasingly larger segments to identify if the document (or portions of it) pertains to the topic of interest, namely, assembly. Knowledge acquired through such processes enables acquisition and reuse of knowledge during any part of the lifecycle of a product.

Keywords: Knowledge acquisition, mechanical assembly, discourse analysis, segmentation.

1 Introduction

In the process of realizing industrial scale products, assembly is a critical and integrative step. If potential assembly issues can be detected during the planning stages, expensive repetitions in assembly planning can be reduced. In order to do so, knowledge of assembly issues is necessary during the planning stage. Knowledge based systems have been explored as a means of providing such knowledge [1]. Knowledge based systems have been in use in a variety of applications for quite some time now.

S. Fukuda et al. (Eds.): PLM 2014, IFIP AICT 442, pp. 417–426, 2014.

The need for using knowledge entities in PLM systems has also been stressed in literature [2, 3]. The ability to manage knowledge generated during a product's lifecycle is key towards automation of design process [4]. Literature indicates the ability [5], importance [6] as well as the limited capability of PLM systems to manage and re-use of knowledge across life-cycles [7].

The acquisition of knowledge for such systems however, remains a bottleneck [8]. Automation of such knowledge acquisition is a larger goal of this research. Specifically, the work reported in this paper is intended to serve as the first step in automatically acquiring diagnostic knowledge pertaining to assembly from documents.

1.1 Background

The research reported here is part of a research work aimed at building a diagnostic system for mechanical assembly. In particular the focus is on the manual assembly of aircraft structures. Aircraft assembly is largely a manual process. The planning of such large scale part-assembly processes is a complex task. After an assembly plan is drawn up, in case there are issues while performing the actual assembly, the assembly plan might have to be revised, and each such revision adds to both cost and time delays. If assembly planners possess prior knowledge of such issues in advance, expensive and time-consuming iterations in the planning- assembly- replanning loop can be reduced. Sources of such knowledge are assembly experts, and documented collections of such issues. We chose documents as the source of knowledge for this research, since they in turn reflect the knowledge of experts who prepared them.

1.2 Documents as a Knowledge Source

In professional organizations, documents can be considered authoritative sources of knowledge, since they are usually prepared by multiple experts and undergo many reviews and revisions. They represent a repository of the experiences of multiple personnel. Documents that would be useful for our purpose are incident reports, standards manuals and best practices. Documents are also a step closer to being machine processible than knowledge that comes directly from experts.

2 Document Segmentation and Classification

Towards acquiring the necessary knowledge from documents, the first step is to identify whether a given document or some sections of the document belong to the relevant domain of interest – in this case, aircraft assembly. For example, a document pertaining to issues in assembly of aft-fuselage is relevant, whereas a document about annual sales of a toy is not. Methods for classifying text are available, notably from the domain of pattern classification and machine learning. However, such methods typically require training data sets to be available for them to work effectively.

However, due to reasons that concern the activities downstream in the knowledge acquisition process (elaborated later in the paper) we chose not to use these methods.

It may not be useful at all times to perform this classification only at a document level – sometimes only some parts of a document may be related to assembly (For example, in a document that contains feedback about workplace difficulties from an organization's employees, only the feedback from shop-floor employees is of interest). The challenge here is to filter such relevant and coherent chunks of text. Relevant chunks of text are those that semantically relate to the domain of aircraft assembly. By coherent chunks, we mean that these are collections of continuous and meaningful parts of a discourse. These pieces of text then serve as input for acquisition of diagnostic knowledge. We concentrate only on the sections of a document, rather than the entire document here. To summarize, the objectives of this paper are,

- To identify coherent sections of a given document
- To classify whether such coherent sections of the document pertain to the domain of aircraft assembly (and it's related domains)

2.1 Current Methods

A number of methods are available to segment given data into meaningful chunks. As mentioned hitherto, machine learning based methods are quite useful [9]. However, such methods usually require large amounts of training data to be available, with the data being manually labeled *a priori*. There are mathematical methods combined with semantics available for text categorization as a standalone application [9]. Also dedicated efforts have been made to link the referred entity to its counterpart in a knowledge base, based on the topic of relevance [10].

The collection of words in a document can be used to determine the topic of discussion in the document, this being termed as a 'bag of words' approach in literature [11]. On a similar note one method uses word-sequences as a means of classification [11]. Document clustering is a popular application of techniques that can work without training data, as opposed to classification methods [12]. There is existing literature about the use of phrases and their semantic relationship, as well as the use of ontology for clustering [13]. Clustering documents based on a graph-based technique by detecting frequent sub-graphs of related terms is another method found in literature [14]. Another method uses sampling to discriminate segments of documents [9]. In this, a probabilistic method called Generalized Mallows Model (GMM) is used to model the topics of a text, and is used for segmentation. As regards to current PLM systems, there exists a piece of work to model and elicit information about key relationships and stakeholders by looking at emails [15].

Another relevant research is based on multi-paragraph segmentation using TextTiling algorithm [16], which divides a given text into predetermined blocks of equal size, and then looks at the semantic relatedness of words between these blocks. Related blocks are chunked together if they are closer than a specified threshold. This method is tested against the method proposed in this paper.

However, use of such methods may not help in the subsequent steps of knowledge acquisition, which demands an understanding of the document.

3 Discourse

Discourses are a common form of communication using natural language. They are considered useful to analyze and track the semantic content of a natural language exchange. Discourse analysis has been the focus of study for quite some time now, and there are different theories and approaches to doing so, see for instance [17]. A discourse can be considered to have a hierarchical structure [18] of segments, each of which is a sequence of clauses. The discourse itself may proceed in various ways, with interruptions, digressions and itemizations amongst the different segments.

3.1 Cue Phrases

One of the means of distinguishing the boundaries between discourse segments is the use of cue phrases, also known as discourse markers [19]. Cue phrases such as "after that" and "by the way" signal the transition from one segment to the other. The type of deviation in the discourse context is associated with the type of cue phrase used.

Since discourse analysis helps to track how the previous sentence in a text influences the understanding of the current sentence [18], it is useful to consider documents as discourses, in which one or more authors try to communicate with the reader. The documents that are intended to be used here are those mentioned in the first section. However, technical documents are usually written in a formal manner, and do not resemble other forms of discourse such as conversations. The presence of discourse markers such as cue phrases is not guaranteed in this case.

4 Proposed Method

4.1 Assumptions

Before discussing the proposed method it is appropriate to state the assumptions that have been made here,

- A document is treated as a one-way discourse between the author and the reader;
- The knowledge represented in documents is correct and valid knowledge;
- Available semantic resources such as dictionaries and lexica are sufficient to cover the range of terminology used in technical documents.

4.2 Comparative Studies

An intuitive means of classifying a document or parts of it is to look at the words used and their frequency. In a preliminary exercise, this approach was tried on documents and the results of such a classification were not always indicative of the content at the sentence level.

As mentioned in Section 2.1, TextTiling is another useful way of segmenting sections from a given text. An implementation of the TextTiling algorithm available as part of the NLTK-tokenizer [20] module was tested on a test document [case study]. Extracts of the text as segmented by the researchers and by the tiling algorithm used are presented in the box below.

The document was 4303 words in length, and was a case study of a wing manufacture [21]. Only a small portion of the entire document was considered. The result was compared with the segmentation of the same portion of the document obtained manually by eight test subjects, including the researcher. During the course of using the algorithm, two parameters needed to be adjusted to get a reasonable number of segments. The parameters that were varied were the block length and the block size. The combination which resulted in maximum number of segments was finally considered. The final number of segments using TextTiling was 39.

Figure 1 shows a comparison of how the TextTiling implementation performed against the manual segmentation.

(Drawing from NASA CR-4735.) Cost is the main barrier to use of carbon fiber composites in aircraft. They can cost from 60*to*400 per pound, compared to 0.33*forsteeland*1.00 for aluminum.4 The main cost element is the fiber. In automobiles and recreational boats, glass fibers are used with epoxies and other polymers. These support much lower stresses but are sufficiently strong and stiff for those applications. They cost much less and are quite economical for those products. Another component of the cost is the molds. These are usually made of Invar or another material with very low thermal expansion coefficient in order that the curing process does not introduce size or shape variations. A third significant cost component is layup, by which is meant placing uncured composite materials onto the mold. This can be done by NC machines if the shape is flat or nearly flat, such as a wing skin, but is mainly done manually. A fourth cost is rework and repair. Composite parts are made in layers, and a major potential failure mode is delamination, or interior separation of the layers due to such causes as gas bubbles or insufficient bonding. Ultrasonic inspection is used to find such flaws, and increasingly they can be repaired even in thermosets. The process is still very costly, however, and the prospect of generating a flawed large assembly that becomes expensive scrap is a deterrent. This is ironic inasmuch as the ability to produce a large assembly all at once is one of the most attractive features of composite construction. Even though large subassemblies can be made all at once in an oven, final assembly still requires drilling holes and installing fasteners. This is just as critical and costly as in metal structures. Furthermore, the structural engineers worry every time a hole is drilled and fibers are cut. In some cases, the parts can be glued together. The parts and subassemblies at this stage are remarkably rigid. If they do not fit properly, it is not feasible to use the fasteners to draw them together. While solid or liquid shims are the only recourse, they reduce the strength of the structure and dilute many of the advantages of the method. Only small errors can be corrected this way. Therefore, part and subassembly size and shape accuracy are essential, and great effort is expended on molds and process control to achieve the necessary accuracy.

Cost is the main barrier to use of carbon fiber composites in aircraft. They can cost from 60*to*400 per pound, compared to 0.33*forste* for aluminum.4 The main cost element is the fiber. In automobiles and recreational boats, glass fibers are used with epoxies and other polymers. These support much lower stresses but are sufficiently strong and stiff for those applications. They cost much less and are quite economical for those products.

Another component of the cost is the molds. These are usually made of Invar or another material with very low thermal expansion coefficient in order that the curing process does not introduce size or shape variations.

A third significant cost component is layup, by which is meant placing uncured composite materials onto the mold. This can be done by NC machines if the shape is flat or nearly flat, such as a wing skin, but is mainly done manually.

A fourth cost is rework and repair. Composite parts are made in layers, and a major potential failure mode is delamination, or interior separation of the layers due to such causes as gas bubbles or insufficient bonding. Ultrasonic inspection is used to find such flaws, and increasingly they can be repaired even in thermosets. The process is still very costly, however, and the prospect of generating a flawed large assembly that becomes expensive scrap is a deterrent. This is ironic inasmuch as the ability to produce a large assembly all at once is one of the most attractive features of composite construction. Even though large subassemblies can be made all at once in an oven, final assembly still requires drilling holes and installing fasteners. This is just as critical and costly as in metal structures. Furthermore, the structural engineers worry every time a hole is drilled and fibers are cut. In some cases, the parts can be glued together.

The parts and subassemblies at this stage are remarkably rigid. If they do not fit properly, it is not feasible to use the fasteners to draw them together. While solid or liquid shims are the only recourse, they reduce the strength of the structure and dilute many of the advantages of the method. Only small errors can be corrected this way. Therefore, part and subassembly size and shape accuracy are essential, and great effort is expended on molds and process control to achieve the necessary accuracy.

Fig. 1. An extract of the text showing segmentation by the researchers (left)and the tiling algorithm (right). Each change of color in a column indicates a shift in segment

Some observations on the results are as follows.

- In the graph, the red blocks on the second row indicate that 50% or more subjects have indicated a discourse segment i.e. where a shift in focus occurs, similar to that indicated in [16]. This is compared against the segmentation provided by TextTiling, which matches up most of the segments as provided by the manual segmentation too. However TextTiling, by default looks at paragraph breaks as a shift in focus. On such instance in the test document, there was an itemization in the document, which was not perceived as a shift by all but one of the subjects. But tiling treated this as four segments as they appeared on different paragraphs.

- For the converse case, where there are multiple segments within a paragraph, tiling had only one exception (due to formatting issues in the input) and performed as expected. Other than these, the segments given by tiling matched with 3 subjects on 4 instances, with 2 subjects on 3 instances, with 1 subject on 4 instances, and with no subjects on 1 instance. Hence the performance for tiling was satisfactory in this case.

4.3 Discourse Context for Segmentation

As seen in the previous subsections, methods such as looking at the frequency of occurrence of words are not useful, since they do not concentrate on the semantic content of the discourse. The semantic content is important from the point of view of future activities in the research, such as identifying the entities in the domain, and extracting diagnostic knowledge that concern these entities.

Although TextTiling has performed segmentation at the most prominent segment boundaries, it identifies other boundaries that are not identified as so by the test subjects. Also, it is a difficult task to keep varying the parameters, namely the block-length and block-size parameters, for every document.

These parameters are important since the number of segments that are recognized are dependent on them. Moreover, since segmentation is only a preliminary step to enable filtering of relevant text portions. More importantly, we need to understand the content of a document and extract diagnostic knowledge from it. By understanding we mean that one should be able to list the entities and events in the text, and the relations among them. An additional case for using discourse analysis techniques is made by the fact that methods that look at words and their meanings do not address the task of resolving pronouns and anaphora. This is important since pronouns implicitly contain references to other words, and may not be captured by such methods.

In such a situation, discourse context is useful. In a given discourse the current context is defined by the entities that are being talked about, the activities that concern them and the relations amongst these entities. The list of entities is called Discourse Entity (DE) list [18]. In the domain of assembly the two important factors are product information and the process information [22]. These translate respectively to the nouns and verbs of sentences in natural language. Nouns would also cover the peripheral but related terms such as tools and the assembly environment. By treating the document as a discourse, it is also possible to find out which fact entails others by means of inference. With this explanation the procedure for extracting relevant segments from a document is proposed as follows:

- Given text from a document, tokenize it into sentences;
- Resolve anaphora and pronouns on a per-sentence basis - This gives a DE list for every sentence;

- Segment the sentences which are both contiguous (i.e. within a certain distance *d*) and share parts of their DE list, within a specified threshold, say N_{common};
- Once the segments are recognized and marked, compare entities in the DE list to determine to how many of them relate to the assembly domain. The basis for comparison here would the set of terms (and their semantic neighbors) from one or more assembly ontologies;
- If, for a given segment, the semantic similarity (as indicated by a certain measure) is greater than a threshold, say D_{sem}, then classify that segment as being related;to assembly. For example, in the WordNet ontology, Jiang-Conrath similarity is one such example of semantic similarity.

4.4 Plan for Implementation

For tokenization, any standard tokenizer (e.g. NLTK Punkt tokenizer [20]) that can split the input into sentences is an adequate choice. To resolve anaphora (back references to entities in previous sentences), pronouns and to perform related discourse analyses, methods of representation such as Discourse Representation Structure (DRS) [23] are available. Once the raw, tokenized text is represented in DRS, existing anaphora and pronoun resolution methods can be utilized. From the DE list, for a combination of *d* (See Section 4.3) and N_{common} (yet to be decided) the related segments can be separated. Alternatively, one could use unsupervised methods of classification such as k-means to automatically infer two groups. Then the DE list for every segment can be compared against one or more assembly (and related) ontologies [24] and classify whether that segment is related to assembly or not, based on the value of D_{sem} (See Section 4.3).

5 Conclusions

This paper has discussed the beginnings of a piece of work to acquire diagnostic knowledge for aircraft assembly from documents. In particular a method for segmenting relevant parts of a document that are related to assembly is proposed. Previous methods have been revised, and one method in particular, namely the TextTiling approach, has been tested on a typical aircraft assembly document with segmentation by human subjects as benchmark. As shown in Figure 2, majority of the subjects' segmentation have corresponded to the segments given by TextTiling. However there have been some specific instances where the desired result has not been achieved. The performance of the existing TextTiling method cannot be conclusively ruled out for our purposes - however, a different approach that is more suited to the future needs of the current research has been proposed. TextTiling does not ensure understanding of the text in the document as natural language and there are no measures such as resolution of pronouns and anaphora being employed to acknowledge their role in segmenting coherent sections.

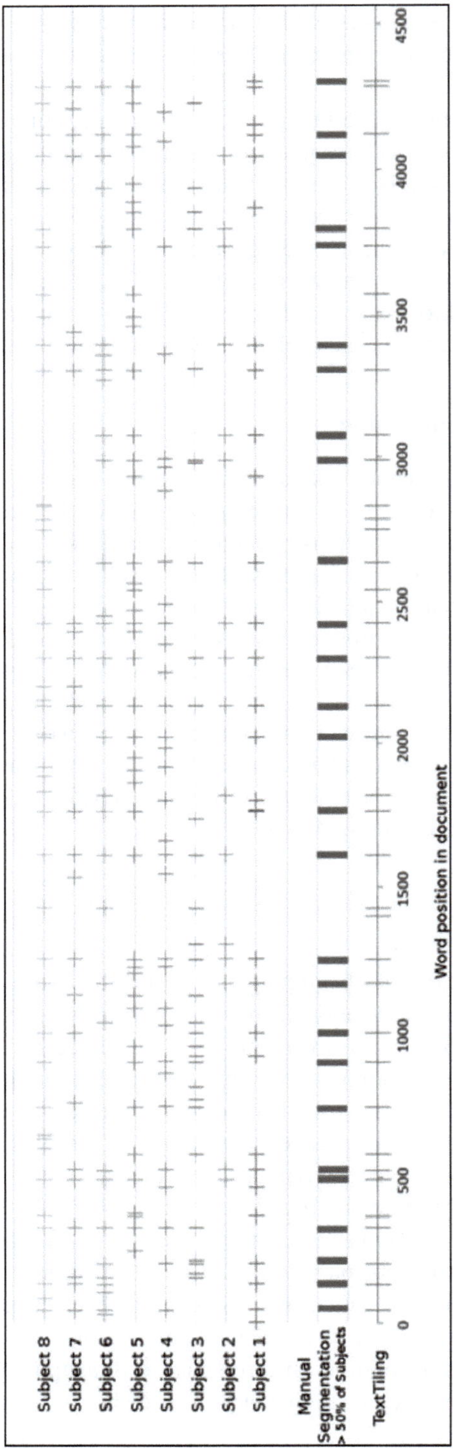

Fig. 2. Comparison of TextTiling vs manual segmentation for eight readers

The proposed approach treats documents as a discourse from the experts to the reader. Techniques from discourse analysis such as pronoun and anaphora resolution can be used to recognize and build coherent sections of a document. The discourse entity list can then be collected from such coherent sections and compared to those from domain ontologies to classify whether each segment is related to assembly or not.

6 Future Work

The paper has described a method for using discourse analysis techniques to classify relevant sections of a document. Some potential directions for implementation have also been touched upon. Future work includes implementing the method as a computer based program. This implementation then needs to be comprehensively tested to evaluate its effectiveness and to obtain feedback. The results of the implementation then have to be compared against the manual segmentation data as shown in this paper.

Acknowledgments. The authors wish to thank the members of IDeaS Laboratory at Centre for Product Design and Manufacturing, Indian Institute of Science, who volunteered as subjects for manual segmentation of the assembly text.

References

1. Madhusudanan, N., Chakrabarti, A.: Implementation and initial validation of a knowledge acquisition system for mechanical assembly. In: CIRP Design 2012, pp. 267–277. Springer (2013)
2. Sadeghi, S., Noel, F., Masclet, C.: Collaborative specification of virtual environments to support PLM activities. In: PLM11 8th International Conference on Product Lifecycle Management (2011)
3. Teng, F., Moalla, N., Bouras, A.: A PPO Model-based Knowledge Management Approach for PLM Knowledge Acquisition and Integration. In: International Conference on Product Lifecycle Management Eindhoven (2011)
4. Pugliese, D., Colombo, G., Spurio, M.S.: About the integration between KBE and PLM. In: Advances in Life Cycle Engineering for Sustainable Manufacturing Businesses, pp. 131–136. Springer, London (2007)
5. Briggs, H.C.: Knowledge management in the engineering design environment. Jet Propulsion Laboratory, National Aeronautics and Space Administration, Pasadena (2006)
6. Penoyer, J.A., Burnett, G.J.F.D., Fawcett, D.J., Liou, S.Y.: Knowledge based product life cycle systems: principles of integration of KBE and C3P. Computer-Aided Design 32(5), 311–320 (2000)
7. Brandt, S.C., Morbach, J., Miatidis, M., Theißen, M., Jarke, M., Marquardt, W.: An ontology-based approach to knowledge management in design processes. Computers & Chemical Engineering 32(1), 320–342 (2008)
8. Savory, S.E.: Some views on the state of the art in artificial intelligence. In: Artificial Intelligence and Expert Systems, pp. 21–34. John Wiley & Sons, Inc. (1988)
9. Chen, H.: Learning semantic structures from in-domain documents. PhD thesis, Massachusetts Institute of Technology (2010)

10. Han, X., Sun, L.: An entity-topic model for entity linking. In: Proceedings of the 2012 Joint Conference on Empirical Methods in Natural Language Processing and Computational Natural Language Learning, pp. 105–115. Association for Computational Linguistics (2012)
11. Li, Y., Chung, S.M., Holt, J.D.: Text document clustering based on frequent word meaning sequences. Data & Knowledge Engineering 64(1), 381–404 (2008)
12. Andrews, N.O., Fox, E.A.: Recent developments in document clustering. Computer Science, Virginia Tech, Blacksburg, VA, Technical Report TR-07-35 (2007)
13. Zheng, H.-T., Kang, B.-Y., Kimp, H.-G.: Exploiting noun phrases and semantic relationships for text document clustering. Information Sciences 179(13), 2249–2262 (2009)
14. Shahriar Hossain, M., Angryk, R.A.: Gdclust: A graph-based document clustering technique. In: Seventh IEEE International Conference on Data Mining Workshops, ICDM Workshops 2007, pp. 417–422. IEEE (2007)
15. Loftus, C., Hicks, B., McMahon, C.: Capturing key relationships and stakeholders over the product lifecycle: an email based approach. In: 6th International Conference on Project LifeCycle Management, PLM 2009, 2009-07-06 -2009-07-08, Bath (2009)
16. Marti, A.: Hearst. Multi-paragraph segmentation of expository text. In: Proceedings of the 32nd Annual Meeting on Association for Computational Linguistics, pp. 9–16. Association for Computational Linguistics (1994)
17. Grosz, B.J., Sidner, C.L.: Attention, intentions, and the structure of discourse. Computational Linguistics 12(3), 175–204 (1986)
18. Allen, J.: Natural Language Understanding, 2/e. Pearson (2011)
19. Fraser, B.: What are discourse markers? Journal of Pragmatics 31(7), 931–952 (1999)
20. Ntlk tokenize package, text tiling module (October 2013), `http://nltk.org/api/nltk.tokenize.html#modulenltk.tokenize.texttiling`
21. Case study of aircraft wing manufacture (October 2013), `http://www.oup.com/us/static/companion.websites/9780195157826/chapter19.pdf`
22. Madhusudanan, N., Chakrabarti, A.: Combining product information and process information to build virtual assembly situations for knowledge acquisition. In: ASME (2011)
23. Kamp, H., Van Genabith, J., Reyle, U.: Discourse representation theory. In: Handbook of Philosophical Logic, pp. 125–394. Springer (2011)
24. Lohse, N., Hirani, H., Ratchev, S., Turitto, M.: An ontology for the definition and validation of assembly processes for evolvable assembly systems. In: The 6th IEEE International Symposium on Assembly and Task Planning: From Nano to Macro Assembly and Manufacturing (ISATP 2005), pp. 242–247 (2005)

Study on Improving Accuracy for Edge Measurement Using 3D Laser Scanner

Kazuo Hiekata[1] , Hiroyuki Yamato[1], Jingyu Sun[1], Hiroya Matsubara[1], and Naoji Toki[2]

[1] Graduate School of Frontier Science, The University of Tokyo, Japan
[2] Graduate School of Science and Engineering, Ehime University, Japan
amatsubara@is.k.u-tokyo.ac.jp

Abstract. A high accuracy edge measurement method of edges of components using point cloud data by 3D laser scanner is proposed in this paper. The proposed method consists of two parts: method for shape measurement of edges by using points of side faces of the components and method for length measurement of edges by attaching the 3D targets. At the experiments with a surface plate and a curved shell plate, the results give suggestions for having possibility of applying this proposed method for actual shipbuilding components.

Keywords: Laser Scanner, Point Cloud Data, Edge Measurement, 3D Target.

1 Introduction

At different manufacturing sites, accurate measurement of large components is of vital importance.

For example, at each manufacturing stage of shipbuilding process, the shapes and sizes of the ship's components are measured and the accuracy is evaluated to reduce the cost of the rework in subsequent manufacturing stages including welding process specifically. Different 3D measurement system is employed for accuracy evaluation of components. Kim et al. suggested the 3D virtual simulation method of shipbuilding blocks using 3D measurement data by total station [1]. According to Shibahara et al., a method of 3D welding deformation measurement based on stereo imaging technique was developed [2].

Because most of the ship's components are very large, it is efficient to conduct measurement by using 3D laser scanner which can measures the whole surface of components at one time as one set of point cloud data. An edge measurement method for shipbuilding blocks was developed [3]. In this existing method, the points of edges are directly extracted from point cloud data based on the distance from a floor panel of the shipbuilding block. However, it is difficult to obtain the accurate shape and the length of edges from the measured point cloud due to intervals existing even in high density point cloud data of the large component.

In this study, a high accuracy edge measurement method of components using 3D laser scanner is proposed. Concretely, the method for edge's shape measurement using the point cloud of the component's side face and the method for edge's length measurement using the feature points of the 3D targets are explained.

S. Fukuda et al. (Eds.): PLM 2014, IFIP AICT 442, pp. 427–434, 2014.

2 Proposed Method

2.1 Overview

Fig. 1 illustrates the overview of the proposed method. The proposed method consists of two parts: method for shape measurement of edges by using points of side faces of the components and method for length measurement of edges by attaching the 3D targets.

In the method for shape measurement of edges, first of all, the component is measured by 3D laser scanner and the point cloud data including the surface part and side faces of the component are obtained. The continuous surface part is extracted using region growing method. To shorten the calculating time, the point cloud data of the surface part is thinned and the points of the thinned points cloud data's boundaries are detected. Using the detected boundary points, the points of the side faces are recognized and plane fitting is carried out locally to-ward the recognized points. Finally, the points on the edges are calculated according to the surface part and the fitted side face planes.

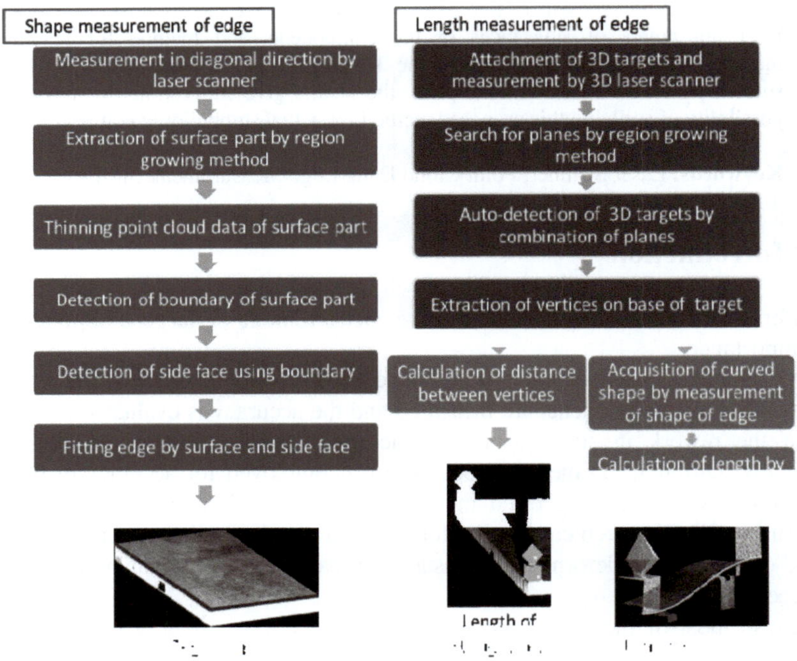

Fig. 1. Overview of the proposed method

In the method for length measurement of edges, at first the 3D targets, whose upper side is regular octahedron and the lower side is cube, are attached on the corners of the component and the component is measured by 3D laser scanner. Firstly, planar domains are detected from the obtained point cloud data and the position and direction information of the targets are recognized by the proper combination of the detected planes. Then, the vertices representing the edge's endpoints on the base of the targets are extracted. If the shape of the edge is a straight line, the length of the edge is calculated by calculating the distance be-tween the vertices. On the other hand, if the shape is curve, the shape is acquired by the shape measurement method of edges mentioned above and the length is calculated by fitting a cubic spline curve toward the calculated edge points.

2.2 Edge's Shape Measurement Method

First, the component is measured by 3D laser scanner and point cloud data including the surface part and the side faces of the component are obtained. An arbitrary point on the surface of the component is selected from the measured data and only the points of surface part are extracted by region growing method [4]. The point cloud except for the extracted surface part including the component's side face is detected at following process.

In order to reduce computational complexity in the following process, the point cloud of the surface part is thinned. The concrete procedure of thinning is described following.

1. Principal component of the surface part is analyzed and it is divided into two equal parts by a plane which is vertical to the first principal component vector.
2. The operation 1 is repeated for the other divided parts until the number of points from each separated part becomes less than a fixed threshold.
3. A set of each part's gravity center is considered as thinned points of the surface part.

Next, the points on the boundary are detected from the thinned point cloud of the surface using edge detecting method from Kalogerakis [5].

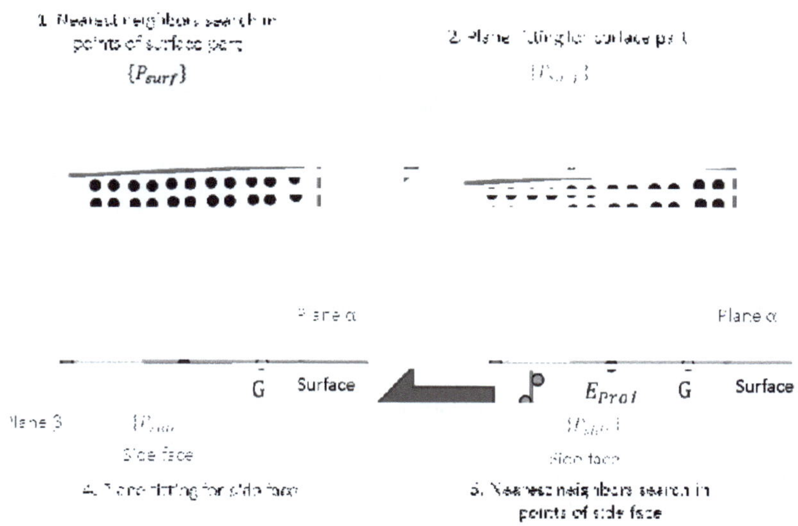

Fig. 2. Procedure of edge fitting

Using the points on boundary (**E**), the shape of edges is acquired. Fig. 2 illustrates how points of edges are fitted. The procedure of edge fitting is described as following.

1. The neighborhood of **E** ({$\boldsymbol{P}_{surf}$}) is searched by k-NN BBF method [6] from the point cloud of the surface part.

2. The gravity center of $\{\boldsymbol{P}_{surf}\}$ (**G**) is calculated and an approximate plane α is fitted to $\{\boldsymbol{P}_{surf}\}$.
3. The projection point of **E** to plane α ($\mathbf{E}_{proj}$) is calculated. The line segment $\mathrm{GE}_{\mathrm{proj}}$ is extended toward $\mathbf{E}_{\mathrm{proj}}$ and a point on the line (**E′**) is obtained. The neighborhood of **E′** ($\{\boldsymbol{P}_{side}\}$) is searched from the points except the surface in the same way as step 1.
4. An approximate plane β is fitted to $\{\boldsymbol{P}_{side}\}$ and the intersection of the line GE′ and plane β is calculated. It is one of the points describing the edge.

The above procedure is conducted for each point on the boundary and the shape of the edge is obtained.

2.3 Edge's Length Measurement Method

First of all, the 3D targets are attached on the corners of the component and measured by a 3D laser scanner. The 3D target is developed by UNICUS Co., Ltd. Fig. 3 illustrates how to attach the 3D targets on the component. The 3D target consists of a regular octahedron and a cube as shown in Fig. 3. They are attached on the corners of the component and a vertex of the target is made to match a corner of the component exactly as shown in the left image of Fig. 3. The component and targets are measured from a certain direction where at least four plane surfaces of the octahedron part and one plane surface of the cube part can be obtained.

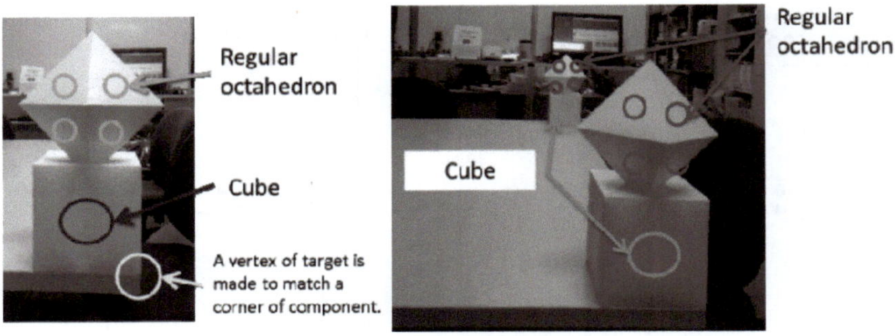

Fig. 3. Attachment of the 3D targets

Here the measured point cloud data is divided into continuous planar domains using region growing method [4]. A seed point for region growing is chosen randomly from the point cloud and all of the planes are recognized one by one.

The position and posture of the targets are recognized by doing proper combination of these recognized planes. Combination of four plane surfaces of octahedron part and one of cube part is found automatically and a target's position can be found uniquely. From the known size of 3D targets, the relative coordinates of the vertices on the base of targets is calculated.

If the shape of the edge is a straight line, the length of the edge is measured by calculating the distance between the selected two vertices of targets representing the corner of the component as shown in the left image of Fig. 4. Otherwise, if the shape of the edge is a curved line, the shape is obtained by the edge's shape measurement method introduced in section 2.2. A cubic spline curve is formed from two selected vertices of targets and the acquired points which describe the shape of the edge. An example of formed cubic spline curve is shown as a white line in the right image of Fig. 4. The edge's length is calculated from the obtained curve.

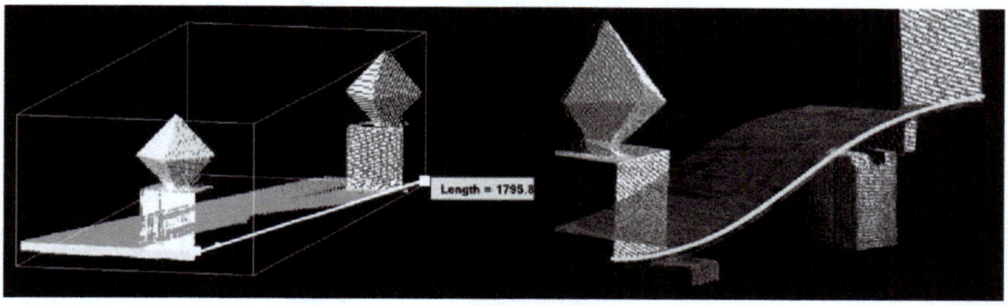

Fig. 4. Calculation of edge length

3 Experiment

Two experiments were performed to validate these proposed methods. The objective of the experiment with the measurement of a surface plate is to confirm the accuracy of measurement by the proposed method. The experiment using the curved shell plate measurement is performed to validate this proposed method with an actual sample of shipbuilding components.

In this study, the experiments are carried out by a FARO Focus3D laser scanner. Its specifications are shown in Table 1.

Table 1. Specifications of FARO Focus3D [7]

Vertical field of view (vertical/horizontal)	305° / 360°
Range	0.6 – 120m
Measurement speed	122,000 – 976,000 points/sec
Ranging error	±2mm@25m
Wavelength	905nm
Beam diamiter at exit	3.0mm

3.1 Edge Measurement of the Surface Plate

As an experiment in a laboratory environment, a surface plate was measured by 3D laser scanner. The surface plate is illustrated in the left image of Fig. 5. The plate and a laser scanner were located as shown in the right side of Fig. 5.

First, the shape of edges was measured by the method proposed in section 2.2. In this measurement, a steel plate was erected along the edge 3 to measure the edges 1, 2 and 3 at the same time as shown in the right image of Fig. 5. Fig. 6 illustrates the measured edge shape. The top image of Fig. 6 shows the whole edge shape and the bottom does an enlarged view of the framed part in the top. This shows that the points describing edges by the proposed method are obtained on the intersection of the surface and side face exactly. The error of distance between the edges 1 and 3 was -1.68mm compared with the measured value with a tape measure.

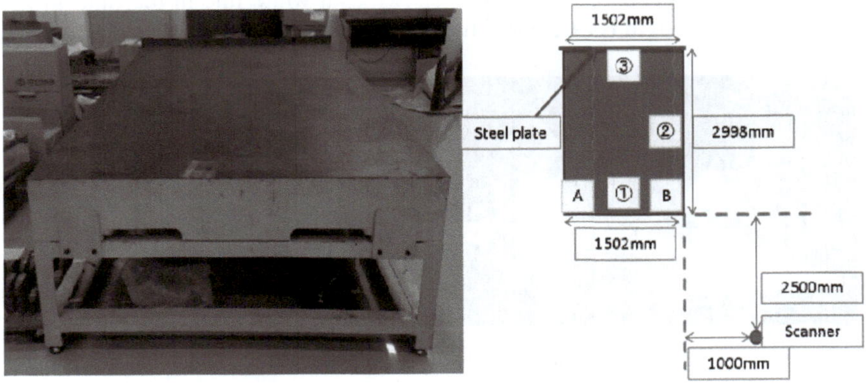

Fig. 5. Measured surface plate and arrangement of objects

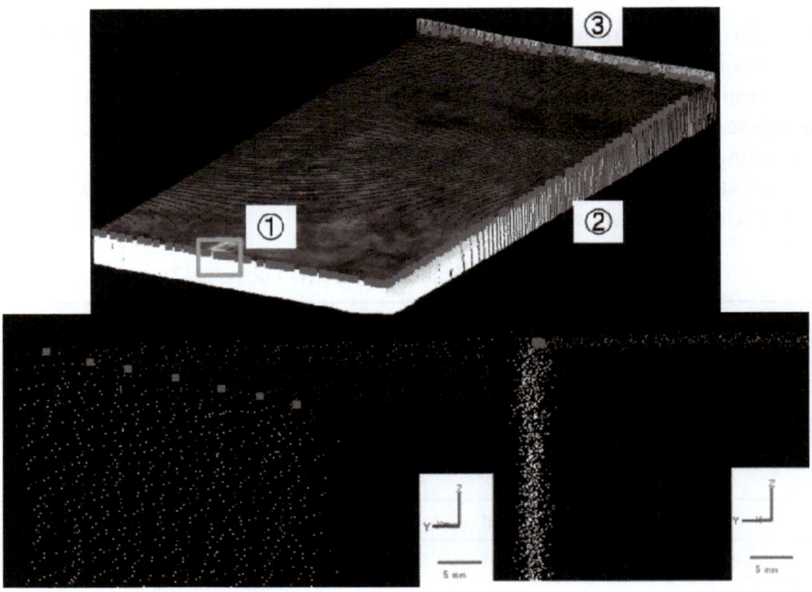

Fig. 6. Result of measurement of edge shape in an experiment with a surface plate

Table 2. Result of measurement of edge length in an experiment with a surface plate

Average value by proposed method	Standard deviation	Value by tape measure	Average of error
1501.85	0.56	1502.0	-0.15

Second, a length of an edge was measured by the method proposed in section 2.3. Two 3D targets A and B were attached on corners of the surface plate as shown in the left side of Fig. 5. The length of the edge 1 was calculated ten times. The result is shown in Table 2. The average of error is -0.15mm compared with the measured value by tape measure and standard deviation is 0.56mm. Two-sigma range is included from -1.27mm to 0.97mm. The accuracy of the error of length measured by the proposed method is less than 2mm.

3.2 Edge Measurement of the Curved Shell Plate

A curved shell plate of ship as shown in the left of Fig. 7 was measured by the proposed method. Its size by tape measure is illustrated in the right picture of Fig. 7. In this case study, the bottom edge of the plate in Fig. 7 was measured.

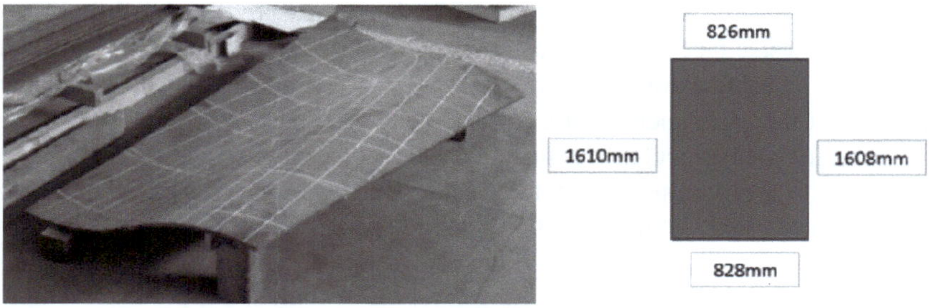

Fig. 7. Measured curved shell plate and its size

Fig. 8. Result of measurement of edge shape in an experiment with a curved shell plate

The result of measurement of edge shape by the method of section 2.2 is shown in Fig. 8. It is confirmed that the obtained white points describing the shape of the edge are in the correct position visually. The length of the same edge was calculated by the method of section 2.3. The error compared with measured value by tape measure was 0.89mm.

4 Discussion

It is necessary to manufacture shipbuilding components with less than 5mm error and detection of the error is required by measurement. In the experiment, the shape and length of edges were measured with less than 2mm error by the proposed method. Improvement in accuracy of edge measurement is achieved by using the points of the component's side face in measurement of shape and the feature points of the 3D target in measurement of length. It is considered that the error of measurement by the proposed method is small enough to evaluate accuracy of manufactured shipbuilding components such as curved shell plate.

In this study, measurement was performed only in a part of edges. There is a possibility of measuring all the shape and length of edges at one time by applying the proposed method to point cloud data obtained by registration of some data scanned from different directions.

5 Conclusion

A high accuracy edge measurement method of components using 3D laser scanner is proposed. Specifically, the method for edge's shape measurement by fitting planes to surface part and side face part of the component locally, and the method for edge's length measurement by using extracted vertices of the 3D targets attached on the component are developed. At the experiment with a surface plate, the shape and length were measured by the proposed method and the results indicated that the error was less than 2mm. At the measurement of a curved shell plate, the results give suggestions for having possibility of applying this proposed method for actual shipbuilding components.

Acknowledgments. UNICUS Co., Ltd. gives us technical supports for employing point cloud data processing platform "Pupulpit". The authors would like to thank that.

References

1. Kim, D.E., Chen, T.H.: A Virtual Erection Simulation System for a Steel Structure Based on 3-D Measurement Data. Journal of Marine Science and Application 11, 52–58 (2012)
2. Shibahara, M., Kawamura, E., Ikushima, K., Itoh, S., Mochizuki, M., Masaoka, K.: Development of 3-dimansional Welding Deformation Measurement Based on Stereo Imaging Technique. Quarterly Journal of the Japan Welding Society 28(1), 108–115 (2010)
3. Hiekata, K., Yamato, H., Kimura, S.: Development of Three Dimensional Measured Data Management System in Shipbuilding Manufacturing Process. In: Proceedings of the 20th ISPE International Conference on Concurrent Engineering, pp. 147–154 (2012)
4. Forsyth, D.A., Ponce, J.: Computer Vision, pp. 539–541. Kyoritsu Shuppan Co. Ltd., Tokyo (2007)
5. Kalogerakis, E., Nowrouzezahrai, D., Simari, P., Singh, K.: Extracting Lines of Curvature from Noisy Point Clouds. Computer-Aided Design 41(4), 282–292 (2009)
6. Beis, J.S., Lowe, D.G.: Shape Indexing Using Approximate Nearest-neighbour Search in High-dimensional Spaces. In: Computer Vision and Pattern Recognition, pp. 1000–1006 (1997)
7. FARO Focus3D Features, Benefits & Technical Specifications, http://www2.faro.com/site/resources/share/944 (accessed February 23, 2014)

Lifecycle-Based Requirements of Product-Service System in Customer-Centric Manufacturing

Jorma Papinniemi[1], Johannes Fritz[2], Lea Hannola[1], Andrea Denger[2], and Hannele Lampela[1]

[1] School of Industrial Engineering and Management, Lappeenranta University of Technology, Skinnarilankatu 34, FIN-53851, Lappeenranta, Finland
[2] Virtual Vehicle Research Center, Inffeldgasse 21/A, A-8010 Graz, Austria
1jorma.papinniemi@lut.fi

Abstract. Managing through-life information of products and services has become an important competitive means in customer-centric industries. The need for managing new types of product-service requirements for sustainability, traceability and performance have widened the traditional perspective of PLM information to integrate new issues, e.g. service information. In this study we examine how the diverse and through-life requirements information could better be integrated in product and business processes of customer-centric manufacturing. The study is based on a literature review and two case interviews. The objective is to elicit requirements information for Product-Service System (PSS). The study introduces the concepts of product-service system, and outlines through-life requirements in customer-centric business. PSS is a new concept for customer-centric business to improve the performance of sustainability, traceability, reusability and repeatability.

Keywords: Requirements information management, lifecycle-based requirements, sustainability, traceability, reusability, product-service system (PSS), product lifecycle management (PLM), customer-centric manufacturing.

1 Introduction

In today's global and competitive market, companies are facing many challenges especially in shortening the time to market, changing regulations, price competition, increasing product complexity and diversity, support and maintenance of products, sustainability and environmental concerns and end of life issues. As response to these challenges, manufacturing companies are striving for accelerating innovation and developing lean supply and product processes through lifecycle.

One related challenge is the effective and efficient management of scattered information on product requirements through lifecycle. Product related requirements and available information is a key factor for business success and competitive advantage. However, requirements are always on the move. Customers often change their mind; market drivers change; authorities keep adding new constraints

S. Fukuda et al. (Eds.): PLM 2014, IFIP AICT 442, pp. 435–444, 2014.

related to environmental or safety concerns; and sometimes the project encounters difficulties that require a revision of the initial targets.

Effective use of through-life information is an important means to response faster to changes in customer needs and product related requirements in customer-centric manufacturing environment [1]. Product lifecycle requirements also include service-based requirements throughout the lifecycle forming the concept of a product-service system (PSS).

In this study, we focus especially in the less studied topic of requirements information, related to the upcoming demand of integrative products and services in the context of customer-centric strategies. We utilize the concept of through-life requirements to describe the integration aspects throughout lifecycle, e.g. sustainability, traceability, reusability and repeatability.

The objective of this paper is to examine:

(1) What are the trends and drivers for managing information of new lifecycle-based requirements in customer-centric industry?

(2) What kind of through-life requirements are to be considered for product-services in project-based business (ETO) and mass-customizing business (ATO)?

This study is based on a literature review on product lifecycle requirements, and the characteristics of customer-centric manufacturing business. The study introduces trends and drivers for managing information [2-3], concepts of product-service system [1, 4-6] and outlines through-life requirements in customer-centric business. PSS is a new concept for business in improving the performance of sustainability, traceability, reusability and repeatability.

A comparative study on requirements information for the PSS was based on interviews in two B2B case companies. The companies represented two different kinds of customer-centric industries: low-volume project-oriented manufacturing mostly based on engineer-to-order (ETO) strategy, and high-volume mass-customization, typically based on assemble-to-order (ATO) strategy [7-9].

2 Literature Review of Related Work

In the following sections, the theoretical background of the paper is introduced from three viewpoints. First, some of the trends and developments leading to new product information requirements and customer-centric PLM are discussed, second a comparison of the typical features of customer-centric manufacturing strategies (ETO and ATO) is presented, and third, the characteristics of requirements management are clarified for this study.

2.1 PLM in Customer-Centric Manufacturing

Product knowledge management throughout the lifecycle of the product and the related services has attracted increasing consideration in research and (mainly manufacturing) company practices in recent years. There is a variety of related concepts and definitions in the literature on product lifecycle management, depending on the focus of the authors. Novel customer needs and the interest of the end customer towards sustainability and lifecycle aspects of both consumer products and business to business investment products has led to increasingly complex information requirements covering the whole value network [10]. However, current practices for product-related information management in manufacturing and service organizations are still mainly focused on developing internal processes and information flows, and are not always adaptable for a larger network of organizations during the lifecycle of the product.

Also from a political view, the tightening environmental legislation in the EU and US sets new requirements for sustainable manufacturing and end-of-life considerations of all kinds of goods produced (e.g. machinery, medicine, chemicals, food, and other sectors) and the responsibility of the manufacturer is emphasized [11]. As a response to these pressures, the concepts and practices of sustainable PSS [12], closed-loop manufacturing/production/supply chains [13] and closed-loop PLM [14-15] have been developed in recent years. These approaches to manufacturing and product information management are based on the ecological ideal of a closed-loop system, which does not exchange any matter outside its boundaries. Similarly, in manufacturing context, the aim of securing the continuous material and information flows between product lifecycle stages and closing the manufacturing loop by end-of-life operations such as recycling or remanufacturing are considered as integral parts of the manufacturing process.

The need for managing new types of product and service requirements for sustainability, traceability and performance have widened the traditional perspective of PLM information to integrate sustainability issues with other PLM information. The systemic nature of the sustainability concept also poses new challenges for the PLM tools and operating processes:

"Despite advances, integration of environmental issues and tools in existing PLM operating procedures is still lacking and a significant challenge..... The 'ultimate' sustainable product life cycle design and management system would contain a variety of product and process design, modelling and analyses modules." [3]

At the same time, companies are increasingly focusing on defining their operations from the customer point of view, and rethinking their strategies in terms of customer-centricity. The concept of customer-centric PLM describes the aim to gather and utilize customer information (e.g. feedback) efficiently to streamline operations and information flows between different lifecycle stages and to create value to customers along the lifecycle of the product [16].

2.2 Customer-Centric Strategies and Business Models

The degree of customer orientation is determined by the customer coupling point and the amount of customer-oriented information [7], [9], see Fig. 1. The more and earlier the customer is involved in the business process (design-fabrication-assembly-distribution), the more customer contact and information is needed.

In pure customization most intensive customer orientation is achieved by engineer-to-order (ETO) strategy and products. ETO production is suitable for unique products that have similar features, and the production is based on receiving a customer order and developing a technical specification accordingly. Customer orders are often organized as projects [17-18].

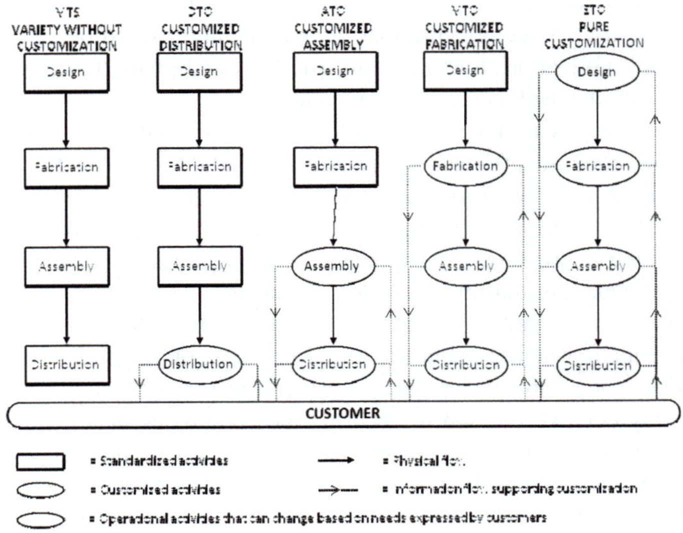

Fig. 1. Scope of customization along customer coupling point (adapted Forza et al. [7], p.10)

Another important customer-centric strategy in this study is the customized assembly (ATO) or customized configuration (CTO). In this case, customer requirements directly influence the assembly activities, not the design and manufacturing process. Products are made with a set of standard components and modules, but the assembly of this set is customized to satisfy specific customer needs. [7]

Managing strategies in manufacturing companies are often too product oriented and pay relatively little attention to services as part of the product offering. Due to the growing servitization of products, manufacturers need to better understand the nature of services and their impact on the design and operation functions [19]. Differences in characteristics of ETO and ATO have been analyzed by Haug et al. [8], especially from the point of transitions in strategy choices and business models. General characteristics of these customer-centric strategies are adapted in Table 1.

Table 1. General characteristics of customer-centric strategies (adapted Haug et al. [8])

Customer-centric strategy	High-volume mass-customizing business strategy (ATO/CTO)	Low-volume project-based business strategy (ETO)
Product variety	Increase variety	Limit variety
Customer view	Create valuable variety	Create adequate variety
Manufacturing cost	Slight increase	Decrease
Business purpose	Increase sales	Optimize processes
Configurator challenge	User interfaces	Knowledge base

2.3 Characteristics of Requirements Management

Requirements management is a critical part of a development process for all products, not only for software [20], where the requirement management practices are traditionally well known. According to Grady [21], perhaps the greatest mistakes in system development performance in industry appears in requirements management. Requirements practices include requirements elicitation, analysis, prioritization, documentation, verification and management. These practices are often discussed together under the umbrella 'requirements management' (RQM). Halbleib [22] states that it is important to treat RQM as a process and not a single event, since requirements change and their status must be tracked throughout the project.

Requirements management support is needed in engineering design [23]. Literature covers several practices, techniques and methods to support the critical process of requirements management. In addition, there are a large number of proposals for managing requirements, and several commercial software tools are available for requirements management [23]. Requirement management methods and tools enable procedures to document requirements and check their progress through the product development project [23].

According to Jiao and Chen [24], understanding and fulfilling customer's requirements individually has recognized as a compelling challenge for companies across industries. Poor understanding and analysis of customer requirements during the elicitation and analysis of requirement information have negative implications on design and manufacturing of a product in terms of quality, lead time, and cost [24]. One of the biggest challenges in requirements management is that the requirements change; customers or other stakeholders require new requirements or want to remove the original ones at any phase of development lifecycle. Other challenges related to requirements management are e.g. inadequate processes, shortage of resources, poor communication (such as a communication gap between customers and developers), complexity of requirements and lack of support from executive management [25].

3 Concepts of Product-Service Systems

Product-service systems (PSS) represent "a marketable set of products and services capable of jointly fulfilling a user's need. The product/service ratio in this set can vary, either in terms of function fulfilment or economic value." [5]

PSS are seen as an excellent mean to enhance the competitive ability "and to foster sustainability at the same time" [6]. This implies a dualistic approach on attracting the customer's attention. The feature-driven product perspective is supported by the more solution-oriented service perspective [26]. Mont summarizes five characteristics for PSS as followed: [27]

- A PSS may consist of products, services, or various combinations of them. Products substituted by services are largely an ideal category without many practical or consistent examples, because any service, even nonmaterial per se, requires material or energy inputs.

- Services, at the point of sale, comprise personal assistance in shops, financial schemes provided to customers, explanations about product use.
- Different concepts of product use consist of two categories: use oriented, where product utility is extracted by the user, and result oriented, where product utility is extracted by the utility provider for the user.
- Maintenance services include servicing of products with the goal of prolonging product life cycle, comprising maintenance and upgrading.
- Revalorization services include offers that aim at closing the product material cycle by taking products back, secondary utilization of usable parts in new products and recycling of materials if reuse is not feasible.

Therefore, Tukker [6] characterizes eight types of PSS in his work – a range from product-related services to a functional result for the consumer.

According to Meier, Roy & Seliger [28], in the domains of mechanical engineering and plant design, "product-related services are usually considered as an add-on to the actual product. Industrial PSS deal with dynamic interdependencies of products and services in production. Research areas cover new concepts and methods which enable the machine producers to design the potential services in an optimal way, already during the development of the machine. This paradigm shift from the separated consideration of products and services to a new product understanding consisting of integrated products and services creates innovation potential to increase the sustainable competitiveness of mechanical engineering and plant design. The latter allows business models which do not focus on the machine sales but on the use for the customer e.g. in form of continuously available machines. The business model determines the complexity of delivery processes. Characteristics of industrial PSS allow covering all market demands." [28]

4 Research Process

Two case studies were employed to illustrate and compare the key characteristics and differences of product-service requirements of through-life information by two different strategy choices. Initial description of the case companies is introduced in Table 2.

Table 2. Description of case company characteristics

Case company characteristics	Company A	Company B
Main business area	Global designer, manufacturer and distributor of agricultural equipment and related parts	Supplier of a complete range of machinery, systems and technology for plywood and veneer production
Strategic choice of Business and product	High-volume mass-customizing ATO/CTO/BTO strategy	Low-volume project-based ETO strategy
Special characteristics	Individual products for individual use by customer order system	Long term installed bases

The primary data was collected by making semi-structured interviews in the case companies. In total, 10 persons were interviewed. Interviewees were chosen from the key functions, representing at least by one person related to both case companies.

The topic areas of the interviews were as follows: Business model/strategy transition; Structuring of product and product related information; Lifecycle related requirements; Role/accountability of services and lifecycle business; Practices of product-service information sharing in company networks; Principles of modularization of products/services/processes/information; Expanded product data (3D+) in design-manufacturing - service; Applying ECM processes in product/service specifications. The elicitation of the requirements information for PSS was based on combining literature results, earlier research in the manufacturing industry, authors' particular experience and insights, and the company-specific results discovered in the case companies.

5 Derived Requirements for Product-Service System

As a result of the interviews, requirements on product, service and product-service in ATO and ETO strategy are identified and classified. Derived requirements are presented in Table 3. The capabilities suitable for each requirements class (product, service, PSS) were selected. The derived requirements were analyzed for ETO and ATO strategies in terms of customer coupling-point, structuring base of product-service and related information, principles of product modularization, sustainability of PSS and managing through-life PLM processes and networks.

Several differences in ATO and ETO strategies were found in the study. For instance, in ATO strategy offered requirements are frozen in the early stage of development which enables better utilization of module-based PSS for customer needs. Respectively, in ETO strategy the challenge is to manage simultaneously frequent requirements changes and through-life requirements related to e.g. sustainability, reusability, repeatability and traceability. The key observation found in this study is that the timing of the customer-coupling point affects strongly on the possibilities of modularity and utilization of through-life requirements.

Table 3. Through-life requirements for product-service systems

Capabilities for PSS	ATO Strategy	ETO Strategy
Product requirements		
Customer coupling-point	Product offering as-designed	As-ideated functionalities, performance proposition
Structuring base of product and related information	eBOM & mBOM structures, Requirements & Features	Design for supply /installation processBOM
Principles of product modularization	Ready-designed modules to be ATO as product variants	Through-life knowledge base of ETO as `reference project-products`

Table 3. (*Continued*)

Managing through-life PLM Processes	Reusability of product information: designs / structures / changes	Repeatability of processes related to `project-products`
Service requirements		
Customer coupling-point	Service order as-maintained	Service contract as-maintained
Structuring base of service and related information	dBOM & sBOM of individual product delivered	ProcessBOM of service & operation
Principles of service modularization	Serviceability of component / module /system /product	Serviceability for usability of machinery and production
Role of services and lifecycle business in company	Accountability for concurrent product & service development	Accountability for lifecycle support of product & service
Product-service requirements		
Customer coupling-point	Combined product-service offering as-ordered	Combined lifecycle support of product-service system
Structuring base of product-service and related information	Global BOM integrated by concurrent product & service eBOM,mBOM,dBOM,sBOM	Global processBOM of `extended project product`
Sustainability of PSS	Closed-loop concurrent design of module based product, components and related services	Closed-loop concurrent design of through-life `project product` and lifecycle services
Managing through-life PLM processes and networks	Through-life traceability of product & service structures	Through-life traceability of extended 'project-product' with service processes

6 Conclusions

This paper combines the knowledge on requirements information management and PLM by examining the research questions through literature and two practical case examples. The questions were answered by a literature overview identifying the trends in the business environment of manufacturing companies and following changes in new product information requirements, mainly focusing on sustainability, traceability and performance. Changes in strategy towards more customer orientation, legislation changes towards environmental sustainability, and closed-loop manufacturing /PLM have had a profound effect on information needs and product information management practices in manufacturing companies.

Eliciting product-service lifecycle requirements in customer-centric business models is based on the literature and empirical findings, confirming the practical relevance of the findings. A comparison between ETO (project-based) and ATO (mass-customized) operating strategies and their influence on the product-service system requirements was presented based on literature and empirical findings from two case companies.

The results of the paper can be utilized in companies planning and developing their product-service offering, and related requirements and processes both on business strategy level and technical information management level. The elicitation of product service requirements acts as basis for comprehensive data structure planning. Although the empirical results of this study are limited on two case studies, they are selected to highlight typical features of different customer-centric manufacturing strategies and thus provide a possibility for adapting the results wider in similar companies.

Further research is needed to develop a framework for data structures in companies following ETO and ATO strategies, as well as for testing the applicability of the findings in other contexts.

Acknowledgments. Research conducted for this paper was coordinated by FIMECC, Finnish Metals and Engineering Competence Cluster, and funded by the Finnish Technology Agency, Tekes and the participating companies.

The Austrian authors would like to acknowledge the financial support of "COMET K2-Research Centres for Excellent Technologies Programme" of the Austrian Federal Ministry for Transport, Innovation and Technology (BMVIT), the Austrian Federal Ministry of Economy, Family and Youth (BMWFJ), the Austrian Research Promotion Agency (FFG), the Province of Styria and the Styrian Business Promotion Agency (SFG).

References

1. Gomez, M., Baxter, D., Roy, R., Kalta, M.: Through-Life Integration Using PLM. In: Proceedings of the 19th CIRP Design Conference – Competitive Design, Cranfield University, March 30-31, p. 155 (2009)
2. Terzi, S., Bouras, A., Dutta, D., Garetti, M., Kiritsis, D.: Product Lifecycle Management, from its history to its new role. International Journal on Product Lifecycle Management 4, 360–389 (2010)
3. Bras, B.: Sustainability and product life cycle management – issues and challenges, Int. J. Int. J. Product Lifecycle Management 4(1/2/3), 23–48 (2009)
4. Baines, T.S., Lightfoot, H.W., Evans, S., Neely, A., Greenough, R., Peppard, J., Roy, R., Shehab, E., Braganza, A., Tiwari, A., Alcock, J.R., Angus, J.P., Bastl, M., Cousens, A., Irving, P., Johnson, M., Kingston, J., Lockett, H., Martinez, V., Michele, P., Tranfield, D., Walton, I.M., Wilson, H.: State-of-the-art in product-service systems. Proceedings of the Institution of Mechanical Engineers, Part B: Journal of Engineering Manufacture 221, 1543–1552 (2007)
5. Goedkoop, M.J., van Halen, C.J.G., te Riele, H.R.M., Rommens, P.J.M.: Product service systems, ecological and economic basis, PricewaterhouseCoopers N.V. / Pi!MC, Storrm C.S., Pre consultants (1999)
6. Tukker, A.: Eight types of product-service system: Eight ways to sustainability? Experiences from SusProNet. Business Strategy and the Environment 13, 246–260 (2004)
7. Forza, C., Salvador, F.: Product Information Management for Mass Customization. Palgrave-Macmillan (2007)

8. Haug, A., Ladeby, K., Edwards, K.: From engineer-to-order to mass customization. Management Research News 32(7), 633–644 (2009)
9. Steger-Jensen, K., Svensson, C.: Issues of mass customisation and supporting IT-solutions. Computers in Industry 54, 83–103 (2004)
10. Seifi, S., Zulkifli, N., Yusuff, R., Sullaiman, S.: Information requirements for sustainable consumption. Social Responsibility Journal 8(3), 433–441 (2012)
11. Messina, J., Simmon, E., Aronoff, M.: Environmental Regulations Impose New Product Lifecycle Information Requirements. In: Complex Systems Concurrent Engineering, pp. 373–438. Springer (2007)
12. Roy, R.: Sustainable product-service systems. Futures 32(3-4), 289–299 (2000)
13. Savaskan, R.C., Bhattacharya, S., van Wassenhove, L.N.: Closed-Loop Supply Chain Models with Product Remanufacturing. Management Science 50(2), 239–252 (2004)
14. Jacopo, C., Tomasella, M., Taisch, T., Matta, M.: A new closed-loop PLM Standard for mass products. International Journal of Product Development 8(2), 141–161 (2009)
15. Kiritsis, D., Nguyen, V.K., Stark, J.: How closed-loop PLM improves Knowledge Management over the complete product lifecycle and enables the factory of the future. Int. J. Product Lifecycle Management 3(1), 54–77 (2008)
16. Schulte, S.: Customer centric PLM: integrating customers' feedback into product data and lifecycle processes. Int. J. Product Lifecycle Management 3(4), 295–307 (2008)
17. Yang, L.-R.: Key practices, manufacturing capability and attainment of manufacturing goals: The perspective of project/engineer-to-order manufacturing. International Journal of Project Management 31(1), 109–125 (2013)
18. Tonchia, S.: Industrial Project Management - Planning, Design, and Construction. Springer, Heidelberg (2008)
19. Zhang, Y., Srai, J., Gregory, M., Iakovaki, A.: Engineering network configuration: transition from products to services. In: Proceedings of the 19th CIRP Design Conference–Competitive Design (2009)
20. Turk, W.: Requirements management, Defense AT-L, 34, 10–3 (2005)
21. Grady, J.O.: System Requirements Analysis. Elsevier (2014)
22. Halbleib, H.: Requirements management. Information Systems Management 21, 8–14 (2004)
23. Baxter, D., Gao, J., Case, K., Harding, J., Young, B., Cochrane, S., Dani, S.: A framework to integrate design knowledge reuse and requirements management in engineering design. Robotics and Computer-Integrated Manufacturing 24, 585–593 (2008)
24. Jiao, J.R., Chen, C.-H.: Customer Requirements Management in Product Development: A review of Research Issues. Concurrent Engineering: Research and Applications 14(3), 173–185 (2006)
25. Hannola, L., Ovaska, P.: Challenging front-end-of-innovation in information systems. Journal of Computer Information Systems 52(1), 66–75 (2011)
26. Vargo, S.L., Lusch, R.F.: Evolving to a new dominant logic for marketing. Journal of Marketing 68, 1–17 (2004)
27. Mont, O.K.: Clarifying the concept of product–service system. Journal of Cleaner Production 10, 237–245 (2002)
28. Meier, H., Roy, R., Seliger, G.: Industrial Product-Service Systems—IPS^2. CIRP Annals - Manufacturing Technology 59, 607–627 (2010)

Product-Service Lifecycle Management in Manufacturing: An Industrial Case Study

Margherita Peruzzini, Michele Germani, and Eugenia Marilungo

Università Politecnica delle Marche, via Brecce Bianche 12, 60131 Ancona, Italy
{m.peruzzini,m.germani,e.marilungo}@univpm.it

Abstract. Product-Service is a recent concept based on a novel product understanding consisting of integrated product and service shares. It represents a new trend for industries to innovate their artefacts and create fresh business opportunities. However, moving from product to services requires the identification of the needed assets to create the new solution and the integration of both product-related and service-related activities into a unique product-service lifecycle. In practice, such an evolution can be defined theoretically but it is hard to implement since supporting tools are strongly product-centred yet. As a consequence, product-service is still a fascinating idea especially in manufacturing sector. This paper tells about a success story of product-service management in manufacturing industry; it describes how a household appliances' manufacturer shifted from traditional product lifecycle towards product-service lifecycle to manage the new service. The study starts from analysis of the AS-IS processes and mapping of the ecosystem tangible and intangible assets, and describes how the company was supported into the definition of an integrated product-service lifecycle.

Keywords: Product Lifecycle Management, PSS (Product-Service System), PLM improvement concept, Collaboration, Virtual Enterprise.

1 Introduction

Numerous manufacturing enterprises are challenged by the transition from a traditional product-oriented model to a new extended service-oriented one, which can be realized by Product-Service Systems (PSS) [1]. This trend mainly consists of adding a wide range of services to increase the value perceived by the customers and better satisfy their needs. In particular, Product-Service Systems (PSSs) consist of the combination of tangible and intangible assets and their integration in Product-Service modules, which are mutually determinant throughout the whole lifecycle [2]. Additional services and added value move the product towards an extended product really tackling the customer's needs and offering a solution. In this context, technical services represent the easiest way to create a PSS in manufacturing industry: from maintenance to training, retrofitting and product monitoring. Indeed, they can be easily realized by improving the product communication capabilities in order to make data flow from product to external systems to realize supporting or differentiating services. This integrated understanding leads to new and customer-oriented solutions, and

S. Fukuda et al. (Eds.): PLM 2014, IFIP AICT 442, pp. 445–454, 2014.

enable innovative functions and result-oriented business models. Furthermore, services can bring great advantages for industry: from the economical viewpoint, services can create higher profit margins and contribute to higher productivity by means of reduced investment costs along the lifetime as well as reduced operating costs for the final users [3]; from an ecological viewpoint, product-services can be more efficient thanks to a more conscious product usage, an increased resource productivity and a close loop-chain manufacturing as reported by some examples [4]; finally, services create socially advanced scenarios, as they secure knowledge intensive jobs and contribute to a more geographically balanced wellbeing distribution [5].

However, producing product-services opens a big issue in enterprise modelling and data management since they overcome the model of traditional products and the boundaries of the single company. Indeed, if tangible assets can found in the manufacturer company and its supply chain, intangible assets require medium-term collaboration with service companies and the creation of the so-called Virtual Ecosystems [6]. These ecosystems are replacing the former single enterprise and take over the lifetime responsibilities for the new PSS; they were also called Virtual Manufacturing Enterprise (VME). As a result, the cohesion between the product, associated services and the life cycle ideas is expressed by the product-service concept. For this reason, product-service requires the management of all assets and entities involved as well as the PSS designed and by modelling the complex the interrelations between products and non-physical services. In this context, the paper describes an industrial case study focusing on product-services in household appliances sector.

2 Product-Service Management for Manufacturing Companies

A product-service consists of proposing a mix of tangible products and intangible services designed and combined to optimize the product use and increase the value for customers [7]. Value creation can be provided through an extended business network involving different stakeholders, which concur to create the services. Product-service idea starts from the concept of extended product [2], where intangible services are incorporated into a core product to add value. The term PSS usually includes the tangible product, the related services, the enterprise network and the infrastructures needed [8]. In manufacturing applications PSS are almost based on technical services for two main reasons: they have a concurrent lifetime to the product to which they relate since they support the product use and interact with the customers during the operation stage [9]; and they can be added to product with low impact for manufacturers since they are usually available at low-cost and have a shorter time-to-market [10]. After-sales services are usually provided as PSS. Here are located the services that ensure and restore the availability of the material good. Furthermore, they can extend the life cycle of the product and reduce consumption, emissions and operating costs [11]. Specifically, after-sales services encompass: maintenance, hotline services, tele-service, spare parts, service and customer training.

There are various forms of servitization with different features and, as suggested by [12], there is a transition line from pure product manufacturers to service providers. At one extreme of the line there are product manufacturers, which produce core products and services purely as an add-on to the product, and services are used as a differentiating factor in product marketing strategy. At the other extreme, there are service providers, whose products are merely an add-on to services since products represent only a small part of total value creation. The transition is based on an extended service business, starting with a few product-related services and ending up with a large number of service offerings. In the evolution of servitization, many manufacturing companies have moved into services and that caused the boundaries between products and services to become blurred [13].

In parallel with servitization, industrial models in manufacturing have recently evolved from rigid, deterministic supply chains, to a next generation of completely flexible, open and dynamic ecosystems with new economic opportunities. In such ecosystems, members share knowledge, innovate and collaborate together, interact or connect with each other, design new products, communicate globally and develop projects [14]. Ad-hoc selection of the most suitable partners for each customer demand is needed in order to become more flexible and reactive on the global dynamic marketplace [15]. In fact, the collaboration between the main manufacturing company and its key partners is fundamental to propose a new value by the right delivery channels and the best strategies by developing new business models.

It is evident that the increasing importance of services represents big challenges for manufacturing companies. However, the biggest challenge is carrying out a reliable management of PSS and a successful coordination of all the activities related. In particular, small and medium businesses often do not have sufficient knowledge and resources to professionalise its service business.

Manufacturing companies have usually a clearly defined product development process, but they lack a sufficiently defined service development process as found in traditional service companies. Many companies recognise that the existing corporate structures and processes do not allow for efficient development and market positioning of innovative services. In addition, they are faced with the problem of being poorly equipped with appropriate approaches, methodologies and tools for an efficient development of services. In addition, due to the often unclear or unstructured portfolio of services in the firms, a lot of time and resources is spent for coordination and consultation work between the main actors.

In a nutshell, services represent an excellent opportunity for manufacturing companies, but companies need to be supported properly to fully catch this new opportunity. Several methods have been recently proposed to manage PSS (from modularization-focused approach, to stochastic and behaviour-focused approach, until lifecycle-focused methods) [16]. However, some of them are very theoretical and hard to implement in practice, while others are too specific and have a limited applicability. Several recent studies focused on requirement elicitation in product-services [17-18]: they highlights the main challenges of requirement engineering in virtual manufacturing ecosystems and proposes an approach based on Business Use Cases (BUC) and Serious Games to elicit PSS requirements and investigate the PSS lifecycle. Moreover, the existing business models in manufacturing are not well suited to servitization and collaboration, which are required to enter new markets [19]. Indeed the company business model must change from product to services: PSS requirements should be satisfied through the analysis of both internal and external factors (i.e. environmental, economic, social, technological and political), and the ecosystem factors. In this context, STEEP analysis well support the identification of internal (related the company structure) and external (related the company ecosystem) requirements and the definition of a new business model for a certain idea. Then, Canvas Business Model can straightforwardly schematize the model by providing a clear definition of how an organization creates, delivers, and captures value throughout its ecosystem [20].

However, companies still have a lot of difficulties in selecting the most appropriate tools for supporting PSS and selecting the partners to create the Virtual Manufacturing Enterprise (VME), as well as to define a valuable business model and a simple but reliable PSS lifecycle to refer their activities and those of their partners in the VME.

3 Methodology to Shift from Product to Product-Service Lifecycle Management

The research methodology provides a set of tools and a straightforward workflow to support manufacturing companies in realizing and managing a product-service idea to innovate their business. The crucial point is the analysis of the company ecosystem and the correlation between the tangible and intangible assets offered and the assets necessary for the new PSS, and the definition of a valuable PSS business model.

The proposed method starts from the analysis of the current situation and the mapping of the company's ecosystem assets to answer these research questions: a) Is the company ready to create a PSS? b) How to select the right partners to realize the product-service VME? c) How to manage the PSS lifecycle?

The method steps are described below.

1. **Analysis of the AS-IS Processes and Assets**: It consists of two main activities; the first is related to the analysis of the current Product Lifecycle Management (PLM) process, from its ideation, through design, manufacturing and delivery, to disposal; the second consists of the mapping all the involved assets of the company and its ecosystem, both tangible (i.e. machines, materials, devices, sensors) and intangible (e.g. competences, skills, knowledge, relations among tangible components needed to realize another product functionality). The first analysis is supported by a modelling tool able to represent the company processes, identify all the activities involved in each process and, for each activity, the related input and output, the needed resources (e.g. human, material or IT), the involved competences and skills, and the control unit (e.g. company's departments, process's managers). The second mapping is supported by interviews and ad-hoc questionnaires, which investigate different aspects of the value creation process. In particular, each question is directly linked to a specific key business activity or resource identified in the company business model.
2. **Analysis of the Servitization Readiness**: It allows understanding if the company ecosystem is ready to create and manage a PSS solution or which areas should be improved. Such an analysis is based on the assessment of four areas

(i.e. lifecycle management capability, ecosystem creation capability, innovation level, network management capability). Different questionnaires are defined to analyse the four areas.

3. **Mapping of Tangible and Intangible Assets**: It is based on the correlation between the new PSS items (i.e. product, services, ecosystem and infrastructure) and the related assets, mapping of the company ecosystem [21]. In fact, the PSS idea is defined by a set of tangible and intangible assets, coming from the specific competences and skills of the ecosystem partners. The mapping consists in tracing the network relations within the ecosystem, in terms of who has a certain knowledge, who provides a certain components, who realize a certain software application, who produces a specific product, who implements a specific service, etc.
4. **Business Model Definition**: It is based on the adoption of the Canvas model and allows clearly defining the company business model according to the previous results. It involves several areas within the company that should be defined in detail in order to identify which are the core areas where action is needed to implement the new business, such as key partners, key resources, key activities, value proposition, customer segments, channels, revenues streams, cost structure, and customer relationship. Business Model Canvas is used to analyse the building blocks of the new business model (service-centred), while STEEP analysis considers both internal and external factors related to environmental, political, economic, technological and social trends.
5. **Definition of the TO-BE Integrated Product-Service Lifecycle and VME**: It finally identifies the new lifecycle to properly manage both product-related and service-related activities and the actors involved. Starting from the previous AS-IS processes modelling, it modifies the core factors individuated in points no. 2 and 3. Moreover, thanks to the definition of the new business model (point no. 4), the company can identify the partners and their own specific knowledge and skills that are necessary to realize the VME and develop the PSS desired.

After step no. 5, the company is ready to create, produce and manage the new product-service solution; in particular, it has defined a certain PSS and a precise VME to support its creation, delivery and operation. At this stage, the quality of the service implemented can be verified in different ways. This research focused on analysing the customer satisfaction and the sustainability index. Satisfaction can be analysed by satisfaction questionnaires and usability testing by directly involving final users, while sustainability is calculated by specific methods (i.e. LCA and LCC applied to the specific PSS solution) to compare the exist product with its related product-service to be developed.

4 The Industrial Case Study in Household Appliances

4.1 The Company Ecosystem

The case study has been realized in collaboration with an Italian company producing household appliances and home care devices. The company ecosystem is guided by the manufacturer and is actually organized in a vertical supply-chain adopting a product-oriented development process. Collaboration between the manufacturer and its partners and suppliers is limited to design stages and components' supply. The leader company recently designs and produces "smart appliances", defined as a manufactured product embedded with a hardware (e.g. sensors, Zigbee module, router Wi-Fi) and software (e.g. web service, data repository, web/mobile application) infrastructure to connect the product to an external network.

The case study focuses on services for smart appliances; in particular, it aims at realizing a new maintenance service, called "Smart Maintenance Service": it consists of providing ad-hoc maintenance services to the consumers for a set of smart appliances connected at home. The PSS involved in the case study consists of the appliances, a web/mobile application able to provide personalized messages for coaching purposes and helping the final users in case of appliances' faults. Figure 1 expresses the underpinning idea of the Smart Maintenance Service and shows the main workflow. Data related to the appliances functioning are monitored by specific sensors and are collected in a database for data storage; here, e set of elaboration algorithms analyse these data according to two policies (i.e. coaching and fault management) in order to recognize the specific use scenario and support the user with personalized and tailored suggestions and advices. For the coaching function, the application gives best practices according to the product usage; for the fault management function, the system controls the appliances' parameters, detects dangerous situations and supports the user when some critical values occur in order to carry out the recommended actions or some specific checking actions.

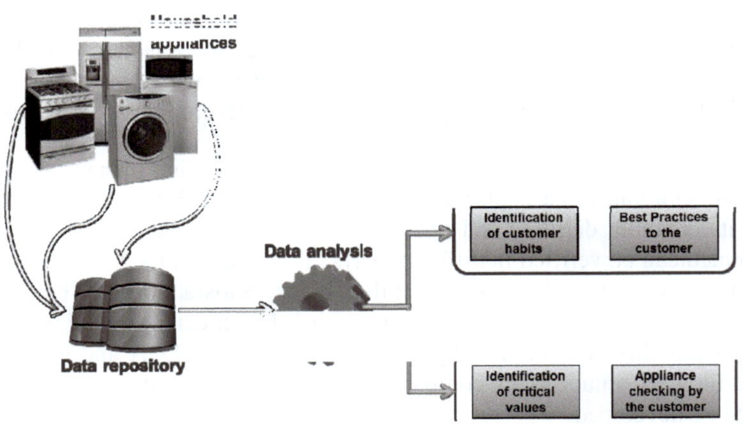

Fig. 1. The Smart Maintenance Service workflow

4.2 AS-IS Process Analysis and Assets

According to the methodology defined before, the company processes has been analysed. In particular, they refer to the following stages: "Product Conception",

"Product Design", "Product Manufacturing", "Product Delivery and Commercialization", and "Product Use". For each process stage, experts from both company and academia detailed the main activities and identified the departments involved, selected the key resources and modelled the activity flows. Moreover, interviews and questionnaires allows tracing the current assets and defining the product items in terms of functionalities, features, number of sensors, brand, production line, materials, any hardware supports (tangible assets) and intangible assets like partners involved in the ecosystem, brand resources, and customer relationships after sales.

	External Information	Customer relationship	PRODUCT Conception	PRODUCT Design	PRODUCT Manufacturing	PRODUCT Delivery&Comm.	Internal Information
STRATEGIC level	Existing appliances- Image of the company	Customer expectations	Business Plann	Methodologies, technical innovations, and partners selection	Choice of development technologies	Choice of the delivery means - Define the partner relationship	Business strategy - WM master planning
TACTICAL level	Existing technologies	Medium term feedback on customer satisfaction	Benchmarking activity; brainstorming for new ideas	Definition of the new product functions and specifications	Definition of production process and related action plan	General planning of the product delivery	Available technologies
OPERATIONAL level	Advertising	Customers orders - Customers claims	Validation of product orders	Detailed design planning	Modification implementation	Short term delivery planning - Measurement of performance	Status of production

Fig. 2. The product maintenance process analysis (AS-IS scenario)

4.3 Analysis of the Servitization Readiness

The analysis shows if the company is ready to implement the specific product-service solution and highlights the strengths and the possible weaknesses of the company in designing and managing the "Smart Maintenance Service" process. In the case study the analysis revealed that the company already has an ecosystem made up of different partners, suppliers, consortia and research centres and theoretically able to support product-service lifecycles, but such ecosystem is still strongly product-centred; services are perceived almost as tools to differentiate the product and do not represent the core business. The analysis also highlighted that the company is interested in understanding how to model and fully exploit PSS innovation projects. The case study defined also those areas (and related processes) to be improved to efficiently move to product-service solutions; they are: "Service Ideation", "Requirements analysis", and "Ecosystem governance and decision making".

4.4 Mapping of the PSS Assets and Creation of the VME

According to the PSS idea to develop (i.e. Smart Maintenance Service), a set of partners in the ecosystem are selected for their competences, skills, supplies, devices and knowledge, and their relationships are mapped in order to identify the better configuration of virtual manufacturing enterprise. The result of this study has given the following VME configuration: a research centre to support the PSS modelling, a technological partners to develop the IT infrastructure, a smart home provider able to share its competences about the household appliances connection into a network, a consortium for disposal, a consortium that studies innovative solutions, a partners to support the company during the delivery phase (e.g. during the best practices proposal) of the PSS, and the customers themselves.

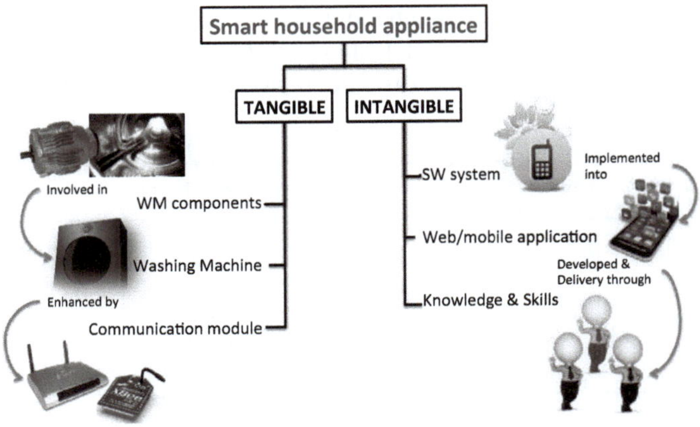

Fig. 3. Example of PSS assets mapping

4.5 Business Model Definition

A value proposition has been identified for the specific case study according to the Business Model Canvas. It consists of monitoring the household appliances and supports the maintenance process by web or mobile application and involving a group of selected partners (i.e. VME) performing the key activities to carry out preventive maintenance and coaching actions, PSS delivery and management. Figure 4 shows the identified business model: it addresses people that love smartness and convenience, and aims at creating making a long-term relationship between the customers and the company through on-line feedback, dynamic proposition and loyalty programs. Such a model can be delivered by local retailers as well as on-line shops, and can be implemented by different payment modes, from leasing contract to mobile payment.

4.6 The Integrated Product-Service Lifecycle and TO-BE Processes

Finally, an integrated product-service lifecycle has been defined to organize and manage all the information gathered in the previous steps. It starts from a recent model proposed in literature [22], that considers how the lifecycle phases are affected by changes due to transition from product to service (e.g. ideation, design, delivery). Figure 4 represents the global view of the TO-BE process by detailing the process activities, data input (e.g. target customer, partners in the ecosystem, competitors analysis), data output (e.g. from the PSS ideated to the creation of the Smart Maintenance), exploited resources (e.g. brainstorming activity, procedures, software infrastructure), and finally the involved competences and skills needed (e.g. coming from company departments, research centre, or technological partners).

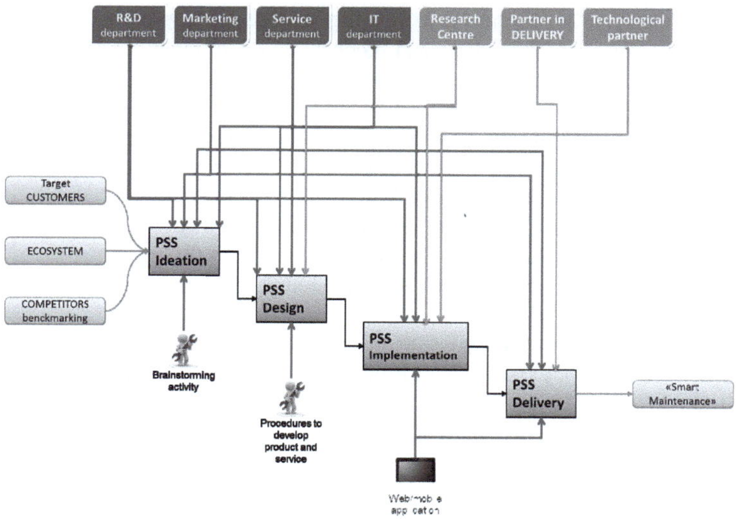

Fig. 4. Product-service lifecycle management process (TO-BE scenario)

5 Conclusions

The paper proposed a methodology to support manufacturing companies to achieve new product-service solutions by managing all the Product-Service lifecycle phases, from ideation to delivery. At the same time, the method allows analysing the company ecosystem in order to identify the virtual enterprise able to develop the specific PSS.

Such a methodology has been applied to an industrial case study focused on realizing services in the household appliances sector, the so-called Smart Maintenance Service. It demonstrated how the shift from a product-oriented to a service-oriented lifecycle can be properly managed and enhancing effective collaboration within the virtual enterprise. The results demonstrated how the Smart Maintenance Service is investigated and modelled, and what are the criticalities to face and solve to move for the AS-IS process until the TO-BE process.

References

1. Goedkoop, M.J., Van Halen, C.J.G., Riele, H.R.M., Rommens, P.J.M.: Product-Service Systems – Ecological and Economic Basic. PWC, The Hague (1999)
2. Thoben, K.D., Jagdev, H., Eschenbaecher, J.: Extended Products: Evolving Traditional Product Concepts. In: Proc. of 7th International Conference on Concurrent Enterprising (2001)
3. Baines, T.S., Lightfoot, H., Evans, S., Neely, A., Greenough, R., Peppard, J., Roy, R., Shehab, E., Braganza, A., Tiwari, A., Alcock, J.R., Angus, J.P., Bastl, M., Cousens, A., Irving, P., Johnson, M., Kingston, J., Lockett, H., Martinez, V., Michele, P., Tranfield, D., Walton, I.M., Wilson, H.: State of the art in Product-Service System. Journal of Engineering Manufacture 221, 1543–1552 (2007)

4. Favi, C., Peruzzini, M., Germani, M.: A lifecycle design approach to analyse the eco-sustainability of industrial products and product-service systems. In: Marjanovic, S., Pavkovic, B. (eds.) Proc. of International Design Conference DESIGN 2012, pp. 879–888 (2012)
5. Stahel, W.: The Utilization-Focused Service Economy, Resource Efficiency and Product-Life Extension. In: Allenby, B., Richard, D. (eds.) The Greening of Industrial Ecosystem, pp. 178–190. National Academy Press, Washington, DC (1994)
6. Camarinha-Matos, L.M.: Collaborative networked organizations: Status and trends in manufacturing. Annual Reviews in Control 33, 199–208 (2009)
7. Furrer, O.: Le rôle stratégique des services autour des produits. Revue Française de Gestion 113, 98–108 (2007)
8. SUSPRONET final report, `http://www.suspronet.org/`
9. Mont, O.K.: Clarifying the concept of Product-Service System. Journal of Cleaner Production 10(3), 237–245 (2002)
10. Aurich, J.C., Fuchs, C., Wagenknecht, C.: Life Cycle oriented design of technical Product-Service Systems. Journal of Cleaner Production 14, 1480–1494 (2006)
11. Homburg, C., Garbe, B.: Towards an improved understanding of industrial services: quality dimensions and their impact on buyer-seller relationships. Journal of Business-to-Business Marketing 6(2), 39–71 (1999)
12. Oliva, R., Kallenberg, R.: Managing the transition from products to services. International Journal of Service Industry Management 14(2), 160–172 (2003)
13. Baines, T.S., Lightfoot, H.W., Benedettini, O., Kay, J.M.: The servitization of manufacturing: A review of literature and reflection on future challenges. Journal of Manufacturing Technology Management 20(5), 547–567 (2009)
14. Tapscott, D., Williams, A.: Wikinomics: How Mass Collaboration Changes Everything. Penguin Books, New York (2006)
15. Windahl, C., Andersson, P., Berggren, C., Nehler, C.: Manufacturing firms and integrated solutions: characteristics and implications. European Journal of Innovation Management 7(3), 218–228 (2004)
16. Garetti, M., Rosa, P., Terzi, S.: Life Cycle Simulation for the design of Product–Service Systems. Computers in Industry 63, 361–369 (2012)
17. Peruzzini, M., Germani, M., Favi, C.: Shift from PLM to SLM: A method to support business requirements elicitation for service innovation. In: Rivest, L., Bouras, A., Louhichi, B. (eds.) PLM 2012. IFIP AICT, vol. 388, pp. 111–123. Springer, Heidelberg (2012)
18. Wiesner, S., Peruzzini, M., Doumeingts, G., Thoben, K.D.: Requirements Engineering for Servitization in Manufacturing Service Ecosystems (MSEE). In: Proc. 4th CIRP IPS2 Conference, Japan (2012)
19. Casadesus-Masanell, R.: Ricart, J.E.: From Strategy To Business Models And To Tactics. IESE Business School, University of Navarra, pp. 1–3 (2010)
20. Osterwalder, A., Pigneur, Y.: Business Model Generation. Modderman Druckwerk (2009)
21. Cassina, J., Cannata, A., Taisch, M.: Development of an Extended Product Lifecycle Management through Service Oriented Architecture (2009)
22. Peruzzini, M., Germani, M., Marilungo, E.: Product-service sustainability assessment in virtual manufacturing enterprises. In: Camarinha-Matos, L.M., Scherer, R.J. (eds.) PRO-VE 2013. IFIP AICT, vol. 408, pp. 13–21. Springer, Heidelberg (2013)

Process Information Model for Sheet Metal Operations

Ravi Kumar Gupta[1,2], Pothala Sreenu[1], Alain Bernard[2], and Florent Laroche[2]

[1] Mechanical Engineering Deptt., National Institute of Technology, Silchar-788010, India
[2] IRCCyN, Ecole Centrale de Nantes, 1 Rue Noë, Nantes 44300, France
{rkgiisc,sreenupothala037}@gmail.com,
alain.bernard@irccyn.ec-nantes.fr

Abstract. The paper extracts the process parameters from a sheet metal part model (B-Rep). These process parameters can be used in sheet metal manufacturing to control the manufacturing operations. By extracting these process parameters required for manufacturing, CAM program can be generated automatically using the part model and resource information. A Product model is generated in modeling software and converted into STEP file which is used for extracting B-Rep which interned is used to classify and extract feature by using sheet metal feature recognition module. The feature edges are classified as CEEs, IEEs, CIEs and IIEs based on topological properties. Database is created for material properties of the sheet metal and machine tools required to manufacture features in a part model. The extracted feature, feature's edge information and resource information are then used to compute process parameters and values required to control manufacturing operations. The extracted feature, feature's edge information, resource information and process parameters are the integral components of the proposed process information model for sheet metal operations.

Keywords: Process Information Model, Process Parameters, Sheet metal Operation.

1 Introduction

Manufacturing planning plays a vital role in determining the effective use of resources and smooth production flow. As a consequence, both the scientific insight into and manufacturing procedures of various sheet metal forming processes have been rapidly developing. Particularly fast progress could be observed in the area of computer simulation methods for the forming operations. A number of specific techniques and simulation programs are now widely in use. Sheet metal forming operations are standard manufacturing processes, which enable to obtain different types of draw pieces. The complexity of these processes leads to numerous techniques to predict or evaluate the formability of the raw materials.

CAD/CAM systems provide flexibility and automation. Even so there is interaction gap between CAD and CAM. The void between CAD and CAM can only be filled by automatic manufacturing and process planning activities. For a given sheet metal component, this involves determination of operations and parameters required to

S. Fukuda et al. (Eds.): PLM 2014, IFIP AICT 442, pp. 455–463, 2014.

obtain a component from a flat sheet metal. Sheet metal forming processes are those in which force is applied to a piece of sheet metal to modify its geometry rather than removing material.

Sheet metal forming depends on numerous interactive variables like geometric parameters, process parameters and material properties. The extraction of process parameters follows extraction of feature information from a sheet metal part model (STEP Format) using feature recognition module and then utilizing extracted feature information, material properties of sheet metal and tool information for extracting process parameters.

The feature reasoning deals with manufacturing information required to produce feature like blank size, location of various features, internal cuts, types of tools required and operation sequence. The work presented in the current paper is for development of process information model for sheet metal operation. The aim of the paper is to explain the extraction of process parameters and their values for sheet metal operation which is the main component of the process information model and is required for automation of the manufacturing process.

2 Literature Review

A survey of literature shows that different sheet metal feature recognition systems have been developed that takes 3D models as input. Review of such methods can be found in papers [1], [2].

Jae-Jun and Gyung-Jin [3] proposed optimization of process parameters (blank holding force and draw bead restraining force) for a sheet metal operation using response surface method, where process parameters are specified manually. Liu and Tai [4] proposed optimal design for flat pattern development by enumerating face adjacency graphs and potential topological unfolding of the structure.

Kannan and Shunmugan [5] proposed feature reasoning method to extract manufacturing information like blank size, types of tools required and operation sequence by using the extracted feature information and topological properties [1]. The flat pattern development is achieved by flattening each feature of sheet metal part model. The tool selection is based on single blow features and multi blow features. The extraction of actual process parameters required for feature operation is not discussed in the paper.

Gupta et al. [6] proposed automated process planning activates for sheet metal bending operations, flat pattern development for sheet metal part and tool geometry for the desired feature. A search formulation and algorithm is developed to optimize operation bending sequence for a sheet metal component. Qiang et al. [7] proposed optimization of sheet metal forming parameters by sequential optimization algorithms. The parameters required for operations are specified interactively. SceToh et al. [8] proposed a feature based flat pattern development system for sheet metal parts by classifying the sheet metal part as plate, wall, bend, design feature and co-feature. By getting the feature and co- feature entities, these features are unfolded in sequential way to obtain flat pattern for sheet metal component.

Papers [1], [2], [9], [10], [11] proposed feature recognition methods for recognizing and extracting sheet metal features from sheet metal part models to extract feature type, size and thickness of sheet metal. Feature recognition methods are well established and are used in commercial feature based modeling software like Geometric Solution [12], CATIA, Pro-E. Available feature recognition methods [1], [2], [9] can extract type and shape of the sheet metal features. But feature reasoning and identification of process parameters for a sheet metal operation from a part model is still an open issue. The extraction of actual process parameters required for manufacturing a sheet metal feature in a manufacturing set up is not addressed in the available literatures.

3 Process Information Model

Process information model for a sheet metal operation requires (i) shape to be produced, (ii) raw material used, (iii) manufacturing operation, (iv) tooling, and (v) parameters and their values for the operation. The information of the shape to be produced can be constructed in the process information model using available feature recognition techniques. Manufacturing and tooling information can be constructed based on the industrial setup and the feature information. The present paper utilizes feature recognition method [2] for extraction of features from a part model. The extracted feature information along with the material and resource information are used for extraction of process parameters. Thus the proposed process information model for sheet metal operations is based on the extracted feature information along with material properties, manufacturing tool used, and manufacturing process parameters and their values. Following sub-section is explaining the terminologies used for reasoning for extracting process parameters.

3.1 Terminology

Thickness (th). It is the minimum of the shortest distance between pairs of faces that lie on the same type of surface having anti–parallel normal (same direction and opposite sense) [2]. The thickness is constant for a sheet metal part [2], [9], [12], [13]. The thickness of a sheet metal part model is shown in Fig.1.

Reference Face (RF). RF is a planar face with maximum surface area among surface area of other faces in the part model. There are two such faces in the part model. Any one of these Faces is considered as reference face (RF). Example of RF in a part model is shown in Fig. 1.

Basic Deformation Features (BDFs). Deformation of the base-sheet or forming of material creates Bends and Walls with respect to a base-sheet or a reference face. These Bends and Walls are referred to as Basic Deformation Features (BDFs) [2]. The BDFs are similar to the Wall and Bend features proposed by Liu et al. [9]. Each pair of planar end faces forms a Wall; each pair of non-planar end faces forms a Bend. Wall and Bend features are shown in Fig. 2.

Exterior Edge (EE). An edge of the reference face is classified as exterior edge if it is outer edge-bound of the face. If an exterior edge is shared with other BDF then it is termed as common exterior edge (CEE) else it is termed as isolated exterior edge (IEE). The types of CEE and IEE in a part model are shown in Fig. 3.

Interior Edge (IE). An edge of the reference face is classified as interior edge if it is inner edge-bound of the face. If an interior edge is shared with other BDF then it is termed as common interior edge (CIE) else it is isolated interior edge (IIE). These types of faces are shown in Fig. 3.

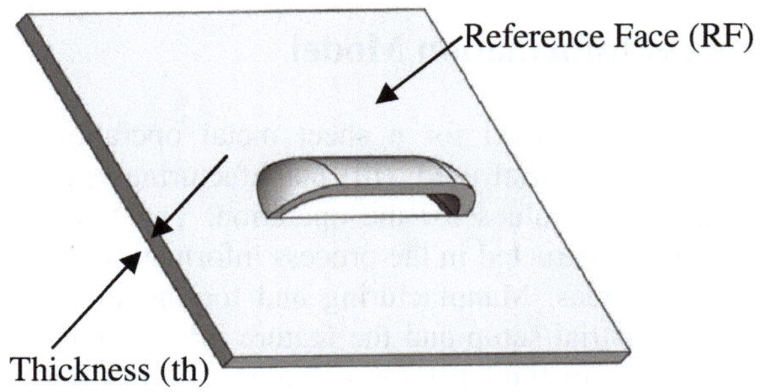

Fig. 1. Reference face and thickness of sheet metal part model

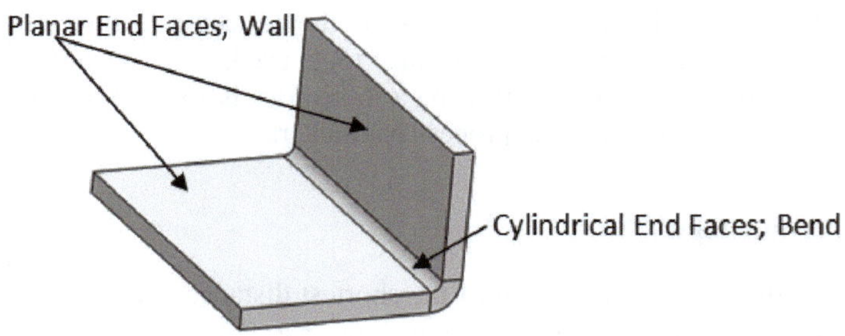

Fig. 2. BDFs (Wall and Bend) in a sheet metal part model

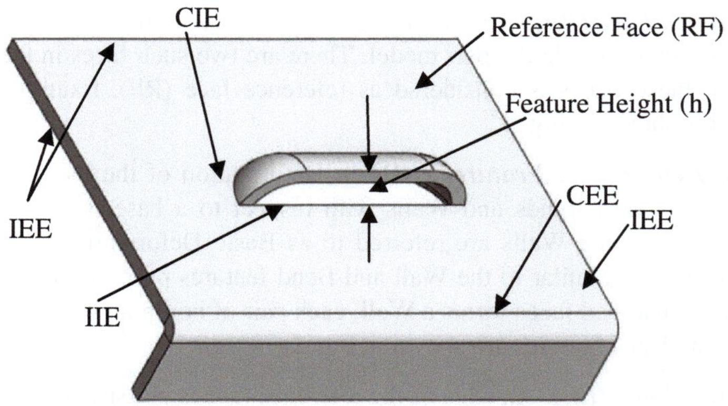

Fig. 3. Type of edges in reference face of a sheet metal part model

Feature Height (h). It is the maximum of perpendicular distances between reference face and feature faces facing in the same direction as RF. Feature height of a feature in part model is shown in Fig. 3.

Force. The amount of force applied to produce the desired feature. This force is classified as shearing force (Fs) and deformation force (Fd) based operation required. Shearing force is the force required to cut the material whereas the deforming force is the force required to deform the material plastically to the desired shape.

Blank Holding Force (Fh). This is the force required to hold the sheet metal during the feature operation and depends on the force required to generate the feature.

Primary Distance Moved by Tool (H1). This is the distance moved by tool through the sheet metal with the required shearing force. It is considered as 1/3 of thickness of the sheet metal [7].

Secondary Distance Moved by Tool (H2). This is the distance moved by tool through the sheet metal with the required deformation force.

3.2 Classification and Extraction of Edges

Edges of the reference face in a part model are classified as CEE, IEE, CIE and IIE as explained in sub-section 3.1. For the given part model (B-Rep), a planar face with maximum surface area is extracted and named as reference face. The edges in the extracted reference face is grouped under exterior edges or interior edges depending upon whether the edge is outer edge-bound of the face or inner edge-bound of the face respectively. These edges are further categorized as common or isolated depending upon whether the edge is shared with other BDF or not shared with other BDF respectively. Finally edges in the reference face are categorized into four groups as CEEs, IEEs, CIEs and IIEs.

The process parameters required for manufacturing a sheet metal operation are obtained from experimental setup. The process parameters with required values for manufacturing sheet metal features are extracted from a sheet metal part model as illustrated in the following sub-section.

3.3 Extraction of Process Parameters

Sheet metal forming is an industrial process that strongly depends on numerous interactive variables like geometric parameters, process parameters, material properties. These process parameters are required for controlling operation and to obtain the desired shape. The process parameters for a sheet metal operation depend on shape feature, material used for sheet metal and operation itself.

The extraction of process parameters for sheet metal feature operation from a sheet metal part model is explained in the following steps using flow chart shown in Fig. 4.

Step 1. STEP file of a sheet metal part model is read to extract B-Rep. Feature recognition framework [2], [14] is used to classify, represent, and extract sheet metal features in the part model. The feature information such as reference face (RF), thickness (th), feature type and feature height (h) are extracted.

Step 2. Edges in the reference face are categorized as CEEs, IEEs, CIEs and IIEs as explained in sub-sections 3.1 and 3.2.

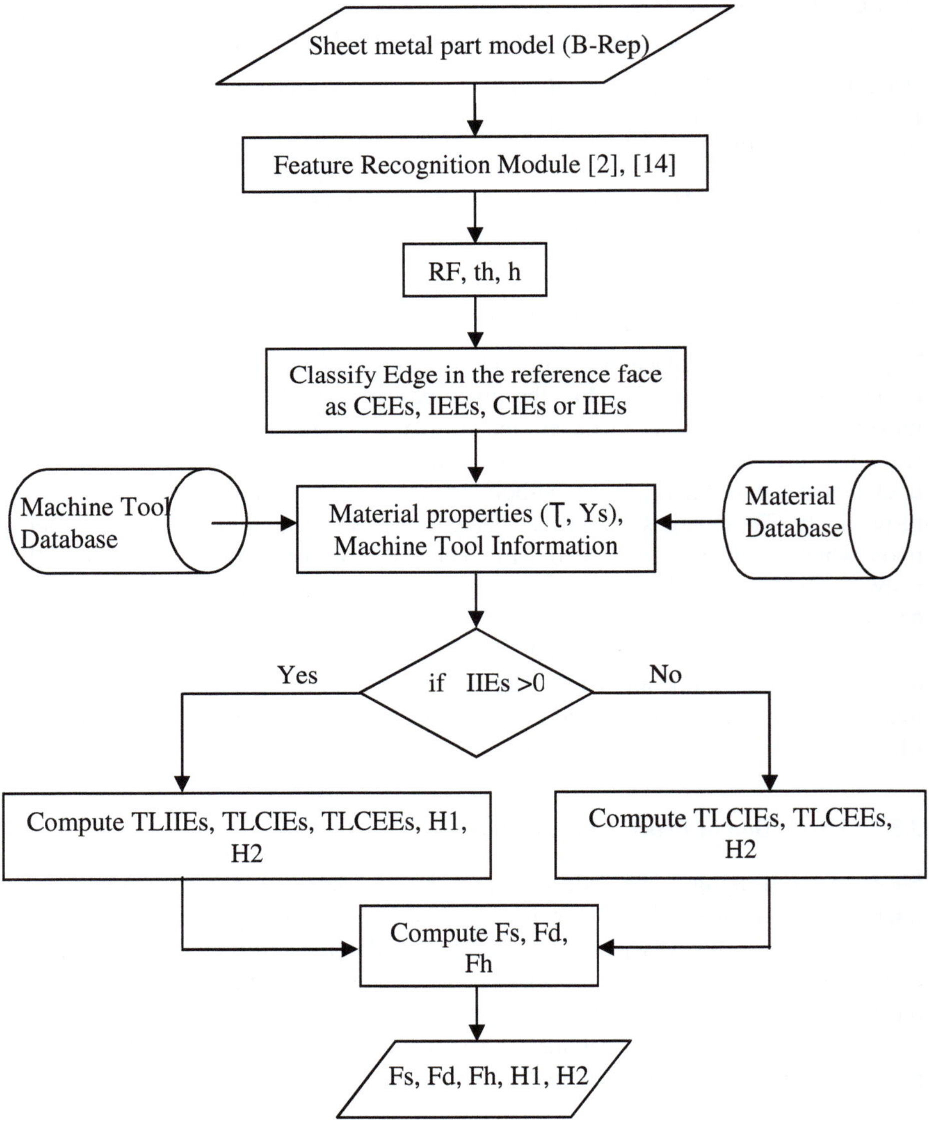

Fig. 4. Flowchart for extraction of process parameters from sheet metal part model

Step 3. Database for material properties can be created [15] and used for selecting the required material's properties such as shear stress (τ) and yield stress (Ys). Steel - Grade 304 (τ = 300N/mm^2, Ys = 210N/mm^2) is used as sheet material for calculations in this paper.

Step 4. Database of machine tool can be created based on the resources available in a manufacturing setup or enterprise and used for selecting machine tool for manufacturing the feature in the part model. Punching press as machine tool is used for calculations for the example presented in this paper.

Step 5. Parameters required for manufacturing are computed using information extracted in previous steps and are given below:

```
if number of IIEs for the feature is greater than zero
        then Calculate the following
        Total length of IIEs (TLIIEs) = Sum of length's of IIEs on the feature;
        Total length of CIEs (TLCIEs) = Sum of length's of CIEs on the feature;
        Total length of CEEs (TLCEEs) = Sum of length's of CEEs on the feature;
        Primary distance moved by tool (H1) = th/3;
        Secondary distance moved by tool (H2) = h-H1;
else
        Calculate the following
        Total length of CIEs (TLCIEs) = Sum of length's of CIEs on the feature;
        Total length of CEEs (TLCEEs) = Sum of length's of CEEs on the feature;
        Primary distance moved by tool (H1) = 0;
        Secondary distance moved by tool (H2) = h;
end
Shearing force (Fs) = τ*th*TLIIEs;
Deformation force (Fd) = Kd*Ys*th*( TLCIEs + TLCEEs);
Blank holding force (Fh) = 0.2*(max(Fs, Fd));
```

Where Kd is a Constant; depends on the design of tool (punch/die) and complexity of the feature geometry. It ranges from 0.33 (for bend radius<2*th) to 0.5 (for bend radius >2*th). The output "Fs, Fd, Fh, H1, H2" with their values are used for generating computer program to run the machine tool. Case studies for extraction of process parameters from part model are presented in the following section.

4 Case Studies

Examples for extraction of process parameters from sheet metal part model are shown in Table 1. Images of the part model are shown in first column of the table. The extracted information from B-Rep is shown in second column (under 8 sub-columns). The process parameters computed using extracted information and material properties (τ = 300N/mm^2, Ys = 210N/mm^2 for Steel - Grade 304) are shown in third column (under 5 sub-columns).

Table 1. Extraction of process parameter from the sheet metal part model

Sheet Metal Part Model	**Information extracted from the part model**								**Process Parameters**				
	th	**Number of**						**h**					
		CEEs	***CIEs***	***IIEs***	***TLIIEs***	***TLCIEs***	***TLCEEs***		***Fs***	***Fd***	***Fh***	***H1***	***H2***
	2	0	1	3	130	30	0	50	78000	4158	15600	0.67	49.33
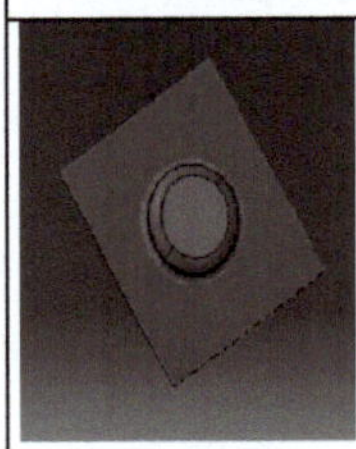	2	0	2	0	0	62.83	0	10	0	8709	1742	0	10
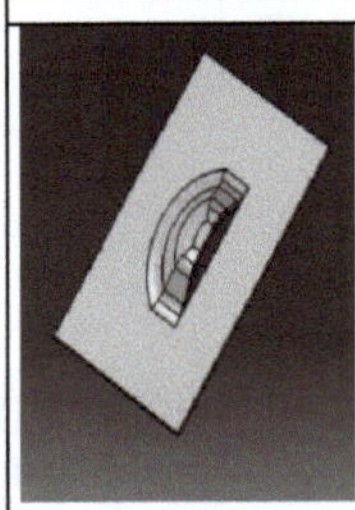	2	0	3	1	50	71	0	10	30000	9841	6000	0.67	9.33
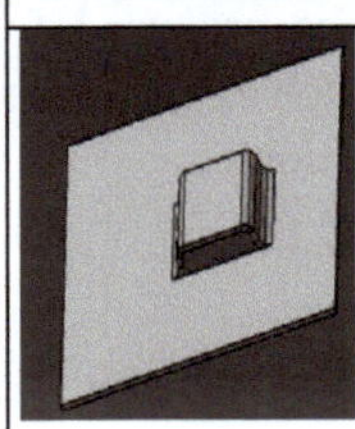	2	0	2	2	100	60	0	10	60000	8316	12000	0.67	9.33

In the above table 1: th, TLIIEs, TLCIEs, TLCEEs, h, H1 and H2 are in millimeter and Fs, Fd, and Fh are in Newton.

5 Conclusion

Process information model for sheet metal operations has been proposed which includes feature information, resource information, sheet material information and process parameters required for manufacturing the features in the part model. These process parameters are seen as to provide integration of manufacturing operation with the design stage. The automatic extraction of process parameters from a sheet metal part model has been demonstrated.

The process parameters can be optimized in actual manufacturing environment. The extracted process parameters can be formulated further for providing signals (electrical or other) to the manufacturing machine tool. So that an integrated design and manufacturing of sheet metal parts can be achieved computationally.

References

1. Kannan, T.R., Shunmugam, M.S.: Processing of 3D sheet metal components in STEP AP-203 format. Part I: feature recognition system. International Journal of Production Research 47, 941–964 (2009)
2. Gupta, R.K., Gurumoorthy, B.: Classification, representation, and automatic extraction of deformation features in sheet metal parts. Computer-Aided Design 45, 1469–1484 (2013)
3. Jae-Jun, L., Gyung-Jin, P.: Optimization of the structural and process parameters in the sheet metal forming process. Journal of Mechanical Science and Technology 28, 605–619 (2014)
4. Liu, W., Tai, K.: Optimal design of flat pattern for 3D folded structures by unfolding with topological validation. Computer-Aided Design 39, 898–913 (2007)
5. Kannan, T.R., Shunmugan, M.S.: Processing of 3D sheet metal components in STEP AP-203 format. Part II: feature reasoning system. International Journal of Production Research 47, 1287–1308 (2009)
6. Gupta, S.K., Bourne, D.A., Kim, K.H., Krishan, S.S.: Automated process planning for sheet metal bending operations. Journal of Manufacturing Systems 17, 5–28 (1998)
7. Qiang, L., Wenjuan, L., Feng, R., Hongyang, Q.: Automated optimization in sheet metal forming process parameters. Journal of Materials Processing Technology 187, 159–163 (2007)
8. SecToh, K.H., Loh, H.T., Nee, A.Y.C., Lee, K.S.: A Feature – based flat pattern development system for sheet metal parts. Journal of Materials Processing Technology 48, 89–95 (1995)
9. Liu, Z.J., Li, J.J., Wang, Y.L., Li, C.Y., Xiao, X.Z.: Automatically extracting sheet-metal features from solid model. Journal of Zhejiang University Science 5, 1456–1465 (2004)
10. Razdan, A., Bae, M.: A hybrid approach to feature segmentation of triangle meshes. Computer Aided Design 35, 783–789 (2009)
11. Byung, C.K., Duhwan, M.: Feature-based simplification of boundary representation models using sequential iterative volume decomposition. Computers & Graphics 38, 97–107 (2014)
12. Geometric Limited, Sheet metal feature recognition, `http://feature.geometricglobal.com/` (accessed on November 17, 2014)
13. Lipson, H., Shpitalni, M.: On the topology of sheet metal parts. Transactions of the ASME Journal of Mechanical Design 120, 10–16 (1998)
14. Gupta, R.K.: Feature-based approach for semantic interoperability of shape models. Ph.D. Thesis. Indian Institute of Science, Bangalore, India (2012)
15. Engineering Handbook. Huyett G.L.: Expy Minneapolis, KS 67467

Skill-Based Asset Management: A PLM-Approach for Reconfigurable Production Systems

Kiril Aleksandrov[1], Viktor Schubert[1], and Jivka Ovtcharova[2]

[1] ISPE/PDE, FZI Research Center for Information Technology, Karlsruhe, Germany
{aleksandrov,schubert}@fzi.de
[2] IMI, Karlsruhe Institute of Technology, Karlsruhe, Germany
jivka.ovtcharova@kit.edu

Abstract. To handle complexity in a modern reconfigurable production system from a strategic and tactical planning perspective as well as to enable operational decision making a skill-based asset management system is introduced. It provides a novel approach of managing assets in the context of the asset lifecycle based on their provided skills. It aims at the vertical integration of higher level management systems with production execution level systems of small and medium sized manufacturing enterprises, using a common skill-based abstraction. Thus the skill-based asset management system can effectively provide digital factory functionality to companies while integrating into their existing IT systems.

Keywords: asset management system, reconfigurable production system, skill-based model, vertical integration, digital factory.

1 Introduction

The increasing external complexity, such as changes in demand or the product, challenges production companies to raise their productivity while making use of the changeability within their asset park [1]. An evident need is recognized to plan the production organization and to utilize the production assets flexibly and efficiently in order to stay competitive in a rapidly changing market [2]. The production resources utilized in a modern production company are highly flexible and adaptable in their skills but there is still a lack in the IT infrastructure to appropriately allow them to use that high variety of operating alternatives in an economic reasonable way. The continuous research in the area of reconfigurable manufacturing systems (RMS) is highlighting the trend toward more flexible and adaptable production systems [1], [3-4]. However those types of production systems are associated not only with large capital investments [5], but rather with high lifecycle cost. They also increase the internal complexity and provide new challenges in terms of management and planning. They often stay underutilized because of the lack of appropriate tool support for overview, planning and reconfiguration. As a result production companies do not

S. Fukuda et al. (Eds.): PLM 2014, IFIP AICT 442, pp. 465–474, 2014.

optimally exploit their changeability provided by the available technical infrastructure. Furthermore on an operational level the production is planned by order-centric enterprise resource planning (ERP) software and its execution is controlled by technical shop-floor control systems such as manufacturing execution systems (MES) or production planning and control (PPC) systems. These systems operate on different levels in the enterprises' IT infrastructure and often lack technical as well as the conceptual integration [6].

This paper presents the ongoing work towards a skill-based asset management system (AMS) by the European project SkillPro [1]. The project aims at the development and utilization of a novel approach for skill-based resource controller architecture in the context of RMS. As one of the main components of the desired project framework the AMS in particular addresses the technological and conceptual gap between upper enterprise level applications and technical processes in the production. It provides a lifecycle approach that combines information both from a technical and a business point of view and via a common skill concept supports an appropriate frontloading towards product development as well as towards asset and factory planning.

Under the consideration of the product lifecycle management (PLM) for manufacturing companies this contribution reviews in paragraph 2 relevant works in the domains of digital factory, enterprise asset management, and skills in production and automation. An overview of the SkillPro framework and a brief introduction of the project's skill concept is presented in paragraph 3. Paragraph 4 describes the skill-based AMS, providing insights on its functionality, its utilization in the IT-landscape of a production company and its main benefits for a modern production enterprise. Finally, paragraph 5 concludes the paper and provides an outlook on future research.

2 Related Works

In the context of the *digital factory* (see [8]) there have been many findings regarding consistent mechatronic approaches to ensure integrated simulation models recently. The Hardware-in-the-Loop (HiL) approach derived from the embedded systems engineering is increasingly utilized within the digital factory [9]. Also aspects of interoperability between IT systems in the digital factory are often addressed besides the designation of virtual models [9]. Different formats for model exchange between computer-aided engineering (CAE) or simulation tools, such as the Functional Mock-Up Interface (FMI) [10] are now discussed regarding the improved simulation of production processes and resources.

Due to holistic simulation approaches as well as the consideration of the lifecycle of assets, the need for robust and consistent product-process-resources (PPR) models as a backbone system for the digital factory is identified. This gradually leads to further transmission of PLM approaches to the systems of the digital factory. Thus the aim is to combine the industrial value creation via a lifecycle-related PPR model [11] as depicted in Fig. 1.

[1] `www.skillpro-project.eu`

Digital factory systems are highly covered in research and even utilized in practice by large enterprises. However, despite their benefits, small and medium sized enterprises (SME) are currently hesitant to utilize them, due to the still poor integration in the preexisting fragmented IT landscape [12-13]. To address this issue, new systems are emerging that handle the data management for planning and operating of production plants similar to the well-known product data management (PDM) concepts. One standard, which is strongly considered for this type of systems, is AutomationML[2] as an open, XML-based interchange format. It can ensure the interconnectivity and interoperability of the systems, connecting especially MES with the digital factory [14].

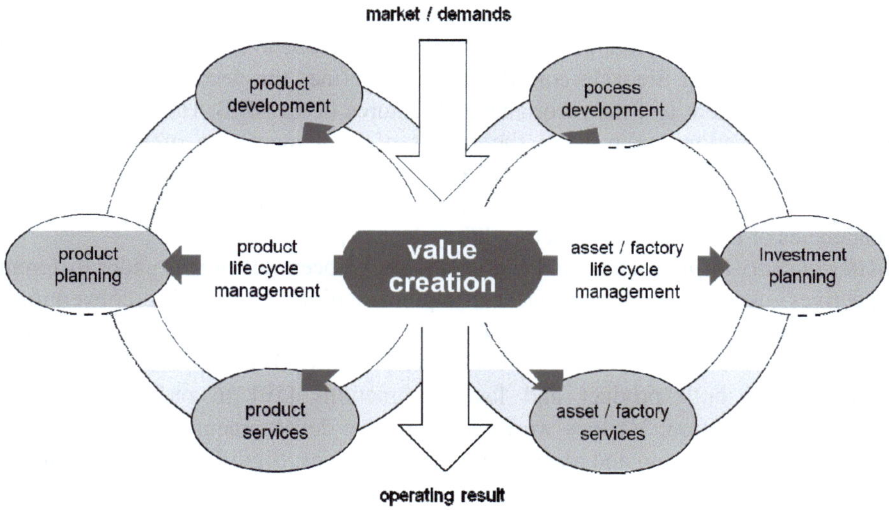

Fig. 1. The alignment of the product lifecycle and the asset/factory lifecycle managements in the value creation (according to [11])

The *enterprise asset management* (EAM) is gaining a lot of research interest in recent years. Initially regarding (technical) assets only from a financial point of view it now focus on different aspects of their lifecycle such as utilization, maintenance, effectiveness, etc. In his work Haider provides an extensive study of the asset management in the context of engineering and infrastructure [15]. Although this work is focused on the asset management of big infrastructure plants (water supply or roads) it summarizes an effective definition of an asset in the production domain as well. An asset is a component with economic life span of more than 12 months that has a value profile, and creates and maintains its value by providing services or certain skill sets [15]. Haider distinguishes between three types of asset management – strategic, tactical and operational – depending on the management horizon and the type of decisions, indicating that asset management is a lifecycle challenge. Cambel, Jardine and

[2] `www.automationml.org`

McGlynn do extensive work on providing a framework for best practices and optimization of maintenance of plants, fleets, facilities or equipment from a lifecycle perspective [16]. They are addressing the complete asset management from a long up to a short-term perspective. Further multiple research projects engage the topics of enterprise assets and their lifecycle management. Kiritsis discusses the research activities of several European projects in the area of asset lifecycle management (ALM) via semantic technologies [17]. Tam and Price present an approach for optimizing the asset maintenance [18], which can be crucial if the given asset is a bottleneck in the production system. By using a generic model for the asset based on three decision dimensions (output cost, risk cost and resource cost), the authors provide a decision support framework for maintenance planning. In February 2014 a new ISO standard for asset management system (ISO 55000) [3] emerged focusing on the management of technical enterprise assets mainly in regards to the financial dimension and still incorporating lifecycle considerations. It defines the necessary activities for the asset management and the recommended features of an AMS. However it neither provides specification nor restricts the means of implementation of such systems. Additionally research efforts are directed towards the factory planning and managing of the factory lifecycle defining "factory as a product" and describing the interdependencies of the product and factory lifecycles [11].

Skill concepts in production and automation have been developed under different perspectives, using different approaches, implementations and naming conventions. Some research activities are focused on the function modelling in the production context. The Function Oriented Product Descriptions (FOPD) approach is used to formally model both product and factory functions [19] in order to conduct performance evaluation. Various works focus on the development and utilization of skill concepts for planning and executing tasks in robotics. Significant work is done in the field of service robotics, robot-human interaction and multi-robot coordination [20-23]. The research in those works is focused on autonomous execution of tasks by means of artificial intelligence. In an industrial context the skill concept is not that highly covered in the research, as the industrial robots are mainly limited in their autonomy [24] and controlled by a central system. Still, Malec et al. describe a skill-based approach for assembly and inspection in robotized work-cells [25]. They propose a dual approach for skill definition – top-down definition of production goals and bottom-up description of machine skills, called capabilities. A follow-up research activity is conducted in [24], [26-27] extending the skill concept of [25] focusing on the knowledge representation of the skill-enhanced PPR model (see [28]) via semantic web technologies. The presented approaches mainly concentrate on skill execution in various application fields. However, they do not consider the skills from a lifecycle perspective of the asset, such as utilization and maintenance profile of the skills, skill evaluation and comparison, asset wear, change possibilities, etc. Furthermore, skill modelling is focused mainly on robot operations and capabilities and although it provides a good common abstraction for the integration of different production-related domains such as manufacturing, logistic or assembly assets, this aspect is still

[3] `http://www.assetmanagementstandards.com/`

not extensively explored. Also, the current research is mainly aimed at interoperability and interactions of technical resources (assets) and not on the high level integration towards ERP and PLM.

The review of the related works shows that a lot of research is dedicated to the topics of digital factory, asset management and skill-based task execution. However, a combined concept for skill-based asset management to support digital factory is not covered sufficiently.

3 The SkillPro Approach

The European project SkillPro aims at the design and realization of a skill-based framework for reconfigurable manufacturing systems. It can be considered as possible implementation of the plug and produce paradigm [29] concentrating not only on physical and asset level changes but also addressing logical and topological changes and long-term planning. Furthermore it provides a skill-centric view of the product-process-resource model [30] as one of its core research activities. The skill concept developed in SkillPro aims at extending the existing skill-based models and frameworks in two aspects. On the one hand it targets a wider scope of assets, focusing not only on industrial or service robotics, but including also logistic assets, CNC (computer numerical control) or DNC (distributed numerical control) machines, other production assets and even human workforce. On the other hand the skill concept is to be utilized not only during execution, but also for operative planning and mid-to-long term asset management.

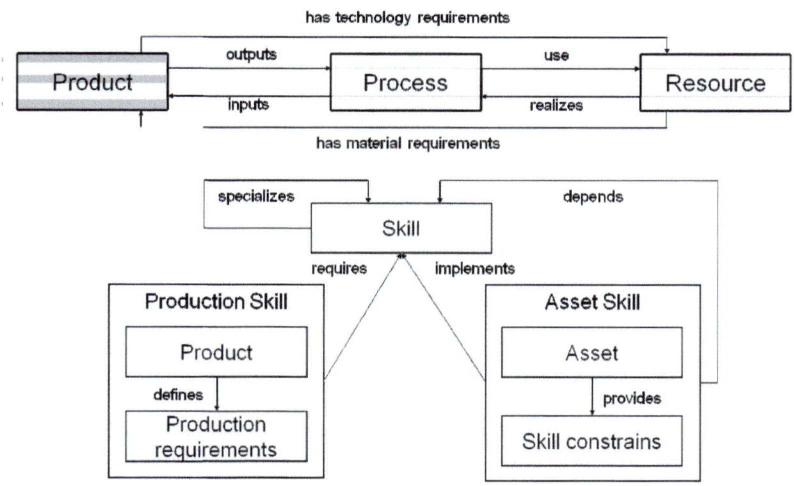

Fig. 2. The Skill concept according to [30] aligned to the classical PPR [31]

The Skill concept is a logical extension of the classical PPR concept in the production context (Fig. 2). Stanev summarizes the PPR dependencies having the asset (resource) as a central element of observation that requires specific properties of the product (such as material) and provides possibilities for its manipulation (via process). Furthermore, a product is an output of the process execution on a certain resource that transforms input products [31]. Another PPR approach that defines the different relations between the objects is the OZONE-model presented in [32]. There however, the product and the resource both provide constraints for the process (called activity) but don't have any direct relation to each other.

The skill concept developed in SkillPro extends the PPR model. It proposes a common abstraction that can be used for production system modeling, production planning and production execution and control, thus allowing a conceptual and technical integration among the production IT systems. Besides the product and the asset that retain their common meaning, the elements of the skill model are:

- *Skill*: A skill is a placeholder for a process providing metadata (parameters) needed for its specification. Skills can have hierarchical structure, thus building skill taxonomies. Thereby the lower skills are specializations, inheriting all parameters of the parent skills.
- *Production Skill*: A production skill is the assignment of specific production requirements for a product based on its properties. The production skill requires a skill with concrete values for all skill parameters in order to fulfill the production requirements.
- *Asset Skill*: An asset skill represents the possibility of an asset to provide a skill. The asset skill implements a certain skill, having restrictions for the skill parameters due to specific skill constraints that are defined by the asset. The asset skill can also have additional dependencies to other skills as pre- or post-conditions for its execution. Those types of relations are then used for different reasoning operations on skills such as skill matching, skill composition, etc.

Each skill type can have structure, thus defining sequential or parallel skill execution.

4 Skill-Based Asset Management System

The goal of this skill concept is to provide a common model that can be used by the three main components of SkillPro. As depicted in the figure (Fig. 3) these are the skill-based AMS managing the enterprise assets, the skill-based MES scheduling and controlling the execution and the skill-based control system (called skill execution engine – SEE) executing skills on the assets. The AMS system conducts high level feasibility check for production orders, creates coarse production plans and plans reconfigurations. The same model shall also be used on the lower control and execution level for exchanging and interpreting instructions. The three components integrate with each other, based on the common skill model, exchanging skill information and conducting certain operations in their level of concerns. These are based on three different time horizons. During the long-to-mid-term planning the AMS is involved by evaluating the production system, managing the lifecycle aspects of the assets and their skills and preparing the production system for new products and product orders. This includes also the "teaching" of previously unknown skills to the execution controller (SEE). The AMS also provides some services (to the MES) during the short-term-planning (operative) such as retooling/reconfiguration instructions and additional feasibility checks. During execution it provides (to the MES or the SEE) the needed models (regarding product and skill), usually before the first execution of a batch as it acts as a central repository for all skill and object models. Via the SkillPro-Framework the AMS gets product and order information from the PLM and ERP systems and persists it in the SkillPro format.

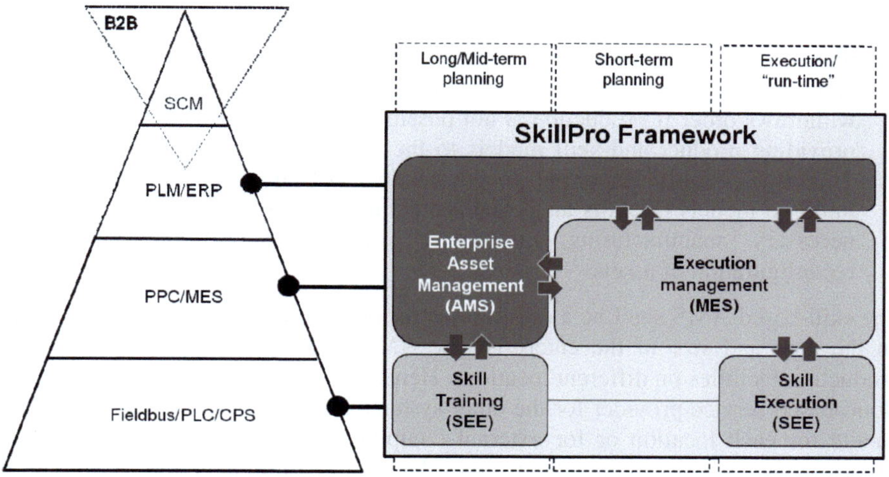

Fig. 3. A bird eye perspective on the SkillPro framework architecture aligned to the different IT-levels in a production company (pyramid on the left) and the different planning horizons (on the top).

The skill-based AMS constitutes an in-house company-specific knowledge base. During production, it gains content by storing correlations between products and resources via the skill abstraction. It is thus further augmented by new skill definitions and skill properties. Hence the previous experiences can be used for production re-planning, estimation of delivery time and strategic planning. In particular the functions of the skill-based AMS are:

- Long-term scope: Manage assets in context of their lifecycle and in context of their skills lifecycle. Each Asset Skill is provided by a certain asset configuration, for example a tool state of a machine, or specific adjustment in an industrial robot. Assets can provide additional Asset Skills in combination with other assets that are otherwise not available if used independently. The skill-based AMS system can manage both asset and skill lifecycle maintaining lifecycle models for both types of entities and evaluating performance indicators such as time, quality, energy consumption, flexibility or responsiveness, etc. to secure a high lifecycle value and minimize the total cost of ownership (TCO).

- The skill-based AMS performs skills matching followed by evaluation for production skills and asset skills. Thereby it identifies different production possibilities for a given asset park and allows for a dynamic assignment of production orders and dynamic generation of the skill-based bill of processes (BoP). By searching for corresponding asset skills to the required production skill (skill matching) the skill-based AMS can perform feasibility checks for new or changed products. Thus it can identify asset bottlenecks, missing assets or outdated assets. It can identify necessity for changes on asset configurations (retooling), topology (changing workflow or communication flow) and topography (layout), based on the currently available and potentially provided skills.
- Short-term scope: When the execution planning and control system (MES) is re-planning due to failure, the skill-based AMS supports the process by providing other production alternatives for the current production system configuration or withdraws order if production is not possible. Also it serves as model repository providing product and skill models to the other components in the framework. This is especially important for embedded SEE that cannot afford to store multiple models of skills and other data simultaneously. In this way it provides necessary manufacturing information on the shop-floor securing the reconfiguration of assets.

The skill-based AMS shall be a central system for a production company. Depending on the type and size of the enterprise the AMS shall be able to support multiple production facilities on different locations. Hence it is intended that the AMS acts as a cloud-based service provider for the other systems in the framework that are installed on-site for each location or for external components such as ERP or supply chain management systems. In this way it serves the purpose of an operating system for the digital factory and bridges the planning and manufacturing layer. The AMS shall store information about skills and assets for each location and consider them while creating coarse production plans or checking the feasibility of orders. Thus it will extend the flexibility of all production facilities of the company.

5 Conclusion and Outlook

In this contribution a novel skill-based asset management system was presented that aims at supporting the lifecycle management of technical assets in long- to short-term planning activities as well as the vertical integration between different IT systems in a manufacturing enterprise. First the need for such a system was highlighted by examining the current research in the fields of digital factory, asset management and skill-based planning. Then the concept of the skill-based AMS was presented as a part of the ongoing work on the European project SkillPro.

In order to realize a real-time decision making support, further research should be focused on both horizontal and vertical integration in realizing PLM-concepts of frontloading from production to product development or to factory planning and vice versa. As shown in fig. 3 this includes the consideration of an appropriate B2B integration of all stakeholders of the factory. Furthermore, a skill-based AMS can be a data management fundament for cyber-physical systems serving as a service integration platform for technology providers and operators.

Acknowledgments. This work has been partially funded by the European Commission through SkillPro project (Grant agreement ICT- 287733). The authors would like to thank the SkillPro partners for the intensive exchange and collaboration.

References

1. Wiendahl, H.P., ElMaraghy, H.A., Nyhuis, P., Zäh, M.F., Wiendahl, H.H., Duffie, N., Brieke, M.: Changeable Manufacturing - Classification, Design and Operation. CIRP Annals - Manufacturing Technology 56, 783–809 (2007)
2. Rogalski, S.: Factory design and process optimisation with flexibility measurements in industrial production. International Journal of Production Research 50, 6060–6071 (2012)
3. Mehrabi, M.G., Ulsoy, A.G., Koren, Y.: Reconfigurable manufacturing systems: Key to future manufacturing. Journal of Intelligent Manufacturing 11, 403–419 (2000)
4. Puik, E., Telgen, D., Moergestel, L.V., Ceglarek, D.: Structured Analysis of Reconfigurable Manufacturing Systems Advances in Sustainable and Competitive Manufacturing Systems. In: Azevedo, A (Ed.), Springer International Publishing, pp. 147–157 (2013)
5. Koren, Y., Shpitalni, M.: Design of reconfigurable manufacturing systems. Journal of Manufacturing Systems 29, 130–141 (2010)
6. Sauer, O.: lnformationstechnik für die Fabrik der Zukunft. Industrie Management 1/2013-Vierte industrielle Revolution 11 (2013)
7. Bracht, U., Geckler, D., Wenzel, S.: Digitale Fabrik. Springer Science & Business (2011)
8. Gu, F., Harrison, W.S., Tilbury, D.M., Yuan, C.: Hardware-in-the-loop for manufacturing automation control: Current status and identified needs. In: IEEE International Conference on Automation Science and Engineering (CASE 2007), pp. 1105–1110. IEEE (2007)
9. Kjellberg, T., Euler-Chelpin, A., Hedlind, M., Lundgren, M., Sivard, G., Chen, D.: The machine tool model—A core part of the digital factory. CIRP Annals - Manufacturing Technology 58(1), 425–428 (2009)
10. Blochwitz, T., Otter, M., Arnold, M., Bausch, C., Clauß, C., Elmqvist, H., et al.: The functional mockup interface for tool independent exchange of simulation models. In: Modelica 2011 Conference, pp. S.20–S.22 (2011)
11. Westkämper, E.: Rahmenmodell der digitalen Produktion. In: Westkämper, E., Spath, D., Constantinescu, C., Lentes, J. (eds.) Digitale Produktion. Springer Vieweg (2013)
12. Rogalski, S., Siebel, J., Aleksandrov, K., Wicaksono, H.: Sustainable Production Planning through Flexibility Measurements in different Manufacturing Organizational Levels. Paper Presented in 10th Global Conference of Sustainable Manufacturing (GCSM) (2012)
13. Himmler, F., Amberg, M.: Die Digitale Fabrik - eine Literaturanalyse. Wirtschaftsinformatik 11 (2013)
14. Schleipen, M., Sauer, O., Friess, N., Braun, L., Shakerian, K.: Production Monitoring and Control Systems within the Digital Factory. In: Huang, G.Q., Mak, K.L., Maropoulos, P.G. (eds.) DET2009 Proceedings. AISC, vol. 66, pp. 711–724. Springer, Heidelberg (2010)
15. Haider, A.: Information Systems for Engineering and Infrastructure Asset Management. Springer (2013)
16. Campbell, J.D., Jardine, A.K.S., McGlynn, J.: Asset Management Excellence: Optimizing Equipment Life-Cycle Decisions, 2nd edn. CRC Press (2010)
17. Kiritsis, D.: Semantic technologies for engineering asset life cycle management. International Journal of Production Research 51, 7345–7371 (2013)
18. Tam, A.S.B., Price, J.W.H.: A generic asset management framework for optimising maintenance investment decision. Production Planning & Control 19, 287–300 (2008)

19. Politze, D.P., Bathelt, J.P., Wegener, K.: Function Oriented Product Descriptions in Product Development and Factory Planning. In: Proceedings of the World Congress on Engineering and Computer Science 2010 (WCECS 2010), vol. II (2010)
20. Browning, B., Bruce, J., Bowling, M., Veloso, M.: STP: Skills, tactics and plays for multi-robot control in adversarial environments. IEEE Journal of Control and Systems Engineering 2004, 219 (2005)
21. Kunze, L., Roehm, T., Beetz, M.: Towards semantic robot description languages. In: IEEE International Conference on Robotics and Automation (ICRA 2011), pp. 5589–5595. IEEE (2011)
22. Tenorth, M., Beetz, M.: KnowRob - knowledge processing for autonomous personal robots. In: IEEE/RSJ International Conference on Intelligent Robots and Systems (IROS 2009), pp. 4261–4266. IEEE (2009)
23. Waibel, M., Beetz, M., Civera, J., D'Andrea, R., Elfring, J., Gálvez-López, D., Häussermann, K., Janssen, R., Montiel, J.M.M., Perzylo, A., Schießle, B., Tenorth, M., Zweigle, O., De Molengraft, R.: RoboEarth. IEEE Robotics & Automation Magazine 18, 69–82 (2011)
24. Björkelund, A., Malec, J., Nilsson, K., Nugues, P., Bruyninckx, H.: Knowledge for Intelligent Industrial Robots. In: Proceedings AAAI (2012)
25. Malec, J., Nilsson, A., Nilsson, K., Nowaczyk, S.: Knowledge-Based Reconfiguration of Automation Systems. In: IEEE International Conference on Automation Science and Engineering, CASE 2007, pp. 170–175 (2007)
26. Björkelund, A., Malec, J., Nilsson, K., Nugues, P.: Knowledge and skill representations for robotized production. In: Proceedings of the 18th IFAC Congress, Milano, Department of Electrical Engineering, Ottawa-Carleton Institute for Electrical Engineering, University of Ottawa (2011)
27. Persson, J., Gallois, A., Björkelund, A., Hafdell, L., Haage, M., Malec, J., Nilsson, K., Nugues, P.: A knowledge integration framework for robotics. In: Robotics (ISR), 2010 41st International Symposium on and 2010 6th German Conference on Robotics (ROBOTIK), VDE, pp. 1–8 (2010)
28. Michel, J.J.: Terminology extracted from some manufacturing and modelling related standards CEN/TC, 310, N1119R2 (2005)
29. Arai, T., Aiyama, Y., Maeda, Y., Sugi, M., Ota, J.: Agile Assembly System by "Plug and Produce". CIRP Annals - Manufacturing Technology 49, 1–4 (2000)
30. Pfrommer, J., Schleipen, M., Beyerer, J.: PPRS: Production skills and their relation to product, process, and resource. In: IEEE 18th Conference on Emerging Technologies & Factory Automation (ETFA 2013), pp. 1–4. IEEE (2013)
31. Stanev, S., Awad, R., Prieur, M., Walla, W., Pölz, S., Ovtcharova, J.: Production-oriented Product Validation Method as Support for the Reuse of Production Lines in the Automotive Industry. In: 3rd International Conference on Changeable, Agile, Reconfigurable and Virtual Production, Munich (2009)
32. Cutting-Decelle, A.F., Young, R.I.M., Michel, J.J., Grangel, R., Le Cardinal, J., Bourey, J.P.: ISO 15531 MANDATE: A Product-process-resource based Approach for Managing Modularity in Production Management. Concurrent Engineering 15, 217–235 (2007)

Sustainable Product Lifecycle Management and Territoriality: New Structure for PLM

Kiyan Vadoudi, Romain Allais, Tatiana Reyes, and Nadege Troussier

ICD, HETIC Department, CREIDD, Université de technologie de Troyes, UMR 6281, CNRS, Troyes, France
kiyan.vadoudi@utt.fr

Abstract. Product Lifecycle Management (PLM) is a business strategy, which aims to streamline the flow of information about products and related processes throughout the whole product's Lifecycle such that the right information in the right context at the right time can be made available. Recently some studies have been presented on general capabilities of PLM to improve sustainability paradigm, but the subject is still not solved completely. In this paper, first a critical review on the recent advances of Sustainable PLM is presented then a new structure for PLM is proposed based on combination of geographical information systems (GIS) and Lifecycle assessment (LCA), to reach an improvement on sustainable development in territorial scale for achieving a more sustainable paradigm in global scale.

Keywords: Product Lifecycle Management, Sustainable Development, Geographical Information Systems, Lifecycle Assessment.

1 Introduction

Company, industrial ecosystem and territory are complex systems in interaction that are organized according to their own specific goal. Although these objectives are usually divergent, sustainable development can be a common target for these embedded systems [1]. Recently, there is a shift to manage the environmental and social impacts of products by PLM across the Lifecycle stages, which is called Sustainable Product Lifecycle Management (SPLM) [2-5]. It requires an in-depth understanding of semantics and structure of product Lifecycle information over the whole Lifecycle from technical, social, cultural and geographical implications. Moreover, it is necessary to know which product Lifecycle information is required from where for each operational issue and each Lifecycle phase, and to classify them into several types depending on their characteristics [6].

Among the tools and methodologies available to evaluate the environmental, economic and social performance of materials and consumer products (including their impact on climate change and natural resources), *Life Cycle Assessment* (LCA) provides a holistic approach that considers the potential impacts from all stages of manufacture, product use and end-of-life [3]. Thus, it could be expectable to have

S. Fukuda et al. (Eds.): PLM 2014, IFIP AICT 442, pp. 475–484, 2014.

different compliance status for a given product cause of different territorial characteristics (proximity to resources, land use, proximity to rivers, etc.) and regulations, which are emphasizing to make link with *Geographical Information Systems* (GIS).

This research purpose is to link GIS and PLM to have a global and systematic approach to improve company sustainable performance and potential improvement of sustainability at territorial scale. It argues on the necessity to take into account local information concerning where the business takes place. Then, from an information system point of view, it argues the necessity to integrate geographical information in the definition of products and processes, and in the whole PLM. It will lead to an integrated data model including geographic and industrial system data.

2 Sustainable Development and Territoriality

Sustainable development issues are manifesting themselves in various forms but an environmental issue is considered as a central point of sustainable development in a spatial setting. It leads to the necessity to specify more precisely the interactions between different resource and industries. Such a more local and regional orientation is mandated not only by the character of the economic and environmental interactions but also by the spatial orientation of policies not only land use. In this regards, some comprehensive impact models based on territory specification have to be developed that encapsulate the complex interacting patterns of regional developments and related consumptions and emissions in relation with social, environmental, economic variables in order to enable industrial decision making. It is noteworthy to mention that the spatial scale of analysis could be handled by Geographical Information Systems (GIS) as a major tool in this field [5]. GIS techniques have been instrumental in developing interactive modes between quantitative modeling and spatial mapping [6] especially when regional development plans have a bearing on the territory, GIS offers a powerful analytical tool for regional/spatial sustainable development [7].

3 The Geographical Information Systems

Geography seeks to understand the Earth with all of its human and natural complexities that puts understanding of social and physical processes within the context of places and regions, recognizing the great differences in cultures, political systems, economies, landscapes and environments across the world, and the links between them [8]. Progress within geography as spatial science and integration with technical advances leads to develop a Geographical Information System (GIS), which integrates hardware, software and data for capturing, managing, analyzing and displaying all forms of geographically referenced information. Globally, there are more than 2 million users of GIS and most companies are still unaware of how this technologies influences upon their daily activities [9].

A GIS is essentially a tool for decision-making and its powerful analytical and visualization capabilities provide the answers to important questions that must be answered in order to make sound and to inform for decision making. A GIS allows us to develop models, create scenarios and ultimately provide solutions for various environmental and socio-economic problems that exist [9]. Although GIS have been used for several years in the natural resources, forestry, and environmental industries, only recently they have begun to be used for a broader array of business and management functions such as logistics, site and facilities management, marketing, decision making and planning. GIS can help a retail business in locating the best site for its next store and helps marketers in finding new prospects [10].

4 Product Lifecycle

Product Lifecycle thinking is an attempt to recognize whole stages of a product within the expected Lifecycle. From production engineering perspective, it is related with the development, production and distribution of the product, which can be defined by three main phases: *Beginning-of-life* (BOL), *Middle-of-life* (MOL) and *End-of-life* (EOL) [11].

BOL stage includes the initial design of a product, its development, testing and initial marketing. During design phase by using many tools, techniques and methodologies, designers, planners and engineers initial design of a product is defined and sent to manufacturing phase, which includes production process, plans, production facilities and manufacturing. The BOL stage is crucial to the sustainable product Lifecycle and elements such as the materials chosen and the processes required to create the product all have a significant impact on the product's ultimate environmental footprint. MOL is including external logistic, use and support (in terms of repair and maintenance). In this phase, the product is in the hands of the final product user/consumer and/or some service providers, maintenance and logistic actors [2]. Finally, in EOL, retired products are re-collected and remanufactured for recovery. The product recovery processes consist in collecting, inspection, disassembly, reuse, remanufacturing, recycling, redistribution, and disposal. During BOL, the information flow is quite complete because it is supported by several information systems like CAD/CAM, product data management (PDM), knowledge management (KM). However, the information flow becomes vague or unrecognized after BOL which prevents the feedback of product-related information such as product usage data and disposal conditions, from MOL and EOL back to BOL. Hence, Lifecycle activities of MOL and EOL phases have limited visibility of the product-related information [12] considering the fact that sustainability in product development is tied with closed-loop flow of information.

5 Life Cycle Assessment

In order to help designers in understanding and translating the environmental constraints into effective actions, Life Cycle Assessment (LCA) methodology has been developed to enable the generation of more Eco-efficient design alternatives [3]. Specifically it is a method to assess the environmental impact of a product during its Lifecycle, from the extraction of raw materials to the production and distribution of energy through the use, reuse, recycling and final disposal. LCA is a tool for relative comparison and not for absolute evaluation, thereby it can be used by decision makers to compare all major environmental impacts in the choice of alternative courses of action [13]. The core phase of an LCA analysis is the Lifecycle Inventory compilation that regards the identification of all input and output flows concurring in the product Lifecycle [14]. The procedures of life cycle assessment (LCA) are part of the ISO 14000 environmental management standards: in ISO 14040:2006 and 14044:2006 [15-16].

Regionalization, in the context of LCA, is the recognition that industrial production characteristics and the environmental impact of environmental flows vary among site-generic, site-dependent, and site-specific assessments. Site-generic is globally valid, site-dependent operates on the regional scale, and site-specific is only locally applicable [15]. During the LCA modeling each subsystem of the Lifecycle is linked together into a chain of processes, in one end extracting resources and in the other giving various types of emissions or waste. This chain of linked processes is referred to as the technical system. In reality a technical system is under some sort of human control and designed for a certain purpose, to deliver a certain benefit or good, which in the LCA is expressed through the functional unit of the system. The processes are also located somewhere, which implies that they can be geographically referenced. Environmental impact caused by a technical system, or its LCA equivalent, the functional unit, is estimated in terms of the negative change implied by the technical system upon the environmental system, as evaluated by the social system. These systems may also be geographically referenced, which is an important starting point for a consideration of the relations between LCA and localized environmental impacts [14].

6 Product Lifecycle Management

Product Lifecycle Management as a business strategy makes it possible to manage the whole Lifecycle of a product. It is ideally an organizationally information and knowledge processing system that integrates information-driven approach comprised of people, processes/practices and technology to all aspects of a product's life and provides a central system to centralize product data, standardize business processes and streamline communication of information across distributed product development teams to shorten development cycles, improve quality and speed time-to-market [21]. To be able to plan the implementation of PLM effectively into an organization, it needs to be understood also the strategic aspect of PLM far more than just an IT system, to develop the company as a whole to integrate all organizational aspects and levels. In this regard, Anneli Silventoinen [21] presented a holistic PLM model that includes five elements of strategies defining main approaches; operational processes of the value chain; structures of product, knowledge and organization; people and culture, and information technology means.

Since Information and Communication Technology (ICT) plays an important role in PLM, the ICT architecture of a company and its dynamic adaptation to new technological developments is necessary for realizing the full PLM potential. ICT is used in running the PLM processes and in up-dating of data and information structures, mainly for creation, acquisition, storing, sharing and application of documented knowledge, but also for collaboration. In this regards different IT tools, platform and systems that are spread through complete Lifecycle of product are dividing in two categories of "ICT tools and systems" and "ICT interoperability and architectures"[2].

Despite progresses in computer-aided design (CAD), computer-aided manufacturing (CAM), computer-aided process planning (CAPP), product data management (PDM), enterprise resource planning (ERP), Lifecycle Assessment (LCA), which help to make decision in the design process, there are still shortcomings in this stage because they were usually separated from a manufacturing company's mainstream operations and they cannot adequately address the need for collaborative capabilities throughout the whole product Lifecycle and they usually focus on special activities in an enterprise, which are not adequately designed to meet new business requirements. Especially, Lifecycle Assessments (LCA) can feed PLM to improve global performance in a sustainable framework, but to have a represent-ability of the model, it may be necessary to have the input data as specific as possible including geographic specificities [2].

7 Sustainable Product Lifecycle Management

During recent years there is a shift to talk about Sustainable Product Lifecycle Management (SPLM) as an opportunity applying scientific knowledge to design and implementing products and processes. N. Duque Ciceri [18] introduced PLM as a platform to provide sustainability by continuous sharing of information among the different product Lifecycle phases. He believes, there are two main challenges for doing PLM as an effective tool for Sustainable Manufacturing; "closing product Lifecycle information loops" and "defining a reference model for the PLM approach to sustainability and Sustainable Manufacturing in particular". Kary Framling [19] by emphasizing more on environmental dimension based on closed-loop PLM, introduced intelligent products as an approach to reduce CO2 emissions, energy usage and environmental damage through the communication between products and other systems. In that paper closed loop Lifecycle management is defined as a basis approach for SPLM to improve environmental sustainability during all phases of the Lifecycle it uses Life Cycle Assessment (LCA) as a methodological framework for estimating and assessing the environmental impacts and "energy informatics" for analyzing the flow of energy between components of the whole system. Martin Eigner [17] proposed a solution for monitoring the sustainability of product development processes based on Integrated Sustainability Triangle. The Integrated Sustainability Triangle, originally introduced as a promising new possibility of quantification and monitoring the Sustainable Development of a national economy, is also an appropriate instrument for the systemization and evaluation of the performance of a company regarding sustainability management. In next section a new structure for PLM is proposed, which tries to be better support of sustainability strategy.

8 Improved PLM structure

This research methodology is based on a mere literature study, evaluating the potential of using GIS in PLM structure by use of LCA as an interrelation tool to improve sustainability in territorial scale, which can be seen as a pre-study to demonstrate and illustrate the impact of taking account of geographic information in PLM to design sustainable systems. Review of related works presented above about SPLM indicate that current PLM solutions for supporting sustainability are often not adequate for the management of product design information beyond BOL, MOL and EOL stages. One of the major problems about implementation and evaluation of the sustainable development is the lack of specificity in concrete circumstances. It means sustainable development, which is implemented in a region, is not necessarily sustainable elsewhere and a large number of small-scale and marginal changes at the local or regional level have clear global dimensions. Thus, accessibility to geographical information can play critical role on quantification and monitoring sustainability in specific area and then running product development process based on results of sustainability assessment. Therefore, it is essentially required to identify and develop a technology for current PLM structure as beginning in company scale to enable product development process based on the result of sustainability in regional scale, in order to solve the issue of sustainability in global scale.

The fact that businesses can start to use GIS within PLM is not surprising, particularly given the fact that much of the data that organizations typically use include significant spatial components (estimates range between 50% and 85%) [9]. Researchers and professionals have seen the potential of using GIS in the planning for a sustainable development; by mapping the same factor in different time spans and spatial areas an overview of changes is created and hence make it easier and more correct to predict future changes and make well founded planning decisions in urban areas [22]. By implementing *GIS*, "Territory" in macro level adds to the structure of

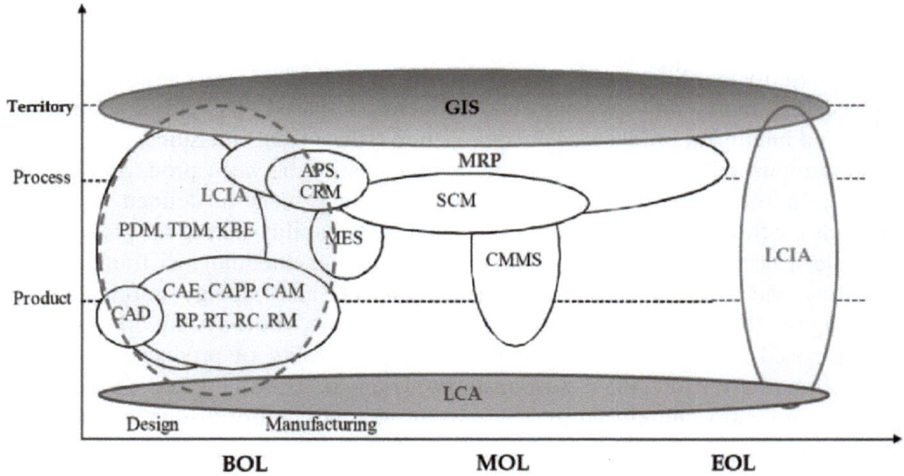

Fig. 1. Improved ICT structure in product lifecycle

PLM and makes it able to provide a proper catalog of the surroundings including environmental impact on natural ecosystems, transportation, community demographics, public safety, utilities, services and accessibility (Fig.1).

The nature of each geographical aspect is presented in the structure of *LCA* as the three subsections of technical, environmental and social systems, which make link between "production" and "process" scales with "territory" through the results of *LCIA*. A technical system generally includes processes which might be geographically referenced, and which are connected via different types of transport systems, such as goods (road, sea, air) or energy ware (pipelines, electricity grid) distribution systems. The geographic location and extension of such a technical system gives relevant information for the modeling and assessment of its environmental impact [23]. By giving the geographical location of the different parts of the technical system, it will be possible to model the dispersion of various agents, so that the varying sensitivity of ecosystems, regions, etc., can be taken into account where this is relevant. A geographically large technical system and the environmental impacts of such a system may cross national, regional and even continental boundaries, and therefore also affects different cultures or groups of people, holding different attitudes towards changes in the environment.

The amassing of these tangible elements of a community goes a long way toward informing the design process, and should always be considered to look at efficiency and sustainability. For instance, by using this new structure it would be possible to develop companies' energy consumption, water usage, CO2 emissions and wastes generation to build scenarios, assess them and make decision. When it comes to model, it will able companies to locate points of water usage, transportation of water from its source to its consumption point, distance of water transportation, climate change, air pollutions, soil-map, location of landfill, customers distribution and other information related with Lifecycle that can be useful in *BOL* to design product, process and plant (Fig.2). It will enable to enhance circular economy and industrial ecology.

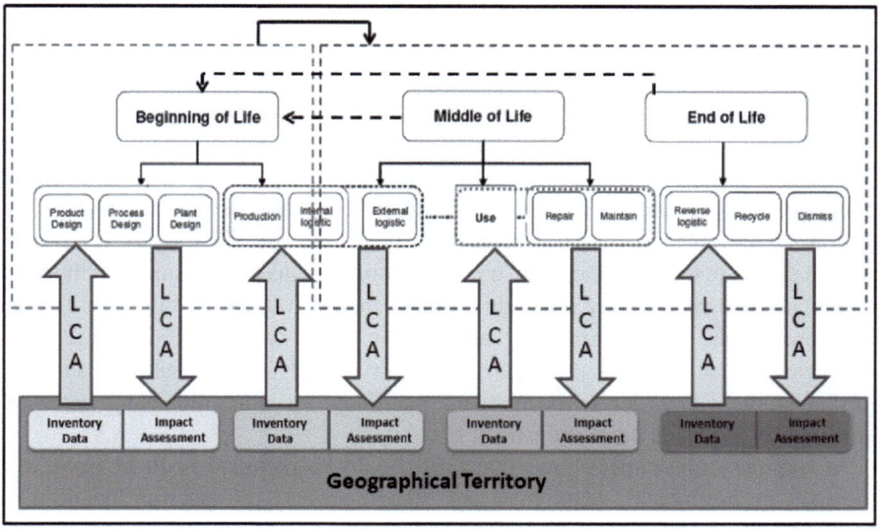

Fig. 2. Interaction between Product lifecycle, GIS, LCA and LCIA

By using sustainability monitoring, it will be possible to analysis the result of this new PLM structure. Several solutions for the monitoring of sustainability of product development processes have been developed but the one that is much more related with PLM, is proposed by Martin Eigner based on integrated sustainability triangle [17] by a weighted aggregation of the single indicators to define the asserted contribution of a respective field. Each field includes several indicators that may contribute to a different extent to the outcome for that field but together all used indicators illustrate 100% of the subject field. The result can present as an Integrated Sustainability Triangle to monitor the sustainability performance and supports communication via graphic elements. There is a shortcoming with this representation as every dimension of this triangle is dependant to another one. Moreover the single score evaluation of the three dimensions of sustainability is a "black box" and data needed locally are not directly reachable.

To overcome this issue of reuse of the information, the French national agency (ANR) founded Convergence project propose a multi-level management system [24]. The three-organization level of a company (i.e. top management, middle management and operations) and their respective domain of action (i.e. strategy, tactics and operation) are connected by a set of indicators dedicated to their daily activities. A dashboard extended to intangibles allows the evaluation and use of local and global indicators to manage the positive and negative externalities of a company (I.E. sustainable performance). A future development is to systematize data collection by connecting to PLM. When available, Convergence enables global performance management for companies.

Thus, it is essentially required to identify and develop a technology for current PLM structure to enable product development process based on the result of sustainability in regional scale, in order to solve the issue of sustainability in global scale.

9 Conclusions

There is no doubt that there is a lot of complexity in the sustainability concept. A possible reduction of this complexity is a proper management, planning and design actions. Therefore, it can be concluded that a holistic management of resources is presented in both consumption and production activities. The goal is to reach from a micro scale of design to macro scale to expand boundary beyond the factory wall to optimize the resources utilization. In macro level businesses measure the sustainability level of same industry or territory to make decision for their design stages and this means they don't think about themselves alone, but there is a higher level entity who is managing the sustainability as a whole. Vertical integration of industries, cross industry mix and community involvement could be subjects for further studies, in order to bring them into PLM structure by using geographical information as driven cross industries.

In summary, the paper shows that GIS should be included in PLM framework to localize environmental, economic and social, related to specific locations when designing green manufacturing systems.

It will lead to the definition of an integrated framework (integration of geographic and industrial data) in order to support decision making, especially in BOL. It will enable both:

- Industrial ecology principles to be applied in BOL reasoning;
- Environmental impact assessment with respect to the local context.

References

1. Capron, M., Quairel, F.: Évaluer les stratégies de développement durable des entreprises: l'utopie mobilisatrice de la performance. l'organisation Responsable (2006)
2. Terzi, S., Bouras, A., Dutta, D., Garetti, M.: Product lifecycle management–from its history to its new role. Int. J. Prod. Lifecycle Management 4, 360–389 (2010)
3. Hart, A., Clift, R., Riddlestone, S., Buntin, J.: Use of Life Cycle Assessment to Develop Industrial Ecologies, A Case Study 83(4), 359–363 (2005)
4. Glavič, P., Lukman, R.: Review of sustainability terms and their definitions. J. Clean. Prod. 15(18), 1875–1885 (2007)
5. Burrough, P., McDonnell, R.: Principles of geographical information systems (1998)
6. Maria Giaoutzi, P.N.: Decision support models for regional sustainable development, p. 304. Avebury, Brookfield, Vt, Ashgate Pub. Co., ldershot, Hants, England (1993)
7. Nijkamp, P., Ouwersloot, H.: A decision support system for regional sustainable development: the flag model. Tinbergen Institute Discussion Paper (1997)
8. Johnston, R.: Geography and GIS. Geogr. Inf. Syst. Princ, pp. 39–48 (1999)
9. Azaz, L.: The use of Geographic Information Systems (GIS) in Business. In: Int. Conf. Humanit., pp. 299–303 (2011)
10. Pick, J.: Geographic information systems in business. IGI Global (2004)
11. Kiritsis, D., Bufardi, A., Xirouchakis, P.: Research issues on product lifecycle management and information tracking using smart embedded systems. Adv. Eng. Informatics 17(3-4), 189–202 (2003)
12. Niemann, S., Tichkiewitch, Westkämper, E.: Design of sustainable product life cycles. Springer (2008)
13. Finnveden, G., Hauschild, M.Z., Ekvall, T., Guinée, J., Heijungs, R., Hellweg, S., Koehler, A., Pennington, D., Suh, S.: Recent developments in Life Cycle Assessment. J. Environ. Manage. 91(1), 1–21 (2009)
14. Mutel, C.L., Pfister, S., Hellweg, S.: GIS-based regionalized life cycle assessment: how big is small enough? Methodology and case study of electricity generation. Environ. Sci. Technol. 46(2), 1096–1103 (2012)
15. ISO, 2006a. ISO 14040 International Standard. In: Environmental Management – Life Cycle Assessment – Principles and Framework. International Organisation for Standardization, Geneva, Switzerland
16. ISO, 2006a. ISO 14044 International Standard. In: Environmental Management – Life Cycle Assessment – Principles and Framework. International Organisation for Standardization, Geneva, Switzerland (2006a)
17. Eigner, M., Von Hauff, M., Schäfer, P.: Sustainable Product Lifecycle Management: A Lifecycle based Conception of Monitoring a Sustainable Product Development. Glocalized Solut. Sustain, pp. 2–7 (2011)
18. Ciceri, N.D.: Product lifecycle management approach for sustainability. In: Proc. 19th, pp. 30–31 (March 2009)

19. Främling, K., Holmström, J., Loukkola, J., Nyman, J., Kaustell, A.: Sustainable PLM through Intelligent Products. Eng. Appl. Artif. Intell. 26, 789–799 (2013)
20. Dyllick, T., Hockerts, K.: Beyond the business case for corporate sustainability. Bus. Strateg. Environ. 11(2), 130–141 (2002)
21. Silventoinen, A., Pels, H., Kärkkäinen, H., Lampela, H.: Towards future PLM maturity assessment dimensions (2011)
22. Walsund, E.: Geographical Information Systems as a Tool in Sustainable Urban Development, Malmö University (2012)
23. Vadoudi, K., Troussier, N., Zhu, T.W.: Sustainable Manufacturing through PLM, GIS and LCA interaction. In: International Conference on Engineering, Technology and Innovation, Bergamo, Italy (2014)
24. Zhang, F., Rio, M., Allais, R., Zwolinski, P., Carrillo, T.R., Roucoules, L., Buclet, N.: Toward a systemic navigation framework to integrate sustainable development into the company. Journal of Cleaner Production 54, 199–214 (2013)

Intelligent Information Technologies to Enable Next Generation PLM

Rainer Stark[1,2], Thomas Damerau[1], Haygazun Hayka[1], Sebastian Neumeyer[1], and Robert Woll[1]

[1] Division Virtual Product Creation, Fraunhofer IPK, Germany
[2] Chair of Industrial Information Technology, Technische Universität Berlin, Germany
thomas.damerau@ipk.fraunhofer.de

Abstract. The steadily growing complexity of products, interfacing processes, value creation networks and IT environments drive today's PLM solutions to their limits. How does this effect engineers? Over 1,400 engineers from the German industry provided feedback in 2011 – with alarming but expected results. Almost two thirds of the respondents can only spend 20% or less time on average for core tasks such as development, design or validation. The study confirmed a lack of time for creative engineering activities caused by a massive coordination and communication overhead. Could engineers and designers be relieved from routine and administrative tasks in product lifecycle management by means of current "intelligent" technologies? In constant dialogue with industry and PLM experts, the Fraunhofer IPK and TUB have investigated the demand for intelligence in product lifecycle management. This paper reflects on the current situation of PLM and introduces a conceptual framework (Engineering Operating System) for next generation PLM. Subsequently, an Engineering Automation Capabilities (EAC) stair step model is proposed and selected research results for "intelligence" in PLM are presented.

Keywords: PLM, Next Generation, Engineering Operating System, Intelligence.

1 Need for intelligent PLM Solutions

Product Lifecycle Management (PLM) is an integrated approach to manage product-related information along a product's entire lifecycle relying on a suitable set of organizational prerequisites, processes and IT solutions [1]. But with an ever growing complexity of products, processes, value creation networks and IT environments, managing all that information becomes an increasing challenge. Figure 1 depicts some of these challenges and drivers, identified by the authors based on experience in industrial and research projects.

To cope with these challenges from the IT perspective, PLM thus has to ensure that massive amounts of information can be stored, searched and used efficiently. Furthermore, PLM must ensure that information from different domains and lifecycle phases is logically and dynamically linked according to variable business intelligences.

S. Fukuda et al. (Eds.): PLM 2014, IFIP AICT 442, pp. 485–495, 2014.

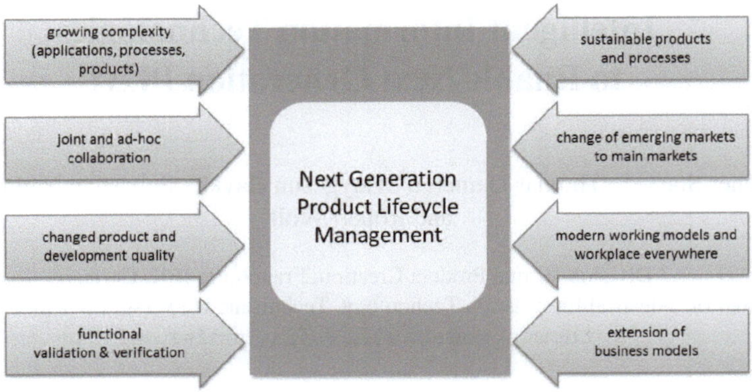

Fig. 1. Challenges and drivers for future PLM

However, current PLM solutions have three essential shortcomings addressed in this paper. Firstly, the underlying data models (describing how information from different engineering disciplines can be linked together) and the actual linking of information are left to the companies implementing a PLM solution into their IT environment. Secondly, PDM/PLM vendors have still not found or proposed a simple way for integrating third-party task-specific solutions besides the ones they offer themselves. And thirdly, almost any kind of "intelligence" in data management today is expected to be provided by the users (engineers, planners, managers). The first stated shortcoming of current PLM solutions calls for standardized, industry-wide accepted high-level PLM data models and for specific solutions that support the modelling of links between data from different domains and the analysis of interlinked data. The second shortcoming may not be obvious at first sight. It must be understood that task-specific solutions and the PDM backbone that they build upon are two types of IT solutions; such implementation oriented separation is necessary to allow for companies to choose the best breed of task-specific solutions and also allow them to develop their individual solutions if needed. In the following, these standalone task-specific solutions will be called PLM solutions, as opposed to PDM/PLM solutions which represent a tightly coupled, combined set of PLM solutions and a PDM backbone that are all offered by the same IT vendor. A future PLM environment has to allow for any PLM solutions to simply be plugged into an already existing PDM backbone. The third shortcoming of today's PLM solutions is characterized by the fact that no sort of intelligence is provided that could relieve engineers from some of the rather dull data-management-centric activities. This leads to an innovation backlog that was confirmed by a survey that 1,400 engineers from the German industry provided feedback to in 2012/2013 [2, 3]. Almost two thirds of the respondents could only spend 20% or less time on average for core tasks such as development, design or validation. The study confirmed a lack of time for creative engineering activities caused by a massive coordination and communication overhead. Due to these shortcomings this paper aims to introduce and review concepts and technologies that will lead to a more intelligent support of engineering activities and an automation of data management related activities in future PLM solutions.

Research Approach. The development of intelligence in PLM solutions demands extensive research activities; a holistic consideration of industrial needs, methodical requirements, technical feasibility and other aspects is necessary for this. To cope with this challenge a research approach was defined in order to answer the research question: How should information technologies be used to best relieve engineers from routine tasks in PLM? The approach contains the following steps:

- proposal and validation of a holistic conceptual PLM framework,
- proposal of a stair step model for "intelligent" PLM solutions, and
- review of existing "intelligent" PLM building blocks and classification according to the stair step model for gap identification.

2 Conceptual Framework for PLM Solutions

This chapter introduces two models; first a conceptual framework for PLM, designated as Engineering Operating System (EOS) [5], proposed by Fraunhofer IPK in 2013, and second, a maturity stair step model, designated as Engineering Automation Capabilities (EAC) model, for PLM solutions. The EOS was drafted with the intention to ensure product creation capabilities in the context of a holistic framework. It is based on four different levels that need to be taken into consideration when PLM processes, solutions or strategies are conceived. The core message of the EOS is that these four different levels must be understood as an integrated system in order to unfold the complete potential of PLM. These four levels are characterized as follows (compare Fig. 2):

- Process and Organization: At this level it has to be ensured that roles, responsibilities, and processes exist that define which value creation activities are to be executed by whom and hence need to be supported by PLM solutions. Furthermore, the information needs of business processes and management must be understood in order to support an effective and efficient information ex-change between engineering activities and management activities.
- Engineering Activities: Engineering Activities generally comprise all activities during the lifecycle that contribute to the generation, verification and validation of a virtual model of a product and to accompany a physical product from its production down to its end of life. While the process and organization layer focusses on the high-level processes, dependencies and responsibilities and thus on the questions of when things are done, in which order and by whom, the engineering activities focus on "how" exactly things are done in detail. From a PLM perspective it must be ensured that engineers have the required access to product-related information when they perform engineering or service activities. In addition it must be ensured that engineers can define and store new information in a way that allows a later reuse of that information (where needed in the lifecycle).

- Data and Information Models: On this layer PLM must thrive to understand the way in which different engineering stakeholders exchange information and data, how they interact with it from their different perspectives and how data is converted and filtered. PLM must ensure that information from different do-mains can be interlinked, that limited views on information can be established according to different application contexts and access policies, and that the lifecycle of data is managed.
- IT-Implementation: In order for all product-related information to be properly managed PLM must ensure that a suitable technological backbone for data management is in place (e.g. servers, networks, service platforms). This comprises the availability of reliable and safe data storages, the use of flexible, efficient and ideally open and standardized data formats, the provision of powerful and user-friendly information retrieval interfaces and the realization of efficient IT system integration mechanisms.

Yet accomplished innovations in PLM solutions were mainly driven from an operational perspective and therefore mostly focused on the top layer "Process and Organization". Examples are the inclusion of project-, workflow management or applications for the conversion of digital models. The engineering activity level is almost not addressed at all. PLM solutions barely support engineers in their key activities such as technical assessment, alternative solution identification and creation, technical system artefact traceability, decision making but mainly address administrative tasks and digital model management.

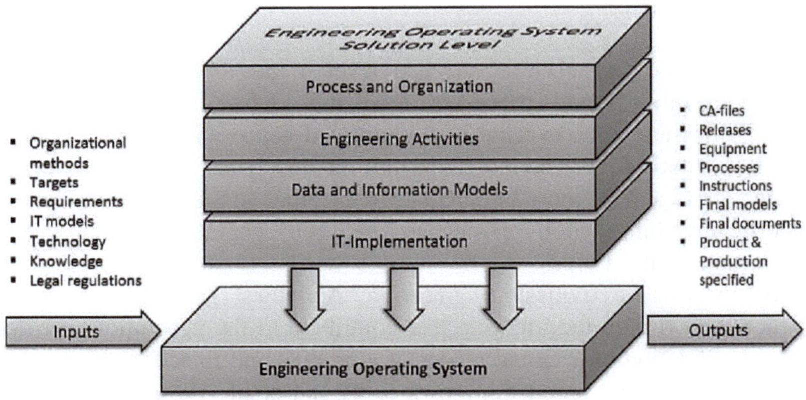

Fig. 2. Solution Layers of the conceptual Engineering Operation System (EOS) model

At the data and information models layer, many PLM solutions, however, still employ proprietary data formats that hinder a fluent information exchange across organizations, and at the "IT-Implementation" layer they usually do not provide open programming interfaces that would allow them to be easily coupled with other PLM solutions. The authors suggest that the use of intelligent information technologies may improve the degree of integration across PLM solutions, have a positive impact on the holistic integration of the two top layers and lead to both, an increased engineering effectiveness and efficiency, and a relief of engineers form routine tasks.

To gain clarity and for the classification of existing and targeted next generation PLM solutions, a stair step maturity model is proposed. The Engineering Automation Capabilities (EAC) model describes the expected and required increments of engineering automation capabilities towards intelligent PLM solutions in four steps (see Fig. 3.)

- User-centered Automation: This step represents today's state of the art in industry. PLM solutions consist of stand-alone PLM applications. Although PLM vendors offer partly integrated solutions e.g. integrated requirements management with linking functionalities to the product structure, these are not widely diffused into industrial practice. Hence, extensive customizing and configuration efforts are made. The engineer is the central source for the intelligent automation of data management centric activities in PLM.
- Assisted Automation: This second level offers developments towards intelligent approaches for data and information management. The engineer is still the single source of intelligence, but is assisted by tools during data search, link-age, usage and other data management centric activities.
- Semi-automated Engineering: Semi-automated engineering means that PLM solutions are able to anticipate engineering activities (e.g. action alternatives and data aggregation for the configuration of a digital mockup). This is the first step towards artificial intelligence (AI) in PLM. Semi automation already uses inherent business intelligences to trigger new engineering tasks or at least information related analysis, synthesis or assessments.
- Automated Engineering: The last step is enabling the automation of routine engineering activities and data management centric activities. Data and information is linked both, vertical through all solution levels of the EOS and the involved domains (mechanic, electronic and informatics), and horizontal along the product lifecycle. Therefore, the anticipation of engineering activities can be enhanced. Furthermore consequences of decisions can be estimated and aligned with business and engineering objectives automatically.

The step "automated engineering" in the stair step model can be seen as the ultimate goal. The next section elaborates present existing research results in context of the EOS and the associated stair step model.

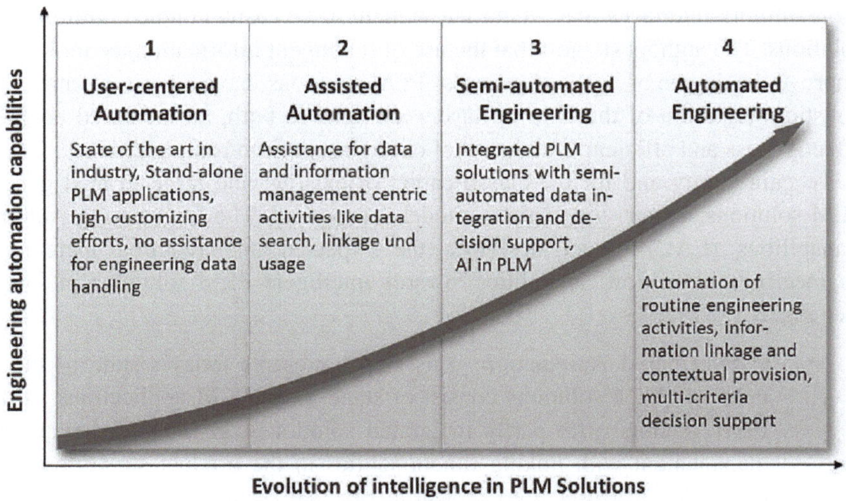

Fig. 3. Evolution steps for intelligent PLM solutions in the context of engineering automation capabilities

3 Research Solutions for Intelligence in PLM

In this section intelligent PLM-solutions are presented that have been developed at Fraunhofer IPK and the Chair of Industrial Information Technology at the Berlin University of Technology.

As described in the previous chapter, past PLM initiatives focused on the layer of "Process and Organization" of EOS. Also the layer of "Data and Information Models" is covered by PLM Solutions, even if the integration of heterogeneous data into PLM still has to be performed by an engineer or by customization and configuration effort in PLM-Solutions. Due to new methods like Systems Engineering (SE), but also due to the increased amount of data and information in the product lifecycle management processes, intelligent PLM-solutions also have to address intelligent solutions for the EOS layer of "Engineering Activities" as well as increased assistance and automation in "Data and Information Modeling" layer. Such solutions and their application in PLM are now presented and allocated in the introduced EAC stair step model.

Visual Analytics for PLM. According to Thomas & Cook, visual analytics is an approach to understand past and current situations, as well as the events that lead to these circumstances. Likewise, visual analytics support the visualization of multiple data layers, the abstraction and integration of data from multiple data sources into a common representation [5]. This especially suits the needs in heterogeneous PLM IT environments, as today's PDM-Systems, which are used as backbone for PLM, including heterogeneous data as well as multiple levels of data layers. But such an amount of data and information can barely be controlled by the engineer.

In Figure 4, an approach developed at the Chair Industrial Information Technology at the Berlin University of Technology is shown, where a potential delay in the development process of a product is analyzed with the support of visual analytics. To analyze or assess such a risk, the data stored in the PDM-System, e. g. the number of design iterations (revisions or engineering changes) done in a past project, is analyzed. By dynamic filtering of the number of iterations (threshold) of an object (see Fig. 4 a, b, c), the engineer receives direct visual feedback of similar challenges within the current project (P1) as well as the past project (P2). By applying a second indicator on the selected data in the PDM System, delay in design, it is possible to identify all those objects with the same level of criticality in the design process (see Figure 4 d). The relevant object, a single part or an assembly, can be further investigated with the retrieved detail information (Figure 4e) and referenced or highlighted for the next risk review.

Other applications of visual analytics are e.g. to understand the chronology of change requests using a 3D product model or the visualization of impacts of changed parameters of a system model on a linked geometrical model. Visual Analytics provides intelligent support to information retrieval and thus fits into the 2nd step "Assisted Automation" of the EAC.

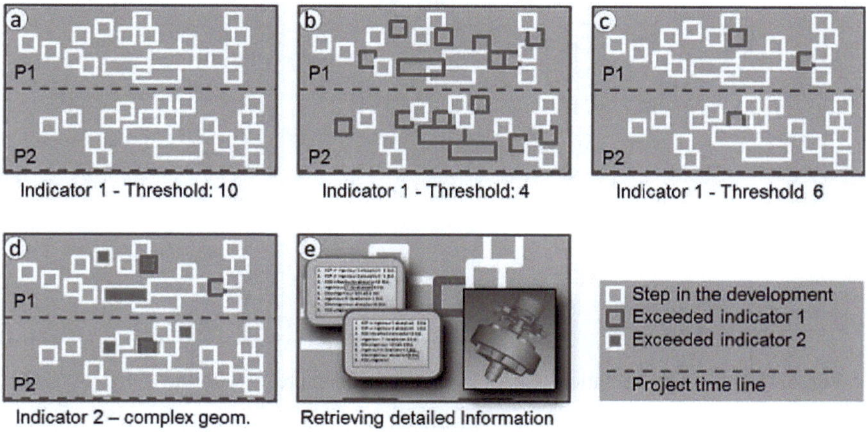

Fig. 4. Example for an indicator based comparison of two projects using Visual Analytics

Traceability in Systems Engineering. Today, the intelligent engineering work in Systems Engineering (SE) covers the task of comprehension of the different domain models as well as the identification of the relevant parameters, requirements and interdependencies between do-main models. To handle this complexity, today's SE approaches propose the creation of tracelinks.

In order to improve the efficiency of tracelink modeling, the "Model Tracer" application has been developed within the research project ISYPROM[1]. This modeler allows the creation and analysis of links between isolated data artifacts (Figure 5) to

[1] Research project ISYPROM. URL: `http://www.isyprom.de/`

ensure consistency and to identify dependencies between data artifacts as well as to estimate the impact of engineering changes. Also other application scenarios like the Fault Tree Analysis, Failure Mode and Effects analysis, Pareto Analysis and tracelink based progress monitoring can be supported using the "ModelTracer" [6].

With a consequent tracelink approach, information on the interdependencies between domain models and other artifacts is made explicit thus allowing for enhanced data analysis. The analysis of such interdependencies would otherwise have to be performed manually by the engineer. Given the amount of different models this is a tedious activity with a high risk of overlooking implicit interdependencies. The "Model Tracer" thus also improves the reliability and efficiency of analyzing model interdependencies. Hence, it mainly addresses the "Data and Information Models" layer of the EOS. Providing intelligent support at data level it also fits step 2 of the EAC.

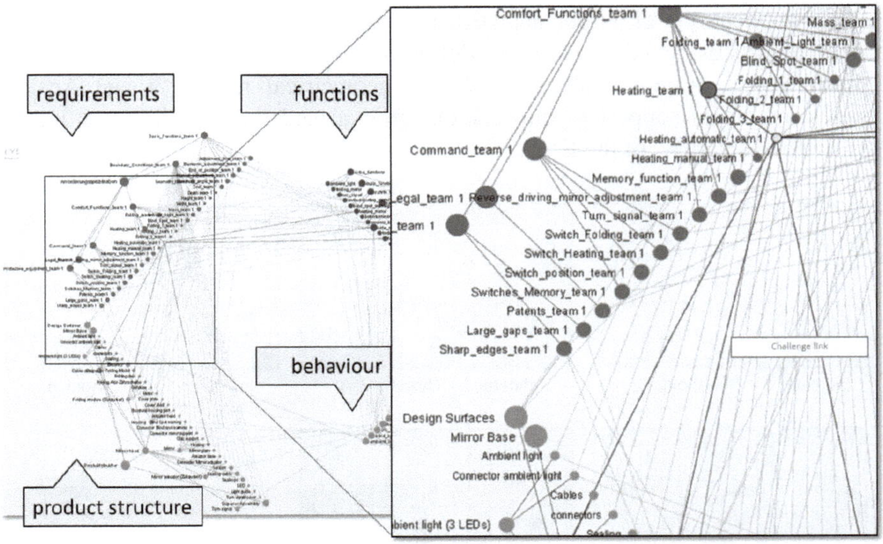

Fig. 5. Graphical presentation tracelinks that have been create with the "ModelTracer"

Ontologies for Semantic Data Integration. An important prerequisite before the ModelTracer can be used, is the definition of a data metamodel that defines which types of tracelinks can be defined between which elements from different data models. In the research field of data integration, a data metamodel that specifies possible relations between heterogeneous data formats is called a "mediated schema". In the EU-funded research project iProd[2] Fraunhofer IPK has investigated the use of ontologies as mediated schemas. The goal of these schemas was not only to allow for tracelink modelling but also for providing a technological foundation that allows for intelligent algorithms (so-called "reasoners") to process existing engineering data. These reasoners shall discover logical links between heterogeneous product data automatically in order to reduce the time for manual tracelinking even further than the ModelTracer allows.

[2] Research project iProd URL: `http: //www.iprod-project.eu`

In the iProd project Fraunhofer IPK has developed ontologies specifying a high-level engineering metamodel for interlinking different engineering artefacts that are generated and used along the Product Development Process (PDP). These ontologies reuse many concepts known from SysML and STEP 233 and they are designed to be easily adaptable for different engineering domains (such as the automotive, aerospace or home appliances domains) [7]. When adapted to the specific vocabulary of one company, an additional ontology-based data integration framework allows for specifying interfaces for different PLM solutions. Through these interfaces, existing engineering data can be linked and subsequently be processed by reasoning algorithms. Using reasoning, not only tracelink modelling can be sped up but also other logical rules can be applied to engineering data. For example, consistency rules between different behavior simulation models could be defined that allow for automatic model checking through a reasoner. Hence, by mapping non-ontological data to an ontology as a mediated schema, additional semantics can be "added" to existing engineering data without modifying it.

Decision Making Support for Sustainable Product Design. For dedicated tasks in engineering, e.g. for sustainable product design, the interdependencies between design decisions during development and sustainability effects of corresponding value creation are so complex, an engineer can't estimate them without support [8]. Currently, at the Chair of Industrial Information Technology at the Berlin University of Technology, an assistance system for semi-automated decision assistance in sustainable product design is under development in the research project CRC1026[3].

For this approach, several concepts for decision support have been investigated. One approach is to use ontologies for interlinking data from different phases in the product lifecycle. The sustainability information handled today in many different IT-Systems and databases are combined with knowledge artefacts based on sustainability related methods (Figure 6). With the help of several data bases, different methods as well as aggregated, sustainability-related knowledge, an assessment of different design alternatives is possible.

Another approach is the usage of a knowledge base, where the core functionality of the support system is the classification of the various properties and characteristics of a product with respect to its sustainability. For this, the environmental and social impacts over the entire lifecycle are considered and information is gathered about the sustainability context areas, e. g. the manufacturing processes and equipment, and about re-use. The system evaluates both designer's intention and the stakeholder's needs and requirements by evaluation criteria. [9].

Such semi-automated solutions enable the engineer to gather all stored knowledge and make the right decisions by pre-defined rules. Nevertheless, even if the 2nd and 3rd step of EAC can be achieved through interlinking the layers "engineering activity" and "data and information models" of the EOS, additional re-search is necessary in order to achieve the 4th step in the EAC model, the "Auto-mated Engineering" as the final evolution in assistance capabilities.

---

[3] Collaborative Research Center 1026 Sustainable Manufacturing – Shaping Global Value creation URL: `http://www.sustainable-manufacturing.net/en_GB/`

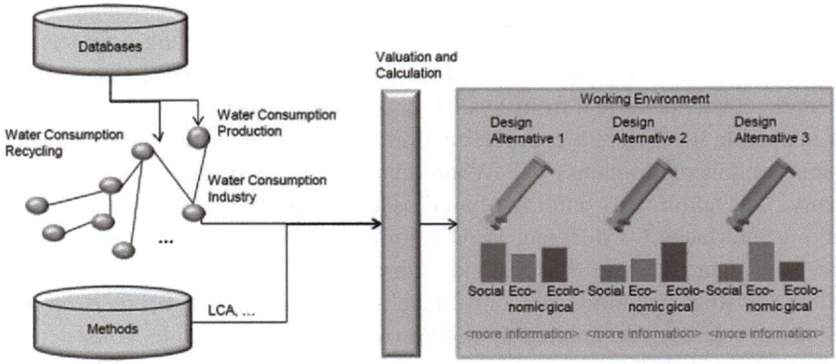

Fig. 6. Approach for integrating sustainability information into an engineer's working environment [6]

4 Conceptual Framework for PLM Solutions

In this paper it has been argued that engineers spend too much time on non-engineering-centric activities. The presented EOS suggests that PLM must always consider four different layers and ensure that these are harmonized. Furthermore, it postulates that PLM must assist engineering activities by providing the necessary information to engineers and that data management centric activities should be automated as much as possible. The EAC stair step model defines the different degrees to which PLM may employ intelligent approaches in order to reach these goals.

Fraunhofer IPK and TUB are introducing technologies and approaches for more intelligent PLM solutions. While a set of promising, existing research results are presented, a coherent vision for, and realization of, future PLM, that addresses all layers of the EOS, is still under development. The essence of that vision is to make better use of artificial intelligence approaches and to build a more integrated PLM IT environment. This future vision can only be reached if research, IT vendors, and industry end users work hand in hand. Towards this, further research steps will be taken by Fraunhofer IPK and TUB:

- Application of a scenario technique [10] to identify major challenges for intelligent data management from the industry perspective and definition of use-cases for the application of intelligent management.
- Implementation of a PLM based simulation environment to quantify and qualify the impact and synergies of presented and further approaches in the context of defined use-cases.

This paper is a contribution to the research field of next generation PLM, in awareness of the need for intensified interdisciplinary scientific discourse. Growing PLM user demands for more intelligence in PLM can be best satisfied by the collaborative research with PLM vendors and PLM users as well.

References

1. Stark, J.: Product Lifecycle Management: 21st Century Paradigm for Product Realisation, 572 p. Springer-Verlag London Limited, London (2011)
2. Müller, P., Pasch, F., Drewinski, R., Hayka, H.: Kollaborative Produktentwicklung und digitale Werkzeuge: Defizite heute - Potenziale morgen, 103 p. Fraunhofer Institut Produktionsanlagen und Konstruktionstechnik, Berlin (2013)
3. Müller, P., Pasch, F., Drewinski, R., Bedenbender, H., Hayka, H., Stark, R.: Study on collaborative product development and digital engineering tools. In: Rivest, L., Bouras, A., Louhichi, B. (eds.) PLM 2012. IFIP AICT, vol. 388, pp. 389–399. Springer, Heidelberg (2012)
4. Stark, R., Hayka, H., Rothenburg, U., Figge, A., Woll, R.: Keynote presentation: Next Generation Smart Product and Systems Engineering; COBEM. In: International Congress of Mechanical Engineering, University of São Paulo, Ribeirão Preto, Brazil (2013)
5. Thomas, J.J. (ed.): Illuminating the path: the research and development agenda for visual analytics, 186 p. IEEE, Los Alamitos (2005)
6. Beier, G., Figge, A., Müller, R., Rothenburg, U., Stark, R.: Supporting Product Development through Cross-Discipline Dependency-Modeling: Novel Approaches for Traceability-Usage. Lecture Notes on Information Theory 1(1), 21–28 (2013)
7. Woll, R., Hayka, H., Stark, R., Geißler, C., Greisinger, C.: Semantic integration of product data models for the verification of product requirements, in: Concurrent engineering approaches for sustainable product development in a multi-disciplinary environment. In: Proceedings of the 19th ISPE International Conference on Concurrent Engineering, pp. 157–168. Springer, London (2013)
8. Pförtner, A., Lindow, K., Hayka, H., Stark, R.: Concept for decision-making support in sustainable product design based on semantic ontology. In: Proceedings: 10th Global Conference on Sustainable Manufacturing Towards Implementing Sustainable Manufacturing, Istanbul, Turkey, October 31 - November 2, pp. 476–480. Springer, Heidelberg (2012); Towards implementing sustainable manufacturing. Proceedings
9. Lindow, K., Heimann, O., Adolphy, S., Hayka, H., Stark, R.: Decision-Making Support for Sustainable Product Development. In: Abramovici, M., Stark, R. (eds.) Proceedings of the 23rd CIRP Design Conference on Smart Product Engineering, Bochum, Germany, March 11-13, pp. 979–988. Springer, Berlin (2013)
10. Gausemeier, J., Plass, C., Wenzelmann, C.: Zukunftsorientierte Unternehmensgestaltung: Strategien, Geschäftsprozesse und IT-Systeme für die Produktion von morgen, 467p. Hanser, München, (2009)

Reframing of Product Position Rescues the Strategy at the Lifecycle Management

Makoto Takayama[1] and Tadashi Takayama[2]

[1] Graduate School for Management of Technology, Graduate School of Modern Society and Culture, Niigata University, Japan; UCLA Medical School, USA
[2] Graduate School of Business Administration, Kobe University, Japan
takayama@econ.niigata-u.ac.jp

Abstract. This paper shows the role of reframing product position at the lifecycle management. From surveys on the products of the leaders, it became evident that win-lose is determined by the competitiveness between a new product and the marketed products of the leaders. The result is that existing products inhibit the development of indirectly competitive new products. To explain win-lose in the NPD, the role of "reframing product position" is proposed. The conclusion is that reframing product position rescues the strategy at the lifecycle management.

Keywords: Reframing, Product position, Strategy, New product development, Lifecycle management.

1 Introduction

We generally believe that incremental product innovations are frequently achieved by strong actors who know the market and technology for new products. Market leaders have the stronger positions to improve products because they have the competitive positions to know the market needs and the seeds of new technologies. When a product changes, it is well known that the incremental product innovation is well managed by the cooperation between the market and technological knowledge [1], [2], [3], [4]. In particular, the technology seeds and marketing needs are generally recognized as the fundamental driving forces for developing the related products in the major markets. The leaders are, therefore, presumed to be able to keep the competitive advantages. The reality is different from the assumption; the leaders are very often replaced when they confront dilemmas [5] or the major products are replaced [6], [7]. There are many discussions on the success factors in product innovation from aspects of technology push and market pull. Technology-push theories highlight the importance of technology in product innovation [8], [9], [10], [11], [12], [13], [14]. On another front, market-pull theories highlight the importance of market needs or customer wants [1], [2], [3], [8], [15], [16]. The push-pull framework has not yet lead to any convincing conclusions. With respect to new product development (NPD), the aforementioned opposing views have, respectively, highlighted the importance of the technological knowledge and market knowledge. At the lifecycle management (LCM), the product profile of a successive product is

S. Fukuda et al. (Eds.): PLM 2014, IFIP AICT 442, pp. 497–506, 2014.

examined from viewpoints of its related-technologies and the market. When a new technology is closely related to a marketed product, the possibility of a new product is evaluated from the estimation of the market size. For maximizing the sales of a new product in a pipeline, the market knowledge assists the accumulation of the technological knowledge. Apparently, both technological knowledge and market knowledge are the key success factors for NPD. Consequently, market leaders can keep the competitive advantages to develop new products related to their marketed products and therefore cannot be easily taken over by newcomers.

For the continuous NPD, the above assumption seems to be true. The concurrent engineering system is thought to be the best way to launch the next product into the market [17]. For the automobile industry and the electricity industry, many authors demonstrated the advantage of the collaboration of technological and marketing capabilities [1], [18]. The reverse is true. Majors often lost the opportunities to develop or launch new products. This paradox has not yet been resolved since in the earlier discussions the key determinants of NPDs had been discussed only from the perspectives of technological and marketing capabilities. Albeit the technological and market knowledge is aligned with the strategy, the discussion so far miss the point of reframing product position.

In this paper, we study the role of reframing product position at the lifecycle management. From the surveys on the products of leaders, it becomes evident that win-lose is determined by the competitiveness between a new product and the marketed products of leaders. The result indicates that the existing products inhibit the development of indirectly competitive new products. To explain the win-lose in NPD, the role of "reframing product position" in NPDs is proposed. If a market player reframes the product position independently from the current market, reframing product position rescues the strategy from the fatal loss in NPD at the lifecycle management.

For demonstrating the role of reframing product position, we focus firstly on the anti-hypertensive market since the final breakthrough products have just replaced the existing products after the market development phase has come to maturity. The finding is that the existing products inhibit the development of indirectly competitive new products that create a new market. In case new products compete indirectly with the existing products, the market leaders are replaced by newcomers. The win-lose is determined by a product position of a new product. To validate the theory, a symbolic case in the win-lose cases in the commodity market is discussed. Tea with high catechins is the biggest selling government-approved food for specified health uses. A commodity firm, Kao Corporation, succeeded in the NPD, although the market leaders had acquired the same knowledge. To explain the win-lose in NPD, the role of "reframing product position" is proposed for the successful product lifecycle management. The conclusion is that reframing product position rescues the strategy from the fatal loss in NPD at the lifecycle management.

2 Win or Loss of New Product Development in the Bio-industry

Many market leaders have failed in promising NPDs. Their intensive R&D investment did not prevent the entry of newcomers. The most typical example is the NPD related by using recombinant DNA techniques. Almost the large firms, as well as in the bio-related industries, had established the bio-tech institutes in 1980s. Although many major players have failed in the NPD, many firms have still believed that bio could strike the gold mines from the huge unveiled markets.

In the bio-industry, win-or-lose results are simple. Major crop firms have continuously succeeded in the NPDs. By the successive launches of recombinant crops, they have maintained the leading position in the market except niche products. On the contrary, major pharmaceutical firms have not succeeded in the NPD of bio-pharmaceuticals. They did not think bio-pharmaceuticals compete directly with the existing products because bio-products were not easy to handle. Major players concluded that bio-products were positioned in the differentiated market. Albeit launched, majors denied the competing possibilities of the bio-products and then declined the opportunity to introduce the bio-products even at a small licensing fee offered by the bio-ventures like Genentech. That proves the major market players have denied the marketability of the new products. Consequently, the major firms in the pharmaceutical industry have lost the bio-pharmaceutical market up to the present. The outstanding winner was Amgen that started by the spin-off researchers from Merck in the US that had lost the top market share in the world and CEO of Amgen became Chairman of the Board of PhRMA (Pharmaceutical Research and Manufacturers in America). The major firms had lost not only the symbolic position but also the upcoming market in the field of the bio-pharmaceuticals.

Table 1 summarized the win-lose of major firms in the new-born recombinant bio-product market. Crop and pharmaceuticals were the biggest industries in the bio-market. The recombinant crops or seeds competed directly with the existing crops. Major multinational crop firms developed the new products by applying the recombinant technology. The major firms have still now excluded the newcomers from the recombinant plant market. In case of the recombinant bio-pharmaceuticals, major pharmaceutical firms did not only succeed in NPD but also rejected the license opportunities of recombinant pharmaceuticals. Pharmaceuticals did not compete directly with bio-pharmaceuticals but some existing products have been gradually replaced by bio-pharmaceuticals in several large markets such as rheumatoid arthritis, cancer treatment/prevention and vaccines. In 2012, the share of the bio-pharmaceuticals has reached 73.5% of the top 10 sellers in the Japanese pharmaceutical market [19]. In case of indirect competition such as recombinant bio-pharmaceuticals, majors failed in the NPD and lost the future market.

Table 1. Win-lose of major firms in the new-born recombinant bio-product market

	Win-lose of Majors	Competition
Recombinant crops	***Win***	Direct
Recombinant bio-pharmaceuticals	***Lose***	Indirect

Table 2 explains the mechanism of win-lose of majors. The author proposed the concept of the product position to existing products. From the viewpoint of the competitiveness, new products are classified by superior point versus differentiated point. If a new product has a superior point to the existing products, it directly competes with the existing products and will replace the market. Major firms decide the NPD and therefore the winner is the major. In case a new product has a differentiated point to the existing products, it indirectly competes with the existing products and will create a new market. Major firms do not need to decide the NPD and therefore lost the opportunity of the NPD.

Table 2. Win-lose of major firms and two types of new products

Type of new product	Superior	Differentiated
Position to Existing products	***Directly competing***	***Indirectly competing***
Mode of Market penetration	Replace market	Create new market
NPD by major firms	***Win***	***Lose***

According to Ansoff's product-market matrix [20], [21], [22], a superior product corresponds to a new product with the same mission that replaces the existing market. A differentiated product corresponds to a product with a new mission that creates a new market.

3 Inevitable Fate of Win-Lose in the Pharmaceutical New Product Development

According to a statistical analysis by Japanese Pharmaceutical Manufacturers' Association [23], the average development cost is approximately 500 million dollars for one product and the average success ratio of NPD was 1/27,090 between 2007 and 2011. The development takes approximately 10 years from the discovery stage to the launch. This means that sufficient skill is required for the NPDs.

Owing to the necessity of the expertise, the market leader can keep the best position to collect the market needs and seeds of new technologies through the network of professionals. Owing to strong contacts with the professionals, the market leaders can often utilize their superior positions to collect the market and technological information on the next product.

Holding the initiative in the corresponding field, the majors lost a new and large market created by an indirectly competitive new product. The market leaders have lost the indirectly competitive new markets, such as anti-hypertensive, anti-ulcer, bio-pharmaceuticals, and other breakthrough pharmaceuticals.

The anti-hypertensive has constituted the largest market which accounts for 10% of the pharmaceutical market in 1990s and has increased the share to 20% of the total market of the leading countries in the early 2010s. Hypertension is one of the lifestyle-related diseases, by which heart failure, cerebral stroke, myocardial infarction, kidney malfunction, diabetes and other dangerous complications are caused. Angiotensin receptor blockers (ARB) were developed from 1990s to 2000s and have reached more than half of the total hypertensive market. For hypertensive medication, two major products, Ca blockers (Ca) and Angiotensine Converting Enzyme Inhibitors (ACE) had been mainly prescribed before ARB was marketed. As Ca shows rapid onset and sharp efficacy, Ca became the first choice for the treatment of the hypertensive patients in the Japanese market. Since ACE is less effective then

Ca but had the organ protection function, ACE is used for the patients who had risks for the organ damage.

The first ARB was launched by Merck & Co. in 1995. According to the industrial reviews, the sales was underestimated around 400 million dollars in the world. After 10 years from the first launch, ARB has replaced the existing Ca market. In 2010, ARB has become the largest product category in the hypertensive market [24]. In 2004, sales of ARB in the Japanese pharmaceuticals market exceeded hyperlipidemia market, which had formerly been the largest product category in the pharmaceutical market and the main target of supplementary food for specified health use as described in the next chapter. ARB has dominated the world antihypertensive market with a share over 70% for the first prescribed patients from the mid-2000s.

Table 3. "Revenge of success" to market leaders of Ca antagonists, a product not competing with ARBs (Source: World Review 1999 by IMS Health, The Pharmaceutical Market) [6], [7]

Company	Market share (%)	Win-lose in the development
Pfizer	33.9	—
Bayer	12.8	—
Hoechst	9.0	(licensed form Sanofi)
Astra	3.7	(licensed from Takeda)
BASF	2.7	—
Monsanto (Searle)	2.4	—
Kyowa Hakko	2.2	—
Yamanouchi	2.0	(licensed from BI after Ca market was replaced)
Takeda	2.0	delayed because the development was discontinued
Ciba-Geigy	2.0	(from an acquired firm, Sandoz)

Particularly in Japan, the "myth of Ca" controlled the antihypertensive market. It claimed the absolute superiority of Ca, the quick onset of the efficacies. Leading firms educated the market through the network of professionals such as professors, prescribing physicians and pharmacists. Due to the strong product position, the leading firms are scarified with the revenge of success not only in Japan but also in the world [6], [7]. The performance of the world top 10 leading firms in the Ca market is summarized in Table 3. Among the top 10 companies, nine had no ARB product and three firms acquired co-marketing rights of ARB after the market became clear. Takeda once discontinued NPD of the world's strongest ARB and therefore lost the chance to sell in the world by its own sales force. Takeda changed the product position and restarted after the sales of the first ARB had exceeded the sales estimation. Takeda's new ARB has now become a breakthrough over 3 billion dollars sales in 2010. Reframing the product position rescued the strategy. Ciba-Geigy merged Sandoz in 1997 (currently named Novartis) and got an ARB. The top 10 firms except Takeda have no self-made or self-developed products in the world market, although ARBs became the global mega breakthrough products in 2010s.

Seven of the top 10 leaders in the ACE market succeeded in the development of ARB ahead of the Ca leaders and the rest, as shown in Table 4 [6], [7]. The reason is that the new products compete directly with their own products. The ACE leaders could use their superior position for developing the new products because they do not need to change the product position and the strategy except of the cannibalization.

Table 4. The achievement of ACE leaders (Source: World Review 1999 by IMS Health , The Pharmaceutical Market)

Company	ACE Market share (%)	The order of the launch dates
Merck & Co.	31.0	1st
Zeneca	13.4	5th (licensed from Tanabe)
BMS	10.7	4th (1st as ACE/NEP inhibitors)
Warner-Lambert	6.4	—
Novartis	5.3	2nd
Hoechst	3.8	3rd (licensed by Sanofi)
Servier	3.7	(2nd as ACE/NEP inhibitors)
Tanabe	1.9	—
Banyu	1.8	1st (Merck's subsidiary in Japan)
Sankyo	1.7	8th (licensed to foreign companies)

ARBs are superior to ACEs and differentiated from Ca. From a marketing viewpoint, ARBs competed with ACEs directly and replaced the ACE market. The leaders in the ACE market needed to develop an ARB to keep the current market position. In contrast, Ca does not compete directly with ARB. Due to the product position of ARB, all of the Ca leaders denied the necessity of the NDPs and lost the market share.

Tale 5 explained the product position as the same manner as shown in Table 2. When existing products directly competed with a new product, the market leaders succeeded in the NPD. When existing products indirectly competed with a new product, the market leaders failed in the NPD.

Table 5. Two types of the market positions of new products

	ACE	Ca
Competition with the new products	Directly compete	Indirectly compete
Position to the new products	Replace the existing products	Create a new market
NPD	Win	Lose

The products for gastrointestinal diseases are the second largest therapeutic area in the world market. Fig. 1 shows the continuous product changes in the Japanese gastrointestinal pharmaceutical market from 1977 to 2012. The products have been changed three times. The first product category was mucosal defense factors, which have still been the basic medicine. The second was H2 blockers, which was the biggest category in 2000. The third is the category of proton pump inhibitors, which sales are presumed to reach the peak in 2020. In accordance with the product changes, the leading firms changed. In the mucosal defenses market, the market leaders were Eisai and Takeda. In the H2 blockers market, Yamanouchi became a top seller in the global market around 2000. In proton pump inhibitors market, Eisai and Takeda have came back to the market leaders. All of the former market leaders did not initiate the NPD since they denied the market of the next products as their strategies of the product position. The product position of the existing products pre-determined the strategy. The existing products inhibited the development of indirectly competitive new products.

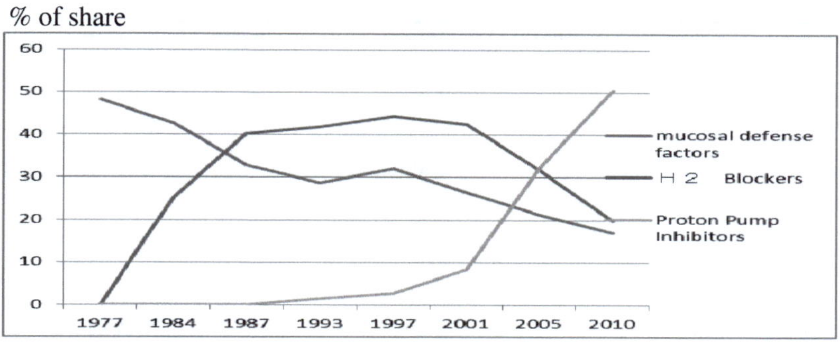

Fig. 1. The product changes in the Japanese gastrointestinal pharmaceutical market

The market leaders did not develop the new product when the market reaches the maturity as far as new products are not directly competing with the existing products. This finding is not limited to the product in case. The same results are obtained in the other pharmaceutical markets such as bio-pharmaceuticals, rheumatoid arthritis, asthma, hypertensive, osteoporosis, cancer and vaccines.

4 Win or Lose in a Commodity Market: A Case of Foods for Specified Health Use

The market of "foods for specified health use" was triggered by a cathechin-rich tea. It is defined as a class of foods which contain specific therapeutic ingredients and are approved by the Ministry of Health, Labour and Welfare based on the test results on the safety and effectiveness. The market is for the life style related diseases and the products claim the same as hypertensives and lipid lowering pharmaceuticals. The difference is not for the treatment but for the prevention. Pharmaceutical firms denied the new market, albeit they had the same category products in the healthy foods market. As shown in Table 6, Foods, beverages and pharmaceutical firms had not initiated the NPD because the new product has a critical disadvantages (bitter, little efficacy) compared to the existing products. Only Kao Corporation, a soap and commodity company, appealed a superior point (health) and accomplished the NPD in 2003. Kao released catechin-rich green tea and its market reached 70 billion yen in 2012 [25].

Catechin is a bitter ingredient of green tea. Itoen Inc. is the market leader after the success of the NPD of canned green tea in 1985 (Itoen HP). Itoen has kept the highest market share for 20 years. Not only beverage leaders but pharmaceutical leaders had known the lipid–lowering function of cathechin. Only Kao did. All of the existing majors denied the marketability. Once the annual sales had exceeded 30 billion yen, they reframed the product position from disadvantageous (bitter and little efficacy) to superior (healthy). The key determinant for initiating the NPD was the position of the new product. If a firm reframe the position of a new product from disadvantageous to superior, the strategy for NPD is transformed from inhibitory to promoting.

Table 6. Win-lose at the start of the governmentally authorized foods market

	Foods or beverages leaders	Pharmaceuticals leaders	Outsiders
Market entry	Lose	Lose	Win (Kao Corporation)
Competitive position	Indirect	Indirect	No related product
New products	Disadvantages (Bitter taste)	Disadvantages (No or little efficacy)	Healthy
Product development	Deny	Deny	Promote

The win-lose fate of major firms was observed likewise in the daily life related markets. In the power-toothbrush market, a small Seattle-based American venture, Optiva Corp., developed the Sonicare sonic toothbrush. Toothbrush manufacturers were skeptical about the future market and neglected the NPD. When Optiva got nearly half of the share (46 percent) of the U.S. power-toothbrush market, Philips Domestic Appliances and Personal Care (DAP), a division of Royal Philips Electronics, acquired the firm in 2000. A million-seller portable power-toothbrush, Doltz, was developed by the same newcomer, Panasonic, in 2010. As well as the former cases, toothbrush majors neglect the differentiated market.

Regarding other products in other markets, the fate of the win-lose of major firms were determined by the same mechanism [26]. In the case of directly competing new products, cassette tape recorder, CD player, digital camera, and DVD are apparently superior to the existing products and therefore the majors won the NPD. In the case of indirectly competing new products, PC, Amazon book store, net securities, and net retailing were not advantageous to the existing products but less superior from majors' perspectives. For transforming the strategic decision, the key determinant for the successful NPDs is reframing the product position by finding the superior points of the new products.

5 Reframing Product Position Rescues the Strategy at the Lifecycle Management

The win-loss was pre-determined by the competitive position of a new product. If a new product apparently has a superior point to the existing products, it competes directly and the majors respond faster and win. If a new product does not have any superior point, it competes indirectly and the majors estimate the market too small or temporary. Therefore, majors will lose the timing for the NPD. The former is "market substitution type" and the latter is "market change type". Although the latter does not compete directly with the existing products, majors could later shift the product position after the market is expected to grow. Kao's success owed to the indifference about the market knowledge [27], [28]. Kao's core capabilities were from lipid and oil, as the base to the soap. Kao's management only decided to make the new product position of the green tea from tasting to the health use. The tea majors' concern was a bitter taste of catechin. After the majors reframed the position of the new products from good taste to good health, they initiated the development of the same categorized products by advertising the superior advantages to green teas. To follow the reframing of the product positions, they turned around the strategies. By reframing the product position, the strategy was rescued not to inhibit the NPD.

Takeda, Sankyo and Yamanouchi re-started the development by reframing the position of new products. The product position of new ARBs was reframed from differentiated to superior in the same manner as cathechin-rich green tea. By shifting the position of the products from differentiated to superior, new products got accepted and the strategy was shifted from inhibitory to promoting.

In the directly competing cases, strategy follows the product position. In indirectly competing cases, majors did not consider the superior point and marketability of new products. Among them, some shifted the strategy by reframing the product position and succeeded in the NPDs. The key for success was the product position. The strong products in the market often freeze the majors' capabilities of NPD. For the market leaders, reframing the product position has released the capability of NPD. In the case of newcomers, reframing the product position is independent from their marketed-products. Reframing the product position rescues the strategy at the life cycle management.

Acknowledgments. The authors acknowledge the contribution of Mr. Takamasa Ishizawa at MOT of Niigata University to the data collection on pharmaceuticals.

References

1. von Hippel, E.: The Source of Innovation. Oxford University Press, New York (1988)
2. von Hippel, E.: Democratizing Innovation. The MIT Press, Boston (2005) ISBN-10: 0262002744
3. von Hippel, E.: Customers as Innovators: A New Way to Create Value (HBR OnPoint Enhanced Edition). Harvard Business Review, Boston (2009) Ansoff, H.I.: Corporate Strategy, vol. 19. McGraw-Hill (1966)
4. Clerk, K.B., Fujimoto, T.: Product Development Performance. Harvard Business School Press, Boston (1991)
5. Christensen, M.C.: The Innovator's Dilemma. Harvard Business School Press, Boston (1997)
6. Takayama, M.: The true reason of failure in new products development, Tokyo Tosho Shuppankai (2002)
7. Takayama, M., Watanabe, C.: Myth of market needs and technology seeds as a source of product innovation. Technovation 22, 353–362 (2002)
8. Rothwell, R., et al.: SAPPHO updated. Project SAPPHO, phase 2. Research Policy 3(3), 258–291 (1974)

9. OECD, Committee for Scientific and Technological Policy, Science, Technology and Competitiveness: Analytical Report of the Ad Hoc Group. OECD/STP (84) 26, Paris (1984)
10. Dosi, G.: Technological paradigms and technological trajectories. Research Policy 2(3), 147–162 (1982)
11. Dosi, G.: Technical Change and Industrial Transformation. Macmillan, London (1984)
12. Dosi, G., et al.: Technical Change and Economic Theory. Printer Publishers, London (1988)
13. Dosi, G.: Cambridge Journal of Economics 34(1), 173–184 (2010a)
14. Dosi, G.: Knowledge Accumulation and Industry Evolution: The Case of Pharma-Biotech [Paperback]. In: Mazzucato, M., Dosi, G. (eds.). Cambridge University Press, Cambridge (2010b) ISBN-10: 052112400X
15. von Hippel, E.: A customer active paradigm for industrial product idea generation, Baker, (ed.) (1979)
16. von Hippel, E.: The user's role in industrial innovation. In: Dean, B., Goldhar, J. (eds.) Management of Research and Innovation. North Holland, Amsterdam (1980)
17. Hammer, M., Champy, J.: Reengineering the Corporation: A Manifesto for Business Revolution. New York Harper Business (1993)
18. Ohno, T.: The Toyota Production System. Productivity Press, Tokyo (1988)
19. Cedium Strategic Data K.K., Uto Brain. Pharma Future (2014)
20. Ansoff, H.I.: Corporate Strategy. McGraw-Hill (1966)
21. Ansoff, H.I.: The New Corporate Strategy. Wiley (1988)
22. Ansoff, H.I., McDonnell, E., Lindsey, L., Beach, S.: Implanting Strategic Management. Wiley (1993)
23. JPMA, JPMA DATA BOOK, Tokyo: Japanese Pharmaceutical Manufacturers' Association (2013)
24. Keizai, F.: Press Release, 2010.5.6 (2010), `http://www.group.fuji-keizai.co.jp/press/pdf/100506_10038.pdf` (accessed February 25, 2014)
25. Toyo Keizai. Toyo Keizai Online 2013.4.21(2013), `http://toyokeizai.net/articles/-/13735?page=2`
26. Takayama, M.: Law of Success or Failure in the High Tech Driven Market– "Revenge of Success" in the Biotech, Nanotech, and ICT Industry In: I. Furstner (ed.) Products and Services; from R&D to Final Solutions, SCIYO, pp.15–36 (2010), `http://www.intechopen.com/articles/show/title/law-of-success-or-failure-in-the-high-tech-driven-market-and-bio-industry`
27. Takayama, M.: Win without Fail and Fail without Win in Bio-Management. Office Automation 25(4), 15–21 (2005)
28. Takayama, M.: Law of success or failure in innovation, Innovation of Japanese Firms. Japan Society of Management, Tokyo (2009) (in Japanese) ISBN-10: 4805109319

How Developers Explore and Exploit Instant Innovation from Experiment to Implementing New Product Development

Masayoshi Fukushima[1], Tadashi Takayama[2], and Makoto Takayama[1]

[1] Graduate School of Modern Society and Culture, Niigata University, Japan
[2] Graduate School of Business Administration,Kobe University, Japan
hnsint@aol.com
takayama-tadashi@arion.ocn.ne.jp
takayama@mot.niigata-u.ac.jp

Abstract. This paper examines the nascent process of how Dynamic Instant Innovation (DII) is created by ambidexterity which is an individual's capacity to be equally skillful with both hands. The influences of DII on new product development are introduced and analyzed through Holtzman's paradox. This premise states that the greatest paradox that surrounds successful new product development is the need for free, unfettered creativity to complement disciplined, systematic processes [1]. Drawing from this paradox, strategies are proposed for new product development exploration and exploitation. A real case of needle-free injection product developed by the first author is presented using the DII concept.

Keywords: Dynamic Instant Innovation, New Product Development, User Specialization. Ambidexterity, Exploration, Exploitation.

1 Introduction

Under the current hyper competitive environment, Instant Innovation is inevitable in order to be successful and compete. Innovation, according to Schumpeter, is defined by carrying out new combinations [2] which have elements of both continuous innovation and incremental innovation. A disruptive innovation is an innovation that helps create a new market and value network, and eventually disrupts an existing market, displacing an earlier technology. Disruptive innovation is typically simpler, cheaper, and more reliable and convenient than the established technologies that it replaces [3]. DII creates products exponentially faster, cheaper, and can instantaneously disrupt current markets [4]. However, under hypercompetition, the competitive advantage created by DII can often be short lived. This is why successful companies are in constant pursuit of DII.

2 What is Dynamic Instant Innovation (DII)?

With the diffusion of more knowledge to more participants in the industry using today's multiplatform communication means, DII can proceed in parallel among

S. Fukuda et al. (Eds.): PLM 2014, IFIP AICT 442, pp. 507–517, 2014.

many open integrated parties and industries. As a result, more parallel experiments are occurring leading to more variety and more choices, which foster more rapid innovation. As such, the concept can be understood as rapid parallel research and development through multi-levels of organizations and individuals across the global spectrum that is loosely integrated by the Internet, thereby leading to Dynamic Instant Innovation. DII differs from user innovation in that user innovation refers to innovation by consumers rather than by suppliers, producers, and/or manufacturers. DII can encompass all of these elements. DII also differs from fusion innovation in that the latter relies on a process by which innovation is fused or comes together over time among the participants in a social system. This concept sometimes comes from happenstance and is not facilitated by formal nor even informal processes. For example, fusion foods have evolved by mixing flavors and recipes from different ethnic foods but not on any wide scale common interest or platform.

Generally speaking, users can experiment, implement and popularize new technology at the same time or instant, which is a form of DII. Its power exceeds that of concurrent engineering and open innovation. DII prevails in the user industries by the following steps:

1. Simultaneous processing of multiple information by reciprocal information exchange,
2. Integration of multiple streams of information into businesses,
3. Specialization of users, and
4. Direct user-created innovation [5]

As von Hippel noted, "Users' abilities to develop high-quality new products and services for themselves are improving radically and rapidly" [6]. The following are examples of DII:

A new scheme of modularization involves adding powerful computations and tabulations for improved efficiency and accuracy to bring about rapid innovation, which is a form of Instant Innovation. Modularization sped up genome sequencing making it possible to sequence 30 billion human genomes in 3 days. Now it is a matter of almost instantaneous sequencing of billions of genomes because of this innovation [4].

This DII is now possible because of exponential convergence of new disruptive innovations. Examples of such converging, disruptive innovations include nanotechnology, wireless sensor, internet, imaging, mobile connectivity, social networking, computing power, data universe, etc., have all contributed to exponential convergence of disruptive innovations.

Another example is DNA arrays that transform genetic sequencing and mapping capabilities. The arrays that are built on the same knowledge domain have limited upside potential whereas those that are built on different complementary knowledge domains could be more valuable as they are not bound by preconceived limitations. This is an indication that DII is also fostering competitive advantages that comes from exploration by ambidextrous employees.

Again, von Hippel noted "Steady improvements in computer software and hardware are making it possible to develop increasingly capable and cheaper tools for innovation that require less and less skill and training to use" [6]. An example of specialization of users by DII is Jack Andraka, a 15-year-old boy who developed a new test for pancreatic cancer. After a family friend died from pancreatic cancer, Jack discovered that there was no useful test to detect pancreatic cancer in the early stages when it can be treated. He researched on Google and Wikipedia to learn as much as possible, then put together a proposal to find a way to develop a test for it. He submitted his ideas to 200 doctors and only one gave him some space in his lab. The results are a test that is non-invasive, costs $0.03, takes only 5 minutes and is 100% accurate [7].

Instant Innovation is enhanced by facilitating user specialization through tailored programming, such as downloadable apps, and by co-creating the development with customers. This power shift is enforced by an open-integrated system instead of open innovation. An example of co-creation is FedEx, a company that lets users further into the shipping process of their packages. The online tracking system is a valuable innovation for FedEx customers [8]. This system empowers users to take more control of the process to enabling the monitoring of the status of shipment. This will lead to customer satisfaction, cheaper, faster, better, easier, smarter, informative, participatory, and predictive Instant Innovation.

Holtzman's research illustrates how to utilize innovation to catalyze efficient and effective new product development (NPD). He emphasizes that a strategic innovation approach is indispensable for organization to be successful. Examples cited include (1) industry knowledge and foresight, (2) seeking to understand its customer, provide insight, pinpoint unarticulated customer needs and delight, and deliver on these unmet needs, and (3) strategic alignment internally and externally, with customers and suppliers, exploring long term possibilities and practical implementation activities[1].

It is also illustrated how product and service development is viewed (Fig. 1) as increasingly important as product and service life cycles have become shorter. Introducing new product and services in an efficient manner gives companies a

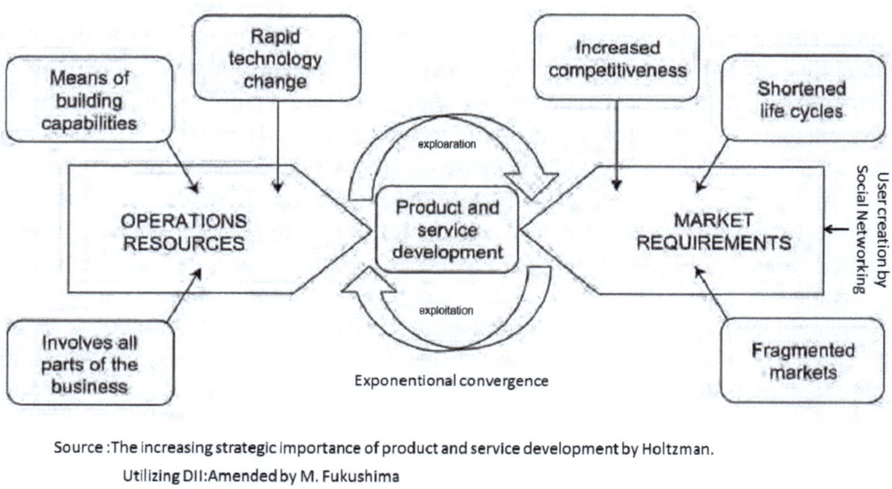

Fig. 1. The increasing strategic importance of product and service development by Holtzman

competitive edge over competition. The general framework advanced here sees dynamic capabilities (DC) and Dynamic Instant Innovation (DII) as the foundation of enterprise-level competitive advantage in regimes of rapid (technological) change. The framework indicates that the extent to which an enterprise develops and employs superior (non-imitable) dynamic capabilities will determine the nature and amount of intangible assets it will create and/or assemble and the level of economic profits it can earn [9].

3 How Dynamic Instant Innovation is Created by Ambidexterity

In the USA, only about 0.10% of firms ever achieve revenues of more than $250 million in sales and only 0.036% of those are successful in attaining over $1 billion in sales. Most of the new startups failed or stayed small [10] [4]. Hannah's study showed many large firms failed and only 20 firms remained between 1912 and 1995. Other research estimated that even large, well-established, companies can only expect to survive between 6 to 15 years [11] [12] [13]. March emphasizes that the ability of a firm to survive is its employees or users' capacity to be equally skillful with both hands, i.e., be ambidextrous by showing its ability to exploit existing assets and positions in a profit-producing way and simultaneously explore new technologies and market to configure and reconfigure organizational resources to capture existing as well as new opportunities [14]. Therefore, DII is created by exploration and exploitation and becomes the heart of successful people and organization.

Why do startups of needle-free injection systems fail? Initial products may not be user friendly and the designs have many flaws. They are more expensive than needle syringes, hard to load, to read, potentially less accurate, requiring an "air shot", and can be potentially misused. Not surprisingly, the initial products needed to be revised or modified until customers are satisfied, which will be very costly for startups if they conduct such implementation without ambidextrous alliances [10]. O'Reilly argues the ability of a firm to be ambidextrous is at the core of dynamic capabilities and further shows that senior management's ability to sense changes in their competitive environment, including potential shifts in technology [15].Therefore the authors argue that senior management's ability to sense changes in their competitive environment, including potential shifts in technology is enhanced by DII. While the authors have not shown any concrete statistics, methodologies, or hypothesis derived from the theoretical analysis of the ambidextrous theory, whether it generally applies to many companies of the world, the authors emphasize its application to one specific company, "INJEX". Gibson and Birkinshaw (2004) conducted 4,195 interviews from 41 companies from all over the world and verified that ambidextrous employees supported their hypothesis. [16] In the past 20 years, during Japan's economic stagnation, Japanese electronics makers were defeated by Samsung. Kawai illustrated the causes of failure of top management of the Japanese makers in fulfilling responsibilities. The causes of failure include (1) failure to sense, (2) satisfaction with status quo, (3) failure to strategize, less resources, and inability to overcome sectionalism and rigidity, (4) lack of flexibility, and (5) lack of concept of "dynamic strategy". Inability to quickly react and forecast are also factors. In contrast, Samsung's top management fulfilled its responsibility and has made Samsung a household name by incorporating factors ignored or not possessed by its Japanese counterparts. Japanese companies were insufficient in fulfilling responsibility concerning both DSC and DRC [17].

Startups need to collaborate with alliances, CVC, and JV, which have specific mechanisms that enable firms to be successful in managing separate "explore-and-exploit" subunits and leveraging common assets in ways that permit the firm to adapt to new opportunities and threats. It is the presence of these characteristics that help startups to be successful. The ability to adapt to change like a chameleon by collaborators may need the ability of the senior leadership to manage the conflicts and trade-offs required by ambidexterity [18].

4 A Real Case of Needle-Free Injection Product Developed by One of the Authors

Medical devices need to be innovated through "Patient Experience Design" and drug or molecular-driven design perspective, which can be thought of as a system or service design perspective. Adapting to unforeseen circumstances require the ability to act decisively, to be both open-minded and confident, and to have a talent for reading messy or hidden data [19]. INJEX has been successful in collaboration with universities and research organizations in Germany, Singapore, Malaysia, Japan and the USA for many years by not focusing on the deal itself but with value-creating relationships. Intel's success was the company's managed relationships with companies that complement their core business, according to Cusmano [20]. Similarly, INJEX uses direct sales via its own exclusive distributors worldwide as well as beauty clinics and anti-aging clinics directly. Direct sales to market via its own distribution make it competitive and self-reliant, which allows Injex to create strong customer relationships. Injex has successfully entered into niche markets with huge profits such as the beauty market where regulatory and government restrictions are milder than those in the medical field. These fields are neglected by the major needle syringe companies such as Becton Dickinson and Terumo [4]. INJEX created the "Shireen" brand for the niche beauty market. Lead users or early adapters of a product or process may become general in the market place in five to ten years. New niche market has been created in collaboration with Injex and beauty practitioners since they are familiar with conditions which lie in the future for most others, they can serve as a need for casting team for INJEX marketing research. Injex has not competed against major syringe companies directly for the reasons outlined in table 1. This is followed by a business case of an innovation developed by the author showing how new product development efficiencies are enhanced through the digitalization of merchandise-flow.

Table 1. Position of existing major to first-generation bio-pharmaceutical and new born bio-pharmaceutical companies

	First-generation bio-pharmaceuticals	New born bio-pharmaceuticals
Business result	Win	Loss
Competition	Direct	Indirect/neutral
New products	Replace existing products	Create new markets
New product development	Promoted	Neglected

5 A Business Case of the Author's Needle-Free Injection Product

Developing new products is time consuming because of the necessity for improving product design to be user friendly and also for the betterment of product quality. Clearly it is preferable to shorten lead-time for developing new products. It follows such cycle as shown in Fig. 2 below when a new product is developed – from trial production stage to finished mass-production stage.

To shorten the total lead-time for new development, it is required to shorten each cycle. While working on an improved trial product, next stage workers have to battle idle time without productive work. So, it is preferable to produce such trial products when normal production is completed, such as at night or during the holidays. But to change work hours, such as labor-shifts, would be a burden to workers. To solve such issues, the idea of using a 3D Printer is a good solution. 3D Printers allow for the creation of 3D products using a material stratified method. By using a 3D Printer, the process can be set up and allowed to run at the end of normal labor hours without idle time. Then in the morning, the process could be finished and it would be possible to start experimenting immediately. So by utilizing 3D printing, it is possible to eliminate or reduce waiting time during work hours and work can proceed effectively with little waste. Furthermore, workers can produce new products easily without any special training for their work. A planner working as an operator by himself can perform as if he himself was a manufacturer and the use of 3D printing will work effectively to reduce the number of personnel necessary for production. In addition to this 3D innovation, instantaneous virtual prototyping is possible under DII. Building Information Modeling (BIM) can impact architecture/engineering/construction (AEC). This can provide a virtually simulated and large integrated database. Another concept similar to BIM is a Digital Mock-up (DMU). This will potentially eliminate the inefficient process of transferring large amount of paper based documents.

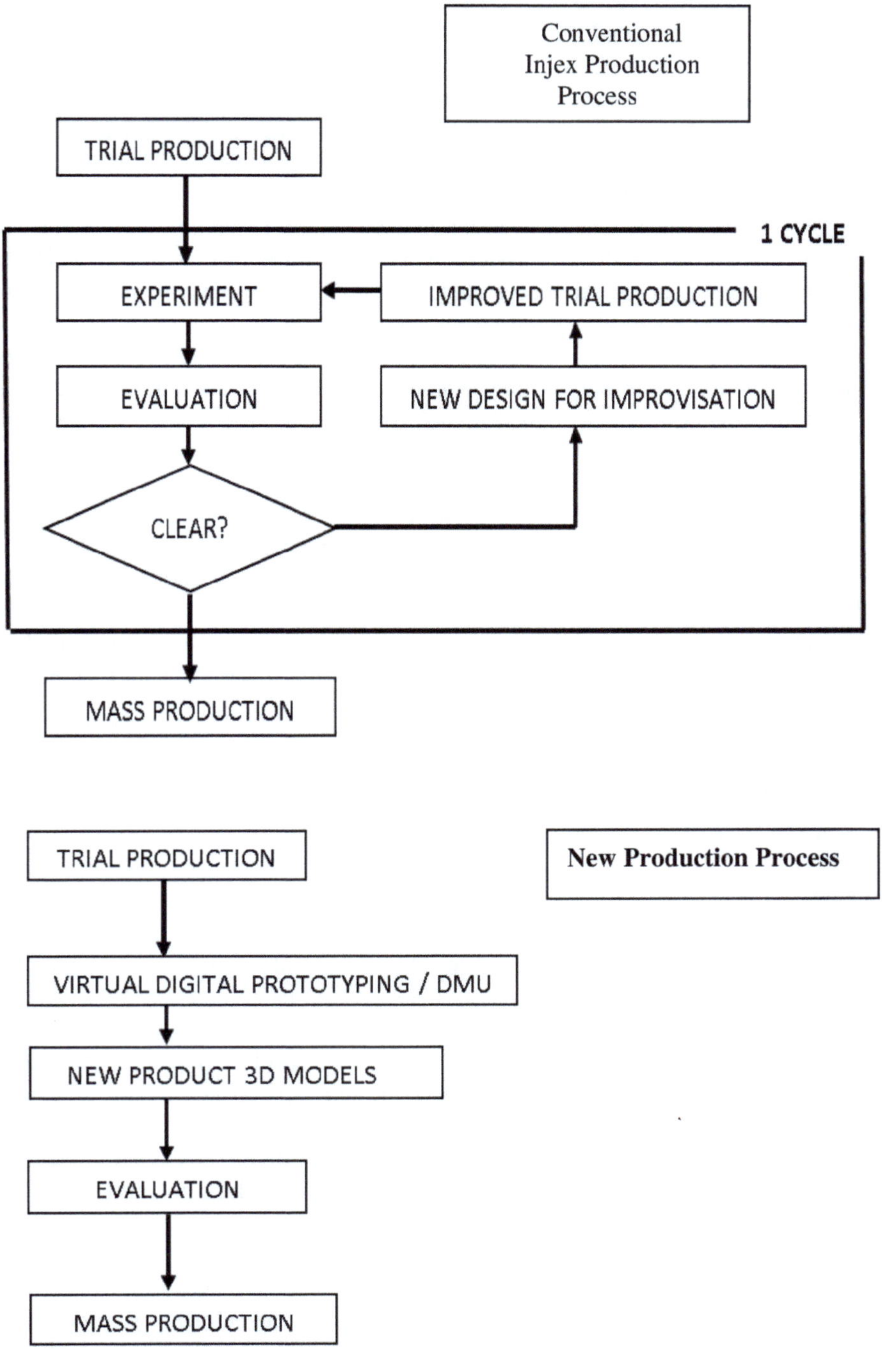

Fig. 2. Flow Chart of New Product Development under DII

6 Digitalization of Merchandise-Flow on Needle-Free Injector in the Future by DII

It is possible to predict different skin hardness for different people, which can cause different volume of drug to dispense under the skin differently even if the same pressure pump is applied to each case (sensing the patient need). That means it is important to individualize each injecting pressure to fulfill proper depth to be achieved (seizing). But it is hard to accommodate such a dynamic requirement with the current fixed mass production system. Therefore, in the near future, if a 3D bio-printer and human genome sequencer could be purchased by each home for general home use, it will be possible to configure or customize an injector for each individual (transforming). For example, a user can scale his own skin-tightness level using a measuring tool to be developed and send data to a manufacturer of needle-free injector (an exogenous technological change that opens up the possibility of new opportunity) [6]. Then the manufacturer produces 3D data for the injector which makes proper depth injection possible. By using such data from the manufacturer, each user can create his or her own injector at home. If this process is established, it would no longer be necessary to manufacture and deliver injectors. Then perhaps only "drug and data" will be necessary in the future. With the present day scientific tools available for genome sequencing, you can know your own genetic makeup. In the future, 3D bio printers assisted by genome analysis, may allow patients to create their own organs and drugs through DII, allowing the patient to make the cure that best fits his or her needs.

7 The Core Mechanism that Discriminates Between "Winner" and "Loser"

Strategy:
Managers should carefully devise a plan of action to efficiently achieve a corporate goal while considering that efficiency as the attainment of maximum value with limited means [21] [22]. INJEX`s strategy is to develop its core competence "needle-free" with patients, medical professionals and distributors. According to von Hippel, innovation is being democratized. A reactive strategy exploits existing knowledge, towards creating stability, consistency and minimizing variation. An innovative strategy uses an explorative approach in order to compete in production innovation [23], yielding disruptive innovation such as NEEDLE-FREE LANCET. Thus, the diffusion process consists of a few individuals who first adopt an innovation then spreads the word among their circles of acquaintances. Such a diffusion process of innovation typically takes a very long time. Since the early Internet era in the 1990s, the use of new technology has spread beyond any imaginable ideas to now allow for experiments and implementations by just about anyone in just about any corner of the world [5]. By reframing the value of a new market such as that of the needle-free injector, the strategy for NPD in the differentiated market is flexible and can be changed due to weak ties. Because of worldwide distributions created in each country,

INJEX's employees run their own contests and invite everyone into INJEX's innovation process, exploring and exploiting to get the best ideas and technologies from others for INJEX business model, and let others use INJEX innovations in each distributor business model. These innovations are based on tacit knowledge which is very difficult to copy and imitate. Since knowledge is the product of an extended learning process and is an intangible asset that is difficult to acquire and copy, it has been considered a strong source of potential competitive advantage [24]. These distributors and cosmetics professionals spend many years and resources to become an exclusive distributor, by getting approval from the Ministry of Health, and by investing their own time and self-generated content. Hence they are less likely to abandon INJEX. The winners in this new economic environment will be those firms that develop strong internal capabilities in a few areas and leverage those capacities by enlisting the efforts of many others in support of their business [8].

Kawai analyzed the failure of Japanese companies, such as Panasonic, Sharp, and Sony, caused by the new DC (dynamic capability) framework. Strategy-changing capability and dynamic resource-reconfiguring capabilities are discussed. Samsung's success is in changing not only corporate and competitive strategies over time in response to environmental changes (i.e. mobilization of DSC), but also resource configurations in response to shifts in strategies (DRC). Japanese electronics makers failed because of their head-strong decision to sticking to the failed strategy of vertical integration and their failure to restructure their business model (DSC, DRC) [17]. The author posits that catalyzing strategy making for growth or survival by Instant Innovation is the single most important task of top management teams (TMT). The main reason is the lack of DII (failure to create new radical innovations) and the "decision speed" of TMT.

How INJEX crossed the bridge (chasm) over the troubled water:
Linking different types of effective alliances to each distinct stage in the new product development process from discovery to commercialization is one of many key success factors. Understanding more fully the role of firms allying along the entire new product development process seems particularly salient [25]. Two key factors managed within the organization that have enabled INJEX to sustain its competitive advantage are as follow.
1) Vision/Design: The product must be needle-free, less painful, no bruising, easy to use, no stigma, disposable, no needle disposal issues, prefilled drug, fewer mistakes of drug injection, no risk of needle sticks, and convenient in emergency room/trauma center especially with elderly patients.
2) Accurate budgeting: Having a good product to sell is absolutely necessary for cash flow and "on target" budgeting. The first thing to consider in product development is defining MVP (the minimum viable product) and most importantly "will it sell?" What kind of product is the easiest to demonstrate to customers and interested investors? Those two objectives are usually obtainable for most startup companies. The most common problem with startups is keeping costs low and having adequate profit to keep producing the MVP on a regular basis. It is important to have a product to sell to generate cash flow. So, the first objective on the product roadmap should be to define the minimum viable product (the MVP).

8 Conclusion

This paper shows that DII can lead to many breakthroughs, foster innovation, and allow us to live healthier and longer. DII, however, can also shorten the product life cycle placing more stress on management to keep pace. Today's firms face enormous challenges with disruptive innovations such as needle-free injection products. This phenomenon illustrates "agnostic marketing", as described by Christensen, in which it is not known "how", or "how much" new innovations are being used. Facing such uncertainty, managers should get out of their laboratories and directly create knowledge for new customers and new applications through discovery-driven research into the marketplace [3]. Therefore, in challenging the "market change type" innovation, an important point is how to reframe the value of the product. Strong products in the market can limit the capability of NPD. Reframing the value of the new products can unleash the capabilities of NPD. The reframing of the product position is made by flexible weak ties through the alliance that rescues the strategy. By reframing the value of a newly created market, such as that developed by the needle-free injector, the strategy for NPD in the differentiated market is flexible due to weak ties. As a result, reframing the product positioning rescues the strategy from fatal loss in life cycle management and helps the organization maintain competitive advantage.

References

1. Holtzman, Y.: Utilizing Innovation and Strategic Research and Development to Catalyze Efficient and Effective New Product Development (2012), `http://www.intechopen.com/download/pdf/31668`
2. Schumpeter, J.A.: The theory of Economics Development: An Inquiry into Profits, Capital Credit, Interest and the Business Cycle. Transaction Publishers (1934)
3. Christensen, C.M.: The Innovator's Dilemma: When New Technologies Cause Great Firms to Fail. Harvard Business School Press, Boston (1997)
4. Fukushima, M.: Enabling Instant Access to Medical Care by Disruptive Innovation Without Patient Barriers: Genome Sequencing Using Tablet PCs disrupt the Medical Industry Symposium (Mobile 2013) (2013)
5. Takayama, M., Fukushima, J.M.: Instant Innovation, From Experiment to Implementing New Technology Through The Tablet PC. In: Asia Pacific Conference on Information Management, (APCIM 2012) (2012)
6. von Hippel, E.: Democratizing Innovation. The MIT Press, Cambridge (2006)
7. Jack Andraka: Promising Test for Pancreatic Cancer from a Teenager, TED 2013, Filmed (February 2013), `http://www.ted.com/` (accessed March 15, 2014)
8. Chesbrough, H.: The Case for Open Services Innovation: The Commodity Trap. California Management Review Spring 53(3) (2011)
9. Teece, D.J.: Dynamic Capabilities & Strategic Management, p. 48 (2009)
10. McFarland, K.: The Breakthrough Company: How Everyday Companies Become Extraordinary Performer. Crown Business, New York (2008)
11. Awarwal, R., Gort, M.: Evolution of Markets and Entry, Exit, and Survival of Firms. Review of Economics and Statics 78(3) (August 1996)
12. Ormerod, P.: Why Most Things Fail. Pantheon Books, New York (2005)

13. Charles, I., Knight, M.: The Case of Disappearing Firms. Journal of Organizational Behavior 27(1) (Feburary (2006)
14. March, J.G.: Exploration and Exploitation in Organizational Learning. Organization Science 2(1) (1991)
15. O'Reilly, C.A., Tushman, M.: Organizational Ambidexterity in Action: How Managers Explore and Exploit. California Management Review Summer 2011 53(4) (2011)
16. Gibson, C., Birkinshaw, J.: The Antecedents, Consequences, And Mediating Role of Organizational Ambidexterity. Academy of Management Journal 47(2), 209–226 (2004)
17. Kawai, T.: Responsibilities of Top Management in the flat-Panel TV Wars: An analysis based on the new DC framework. The International Academy of Strategic Management (September 21, 2013)
18. Gilbert, C.: Unbundling the Structure of Inertia. The Ambidextrous Organization. Harvard Business Review 82(4) (April 2004)
19. Pisano, G.: Can Science Be a Business: Lesson from Biotech. Harvard Business School Press (October 2006)
20. Cusumano, M., Gawer, A.: Platform Leadership: How Intel, Microsoft, and Cisco Drive Industry Innovation (2010)
21. Mintzberg, H.: The Rise and Fall of Strategic Planning. The Free Press, New York (1994)
22. Steiner, C., Perry, P.: Achieving Emotional Literacy. London Bloomsbury Publishing (1997)
23. Benner, M.J., Tushman, M.L.: Exploitation, Exploration, And Process Management: The Productivity Dilemma Revisited. Academy of Management Review 28(2), 238–256 (2003)
24. Teece, D.: Economic Performance and the Theory of the Firm (1998)
25. Griffin: Design of Landfills and Integrated Solid Waste Management (1977)

Author Index

MIX
Papier aus verantwortungsvollen Quellen
Paper from responsible sources
FSC® C105338

If you have any concerns about our products,
you can contact us on
ProductSafety@springernature.com

In case Publisher is established outside the EU,
the EU authorized representative is:
Springer Nature Customer Service Center GmbH
Europaplatz 3, 69115 Heidelberg, Germany

Printed by Libri Plureos GmbH
in Hamburg, Germany